AF660268

Ethics in Counseling and Psychotherapy

Standards, Research, and Emerging Issues

SIXTH EDITION

Elizabeth Reynolds Welfel, Ph.D.
Cleveland State University

CENGAGE

Australia • Brazil • India • Mexico • Singapore • United Kingdom • United States

CENGAGE

Ethics in Counseling and Psychotherapy: Standards, Research, and Emerging Issues, Sixth Edition

Elizabeth Reynolds Welfel

© 2016, 2013 Cengage Learning®

This edition is reprinted with license from Cengage Learning, for sale in India, Pakistan, Bangladesh, Nepal, Bhutan, Sri Lanka and Maldives.

ALL RIGHTS RESERVED. No part of this work covered by the copyright herein may be reproduced, transmitted, stored or used in any form or by any means graphic, electronic, or mechanical, including but not limited to photocopying, recording, scanning, digitizing, taping, Web distribution, information networks, or information storage and retrieval systems, except as permitted under Section 107 or 108 of the 1976 United States Copyright Act, without the prior written permission of the publisher.

ISBN-13: 978-93-5350-338-3
ISBN-10: 93-5350-338-8

Registered Office:
Cengage Learning India Private Limited
T-303, 3rd Floor
DAV Complex, Plot 3
Mayur Vihar Phase 1
Delhi-110091
Email: asia.infoindia@cengage.com

Cengage Learning is a leading provider of customized learning solutions with office locations around the globe, including Andover, Melbourne, Mexico City, Stamford (CT), Toronto, Hong Kong, New Delhi, Seoul, Singapore, and Tokyo. Locate your local office at:
www.cengage.com/global

Cengage Learning Products are represented in Canada by Nelson Education, Ltd.

For product information, visit our website at **www.cengage.co.in**

Printed in India
First Indian Reprint 2020

Disclaimer:
This book contains link to resources which are a part of the US edition. The same may not be available with the Indian edition. The buyer needs to purchase a copy of the US edition to have full access to those resources.
In no event the publisher shall be liable for any limitation or performance due to unavailability of these resources.

To F.M.W.—42 years is not enough.

About the Author

Elizabeth Reynolds Welfel is Professor Emerita of Counseling at Cleveland State University. She has also served on the counseling faculty at Boston College and was a teaching fellow at the University of Minnesota prior to receiving her doctorate there in 1979. In addition to this book, Dr. Welfel has co-authored *The Counseling Process*, co-edited *The Mental Health Desk Reference*, and co-edited *The Duty to Protect* and has written numerous articles and chapters on ethical issues in professional practice. Her special interests include the process of ethical decision making, the ethical use of technology in counseling practice, a professional's responsibility when clients are dangerous to self or others, and the design of ethics education to promote responsible practice. She has also written extensively about a professional's responsibility once he or she recognizes that an ethical misstep has occurred, because no professional is infallible. Dr. Welfel's involvement in these topics began when she was a graduate student at the University of Minnesota, doing research on moral and intellectual development in adulthood. Her fascination with the process by which adults sort through moral and intellectual dilemmas in their lives eventually focused on the unique moral dilemmas that the practice of counseling and psychotherapy presents to those who work in these professions. She earned a Distinguished Faculty Award at Cleveland State for the excellence of her teaching in counseling and for her scholarship on professional ethics.

Ethics is nothing else than reverence for life.

Albert Schweitzer

Contents

CHAPTER 8 Nonsexual Multiple Relationships and Boundary Issues: Risking Objectivity and Client Welfare 214

CHAPTER 9 Interventions With Groups, Couples, and Families: Unique Ethical Responsibilities 243

CHAPTER 10 The Ethics of Assessment: Using Fair Procedures in Responsible Ways 266

Preface

The goal of the sixth edition of the book has not wavered from any prior edition—it is to sensitize readers to a wide range of ethical and legal issues in the practice of counseling and psychotherapy and to provide them with resources upon which they can rely to help them deal responsibly with these crucial issues. The book uses the codes of ethics and guidelines of the major professional associations (the American Counseling Association, American Psychological Association, American School Counselor Association, National Association of Social Workers, and American Association of Marriage and Family Therapists) to familiarize readers with the fundamental standards for responsible practice, and it also includes analysis of the writings of ethics scholars and citations of relevant research. Ethics codes alone do not answer many ethical questions practitioners face, but the writings of scholars and the relevant research can help them respond appropriately to complex and confusing ethical issues not directly discussed in the codes. Underlying the book is the conviction that all mental health professions can learn from each other, and therefore that inclusion of literature from a range of disciplines is vital for successful therapeutic work. I have also endeavored to include both complex topics and emerging issues in professional practice, and I have added additional references to legal cases and statutes affecting practice in mental health and school counseling.

The book also offers numerous additional examples of case law, regulations, and administrative rulings to give readers a fuller sense of the relationship between professional ethics and the law. The book presents my 10-stage model of ethical decision making and shows its application to a variety of ethical dilemmas. My goal in developing this model was to guide readers through complex dilemmas in a systematic way. Coping with ethical issues in practice can be an intense emotional experience. The availability of a systematic model for analyzing ethical issues and for getting consultation from others helps practitioners make decisions that are reasoned and client centered, even when they feel strong emotions. Numerous cases for discussion are also offered, many of which include extensive analysis using the codes and related literature. Additional cases for independent analysis are available both in the text and in the supplemental *Instructor's Guide* available from Cengage. The case examples used in this book tend not to have simple answers. Instead, they have been designed to present realistic, complex, and sometimes confusing scenarios that mirror the types of situations practitioners encounter. In my experience, these cases challenge students and spark stimulating discussion in class and in online discussion boards.

The sixth edition includes several important additions to the content. For example, Chapter 1 now includes attention to the relationship of neuroscience to ethics and the role of personal values, positive ethics, and risk management in professional practice. It delves into greater detail on social constructivist and virtue-based ethics, and includes substantially more attention to these approaches to ethical decision making throughout the text. Chapter 3 includes more attention to issues of diversity unrelated to ethnicity, such as ageism, disability, prejudice, and discrimination based on religion. It also includes several new cases and a new discussion of the ethical issues that emerge when clients express prejudicial ideas during counseling. Chapter 4 addresses the ethical implications of the competency movement in counseling and psychology. Chapter 5 discusses the challenges to confidentiality in online communications and social networking in greater detail. Chapter 11 reviews the "what next?" question—what should mental health professionals do when they realize they have made an ethical mistake? It elaborates a three-part process for personal accountability and recovery, because most ethical missteps do not come to the attention of disciplinary bodies and because ethics is at its core a matter of personal responsibility. Chapter 12 now examines ethical issues in coaching, in addiction to counseling, in professional contacts with the pharmaceutical industry and other organizations that pose a potential conflict of interest; psychologist involvement in military interrogations; and college counseling in the post–Virginia Tech era. In addition, Chapter 13 discusses the implications of cyberbullying, sexting, school violence, and recent court decisions for the school counselor.

Another major goal of the book is to devote comprehensive attention to major ethical issues that confront practitioners—such as confidentiality, informed consent, multiple relationships, and competence to practice—and the ethical issues that practitioners experience in special settings. Thus, the book addresses the unique concerns of school counselors, college mental health professionals, clinical mental health counselors, group and family therapists, clinicians in private practice, researchers, and counselor and psychology educators. Because multicultural competence is so crucial in responsible practice, that topic is interwoven throughout nearly every chapter and is discussed in more depth in Chapter 3.

Lastly, the book aims to help readers understand the philosophical and historical underpinnings of current ethical standards and to tie ethical standards to important legal rulings and statutes. The literature on ethical principles and virtue-based practice forms the core of my perspective on ethical practice. I do not shy away from addressing controversies in the profession, and in these discussions I attempt to provide insight into each side of the argument. My approach to the text is not relativistic, however. The standards of the profession were not arbitrarily determined, and I show readers the reasoning and values underlying those standards. The codes and guidelines are not dry, intellectual documents, but rather, they represent the passion and commitment of the profession to serve the public well.

It is also important to clarify that this is not a text on risk management, though clearly the best protection from liability claims and disciplinary actions is a thorough understanding of the ethical standards of the profession. Once counselors and therapists turn their attention to protecting themselves and managing risk to themselves, two things happen—they have less energy to devote to promoting the welfare of the client, and they tend to view clients as potential adversaries. Neither of these outcomes is likely to help them or their clients in the long run. At its heart, ethical practice is about caring what happens to clients and demonstrating a commitment to the best practice the discipline has to offer them; consequently, what I aim to do in this book is to encourage readers to see the connection between those values and the ethical and legal standards of practice. My approach to ethics aligns with the positive ethics movement and encourages professionals to aspire to do what they believe is best in the situation—to think in terms of ethical ideals and to act with moral courage.

THE INTENDED AUDIENCE

The book has several potential audiences. Graduate students in counseling and psychology are likely to be the primary audience, but the book will also be useful in continuing education for practicing professionals, advanced undergraduate students, and graduate students in related professions, such as social work and pastoral counseling. Consumers of psychotherapeutic services may also find its contents helpful in their search for a responsible professional. Its comprehensive approach to the subject matter and its inclusion of codes of ethics as appendixes make it appropriate for use as the main text in courses in professional ethics or professional issues courses. The book contains an extensive reference list, online resources, cases for discussion, and recommended readings for each chapter, so readers who want to explore the ethics scholarship in greater depth are directed to the proper resources.

THE STRUCTURE OF THE BOOK

The book contains four parts. Part 1 provides a framework for understanding ethical decision making and gives readers a grasp of the process and procedures for redressing ethical violations by mental health professionals. In this section, I describe the relationship of professional ethics in counseling to the broader discipline of ethics, integrate relevant literature from developmental psychology, and present my model of ethical decision making. I also analyze the relationship of multiculturalism to ethical practice. Part 2 reviews the fundamental ethical issues for counselors and therapists, including the ethics of competence to practice, confidentiality, informed consent, multiple relationships, responsible assessment, and multiple-person therapies. What happens when prevention fails is the focus of Part 3. It deals with an often neglected topic: the ethical responsibilities of those who recognize that they have violated the ethical standards of their profession.

Because self-monitoring and personal accountability are at the core of the profession's values, the book discusses the steps professionals can take to redress their own misconduct and to reduce the likelihood that mistakes will recur. In that way, it is unique among the professional ethics books currently published. The topics in Part 4 include the ethics of supervision, teaching, research, clinical mental health and private practice, forensic activities, consultation, and school and college counseling. This portion of the book deals extensively with the emerging ethical dilemmas in the profession, such as the ethical dimensions of managed care, social networking, the impact of school and workplace violence, and therapy mandated by the courts. Each of the 15 chapters also includes a set of questions for further discussion, several online resources, and a list of recommended readings.

The chapters are presented in a logical order, but readers who choose to follow a different sequence will not be at a disadvantage. Also, those who find particular chapters irrelevant to their purposes may omit that material without compromising their comprehension of other parts of the book.

ACKNOWLEDGMENTS

I wish to thank the many individuals who assisted me in this project. First and foremost, I owe a huge debt of gratitude to the students to whom I taught ethics for over 35 years. They inspired and challenged me to write this book. I also thank my colleagues at Cleveland State who have encouraged me, offered valuable insights into the content, and took on extra work to free me to make a full commitment to this book. Carl Rak deserves special recognition for his support, as does Lew Patterson, without whose mentoring I would not have had the courage to embark on so ambitious a task. The following reviewers offered perceptive and extensive feedback on the chapters: Jobie Skaggs, Bradley University; Farrah Hughes, Francis Marion University; Adam Hill, Sonoma State University; Saundra Tomlinson-Clarke, Rutgers University–New Brunswick; Henry Harris, University of North Carolina–Charlotte; Lydia Boldt Smith, University of North Carolina–Charlotte; Suzanne Mudge, Texas A&M University–San Antonio; Marjorie Shavers, Morehead State University. The feedback from this distinguished group of scholars was a gift that I believe strengthened the structure and content of this edition.

The editorial staff at Cengage provided just the right combination of support and challenge for the project. I owe a debt to Julie Martinez of Cengage, Lori Bradshaw of S4Carlisle, Jitenda Kumar of MPS Limited, and copy editor Jill Pellarin for her attention to the many last-minute details in production. I am also especially grateful for the excellent work of Marissa Patsey on the student materials.

Most of all I extend my thanks to my family—to my husband, who always provided a calm and thoughtful response to my frequent worries about the progress of the book and whose careful eye was an enormous help with the manuscript, and to my son, whose fundamental decency is my ultimate guide to what is ethical.

Elizabeth Reynolds Welfel

PART 1

A Framework for Understanding Professional Ethical Values and Standards

CHAPTER

1 Introduction to Professional Ethics

A Psychology and Philosophy for Ethical Practice

Over the last 60 years, irrefutable evidence has emerged that participation in counseling and psychotherapy is an effective intervention for relieving emotional distress, improving interpersonal relationships, and increasing general satisfaction with life (Duncan, 2010; Lambert, 2013; Seligman, 1995). Wampold (2010), for example, concludes that 80% of those who attend psychotherapy are better off than those who elect not to seek help, based on his meta-analysis of the research that psychotherapy has an effect size of 0.80. Moreover, evidence indicates that therapeutic change is not temporary, but is well maintained (Lambert, 2013). In addition, the stigma long associated with seeing a mental health professional has also noticeably decreased (Duncan, Miller, Wampold, & Hubble, 2010). Recent data from educational settings also support the view that school counselors and school psychologists provide effective services to students (Carey, Dimmitt, Hatch, Lapan, & Whiston, 2008; McGannon, Carey, & Dimmitt, 2005).

However, the news is not all good. This same body of research has demonstrated that some mental health services do more harm than good (e.g., Lambert, 2013). Lambert (2013) also concludes that from 5% to 10% of adult clients who attend therapy end up feeling worse, and up to 14% of child and adolescent clients deteriorate. What accounts for this deterioration? Of course, one factor in client deterioration may be an unavoidable exacerbation of the client's problems that even highly competent professionals could not have prevented. Sometimes, though, those deterioration effects are tied to professionals' incompetent services, insensitivity to the ethics of practice, or disregard for the welfare of their clients. These findings about clinicians who make clients' symptoms worse, along with the findings that clinicians' simply fail to help those who can be helped (Lambert, 2013), are at the core of the rationale for developing and enforcing ethical standards and competency requirements for professional practice. We can hardly call ourselves professional helpers deserving the privileges that come with licensing unless our profession is fully committed to making services helpful, and not harmful, and offering practitioners extensive guidance about what they need to do (as well as what they need to avoid doing) to provide beneficial services.

Preventing unethical and incompetent practice that risks harm requires more than the publication of a code or sanctions of unethical practitioners: It demands the profession's sustained commitment to ethics education. It also demands that the individual professional develop an understanding of the factors that produce and maintain ethical and competent practice. At its core, it requires that professionals appreciate the philosophical rationale and moral values that undergird the ethical standards. We turn to philosophy and the psychology of moral behavior to identify crucial foundational factors.

FOUNDATIONS AND RESOURCES FOR ETHICAL PRACTICE

Professional ethics encompasses five dimensions that, when brought together, represent the positive ethical ideals and values of the professions:

1. Having sufficient knowledge, skill, judgment, and character to practice competently
2. Respecting the human dignity and freedom of the client(s)
3. Using the power inherent in the professional's role responsibly
4. Acting in ways that promote public confidence in the profession
5. Placing the welfare of the client(s) as the professional's highest priority

Pared down to those five essentials, acting ethically sounds fairly simple. The first ingredient seems to be a quality education (including supervised practice) so that one is knowledgeable and skilled. All states and provinces require counselors and therapists to pass a licensing examination and have supervised work experience, and nearly 90% of jurisdictions require continuing education to prove their knowledge and skill (Adams & Sharkin, 2012). The other components of ethical practice are consideration of the client's needs and rights as the highest priority, avoidance of self-advancement at the cost of the client, and transaction of one's business in a way that is above reproach. In practice, however, determining the combination of factors that render counseling most effective, most respectful of clients, and most in keeping with the good reputation of the profession is more complicated. Likewise, staying committed to promoting client welfare even when uncomfortable or financially disadvantageous is not easy. Sometimes little is known about which interventions will be most helpful, and at other times even interventions with demonstrable effectiveness fail with a given person. In our rapidly changing profession, keeping knowledge and skills current is a difficult task. If a professional has neglected to keep up with the literature, can he or she still provide effective service? How current does one's knowledge need to be to do effective therapeutic work? Because no one is infallible, even the most diligent and well-trained professional will on occasion act incompetently—how can the professional (and the public) cope with this reality?

Similarly, when counselors and therapists honor the dignity of clients by giving them free choices about their lives, they sometimes make choices contrary to their own best interest. Naturally, when a client is considering a counterproductive choice, the counselor works to help the client see its negative potential. Sometimes this discussion changes the client's mind, but at other times, it is ineffective. Is it acceptable for clinicians to use their power to limit a client's freedom by preventing the client from making a choice that will be regretted later? Is that an abuse of power or an appropriate extension of professional influence? How do cultural and social factors influence the determination of which choices are in a client's best interest and which are not? How reliably can a professional make this judgment when the client's social and cultural background differs dramatically from that of the therapist?

At times, the very actions that help individual clients are actions that the public does not understand. For example, professionals are often legally and ethically bound to maintain the confidentiality of disclosures about a past crime (if that person is in an ongoing professional relationship) unless the client releases them from their obligation or a court orders disclosure. This refusal to betray the client's trust often dismays and frustrates the public. Does this loyalty to the client result in greater or lesser public confidence in the profession? This, too, is not a simple matter. Finally, because clinicians must earn a living in an occupation in which almost no one gets wealthy, determining the balance between a fair interest in compensation and the best interests of the client may also be difficult. Fortunately, there are a number of resources to help mental health professionals wrestle with these issues and ultimately act ethically. Of course, each practitioner must have the character and commitment to do the personal and professional work to take advantage of these intellectual, emotional, and social resources. After all, ethical action is not just about what we think or how we feel, it is about *who we are*. We begin with the intellectual resources while keeping in mind that responsible and competent practice cannot occur consistently in isolation from the social support of other professionals (Johnson, Barnett, Elman, Forrest, & Kaslow, 2012). Our capacity to think productively about complex ethical issues and sustain the values and ideals that brought us into this profession is dramatically enhanced by peer consultation; such consultation is essential, in fact. Why is consultation so necessary? Gottlieb, Handelsman, and Knapp (2013) identify three reasons: First, complex or confusing ethical questions can arise without warning; second, the issue may be a "high stakes" issue where substantial harm can come to the client if the issue is not handled appropriately; and finally, ethical issues often engender substantial emotion, making it more challenging to think clearly about resolutions. (The case of Archie and Annette, described in this chapter, fulfills all these criteria for requiring consultation.)

LITERATURE FROM DEVELOPMENTAL PSYCHOLOGY

The first resource is the abundant literature on morality and moral reasoning that helps clinicians understand professional ethics and ethical decision making as a subset of the broader category of morality and moral decision making. It places professional codes of conduct into a context of fair, decent, and responsible human behavior and provides a framework for explaining what has gone wrong when misconduct occurs. Unlike other resources that focus on the content a person should consider in dealing with an ethical question, the literature from developmental psychology gives a framework for conceptualizing the process of ethical decision making and gives a view of the psychology (and social psychology) of ethics. From this information, professionals derive methods to improve the quality of their own ethical decision making and find better ways to consult with others and to teach ethics to students and practitioners. As we begin this discussion, it is important to reiterate, that ethical decision making is *not* an exclusively intellectual or isolated activity—emotions and social experiences also play a crucial role. Still, ethics always includes thinking about what should be done or, often in the case of unethical action, the repression of thinking about what should be done.

Components of Moral Behavior

When a person faces a moral decision, what provokes him or her to behave morally or immorally? Mental health professionals often raise this question when they hear of a courageous or outrageous act by another professional. Rest (1983, 1994) has provided a useful framework for understanding that process. First, he defines a moral action as any behavior that can affect the welfare of another. For instance, if a person observes someone breaking into a neighbor's home, what he or she does when watching this burglary is defined in moral terms because it affects the neighbor's well-being. (Of course, the robber's actions also have a moral dimension, for the same reason.) If the person acts to benefit the neighbor, by calling the police or trying to scare the burglar away, then that action is moral. Clearly, any attempt to help may backfire, but an action need not be successful to be moral. What makes the action moral is that one makes a good-faith effort to help the neighbor. Conversely, if one does nothing, that inaction could not be labeled moral unless the individual were endangered in some way by this burglar. Morality does not require us to risk our own welfare for another. That's why we label as heroes people who risk their own safety to help others; they have gone beyond their ordinary moral duty to ensure another's well-being.

Rest identifies four components of moral behavior that must take place if a moral action is to result. The first of these is called *moral sensitivity*, the process of recognizing the situation as one with implications for the welfare of another. It involves sensitivity to the cues that a context offers to its moral dimension (Narvaez & Rest, 1994). In the situation just described, it is possible that a person could see this intruder trying to break the lock on the neighbor's door and think about nothing more than the burglar's skill with the crowbar. Or the person might just feel grateful that the burglar chose someone else's home. These reactions indicate no assumption of responsibility to intervene on behalf of the neighbor and exclusive concern with one's own welfare. In this situation, Rest would say that the person lacks moral sensitivity.

Translated into professional ethics, moral sensitivity means realizing the implications of one's behaviors on clients, colleagues, and the public. If a psychologist at a social gathering repeats a funny story about a client, that professional did not consider the welfare of the client or the impact on the reputation of the profession before speaking. This person has missed the moral meaning of her action. She did not need to have a malicious *intent* to act immorally. In fact, immoral and unethical actions frequently result from distraction from the moral implications of actions or even from good intentions. At other times the level of emotional, social, intellectual, and moral development of the professional may prevent awareness of ethical dimensions of professional practice (Foster & Black, 2007).

To illustrate in another way, consider the counselor's actions in the following case:

The Case of Mitchell and Maria

Mitchell, a licensed clinical counselor, decides not to explain the limits of confidentiality at the initiation of services because he considers that approach bureaucratic and distracting from the client's purpose for coming. He hopes to help by immediately focusing on the "issue at hand." One day at the beginning of a session, Maria, a 17-year-old client, tells Mitchell that she has suicidal thoughts, mistakenly assuming that *everything* she says to him is confidential. In reality, if any clinician believes a minor to be at significant risk for suicide, he or she may be obligated *not* to keep this material confidential from parents. When Mitchell explains the limits of confidentiality to Maria after she has already blurted out her secret, she feels betrayed, an outcome clearly detrimental to her already compromised welfare. She feels her lack of knowledge about the limits of confidentiality robbed her of the choice of whether or when to disclose this private material.

Mitchell's notion that explaining the limits of confidentiality to a client is merely "bureaucratic" shows his ethical insensitivity and resulted in unethical behavior. Obviously, sharing suicidal thoughts with a therapist is very important, and professionals have an ethical duty to encourage clients to express such thoughts. However, when the client does not understand the implications of this disclosure, feelings of betrayal occur, and the suicidal impulse may escalate when trust is broken in this way. No such negative consequences ensue when the client discloses such information after building trust and gaining some understanding of what may happen after such a revelation.

Rest's second component of moral behavior is *moral reasoning*. Moral reasoning is the process of thinking through the alternatives once a situation has been recognized as having moral dimensions. At first glance, moral reasoning sounds like a methodical, logical process, but it typically takes place rapidly and without great deliberation. It has both an emotional and a cognitive aspect. When a person sees a burglar at a neighbor's door, one must act quickly, so the process of thinking about what action(s) would benefit the neighbor is completed in seconds. Sometimes only one alternative comes to mind—call the police. At other times, the person weighs the merits of two or more alternatives such as going outside, calling another neighbor, or getting the gun kept for protection in the bedroom. Moral reasoning is the process of evaluating the choices and deciding which is best.

The research by Kohlberg (1984), Gilligan (1982), and others suggests that not all adults reason about moral issues with the same moral maturity. In fact, these researchers posit stage models of moral development based partly on biological maturity and partly on social experience. Some research suggests that counselors at higher stages of moral development make ethical decisions more in keeping with the standards of the profession (Bombara, 2002; Linstrum, 2005;

Uthe-Burow, 2002; Welfel & Lipsitz, 1983), but other studies contradict this finding (Doromal & Creamer, 1988; Fox, 2003; Royer, 1985). Recent research offers preliminary evidence that there is a relationship between scores on a measure of social-cognitive development and gains in ethical decision making after training (Lambie, Hagedorn, & Ieva, 2010).

According to Rest, the third component of morality is *moral motivation*. Once a person has evaluated the options and determined which is most moral, then that person must decide whether to act. For example, a counselor may have observed a colleague who is missing appointments, neglecting paperwork, and showing signs of intoxication at work. The counselor recognizes this as a moral dilemma because the welfare of clients and the counseling service are at stake. The ethics codes also identify this as her ethical responsibility (American Counseling Association [ACA], 2014, Section I.2.a; American Psychological Association [APA], 2010a, Standards 1.04, 1.05). She has weighed the moral alternatives and has concluded that the best course of action is confronting the colleague and insisting that he modify his behavior with clients and seek help.

Essentially, at this point the therapist asks herself, "Will I *choose* to do that which I now *know* I should do?" If she answers affirmatively, she is one step closer to an ethical action, but if not, then no ethical action will take place. At this point, competing values may interfere. Professional ethical values are not the only values operating in a person, and values that compete with ethics may take priority. These other values may be admirable—such as the commitment to earning a salary sufficient to support one's children—or they may be contemptible; self-interest is one such ignoble value. The therapist may realize that if the dysfunctional colleague deteriorates further, he may leave the practice, resulting in more clients and more income for her. Or she may value harmony in the workplace more than ethics and may decide not to risk conflict among the staff. In short, this is the point in the process where the power of the professional's ethical values is balanced against other values, the point at which a professional's commitment to the best interest of the client is tested. If the ethical values take precedence, then ethical action follows. Research has found that when presented with hypothetical ethical situations, graduate students in psychology indicate that they *would* do what they know they *should* do approximately 50% of the time (Bernard & Jara, 1986). Studies by Betan and Stanton (1999), Fox (2003), and McDivitt (2001) report similar percentages of graduate students and practicing school counselors who would do less than they believe they ought to do. Betan and Stanton (1999) also found that emotions played a significant part in these decisions: those who were more anxious about taking action and less optimistic about its effectiveness were less likely to report a colleague. Practicing psychologists do somewhat better. In a related study, Bernard, Murphy, and Little (1987) found that two-thirds of psychologists chose the ethical value. Two other studies (Smith, McGuire, Abbott, & Blau, 1991; Wilkins, McGuire, Abbott, & Blau, 1990) reported a similar pattern. These statistics show how strong competing values can be and how they can operate both on intellectual and emotional processes.

Of course, ethical decision making is not always fully conscious. Mental health professionals often experience cognitive dissonance when choosing not to carry out the most responsible choice. Because they like to view themselves as ethical, their dilemma becomes how to retain that positive self-evaluation if they are rejecting the ethical choice. To reduce their mental discomfort, they may redefine the problem. In the case of the intoxicated colleague, the therapist might hypothesize that the colleague is not really drunk or that the missed appointments are not as frequent as they seem. She may even convince herself that this colleague may be on medication that affects his behavior. Of course, that may be true, but when the professional's goal is to extricate herself from the ethical responsibility, the facts of the case are not explored. Instead, she rationalizes, and thus her definition of her ethical responsibility has changed and her motivation to act declines. With this distortion of the facts, the counselor gets to avoid painful confrontation with the colleague and continue to define herself as ethical. In some cases, the cognitive dissonance operates in the opposite way, making professionals who have engaged in an unethical practice more critical of colleagues than those who have not committed that violation. (See Barkan, Ayal, Gino, and Ariely [2012] for a fascinating research study on this phenomenon.)

If the professional works in an environment that places a high priority on professional ethics, the risk of self-deception is reduced. Those in supervisory positions facilitate responsible behaviors when they make it known to their subordinates that ethics matter and that employees will be rewarded for taking an ethical path. In business, such leadership is called "creating an ethical culture in the organization." The competing values have less pull then, and the person who pursues the ethical action is likely to be supported and not isolated. In parallel fashion, if a professional is involved in regular peer consultation and is committed to using such social support, the capacity to decide to do what is right is also likely to be strengthened (Johnson, Barnett, Elman, Forrest, & Kaslow, 2013).

The research of Wilkins et al. (1990) also shows that mental health professionals deviate from the ethical value more frequently when ethical and legal standards governing an issue are not clear. If, as sometimes happens, work climate is hostile to ethical action, Vansandt's research (1992) suggests that organizational culture can actually suppress an individual's inclination to act ethically.

Social and political factors also affect a person's capacity to make an ethical choice. Social norms sometimes render ethical action more difficult. A high school student may believe that he or she ought to intervene to assist a gay student who is being harassed, but may decline to do so because of fear of social alienation. For the same reason, a citizen in a small, homogeneous community may support legislation he or she thinks is morally wrong for fear of social reprisals. Or a counselor may go along with a supervisor's suggestion to change a diagnosis for reimbursement purposes because it seems to be good for the agency, even if it deceives the insurer and misrepresents the client's problem.

Cultural definitions of what is ethical also vary (Knapp & VandeCreek, 2007; Pedersen, 1994, 1997). The high priority given to individual autonomy in Western cultures is not universally endorsed by other societies. Thus, culture affects not just the values that compete with ethical values, but the very definition of what is ethical to some extent. Similarly, definitions of appropriate gender roles and parenting practices can differ substantially from culture to culture. (Chapter 3 discusses the dilemma of a client whose parents have arranged a marriage that he does not want but which his cultural and religious tradition makes it difficult for him to refuse.)

Moral character is the final component of the process in Rest's model. Betan and Stanton (1999) use the term *resoluteness* to refer to this aspect of moral behavior. One must carry out the moral action to its conclusion. Doing so typically requires virtues such as compassion, integrity, and conscientiousness. People who lack these characteristics may change their minds or withdraw when they encounter resistance. In the case described in the last section, the therapist may express her concerns about the colleague's erratic behavior, but if she receives an angry response or a revelation about personal troubles, she may back down. A moral action cannot take place if it is not implemented. Sometimes, persevering with the moral plan has personal costs; that's where integrity, character, and social support are critical. Keeping one's eyes on the goal and on the welfare of clients in spite of other pressures is often a difficult task, though ultimately it is the most rewarding. Collaborating with other professionals who are committed to the ethical ideals of the profession eases the difficulty of implementing the moral action. Colleagues can also assist in mitigating any negative consequences of implementing the ethical action.

CODES OF ETHICS

The second resource for ethical decision making is the code of ethics of the professional associations. These codes have a variety of names, but they all specify the standards of care and the rules of conduct for members, and they represent "both the highest and lowest standards of practice expected for the practitioner" (Levy, 1974, p. 267). Licensed professional counselors rely on the *Code of Ethics and Standards of Practice* of the American Counseling Association (2014); psychologists, on the *Ethical Principles of Psychologists and Code of Conduct* of the American Psychological Association (2010a); and social workers, on the *Code of Ethics* of the National Association of Social Workers (2008). (Throughout this book these codes documents will be referred to as the ACA Code and the APA Code). Marriage and family therapists are bound by the *Code of Ethics* of the American Association of Marriage and Family Therapy (2012); and school counselors, by the *Ethical Standards for School Counselors* (American School Counselor Association [ASCA], 2010). Because many mental health professionals are members of more than one professional association, they often can refer to two or more of these codes of ethics to guide them through ethical dilemmas. In addition, professional associations supplement the codes with casebooks (Nagy, 2005), commentary (Campbell, Vasquez, Behnke, & Kinscherff, 2010; Herlihy & Corey, 2014), and guidelines for practice related to specific populations that have come to their attention. For example, the American Psychological Association has published ethical guidelines for providing services via telepsychology (APA, 2013b), for undergraduate psychology majors (APA, 2013c), and for working with older adults (APA, 2014a). Other organizations have similar specialized codes; a sampling of these, along with additional guidelines from ACA and APA, is contained in Appendix D.

These codes represent the official statements of the professions about what is expected of members, and all members are held accountable for actions that violate the code. When they accept membership in the professional association or a credential from a licensing agency, members are agreeing to abide by the stipulations of the code, even if the values of the code contradict in some way the moral values that guide their personal lives. Each national professional association has established an ethics committee and empowered it to enforce its code. (Most state associations also have ethics committees and standards, but they rely heavily on the national codes to determine their rules of conduct.) The American Counseling Association first published its code of ethics in 1961 and has revised it five times since (most recently in 2014). The American Psychological Association produced its first code in 1953 and published revisions in 1959, 1981, 1992, 2002, and 2010.

The intent of a code is to identify the ethical goals and values of the profession and to guide the professional through the most common pitfalls in practice. Thus, codes of ethics define prescribed (required) activities such as explaining the benefits and risks of services to clients, as well as prohibited activities such as having a sexual relationship with a current client or student. Codes also define the conditions under which certain other behaviors are permissible. For example, the ACA and APA Codes both elaborate on the circumstances under which a professional can accept barter rather than money for services (ACA, 2014, Section A.10.e; APA, 2010a, Standard 6.05). Moreover, codes include "aspirational statements" that clarify the fundamental ethical values of the profession. These statements are typically included in the Preamble or Introduction to the code. (Appendix A, pp. 489–490, for the wording of these statements in the ACA Code and pp. 534–537 for the Preamble of the APA Code.)

Codes of ethics from professional associations are frequently included in state regulations governing the practice of counseling and psychotherapy. It is important to note, though, that licensing boards frequently have additional ethical standards for professionals that are binding on all licensees. Ignorance of the codes and regulations does not excuse problematic behavior. The professions assert that if practitioners are benefiting from their professional identity, they have a duty to know and respect ethical standards and to work to enforce them. Each of the codes stipulates that ignorance of their provisions does not relieve a professional of these responsibilities (see APA Code, Introduction [2010a], and ACA Code, Section I.1.a).

Advantages and Limitations of Codes of Ethics

For the individual practitioner, the major contribution of a code is the support it gives the professional faced with an ethical question. A prudent professional always refers to the code because it often reveals the responsible action, and no further deliberation is necessary. No code of ethics provides a blueprint for resolving all ethical issues, nor does the avoidance of violations always equate with ideal ethical practice, but codes represent the best judgment of one's peers about common problems and shared professional values. The existence and enforcement of codes of ethics also demonstrate that mental health professionals take seriously their responsibility to protect the public welfare. The lengthy process of obtaining input from members about revisions of the code and educating them about those changes keeps the code in the limelight so that members know its importance. The inclusion of statements of aspirational ethics also furnishes members with a definition of what their colleagues consider the fundamental ethical values of the profession.

Codes also have limitations. First, the members of a professional organization typically work with diverse populations in a variety of settings and engage in different activities. This variability means that a code must be written broadly, and its application to any one setting is limited. Second, because the profession changes rapidly, with new forms of practice and new populations emerging constantly, parts of the codes may be outdated as soon as they are published, despite the best efforts of their writers. Codes, therefore, do not uniformly address cutting-edge issues (Mabe & Rollin, 1986) such as professionals' use of social networking sites or their responsibilities when clients operate motor vehicles while impaired. Clinicians wrestling with such dilemmas must find support elsewhere, typically from peer consultation. In addition, codes are developed within organizations that also have other values and priorities, so the resulting documents sometimes represent what the board of directors can agree to, rather than an ethical ideal. For example, the first 15 drafts of the 1992 APA Code banned all sexual intimacies with former clients, but the version that the governing body approved (and that is included in the current APA Code) allowed sexual contact with former clients after two years, under limited conditions. Gabbard (1994) characterized this change as a result of compromise and self-interest rather than concern about the public welfare. Ladd (1991) makes another important point about the limitations of a code of ethics—it can focus so much attention on the minor issues of the profession (such as the permissibility of barter) that it distracts professionals from the major questions (such as the ethical responsibility to promote social justice).

Most important, though, codes of ethics are not cookbooks for responsible behavior (Kitchener & Kitchener, 2012). To take the cookbook analogy further, codes fail to provide recipes for healthy ethical decision making, although they do offer two essential components of cookbooks—goals for good ethical nutrition and, as Handelsman has noted, lists of ethical poisons (Kuther, 2003). Largely because of these limitations, they provide unequivocal guidance for only a few problems. For example, there is no doubt about the prohibition of a sexual relationship with a current client. The codes state that it is *never* appropriate. For many other issues, though, the guidance is not so clear. The following situation illustrates this limit:

The Case of Dr. Remmard and Ms. Harks

Ms. Harks serves on a civic committee with Dr. Remmard, a counseling psychologist, and approaches him for help with depressive feelings. She says that she feels comfortable with him now that she's gotten to know him on this committee and hears that he has a good reputation in the community. May Dr. Remmard accept her into counseling while they are serving together on the committee?

The codes address this matter but do not make the decision clear cut. (Note that the term *multiple relationship* means having a second or overlapping relationship with a client in addition to the counselor–client relationship). The APA Code specifies in Standard 3.05 that any such relationship that impairs objectivity, effectiveness, and presents a risk to the other person should be avoided.

Dr. Remmard must interpret the relevant code and apply its provisions. The code does supply the questions he must ask, such as, "Is this a social or close personal relationship?" "Can I avoid it?" "If I cannot, how do I ascertain that I will be objective with a client whom I see periodically in another setting?" However, in the end, Dr. Remmard must sort out the ethical considerations and use his best judgment. He must deliberate about the nature of the connection with this woman, the degree to which objectivity may be compromised, and the client's best interests served. The client's access to other qualified professionals is also a consideration.

On other ethical issues, the code provides even less guidance. Consider a counselor who works primarily with children and adolescents. This professional needs support in determining how much material from counseling must be shared with parents and guardians and what the disclosure of that material means to the progress of the counseling relationship with the child. The ACA Code (2014) advises counselors to seek the assent of minors (or anyone else who cannot provide legal consent) and to appreciate both their rights and parents' rights and responsibilities (see Section A.2.d, Appendix A, pp. 492–493).

These statements are general and provide limited help to a counselor struggling with an adolescent client who feels alienated from his chaotic family and wants the counselor to keep his violations of curfew and experimentation with alcohol secret from his parents. The APA Code makes even less reference to this topic in Standard 3.10b (Appendix B, p. 543). Here, the burden of analyzing ethical issues falls squarely on the professional and requires careful reasoning to judge the best solution. The professional must turn to other resources to guide this decision-making process.

In short, ethics codes do not provide easy answers to complex questions. They serve instead as the critical starting point for developing independent judgment based on the shared wisdom of the profession. Professionals who ignore them do so at their own peril; those who view them as the prescription for all ethical issues are equally at risk.

LITERATURE FROM PHILOSOPHY

The third resource for making responsible ethical judgments is the growing body of literature that ties professional ethics to philosophers' writings on ethics and explains the philosophical underpinnings of the codes. This scholarship defines the ethical principles, virtues, and theories that form the rationale for the standards in the codes. In essence, these writings connect the codes to the wisdom of the ages and are of greatest use in coping with the most difficult and confusing ethical dilemmas. The philosophical literature also clarifies the values and virtues underlying the actions of responsible professionals and highlights that ethical practice always requires value judgments on the part of the professional. Some authors (e.g., Birrell, 2006; Kitchener & Kitchener, 2012; Sommers-Flanagan & Sommers-Flanagan, 2007; Urofsky & Engels, 2003) make a strong argument for integration of moral philosophy into the ethics education of mental health professionals.

Consider the following situation:

The Case of Annette and Archie

During his fourth counseling session, Archie, a 17-year-old, tells his high school counselor that the claim he made of sexual abuse by his stepfather is not true. He now says that he fabricated the story because he wanted his mother to leave his stepfather, who has punched her many times. Archie made the statements about abuse to his coach, who reported them to authorities. As his school counselor, Annette was then informed of the report when she began individual counseling with Archie. They have had four sessions.

Should Annette maintain confidentiality if the client does not agree to release this information? The counselor here is in a true ethical dilemma because there are potentially harmful consequences no matter what she does. The welfare of the boy, his mother, and his stepfather are all at stake. Reference to the ethics codes does not resolve the question, although it does provide relevant information. The codes stress the importance of confidentiality as a protection of the client's right to privacy. They also indicate an exception to that right when laws demand and in situations of serious and foreseeable harm to the client or others. The codes inform the counselor that the decision to violate confidentiality should not be taken lightly, and then broadly define the exceptions. Does the law require disclosure? Consultation with an attorney may be necessary to answer that question. Is there serious and foreseeable harm? There would be if the boy were talking of shooting the stepfather or committing suicide because he felt so hopeless. But is subjecting the stepfather to an investigation by children's services, and possibly causing the stepfather to leave the home, the same kind of harm? If criminal charges were brought against the stepfather and he faced incarceration, would that be serious and foreseeable harm? Is it Annette's responsibility to bring this information to the investigators from children's services, or is it their responsibility to ascertain the facts of the case? Is disclosing the confidential information ethical if it results in the boy terminating the counseling relationship when he is in serious psychological distress and feels alienated from his family? Should the boy's age influence the counselor's decision?

In this situation, the counselor obviously needs more information than the codes provide. An understanding of how philosophers conceptualize and prioritize ethical obligations can shed light on the problem and provide more structure to the decision-making process (we return to this case in the next chapter). As Chapter 2 also describes in detail, the ethics codes spring from several ethical principles. By thinking through these ethical principles, professionals can better evaluate their options in such complex situations. For example, Kitchener (1984) suggests that five ethical principles underlie the ethical standards in human service and medical professions. These principles include respect for autonomy, beneficence (the obligation to do good), nonmaleficence (the avoidance of harm), fidelity to promises made, and justice. In confusing dilemmas, professionals should weigh the alternatives according to these broader ethical principles. Beauchamp and Childress (2012) add the principle of veracity, the obligation to be truthful in professional interactions, to this list.

Philosophers go on to describe another level of ethical reasoning that they term *ethical theories* (Freeman, 2000; Kitchener, 1984). Consideration of ethical theories is needed when the ethical principles do not resolve the problem. As noted above, the next chapter elaborates on both ethical principles and ethical theories in the context of professional practice.

Other philosophers offer an alternative way to think about ethics. They talk not about ethical principles or rules or about ethical problem solving, but about an *ethics of virtue*. They are not interested so much in how professionals behave as in who they ought to be (May, 1984). This scholarship centers on the qualities professionals should develop and the habits of character they need. Reference to such scholarship keeps the profession's attention not just on the rules of behavior and the criteria for applying those rules but also on the person of the counselor in connection with others (Cohen & Cohen, 1999; Jordan & Meara, 1990; Meara, Schmidt, & Day, 1996). The five virtues most commonly referred to in this literature are *integrity*, the capacity to act consistently upon deeply held personal values; *prudence*, the ability to act with discernment; *trustworthiness*, the capacity to follow through on promises and commitments; *compassion*, deep concern for another's welfare and sympathy with his or her pain; and *respectfulness*, an attitude that recognizes others' concerns and respects their dignity. Beauchamp and Childress (2012) refer to five focal virtues in human service that differ slightly from other such lists: compassion, conscientiousness, integrity, trustworthiness, and discernment. Regardless of the particular virtues cited as most applicable to practice, they all highlight the critical role that virtue plays in the motivation of a professional to act responsibly and to be accountable for the outcomes of his or her actions and decisions.

Another major philosophical perspective on professional ethics comes from feminist theory (Brabeck, 2000; Hill, Glaser, & Harden, 1998; Lerman & Porter, 1990; Nodding, 1984). This view emphasizes systemic variables such as the power of the participants within the system and the impact of race, class, and oppression on the decision-making process. Feminist theorists advocate for attention to the uniqueness of each client and equality in decision making between the client and the professional. The focus is on care for the client as the central value of therapeutic service (Birrell, 2006). A recent addition to the literature on philosophical influences on ethical standards comes from the writings of Cottone (2001) and Guterman and Rudes (2008), who advocate a social constructivist model of ethical decision making in which ethical choice is viewed as primarily a socially interactive process and not a process that is internal to the individual. This approach is consistent with the view that responsible and competent practice by an individual should be thought of as inextricable with the professional support system in which he or she is embedded (Johnson et al., 2013).

The positive ethics perspective represents the most recent shift in thinking about fostering ethical practice. According to Handelsman, Knapp, and Gottlieb (2005) mental health professionals and their clients are not well served by an approach to ethics that emphasizes avoiding breaking rules and following standards. Instead these authors advocate for an approach to ethics that encourages practitioners to frame ethical action according to ethical ideals; to begin with the question: What action is most consistent with the ideals the profession professes and most consistent with the values I espouse as a mental health professional? Borrowing from the work of Berry and Sam (1997), Handelsman et al. (2005) conceive of the promotion of ethical practice as a process of *ethical acculturation*, a process that involves the integration of personal moral values with professional ethical values, to develop an ethical identity. Such an identity fosters a focus on ethical ideals rather than ethical rules and integrates the intellectual, emotional, and interpersonal components of ethical action.

LITERATURE FROM NEUROSCIENCE

The relationship between the functioning of the brain and the individual's moral judgments has been a recent topic of research, and its findings help clarify the areas of the brain that are activated during the process of making moral judgments (Sinnot-Armstrong, 2008; Farah, 2012; Young & Phillips, 2011). The first publicized case of damage to moral judgment from a neurological injury predates this literature by nearly one hundred years. In this case Phineas Gage suffered a severe neurological injury (a metal pole through his head) in which much of his medial frontal cortex was destroyed. Surprisingly, he recovered all his mental capacities except moral judgment. After the injury he changed from a pillar of the community to a lawless anti-social individual (Greene, 2005a). The current research also offers some intriguing and controversial findings: It suggests that moral functioning may be affected by changes in the brain caused by early experience and supports the deep connection between emotions and moral judgments (Greene, 2005b).

This research also highlights the relationship between some forms of brain damage and misbehavior, especially damage to the prefrontal cortex (Damasio, 2007). In similar fashion, this research is exploring the connections between emotion, reasoning, and brain function when people are dealing with moral issues. For example, a recent study explored differences in brain activity when people deal with acts of ethical omission (failing to do the right thing) in contrast to acts of ethical commission (engaging in a clearly immoral act) (Greene & Paxton, 2011).

Truscott summarizes this research well when he writes:

> [W]hen people consider moral dilemmas, a number of different neural networks in our brains are active. The medial frontal lobes are actively processing how we feel about other people, while the dorsolateral surface of the frontal lobes are engaged in ongoing mental computation … and the anterior cingulated cortex is dealing with conflict between impulses emanating from one part of the brain and inhibitions coming from another. (Truscott, 2013, p. 3)

There is even some research that suggests that moral functioning can be enhanced by surgical, electrical, or chemical interventions to the brain (Narvaez & Vaydich, 2008). This body of research is clearly in its infancy, but findings thus far demonstrate that making moral judgments is not a purely conscious process and that there may be an interaction between genetics, brain chemistry, emotions, and environment on moral and ethical behavior.

RESEARCH ON PROFESSIONAL ETHICS

Another important source of information is the professional literature that examines specific ethical issues such as the limits of confidentiality with children and the ethical considerations in advertising professional services. Over the past 40 years, published materials on ethics have increased dramatically. These books and articles are particularly helpful for professionals trying to cope responsibly with emerging areas of practice where the codes are less likely to offer specific guidelines for ethical conduct. In controversial areas, such as sexual contact with former clients or confidentiality with clients whose actions place other adults at risk, these writings give practitioners a sense of the dimensions of the debate and the critical factors that influence experts' views on the issue. These resources are also relatively free from the external pressures that often influence the development of ethics codes. They usually encourage professionals to practice in the most responsible way possible.

In the case of Archie, the boy who says he lied when he disclosed sexual abuse, this literature can assist the counselor in several ways. It more fully defines the meaning of "serious and foreseeable harm" from the code (e.g., Swenson, 1997), clarifies the limits of confidentiality with adolescents (Ellis, 2009; Gustafson & McNamara, 1987; Lawrence & Kurpius, 2000; Taylor & Adelman, 1998), and explores the potential effects of breaking confidentiality on the future of the counseling relationship (Baird & Rupert, 1987; Fisher, 2012; Nowell & Spruill, 1993; Pipes, Blevins, & Kluck, 2008; Rokop, 2003). Used in conjunction with the codes and ethical principles, this literature offers the counselor an opportunity to consult with the most knowledgeable and experienced scholars in the profession on a given ethical issue.

The Scope of Unethical Practice

Ethics scholars have also researched the most common types of ethics offenses and the practitioner characteristics associated with them. Their findings warn about red flag issues and the circumstances under which others have fallen short. Specifically, researchers have studied the pattern of complaints to licensing boards and professional associations, the nature of malpractice suits filed against counselors and psychologists, and the self-reports of professionals in national surveys. In addition, ethics committees publish annual accounts of their activities and the outcomes of the cases they handle (see, e.g., APA, 2014b; Ponton & Duba, 2009). Moreover, when the APA and ACA terminate members for unethical behavior, the committees send notice of the termination to all members with their dues statements. The APA also publishes the names of all individuals found guilty of less serious offenses and the punishment imposed. Many state licensing boards are also posting disciplinary actions on their websites. California, for instance, provides the specific rulings against psychologists disciplined in the last several years at http:/www.psychology.ca.gov/consumers/actions.shtml. The U.S. Department of Health and Human Services publishes reports annually regarding actions and inquiries against health care professionals. The most recent version online is available at http://www.npdb-hipdb.hrsa.gov/resources/npdbstats/npdbStatistics.jsp#contentTop.

From all these data, several important findings emerge. First, although some variation occurs depending on the source of the data, the same problems recur—sexual misconduct; improper and incompetent practices (including financial misconduct); and multiple relationships, also commonly referred to as boundary violations. Ethics complaints about psychologists are related primarily to sexual misconduct and other boundary violations and insurance or fee problems. In 2010, for example, 38.5% of the cases opened for investigation involved sexual misconduct by psychologists, and another 15.4%, nonsexual dual relationships (APA, 2013d). In the prior year, 55.6% of the cases opened by the APA Ethics Committee involved sexual misconduct (APA, 2012a). Complaints related to improper child custody evaluations have occurred more commonly since 1995, but they still represent a fairly small percentage of the investigations. Many complaints are forwarded by a state licensing board after the psychologist lost his or her license to practice in that state. In such a circumstance, the APA Ethics Committee investigates and makes a separate ruling on the case. Because of rule changes that require complaints to be heard by regulatory bodies prior to consideration by the Canadian Psychological Association, that group has received only nine complaints since 2001 (Pope & Vasquez, 2011). Only one of these complaints, which was related to child assessment, resulted in adjudication (Pope & Vasquez, 2011).

The formal investigations opened by the ACA's Ethics Committee also center on violations related to the counseling relationship, such as sexual misconduct (e.g., ACA, 2013). The pattern is somewhat different for informal inquiries brought to the committee. Of the 2425 informal inquiries brought forward in 2009–2010, nearly half (49%) of these involved issues of confidentiality. ACA also notes a substantial increase in the number of complaints related to child custody evaluations (ACA, 2013). An analysis of the complaints to the National Association of Social Workers (NASW) and social work licensing boards shows frequent violations of dual relationship standards, both sexual and nonsexual (Boland-Prom, 2009; Strom-Gottfried, 1999, 2003). The most common violations appear to be relations to the general category of commitment to clients (NASW, n.d.).

The number of complaints filed each year is small when compared to the number of members of each organization. Data from 2011 show that APA has 84,339 members but opened only 141 cases between 2004 and 2009. The ACA, with membership of almost 45,000, received only nine complaints between 2009 and 2010 (ACA, 2011a). That means that in a five-year period, the number of active cases per member for the APA was 1 per 655, or 0.00167% of the membership; for the ACA, the percent of cases per member was 0.0002%. Phelan (2007) reported very few expulsions of members from professional associations for ethics violations. According to Phelan, in a 10-year period ending in 2005, only 17 marriage and family counselors were expelled from AAMFT, 21 social workers from NASW, four counselors from ACA, and 126 psychologists from APA.

Data from state licensing boards also suggest that very few mental health professionals are likely to have an ethics complaint filed against them. California, with more psychologists than any other state, launched 382 investigations of psychologists between 2004 and 2008, representing 2.4% of those with active licenses. National data parallel the California experience. The Association of State and Provincial Psychology Boards (ASPPB, 2012) reports an average of 227 disciplinary actions taken against licensed psychologists in the period between 2008 and 2012. Sexual misconduct was among the top four reasons for discipline in every year in that report. Neukrug, Milliken, and Walden (2001) indicate that less than 1% of the 103,600 licensed counselors in the United States experienced an ethics claim to a state board. In Ohio, for example, 30,067 counselors, social workers, and marriage and family therapists held active licenses in 2007, but between 2006 and 2008, only 91 professionals were disciplined by the board. The Canadian experience has been similar—between 1983 and 2006, 109 Canadian psychologists were disciplined by their provincial licensing boards (Pope & Vasquez, 2011). Currently, however, the Canadian Psychological Association rarely receives complaints because the organization entered into an agreement with licensing boards for the boards to adjudicate complaints.

The consensus in the professions is that these numbers substantially underestimate the number of violations that occur. Most authors suggest that the actual number of ethical violations is much higher (Biaggio, Duffy, & Staffelbach, 1998; Pope & Vasquez, 2011). Why is this so? Several reasons seem to operate: Clients do not know their rights or do not feel empowered enough to complain, or don't want to cost the professional a job in spite of the harm caused to them. In addition, frequently colleagues knowledgeable about the infraction do not want to get involved or fear reprisals if they do.

State licensing boards for counselors indicate that the most common complaint they receive is for negligence followed by an inappropriate dual relationship, that is, inappropriate contact between the client and the clinician outside of the therapeutic sessions (Wheeler & Bertram, 2012). Of all complaints, 53% are characterized as negligent practice. Annual data regarding the number of complaints per year are compiled by the American Association of State Counseling Boards (AASCB, 2008). These data show that in 2008 there were 81,309 licensed counselors in the United States and that 1065 complaints were filed against them, resulting in 397 individuals found guilty of violations, representing 0.49% of the population of licensed counselors. Certification boards that oversee addiction counselors indicate that complaints about sexual misconduct are most frequent, with claims of impairment related to substance use and practicing without a certificate given as the next most common types of complaints (St. Germaine, 1997). Not surprisingly, psychologists who practice in "high-risk" areas such as child custody evaluation, divorce, supervision, and other kinds of third-party evaluation experience the greatest frequency of complaints filed, though most are ultimately dismissed (Thomas, 2005). The research of Schoenfeld, Hatch, and Gonzales (2001) illustrates the distress and distraction that complaints cause all those accused, as well as the ways in which that distress is intensified when the professional is found to be at fault. The psychologists in their sample found guilty of one or more violations of state regulations suffered symptoms of depression, anxiety, sleep disturbance, disruption in interpersonal relationships, and medical problems. All the accused lost time at work and spent money to respond to the claim.

Financial Costs of Unethical Practice The ACA Insurance Trust reports that for the period between 1997 and 2001, negligent failure to prevent client suicide or other violent behavior emerged as the costliest category of legal claim, representing 55% of the dollars paid out but only 8% of the claims made. The most common type of claim arose from a breach of confidentiality; the second most common was from a boundary violation. More recent data from the ACA Insurance Trust show a nearly identical pattern of claims, with 53% of the claims for professional negligence (Wheeler & Bertram, 2012).

The 20-year pattern of malpractice claims against social workers shows a significant proportion of claims in two areas: incorrect treatment (18.6% of all claims) and sexual misconduct (18.5% of all claims) (Reamer, 1995). The largest settlements were focused on sexual misconduct, amounting to 41% of the total money paid in claims. As is true in other professions, a small percentage of social workers have malpractice claims filed against them. There are 155,000 current members of the National Association of Social Workers and 180,000 licensed social workers in the United States, but in the 20-year period ending in 1995, only 634 malpractice claims were filed (Reamer, 1995).

Legal and ethics claims against mental health professionals also have indirect costs. Those who are sanctioned may be excluded from insurance panels, lose hospital privileges, and experience higher malpractice premiums (Bricklin, Bennett, & Carroll, 2003).

Ethical Missteps in Day-to-Day Practice Because ethics complaints and malpractice claims do not provide data about unreported ethical violations, researchers have surveyed mental health professionals about misconduct they have engaged in or observed. The most common intentional violation of ethical standards described in this research involves breaches of confidentiality. In one major study of psychologists (Pope, Tabachnick, & Keith-Spiegel, 1987), 8% of the sample indicated that they had discussed a client by name with a friend. In that study, more than half admitted that they had also unintentionally violated confidentiality; however, a smaller study 14 years later found that fewer professionals (40%) admitted unintentional violations of confidentiality (Tubbs & Pomerantz, 2001). This change represents a statistically significant change from the 1987 data but still shows a high percentage of psychologists who have violated client privacy at least once.

Researchers have tried to determine which professionals are most vulnerable to misconduct. The goal is to find predictors of unethical behavior so that preventive strategies can be devised. However, studies that examine demographic characteristics of ethics violators have found only one significant correlate: Male therapists and educators are more likely to engage in sexual misconduct than are female therapists (Pope, 1994; Tabachnick, Keith-Spiegel, & Pope, 1991; Thoreson, Shaughnessy, Heppner, & Cook, 1993). (It is important to note, however, that several egregious cases of sexual misconduct have involved female therapists.) In addition, those who engage in sexual misconduct are likely to have done so more than once. No other clear pattern links other forms of unethical practice to demographic or educational characteristics. Even professionals honored for their scholarly and professional accomplishments, elected to high office in professional associations, and appointed to ethics and licensing boards are not immune from convictions for unethical conduct (Pope & Vasquez, 2011).

Client Threats of Legal Action What is the risk that a client who threatens a complaint will actually file one? Montgomery, Cupit, and Wimberley (1999) and Schoenfeld et al. (2001) reported that 71.5% of the psychologists they surveyed reported that they knew someone who experienced a complaint filed to a state licensing board. A much smaller percentage (14.4%) had been threatened with a complaint by a client, but in those cases only 39% of the clients had followed through with the filing of the complaint documents. Montgomery et al. also explored the respondents' experience with malpractice claims, with 38.7% of the sample indicating that they knew a professional against whom a lawsuit had been filed, but only 7.4% of them had personally experienced a threat of legal action against them. Slightly more than half of these threats (57.1%) resulted in the filing of a lawsuit. Others had no prior warning about the lawsuit. In all, 17 of 284 respondents had gone through a malpractice lawsuit, and 21 psychologists had dealt with a licensing board complaint. These figures are slightly higher than data from professional associations and licensing boards, suggesting that professionals may hear threats from upset clients and worried colleagues more frequently than those threats are acted upon.

Ethical Questions in Day-to-Day Practice Counselors and psychologists have been asked what kinds of ethical dilemmas they face in their work. The focus in this research is not on violations, but on the ethical questions that arise in the ordinary course of events. They report that the most frequent dilemma concerns confidentiality and its limits. Specifically, Pope and Vetter (1992) found that 18% of their sample listed this topic more than any other. The same pattern was evident in recent research by Cruz (2007) with a sample of mental health counselors and from Helbok, Marinelli, and Walls (2006) with a sample of rural psychologists. These findings are consistent with reports from the ethics committees regarding questions they receive from members (APA, 2013d; ACA, 2013). A study of British psychotherapists reported a similar pattern of results, with 73% of the sample indicating that they had experienced an ethical dilemma during the past year, most of which related to confidentiality (Lindsay & Clarkson, 1999). Emerging issues also appear frequently in queries to ethics committees. For example, in 2009, the APA Ethics Committee experienced inquiries regarding executive coaching, Internet-based services, and consultation to reality television (APA, 2010c).

Unfortunately, a national survey of ethical practices of counselors has not yet been published (although two national surveys of counselor beliefs about the ethics of a wide range of behaviors have been completed; see Gibson and Pope, 1993, and Neukrug and Milliken, 2011). A similar survey of ethics beliefs of human service professionals has also appeared in the literature (Milliken & Neukrug, 2009). Only the most notorious of ethical violations, sexual misconduct, has been studied with a sample of counselors. Thoreson et al. (1993) reported that 1.7% of the male counselors responding admitted sexual misconduct with clients during a professional relationship. However, when sexual intimacies with supervisees and former clients were included, the prevalence rate increased to 17%. In a parallel study, Thoreson, Shaughnessy, and Frazier (1995) found that less than 1% of female counselors reported a sexual relationship with a current client or supervisee, but 4.6% reported engaging in a sexual relationship with a former client or supervisee after the professional relationship ended. Obviously, more research is needed to understand the other forms of misconduct and the types of ethical issues counselors face regularly.

Unaware and at Risk for Unethical Practice

Some of the ethical problems that counselors and therapists encounter in their work are not in their awareness or are not identified as ethical problems. Two examples illustrate this situation. One is a study by Hansen et al. (2006) that examined the extent of psychologists' implementation of the competencies for multicultural practice developed by the professional associations. These researchers found that although 51% of those they surveyed self-identified as extremely competent on most dimensions of effective multicultural practice, only 14% of them reported actually practicing what they espoused, in spite of the fact that 36% of the clients they saw were likely to be from diverse backgrounds. Similarly, Pabian, Welfel, and Beebe (2009) found that although psychologists were confident that they understood their legal and ethical obligations with clients at high risk for violence to others, 76% of the respondents were inaccurate in the interpretations of those standards. In such circumstances, the potential for improper practice is high, but professionals seem ignorant of the ethical lapses they may be committing.

The Impact of Unethical Practice

Because it is the most prominent violation, much empirical evidence on the negative effects of specific violations is concentrated on sexual misconduct. Clients of therapists who have sexually exploited them show significant negative effects (Bouhoutsos, Holroyd, Lerman, Forer, & Greenberg, 1983; Brown, 1988; Lamb, Catanzaro, & Moorman, 2003; Nachamani & Somer, 2007; Williams, 1992). Some have committed suicide or undergone hospitalization, and most others suffer additional psychological distress in addition to their preexisting problem. Research demonstrates that these problems are not simply acute reactions that abate with time (Nachamani & Somer, 2007). Instead, they tend to be long lasting and can become chronic. Bates and Brodsky (1989) present a detailed case example of the devastating effects of sexual abuse. Moreover, an experience with one exploitive mental health professional tends to make clients wary of all mental health professionals and reluctant to seek professional help for mounting problems. Sometimes it shatters trust in those beyond the professional community, as this participant in Nachamani and Somer's (2007) study stated: " [I experience] ... a sense of having lost trust in humanity, if one cannot trust her therapist then who can one trust" (p. 11). In 15 states, criminal penalties (typically a felony charge) are imposed for sexual contact with clients (Haspel, Jorgenson, Wincze, & Parsons, 1997).

Unethical behavior also undermines the willingness of others who may benefit from counseling or psychotherapy to seek professional help. Its legal ramifications are substantial: Some clinicians end up in civil court in malpractice suits or in criminal court for libel, slander, or abuse (Crawford, 1994). The true frequency of violations is unknown, but it is probably a rare professional who practices an entire career without a single minor ethical misstep. Ignorance of ethical standards or distraction from the ethical dimensions of practice is likely to cause harm more frequently than can be seen from ethics committee reports or licensing board sanctions.

Some professionals appear to make a regular habit of such behavior (Pope et al., 1987). Others make real personal sacrifices to honor the values and standards of the profession and consistently protect clients. What follows in the other chapters in the book are ideas and practices to help you join the latter group.

ETHICS AND THE LAW

Both professional ethics and the law have a set of values at their core: For the law, they are the values the society agrees upon; for the professions, they are the central values that its members have endorsed. Professional ethics puts into operation those values in the way it defines the actions professionals ought to take in relation to each other, to those who seek their services, and to the public. Ethics codes are the standards adopted by national professional associations to govern the definitions of ethical behavior for their members. Also referred to as codes of conduct, they lay out the penalties for misbehavior. As noted, they also include comments about the profession's ethical ideals and central values. The most severe penalty a professional association can inflict is expulsion from membership.

In contrast, statutes that govern professional practice are enacted by state or federal legislatures, and case law is handed down by state or federal courts. Moreover, laws vary by jurisdiction, but codes apply to the whole membership of a national association. Even when all states and provinces have laws governing the same issue, such as those relating to child abuse and neglect, variations in the exact wording of the laws result in varying interpretations in different jurisdictions (Foreman & Bernet, 2000). Thus a behavior considered legal in one place may be illegal in another. Violations of the law carry stiffer penalties than codes, of course, ranging from limitations placed on one's license to practice and vulnerability to being sued, to criminal liability for the most egregious actions.

Ethical standards cover a wider range of behaviors than do laws and generally include introductory comments written to inspire professionals to do their best. In other words, they help define the "best practices" of a profession. Laws and regulations deal only with the "do's and don'ts" of practice and tend to limit their attention to a threshold level of behavior for professionals. State regulations and the codes of ethics may overlap considerably. For instance, most regulations indicate a duty to avoid discrimination, and codes contain similar wording. However, some areas of conflict appear between the guidelines of the code and any given state's regulations or court rulings (common law). The ethics codes indicate that mental health professionals are bound to make reasonable efforts to resolve the issue without violating ethical standards (see Standard 1.02 of the APA Code and Section I.1.c of the ACA Code).

Professionals are encouraged by their professional association to abide by the laws governing their profession. Usually, this guideline is easy to follow, but sometimes practitioners believe that what is truly in their client's best interest conflicts with the law. For example, Pope and Bajt (1988) found that 57% of psychologists intentionally violated a regulation because they believed compliance would injure their clients. The failure to comply with the law can be merely a part of the self-deception that takes place when other values compete with ethics, but on occasion, the practitioner may feel morally compelled to act according to what he or she perceives as a higher standard. Defying the law and/or code is an act of civil disobedience and is a serious matter. Those taking this path are still accountable to the state and the profession. Thus, any professional entertaining such an option should consider it carefully, consult with colleagues and an attorney, and be willing to suffer the legal penalty if discovered.

Another reason that laws and ethics sometimes conflict is that they derive from different philosophical perspectives or different cultural worldviews (Rowley & MacDonald, 2001). According to these authors, the law focuses on order, rationality, fact-finding, and stability, while mental health professions focus on the subjective needs of the individual and place the greater good in a secondary position if it is achieved at the expense of the individual. Professionals who understand these cultural differences are able to interact with the legal system and appreciate laws in a fuller way, though the essential conflict is not resolved even with this understanding.

How is a professional to proceed when he or she feels caught between conflicting ethical and legal obligations? Knapp, Gottlieb, Berman, and Handelsman (2007) offer a useful strategy for coping with this distressing circumstance in a reasoned way, suggesting careful reflection on personal values and consultation with a knowledgeable professional on ways to comply with the law that are least likely to be detrimental to ethical values involved. They also emphasize that because these conflicts occur from time to time in professional practice, clinicians are best advised to anticipate them to avoid unnecessary complications. As Franklin's old adage advises, "An ounce of prevention is worth a pound of cure."

WHEN PERSONAL AND PROFESSIONAL VALUES CONFLICT

No one enters mental health practice as a blank slate. All professionals have values and beliefs that have served as major influences on the way they have lived their lives and the choices they have made. Some of these values are rooted in a religious identity, while others derive from upbringing or educational experiences. Some are quite admirable, such as devotion to helping others or a commitment to be a responsible citizen in a democracy, and other are not, such as the belief that all people are self-interested and will take advantage of anyone who lets them. Many admirable beliefs and values are highly consistent with the values of the mental health professions, and integrating those values into one's identity as a professional happens smoothly. Other personal values may be at odds with professional values. For example, some professionals have a personal belief that they have a duty to share the message of their religion with others, or some may believe that no one has a right to make any decision that would hasten death. These beliefs conflict with the stance of the profession that endorses the principle of respect for autonomy; no practitioner has the right to proselytize or work to convince someone that his or her belief that it is morally acceptable to hasten death is wrong. Similarly, a trainee may have a deeply held conviction that homosexual activity is morally wrong. When these conflicts occur, they can be a source of substantial stress for the new professional. What is most important for the professional is to confront the conflict honestly and openly and to seek multiple sources of consultation and education. Such a process takes time and patience. In rare cases a novice may decide that the conflict is so great that this career is impossible. Most of the time, however, a way forward is found to make a commitment to professional values that does not negate personal beliefs. What is unacceptable and unethical is to feign agreement with professional values and continue in the work with the aim of imposing personal beliefs on clients.

POSITIVE ETHICS AND RISK MANAGEMENT

In recent years, mental health professionals have expressed increasing concern about being disciplined by licensing boards or being sued by clients. Presentations at professional conferences on avoiding malpractice claims are well attended. Special seminars on legal issues in counseling and psychotherapy have attracted thousands of participants eager to learn the path to a lawsuit-free work life. The first online course the ACA offered dealt with legal issues for counselors and ways to avoid malpractice claims. Although such knowledge is important, scholars repeatedly tell attendees that the single best way to avoid a malpractice suit or discipline by a licensing board is to know and follow the profession's code of conduct (e.g., Bennett, Bricklin, Harris, Knapp, VandeCreek, & Younggren, 2006). Acting ethically offers all professionals the best protection from legal problems. Consequently, in this book the focus is on the ethical guidelines of the professions. Legal issues are certainly addressed, but starting with legal issues implies more self-interest than devotion to client welfare. At its worst, risk management degenerates into viewing the client as an adversary who is aiming to take advantage of a professional at the first misstep; such a view is not only inaccurate, it is counterproductive and inconsistent with the profession's values. By aiming higher to understand the contents of the code and the reasons for its contents, practitioners and the general public gain both ethically and legally. This author concurs with the view of Handelsman, Knapp, and Gottlieb (2005) that a professional's exclusive focus on avoiding discipline is akin to giving attention only to the psychopathology in clients. It ignores the resources, ego strength, and sociocultural context in which clients' problems have arisen and thereby increases the chance for a negative outcome. It also ignores the good in the professional, who almost always wants to do the right thing and benefit the client. Handelsman et al. (2005) encourage the mental health professions to adopt a "positive ethics" philosophy that inspires professionals to aim for the ideal, identify ways to integrate their personal values with professional standards, broaden the discussion of ethics beyond avoiding risk to an emphasis on strategies to promote positive client change, and encourage the professional to understand the relationship between self-care and the capacity to act ethically in practice (pp. 736–737). That philosophy undergirds what follows in this book. Rules, laws, and codes must be fully understood to act responsibly, but they are the starting point of truly ethical action, not the end point.

SUMMARY

Because counselors, psychologists, and other mental health professionals boldly claim to be professional helpers, they have a duty to fulfill their promise of help and to protect the public from unscrupulous professionals. Acting ethically means being as competent as professed, considering the client's welfare as predominant, using power responsibly, and conducting oneself so as to enhance the reputation of the profession. When faced with an ethical dilemma, a counselor has four primary intellectual resources. The first is the literature from developmental psychology, which provides a framework for understanding the components of moral behavior. The second is the code of ethics of the professional association, which includes the standards one's colleagues have set for the profession. Next is the philosophical literature, which helps counselors understand the ethical principles and theories that underlie professional codes of conduct. Finally, counselors can rely on books and articles by their colleagues who are experts in professional ethics. These scholars discuss ethical dimensions of emerging types of practice and debate the critical controversial ethics topics. These resources can guide the professional through many agonizing dilemmas. Ultimately, however, individual professionals must take responsibility for their own actions and use their commitment to ethical values to carry out the action.

The documentation of unethical behavior shows that sexual contact with clients is a frequent violation for which counselors and psychologists are brought to ethics committees and court. Other kinds of multiple relationships that compromise objectivity also occur repeatedly. Incompetent practice, including violations of confidentiality, negligence in responses to suicidal clients, and inappropriate fees are also recurrent problems. There is little correlation between types of unethical practice and the characteristics of mental health professionals, with one exception. Male therapists are more likely than female therapists to engage in sexual misconduct with clients, former clients, students, and supervisees.

Codes of ethics and laws related to counseling and psychotherapy overlap substantially, but some conflicts arise. Moreover, laws seek to eliminate problematic behaviors, while codes also define good and desirable behaviors. Sometimes practitioners disregard state laws because they feel compliance would harm their clients. Such civil disobedience should be carried out only after serious deliberation and comprehension of the possible consequences. The best insurance for avoiding legal problems is knowledge of the codes of ethics and their underlying principles and acting in accordance with them. However, professional ethics is not a matter of minimal compliance with codes and laws; it represents a deep personal commitment to be a virtuous clinician who strives for the ethical ideal.

Discussion Questions*

1. Only a tiny proportion of unethical practice is reported. Why do you think this occurs? Does this low level of reporting hurt or benefit the professions?
2. What competing values may be operating when professionals decide to do less than they know they ought to do?
3. The reports of practitioners about the ethical dilemmas they most commonly face in their work do not match the ethical violations reported to ethics boards or used in civil suits. What do you think accounts for this discrepancy?
4. One alternative to the general ethics codes currently published by the mental health professions is a lengthier document that addresses ethics for specific kinds of practice. Should the professions retain the current form of the codes or change to another format to make them more relevant to specific settings? What advantages or disadvantages would accompany such a change?
5. When ethics codes conflict with laws, the codes indicate that the professional may follow the law. Do you agree with that position? Why or why not?

---

*Note to course instructors: The *Instructor's Guide* for this book includes other discussion questions, class exercises, cases, and multiple-choice and essay test items for this chapter.

6. How do you think the professions should deal with professionals who violate codes and laws because they have a different personal morality?
7. Have you ever known anyone who experienced an unethical action by a mental health professional? Was his or her response similar to those documented in the professional literature?
8. Based on what you have read, go back to the case of Annette and Archie to determine what you think Annette should do in this case. What do you notice about both your emotional and intellectual response to this case?

Recommended Readings

American Psychological Association (APA) Committee on Professional Practice and Standards. (2003). Legal issues in the professional practice of psychology. *Professional Psychology: Research and Practice, 34*, 595–600.

Bricklin, P., Bennett, B., & Carroll, W. (2003). *Understanding licensing board disciplinary procedures*. Washington, D.C.: American Psychological Association.

Fisher, C. B. (2012). *Decoding the ethics code: A practical guide for psychologists* (2nd ed.). Thousand Oaks, CA: Sage.

Freeman, S. J. (2000). *Ethics: An introduction to philosophy and practice*. Belmont, CA: Wadsworth.

Gibson, W. T., & Pope, K. S. (1993). The ethics of counseling: A national survey of certified counselors. *Journal of Counseling & Development, 71*, 330–336.

Gottlieb, M. C., Handelsman, M. M., & Knapp, S. (2013). A model for integrated ethics consultation. *Professional Psychology: Research and Practice, 44*, 307–313.

Herlihy, B., & Corey, G. (2014). *ACA ethical standards casebook* (7th ed.). Alexandria, VA: American Counseling Association.

International Union of Psychological Science. (2008). *Universal declaration of ethical principles for psychologists*. Retrieved from http://www.sagepub.com/cac6study/pdf/UniversalDeclaration.pdf.

Kahneman, D. (2011). *Thinking fast and slow*. New York, NY: Farrar, Straus & Giroux.

Keith-Spiegel, P. (2014). *Red flags in psychotherapy: Stories of ethics complaints and resolutions*. New York, NY: Routledge.

Kitchener, R. F., & Kitchener, K. S. (2012). Ethical foundations of psychology. In S. J. Knapp, M. C. Gottlieb, & L. D. VandeCreek (Eds.), *APA handbook of ethics in psychology,* Vol. 1 (pp. 3–42). Washington, D.C.: American Psychological Association.

Knapp, S., Gottlieb, M., Berman, J., & Handelsman, M. M. (2007). When laws and ethics collide: What should psychologists do? *Professional Psychology: Research and Practice, 38*, 54–59.

Neukrug, E. S., & Milliken, T. (2011). Counselors' perceptions of ethical behaviors. *Journal of Counseling & Development, 89*(2), 206–216.

Pope, K. S., Tabachnick, B. G., & Keith-Spiegel, P. (1987). Ethics of practice: The beliefs and behaviors of psychologists as therapists. *American Psychologist, 42*, 993–1006.

Tjeltveit, A. C. (1999). *Ethics and values in psychotherapy*. New York, NY: Routledge.

Truscott, D., & Crook. K. J. (2004). *Ethics for the practice of psychology in Canada*. Edmonton, Alberta: University of Alberta Press.

Wheeler, A. M. N., & Bertram, B. (2012). *The counselor and the law: A guide to legal and ethical practice* (6th ed.). Alexandria, VA: American Counseling Association.

Additional Online Resources

American Counseling Association. Ethics Knowledge Center: http://counseling.org/knowledge-center/ethics.

Ethics Codes & Practice Guidelines for Assessment, Therapy, Counseling, & Forensic Practice: http://kspope.com/ethcodes/index.php.

Association for Practical and Professional Ethics: http://www.ethicsweb.ca/resources/bioethics/institutes.html.

United Kingdom Clinical Ethics Network: http://www.ukcen.net.

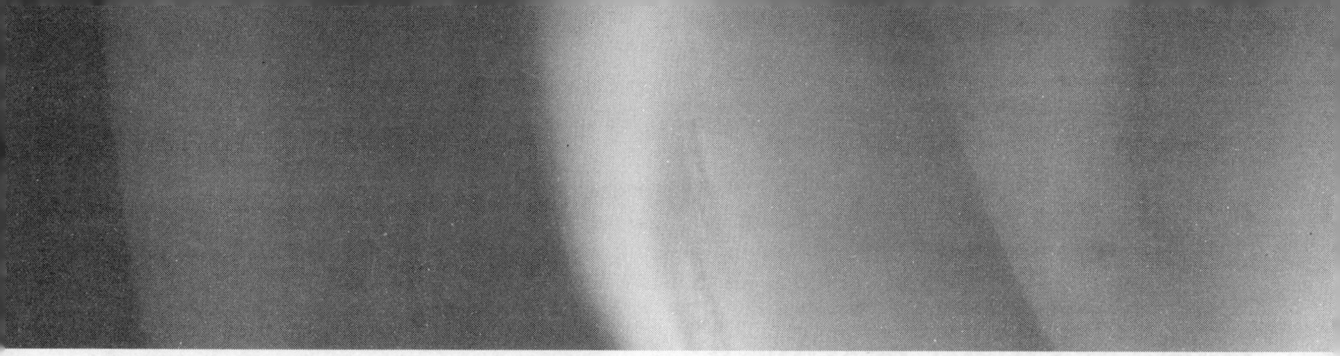

A Model for Ethical Practice

CHAPTER 2

Using Resources to Enhance Individual Judgment and Ethical Resolve

The first chapter explored the importance of ethical standards in counseling and psychotherapy as the representation of the profession's common moral vision and a manifestation of its endorsement of its public responsibility to be of service. Chapter 1 emphasized the critical role of virtue and commitment to the values of the profession as the foundation upon which judgment rests and highlighted consultation and consideration of the social context as essential components of ethical action. The first chapter also identified resources to guide professionals to responsible ethical decisions and described common ethical pitfalls. Chapter 2 presents a systematic 10-step model of ethical decision making that incorporates intellectual, emotional, scoiocultural, and consultative aspects of ethical choices. This model is most useful when ethical questions arise, but it also has substantial value in identifying the broader ethical issues inherent in the context in which one works. Usually ethical decision-making models are viewed as reactive to problems (e.g., Verges, 2010), but they need not be. A model of decision making can and should be proactive and has its best use as a preventive of problems. A new professional can use this model as an aid to identifying the ethical issues likely to emerge in a new work or training setting.

The most complex dilemmas require completing each step, but the more obvious questions can be resolved with an abbreviated approach. Although the model begins with the cognitive components of ethical choices, its steps are embedded in the conviction that a truly ethical decision occurs only when a professional possesses a personal commitment to the ethical values of the profession (i.e., an ethical identity), integrates the social and cultural context from which the ethical question arises, copes with the emotional stress associated with many ethical issues, and is resolute enough to implement an ethical choice. In addition, the professional recognizes that no ethical decision is made in isolation and that every ethical decision is necessarily grounded in consultation with others—either colleagues, supervisors, or scholars and researchers of professional ethics by their reading of the professional literature. The chapter begins by clarifying the varying forms of ethical reasoning that make up one of the major components of ethical behavior. Ethics at its foundation requires thinking, so that is where we start.

FORMS OF ETHICAL REASONING

Kitchener (1984) has suggested that there are two distinct forms of ethical reasoning: intuitive and critical-evaluative. The following sections define these terms and illustrate their roles in ethical decision making.

Intuitive Ethical Judgments

When people make most moral or ethical judgments, they tend to be spontaneous and motivated by emotion or by a person's ordinary moral sense. In applications to human decision making in general, Kahneman (2011) referred to this phenomenon as "thinking fast"—a crucial system for operating in the world, of course, but one that tends to use metaphor and association to make a judgment and may not fully account for the complexity of the situation. Recent research from neuroscience and genetics also suggests a fundamental biological and evolutionary component of ethical behavior (Bloom, 2013). Anderson and Handelsman (2010) refer to this form of ethics as the "ethics of origin." According to Kitchener and Anderson (2011), a person's ordinary intuitive moral sense derives from past learning about being moral and from a person's character and level of cognitive complexity. Rarely are the reasons for intuitive moral judgments in full conscious awareness. For example, when reporters interview people who risked their lives to save others, these heroes are notably inarticulate about what made them act courageously. Many say that the thought of doing anything else never entered their minds. Others say they didn't think; they just acted. If pressed, they may refer to their upbringing or spiritual beliefs as a motivation, but virtually no one provides a philosophical justification for his or her heroism, even after the fact. To apply Rest's model of morality (1983, 1994), these heroes had immediate moral sensitivity, used good intuitive moral reasoning, had strong moral motivation, and were resolute in following through on their commitment to do what they sensed was right.

Needless to say, not all people have such admirable moral intuitions. Those who walk away from people in trouble also tend to be inarticulate about their motivation. For example, many soldiers who witnessed the abuse of detainees at the Abu Ghraib prison in Iraq failed to intervene or report the abuse to senior officers and offered no justification for their behavior (Hersch, 2004). Moral insensitivity is not limited to the general citizenry or the military, however. The history of the helping professions offers ample testimony to the problematic nature of some professionals' ethical intuitions. For example, in the 1960s and 1970s, some mental health professionals (e.g., McCartney, 1966) argued that sexual intimacies with clients were desirable actions for therapists and that sex with clients constituted a legitimate *treatment*. Similarly, in the mid-nineteenth century a new medical diagnosis called *drapetomania* was coined by Samuel Cartwright, a Louisiana physician, and added to the psychiatric nomenclature. It meant "running-away-from-home disease" and was used to diagnose slaves who tried to run from their masters (Szasz, 1971). By this definition, any slave who chose freedom over enslavement was considered mentally ill. The treatment Cartwright recommended was to beat the slaves who were caught trying to run away. In these and other cases, professionals lacked ethical sensitivity or rationalized an unethical act as ethical. Much of this lack of ethical sensitivity stems from cultural norms and political or social pressures at the time. Thus, relying on the uneven and unpredictable intuitions of some professionals to provide guidance for a responsible ethical choice has proved inadequate to protect the public welfare. As Anderson and Handelsman (2010) point out, sometimes poor intuitive judgments stem from an inaccurate or incomplete understanding of the facts of the situation. In this circumstance, the individual's process of responding to the ethical issue has become a conscious process, and not entirely intuitive, but is flawed because of deficiencies in the analysis of the particulars of the case. Consequently, our profession demands that we be able to *justify* our ethical decisions based on careful consideration of the facts involved as well as consistency with professional values and standards for practice. This is not simply a matter of finding reasons to support our intuitions and impulses, but rather an openness to discover what action is best through a comprehensive process that is both intellectual and emotional (Truscott, 2013). It is important to note that the view that intuition is insufficient in itself for making ethical decisions does not imply that it should be ignored. Ethical decision making should take into account an individual's immediate ethical impulse along with contextual factors such as culture and interpersonal relationships (Betan & Stanton, 1999). What is likely to be problematic is a reliance on intuitive judgment to the exclusion of a more deliberate process of judgment and consultation. Just as there are heroes in ordinary settings who rely on their moral intuition to make courageous decisions, so, too, are there times when the intuitions of mental health professionals are just as admirable. Unfortunately, those occurrences are insufficiently predictable to be reliable.

Critical-Evaluative Ethical Judgments

To make adequate ethical decisions on a reliable basis, Kitchener and Anderson (2011) recommend deliberately analyzing the ethical issue in a process that includes considering professional standards and the wisdom of ethics scholars and colleagues, followed by intensive problem solving based on ethical principles and consultation as needed. This analysis must also be grounded in a commitment to the moral vision and the virtues that the profession values (Cohen & Cohen, 1999; Hill, 2004b; Meara et al., 1996; Radden & Sadler, 2010). Otherwise, the process degenerates into an empty intellectual exercise. It cannot be overstated that ethical practice is not just about what counselors and therapists think but also about who they are (Meara et al., 1996). Nevertheless, thinking carefully about ethical questions is essential for those fully committed to ethical values.

Kitchener (1984) named this method of analysis the *critical-evaluative* level of justifying an ethical decision. When ethical issues are critically examined in this way, the public is less vulnerable to the idiosyncratic intuitions of a given professional. Preliminary evidence suggests that the use of ethical justification improves clinical decision making more than other pedagogies (Dinger, 1997). The following model of ethical decision making builds upon the work of Kitchener (1984) and Kitchener and Anderson (2011) and provides a step-by-step method of deliberating about ethical issues. It both guides the individual's thinking process and encourages a consultative and contextual approach to resolving ethical questions. Figure 2.1 graphically represents the model.

A MODEL FOR ETHICAL DECISION MAKING

At first glance, this model seems to suggest that ethical decision making is unavoidably time consuming and that at the first hint of an ethical issue, a professional must immediately proceed through all the steps of this elaborate process. A model that required so much time would be neither realistic nor useful. Counselors and therapists do not regularly have extended periods of time in which to deliberate about ethical problems, nor are their colleagues always immediately available for extensive consultation. Some ethically sensitive situations require immediate action. For example, a school counselor who sees a teacher supplying correct answers to students during a standardized test must act quickly, or the test results will be invalid. Similarly, when a child psychologist learns that a 13-year-old client is about to meet an adult she met on a social networking website on a "date," there is little time to deliberate about how to intervene because of the immediate risk to the child. Even when a professional need not make an instantaneous decision, there is still pressure to act expeditiously. How do professionals apply the decision-making model in such situations? Quite simply, they comply by having done their ethics homework and by prior integration of the ethical values of the profession. In addition to a firmly grounded commitment to ethical ideals, counselors and therapists must have sufficient knowledge to arrive at a decision based on more than intuition. They advance the process by being well studied in the ethics codes and guidelines and by having prior practice in applying the standards to real (or realistic) situations. Prudent professionals keep a copy of the code within easy reach. Similarly, when working in specific settings such as addictions treatment or inpatient care, clinicians expedite decision making by keeping up with the ethics literature for their setting. Experience in using a systematic process or model with hypothetical cases also hastens the process (see Cottone [2012] for a review of this model and eight other systems for ethical decision making).

There is a second benefit to this preparation and experience. Confronting an ethical dilemma is a highly stressful experience. For example, Holland and Kilpatrick (1991) found that a sample of social workers experienced "a poignant sense of loneliness or isolation in their struggle with moral questions" (p. 140). Figuring out how to respond to the dilemma of a teenager who now asserts he was lying about prior disclosures of sexual abuse, for example, is both intellectually challenging and emotionally agonizing. The potential harm from a wrong choice is obvious, and practitioners feel tremendous anxiety about their responsibility in such situations. Comprehension of ethics standards, familiarity with the literature, and background in sorting out other complicated dilemmas all help to keep the stress manageable and let the decision making proceed with a clearer head.

For counselors, a final reason for adopting a formal model of ethical decision making is that the ACA Code requires the use of such a procedure in its Purpose

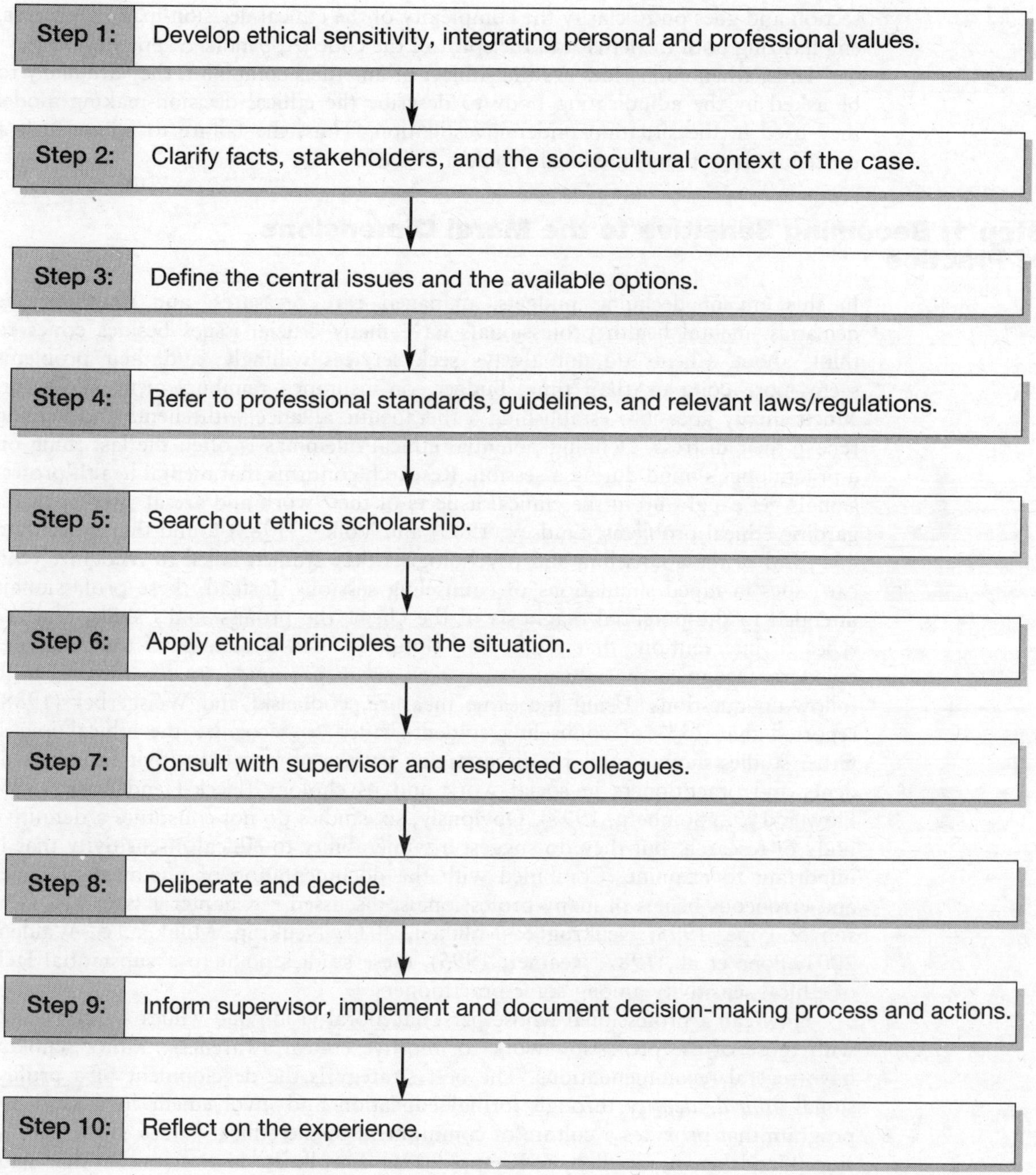

Figure 2.1 A Model for Ethical Decision Making

© Cengage Learning 2013

section and goes on to clarify the complexity of the ethical decision-making process, emphasizing both the letter and the spirit of the code (Appendix A, pp. 490–491).

Thus, when counselors are the subject of an ethics complaint, they are likely to be asked by the adjudicating body to describe the ethical decision-making model they used in the situation under investigation. Thus, the failure to adopt such a procedure represents an ethical problem in itself.

Step 1: Becoming Sensitive to the Moral Dimensions of Practice

In this era of declining budgets, managed care pressures, and multiple role demands, mental health professionals have many crucial issues besides ethics to think about. Clients do not always seek services willingly, and their problems seem more complex than time, budget, or insurance reimbursement allow for. Much energy goes into establishing a therapeutic alliance with clients and helping relieve their distress. Defining potential ethical dilemmas is often the last thing on a practitioner's mind during a session. Research confirms that mental health professionals get caught up in the clinical aspects of their work and are at risk for disregarding ethical problems. Lindsey (1985) and Volker (1983) found that more than one-third of the counselors and psychologists they studied failed to recognize ethical issues in taped simulations of counseling sessions. Instead, these professionals attended to the potential diagnosis of the client, the professional's skills, and the types of interventions that might be helpful. In fact, a quarter of their samples failed to recognize the ethical issues *even when prompted by the researcher* in follow-up questions. Using the same measure, Podbelski and Weisgerber (1988) reported that 25% of counseling students failed to recognize the ethical issues. Other studies show a similarly discouraging pattern of moral sensitivity among students and practitioners in social work and psychology (Fleck-Henderson, 1995; Flower, 1992; Somberg, 1997). Obviously, six studies do not constitute a definitive body of research, but they do suggest a vulnerability to ethical insensitivity that is important to examine. Combined with the documentation of unethical practices and erroneous beliefs of many professionals, discussed in Chapter 1 (see, e.g., Gibson & Pope, 1993; Neukrug & Milliken, 2011; Neukrug, Milliken, & Walden, 2001; Pope et al., 1987; Reamer, 1995), these studies point to a substantial lack of ethical sensitivity among some practitioners.

How can a professional whose personal moral vision and values are consistent with those of the profession work to improve ethical awareness? Ethics scholars have several recommendations. The best strategy is the development of a professional *ethical identity* through formal education and involvement in a graduate program that provides a culture of commitment to the ethical values of the profession (Handelsman, Gottlieb, & Knapp, 2005). Enrollment in courses that deal with both the content of professional standards and processes for moral decision making heightens the likelihood that trainees will be aware of the ethical dimensions of their practice (Dinger, 1997; Eberlein, 1987; Wilson & Ranft, 1993). Educators obviously endorse this view; the number of ethics courses available over the past 30 years has increased dramatically (Hill, 2004a; Urofsky & Sowa, 2004; Vanek, 1990; Wilson & Ranft, 1993). When ethics courses include a pedagogy that transcends indoctrination into the rules of the profession and offers students the space to integrate professional values into their own belief system, they are more likely to be effective in promoting ethical sensitivity (Handelsman et al., 2005; Welfel, 2012). After completing graduate school, professionals foster ethical sensitivity through continuing education and dialogue with colleagues. The perspectives of colleagues counterbalance the professional's sometimes one-sided view. In fact, consultation about ethical questions appears to be the preferred mode of seeking help when school counselors and community-based professionals are grappling with an ethical issue (Bombara, 2002; Cottone, Tarvydas, & House, 1994). Next, as noted, prior experience in dealing with ethical dilemmas seems to make a professional more alert when a new ethical issue arises. Therefore, much ethics training focuses heavily on case analysis and class discussion (Welfel, 2012).

Professionals also need insight into their own values and motivation for entering the mental health field. Ethical sensitivity assumes not only knowledge and background in professional ethics but also personal principles and philosophy consistent with the profession. A person motivated exclusively by narrow self-interest has little likelihood of achieving ethical sensitivity. Consistently doing the right thing demands altruistic motives and resoluteness in the face of obstacles to good conduct. As Jordan and Meara (1990) suggest, an ethical professional is first a person of virtue committed to social service and social justice. People at the start of their careers ought to frankly assess their reasons for choosing this profession, and those at mid-career should periodically conduct the same kind of self-analysis. Experienced clinicians need to take care so that they avoid burnout and emotional exhaustion from their work, as these factors diminish real empathy for clients and put professionals at risk for inadvertent violations or outright disregard of professional standards. The ethical standards of the ACA (Section A.4.b) and APA (Principle A) both highlight the importance of not allowing personal values or emotional distress to compromise service to clients.

Finally, a shift in one's mental set about ethics is needed. Because so much of what is presented about ethical violations deals with sensational cases, many new professionals mistakenly conclude that only those who are unscrupulous or naive act unethically. As Hill (2004b) notes, mental health professionals sometimes view ethics as a secondary, peripheral concern with rules and regulations, when ethics is, in reality, the core of the life of a professional's work life and professional identity. A corollary misperception is that ethical dilemmas rarely occur, but if they do, they are immediately visible. All of these conclusions are mistaken. Instead, practitioners need to recognize the commonness, complexity, and subtleties of ethical dilemmas. Without vigilance, even well-intentioned and fundamentally virtuous professionals can sometimes end up harming clients. As a practical step to heighten ethical sensitivity, clinicians need to establish a protocol for examining the ethical dimensions of every intake and ongoing session. The simple step of adding a question about potential ethical issues to the intake form or the outline for case notes may help alert the professional to issues he or she might otherwise overlook. Similarly, a regular consultation network is critical to responsible practice. It is naïve in this stressful profession to imagine that we don't need the support of other professionals.

A corollary of sensitivity to the ethical issues that clients and colleagues may present is sensitivity to ethical issues that may emerge from the personal history and current experience of the professional. A professional who witnessed episodes of domestic violence between her parents, for example, may have a powerful emotional reaction to a report like Archie's, and would need to take extra steps to ensure that her response to the case was not unduly affected by her own history. Similarly, a counselor whose childhood was harmed by his parents' nasty divorce may have difficulty being objective and fair with an adult client seeking to end a marriage and feeling great anger at a spouse.

Step 2: Identify the Relevant Facts, Sociocultural Context, and Stakeholders

Once a professional knows that a situation with ethical dimensions exists, has taken steps to manage the associated anxiety, and has consultation resources available as needed, he or she must organize relevant case information, including the cultural and social context in which the case emerges. Consider Archie's case from Chapter 1:

The Case of Archie and Annette

Archie, a 17-year-old, tells his high school counselor in a counseling session that the claim he made of sexual abuse by his stepfather is not true. He now says that he fabricated the story because he wanted his mother to end her relationship with his stepfather, who has punched her many times.

Archie made the statements about abuse to his coach, who reported them to authorities. As his counselor, Annette was then informed of the report and began individual counseling with Archie. They have had four sessions.

Annette's initial task here is to ask herself whether all relevant information about the particulars of the situation is available. Fact-finding is the foundation upon which all subsequent reasoning is built. Neglect of pertinent facts can lead a professional (and those with whom he or she is consulting) to a mistaken line of reasoning or unsatisfactory ethical outcome. In the case of Archie, here are some of the relevant facts Annette should attempt to learn:

- What are Archie's wishes about the confidentiality of his disclosure? Has he discussed his retraction of the charges with anyone else?
- What is Archie's current emotional health, and what is his mental health history?
- What is his history of making responsible choices about other matters; that is, what is his intellectual maturity level?
- Has an investigation been initiated by children's services? If so, what is the current status of that investigation?
- What is the current status of Archie's relationship with his mother and stepfather? What can Archie reveal about their current level of distress?
- How strong is Archie's counseling relationship with Annette, and how much influence does she have on his thinking and behavior?

- Are there other stakeholders in addition to Archie, his mother, stepfather, and biological father? Are there siblings or other relatives living in the home, for example, a disabled grandparent, who are also affected by these events?
- What is known about Archie's cultural and social background and worldview that may be influential to the ethical options for this situation or his perception of the situation (Garcia, Cartwright, Winston, & Borzuchowska, 2003)?

A great deal of this information comes from the client or from the counselor's assessment of the client. In this case, Annette is likely to obtain reasonably reliable responses from Archie about most of these questions and can rely on her professional judgment and prior therapeutic contact with the client for additional data. In the event that important information is not available, the counselor should explore avenues to obtain that information without compromising client confidentiality. The next important aspect of the delineation of important facts is the identification of other stakeholders in the situation in addition to the client. A stakeholder is defined as a person or group of people likely to be helped or harmed by the counselor's actions (Garcia et al., 2003; Treppa, 1998). Whenever working with a minor, parents or guardians are crucial stakeholders because they are ultimately responsible for the welfare of their child. The welfare of the other stakeholders cannot take priority over the welfare of the client, but the goal of the professional is to consider possible ways in which the welfare of all stakeholders can be protected. The obvious stakeholders here are Archie's mother, stepfather, siblings (if any), and other members of the household.

Step 3: Define the Central Issues in the Dilemma and the Available Options

Once the facts of the case, its sociocultural context, and the relevant stakeholders are sufficiently clear, the professional attempts to classify the fundamental ethical issues or the type of ethical problem involved. In this case, the main issues deal with (1) the promotion of the welfare of the client when his best interest is not clear, (2) the degree of confidentiality a school counselor owes a minor when the welfare of other family members is also at stake, and (3) the question of the counselor's legal obligation to communicate with child welfare professionals investigating the abuse claim if a client's subsequent counseling disclosures do not constitute claims of abuse. Some situations may present even more ethical issues. Defining the broad type of problem allows a professional to utilize the ethics codes and the literature more effectively and access prior training on the topic. Because ethical questions do not arise in a vacuum, professionals should also consider how the context of the situation may affect the decision (Treppa, 1998). For example, Annette's role obligations as a school counselor should be a component of thinking about the issue. Annette must also reflect on her own assumptions, values, and sociocultural history to be certain that the assessment of the facts that she has just conducted is not arbitrarily influenced by her beliefs or her social privilege as an educated person in a position of authority. All such decision making is socially constructed, and it is important for professionals to be fully aware so that no judgment is made in isolation from its interactional and cultural context (Burke, Harper, Rudnick, & Kruger, 2007; Cottone, 2001, 2012).

Next, the professional needs to brainstorm the potential courses of action that come to mind—naming options without censorship. Evaluating and eliminating options comes later. This brainstorming is important to ensure that the analysis goes beyond the one or two choices that might emerge from a professional's ordinary moral sense. In this process, professionals should acknowledge which options are intuitively appealing and recognize the ways in which their personal moral values are influencing their decision making. Treppa (1998) advises that mental health professionals actively challenge their own assumptions and preferences to improve their openness to all reasonable alternatives. Groopman's (2007) advice to medical patients to ask, "What else might this be?" can be applied to the process of ethical decision making as well, with a slight modification—"What else might be ethical?" On a practical level, this may mean consciously evaluating how emotionally difficult each alternative may be to implement because of competing values, environmental pressures, or personal moral philosophy. As Hill (2004b) recommends, a professional facing an ethical dilemma is wise to ask, "What would this action say about me as a person as well as a counselor?" In this case, Annette's alternatives are as follows:

- Tell no one and maintain confidentiality, letting the client decide what to do next.
- Inform Archie that she needs to break confidentiality to tell his parents, even if he is uncomfortable with this option.
- Call the investigator from children's services in the case, and tell him or her about Archie's disclosure, even if Archie is uncomfortable with this action.
- Encourage Archie to tell either his mother or the investigator himself, but do not disclose the information without Archie's consent.
- Advise Archie that continued counseling is contingent upon his disclosing this information himself or allowing her to do so.
- Wait until the next appointment to see whether Archie maintains or withdraws his retraction or his request for confidentiality, and then decide about a breach of confidentiality.

Thus, at the end of step 3, the professional has broadly defined the type of ethical dilemma and listed the potential responses available. Further reading and consultation may produce additional options, of course, but at least a workable list now exists. In Archie's case, Annette also acknowledges that her worry about legal problems, her personal moral intuition, and ordinary moral values lead her to want to disclose this information to Archie's mother or the social worker investigating the case. She decides to postpone acting on this intuition until she has studied the issue further (a demonstration of the virtue of prudence) and talked it over with her network of consultants. Evaluating the merits of each alternative takes place through the next several steps in the process. Professionals who have any doubt that they have developed an adequate list of alternatives are wise to share their ideas with trusted colleagues to ensure that they have not overlooked something important. In virtually all cases, consultation is valuable in this process. Keeping a written record of the alternatives is obviously useful, as is documenting the reasoning process, the results of the consultation, and actions taken throughout the steps (see step 9 for more on documentation).

Step 4: Refer to Professional Ethical Standards, Guidelines, and Relevant Laws and Regulations

Once a person identifies an ethical issue and his or her options, the next step is to refer to the code of ethics to determine how it applies. If Annette is a member of more than one professional association, she should consult more than one code. As Chapter 1 discusses, the code states that confidentiality is important but is limited by laws, by Archie's status as a minor, and by situations of serious and foreseeable harm. Please review the ACA Code, Section B.1, in Appendix A, p. 498).

The code provides Annette with relevant questions to ask, such as, "Would revealing Archie's retraction be a warranted or unwarranted disclosure? Does this situation constitute serious and foreseeable danger, and if so, to whom? Is it appropriate to include the parents, and is it in Archie's best interest to do so?" Ultimately, though, the code sets only the path for her thinking and does not offer a resolution to the dilemma. For example, the code does not define what foreseeable and serious danger really means. Because she is working as a school counselor, Annette should also refer to the *Ethical Standards for School Counselors* (ASCA, 2010). ASCA standards echo the provisions of the ACA Code, emphasizing the primacy of her duty to the confidentiality of the student as well as her responsibilities to parents (see Appendix C, Section A.2). These codes also suggest that whatever she decides, she needs to keep Archie informed and to seek his assent if possible. Ultimately, though, neither the ACA nor the ASCA Code offer a full resolution, so this counselor must proceed to the next step of the decision-making model to determine what is most ethical (see Appendix C, p. 560, for the ASCA Code).

Fortunately, for many other problems review of the codes does provide a reliable answer. The following case illustrates an ethical problem that can be resolved at this stage:

The Case of Yolanda and Justine

Yolanda, a supervisor of counseling psychology interns, has been supervising Justine, an exceptionally skilled and mature trainee, for several months. In various conversations during internship meetings, Yolanda has discovered that she and Justine share a number of mutual interests. Both play the cello and ride horses in their free time. Yolanda wants to ask this intern to audition for the open cello seat in the community orchestra to which she belongs and to join her in horseback riding one weekend soon. She wonders if it would be ethical to offer Justine these invitations.

Yolanda shows ethical sensitivity insofar as she recognizes that the behavior she is entertaining has an ethical dimension (step 1). Organizing the facts of this case is fairly simple because this dilemma came from Yolanda, not from an interaction with a client or colleague. Three facts are clear from step 2. First, Justine is under her supervision (along with other interns she is supervising) and will be until the end of the academic year. Second, in addition to the verification of successful completion of internship at the end of the year, Justine may also need reference letters from Yolanda from time to time. Third, Yolanda is unlikely to supervise this intern again or be in any other evaluative role with her. Justine is the primary stakeholder, but the other interns and the counseling center also have a stake in this supervisory relationship. The case gives no information about the cultural and social variables involved, but it would be helpful to explore whether some shared cultural or social background is an influence in Yolanda's interest in this social contact with Justine. To complete the consideration of the content of step 2, Yolanda then identifies the category of ethical issue involved. She thinks these outside contacts might represent an inappropriate relationship with her intern, a kind of multiple relationship, and has identified three possible courses of action (step 3). The first is to go ahead with the invitations. The second option is to withhold the invitations until Justine's internship is completed, and the last is to ask Justine to do just one of the two activities with her.

The fourth step in the process is for Yolanda to refer to the ethics code to weigh the merits of her options. As mentioned in Chapter 1, Standard 3.05, of the APA Code (2010a) stipulates that a multiple relationship should be avoided when a reasonable evaluation would indicate a risk of inadequate service related to a lack of objectivity, competence, or effectiveness. In the absence of such risks, a multiple relationship is permitted.

This section of the code has no unmistakable directive but suggests that if Yolanda were to extend the invitations, she would be at risk for reducing her effectiveness as Justine's supervisor and for impairing her objectivity about the intern's work. Some risk of harm or exploitation is also possible. On this basis, Yolanda also reasons that riding together would be the more problematic of the two situations because it would set up a personal relationship that blurs the boundaries in their supervisory relationship. Inviting this intern to audition for the orchestra is a less obvious violation because there is no guarantee that the supervisee would pass the audition, and no one-on-one relationship would necessarily follow if Justine were accepted. However, belonging to the same orchestra could be uncomfortable for Justine, and if the invitation to audition came from Yolanda, Justine might feel she had no choice but to audition and that refusing her supervisor's invitation could negatively impact her internship evaluation. If Justine learned of the orchestra opening in some other way and independently decided to try out, there would be no inherent ethical problem with belonging to the same arts organization, provided Yolanda did not develop a separate personal relationship with her during the internship.

Because Yolanda is also a member of ACA, she consults that ethics code and finds guidance in Section F.3.a. She must ensure that she will not act in an exploitive way and that her judgment will not be impaired. She must also understand the risks and benefits of the boundary extension and avoid a nonprofessional relationship that may compromise supervision. There is little doubt that regular personal contact with Justine at the riding stables would constitute a nonprofessional relationship.

Having reviewed both codes, Yolanda decides to refrain from inviting Justine to join her in either social activity because doing so makes it harder for her to objectively evaluate the student's work and sends confusing messages to other interns. Moreover, Justine might misunderstand the invitations and may feel awkward in supervision. For these reasons, Yolanda decides she will consider a social relationship with this (or any other) intern only when she no longer has an evaluative role in the intern's professional development.

This case illustrates how carefully interpreting the code of ethics and consulting related codes can help a mental health professional resolve an ethical problem. When a professional is so familiar with the codes that he or she can quickly locate the appropriate section, a decision can be made without delay. Then the professional may skip steps 5–7 of the model and can move directly to the last three steps as appropriate.

The codes of the ACA, APA, and other mental health professions differ somewhat. This divergence sometimes presents a problem to those belonging to more than one organization. For example, the APA forbids all sexual contact with any former clients for at least two years after the termination of services (Standard 10.07), while the 2014 ACA Code, Section A.5.c, forbids sexual contact with former clients for at least five years after professional services have been completed. Professionals motivated by narrow self-interest might decide to review the codes to find the least demanding standard and follow that one. Such a rationale is shortsighted and ignores the aspirational parts of the codes and the fundamental values of the profession. The wisest course is to abide by the strictest mandate. All members are obliged to follow the dictates of the organizations to which they belong.

Professionals also need to be aware of other official statements of ethics committees. From time to time, ethics committees publish special guidelines to inform members about emerging ethical issues or to respond to an issue brought to the committee by many members. In 2001, for example, the APA published *Guidelines for Test User Qualifications* (Turner, DeMers, Fox, & Reed, 2001) to address questions about the training and background that are essential for the competent use of psychological tests. More recently, it issued its *Guidelines for Psychological Practice with Girls and Women* (APA, 2007a) and the *Guidelines for the Practice of Telepsychology* (2013a) to help psychologists practice responsibly. An extensive list of special guidelines and statements is included in Appendix D of this book.

Mental health professionals employed by agencies and institutions may also need to consult with employer policy manuals for statements regarding professional ethics. Manuals may provide additional guidance about confidentiality, informed consent, record keeping, and procedures for reporting unethical conduct by coworkers (Hansen & Goldberg, 1999). Institutional policies do not take precedence over ethics codes or regulations, but they offer additional guidance to clinicians in circumstances where the codes and regulations are ambiguous or nonspecific.

Finally, all codes direct members to act in accordance with existing laws as long as they don't violate human rights. This means that the professional must refer to relevant federal and state statutes and regulations governing an issue. Case law, the rulings of courts in cases that come to trial, may also apply. (One benefit of membership in a state or national professional organization is that those groups monitor legal developments and inform members of changes in statutes and case law that affect practice). The laws in Yolanda's state may make no reference to a social relationship between a supervisor and an intern. However, the state's regulations governing licensed counselors may specify that all should abide by the ACA Code. Currently, 17 states have embedded the ACA Code into state regulations, and 3 other states refer to them and advise licensees to use them (see http://counseling.org/docs/ethics/aca-code-of-ethics-2010-%2812-22-09%29.pdf?sfvrsn=2 for a list of these states).

Archie and Annette Revisited Annette's next task in ethical decision making is to explore whether any legal rulings or statutes are relevant to her actions. This is particularly important because the laws about confidentiality with minors differ from jurisdiction to jurisdiction. Moreover, even within the same state or province, statutes and court opinions about confidentiality with minors may be conflicting. Of particular relevance are the laws related to reporting child abuse and the right of minors to have secrets in therapy that are not disclosed to parents. Also important are the legal issues related to a counselor's responsibility when a client reveals a false claim of abuse. In a number of situations, both the law and the codes are not definitive or are mute on a subject. When that happens, the professional should move to step 5 in the process. In most situations when laws and codes conflict, professionals are not required to violate laws to comply with a code. (See http://www.apa.org/news/press/releases/2010/02/ethics-code.aspx for a discussion of the modifications APA made to its ethics code on this issue in light of the involvement of some psychologists in military interrogations that violated detainee human rights. Also see Stone and Zirkel, 2010, for a discussion of aspects of such conflict for school counselors.)

Step 5: Search Out the Relevant Ethics Literature

This step involves consulting the professional literature that explores the thinking of other clinicians and scholars who have grappled with the same ethical issues. Researching this literature provides the perspectives of experts and helps the professional become aware of previously unconsidered aspects of the situation. Reading also has the added benefit of removing the emotional isolation involved in making a tough ethical decision. Unfortunately, some evidence suggests that the abundant literature on complex ethical issues is underutilized by professional counselors, though those with formal courses in ethics appear to refer to it more frequently (Bombara, 2002).

In the case of Archie, Annette can locate literature that suggests how to determine the circumstances under which a child's disclosures should be kept confidential (e.g., see Behnke & Warner, 2002; Glosoff & Pate, 2002; Gustafson & McNamara, 1987; Koocher, 2003; Mannheim, Sancilio, Phipps-Yonas, Brunnquell, Somers, & Farseth, 2002; Moyer & Sullivan, 2008; Stone & Isaacs, 2003; Stone, 2005; Strom-Gottfried, 2008; Taylor & Adelman, 1998). This literature, which is less general than the ethics codes, suggests that the degree of confidentiality that must be maintained is related to the child's maturity (and gives criteria for maturity) and more fully defines the child's best interests (Koocher & Keith-Spiegel, 1990). It also underscores that Archie's request for confidentiality is not unusual—other researchers have found that confidentiality is one of the most salient issues for adolescents who seek mental health care (Kaser-Boyd, Adelman, & Taylor, 1985; Society for Adolescent Medicine, 2004) and that adolescents believe that their rights of confidentiality should be respected to virtually the same degree as adults (Collins & Knowles, 1995). Several state courts have also ruled that records of services to adolescents may be kept confidential from parents (Ellis, 2009). From this literature, Annette concludes that Archie's age (17) is relevant and that his right to decide to keep disclosures private from his parents is greater than if he were several years younger but is not guaranteed. Other writers provide suggestions for dealing with parents to encourage them to waive their right to information and affirm the privacy of the interactions between therapist and client (e.g., see Taylor & Adelman, 1989). Annette decides that immediately communicating his disclosure to parents or investigators would probably fail to acknowledge his age and maturity. Annette concludes that the options that involve breaking confidentiality immediately must be revised to allow disclosure after additional discussion with Archie. She is still unsure about whether her other options are ethical. The literature has reminded her about attending to Archie's preferences and has affirmed that her primary responsibility is to him, not his parents. However, she cannot disregard his parents' rights and their responsibility for Archie or the suffering they are enduring because of Archie's revelation about abuse.

The literature on a wide variety of common ethical issues has mushroomed in the past 40 years. (Prior to that time, publications on professional ethics were fairly rare.) Especially valuable is the literature that puts ethical decision making in the context of a multicultural society and in the context of the values and virtues of the professional and the profession. The following chapters introduce readers to the extensive scholarship on issues such as confidentiality, informed consent, multiple relationships, diagnosis and testing, group and family counseling, and special ethical concerns for professionals employed in schools, agencies, private practice, and other health care settings. This body of work is a rich resource for students and practitioners who feel vulnerable and isolated in their ethical decision making. When familiar with this literature, they can better justify their decision to superiors, clients, or legal bodies and can trace their own reasoning to that of the experts. One can also argue that knowledge of this literature is a necessity, not a luxury, for competent professionals, especially when dealing with an ethical issue that is common to the population or setting in which they work. To function without knowledge of this literature could be seen as acting incompetently, especially now that electronic media make published works so easily accessible.

Of course, review of the literature is no panacea for all ethical issues. It will not always be definitive and does not reduce the responsibility of the professional for the choice taken. Many times additional deliberation or consultation about the issue will be required. Professionals then move to step 6 in the process.

Step 6: Apply Fundamental Ethical Principles and Virtues to the Situation

At this point, the professional applies the fundamental philosophical principles and virtues that underlie the codes to the situation. The professional literature narrows and clarifies the options, but it does not always point to a single path. By thinking in terms of ethical principles and virtues, professionals can bring "order and coherence" to the discussion of particular cases (Beauchamp & Childress, 1983, p. 1). In addition, by understanding ethical principles, they can better see the patterns among seemingly unconnected situations and better understand their own ethical intuitions. Building on the work of Beauchamp and Childress (1983) and Drane (1982), Kitchener (1984) identified five primary ethical principles governing human service professions. None of these principles is absolutely binding. For example, involuntary commitment violates autonomy but serves a greater good of protecting human life. Most philosophers describe ethical principles as *prima facie binding*, which means that they are binding in all situations except when in conflict with equal or greater duties (Beauchamp & Childress, 2012). Ethicists argue that principles must always be reckoned with: "Principles count even when they don't win" (Beauchamp & Childress, 2001, p. 47). In the next section, each principle is defined and applied to the case of Archie.

Respect for Autonomy Respect for autonomy means respect for the inherent freedom and dignity of any person. In other words, because all people possess inherent dignity, they should be free to make choices for themselves. This principle derives from philosopher Immanuel Kant's notion that people are ends in themselves and should not be treated only as a means to another end (Kant, 1785/1964). Implicit in autonomy is the concept that the person is responsible for him- or herself. To respect autonomy means that "a person's choices should not be constrained by others" (Beauchamp & Childress, 2001, p. 62). Paternalism, the opposite of autonomy, means acting as a parent to another, determining that person's best interest.

Respect for autonomy does have limits, of course. One's actions cannot interfere with the freedom of others, and autonomy must be based on an understanding of the meaning and implications of one's choices. The actions do not need to be rational in the sense that they need not seem sensible to others. A person is free to act foolishly, even in ways that harm him- or herself, if that person is capable of understanding the implications of the choice and if others are not hurt by those actions. Children, people with severe developmental disabilities, or people in a psychotic state do not have autonomy of action because they are (at least at the moment) unable to understand the implications of their choices. In these circumstances, others must act paternalistically on their behalf.

The right to privacy is coupled with freedom of choice as a part of respect for autonomy. A person should have the power to decide what information about self to share, a right to control what others know about his or her private life. As with autonomy, without privacy there is no dignity. In the United States and Canada as well as many other countries, a person's right to privacy is also guaranteed by the country's laws.

The connection between respect for autonomy and the codes of ethics is obvious in nearly every section. The duties to obtain informed consent for professional services and to maintain confidentiality of therapeutic disclosures derive directly from this principle. Similarly, many aspects of research ethics and the ethics of diagnosis and testing relate to respect for autonomy. This principle also implies that people have the right to relinquish or suspend their own autonomy to achieve some other aim they see as beneficial. For instance, an adult may surrender autonomy by agreeing to a marriage arranged by parents, because that practice is consistent with the adult's cultural and social beliefs.

Professionals trying to resolve an ethical dilemma use the principle of respect for autonomy by asking which of the alternatives under consideration is most consistent with this principle. In Archie's case, respect for autonomy is crucial. If he can be granted the same measure of autonomy as an adult, then Annette must honor his wishes for confidentiality to the extent that those wishes do not substantially harm others. Immediately, two questions arise: Can he be granted the same measure of autonomy as an adult? How much harm does his action cause others? (The counselor, at this point, is probably wishing that Archie had waited until his 18th birthday to share this information with her.) Most children have limited competence, and as they mature, the limits on their competence decrease. The ethics literature explains the relationship between competence and maturity and suggests that an adolescent at 17 probably is mature enough to act autonomously (e.g., Gustafson & McNamara, 1987). It suggests that a counselor or therapist with a client so near adulthood should start by assuming maturity and autonomy unless there is evidence to the contrary. Given her knowledge of Archie, Annette decides that he can be granted a nearly full measure of autonomy. Her analysis of the potential harm inflicted is another important consideration. An allegation of sexual abuse may affect his stepfather's work, his emotional stability, his marriage, his ability to parent his stepson, and perhaps his personal freedom. His mother may also suffer psychological distress and be affected by the harm her husband experiences. In other words, Archie is not the only stakeholder in the situation.

If Archie is now telling the truth, then his refusal to admit his prior lie to anyone else violates the stepfather's rights. Of course, Archie may be lying *now*, feeling uncomfortable with his earlier revelation. Young people sometimes recant revelations of abuse because they fear the consequences. This later denial may be an effort to reduce the present distress. If so, disclosing his denial would not be in his best interests. The stepfather might even be free to abuse him again. The process of applying the principle of respect for autonomy to this case reveals the importance of the specific facts of the case. Annette's ethical analysis depends on the skill and quality of her assessment of the boy and his family. Her knowledge about the client is crucial in helping her evaluate which is the real lie and what the consequences of disclosure (or nondisclosure) are likely to be. The principle of respect for autonomy requires that Archie's wishes figure prominently in Annette's decision, and that if substantial doubt exists about the harm to others, the client's right to make his own choice about what is revealed should weigh heavily in the counselor's decision.

The virtue most closely related to this principle is *respectfulness*, "the willingness to take into consideration the particular concerns of others, especially when our actions affect them" (Kitchener & Anderson, 2011, p. 66). This virtue is tied to what Nodding (1984) referred to as an *ethics of care*, in which the professional evaluates ethical choices not just on the basis of principles and rules but also includes compassion and real care for the client at the core of decision making.

Nonmaleficence The second ethical principle has its roots in medical ethics and is often associated with the Hippocratic oath, to which physicians swear. This oath admonishes physicians to heal the sick and never injure or harm them. This is derived from the principle called nonmaleficence and is often seen in its Latin form, *primum non nocere*. Its specific translation is "First, do no harm," and it has been called the most fundamental ethical principle for medical and human service professionals. This principle also includes avoiding preventable risks.

Professionals have a duty to use only those interventions that they know are not likely to harm clients. This duty means that they must recognize and assess the risks of treatment for their clients and act accordingly. The duty to avoid harm also applies to the other roles of mental health professionals. For example, researchers are prohibited from conducting research that will hurt participants; educators may not use teaching methodologies that damage students; and consultants may not employ interventions that harm the people they were hired to help. Professionals cannot always foresee all consequences of their services, because unexpected events happen. The duty to nonmaleficence does not require omniscience—just careful, prudent, and competent judgment.

The concept of avoiding harm must be put into context because many aspects of counseling and psychotherapy can be uncomfortable, and clients may temporarily feel worse before they feel better. A person trying to cope with a history of physical abuse may be more distraught after sessions that examine the impact of those past experiences on current functioning than he or she was at the start of the sessions. This would constitute harm if the intervention had no evidence of benefit in the long run or if the client had not consented to a treatment including temporary negative effects. If a professional is competent in the use of a treatment that is known to have positive effects, and has evaluated the effectiveness of this approach with this client, that professional is complying with the principle of nonmaleficence. The professional's additional duty is to monitor the client's progress in order to identify and handle unanticipated negative effects of the intervention.

Another aspect to the principle of nonmaleficence implies that doing nothing is preferable to engaging in an action that would be likely to cause harm. For example, a family physician untrained in cardiac surgery would not attempt a cardiac bypass operation. The ethical rationale is clear. A family physician is likely to do great harm engaging in a procedure in which he or she is untrained. That harm is avoidable because other doctors with that training are available. Consequently, the only ethical stance is for the physician to refuse the patient's request. Except in the most extreme emergency, the risk of death from surgery by an untrained physician is greater than the risk of death by no treatment. Similarly, mental health professionals cannot engage in actions that they know or should know are likely to do harm—even if they are asked to by clients or colleagues and even if it means they do nothing instead. The harm they would cause is probably not as visible and dramatic as in the medical example just given, but the psychological injury can be just as real. Nonmaleficence demands that clinicians untrained in powerful techniques do nothing rather than engage in procedures that are likely to do harm in inept hands.

The principle of nonmaleficence is the basis for the ethical standards concerning competence to practice, informed consent, multiple relationships, and public statements. It also is the foundation for the sections of the code dealing with appropriate use of psychological tests and research methods with animals. This principle is most related to the virtues of prudence, trustworthiness, and compassion.

When we apply this principle and these virtues to the case of Archie, we realize that we must consider the harm that can come from each alternative, beginning with the harm to Archie if Annette discloses the information without his agreement. Because the counselor's primary duty is to the client, the analysis starts with

Archie. So Annette must carefully weigh the young man's mental state, emotional stability, and tendency to impulsive or destructive behavior, along with the effect disclosure would have on each of these facets of functioning. She also needs to acknowledge that revealing the confidence may cause Archie to drop out of counseling or, at the least, lose trust in her and refuse to reveal other personal information. She must consider the harm the loss of a trusting counseling relationship could cause her client. Then she should evaluate the harm that comes to Archie's family members from each of her options. In different ways, both the mother and stepfather are harmed if the allegation goes forward but is not true. Finally, the counselor needs to weigh the injury her client would suffer against the injuries his family members would suffer. If Archie is likely to experience minor, brief discomfort, but his stepfather is likely to have a criminal conviction or his mother to file for divorce, that information should be part of Annette's deliberation. The principle of nonmaleficence asks professionals to use their power wisely so that the client, student, or research participant leaves the experience at least no worse off than he or she began. A counselor who did not carefully consider possible risks would not be prudent, nor would she be trustworthy, or if she used her own worries about getting harmed as the basis for action, she would not be demonstrating personal or professional integrity.

Beneficence The third ethical principle is beneficence, which is defined as the responsibility to do good. Because counselors and therapists advertise themselves as professional helpers, they have a duty to help those who enlist their services. As mentioned in the last chapter, this responsibility is grounded in our contract with society that offers us special privileges and status. Beneficence also includes a duty to help society in general and people who are potential clients. This duty is not imposed on all workers who sell their services to the public. People who manufacture shoelaces, copiers, or potato chips do not market themselves as helpers, and so ethically they have no obligation to help, only to produce the goods without causing harm to the public. Of course, it is *desirable* for such workers to help others. The distinction is that helping others is not a duty imposed by the nature of their work.

The principle of beneficence also underlies the provisions in the code requiring professionals to work within the limits of their competence and to promote the public welfare. Acting in an incompetent way means that the professional will not be able to give the help that has been promised (and paid for) and that a client has the right to expect. The obligation to help is rooted in the virtues of trustworthiness and integrity.

Of course, not all professional service ends up benefiting the client. Sometimes services are ineffective, and less often, they may inadvertently leave the client feeling worse. Moreover, counseling and psychotherapy can help only those who agree to participate in the process. The ethical obligation of beneficence is not to a guaranteed positive outcome; rather, the obligation is to do one's best to help and to offer alternatives when treatment does not appear to be succeeding. When professionals consistently leave clients no better off at the end of service than at the beginning, they are violating the principle of beneficence. They are also failing to demonstrate the virtue of trustworthiness, because clients have the right to expect experts to be honest about offering beneficial services.

Beneficence also requires clinicians to engage in professional activities that provide general benefit to the public. Thus, determining the benefits in each possible course of action is important in resolving an ethical dilemma. Beneficence asserts that it is insufficient for professionals simply to avoid injuring their clients. Interventions should be based on avoiding harm as a first requirement and on doing good as a second requirement.

Applied to Archie's case, beneficence means being committed to a resolution that not only avoids preventable harm to Archie but also leaves him better off after counseling. Moreover, beneficence means that Annette ought to evaluate what course of action would most help the whole family. She also must examine the impact of breaking confidentiality on her role as a school counselor. If other students learn that she disclosed Archie's statements outside the counseling office, perhaps they would refrain from using the counseling service, even when they might benefit. In other words, she should seek a solution that increases her likelihood of continuing to help all those she serves. Again, her responsibility to do good for Archie takes precedence over other considerations, but all aspects of beneficence need to be explored.

Justice Justice is the obligation to act fairly. This principle calls for professionals to recognize the dignity of all people and avoid bias in professional action, and it is best expressed in a statement attributed to Aristotle: "Justice means treating equals equally and unequals unequally, in proportion to their inequality" (cited in Kitchener, 1984). Justice means being nondiscriminatory. When Oscar Wilde defined morality as "the attitude we adopt towards people we personally dislike," he was emphasizing the justice component of morality. The risk of violating this principle is greatest when one stereotypes a group. Professionals are ethically obligated not to show bias on the basis of race, age, gender, culture, disability, or any other variable irrelevant to the real matter at hand, because doing so is inherently unfair. Clearly, this principle is tied most closely to the virtue of respectfulness and requires both personal and professional integrity.

Justice is more than avoiding prejudice, however. It also means offering additional services to those whose difference is relevant. For example, an educator in a mental health profession has an obligation to evaluate all students' performances, using the same criteria. However, if one student is deaf, the educator would be unfair to treat that student exactly the same as the others. Instead, justice dictates that adaptations to the teaching environment be made so that the student can understand what is being communicated. Once those adaptations are in place, however, fairness also demands that equal performance standards be used. A faculty member would be unethical to grade that student's work more leniently based solely on the hearing impairment.

The principle of justice also obliges professionals to be sure their services are accessible to the public. For instance, it is unethical to deny those who are poor access to counseling and psychotherapy because they cannot pay or to deny services to people who do not speak English because their language is different. Justice does not require that practitioners accept so many nonpaying clients that they cannot support themselves or that they become multilingual, but it does require them to make reasonable accommodations so that factors that are really irrelevant to a person's ability to benefit from therapy do not determine that person's access to therapy. This principle also implies that professionals should advocate for social policies that serve the mental health needs of the public.

This principle is at the root of statements in the codes against discrimination and sexual harassment as well as those supporting pro bono work and public service. It is also the foundation for the obligations to protect the public welfare and to actively combat discrimination whenever found.

Applying this principle to Archie's case suggests that Annette should deal with Archie as she would with any other adolescent client of hers, insofar as she should not let extraneous variables enter into her ethical reasoning. Archie's parents' position in the community, for example, should have no bearing on her actions because their social status is irrelevant (demonstrating the virtues of integrity and respectfulness). Similarly, if Annette dislikes the stepfather or sees parallels between Archie's mother and her own mother, justice demands that she give these personal feelings no weight in the decisions she makes about confidentiality with Archie. If Annette is unable to treat Archie and his family fairly, she should arrange for Archie to work with a professional who can. If in doubt, she should obtain consultation on this issue.

Fidelity The fifth ethical principle is fidelity, and it deals with faithfulness to promises made and to the truth. Fidelity is loyalty. Counselors must place clients' interests ahead of their own and be loyal to clients, even when such loyalty is inconvenient or uncomfortable. Fidelity derives from the central role of trust between counselor and client. Trust becomes impossible if a counselor's words or actions are unreliable. In addition, fidelity is necessary because clients are vulnerable, and the role of the counselor/therapist holds inherent power. Truthfulness is an essential aspect of fidelity in counseling and psychotherapy because the primary medium of the service is verbal communication. Clients expect to be able to believe what professionals say—the whole enterprise would likely crumble without trustworthiness. (It goes without saying that this principle is tied to the virtue of trustworthiness). The emphasis is on avoiding deception and on trust, however, not on brutal honesty. Obviously, a professional who finds a client's style of communication boring or who disagrees with a client's political views has no obligation to share these reactions with a client. Honesty must be tempered with consideration for the effects of such information on clients. In this case the virtue of prudence comes into play. Still, the prima facie duty is to truthfulness, unless overruled by another principle or virtue.

The principle of fidelity also implies loyalty to colleagues and the profession. It obliges us to do what we have agreed to do. Because professionals have a contract with their employers to give professional service in exchange for compensation, they should be loyal to that agreement as long as they are collecting a paycheck. Counselors and therapists have a similar contract with the professions. In exchange for the benefits of their professional status, they have agreed to act according to the rules of the profession and to respect other professionals. These agreements sometimes take the form of written contracts, but at other times they are informal or implied.

Fidelity is the principle underlying the statements in the codes regarding the structure of the counseling relationship and relationships with colleagues, employers, and professional associations. Fidelity is also the foundation for the caution about the use of deception in research designs. Professionals wrestling with an ethical dilemma need to ask themselves which of the courses of action under consideration is most faithful to the promises that have been made or implied.

In Archie's case, fidelity demands that Annette remain loyal to Archie and to promises made to him. If promises have been made or implied to Archie's parents and the school district, then she also has a duty to be loyal to those promises. If the loyalties conflict, then her first obligation is to her client. Annette cannot abandon her client, making excuses to refer him elsewhere just because the situation is now difficult for her. Fidelity means keeping commitments.

When Ethical Principles Conflict Applying ethical principles to a particular dilemma can reveal internal conflicts between principles. In Archie's case, different principles lead to incompatible conclusions. The principle of respect for autonomy emphasizes Archie's freedom and responsibility for his decision, while the principle of nonmaleficence uses harm to Archie and others as the measure of what is right. The principle of fidelity implies loyalty to the promise made to keep disclosures private, while the principle of beneficence suggests that disclosure may be best for the whole family.

How are these conflicting recommendations reconciled? As noted earlier, some philosophers argue that nonmaleficence is the most important ethical principle and that its requirements take priority over the claims of other ethical principles (Beauchamp & Childress, 2012). The central issue is the nature and intensity of harm to the client if disclosure is made without his or her consent. The principles of autonomy, beneficence, fidelity, and justice play secondary roles. The counselor's ultimate goal is to find a way to abide by all the ethical principles, but his or her first task is to ascertain as best as possible the probable injury to the client.

Returning to Archie, the crux of the issue then becomes whether Archie is telling the truth now or when he made the initial disclosure about abuse. If the client is acting out of fear now, and the abuse actually happened, then the harm from disclosing this current denial could be significant for the boy. If he was really fabricating the abuse in a misguided attempt to help his mother, then the harm to Archie from disclosure may be of a different nature and severity. In any case, Annette should consider the potential injury to Archie if he abandons counseling if she breaks confidentiality. Clearly, others are at risk for injury here. If the abuse never happened, then the parents are also being unnecessarily harmed.

The principle of nonmaleficence suggests that the counselor has a duty to be as sure as possible about what the real truth is. That probably means that Annette needs more discussion with Archie to get a better sense of his motivation for retracting his prior claim of abuse. Annette needs a fully informed judgment about what really happened in order to decide on the least harmful alternative. Caution in proceeding also fits with the virtue of prudence and with three other principles. If the abuse did not occur, respect for autonomy, in conjunction with nonmaleficence, might lead Annette to help Archie disclose the lie himself, either to his family or to the investigator from children's services. By exploring the implications of his behavior with Archie, Annette may assist Archie to gain enough insight that he himself decides to undo the harm he has caused. Such an approach is consistent with the duty to beneficence. Helping Archie take responsibility for his actions helps him behave in a more mature and self-sufficient way—clearly a desirable outcome. Supporting Archie in communicating about the frustrations and fears that led him to lie might be an outcome that benefits the whole family and gets them intervention for the real domestic violence. Obviously, if Archie chose to disclose the fabrication himself, then Annette would not be breaking any promises to Archie or to his family.

Ethical Theories There are even thornier dilemmas than the one Archie presents. For instance, a client whose medical condition is terminal and who is experiencing overwhelming pain may seriously consider hastening death by taking an overdose of medication. Is this action always wrong? Does the counselor have a duty to prevent this hastening of death, too? (See Chapter 5 for a discussion of ethical standards for end-of-life situations.) This is an agonizing problem. In such situations, the principles conflict, and the harm seems equal no matter which alternative is chosen. Under those circumstances, professionals can turn to ethical theories that are broader than ethical principles. Ethical theories are at the very foundation of Western societies' beliefs about morality. Ethical theories represent the perspectives of great Western ethicists throughout history. A full discussion of ethical theories is beyond the scope of this book, but the following material gives a sense of the scholarly thinking (see Kitchener & Kitchener [2012] or Sommers-Flanagan and Sommers-Flanagan [2007] for an analysis of this topic).

These theories are at the core of our religious, social, and political institutions. One is the moral law theory, which argues that there are universal moral values that must be absolutely followed. A similar theory is what Newton (1989) describes as biblical theory, encompassing absolute laws for human behavior expressed in the holy writings of the great religions of the world. In either case, the rules are treated as moral laws and are held to be universally binding. At the other end of the continuum is utilitarianism, a theory that defines morality in terms of the benefits an action provides for society. In the simplest terms, utilitarianism defines morality as the action that brings the greatest happiness to the greatest number. No action is inherently good or bad in utilitarianism; an action's effects on the happiness of the larger group determine its morality.

Ethical theories describe different assumptions about the central essence of moral behavior. For the most complex dilemmas, in which a professional agonizes about the process and in which each alternative seems to have negative consequences, thinking about how he or she defines morality at the most basic level may help in resolving the dilemma. Counselors and therapists are well advised to consult with ethicists when analyzing the relationship between moral theory and the facts of a particular case.

Step 7: Consult With Colleagues About the Dilemma

Ethical issues can be intellectually overwhelming and emotional distressing for both the client and the professional. Objective feedback from trusted colleagues can provide a wider view of the problem, a new focus on unconsidered facts, or additional relevant literature. Consultation can assist in how one thinks about a problem and how one acts, in other words, by helping with both motivation to act responsibly and willingness to fully implement the ethical choice (Kempwith, 2005). Research by Cottone et al. (1994) suggests that consultation frequently results in reconsideration of an ethical decision. Consultation may also reduce distress as well as the moral and emotional isolation that clinicians often feel. This reduction in distress doesn't just help professionals feel calmer; it helps them avoid the tendency to overestimate potential losses and to take impulsive action simply to avoid the feeling of distress.

Colleagues do not often have easy answers, but they do have insight, experience, and compassion to share. It is critical to emphasize that consultation should take place *at any point in the decision-making process* and need not be limited to this step. For instance, one might seek input from a colleague about interpreting a confusing section of an ethics code or clarifying the relevant facts of the case. Research suggests that psychologists underutilize consultation to assist them with ethics questions, and this failure sometimes diminishes the quality of the care clients receive (Clayton & Bongar, 1994). In one study, only 65% of licensed counselors indicated that they would consult with colleagues and supervisors about serious ethical issues related to interactions with managed care companies (Danzinger & Welfel, 2001).

Whether a colleague can be approached with information that identifies a specific client depends on the consent to consultation a professional has obtained from the client. Identifying information can be released with client consent or, in the absence of consent, with legal authority. In the absence of consent, professionals may discuss the case only in a way that protects the client's identity. Usually that means disguising both the name and any other information that might make the client identifiable.

When consulting with colleagues at this point in the process, professionals should describe the facts of the situation, their understanding of the relevant ethical standards, their interpretation of how the ethics literature and ethical principles apply to the case, and their current assessment of which alternatives are most responsible. In other words, the professional should summarize the decision-making process thus far and ask the colleague the following questions:

- Which facts of the case seem most important?
- What have I not considered? What do you think my blind spots may be here?
- What sociocultural considerations am I overlooking or misunderstanding?
- How is my background and sociocultural context influencing my thinking?
- Am I appropriately considering the client's sociocultural context?
- Is my interpretation of the ethics code accurate?
- What other parts of the code may be applicable?
- What laws or legal rulings may apply?
- What books and articles do you know of that are relevant to my decision?
- Does my analysis of the ethical principles or virtues appear sound?
- Is my evaluation of the most responsible options consistent with your judgment?
- How would you resolve this dilemma? Why would you make that choice?

The number of colleagues one consults will vary with the nature of the issue and a practitioner's prior experience, but some consultation is always advised in complex cases. Of course, not all the feedback will be useful, and conflicting advice is not uncommon. It is important to note that a professional is not obliged to follow a consultant's advice if it is clearly improper. Even when the feedback is disappointing, the endeavor is worthwhile. The process of articulating one's thinking clarifies that thinking and brings ideas that may have been at the periphery of awareness into full view. Just as the process of self-disclosure helps clients to see their problems more clearly, so, too, discussing ethical questions with colleagues provides a fuller vision of the issues. It is important to note that whenever a consultant's advice is not followed, a clinician should document the rationale for disregarding that advice along with the documentation for a second consultation that provided recommendations more in keeping with current practice.

What are the responsibilities of the clinician who is called to consult with a peer? Gottlieb, Handelsman, and Knapp (2013) have presented a model for peer consultation that offers professionals an excellent resource to ensure that they are effective and ethical in the feedback offered. They identify four levels of intervention, based primarily on the complexity of the ethical questions involved and the circumstances of the professional seeking consultation. They also present recommendations for consultants to set boundaries, manage confidentiality, handle the time commitment and record keeping responsibilities, and work within the scope of their practice.

If a mental health professional is under supervision to obtain a professional license or as part of a training experience, consultation with supervisors is mandatory. Discussion with one's supervisor should take place at the first opportunity, and in making the final decision, the feedback from one's supervisor should be weighed more heavily than any from colleagues. In practice, supervisors usually advocate for the trainee, supporting him or her and providing practical advice. Of course, those not yet licensed for independent practice are obligated to act in accordance with the standards of the profession, so any advice contradictory to the standards may not be followed, even if it originates with a supervisor. The supervisee is still accountable and may not claim that "a supervisor made me do it." More explanation about responding to such dilemmas in supervision follows in Chapter 14.

Consultation with colleagues can include discussion with members of professional ethics committees to get their advice. National associations are accessible to members through a toll-free phone call. The ACA's toll-free telephone number is (800) 347-6647, ext. 314; the APA's number is (800) 374-2721 or direct to the Ethics Committee (202) 336-5930. Counselors may also e-mail the ACA Ethics Office at ethics@counseling.org. Many state and provincial organizations also have ethics committees who can discuss these matters with members. Moreover, liability insurers and licensing boards typically provide access for eligible professionals seeking ethics advice. The role of these bodies is to help professionals understand the standard of care based on codes, regulations, and published guidelines. Because none of these committees will have the full facts of the case, they do not provide members with recommendations guaranteed to comply with their standards. Rather, they help members understand the professional standard of care and assist them in raising relevant questions. In other words, they do not take the responsibility for the decision, but they offer guidance about how others have dealt with similar situations.

Step 8: Deliberate Independently and Decide

At this step, the data collection process has ended, and the private, individual process of sorting out the information begins in earnest. Through this personal deliberation, the professional decides which alternative is most ethical and develops a plan for implementing that action. For example, in Archie's case, Annette's deliberations might result in calling Archie back for another session later that same day to explore his new disclosure more fully in order to ascertain, to the degree possible, what the real events were. She decides that if Archie was fabricating the story of the abuse, the counseling must focus on helping him understand the implications of his action and how he can undo some of the damage already done. She will not threaten or coerce him into disclosing his lie, but she will engage in a respectful process of helping him face the meaning of his actions and take responsibility for making things right. She will maintain confidentiality for the immediate future. If Archie refuses to change his position after additional counseling, she will need to reconsider her decision. She may still honor the confidentiality but will want to go through the decision-making process again at that time. If Annette believes Archie is now lying for fear of the consequences of admitting abuse, she has a duty to maintain confidentiality, but will work with him to find alternative ways to cope with his obvious distress.

Essential to this personal deliberation is an examination of the competing values and blind spots that may make implementing the ethical choice more difficult. As noted in Chapter 1, competing values are other personal values that influence a person's behavior. All people have other values, and there is nothing inherently problematic about them. In themselves, many competing values have considerable ethical merit. A professional's commitment to provide financial support for his or her family and to have a harmonious relationship with co-workers are good values to have. These values become problematic only when they override a counselor's ability to choose the professional ethical value. What motivates individual counselors and therapists not to implement ethical choices differs in each case, but worry about negative consequences to self, lack of support from colleagues or supervisors, or fears that doing the right thing will complicate one's life are frequent competing values. Sometimes personal religious values come into conflict with the ethical values of the profession. Professionals have an obligation to identify potential conflicts between personal moral values and professional values while in training and to consult with faculty and supervisors to find responsible ways to manage such conflicts. APA has recently offered some guidance to students and graduate faculty on this matter (APA, 2014b). When professionals become aware of the factors that pull them in another direction, they can devise a plan to counteract these pressures and increase the likelihood of acting responsibly.

Ethical choices have costs and benefits that must be addressed. Sometimes complying with ethical standards results in more work, pressure, and anxiety. For instance, Annette will need to schedule extra sessions with Archie to ascertain the truth, and if she maintains confidentiality, she risks angering the parents, investigators, and even school administrators. In rare cases, acting ethically means defying supervisors or even risking one's employment or income. By frankly confronting these possible costs, the professional may discover ethical ways to minimize or eliminate them or, at least, to protect him- or herself from an unexpected cost. In addition, the professional can muster strength for uncomfortable consequences of an ethical choice.

The benefits of ethical action are just as real but are sometimes overlooked. Clinicians who believe they have come to an informed decision about the problem often feel a sense of professionalism and allegiance to the highest values of the profession. They take pride in their moral courage and gain confidence to face future problems. The ethical climate of the profession and the workplace also influence the feelings about implementing an ethical action. The past 40 years have spawned greater awareness of the major ethical issues, and those trained in recent years have more formal education in ethics (Welfel, 1992, 2012; Hill, 2004a). When one knows colleagues are committed to ethical practice, the lure of competing values lessens, and support from those co-workers increases. Professionals gain the respect of their colleagues and also have the satisfaction of knowing that they are modeling ethical behavior for others in the workplace. Most important, they have the satisfaction of knowing that even under pressure, they considered the welfare of the client above their own needs.

Step 9: Inform Appropriate People, and Implement and Document the Decision

This step sounds deceptively simple but it may be more difficult to carry out the decision than it is to make it, even in a case as complicated as Archie's. When resistance is encountered in implementing the ethical choice, the professional should remember to engage the supports outlined in the last step. One may benefit from a follow-up consultation or from rereading the codes or literature to help one shore up resolve to stick with the choice. Ethical courage has several sources. One's moral character is one piece of it; awareness of the consequences of failing to act and structuring the environment to minimize temptation are others. A fourth aspect is habit—people are more likely to act morally in major issues if they have made a habit of acting responsibly in the less important matters.

When a professional is ready to carry out an ethical decision, he or she needs to inform supervisors. Supervisors have a legal and ethical right to hear the choice and the rationale for it (Thomas, 2010). Then communication with other people may be needed. Needless to say, the client is the first person to consider. If Annette decided to break confidentiality with Archie, then Archie should be informed. He should also hear her rationale and be given the opportunity to discuss the issue with her. Informing the client is necessary because of the principle of autonomy and is mandatory unless a greater ethical good is at stake. For example, sometimes when clients are violent, mental health professionals may break confidentiality to warn the intended victim. Under these circumstances, the client should be told only if the disclosure does not put the victim (or the professional) at greater risk for harm. If the client is a child, parents or guardians may need to be informed. In each case, only people who truly have claim to the information should get it. The client's right to privacy must still be honored to the fullest extent possible.

Formal documentation of one's decision in records, case notes, or other files is the final portion of this step. Written information about the choice taken and the rationale for that decision offers a mental health professional the best available protection from later challenges to that decision. Process notes ought to begin at step 2 with the list of options to consider and then include the outcomes of each step of the decision-making process. Remember, if it isn't written down, it didn't happen. Additional discussion of the ethics of documentation follows in Chapter 12.

Step 10: Reflect on the Actions Taken

Experience without reflection is wasted. Only when coupled with reflection can experience provide insight. Such reflection offers an opportunity to acknowledge the responsible way in which a person behaved and a chance to evaluate the flaws in thinking and actions that should be avoided when the next dilemma comes along. Now that the pressure is lessened, the mind may be able to see what the emotions had clouded. Reflection also increases ethical sensitivity so that the next ethical issue that arises will be noticed more quickly and addressed more effectively. Specifically, at this step the following questions need attention:

- Did I attend to the ethical dimensions of the situation as soon as they arose?
- Did I carefully sort out the relationship between the clinical issues and ethical issues and between legal and risk management issues (Behnke, 2014)?
- Did I know enough about the ethics codes and laws to use them effectively?
- What ethical literature do I need to keep in my personal library for easier access the next time it is needed?
- How effectively did I consult? What could I have improved?
- How well did I identify the competing values, cultural influences, and other pressures affecting my decision making?
- What else could I have done differently?
- What am I proud of doing? In what ways did I behave virtuously? How has this situation changed me as a professional and a person?
- How can I use this experience to assist others faced with similar problems?

This period of reflection begins after the decision is implemented and its consequences are known. Thus some delay may occur between the last two steps. Professionals must take care to engage in this step so that they gain the full benefit of the experience.

SUMMARY

When counselors and therapists make ethical decisions that impact others' lives, these decisions should not be intuitive, but instead should be made after careful deliberation about the ethical justification of various potential actions. A 10-step model for justifying ethical decisions begins with (step 1) recognizing the ethical dimensions of the situation and moves to (step 2) examining all the relevant facts (including the sociocultural context of the situation), the stakeholders, and categorizing the type of ethical dilemma involved. In step 3, professionals define the central issues and their options. Step 4 examines the standards, laws, and regulations relevant to the issue. Step 5 involves review of the relevant ethical literature to learn the views of experts in applied ethics. Step 6 entails analyzing the five ethical principles that govern human service professions: respect for autonomy, nonmaleficence (avoiding harm), beneficence (doing good), justice or fairness, and fidelity to promises made. If analysis of these principles does not resolve the dilemma, a practitioner may need to move to a deeper level of ethical justification—ethical theories. At step 7, consultation with supervisors and respected colleagues obtains alternative perspectives. In step 8, once all the data are obtained, the process of individual deliberation and decision making takes place. Deliberation requires acknowledging pressures and practicalities that may make implementing the decision more difficult. Step 9 involves informing supervisors and other relevant individuals, usually including the client, and then implementing and documenting the chosen action. Step 10 is a period for reflection on the experience that allows one to take pride in one's honest effort to act responsibly and to identify ways in which the process could be improved when the next similar dilemma occurs.

Not all ethical issues require progressing through all 10 steps. Some are resolved expeditiously. When ethics codes or laws are definitive, a counselor can move immediately to the final three steps of the model. In addition, although the process appears time consuming, it can be shortened by a familiarity with the ethics codes and the relevant ethics literature and by ensuring ready access to a set of knowledgeable colleagues with whom to consult. Up-to-date ethics knowledge and prior experience with ethical problems also speed up decision making.

Discussion Questions*

1. Do you agree with the view that nonmaleficence should be the primary ethical principle governing the human service professions? Why or why not?
2. Are there other virtues you think important for a counselor to demonstrate?
3. Which aspect of the codes of ethics seem most definitive to you? Why?
4. How would you determine which colleagues to consult about an ethical problem?
5. How would you define your own implicit theory of morality? What fundamental assumptions do you make?
6. Do you see any potential conflicts between your personal moral or religious values and the ethical values of the profession? If so, how do you think you should address them?
7. Do you agree with the way Annette and Yolanda resolved their ethical dilemmas? Why or why not?

Cases for Discussion

Benita is a 54-year-old executive in an international company that manufactures athletic shoes. Before she became successful in business, she was an Olympic-caliber runner, winning medals in two consecutive Olympics and other national and international titles. After retiring from competition, she earned her MBA, joined the company, and quickly rose to the top of the organization. She is now a wealthy woman who donates much of her income to charity. In fact, she has set up a foundation to help give girls in poor countries an opportunity to compete athletically. Eighteen years ago, Benita adopted a child from Kenya; she has been a good parent to that child, who is now enrolled in college. Recently, Benita has been diagnosed with a stage II melanoma; her chances of survival for more than three years are about 30% with aggressive treatment. Benita has

*Note to course instructors: The *Instructor's Guide* for this book includes other discussion questions, class exercises, cases, and multiple-choice and essay test items for this chapter.

decided to forego treatment and has come to see a counselor to get advice about how to tell her family of her decision and get them connected to professional support as she becomes ill and dies. Benita is convinced that she does not wish treatment, that she has lived a full life, and that she does not want to sacrifice the quality of the time she has left for an uncertain prospect of cure. Your assessment shows no evidence of depression or other mental illness or cognitive deficit. Can you ethically agree to her request? Do you have an ethical obligation to do anything to get her to reconsider her decision about refusing a treatment with a reasonable chance of success? What do you think you ought to do if Benita tells you that she is considering suicide when she begins to get debilitated by her cancer?

Jonah is a well-known counseling psychologist who is approached by a major retailer to provide counseling to employees. The executive at the corporation explains to Jonah that personal problems of employees are causing much absenteeism and that some support at the workplace may help the organization avoid the expense of absenteeism and increase employee productivity. It will also be seen as a benefit by the employees. Jonah is intrigued by the offer and believes that as long as he sets clear boundaries for confidentiality of employee disclosures, he will be able to follow professional guidelines. Do you think Jonah has other ethical issues to consider before accepting the offer?

Recommended Readings

Beauchamp, T. L., & Childress, J. F. (2012). *Principles of biomedical ethics* (6th ed.). Oxford, England: Oxford University Press.

Bloom, P. (2013). *Just babies: The origin of good and evil*. New York, NY: Crown.

Cottone, R. R., & Claus, R. E. (2000). Ethical decision-making models: A review of the literature. *Journal of Counseling & Development, 78*, 275–283.

Freeman, S. J. (2000). *Ethics: An introduction to philosophy and practice*. Belmont, CA: Wadsworth.

Gibson, W. T., & Pope, K. S. (1993). The ethics of counseling: A national survey of certified counselors. *Journal of Counseling & Development, 71*, 330–336.

Jordan, A. E., & Meara, N. M. (1990). Ethics and the professional practice of psychologists: The role of virtues and principles. *Professional Psychology: Research and Practice, 21*, 107–114.

Kitchener, K. S. (1984). Intuition, critical evaluation and ethical principles: The foundation for ethical decisions in counseling psychology. *The Counseling Psychologist, 12*, 43–55.

Kitchener, K. S., & Anderson, S. K. (2011). *Foundations of ethical practice, research and teaching in psychology* (2nd ed.). Mahwah, NJ: Lawrence Erlbaum.

Milliken, T. F., & Neukrug, E. S. (2009). Perceptions of ethical behaviors: A survey of human service professionals. *Human Service Education, 29*, 35–48.

Pedersen, P. B. (2001). Cross-cultural ethical guidelines. In J. B. Ponterotto, J. M. Casas, L. A. Suzuki, & C. M. Alexander (Eds.), *Handbook of multicultural counseling* (2nd ed.) (pp. 34–50). Thousand Oaks, CA: Sage.

Welfel, E. R. (2012). Teaching ethics: Models, methods, and challenges. In S. Knapp & M. M. Handelsman (Eds.), *APA handbook of ethics in psychology*, Vol. 2, (pp. 277–305). Washington, D.C.: American Psychological Association.

Additional Online Resources

Ethical Decision Making: http://josephsoninstitute.org/MED/index.html.

A Practitioner's Guide to Ethical Decision Making: http://www.counseling.org/docs/ethics/practitioners_guide.pdf?sfvrsn=2.

Pennsylvania Psychological Association Ethics Blog: http://www.papsyblog.org/.

There are, in every age, new errors to be rectified and new prejudices to be opposed.
Samuel Johnson, 1735

Ethical Practice in a Multicultural Society

CHAPTER 3

The Promise of Justice

Western society has always been culturally diverse, but for nearly a century mental health professions largely ignored the impact of that diversity on their work, and research into human behavior typically did not even account for culture, gender, or ethnicity as a variable. Wrenn (1962, 1985) aptly described counseling and psychotherapy as "culturally encapsulated." In recent years, however, the topic of diversity has moved from the periphery of the profession's consideration toward the center. Attention to diversity has become so intense that some have called this movement psychology's "fourth force" (Pedersen, 1991a). Many scholars contend that the issue has not yet achieved the attention it deserves (e.g., see Pedersen, Draguns, Lonner, & Trimble, 1996; Sue & Sue, 2012) and that the ultimate goals of full sensitivity to the role of culture in therapy and skill in working with diverse populations are far from achieved, but the progress in awareness of diversity as a factor in virtually every aspect of professional practice is clear.

Several factors account for this shift. Demographic changes are the most obvious cause. Racial and ethnic groups once referred to as "minorities" now make up a larger percentage of the population and the labor force than ever. Groups that were numerical minorities in the U.S. population now constitute a majority of the population in California, Texas, New Mexico, the District of Columbia, and Hawaii and more than 40% of the population of five other states: Arizona, Georgia, Florida, Maryland, and Nevada (U.S. Census Bureau, 2010b). Asians were the fastest growing ethnic population in the United States, followed closely by the Hispanic population (U.S. Census Bureau, 2013). In fact, growth in the Hispanic/Latino population accounted for more than half the growth of the total U.S. population between 2000 and 2010. Projections are that by the year 2043, those who have been numerical minorities will become a majority of the United States population (U.S. Census Bureau, 2010b). In many communities, that transformation has already occurred. When analyzed by county, in 1 out of every 10 U.S. counties, 50% of its residents are members of diverse groups (U.S. Census Bureau, 2010b) and this number has increased between 2010 and 2012 (U.S. Census Bureau, 2013).

Moreover, it is not just urban communities that are increasingly diverse; rural communities are experiencing the same phenomenon (Sawyer, Gale, & Lambert, 2006). Diverse populations of that size garner attention not only for their magnitude but for their expanding political and social power as well. A related factor is the increase in the number of people with multiple racial and ethnic histories. Between 2000 and 2010, there was a 32% increase in the number of individuals reporting more than one racial identity (U.S. Census Bureau, 2010b). Additionally, immigration into the United States, Canada, and Western Europe has increased substantially. For example, immigration of foreign-born people into Minnesota more than doubled in the 1990s, with 83% of these immigrants from Asia, Latin America, and Africa (Minneapolis Foundation, 2004). Almost 21% of the U.S. population speaks a language other than English at home, and there are 381 different languages identified in these data (U.S. Census Bureau, 2011). The number of persons with disabilities is also probably higher than most people realize. It has reached 54 million in the United States, a figure representing 18.7% of the population (U.S. Census Bureau, 2010a). Thirteen percent of the population is age 65 or older (U.S. Census Bureau, 2010a).

The second factor that has affected professional awareness of diversity is the passage of federal statutes such as the Civil Rights Act of 1964, Title IX of the Education Amendments of 1972, and the Americans with Disabilities Act of 1990 (Public Law 101-336). The recent rulings by the U.S. Supreme Court on marriage equity for gays and lesbians (spurred by the passage of marriage equity laws in the 19 states) have also enhanced awareness of diversity. Taken together these laws offer better protection against unfair treatment. Not all efforts to increase rights for populations vulnerable to discrimination have been successful (note the failure of the Equal Rights Amendment in 1982), but the momentum has clearly been in this direction. Third, as professional education became more available to groups previously denied access, the professions themselves included more members of diverse populations. However, ethnically diverse mental health professionals still constitute less than 10% of practicing counselors and psychotherapists (Koocher & Keith-Spiegel, 2008). Currently, however, approximately 12% of faculty and 20% of doctoral students in psychology come from diverse backgrounds (APA, 2005). Many of these scholars have provided leadership in the profession's consideration of multicultural issues. They have also pushed the profession toward a fuller acknowledgment of its own history of failures in providing effective services to diverse groups and of the harm that ageist, racist, homophobic, and ethnocentric attitudes can cause others (e.g., see Danzinger & Welfel, 2000; Ridley, 2005; Sue & Sue, 2012). In addition, scholarship in cross-cultural psychology has blossomed in this period, providing a rich conceptual base for that agenda. Finally, the reemergence of interest in professional ethics over the last two decades has also played a small role, placing the profession's fundamental ethical principles and virtues at the forefront of professional concern. Attention to multicultural issues is a natural outgrowth of discussions of respect for autonomy, justice, and the obligation to do good for others. At its core, professional ethics is about commitment to reducing the suffering of other people, advocating for social justice, and helping clients flourish, that is, reach their full human potential (Fowers & Richardson, 1996; Fowers & Davidov, 2006). One cannot honor that commitment without working to eliminate racism, oppression, and stereotyping, which cause much suffering in modern society and play a significant role in the development and persistence of emotional distress (Carter, 2007).

In this context, it is not surprising that the ethical implications of the multicultural movement on mental health practice have been extensively discussed. The most recent versions of the ethics codes of the ACA and APA show an unprecedented concern for this topic. Moreover, the associations have published additional guidelines to enhance responsible practice with diverse clients (e.g., the APA's *Guidelines on Multicultural Education, Training, Research, Practice, and Organizational Change for Psychologists*, 2003; the *Guidelines for Assessment of and Intervention with Persons with Disabilities*, 2011a; and ACA's *Competencies for Counseling Transgender Clients*, 2009). This chapter reviews those materials, discusses the relevant scholarly literature, and examines emerging aspects of professional ethics in a multicultural society. Its central theme is that ethics requires professionals to break free from cultural encapsulation and develop a set of competencies and commitments for productive work with diverse populations. It also requires professionals to reject simplistic notions of culture and diversity, recognize that few counseling interactions are monocultural, and appreciate that all professionals are affected to some degree by what Sue (2005) calls institutional and cultural racism. Achieving this goal for all professionals is crucial if the ethical ideals of the profession are to be met, especially because the history of the profession is marred with incidents of ignorance, insensitivity, and ethnocentric bias.

THE LANGUAGE OF MULTICULTURAL COUNSELING

A set of definitions of terms used in this chapter is a necessary preamble to the discussion:

- *Culture* is the "set of shared meanings that make social life possible" (Fowers & Richardson, 1996, p. 610). These meanings form the structure of social interaction and give members of the culture a set of standards and norms for behavior. In this chapter, *culture* is used broadly, including not only ethnicity and nationality but also encompassing demographic variables (such as age, gender, sexual orientation, and physical disability) and affiliations (such as religion).
- *Ethnicity* is a shared identity derived from shared ancestry, nationality, religion, and race (Lum, 1992). Individuals may have multiple ethnic identities that operate at different times. For example, a child of Romanian heritage adopted by Mexican American parents may identify with both ethnicities. In the most recent U.S. Census (2010b), approximately 3% of the population identifies in this way.
- *Multiculturalism* is a "social-intellectual movement that promotes the value of diversity as a core principle and insists that all cultural groups be treated with respect and as equals" (Fowers & Richardson, 1996, p. 609).
- *Culture-centered practice* is a term endorsed by psychology to refer to the "cultural lens" psychologists should use as a central focus in their work.

It encourages psychologists to consider the multiple sources that may shape behavior—culture, group memberships, and cultural stereotypes (APA, 2003).

- *A minority* has long been identified as a group that has suffered discrimination or been oppressed. It is typically smaller in size and has less power than a majority cultural group, but it need not be small to be considered a minority. Minority status is primarily a function of access to power and history of oppression. Women, though they are a numerical majority of the population, have long been considered a minority group because of the discrimination they have suffered. This term is infrequently used in the current professional literature.
- *Culturally diverse clients* are clients from any group that is represented in the preceding definition of minority or are otherwise of a different cultural tradition from the professional or from those who hold a more dominant position in the society. Diverse clients are those at risk for discrimination or stereotyping based on age, gender, gender identity, race, ethnicity, culture, national origin, religion, sexual orientation, disability, language, and socioeconomic status.
- *Multicultural counseling or multicultural psychotherapy* is any service in which the cultures of the client and the professional differ in ways that are likely to influence communication and therapeutic content and progress. In some writings, the terms *cross-cultural, transcultural counseling*, or *transcultural psychotherapy* are used.
- *Prejudice* is "the positive or negative evaluation of social groups and their members" (Sherman, Stroessner, Conrey, & Azam, 2005, p. 1). It is important to note that a prejudice can be positive (e.g., one group is intelligent) or negative (another group is unintelligent).

THE FOUNDATION OF ETHICAL PRACTICE IN A DIVERSE SOCIETY

Gallardo (2009) speaks to the central rationale for culturally sensitive practice when he raises the following questions: "What is our interest in multiculturalism, diversity, culture, and so on? Are we invested because we 'should' be, or are we invested because we have a genuine interest in understanding the 'other'?" (p. 428). Appreciating diversity and our personal culture and responses to those different from us is essential for truly understanding and helping others. Empathy is not possible without awareness of the sociocultural context in which a client is describing the reasons for seeking help. When focused on getting a clearer sense of the context in which we and our clients function, professionals move beyond seeing cultural sensitivity as only a professional duty and begin to see it as an absolutely fundamental characteristic of professional service. To quote Gallardo again, "[T]o be culturally responsive is not a concept at which one arrives, but more a process that is life-long and ever evolving" (p. 428). When mental health professionals are acting in a culturally responsible way, they not only begin to appreciate the context of the individual, they begin to understand the relationship between the individual's circumstances and social justice issues or, as the case may be, the social injustices to which a client may have been vulnerable. A professional then expands his or her definition of responsible practice to include advocacy for social justice at the institutional and societal level along with assistance to individual clients to help them advocate more effectively for themselves.

As Vasquez (2012) notes, commitment to competent service to diverse populations is part of the professions' broader value of the promotion of social justice. For example, in 2009 the APA identified the following as a central part of its vision for the organization: "an effective champion of the application of psychology to promote human rights, health, well being and dignity" (APA, 2009b). In parallel fashion, the ACA notes its mission on its website as follows: "to enhance the quality of life in society by promoting the development of professional counselors, advancing the counseling profession, and using the profession and practice of counseling to promote respect for human dignity and diversity" (http://counseling.org/about-us/about-aca/our-mission).

THE CONTEXT OF THE CURRENT ETHICAL STANDARDS

To fully appreciate the ethical standards for mental health services in a multicultural society, one must acknowledge not only that there are many cultural traditions beyond one's own, but even more importantly, that not all groups have equal power in our society. Many groups have been subject to oppression and discrimination on an individual, institutional, and societal level, and the prejudicial attitudes and behaviors that allowed such violations of human dignity to occur are far from extinct. One only needs to read a newspaper or peruse an online magazine to find reports of religious, ethnic, sexual, and gender violence in many places in the world. (Note the recent expansion of laws across the world that criminalize homosexual behavior in Russia and Uganda.) Furthermore, professionals need to recognize that they themselves are not immune from prejudicial attitudes and that they can inadvertently perpetuate oppression and discrimination, even if they abhor prejudice and want to practice sensitively (Sue, Ivey, & Pedersen, 1996; Sue & Sue, 2012). Counselors and psychotherapists internalize society's biases, just as other citizens do, and these biases frequently play themselves out in unconscious ways. For example, if a private practitioner locates a practice so as to be inaccessible to public transportation, he or she is probably not deliberately discriminating. Nevertheless, the effect is still discriminatory insofar as it denies access to people without their own cars—a group likely to contain a greater proportion of diverse clients. Or, to cite a different example, a school counselor might accept without challenge a Latina's request to drop out of an advanced placement physics class because it's too demanding, when that same counselor might actively encourage a European American boy to persevere or help him get tutoring. The counselor need not have a conscious belief that Latinas are less intelligent or less deserving; he or she may just have lower expectations for Latinos (or for girls), without ever being aware that that assumption is operating.

Similarly, Hays (2008) recounts an example of a conversation with a faculty member who explained that the low representation of diverse professionals on the faculty was probably related to the university's research agenda, implying that diversity recruitment and rigorous research goals were not compatible.

Here are other examples:

"Gee, you don't look or dress like you are gay."

To an Asian American student new to the program: "Can you help me with the stats class?"

"You'd be pretty if you lost some weight."

"You're so articulate (to an African American at a job interview)."

"It must be hard never to have any sex" (to a person in a wheelchair).

To a 40-year-old single woman: "How do you deal with the loneliness?"

Ridley (2005) refers to such acts as *unintentional* racism or sexism. Salter and Salter (2012) refer to other terms for nondeliberate comments and attitudes, such as ambivalent racism or modern racism. The harm such actions cause is no less real because they are unintended, however. Sue, Bucceri, Lin, Nadal, and Torino (2007) refer to acts that are often unintentionally prejudicial as *racial microaggressions* and define them as "brief and commonplace daily verbal, behavioral, and environmental indignities that communicate hostile, derogatory, or negative racial slights and insults to the target person or group" (p. 72). Two subtypes of this phenomenon are termed *microinsults* and *microinvalidations* (Sue et al., 2007). In the years since Chester Pierce first coined the term *microaggression* it has been used to describe insults based on age, gender, religion, sexual orientation, and other types of diversity. Crethar, Rivera, and Nash (2008) aptly name such behaviors and attitudes as *unintentional injustices*. The fact that such actions are unconscious and unintended does not erase their harm or render them any more ethical than deliberate actions. Another manifestation of unintentional injustice comes from the discrepancy between the multicultural competencies professionals think they are implementing and their actual behaviors, which often fail to demonstrate such competency (Hansen et al., 2006; Sehgal et al., 2011). This literature clearly shows that mental health professionals do not routinely implement the cultural competencies that they report that they have. It may be that they are unaware of this discrepancy or that they want to put their best foot forward in responding to researchers who ask such questions.

What complicates the picture even further is the difficulty the listener to microaggressions has in responding. Pointing out the insult usually results in defensiveness because the speaker was unaware that the comment showed bias, and instead consciously thought it was a compliment (e.g., "You are so articulate"). However what a microaggression really reveals, according to Sue (2010), is an underlying message of discrimination. In the example just mentioned, the biased message is that "for your race you are an exception; I expect African American people to be inarticulate." In the last decade, research has been emerging on the impact of microaggressions on marginalized populations. For example, Nadal, Griffin, Wong, Hamit, and Rasmus (2014) have found negative effects on the mental health of individuals who experience frequent microaggressions. They are significantly more likely to experience depression and anxiety than those who do not encounter such behaviors frequently.

Of course, unintentional bias is not the only form of bias mental health professionals may exhibit. Sometimes they consciously endorse prejudiced beliefs and attitudes. As late as 1993, 14% of counselors still equated homosexuality with psychopathology, even though the professions had definitively asserted 20 years before that homosexuality was not a psychological disorder (Gibson & Pope, 1993). Similarly, Ruebensaal (2006) reported that school counselors in her study expressed discomfort at working with homosexual students. Endorsing such beliefs and attitudes directly contradicts the provisions of the ethics codes of every major mental health association.

THE CODES OF ETHICS ON MULTICULTURAL PRACTICE

The 2014 ACA Code speaks to the topic of multicultural counseling in the first paragraph of its preamble and in the Introduction to Section A (see Appendix A, pp. 489–490). In addition, the ACA Code contains another 24 references to multicultural diversity issues, divided among nearly all sections of the code. The 2010 revision of the APA Code also includes numerous references to diversity issues, emphasizing the need for psychologists to be just and unbiased and to recognize the role of social factors in people's psychological distress. The other sections of the codes that refer to multicultural issues deal with the promotion of client welfare, competence to practice with diverse populations, avoidance of discriminatory behavior, fair use of assessments, and training and research issues.

Every reference to diversity and culture in the ACA Code highlights the degree to which counseling cannot be separated from personal values and beliefs, These statements are grounded in the recognition of the power of the professional and the social forces at work for both the counselor and the client. This language also reminds professionals that this occupation is one of service to others, not self-service. When counselors and psychotherapists fail to operate in a culturally sensitive way, they are serving their own needs, not those of their clients. Here are examples of professionals who are unintentionally exhibiting behaviors that conflict with these standards:

Penny and the Interpreter

Penny, a hearing-impaired client, enters counseling for post-traumatic stress. Recently, her apartment was robbed while she hid in a closet. Penny brings an interpreter with her to the first session to help her communicate with her therapist. Barbara, her psychologist, has difficulty keeping focused in the session with Penny. She finds herself uncomfortable with the presence of the interpreter. After the session is completed, Barbara sends Penny a letter, asking her to come to the next session alone and to rely on her skills in lip reading. Barbara reassures Penny that she will speak slowly and clearly in that session and that her purpose in making this request is to be able to give her undivided attention to Penny.

Linda's Approach to College Counseling

Linda is a college counselor who works in the counseling center of a prestigious college with a large number of international students. She says that she could never really learn enough about the varied cultures from which many of her clients come, so she relies on the clients to teach her about their cultural backgrounds. When, for example, she had a client from Indonesia, she asked that young man directly about the ways in which he thought his culture affected his thoughts, feelings, and behavior. Linda says that because her clients are all gifted students, they have good insight into their culture, and she relies heavily on their interpretation of the role of culture in their lives. She is content that she needs no other knowledge base.

Roger's Dilemma

Roger, a clinical social worker, has an appointment with a 24-year-old male named George who is seeking service because of mild depression and dissatisfaction at work. His fiancée recently broke off their engagement, and although he was also having serious doubts about the relationship, he still feels lonely and hopeless about finding a satisfying, committed relationship. The young man and his family are members of a conservative religious group that has long been skeptical of mental health services, but when George requested services, his family was willing because nothing else seemed to be helping. When the client arrives for services, he is accompanied by his parents, who assume they will fully participate in the sessions. Roger is surprised by this situation and asks George whether he wants an individual or family session. The young man just shrugs his shoulders and looks at the floor. His father replies that there is no doubt that George wants his parents in the room. Roger suggests a brief individual meeting with George first, but the family is obviously upset by this arrangement and fails to return for any further appointments. Roger wonders whether he could have handled the situation differently in light of the young man's passivity and the parents' determination to be a part of George's treatment.

In the cases of Penny and Linda, the ethical violation appears to be fairly obvious. It is impossible, for example, for Linda to approach each client with an entirely open mind, because it is impossible to assume nothing about a client. Hays (2008) suggests the absence of knowledge acts like a vacuum that gets filled with dominant cultural messages (or specific messages from family or locale) if no accurate knowledge is there to supplant it. To impose on the client the responsibility of educating a professional about every cultural influence about which he or she may be aware is unacceptable. Roger's situation is more complex. Because George is an adult, Roger had an obligation to offer him privacy and freedom to decide the type of service he wanted, based on the ACA Code B.1.b and APA Code in Principle E, which reads in part, "Psychologists respect the dignity and worth of all people, and the rights of individuals to privacy, confidentiality, and self-determination."* However, Roger also had an obligation to understand the client behavior in its sociocultural context ACA Code B.1.a. His client would have been better served had he first met with all the parties, gotten a sense of the dynamics, and worked to build sufficient trust so

*Source: Copyright © 2010 by the American Psychological Association. Reproduced with permission.

that the parents might consider an individual session between Roger and the son if George were amenable to that at some point. It is undoubtedly clear from this discussion thus far that ethical practice with diverse populations requires more than a rule-bound view of the ethical standards. In these sections of the codes, perhaps more than in any other, the standards are asking professionals to act in ways consistent with the highest ideals of the profession.

COMPETENCE WITH DIVERSE POPULATIONS

As will be discussed in Chapter 4, competence to practice means a professional has the knowledge, skill, and diligence required for the tasks he or she undertakes. Multicultural competence is a subset of clinical competence. There are two references to multicultural competence in the ACA Code. The first is in the section explaining the boundaries of one's competence, and it states, "Counselors gain knowledge, personal awareness, sensitivity, and skills pertinent to working with a diverse population"* (ACA Code, Section C.2.a). The second reference extends that responsibility to continuing-education experiences and advises counselors to continue to update their knowledge of work with diverse groups (ACA Code, Section C.2.f). The APA Code addresses the topic in Standard 2.01 in its provision that psychologists should engage only in those professional activities in which they are competent.

Sue and Sue (2012) laid out three broad dimensions of multicultural competency: (1) self-awareness, so that one's values, biases, personal beliefs, and assumptions about human nature are known; (2) an understanding without negative judgments of the worldviews and assumptions of culturally diverse clients; and (3) skill in using and developing counseling interventions appropriate with diverse clients. Other authors have organized the necessary multicultural competencies as appropriate beliefs and attitudes, cultural knowledge, and practical skills. Toporek and Reza (2001) emphasize that the institutional context of the professional plays an important role in multicultural competence, and Sue et al. (1998) offer an extensive discussion of approaches to institutional development to promote more culturally sensitive counseling. The ACA has endorsed competency guidelines for counselors and counselor educators, entitled *Multicultural Counseling Competencies and Standards* (Arredondo et al., 1996). Owen, Tao, Leach, and Rodolfa (2011) emphasize that competence in serving diverse populations may be better described as a *multicultural orientation* in which specific competencies are embedded. The term *orientation* more clearly links the values of the professional regarding multiculturalism to the specific competencies.

These guidelines identify four major components of competency. The first is awareness of the influence of one's own cultural heritage on his or her experiences, attitudes, values, and behaviors as well as the ways in which that culture limits or enhances effectiveness with diverse clients. Next comes comfort with cultural differences and with clients from diverse cultures, developing an attitude that values and appreciates cultural difference rather than disparages or tolerates it. Honesty with self about negative emotional reactions and preconceived notions about other cultures, recognition of the harmful effects such reactions can have on clients, and commitment to work on changing such attitudes is the third competency. Finally, the

*Source: Reprinted with permission from American Counseling Association.

guidelines identify respect and appreciation for culturally different beliefs and attitudes as the last component. This can be accomplished, for example, by honoring natural community support networks and valuing bilingualism. More recently ACA and the Association for Lesbian, Gay, Bisexual, and Transgender Issues in Counseling (ALGBTI) have published *Competencies for Counseling with Lesbian, Gay, Bisexual, Queer, Questioning, Intersex and Ally Individuals* (2012).

These documents also detail an extensive knowledge base for counselors that includes a strong foundation of self-knowledge and a solid background in the particular cultures of one's clients:

- Comprehension of how one's own culture affects one's definition of normality–abnormality (including definitions of healthy interpersonal relationships and responsible parenting practices) and the ways in which one's cultural heritage affects the process of counseling.
- Understanding of the implications of racism, oppression, and stereotyping on a personal and a professional level, including acknowledgment of one's own racist, ageist, and homophobic attitudes.
- Familiarity with the literature on social impact on others, with special attention to the effect of one's communication style on diverse clients and the complications that language disparity bring to counseling and psychotherapy. (See Schwartz, Rodrguez, Santiago-Rivera, Arredondo, and Field [2010] for an excellent review of cultural and linguistic competence.)
- Appreciation of the cultural heritage of diverse clients with whom one is working and the impact that cultural identity development may have on clients
- Sensitivity to the ways in which culture may affect specific client attributes such as personality development, career choice, help-seeking behavior, and manifestation of psychological distress.
- Comprehension of the influence of social and political factors on culturally diverse clients, with appreciation of the harm that institutional and cultural racism can inflict on individual functioning.
- Knowledge of the aspects of traditional counseling that may clash with a particular client's culture, including assessment tools, intervention strategies, and attitudes toward family involvement in services.
- Appreciation of institutional barriers that impede access to counseling and psychotherapy for many diverse clients (see the National Healthcare Disparities Report [2005] for specific data regarding the difference in access to service for African American and Asian American clients).
- Familiarity with cultural norms and practices regarding family structure and understanding of how the cultural group uses family and community resources to help people in distress.
- Appreciation of the ongoing problems of discrimination and oppression that may have particular impact on culturally diverse clients in a given community.

Finally, the document elaborates on a number of skills or activities that counselors should acquire to be effective multicultural counselors (the theme of this section is active engagement in activities that enhance skills):

- Pursuit of activities that enhance understanding of one's own culture and decrease the degree to which the prejudiced attitudes of the culture affect one's behavior, along with active involvement in activities that expand knowledge of cultural groups. These activities should be both intellectual and experiential to gain full understanding. A fuller description of specific strategies for helping professionals developing these skills can be found in Constantine and Sue (2005). A model for training programs in developing cultural skills is outlined in Pack-Brown, Thomas, and Seymour (2008).

- Versatility in verbal and nonverbal helping responses and judgment about when to use each appropriately.
- Skill in helping clients intervene effectively with respect to institutional barriers to their goals, as well as a capacity to use community resources, such as traditional healers, when appropriate.
- Bilingualism, or at least a willingness to appreciate the client's desire to use a first language in counseling; acceptance of interpreters when required; and resources to make an appropriate referral if language barriers cannot be overcome.
- Expertise in the responsible use of assessment tools with diverse populations (Suzuki, Ponterotto, & Meller, 2008).
- Active involvement in activities meant to reduce prejudice and enhance cross-cultural knowledge in the community—in other words, participation in actions that promote social justice, including advocacy on behalf of clients when permissible. The ACA Code Section A.6.a speaks directly to this issue when it advises counselors to take advocacy roles for clients as needed.
- Skill in educating diverse clients to the counseling process in ways that make sense to them, including a collaborative approach to counseling plans, with a willingness to adapt interventions to client needs.

The APA's *Guidelines on Multicultural Education, Training, Research, Practice, and Organizational Change for Psychologists* (2003) echo the same themes, with somewhat greater emphasis on the impact of bias on diagnosis and assessment. This document also provides examples that help flesh out the concepts embedded in both sets of guidelines, such as the "healthy paranoia" of oppressed groups, to illustrate the ways in which diagnosis must take cultural factors into account if it is to be accurate. All too often that suspicion is treated as pathological when it is indeed functional to the environment of that client. Here are the five guidelines in that document (APA, 2003):

> Guideline 1: Psychologists are encouraged to recognize that, as cultural beings, they may hold attitudes and beliefs that can detrimentally influence their perceptions of and interactions with individuals who are ethnically and racially different from themselves.
>
> Guideline 2: Psychologists are encouraged to recognize the importance of multicultural sensitivity/responsiveness, knowledge, and understanding about ethnically and racially different individuals.
>
> Guideline 3: As educators, psychologists are encouraged to employ the constructs of multiculturalism and diversity in psychology education.
>
> Guideline 4: Culturally sensitive psychological researchers are encouraged to recognize the importance of conducting culture-centered and ethical psychological research among persons from ethnic, linguistic, and racial minority backgrounds.
>
> Guideline 5: Psychologists strive to apply culturally appropriate skills in clinical and other applied psychological practices.

Several objective measures to help professionals assess their level of multicultural competency have been developed. The test with the most evidence of reliability and validity is the *Multicultural Counseling Inventory* constructed by Sodowsky, Taffe, Gutlin, and Wise (1994). These instruments examine the skills, knowledge, and attitudes of counselors toward multicultural populations. Professionals who are unsure about their current competency might find one of these measures useful and should consult Hays (2008), Pope-Davis and Coleman (1998), or Suzuki, Ponterotto, and Meller (2008) for a review of the literature on these instruments. Some of these instruments are appropriate for research and some for self-assessment.

Research on the beliefs of professionals about the importance of the multicultural competencies of mental health professionals has shown some promising results. Zayas, Torres, Malcolm, and DesRosiers (1996) found that mental health practitioners endorsed the same components of culturally sensitive counseling as the scholars named in the literature. Manese, Wu, and Nepomuceno (2001) reported in a 10-year study that intensive multicultural training was an effective way to increase competencies during internship. Finally, Holcomb-McCoy and Myers (1999) indicated that professional counselors perceive themselves as culturally competent and rate their graduate training in this area positively. Unfortunately, because most research on the endorsement of multicultural competencies relies on self-report, and little evidence exists from other observers of behavior, as mentioned already, other measures of competence do not report such optimistic findings either among practitioners or students (Cartwright, Daniels, & Zhang, 2008; Hansen et al., 2006; Sehgal et al., 2011). It is also important to note that cultural competence is subject to the same level of erosion over time as other competencies because of the advancement of professional knowledge. Therefore, no one maintains this competency without continued professional education. Some states, including Ohio, are asking professionals to identify their competence to work with diverse populations on their license renewal forms, another indication that cultural competence is valued and that it needs to be maintained. If a complaint was submitted to the psychology board that alleged improper service to a client from a diverse population, one aspect of the investigation would be a review of the claims of cultural competence on the license renewal to determine whether those claims were legitimate.

A CRITIQUE OF THE CURRENT ETHICS CODES

Critics of the ethics codes note that the ethical principles that underlie their tenets are not universally endorsed by all cultures (e.g., Pedersen, 1997; Sadeghi, Fischer, & House, 2003). The emphasis on respect for the autonomy of the individual that girds the entire social and political structure in Western societies is much less dominant in some Eastern and African cultures. Instead, those cultures give primacy to the health and well-being of the group or the family. (For an excellent review of professional ethical decision making in non-Westen cultures see Houser, Wilczenski and Ham [2006].) In this and other ways, the codes, the critics say, have abrogated their responsibility to acknowledge this diversity in ethical values and have failed to help practitioners deal responsibly with cultural conflicts in fundamental ethical values. Others have reframed the dilemma, suggesting that providing culturally responsive treatment can be consistent with ethical standards and with the notion of clinically responsive treatment (Gallardo, Johnson, Parham, & Carter, 2009), though these authors also note that work with diverse clients can often present complex dilemmas, especially in regard to boundary issues that the profession needs to address more fully in the future. For example, Carter, in her portion of the article, suggests that a more helpful way to conceive of the boundary issue is to substitute the notion of the wall of a living cell for the notion of a boundary. "A cell wall defines what it keeps inside and what it does not. It is permeable and flexible, which allows for growth and change, and it can take in new and different information while still maintaining its essential being" (Carter, p. 434).

This debate on the value of the current codes with diverse populations highlights some of the thorniest ethical dilemmas that mental health professionals confront in their work. Consider the following case:

Daniel's Concern

Daniel is a 23-year-old Muslim man whose family has arranged a marriage for him, the accepted practice in his community. His reaction to this marriage has caused him so much distress that the imam recommended counseling. In session, Daniel reveals that he is ambivalent about the marriage. On the one hand, he wants to follow the tenets of his religion, which place strong emphasis on the importance of marriage for a Muslim man, but on the other, he knows he feels nothing for the woman his family has chosen. Daniel says he wants to marry eventually but feels completely unready now. He feels trapped. To violate his parents' choice would be inconsistent with the expectations of his religion and would risk his family's goodwill and his community's acceptance, but he feels strongly unsuited to this woman at this time. He asks his counselor to help him find a way to be more accepting of his parents' and community's choice for him.

How should one respond when the situation of the client seems to compromise his or her personal freedom and dignity, yet is condoned or encouraged by his or her culture? Here, Daniel seems caught between strong religious and cultural values that he generally endorses and his own hesitance about this particular value (see the material at the end of the chapter for an analysis of this case). What are the professional's ethical choices here? In other examples, what is the ethical response when a client's culture refuses to allow girls to attend school or condones a kind of indentured servitude of some classes that is not far removed from slavery? Is there a point at which respect for the cultural tradition of the client gives way to universal human values? If so, who makes the decision about which values are universal? Does that come from the individual practitioner or from somewhere else? Sadeghi et al. (2003) report that such a conflict between the desires of the individual and the sociocultural fabric in which that person lives are the most common multicultural dilemmas that practicing mental health counselors face.

LaFromboise, Foster, and James (1996) wrestle with these questions, suggesting that professionals must avoid both ethical absolutism (a rigid, dogmatic adherence to a particular set of ethical values) and ethical relativism (an equal acceptance of all ethical values). Instead, they recommend a middle position that allows for diversity in values, but is not so relativistic as to deny the existence of any universal human principles. The themes by Fischer, Jome, and Atkinson (1998) echo this view as they discuss multicultural counseling as a "universal healing process that takes place in a culturally sensitive context" (p. 525). They remind professionals to attend to the common factors that make therapeutic work effective: a strong therapeutic relationship, a shared worldview, a client with expectations of positive results from treatment, and a set of interventions that both people accept as healing.

James and Foster (2006) make two additional important points that can assist professionals in responding to difficult ethical questions. First, they encourage mental health professionals to be aware of the difference between rights-oriented societies and duty-oriented societies. In rights-focused societies, the emphasis is on protecting individual entitlements; in duty-oriented societies, the emphasis is on carrying out one's obligations to the larger group. Professionals working with clients from duty-bound cultures ought to first assess the likelihood that part of the struggle the client is experiencing may be related to the conflict between a duty-bound cultural tradition and the expectations of the society in which the client resides. Second, James and Foster recommend that professionals strive to develop what Aristotle referred to as *practical wisdom*, which is the capacity to use rules, norms, and standards in a contextual way, interpreting them rather than attempting to apply them in a rigid or unvarying way.

Consider the following cases that also present complex issues and that highlight the importance of self-awareness on the part of the professional:

The Unhappy Couple

A couple who have just celebrated their 50th wedding anniversary come to counseling because the satisfying sexual relationship they have had for their entire marriage is now more difficult to maintain as a result of health problems. Both people are feeling depressed and anxious, and they are arguing with each other more frequently than at any prior time in their marriage. Their physicians have advised them to "look for other satisfactions in life" and indicated that it was entirely normal and expected to have to give up sexual activity at their ages. They reject that alternative but don't know what else to do. They hope that the psychologist can help them find a way to resume some sexual activity.

A Religious Request

A graduate student in clinical counseling approaches her site supervisor at the start of internship to ask for five days off for the Jewish holidays that will occur during the internship, as well as permission to leave in time to get home before sunset on Fridays during the winter months. The site supervisor tells the student that five days off is too much time and that she will only be able to take two days off. The supervisor agrees with the schedule change on Fridays as long as the student makes up the time on other days.

In both cases, the professional's lack of knowledge and sensitivity complicated the problem. In the case of the couple, the psychologist needs to be aware of how ageism and how his views about same-sex couples (did you assume they were heterosexual?) may affect his thinking. He also needs medical knowledge and/or accurate information about sexuality in older adults in order to evaluate the problem. In the case of the student, the supervisor appeared ignorant about the importance of holy days in the Jewish calendar and about how to balance what may be legitimate needs of the organization against the religious commitments of the intern.

MISINTERPRETATIONS OF MULTICULTURAL COMPETENCE

There are two extremes to be avoided if one is to become culturally competent. One extreme is obvious from the preceding discussion, that is, the failure to take culture into account in the therapeutic process. The second extreme to be avoided is the failure to acknowledge intra-cultural variations and individual differences. Within the African American community, for example, are many subcultures, and it is a mistake to assume uniformity in culture that simply does not exist. Not all people from the same cultural group are identical, even if they share a culture. Their individual beliefs, values, practices, and assumptions may vary substantially from those that typify their culture in general. Cultural groups overlap, too, as indicated by the dramatic increase in U.S. residents with multiple ethnic identifications in recent years (U.S. Census Bureau, 2006). A man may have an Asian mother, an African American father, and a Latina stepmother, and be gay. In this situation, many cultures have contributed to his development and current functioning, and it would be inappropriate to single out any one group as "his culture." Pedersen (1991b) makes the point that each interpersonal encounter is a multicultural encounter. Cultural traditions, then, must be seen as hypothetical influences on individuals until evidence shows that they are operative. In other words, a balance is to be achieved that gives cultural variables their appropriate consideration without either overemphasizing or ignoring their influence on human behavior. Professionals who find themselves thinking thoughts such as, "She's Native American, so she must feel ..." or "He's Latino, so he must think..." are falling victim to the very prejudicial behavior they may be trying to avoid. Implicit in this view is the recognition that culture is dynamic, not static. Cultures change over time as circumstances change, and as contact with other cultures increases or varies (Gallardo et al., 2009). A developmental component also exists in cultural identity, especially as it relates to groups that experience oppression (Buckard & Ponterotto, 2008). Consequently, one's worldview and sense of self in the cultural context are also dynamic over time.

Finally, scholars on this topic note that the need for attention to issues of cultural diversity is not limited to professionals from European backgrounds or others in privileged groups. They are not the only cultural group that has internalized prejudicial messages from the society, and they are not the only professionals who will encounter clients whose cultural background differs from their own. Any cultural group can stereotype or assume that its cultural tradition is the best or the only way to organize social reality. Of course, European American practitioners, as the majority in the professions and as the beneficiaries of privilege in the current social structure, have an especially strong obligation to develop and maintain multicultural sensitivity. A commitment to multicultural sensitivity and competence is a necessity for all professionals, however.

WHEN CLIENTS EXPRESS PREJUDICIAL IDEAS

The following case illustrates that professionals are not the only people in the room who express prejudicial ideas.

Parents' Request for Help

A couple seeks out the services of a clinical counselor in a rural city in the United States for their teenage daughter. She has been neglecting her school work, ignoring curfew, and acting defiantly toward them. When queried about when this pattern of problems began, they reply that the difficulties all started two months earlier when the girl began dating a boy from school. They had forbidden her to see this boy because "people should stay with their own kind." (One teen was European American and the other was African American.) They then asked the counselor if he could help them get their daughter to stop seeing the boy and behave more appropriately at school and at home.

This scenario places the values of the profession regarding social justice against the parents' request for assistance. The professional's needs, on one hand, to be respectful of the parents and find a way to be helpful to them and their daughter, and on the other, to avoid endorsing their view of interracial dating and defining the problem as they do. The situation may be made more difficult by the reluctance of most people in the United States to directly confront racial issues (Salter & Salter, 2012) and by the implicit assumption of the parents that a counselor of the same ethnicity as them would be likely to agree with them or acquiesce to their request. Clearly, the ethics of the profession are inconsistent with agreeing to the parents' goal regarding the daughter's dating, as stated in the Preamble to the ACA Code. However, in Section A.4.a, the ACA Code also advises counselors not to impose their values on clients. When viewed from the lens of the ethical principles and virtues, the counselor must balance respect for the autonomy of the parents against the principles of nonmaleficence and beneficence. If he submits to their request, he may ultimately harm and not help the girl, but if he does not respect their autonomy and rights as parents, he may never get the opportunity to counsel the girl at all. If he is to act in ways that show virtue, he must show integrity to the profession's values and honesty in his remarks, but he must also show compassion for the parents' situation and prudence in his response.

Is there a way forward here that is consistent with ethical values and that respects the parents? Perhaps—if the counselor suggests that he sees some of their goals for their daughter's counseling as workable, and some as not. Employing the full measure of his counseling skills, he probably needs to respectfully tell them that they may not want him as their daughter's counselor because he does not see interracial dating as inherently wrong, immediately following up with an offer to refer them to another counselor and an explanation of the help he may be able to offer them and their daughter on the other issues. It is important that he not deride their personal values or offer a long explanation about racial bias or the profession's values. Ultimately, the counselor must not contradict the fundamental professional value of respect for human dignity.

In other situations, someone may enter a professional's office to ask for help in changing someone's sexual orientation. Parents sometimes mistakenly think that sexual orientation is a choice, or a consequence of the media or the influence of friends. Sometimes clients also ask for a referral to reparative therapy that aims at changing their orientation because of the distress that not being heterosexual in most societies can cause. In these circumstances, the professional has an obligation to present to clients the data that indicate that such interventions are likely to be ineffective and can be harmful (e.g., APA, 2009a; Forstein, 2001; Nicolosi, Byrd, & Potts, 2000). Based on the scientific evidence, both the ACA and APA have adopted resolutions indicating that professionals should avoid endorsing strategies to change sexual orientation (APA, 2009a; Whitman, Glosoff, Kocet, & Tarvydas, 2006). The codes of ethics also clearly indicate that professionals base their interventions on scientifically established principles and evidence (ACA Code G.3.b. and APA Standard 2.04). Thus, the task of the professional in this circumstance is to educate the client about the evidence in a respectful and understandable way, explore the alternatives available to help reduce the distress, and offer additional social support.

CASES FOR DISCUSSION AND ANALYSIS

Consider the following questions for each case:

- How important is the client's cultural context in assessing the client's issues and determining treatment options?
- What is your emotional reaction to the problem the client presents?
- How do you think your personal values and cultural background would affect your capacity to provide services to these clients?
- What multicultural competencies do you think are necessary to provide effective service in each of these cases?

Worries about Roberta

Roberta has come to counseling with her aunt, Mary Begay. Roberta is a 14-year-old Navajo who lives on the reservation with her father, stepmother, and four stepbrothers. She has been detached from the family and acting in ways that are very atypical for her. They are all worried about her, especially her aunt. Ms. Begay tells of a recent episode that she calls "moth madness," and Roberta acknowledges that this occurred.

The counselor wonders if Roberta has developed an insect phobia and questions her extensively about her fears. Her responses do not point to a phobia. The counselor is unsure of how counseling ought to proceed, but the client is willing to return to counseling again to explore the matter further. The counselor tentatively diagnoses an adjustment disorder but is unsure of the cause of Roberta's distress.

Mervin's Request

Mervin is a 17-year-old African American teenager who was found living on the streets and sent to counseling by the courts. He is now in a foster home. His mother and father died recently of AIDS complications. His father was a hemophiliac who infected his mother with the virus before he was diagnosed. Mervin does not establish eye contact easily with his European American psychologist and has trouble sitting still for a whole session. The boy says that he wants to be left alone to finish high school, get a job, and earn enough money to live on his own. He resists discussing his feelings about his parents' deaths or his current situation. He seems skeptical about the psychologist's intentions and may well have concluded that counseling is something to be patiently endured until the psychologist gets tired of it.

Calvin's Career Dilemma

Calvin is a 20-year-old architecture student who comes to counseling because of his tendency toward procrastination. Calvin is of Korean ancestry, and his father is a scientist. As the counseling session progresses, Calvin's problem becomes clearer. He procrastinates because he has little interest in architecture. He loves to sculpt and has taken several elective courses in art. His behavior and affect reveal that sculpture is his true interest, but Calvin resists the suggestion that he may want to consider another major besides architecture. Instead of talking about his own interests, he discusses the long line of scientists in his family and his need to choose a profession with at least some relation to science. He asks the counselor to focus on the procrastination problem, because he cannot really consider other majors.

Daniel's Concern (Repeated)

Daniel is a 23-year-old Muslim man whose family has arranged a marriage for him, the accepted practice in his community. His reaction to this marriage has caused him so much distress that the imam recommended counseling. In session, Daniel reveals that he is ambivalent about the marriage. On the one hand, he wants to follow the tenets of his religion, which place strong emphasis on the importance of marriage for a Muslim man; but on the other, he knows he feels nothing for the woman his family has chosen. Daniel says he wants to marry eventually but feels completely unready now. He feels trapped. To violate his parents' choice would be inconsistent with the expectations of his religion and would risk his family's goodwill and his community's acceptance, but he feels strongly unsuited to this woman at this time. He asks his counselor to help him find a way to be more accepting of his parents' and community's choice for him.

Analysis of the Cases

In each of these cases, understanding the client's culture is a crucial component of ethical and effective professional service. Daniel, for example, lives in a religious community whose values, traditions, beliefs, and goals probably define almost every aspect of his life. He is part of a group that has been victimized by discrimination and oppression. His problem stems from a clash between personal wishes and cultural norms, or to use the framework James and Foster (2006) describe, he is caught between a duty-bound culture and a rights-oriented culture. Similarly, Roberta comes from a community that has suffered discrimination and oppression and has learned to be careful in interactions with non-Indians. The cultural norms of her tribe have probably defined her values and beliefs. She may view counseling as a last resort and be skeptical about its capacity to help. She is also an adolescent in the midst of forming her personal and cultural identity. The particular problem she mentions, "moth madness," is specific to her culture and is not part of most formal diagnostic systems used in mental health, so it is not meaningful outside the client's culture unless others (e.g., the clinician) have been taught its definition. In the next case, Mervin may have learned not to trust white Americans easily and to be uncomfortable with other people involving themselves in his personal affairs. Finally, Calvin has placed his family's expectations for his profession above his personal desires, a frequent choice in Asian American culture (Sue & Sue, 2007), but one that conflicts with the dominant U.S. cultural values of individual freedom of choice and action.

Thus, culture is a major influence on the development and definition of the problems these people are experiencing and has an impact on the selection of an appropriate treatment strategy and the development of a working alliance with the professional. A clinician who is unfamiliar with the Navajo concept of moth madness will have little sense of what Roberta is experiencing, and without asking questions and consulting with others will likely misdiagnose and mistreat this girl. (Moth madness is a seizure-like experience that typically follows incestuous dreams or thoughts in Navajo culture.) Similarly, a professional who frames Daniel's or Calvin's problem as depression and anxiety stemming from a lack of assertiveness or a failure to appropriately separate from family may create greater pain and will have little success in selecting an intervention that alleviates their pain. Mervin might be misunderstood as hostile, unfeeling, or unable to form close social bonds if his counselor fails to take the cultural context of his behaviors into account. Under such circumstances, his real difficulties are unlikely to be remedied.

Each of these cases probably stirs an emotional reaction in those who imagine themselves in that professional's position. The view that one's family has the right to choose one's marriage partner is a perspective that few in Western society hold and that seems contradictory to the central concept of individual freedom and a rights-entitled culture. It may evoke confusion, anger, and negative judgment in practitioners from Western cultures. Roberta's counselor may react with puzzlement and discomfort, or may approach her with benevolent condescension for her use of such quaint language. The implication in the case description, that the counselor failed to ask the client the meaning of moth madness, suggests either a discomfort with such a strange wording or a naive assumption that it is equated with an insect phobia. Such behavior epitomizes what Wrenn (1962) termed "cultural encapsulation."

Mervin's counselor may react to his behavior and attitude with frustration and may misinterpret the client's response as showing a personal dislike of the counselor or disdain for services. The counselor might assume that Mervin's parents were infected with the HIV virus through intravenous drug use because of a stereotype about heterosexual African Americans who are HIV infected. Mervin may have experienced this reaction previously from those who did not know his family.

Finally, in the case of Calvin, some of the same emotions may emerge. Some professionals may feel angry with the cultural value that minimizes the importance of individual career choice. They may even disbelieve the family influence as a primary factor and wonder if Calvin has some deeper psychological problem that prevents him from doing what he wants. In this instance, too, some may believe that the family is morally wrong to impose a career choice on a young adult. In any of these cases, a clinician can also feel the urge to rescue the client and show him or her a different (better?) way of understanding self and relating to family and others.

What follows are two cases in which the professional acts without sufficient awareness of the impact of disability and ageism on his or her actions.

Bernadette's Diagnosis

Bernadette was recently discharged from the Marines after service in Iraq, having suffered a traumatic brain injury (TBI) from a roadside bomb. Bernadette's language skills and cognitive abilities were not significantly affected by the explosion, though her judgment and emotional responsiveness were greatly harmed. In addition to the TBI, Bernadette is also experiencing mild symptoms of post-traumatic stress disorder (PTSD). The therapist her family has found for her does not regularly work with veterans or with individuals with brain injuries, but she is very experienced in working with PTSD from other causes. Because conversation with Bernadette appears normal in the initial session (and the client does not appear to have any physical injuries), the therapist proceeds with her typical process for clients with mild PTSD.

Dorian's Decision

Dorian, a clinical psychologist, has a 79-year-old client named Glenda who has come to counseling at the insistence of her children. Glenda wants to maintain her own home, but her children and neighbors are convinced that she can no longer care for it properly. Glenda begins the interview by stating that if anyone forces her to move, she will commit suicide because she has nothing else to live for. In the course of the session, Glenda admits some problems with independent living and seems to be distracted and unfocused in her comments. However, she does not seem disoriented or unable to meet her own needs. After several sessions, Dorian concludes that Glenda would probably be better off not having the responsibility for a large home. Dorian also concludes that although her mental capacities are not as strong as they once were, this woman is competent and in touch with reality. Whatever suicide risk that existed before has diminished. When the family calls Dorian to ask about Glenda's progress in therapy, he decides to reveal this information to them, even though he has not received prior permission from Glenda to do so.

MULTICULTURAL COMPETENCIES: CASE APPLICATION

The competencies essential to avoid the many pitfalls just described include *an attitude of openness* toward other worldviews. Understanding the influence of one's cultural heritage on a person's own development, values, beliefs, and social behaviors is a prerequisite for this attitude. When professionals see the roots of their own behaviors in culture, they are less likely to assume their universal truth or generalizability. This attitude of openness also encompasses a caution about applying heuristics, that is, "rules of thumb," about diagnosis or treatment too quickly. In Daniel's case, a therapist would need a willingness to understand the history and function of the arranged marriage tradition in that culture and to identify its origins in a different philosophy of individual freedom. He or she should also be familiar with the implications of the choices Daniel is considering for his social, occupational, and individual functioning. If the therapist is tempted to encourage the client to refuse the marriage at this point, he or she should understand that such a path may carry with it enormous costs for Daniel and may therefore not be in his best interests. That open mind is a prerequisite for helping a client sort out available alternatives and come to a free, self-made choice. Without it, the therapist has a hidden agenda of pushing the client toward a particular action. In the end, it is the client who must live with the consequences of the decision, not the counselor. Another way to conceive of the attitudinal components of competence is to apply the term Pedersen, Crethar, and Carlson (2008) use—*inclusive cultural empathy*. Among the other meanings of this construct is the assertion that effective multicultural service is embedded in an empathic relationship in which the professional diligently works to experience the world as the client views it.

Second, a professional must have *knowledge of the specific culture*. This is especially obvious in the case of Roberta. Ignorance of common cultural phenomena seems to be causing the counselor to badly misdiagnose the problem. Knowledge of the culture is also crucial when clients are torn between following the path typical of their culture and breaking off in a different direction. Knowledge would prevent Calvin's counselor from minimizing his parents' role in career decision making or underestimating the difficulty of violating that expectation.

Third, a professional must be *competent in involving other support people* from the culture. Knowing when and how to engage the imam in Daniel's decision making (assuming, of course, that Daniel agrees) could be a crucial factor in resolving the dilemma. In Roberta's case, the counselor did not seem to understand the aunt's role or availability as a resource, nor did she seem to know to contact a healer from the tribe who might shed light on the situation. In these scenarios, all clients spoke English, but if they did not, this competency also implies the capacity to use the client's language, select a competent interpreter, or make an appropriate referral. Mental health professionals should know how to seek out support for themselves, through consultation with peers and supervisors, to become better informed about the client's culture. Section A.1.d. of the ACA Code (2014) speaks directly to the importance of utilizing client supports to make counseling effective.

Fourth, the clinician needs to *modify interventions* or use interventions designed for cross-cultural counseling. Standard approaches to decision making or problem solving do not sufficiently account for the cultural aspects of situations such as Mervin's or Calvin's. Professionals must be skilled enough to adapt them or to use alternative approaches developed for cross-cultural counseling. For example, if Daniel decides to express his feelings about the marriage to his parents, the counselor must be competent in adapting traditional methods for effective interpersonal communication or assertive self-statements to this cultural context. The work of Pedersen and colleagues (e.g., see 2007 and 2008) and the book edited by Ponterotto, Casas, Suzuki, and Alexander (2009) are important resources in developing such competencies.

Professionals must also *develop a tolerance for ambiguity and divergent views of right and wrong*. When counseling clients such as Daniel, Calvin, or Mervin, counselors need the ability to accept that others do not have the same philosophy, worldview, or system of morality. Professionals accustomed to Western-style marriage based on romance must be able to tolerate the discomfort that watching a young person enter into an arranged marriage may elicit. In parallel fashion, they must learn to accept Mervin's choice not to participate fully in counseling, if that is his decision. In essence, this competency springs from the principle of respect for autonomy. If clients freely elect a path and have considered its alternatives, psychotherapists have a duty to respect that choice—provided, of course, it is not a serious risk to the client or others.

Some cross-cultural counseling situations are extremely difficult for professionals to deal with competently. These circumstances arise when, for example, the cultural values of the client seem to contradict more universal human values, for example, the right of all children to education (as affirmed in the United Nations' Universal Declaration of Human Rights, 1948). Consider the following case:

Chantu's Distress

The school counselor refers a family to a community mental health center for services because the father wants his 16-year-old daughter, Chantu, to quit school to manage the household and help care for her three younger siblings. Her father has offered her the option to finish her education through an online school if she wishes. Her mother is ill and can no longer carry out those responsibilities. The family emigrated from Cambodia nine years ago, and the daughter appears to have adapted to American schooling and culture quite well. She has told the school counselor that she is very distressed about having to quit regular school, but her father has been firm that no other choice is possible. Chantu has been very active in sports, debating, and Student Council and doesn't want to relinquish these activities. The girl has started to rebel and seems depressed.

In such cases, the professional should seek consultation from a professional with expertise in counseling South Asian clients, to better appreciate the father's perspective and get recommendations about how to assist both the girl and the father in the current situation. In fact, whenever a professional faces a complex ethical question, consultation is essential, as the ACA Code states in Section C.2.e.

CONFLICTS BETWEEN RELIGIOUS VALUES AND SERVICE TO DIVERSE CLIENTS

Consider the following situation:

An Unusual Applicant

An applicant to a counseling program makes an appointment with a faculty member to discuss her application. The applicant is a member of a religious community that rejects modern ways and lives without modern conveniences such as electricity and automobiles. She says she wants to stay in her community and offer them mental health services. She says these services are needed and that people in her community do not want to see a mental health professional from outside. The applicant also indicates that she wants as little interaction with other parts of society as possible once she finishes her degree. She is asking the faculty member whether all of her field experiences can be within her community and that she not be asked to learn how to counsel people from other segments of society in her training program. The faculty member is unsure of what to say and tells the applicant that the program includes role-playing with other students, a group counseling experience, and other activities that require the applicant to interact with other students. The applicant agrees to these training experiences but wants all of her community-based placements to be within her religious community and for her competence to be judged on the basis of her work there. The faculty member tells her that he will consult with the other counseling faculty and get back to her. The faculty have an extensive and heated discussion of the request of this otherwise competent applicant. Some are in favor of allowing the request because this community is indeed underserved, but others say that the license for which they are preparing this student is a general license, and they need some assurance of that before they can endorse this person as competent for licensing. The faculty vote is very close, but they grant admission.

In recent years, one issue related to cultural competence has come to the forefront: Is it ethical for someone whose religious beliefs conflict with client values/behaviors to refuse to counsel these individuals? For example, can a psychologist whose religious beliefs posit that homosexual acts are immoral refuse to counsel a lesbian client regarding the difficulties she is having in her relationship? This is an important question because all the codes of the professional associations prohibit clinicians from imposing their personal values on clients. The courts have become involved in some situations. For example, in *Bruff v. North Mississippi Health Services* (2001) a counselor in an employee assistance program refused to counsel a lesbian client regarding relationship issues, explaining to the client that such counseling was inconsistent with the counselor's religious beliefs. The client did not return for any appointments and filed a complaint against the counselor. In the meantime, the agency attempted to find a way to accommodate the counselor's beliefs and still provide fair service. When the counselor indicated that she would continue to refuse to counsel any client about matters that conflicted with her religious beliefs, the counselor was fired. The counselor filed suit for discrimination and violation of her rights. The Appeals Court ruled that even though employers have a responsibility to make a reasonable accommodation to an employee's religious beliefs, in this case the employee's demands were not reasonable. Therefore, the court supported the employer's right to terminate the employee. Another case resulted in a similar finding. In *Walden v. Centers for Disease Control and Prevention* (2010), the court upheld the termination of a counselor in an employee assistance program when that counselor not only refused to counsel LGBT clients regarding matters related to their sexual orientation but also insisted on disclosing to clients her negative judgment of LGBT orientations (or any other behavior prohibited by her religious beliefs). Once again the court held that the counselor's stance was unreasonable. Both of these cases affirmed the need for employers to make adjustments based on counselors' religious values, but they also indicated that such requests cannot be inflexible. (For more discussion of the impact of this issue on training programs and a full discussion the *Ward v. Wilbanks* [2010] case involving a training program, see Chapter 15.)

ADDITIONAL CASES FOR DISCUSSION

Jeremy is a clinical counselor from a Hopi tribe. He spent his developing years partly on a reservation and partly in a small town. He had no access to mental health services until college. After a college counselor helped him succeed in college, he decided to go to graduate school and become a counselor himself. When he opened his practice, Jeremy knew that he wanted to provide services to people in rural areas who were probably not getting their mental health needs met. He also hoped to be of service to American Indians. To achieve this goal, Jeremy decided to develop an Internet-based counseling service in addition to his regular practice. On this website, Jeremy offers clients email exchanges with him for very low fees. Some of the clients who use this website are depressed; others are anxious, and still others are dealing with substance abuse issues. A number of them are just lonely. Currently Jeremy has contact with approximately 30 people each week who use his website. Several of them are American Indians, and most live in small towns or rural areas. Jeremy feels grateful that he has accomplished his goal of helping rural and American Indian people cope better with their problems. Discuss the ethical risks and merits of Jeremy's actions. If he came to you for advice about his online practice, what would you advise him?

Tyrone is an African American counselor who has devoted his life to improving the civil rights for his race. He has pictures of several African American civil rights leaders in his counseling office, including Martin Luther King Jr., Malcolm X, and Medgar Evers. He has recently added the picture of a highly controversial African American to his collection. This man has been widely quoted in the media, making comments that many interpret as anti-Semitic. The director of the agency has asked Tyrone to remove the latest picture because she believes it may offend some clients. Tyrone has refused, and the director is trying to get him to change his mind about the picture. In the meantime, the director orders the intake workers not to schedule any Jewish clients with Tyrone. Was it ethical for Tyrone to bring a picture of this controversial man into his office? Should he have agreed to remove it? Were the director's actions in response ethical? What do you see as the ideal ethical solution to this conflict?

SUMMARY

American society has never been culturally homogeneous, but recent and projected changes in population demographics will render it truly heterogeneous. In fact, by middle of the twenty-first century, ethnic groups that have long been labeled *minorities* will collectively outnumber the rest of the population. These changes mean that mental health professionals will need skills, beliefs, and attitudes that equip them for providing effective service to diverse clients. The current versions of the codes of ethics place substantial emphasis on multicultural issues. Commitment to principles of equality and justice has never been more important. Along with the desire to be fair and accessible, one must have specific competencies in multicultural counseling to achieve that goal. These competencies include self-awareness that encompasses understanding of one's own cultural heritage and the impact of racism and discrimination on self and others. They also include knowledge about other cultures and the impact of culture on human behavior, with special emphasis on cultural effects on expressions of distress and dysfunction and on responses to counseling. Finally, competent counselors and therapists in a multicultural society will also possess skills in transcultural interventions and in adapting other counseling interventions to meet the needs of a diverse clientele.

In the course of their work with diverse populations, practitioners will confront dilemmas that are exceptionally difficult to resolve because some of them involve conflicts about deep personal values and beliefs. When this happens, they should act cautiously, seek consultation from those more knowledgeable about the client's culture, and refer to the abundant literature on responsible multicultural counseling and therapy.

Discussion Questions*

1. Do you believe the competencies outlined in this chapter are sufficient to equip mental health professionals to work with clients from different backgrounds? Are there other competencies you think should be added to this list? Explain.
2. Racism, sexism, and other forms of stereotyping are certainly not extinguished. Sometimes they even seem to be getting worse. What is the responsibility of a professional in the face of such eruptions of prejudice?
3. Some scholars suggest that all therapeutic services should be seen as cross-cultural. Does this view make sense to you? Why or why not?
4. Language barriers have been one important reason that diverse populations have had less access to mental health care. To address this problem, should competency in a second language be added as a requirement of professional training? Is using an interpreter a good solution to this deficiency?
5. Racist, ageist, sexist, and homophobic professionals still practice, and otherwise well-intentioned professionals still act in prejudicial ways sometimes. How do you think a professional should react when he or she encounters such behaviors in colleagues?
6. Do Asian, African American, and Latino professionals need to be as vigilant about self-monitoring for unconscious racism as European American counselors? Why or why not?

*Note to course instructors: The *Instructor's Guide* for this book includes other discussion questions, class exercises, cases, and multiple-choice and essay test items for this chapter.

7. Owen, Wong, and Rodolfa (2009) suggest that the mental health professions have operated on the good-hearted assumption that professionals can counsel either gender. They propose that perhaps gender competence should be analyzed more carefully. What do you think?

Recommended Readings

American Psychological Association. (2003). Guidelines on multicultural education, training, research, practice, and organizational change for psychologists. *American Psychologist, 58,* 377–402.

American Psychological Association. (2007a). Guidelines for psychological practice with girls and women. *American Psychologist, 62,* 949–979.

American Psychological Association. (2011a). Guidelines for assessment of and intervention with persons with disabilities. Retrieved from http://www.apa.org/pi/disability/resources/

American Psychological Association. (2011b). Guidelines for psychological practice with gay, lesbian, and bisexual clients. Retrieved from http://www.apa.org/pi/lgbt/resources/guidelines.aspx

Arredondo, P., Toporek, R., Brown, S. P., Jones, J., Locke, D., Sanchez, J., & Stadler, H. (1996). Operationalization of the multicultural counseling competencies. *Journal of Multicultural Counseling and Development, 24,* 42–78.

Artman, L. K., & Daniels, J. A. (2011). Disability and psychotherapy practice: Cultural competence and practical tips. *Professional Psychology: Research and Practice, 41,* 442–448.

Association for Lesbian, Gay, Bisexual and Transgender Issues in Counseling (ALGBTIC). (2012). Retrieved from https://www.ceunits.com/trainings/pdf_download/182/

Carter, R. T. (2007). Racism and psychological and emotional injury: Recognizing and assessing race-based traumatic stress. *The Counseling Psychologist, 35,* 13–105.

Cornish, J. A. E., Gorgens, K. A., Monson, S. P., Olkin, R., Palombi, B. J., & Abels, A. V. (2008). Perspectives on ethical practice with people who have disabilities. *Professional Psychology: Research and Practice, 39,* 488–497.

Gallardo, M. E., Johnson, J., Parham, T. A., & Carter, J. A. (2009). Ethics and multiculturalism: Advancing cultural and clinical responsiveness. *Professional Psychology: Research and Practice, 40,* 425–435.

Herlihy, B. J., Hermann, M. A., & Greden, L. R. (2014). Legal and ethical implications of using religious beliefs as the basis for refusing to counsel certain clients. *Journal of Counseling & Development, 92,* 148–153.

LaRoche, M. J., & Maxie, A. (2003). Ten considerations in addressing cultural differences in psychotherapy. *Professional Psychology: Research and Practice, 34,* 180–186.

Pedersen, P. B. (2000). *A handbook for developing multicultural awareness* (3rd ed.). Alexandria, VA: American Counseling Association.

Pedersen, P. B., Crethar, H., & Carlson, J. (2008). *Inclusive cultural empathy: Making relationships central in counseling and psychotherapy.* Washington, D.C.: American Psychological Association.

Pedersen, P. B., Draguns, J. G., Lonner, W. J., & Trimble, J. E. (2007). *Counseling across cultures* (6th ed.). Thousand Oaks, CA: Sage.

Ponterotto, J. G., Casas, J. M., Suzuki, L. A., & Alexander, C. M. (Eds.). (2009). *Handbook of multicultural counseling.* Thousand Oaks, CA: Sage.

Ridley, C. R. (1995). *Overcoming unintentional racism in counseling: A practitioner's guide to intentional intervention.* Thousand Oaks, CA: Sage.

Sue, D. W. (2010). *Microaggressions in everyday life: Race, gender, and sexual orientation.* Hoboken, NJ: Wiley.

Sue, D. W., Capodilupo, C. M., Torino, G. C., Bucceri, J. M., Holder, A. M. B., Nadal, K. L., … Esquilin, M. (2007). Racial microaggressions in everyday life. *American Psychologist, 62,* 271–286.

Vasquez, M. J. T. (2012). Social justice and civil virtue. In S. J. Knapp, M. C. Gottlieb, M. M. Handelsman, & L. D. VandeCreek (Eds.), *APA handbook of ethics in psychology* (Vol. 1), (pp. 75–97). Washington, D.C.: American Psychological Association.

Additional Online Resources

Association for Multicultural Counseling and Development, 2008. Multicultural Counseling Competencies: https://www.counseling.org/docs/competencies/multcultural_competencies.pdf?sfvrsn=5.

The Universal Declaration of Ethical Principles for Psychologists: http://www.apa.org/international/pi/2008/10/gauthier.aspx.

National Center for Cultural Competence: http://nccc.georgetown.edu/.

National Healthcare Disparities Report, 2011: http://www.apa.org/international/pi/2008/10/gauthier.aspx; www.ahrq.gov/research/findings/nhqrdr/nhdr13/2013nhdr.pdf.

Notes from the APA's Multicultural Conference and Summit: http://www.apa.org/international/pi/2008/10/gauthier.aspx; www.apa.org/monitor/mar07/ethics.aspx.

PART 2

Major Ethical Issues for Counselors and Therapists

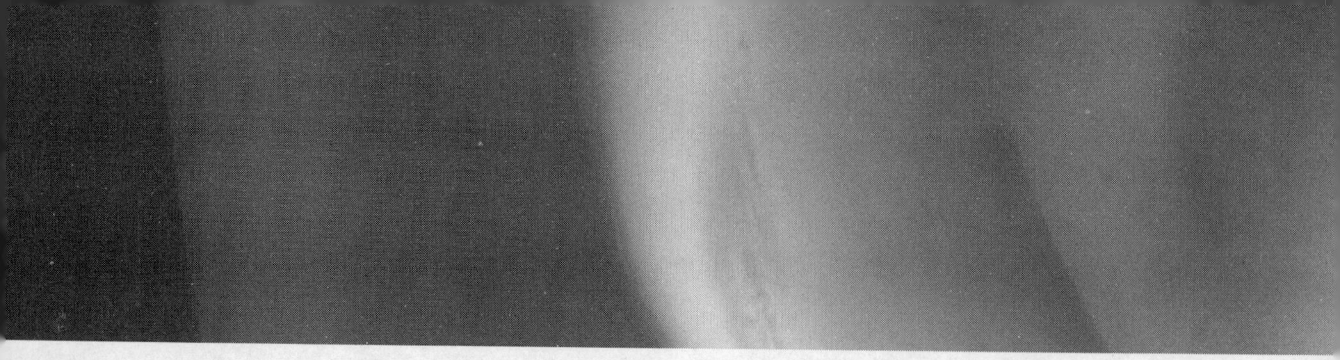

CHAPTER 4 Competence to Practice

Building and Maintaining a Foundation for Doing Good and Avoiding Harm

Competence is the most obvious ethical obligation of the practitioner, since incompetent practice dramatically increases the likelihood of harm to a client. Nevertheless, professional competence defies easy definition, but three major components capture its essence: *knowledge*, *skill*, and *diligence*. This chapter opens with an explanation of each element, reviews the relevant standards in the ethics codes, and offers guidelines for determining their limits and expanding areas of competency. It concludes with an analysis of the impact of distress and dysfunction on competence and provides strategies for coping with the challenges of professional practice, with special emphasis on the role of a professional support network.

COMPONENTS OF PROFESSIONAL COMPETENCE

Knowledge

To be knowledgeable means being schooled and up to date in the theory and research of one's field and cognizant of the limits of current understanding. Knowledge includes both comprehension of the relevant content and the capacity for judgment to make an informed choice about what knowledge and interventions apply in a given situation. To be knowledgeable also means that a professional has a set of objective and scientifically validated criteria for evaluating new theory and research (Spruill et al., 2004). The latter is especially important in counseling and psychotherapy because theory and research are always evolving. Pope and Vasquez (2011) refer to this component as intellectual competence, or in more simple terms, *knowing about*. In mental health professions, knowledge is first achieved by completing a credible graduate program in a mental health discipline. The most direct measure of the quality of a training program is accreditation by its discipline, because accredited programs have been judged to meet standards for assuring that their graduates have essential competencies to practice. Counseling (through the Council for Accreditation of Counseling and Related Educational Programs), psychology (through the APA's Office of Program Consultation and Accreditation), marriage and family therapy (through AAMFT), and social work (through NASW) all set high standards for graduate programs that seek accreditation. For counseling, marriage and family therapy, and social work, the entry-level degree is the master's, but psychologists in the United States have defined their entry-level degree as the doctorate. (In Canada and many other countries, the master's degree is the entry-level training for licensing as a psychologist). In recent years, graduate programs in psychology have devoted much attention to developing criteria for more accurately evaluating the competencies of students and their readiness for professional practice (e.g., Fouad et al., 2009). However, because knowledge is not static, and research on human behavior is evolving, a graduate degree, even from an accredited program, is only a starting point for intellectual competence. Without continued study, a professional's knowledge base quickly erodes. In fact, Dubin (1972) and Jensen (1979) conclude that approximately half of what a mental health professional learns in graduate school is obsolete within a decade of graduation. More recent research in professional psychology has reduced the half-life of knowledge related to clinical practice to approximately seven years, and practice in specializations such as clinical health psychology to less than six years (Neimeyer, Taylor, & Rozensky, 2012; Neimeyer, Taylor, Rozensky, & Cox, 2014). Unfortunately, research evidence suggests that a sizeable minority of practitioners fail to update their knowledge and do not participate in continuing education or stay current with the literature (Morrow-Bradley & Elliott, 1986; Neimeyer, Taylor, Zemansky, & Rothke, 2013). In jurisdictions that do not require professionals to participate in continuing education experiences, they are less likely to attend such programs (Neimeyer, Taylor, & Philip, 2010). For this reason, many state licensing boards have mandated continuing education for licensees. For example, 45 states and the District of Columbia require 20 or more hours of continuing education for psychologists every two years, though the number of hours required and the content of those hours vary significantly. Twenty-nine states stipulate completion of two to six hours of continuing education in ethics and legal issues for psychologists every biennium (Wise et al., 2010). Whether the licensing boards' requirement for regular continuing education reverses clinicians' erosion of knowledge remains to be determined by research (Sharkin & Plageman, 2003), although evidence suggests that participation has no effect on disciplinary action by licensing boards (Neimeyer, Taylor, & Orwig, 2013). However, professionals find the programs quite helpful in advancing their knowledge (VandeCreek, Knapp, & Brace, 1990; Neimeyer et al., 2010), regardless of whether they are mandated to attend or attend voluntarily (Neimeyer, Taylor, & Wear, 2011). Neimeyer et al. (2011) also noted that nearly two-thirds of psychologists report actually using the knowledge gained in continuing education experiences in their professional practices. The American Association of State Counseling Boards (AASCB) indicates that 23 states have continuing education requirements for licensed counselors, ranging from 20 to 40 hours per renewal cycle (AASCB, 2009).

Skill

The second component of competence is skill in successfully applying interventions with clients, or as Pope and Vasquez (2011) term it, *knowing how*. Norman (1985) and Overholser and Fine (1990) divide this component into two kinds of skills: *clinical skill* is the counselor's appropriate use of basic interviewing skills, and *technical skill* concerns effective use of specific therapeutic interventions. Clinical skills include the capacity to build a productive therapeutic alliance, experience empathy, communicate effectively, and sensitively explore a client's problem. Spruill et al. (2004) identify cultural competence, knowledge of ethical and legal guidelines, and the ability to think critically as additional foundational clinical skills, a designation fully endorsed in current ethical standards of all the mental health professions. The language in the ACA Code (2014) clearly illustrates this endorsement of cultural competence, as it states in C.2.a: "Counselors gain knowledge, personal awareness, sensitivity, and skills pertinent to being a culturally competent counselor in working with diverse populations."

The APA Code communicates a similar message in Principle E, which delineates the obligation of psychologists to respect cultural differences and eliminate bias in their work with diverse populations (Appendix B, pp. 537–538).

Technical skills are exemplified by the ability to conduct desensitization for a client with test anxiety or to administer an individual intelligence test. Implicit in the general concept of skill is the capacity of the professional to make judgments about which interventions are appropriate in which situations. These judgments should be informed by the current research on evidence-based practice (e.g., Lambert, 2013; Norcross, 2011), which includes the data from clinical trials and naturalistic studies of interventions, evidence regarding the role of the therapeutic relationship, client values and preferences for services, and the judgment and skill of the professional (Levant, 2005; Norcross, Beutler, & Levant, 2005).

To help students develop clinical judgment and intervention skills, all mental health training programs require field experiences such as practica and internships as major parts of their degree requirements. Applying knowledge with a client is a higher-order process than comprehending that information, and no one is competent until he or she has mastered both. For example, graduate students typically learn about communicating empathy and treating phobias in their classes, becoming familiar with both the theory and the research on these actions. They may read transcripts of sessions, view videotapes of model sessions, and practice these skills in role-plays with each other. Then students are evaluated on their grasp of the material. However, even students who succeed in the classroom are not competent unless they can skillfully apply this knowledge to appropriate clients. Because of the complexity of skill building in counseling and psychotherapy, many hours of closely supervised field experience are necessary to achieve competence.

The importance of competent practice has been highlighted by the increased attention of accrediting bodies on the thoroughness of training programs in assessing students' development of therapeutic knowledge and skill. In fact, assessing student competencies has emerged as a major consideration in determining whether training programs achieve accreditation (Fouad et al., 2009; Kaslow, Rubin, Bebeau, et al., 2007; Nelson, 2007). The profession of psychology, for example, has devoted much attention to strategies for developing a "culture of competence" in training programs and for more extensive assessment of students' readiness for professional practice (Fouad et al., 2009; Kaslow et al., 2009. The accumulation of hours in placement is no longer viewed as the best criterion for assessing a student's capacity to provide acceptable levels of clinical service.

Additional supervised experience after the awarding of a degree is also typically required before states will license mental health professionals for independent practice. Many states require two years of full-time supervised work experience before granting a license to a master's level professional and one year of full-time supervised practice for doctoral-level psychologists. Even in the jurisdictions that forego post-doctoral supervision for psychologists (Alabama, Arizona, Connecticut, Indiana, Kentucky, Maryland, North Dakota, Ohio, Puerto Rico, Utah, Washington, and Wyoming), extensive practica and predoctoral internship experiences are mandatory. In Canada, three provinces require post-degree training for psychologists: Manitoba, Nova Scotia, and Ontario (see http://www.asppb.org/HandbookPublic/Reports/default.aspx?ReportType=SupervisedExperience for a detailed description of licensing requirements in psychology).

The complexity of counseling and psychotherapy also means that no single individual will be skillful in all interventions, either at graduation or at any point in his or her career. The staggering range of human problems, coupled with the diversity of client backgrounds and therapeutic interventions, renders universal competence impossible. All practitioners must limit their work to some subsample of problems and populations. A clinician's limits of competence are also referred to as the *scope of practice*. Some professionals elect to focus on particular problems such as depression or career indecision, whereas others focus on particular age groups, such as college students or older adults. Still others limit their practice to group or family counseling or to specific services for particular populations, such as therapeutic interventions for survivors of torture or rehabilitation counseling for individuals with traumatic brain injuries. Beware the professional who claims to do everything well: Either some of those skills are underdeveloped, or that person is a fraud.

Diligence

Diligence, the third component of competence, has two aspects. The first is a consistent attentiveness to the client's needs that takes priority over other concerns. A diligent professional gives deliberate care to appropriate assessment and intervention for a client's problem and maintains that care until services are completed. He or she also plans for follow-up and evaluation of the quality and endurance of treatment effects. Diligence means that the professional is willing to work hard to benefit a client and is ready to refer the client elsewhere if unable to give competent help.

The second aspect of diligence is self-knowledge, rooted in self-reflection and humility about the accuracy and comprehensiveness of our own strengths and limitations. This aspect of competence has been called *emotional competence*, a term from Pope and Vasquez (2011) that refers to capacity of the individual for "self awareness and respect for ourselves as unique, fallible human beings" (p. 62). It also encompasses a professional's commitment to self-care and self-monitoring so that developing problems in competence are identified long before they affect work with clients. We must be humble about our ability to accurately identify our strengths and weaknesses because research shows, rather convincingly, that mental health professionals are often less knowledgeable than they think about how clients are experiencing counseling and therapy and whether their interventions are helpful. For example, Lambert and his colleagues have demonstrated that therapists typically overestimate client progress in counseling and that these misjudgments sometimes lead to client dropout and treatment failure (Lambert, 2010a). Walfish, McAlister, O'Donnell, and Lambert (2012) reported that 25% of the mental health professionals they sampled believed they were at the 90th percentile compared to other professionals, and none indicated they were below average. Other evidence shows that psychologists think they understand their legal and ethical duties with clients when they are, in fact, in error (Pabian, Welfel, & Beebe, 2009). This reality means that diligent practice cannot be achieved in isolation—only those who systematically consult with others about the quality and effectiveness of their work can be called diligent (Johnson et al., 2012). In other words, these authors propose that it is time for the profession to endorse a communitarian view of competence.

Evidence of a diligent attitude emerges in several ways. It is present in the thoroughness of services. A diligent professional wants to be as sure as reasonably possible about the diagnosis and the treatment. (Note the words *reasonably* and *sure*; diligence does not require obsessive concern with detail.) Diligence is also present in one's willingness to engage in additional research and consultation about a client's diagnosis and treatment. A diligent professional is also interested in following up with clients who complete services, to gather data on the long-term effectiveness of their interventions. Such information can help both the former client and future clients. A diligent professional is willing to ask the hard questions and face the instances in which service did not prove helpful. In discussing responsible medical diagnosis and treatment, Groopman (2007) advises clinicians and patients to ask, "What else might this be?" Clearly, the entire evidence-based practice movement requires no less than a diligent approach to planning, administering, and following up on services once they are completed (Norcross, Beutler, & Levant, 2005). APA has defined evidence-based practice as "the integration of the best available research with clinical expertise in the context of patient characteristics, culture, and preferences" (Levant, 2005, p. 7).

The Competence Continuum

Thus competence takes intellectual and emotional energy and is both a goal and a reality for the individual and the profession. The competence continuum runs from incompetent to exceptionally competent (Koocher, 1979). Spruill et al. (2004) used a similar model developed by Dreyfus to delineate five levels of competence from novice to expert. A competent professional is always seeking to enhance current skills and knowledge but the aim is not perfection. Instead, competence implies, at a minimum, adequate care and is partially measured in a comparative fashion. One is competent when one's knowledge and skills are as well developed as those of other professionals previously demonstrated to be competent in the specified area. In other words, one is deemed competent if, after education and supervised practice, one can carry out an intervention at least as well as supervisors or colleagues.

A comparative criterion has its perils, however—one might settle for being as ineffective as one's colleagues. A preferable criterion for competence is one's effectiveness in helping clients, in developing plans for counseling, in implementing those plans, and in evaluating the outcomes of services (Spruill et al., 2004). Care that benefits the client and avoids unnecessary risk is the more fundamental measure of competence. Sometimes a third criterion exists—attainment of the standards established by a professional association for a particular type of practice. For example, the American Psychological Association has produced specialty guidelines for providing services in clinical, counseling, school, and organizational psychology (APA, 2003) that identify skills essential for competence with multicultural clients. Similarly, the American Association for Marriage and Family Therapists (AAMFT) has established criteria for competence in that discipline (Everett, 1990). Another way to think about aiming toward competent counseling and psychotherapy is to practice as Gawande (2007) advises his medical students—to be a "positive deviant," to avoid settling for minimally acceptable work and seek instead to provide services to clients that would be of the quality one desires for a loved one.

Competence refers to a person's professional performance, not to abilities. One may have the *ability* to perform competently, but competence is judged in the *performance* of the task itself (Jensen, 1979). Many factors can interfere with a capable person's performance. These factors range from environmental circumstances (such as impossible work demands) to unpredictable events (such as a sudden illness in the middle of a session) to a therapist's mental health problems (such as depression or burnout). Ability is a prerequisite for competence but is not identical with it.

Competent performance probably also varies from client to client and day to day. No mental health professional performs at the identical level of skill and diligence with every client. Fatigue, distraction, and stress are typical problems that compromise competent performance. A more realistic standard is a set threshold level for competent practice, defined as service that provides the client with the likelihood of benefit. If professionals give service less competent than that, they need to rectify the problems they created. For instance, one may invite a client back for another session without charge, or may consult a colleague or supervisor to deal with the stress that caused the lapse. (A later section of this chapter discusses service made persistently inadequate by dysfunction or distress.)

PROFESSIONAL STANDARDS FOR PRACTICE

All the major codes of ethics governing mental health professions contain statements about competence. Both the ACA and APA codes make lengthy comments on the topic, underscoring its importance. These standards derive from the ethical principles of beneficence and nonmaleficence, the duty to do good and avoid harm. As mentioned in Chapter 1, genuine skill at helping people in distress is essential for professions that publicly proclaim their expertise in this area. Offering anything less constitutes dishonest advertising. Both codes acknowledge the impossibility of universal competence and emphasize the importance of working within the boundaries of one's knowledge and skill. The codes designate the duty to monitor one's competence and make improvements as the responsibility of the individual professional. Finally, the codes stipulate that competence results from a combination of formal education, supervised practice, and continuing education, and indicate that competence is a career-long endeavor not to be left to chance or incidental encounters. Not all activities to enhance competence need to be as structured as a course; informal activities may also be helpful, as Lichtenberg and Goodyear (2012) suggest. See Appendix A, ACA Code, Section C.2, pp. 503–504, and APA Code, Appendix B, Standard 2, pp. 539–541, for the specific code language.

Expanding the Scope of Practice

Professionals seeking to extend their competence to a new area should develop a systematic and comprehensive plan consistent with existing standards. The APA Code also offers guidance for establishing competence in emerging areas of practice. This standard imposes a duty to act to become competent and to protect clients and other consumers of such untested approaches. It is important to note that professionals need not exclude new procedures from their practice, but rather they should be cautious and prudent in their use to protect client welfare. If a treatment approach with demonstrated effectiveness for a given population or problem exists, the use of an unproven intervention is difficult to justify.

Some of the most egregious violations of ethical practice have occurred when professionals have failed to examine the scientific basis for their interventions and have used experimental interventions without attending to their risks. The case of Candace Newmaker, the 9-year-old girl who lost her life in a “rebirthing” treatment for an attachment disorder, is the most outrageous example of therapists who were so convinced that they were justified to use this highly risky intervention that they allowed this girl to suffocate in the constricting blanket that they used to simulate rebirth. Other less egregious examples can be found in the literature and media reports that illustrate the faddish nature of some innovations.

Emergency Situations

Sometimes no one else is immediately available to offer service to a client. The APA Code, Standard 2.01e, clarifies the responsibility of professionals in situations where alternative service is not reasonably accessible. It advises professionals that if their competence is in an area closely related to the service the client needs, professionals may proceed with treatment, provided that they make efforts to become competent through training, consultation, and supervision. The APA also advises professionals about the ethics of competent service in emergency situations in Standard 2.02, stating that it may be permissible to provide care beyond the scope of one’s competence in an urgent situation, but that the duty is also to refer to a qualified person as soon as feasible.

This standard frees professionals from undue concern about an ethics violation when they are attempting to respond compassionately to an urgent situation. It also highlights the promotion of the welfare of the client as the highest ethical priority. At the same time, when professionals are providing emergency care outside the customary of their competence, they must intervene as conservatively as possible and work diligently to obtain more competent care as soon as possible. The ACA Code does not address this issue.

The Relationship Between Competence and Professional Credentials

Licenses and certificates are designed to protect the public from frauds and charlatans (Vaughn, 2006). Procidano, Busch-Rossnagel, Reznikoff, and Geisinger (1995) capture the function of licenses well when they write: "What the states license is the absence of deficiencies, rather than the presence of competencies" (p. 427). Certifying bodies extensively review only the knowledge component of competence. These boards weed out the least knowledgeable by preventing those who lack appropriate graduate degrees from becoming licensed or certified. A graduate degree is, after all, the primary credential for professional competence; licenses and certificates are secondary (Koocher, 1979). Because clinicians typically need to pass a state examination to get a license, individuals who managed to receive a degree without learning much are not likely to succeed in getting licensed.

Credentialing bodies in the United States evaluate the skills component rather indirectly, through the requirement that candidates for licensing amass a substantial number of hours of supervised experience in the field, although there is discussion about including direct evaluation of skills both at entry to a profession and at re-licensing (Rodolfa et al., 2012). Some other countries already use this approach to licensing and re-licensing (Welfel & Khamush, 2012). Licensing bodies tend to measure diligence minimally, using inquiries about prior ethics violations, criminal convictions, or personal problems that may compromise practice. Some states require professionals to meet character and fitness requirements, but other jurisdictions prohibit queries about character for mental health professionals (Johnson, Porter, Campbell, & Kupko, 2005). The continuing education requirements built into most mental health licenses aim to protect the public from practitioners whose knowledge and skills are obsolete. Finally, licensing boards usually require applicants to specify their areas of competence and continue to request this information at each license renewal. This is also referred to as defining one's *scope of practice*. In a small way, this process forces practitioners to identify the boundaries of their competence and reminds them that the limits they specify are a matter of public record. Working outside those boundaries carries a risk to their license. Some states such as Ohio are also requiring licensees to describe their competencies in multicultural counseling and psychotherapy in an effort to ensure competent practice with diverse populations, and a few states mandate regular continuing education in sociocultural issues. (For more discussion of multicultural competence, see Chapter 3.)

Professional organizations that branch off from the national associations have been formed to provide more stringent measures of competence and more direct assessment of therapeutic judgment and skills. One such organization is the American Board of Professional Psychology (ABPP). Practitioners may apply to this body to be certified as "diplomats" in their field. If applicants pass the rigorous review process for this status, they have demonstrated a well-recognized level of professional accomplishment. The National Board for Certified Counselors (NBCC) provides the same service for counselors. These certifications go a step beyond a professional license to practice, although they are also categorized as secondary credentials. Koocher and Keith-Spiegel (2008) classify membership in professional associations and listings in the National Register of Health Care Providers as tertiary credentials.

However, the accumulation of credentials is not in itself a guarantee of competence in practice because of the inherent weaknesses in the procedures used to evaluate candidates. Nor do credentials imply future competence. Without continued effort to maintain knowledge and skill, competence still erodes, no matter how firmly established it has been in the past.

Woody (1997) points out that some "dubious and bogus" credentials have emerged in mental health partly because of increased competition in the marketplace for clients and reimbursement (p. 337). Practitioners "earn" these credentials by paying the requisite fees; little additional verification of their training or qualifications is required. Such credentials offer little more than an ego boost and are dangerous insofar as they deceive the public about the expertise of the practitioner. Academic institutions touting degrees in counseling or psychology in six weeks (or less) still exist, as any Web search will reveal, though none of these institutions are accredited and therefore would not be recognized by any state or provincial licensing board.

CHALLENGES IN DEFINING THE LIMITS OF COMPETENCE

How do professionals determine the areas in which they are competent, and how do they develop new areas of competence during the years they are practicing? The codes give reasonable direction in this area in Sections C.2.a and C.2.b (ACA, 2014) and APA Code, Standard 2.01 (2010a). Before one can claim competence in any new procedure, population, or assessment tool, formal training is necessary. Formal training typically entails structured learning, reading, and discussion with experts. The length and intensity of instruction depends on the complexity of the new competence, its potential to help or harm, and the prior background of the professional. For example, someone who is well trained in play therapy with school-age children and wants to become competent in a new form of play therapy requires less formal instruction time than a therapist unschooled in play therapy. The latter person would require in-depth instruction in the history, theory, procedures, and research of play therapy, along with supervised practice in established interventions, before he or she could implement the new technique. Both would need supervised experience in the new technique, but the amount of supervised experience would differ; the criterion for success is the capacity to use appropriate clinical judgment and to apply the knowledge skillfully. If the new play therapy technique has been demonstrated to be a powerful therapeutic intervention (i.e., one that can offer substantial help when used properly or cause substantial harm when used improperly), the standard for competence should be set very high. Practically, this translates into longer and more intensive training and practice with the technique. It is important to remember that the requirements for competence in new areas are not different for those who are already competent in other interventions. What may be different is the speed with which a practitioner can proceed through the requirements because of his or her history and background.

Some weekend workshops and brief seminars are advertised as training for professionals in new interventions. Recently, this author received a brochure for a one-day seminar that claimed to teach a new therapy that treats all personality disorders, addictions, and repetitive criminal behaviors. The presenter was described as a trained psychotherapist with a private practice who is currently writing a book about this new therapy. No other information about the scientific basis for the intervention was provided, nor did the schedule for the seminar include time for assessing the skills of the attendees in this new therapy. However, the presenter did offer to sell tapes and videos to interested professionals. Because such workshops seldom offer time for reading, research, and supervised practice with actual clients, they are unlikely to produce participants who are truly competent in the technique. By the same token, presenters have a responsibility to clarify the goals and limitations of their seminars and describe the possible benefits of attendance. They are also accountable for avoiding actions that risk harm to clients. Moreover, the definition of competence includes scientific value. Independent research demonstrating the efficacy of the approach is the cornerstone of such evidence. In its absence, new interventions are considered experimental or innovative, and claiming competence in such situations is premature. Thus, when looking for continuing education experiences to expand their competencies, professionals need to ascertain whether the proposed training (1) is based on scientific evidence, objectively obtained; (2) includes sufficient classroom time for learning; (3) is offered by a professional with expertise in the area; and (4) provides opportunities for supervised practice and recommendations for obtaining additional supervised experience. Sometimes direct inquiries to the workshop organizers are necessary to obtain this information. The wording of the APA Code as expressed in Standard 2.01e reflects this interpretation with its emphasis on sufficient competence in emerging areas to protect the client, along with appropriate informed consent. The ACA Code offers similar requirements for counselors in Section C.7.b and for counselor educators regarding the teaching of innovative theories and techniques in Section F.7.h.

Limits of Competence With New Client Populations

The boundaries of competence extend not just to interventions such as play therapy or career counseling but also to new populations. A person may be skilled in career counseling for one cultural group or age group but may be insufficiently competent to use that intervention with other age groups or cultural groups. This happens because these contexts can alter both the way the intervention is received and its effectiveness. Competent work with particular populations also assumes knowledge of the group and demonstrated skill in working with that group. A college counselor who applies the career counseling approaches he uses with university students to middle school students is unlikely to help those children. The counselor has failed to adapt his intervention to their developmental level and may thereby have inflicted unintended negative effects on the children. Similarly, helping a recent Cambodian immigrant to the United States deal with depressed feelings may demand additional competencies from those needed to treat a depressed client raised in the United States. In this situation, knowledge of the impact of culture, national origin, and immigration status on the etiology and symptoms of depression is important. Professionals competent in treating depression have a responsibility to recognize the unique parameters of this case and to seek additional training or consultation to help the client or refer him to another professional already competent with these issues (see Chapter 3 for a more extensive discussion of competence with diverse clients).

The professional associations recognize the need for knowledge and skill in working with different populations in two major ways. First, in addition to its statements in the ethics code, the APA has published numerous guidelines for working with diverse populations (see Appendix D for a list). *Guidelines for Psychological Practice With Girls and Women* (APA, 2007a), *Guidelines for Providing Services to Ethnic and Culturally Diverse Populations* (APA, 1993, 2003), and *Guidelines for Psychological Practice With Older Adults* (APA, 2014) are three representative examples. These documents are a crucial resource for practitioners seeking to evaluate their competence with clients from these populations. Second, the ACA has addressed the topic in its ethics code in Sections C.2.a and C.2.f, cited above. In addition, the ACA also publishes its criteria for competent service to diverse publications (Arredondo et al., 1996) and competency statements for working with LGBT populations and for advocacy activities. See http://www.counseling.org/Resources/ for a list of all of ACA's competency statements.

Limits of Competence in Rural Environments and Small Communities

One challenge in working within the boundaries of competence arises from the geographical location of a given professional practice. Professionals in urban and suburban settings tend to have many local referral sources when they are not competent to offer services, and they also tend to have easier access to face-to-face consultation and supervision (Helbok, 2003). Thus, urban and suburban practitioners have relatively little difficulty limiting their scope of practice and may focus on areas in which they have developed significant expertise. In contrast, practitioners in rural areas and small communities do not have many referral sources nearby. Traveling to see another professional is frequently an inconvenience for a client. Sometimes the local mental health professional is the only available source of services. If he or she cannot provide services, clients may not seek further help and may try to cope on their own. Consequently, out of necessity, professionals in rural areas usually practice as generalists. Clinicians who focus on counseling clients from small cultural/ethnic communities, the deaf community, LGBT communities, faith-based communities, the military, and in corrections settings experience the same complications (Schank, Helbok, Haldeman, & Gallardo, 2010).

The ethical challenge for rural and small community professionals is to provide competent service across a wide range of issues, age groups, and populations while acknowledging that they are not omnipotent (Curtin & Hargrove, 2010; Schank & Skovholt, 2006). What criteria should rural practitioners use when deciding whether a given client request is beyond the limits of their competence? The major determination evolves from the principle of nonmaleficence—avoiding harm to clients. Clients who are at risk for significant harm from an incompetently administered intervention are better served by a referral, in spite of the inconvenience. Second, professionals should evaluate the opportunity to do good and compare the risk of harm to the opportunity to help. If the risk of harm is high and the chance to help is low, then one should refrain from intervention. If the risk of harm is low and the opportunity to benefit the client is significantly greater, then the intervention can be considered. Access to alternative service is an important variable to consider because there is shortage of practitioners in small communities. Over 85% of the designated shortage areas in the United States are rural (U.S. Department of Health and Human Services, 2006). Moreover, the demand for practitioners with multicultural competencies is growing in rural areas as the populations there have become more ethnically diverse (Sawyer, Gale, & Lambert, 2006). This deficit of service places an added responsibility on these professionals to use inventive strategies to enhance their competence and gain access to appropriate supervision. Thankfully, the advent of the Internet has provided easier access to a variety of educational and consultation resources for rural mental health professionals. It has also offered consumers online treatment options (see Chapter 5 for a fuller discussion of the ethical issues in using electronic media for communication about particular clients). Finally, small community practitioners should monitor client progress and aggressively intervene when the client seems not to be benefiting. If professionals see a pattern of client problems at the boundaries of their competence, they have an obligation to gain additional education to become more competent in serving this community need. (Needless to say, informed consent takes on even greater importance when the intervention approaches the boundaries of a professional's competence. Clients should be informed about the level of their provider's skills and give written consent to services.)

Haas and Malouf (2005) recommend that mental health professionals ask themselves two other questions when they are unsure about their competence with a particular client. The first question is, "Are you emotionally able to help the client?" (p. 28). They suggest that counselors and therapists ask themselves whether they can maintain objectivity in the situation. Perhaps the nature of the client's problem is too close to the clinician's own experience to avoid countertransference. To maintain objectivity, professionals need to have insight into their behavior and have a professional support system available to double-check the accuracy of their own interpretations of the client. Even then, some client issues can be strong triggers for some practitioners, and those safeguards are insufficient. Referral is then the safest choice. Taking these steps helps the professional maintain what Pope and Vasquez (2011) refer to as *emotional competence*.

The second question Haas and Malouf suggest is, "Could you justify your decision to a group of your peers?" (2005, p. 30). They also refer to this as the "clean, well-lit room standard," which means that any action that a practitioner would feel comfortable describing in an open discussion with his or her peers is likely to be appropriate. Conversely, any activity that a professional would like to hide or would be ashamed to admit to peers is probably not a responsible action. This standard applies not only to questions of competence to treat but also to other ethical issues in practice, especially boundary violations. For example, if a professional is wondering whether it would be ethical to ask her client for retirement planning advice because he is a financial planner, that counselor can obtain a sense of the ethics by imagining describing to other staff a plan to work with a current client on a financial plan for retirement. For all but the most insensitive professional, such an exercise is likely to result in uneasy feelings, and that uneasiness itself is a signal to reevaluate the plan.

The Limits of Competence: Case Examples

Consider the following cases, both of which illustrate the challenges of defining the limits of one's competence as a professional.

The Case of Mrs. Varos

A couple makes an appointment with Mrs. Varos, a licensed professional clinical counselor with 10 years of experience in private practice. This couple is requesting sex therapy, and the initial assessment suggests that they have accurately identified the major difficulty in their relationship. In fact, the sexual dysfunction they describe is very common and is typically responsive to therapy. Mrs. Varos had no formal courses in sex therapy in graduate school, but has read several books on the topic and attended a two-day workshop on treatment of sexual dysfunctions nine months ago. She also has attended a national conference on sex therapy. Mrs. Varos has a colleague with extensive training and experience in this area; he is willing to supervise her for this case. In this situation, can Mrs. Varos consider herself competent to offer professional services to this couple?

The first step in determining whether Mrs. Varos should accept this couple as clients is to ascertain whether she has the requisite knowledge of sex therapy. Knowledge usually means formal education, which she lacks. However, if Mrs. Varos can demonstrate that her independent reading and attendance at professional programs are equivalent to what others receive in formal courses, then she could meet the knowledge requirement. The second issue is whether she has enough supervised experience in sex therapy to be skillful in its application. She has no such experience, which is a significant obstacle to demonstrating competence in sex therapy. If her experience as a professional counselor includes marriage and family therapy, and she is competent in this related field, she may not need extensive hours of supervised experience in sex therapy to become competent. However, the absence of supervised experience probably renders her incompetent to serve independently as a sex therapist at this time, even though this couple's problem usually responds to therapy. Her colleague's offer to supervise her work with this couple is an important factor to consider, but it is only sufficient if he is willing to provide close supervision and she is willing to do any additional work that he recommends to upgrade her knowledge. On the other hand, the availability of a colleague with expertise to help this couple may constitute an argument for referral. Why risk harming or simply not helping this couple when another professional with proven skill is easily accessible? The clean, well-lit room standard also can be useful in evaluating the situation. Mrs. Varos probably would not be comfortable reporting to respected colleagues that she treated this couple unless she could demonstrate that she was receiving close supervision or gaining additional knowledge.

Regardless, if Mrs. Varos is to continue as their counselor, the clients must be informed of her novice status (in this intervention) and of the close supervision she is receiving. If they agree to service under these conditions, then it would be ethical to continue working with them. She would have the responsibility to fill gaps in her knowledge, to monitor their progress closely, and to use supervision wisely. The couple should also be informed of the identity of the supervisor in the event that they have questions about her effectiveness.

The Case of Dr. Marcello

Dr. Marcello is a licensed psychologist who has worked in a community mental health agency for five years. His parents immigrated to the United States from Italy when he was a child. He specializes in family therapy, an area in which he has had considerable academic training and supervised experience. Dr. Marcello views himself to be competent as a family therapist. Mr. and Mrs. Turner make an appointment to see him because they are concerned about their teenage son, who frequently skips school and has been ignoring curfews and other family rules. The Turners are African Americans. Dr. Marcello has little experience in counseling African American families, and his cultural background does not match that of the Turners. He did have formal courses in multicultural issues in graduate school and has kept up with the literature in this area. In fact, the mental health center has very few African American clients and no other staff member at the agency has better training in family therapy. Does Dr. Marcello's experience make him competent to work with the Turners?

The case of Dr. Marcello is more complicated than the first case. There is no doubt of his competence in family therapy. His knowledge base on multicultural issues may also be adequate. The cultural difference between the therapist and the potential clients here, coupled with Dr. Marcello's lack of experience in family therapy with African American families, is the central issue. Should his lack of experience with African American families prevent him from accepting this family as clients? To resolve this question, several other questions must be addressed:

- To what degree does the literature suggest that family dynamics in African American families differ significantly from those in other cultures?
- To what degree have the approaches to family therapy in which Dr. Marcello has been trained been shown to be effective for African American families?
- What evidence exists that these approaches have harmed or failed to benefit African American families?
- What is the attitude of this family to this psychologist, and what are their views about whether the cultural differences between them will inhibit effective therapy?
- Exactly how much prior experience has Dr. Marcello had with African American families and individuals during his training? Can he arrange for competent supervision/consultation for this case?
- Are there other competent professionals in the community to whom Dr. Marcello can refer this family?

By reviewing the requirements for competence, knowledge, experience, and diligence to resolve this dilemma, we can surmise that Dr. Marcello's knowledge is probably adequate, given his education and continued reading. His commitment to stay current in the literature on multicultural issues and his demonstrated competence as a family therapist also are positive signs of diligence and cultural sensitivity. His limited supervised experience is the problem, which is further complicated by the unavailability of an appropriately trained professional at his agency. At the very least, because of this deficit, Dr. Marcello cannot proceed in a business-as-usual way. He has two ethical alternatives. He may refer the family to a competent professional at another agency, or he may make arrangements for supervision/consultation from a professional outside the agency and then obtain the Turners' consent to such supervision. In the latter case, the Turners would understand Dr. Marcello's strengths and weaknesses as their family therapist and would agree to the supervisor's involvement in the case.

Of course, referral to a professional who is competent in this area is not always practical. If obtaining a competent referral is problematic, and the Turners are willing to work with him and likely to benefit from intervention, the argument in favor of Dr. Marcello's taking on this case is significantly stronger. As in the case of Mrs. Varos, the family's progress must be carefully monitored. In the end, the central consideration is doing good for the clients and avoiding harm to them—both the harm that derives from incompetent practice and the harm that derives from failing to provide them with access to services likely to be beneficial.

DISTRESS, BURNOUT, AND OTHER COMPETENCE PROBLEMS

One of the hallmarks of clinical work is the pervasiveness of ambiguity and uncertainty. As Skovholt and Starkey (2010) suggest, no Holy Grail of counseling exists and no amount of experience guarantees perfectly competent service. Reed (2006) indicated that at least 33 variables are active in the counseling and therapy session, resulting in 1089 possible combinations of variables in a session! (The good news in these realities is that the practice of counseling/psychotherapy never gets boring for those who continue to aim at positive outcomes for their clients.) In addition to the substantial intellectual and technical demands of their jobs, the work includes some occupational hazards that arise from the emotional power of the work (Norcross & Guy, 2007; O'Brien, 2011; Webb, 2011). We repeatedly see the pain and destructiveness of people, and although we can usually offer help and hope to those in need, we have no magic wand to cure suffering. The cumulative effects of witnessing so much human suffering can wear down even the most competent professionals unless they are committed to self-care. We also have the increasingly burdensome responsibility of dealing with institutions and governmental agencies indifferent or hostile to mental health and counseling services, or with third-party payers whose demands for short-term treatment for lifelong problems frequently seem absurd and counterproductive. Interestingly, several studies suggest that clinicians with a greater proportion of managed care clients feel more work stress and are at greater risk for emotional exhaustion than those with fewer managed care clients (Rupert & Baird, 2004; Orr, 2000; Thompson, 1999). Practitioners are being asked to do more with less, and there is no end to that trend in sight. Factors within the workplace also appear to contribute to the risk of burnout. A workplace perceived as stressful or unsupportive has also been associated with higher risk of burnout and a greater risk of compassion fatigue (Thompson, Amatea, & Thompson, 2014).

The good news here is that the Patient Protection and Affordable Care Act offers mental health patients more rights and greater parity with treatment for other health problems. However, that legislation is not a panacea for the external pressures that sometimes leave professionals emotionally exhausted by the work. In its most extreme form, this emotional exhaustion becomes burnout, a syndrome that significantly compromises the competent performance of mental health professionals. A true burnout syndrome consists of emotional exhaustion, the loss of a sense of accomplishment in one's work, and a depersonalization of those served (Maslach & Jackson, 1986).

Research shows that burnout affects a small but significant number of mental health professionals (Fortener, 2000; Jenaro, Flores, & Arias, 2007; Lee, Lim, Yang, & Lee, 2011; Lent & Schwartz, 2012; Raquepaw & Miller, 1989), school counselors (Rovero, 2004), marriage and family therapists (Tziporah & Pace, 2006), and school psychologists (Wylie, 2003). Recent studies show that between one-third and nearly one-half of psychologists had high scores on emotional exhaustion (Mahoney, 1997; Rupert & Morgan, 2005; Rupert & Kent, 2007). Lent and Schwartz (2013) reported that licensed counselors in community mental health settings experienced significantly higher levels of emotional exhaustion than those in private practice. Jevne and Williams (1998) suggest that mental health professionals may be at the initial stages of burnout when they begin to feel less of everything—less valued, enthusiastic, competent, connected, idealistic, involved, energetic, and creative.

Professionals who regularly work in crisis situations with those traumatized by violence, war, and natural disasters sometimes experience a form of trauma themselves. They may suffer from the very symptoms of post-traumatic stress that they are treating, a phenomenon labeled in the literature as *compassion fatigue, vicarious traumatization*, or *secondary post-traumatic stress disorder* (Figley, 1995; McCann & Pearlman, 1990). Counseling support for those who help victims of crises such as the attacks on September 11, 2001, or the 2012 Newtown, Connecticut, shootings is being recognized as a necessary component of crisis intervention services. (See Creamer and Liddle [2005] for findings on the traumatic effects of responding to the September 11 attacks on mental health disaster workers.) Not surprisingly, clinicians who see a high proportion of survivors of trauma tend to experience higher levels of symptoms themselves (Brady, Guy, Poelstra, & Brokaw, 1997; Trippany, Wilcoxon, & Satcher, 2003). According to VandeCreek and Jackson (2000), the primary manifestations of compassion fatigue include withdrawal and isolation from others, inappropriate emotionality, loss of pleasure, loss of boundaries with the client, and a sense of being overwhelmed or pressured. Some therapist beliefs seem especially predictive of burnout and vicarious traumatization according to research by McLean, Wade, and Encel (2003). They found that therapists who feel a very high level of responsibility for their clients, avoid strong emotions, rigidly adhere to a preferred clinical model, and have strong allegiance to the stance of the therapist as an agent of change have higher levels of these problems. On a positive note, Thompson, Amatea, and Thompson (2014) found that a supportive work environment reduced the intensity of compassion fatigue in mental health workers when treating trauma.

Counselors and therapists have their share of emotional challenge in their personal lives, too. They simultaneously juggle careers, family responsibilities, relationships, and civic duties, and sometimes get hit broadside by unexpected problems. If the distress is temporary, the usual coping mechanisms of taking time off, restructuring responsibilities, or getting support from colleagues and loved ones usually prevent any compromise in competent performance (Coster & Schwebel, 1997). Sometimes, however, the usual strategies fail, and work is compromised. Pope et al. (1987) found that 62% of psychologists reported working when overwhelmed by stress, and most of these (85%) recognized that it was unethical to do so. In another study, Guy, Poelstra, and Stark (1989) found that more than one-third of their sample of mental health providers admitted giving substandard care while distressed, although only 5% of those thought the care was poor enough to be defined as incompetent. A 2009 survey of psychologists indicated that 49% to 60% experienced at least mild disruption in professional practice because of burnout, anxiety, or depression (APA, 2010d). Counseling and psychology trainees also experience substantial levels of distress, and their distress frequently results in problems in competence (Gizara & Forrest, 2004; Gaubatz & Vera, 2006; Huprich & Rudd, 2004). Psychology trainees are also aware of fellow students with problems in professional competence. According to Shen-Miller et al. (2011), 44% of students were aware of other trainees with such problems. Unfortunately, few data exist regarding the incidence of distress and dysfunction in practicing licensed counselors (Stadler, Willing, Eberhage, & Ward, 1988).

Of course, mental health professionals are not immune to substance abuse and other psychological disorders. Thoreson, Miller, and Krauskopf (1989) found that drinking was a problem for 9% of the psychologists they surveyed, and 20% of counseling psychologists indicated daily or almost daily use of alcohol (Good, Thoreson, & Shaughnessy, 1995). Substance abuse has been cited as the most frequent cause of impairment in physicians (Bissell & Haberman, 1984). In a rare study that included master's level counselors along with other therapists, Deutsch (1985) found that 10% of her sample reported substance abuse difficulties. The rates of depression and other emotional problems do not appear different from rates in the general population, with about 10% of psychologists reporting depression (Gilroy, Carroll, & Murra, 2002; Thoreson et al., 1989) and about 15% of psychiatrists showing evidence of emotional problems (Herrington, 1979), although some surveys show much higher rates of depressive symptoms (see Kleespies et al. [2011] for a review of this literature). When trainees experience emotional difficulties that impede learning and competence with clients, faculty report that the most common problems can be defined as adjustment disorders, alcohol problems, symptoms of anxiety and depression, or personality disorders (Huprich & Rudd, 2004).

Another common cause of distress among practitioners is dissatisfaction with their intimate relationships (Deutsch, 1984; Sherman & Thelen, 1998). Guy et al. (1989) reported this difficulty as the second most frequent one identified by psychologists. Sherman and Thelen (1998) added major medical illness or injury and work issues such as malpractice claims by clients, demands of third-party payers, and time pressures to this list.

In the face of all this discouraging information about the stress of professional practice, it is important to note that *no counselor or therapist is doomed to experience any of these problems.* Evidence also suggests that professionals who engage in career-sustaining behaviors and are committed to personal emotional wellness are better protected from feeling burnout or secondary traumatization (Rupert & Kent, 2007). They are also better able to self-monitor and take action to prevent incompetent service to clients. International research by Orlinsky and his colleagues (1999) suggests that 60% of the psychologists they surveyed would describe the overriding character of their work as a *healing involvement* and not a stressful involvement. Further, few psychologists across the globe describe their practice as disengaged or distressed, so in spite of the many challenges just described, it is more than possible to be compassionate, committed, and enthusiastic about work with clients throughout a career. What it takes is self-awareness, openness to learning, and a willingness to seek support and consultation (Skovholt & Starkey, 2010). Wise, Hersh, and Gibson (2012) identify an even more comprehensive model for self-care that focuses on four principles: an emphasis on flourishing, intentionality in action, awareness of reciprocity in care of self and others, and the incorporation of deliberate self-care strategies into daily professional and personal activities (p. 487). This model emphasizes that self-care is not simply a matter of avoiding burnout: it is, as already mentioned, an ethical duty. Thompson et al. (2014) also suggest that *compassion satisfaction*, a term they apply to the experience of feeling satisfaction from helping clients and seeing them recover from distress and trauma. These authors also indicate that compassion satisfaction may occur more in counselors who deliberately attend to their role in positive change in clients.

The codes of ethics comment directly on the phenomena of distress and dysfunction and the responsibility of a professional to monitor the stress of practice. The APA Code offers illustrative language mandating that psychologists restrict professional activities when they are aware of the likely negative influence of personal problems on their professional practice (Appendix B, Standard 2.06, Appendix B, pp. 540–541). The language in the ACA Code on self-monitoring is found in Section C.2.g, Appendix A, p. 504.

The professional must then take steps to amend or interrupt practice, if necessary, to prevent harm to clients. Both codes imply that professionals ought to seek counseling and psychotherapy as appropriate or to engage in other activities that will help the professional regain his or her prior level of professional functioning. The ethical principle underlying the comments in the codes is nonmaleficence. Phillips (2011) reported that most mental health professionals seek therapy at least once in their career, though compliance with this standard for self-care is less than universal. Bearse, McMinn, Seegobin, and Free (2013) have identified a number of barriers that interfere with psychologists' willingness to seek therapy: problems in finding the right therapist; lack of time, money, or both; the stigma of being less than fully stable; and difficulty in admitting personal distress.

Avoiding Harm to Clients From Distress and Emotional Exhaustion

In addition to monitoring their own emotional status and stress levels, counselors and therapists can take additional actions to prevent a level of distress that compromises work performance (Baker, 2003; Barnett, Baker, Elman, & Schoener, 2007;

Brems, 2000; Brems & Johnson, 2009; Norcross, 2000; Skovholt, 2001; Smith & Moss, 2009; Trippany, Kress, & Wilcoxon, 2004; Wise, Hersh, & Gibson, 2012).

1. Recognize the risks of mental health practice, and celebrate its rewards. In the face of external stresses such as managed care, budget cuts, and unsympathetic administrators, clinicians need to work in a cross-disciplinary way to fight structural changes that harm clients and to get support from colleagues. Isolation increases the risk of compromised competence. Conversely, practicing professionals consistently report that their profession is a significantly positive influence on their sense of well-being and mental health (Radeke & Mahoney, 2000). Many flourish! They feel wiser, more aware, and more able to enjoy life because of their profession. In the face of the stresses of the work, professionals need to maintain focus on the less tangible benefits it provides them. Stevanovic and Rupert (2004) and Lawson and Myers (2011) have identified several career-sustaining behaviors that focus on a balanced professional and personal life. These behaviors, such as finding time for relationships and generativity outside of work, appeared to increase career enjoyment and reduce the negative impact of work stress. Wise et al. (2012) emphasize the role of mindfulness, whereas Johnson, Barnett, Elman, Forrest, and Kaslow (2012) highlight the role of a professional support system. Brems (2009) discusses strategies for managing the stress that suicidal and violent clients bring to the professionals who treat them.
2. Set clear limits about how much help you can humanly give. Out of misguided good intentions, mental health professionals sometimes overpromise and overcommit. This tendency may be related to the personality characteristics that initially drew these professionals to this work—a heightened capacity for empathy with people in need, a perfectionism about work tasks, and a sense of self-doubt that encourages one to keep doing more to be worthy of others' good judgments. However, if not kept in check, the tendency to give until depleted leaves one exhausted and ill-equipped for competent work.
3. Use the advice you give to clients about self-care. All too often counselors fail to take time for themselves even as they admonish client after client about the importance of self-care. Brems (2000, 2009) divides self-care into two major components: professional self-care, including continuing education, consultation and supervision, networking, and stress management; and personal self-care, including healthy personal habits, attention to relationships, opportunities for relaxation and centeredness, and self-exploration and awareness. Norcross and Guy (2007) and Skovholt (2001) provide excellent resources on self-care for clinicians.
4. Recognize your vulnerability, and seek support when overwhelmed. The combination of work stress and life's complexity often leads to emotional difficulties. Acknowledging these difficulties is a strength, not a weakness. A self-help network for psychologists has been available for more than two decades (APA, 2009c; Smith & Moss, 2009) and 20 of 60 states and Canadian provinces operate a formal program for colleague assistance (APA, 2003). Interestingly, this number has declined from prior years, partly as a result of liability concerns and lack of volunteer support. Through the APA network, psychologists

can find colleagues who volunteer to help other psychologists with drug and alcohol problems, although utilization of such services is limited (Floyd, Myszka, & Orr, 1999). State-level programs typically seek to rehabilitate professionals who have been disciplined by the licensing board or who come to their attention through referrals from other professionals. The APA has published a monograph and a toolkit on colleague assistance to help professional organizations that wish to develop or improve their colleague assistance programs (APA, Practice Directorate, 2006; APA, 2009b). The ACA established a task force on counselor impairment in 2003 that issued a report on risk factors and prevention efforts (Lawson & Venart, 2003). ACA also identifies three states with comprehensive programs for counselors with competence problems: Michigan, Minnesota, and Virginia (http://www.counseling.org/wellness_taskforce/tf_resources.htm).

5. Consider counseling or psychotherapy for personal problems, even if not overwhelmed by them. Practicing clinicians might also consider occasional returns to therapy, perhaps for just a session or two, to bolster their current functioning and redress any emerging problems. Clinicians who have been in therapy consistently report that it was helpful in maintaining empathy for clients, respecting client dignity, boundaries and pacing, and gaining the confidence to work at a deeper level (Marcan & Shapiro, 1998; Norcross, 1997). In Great Britain and in some training programs in the United States, personal counseling is required (Marcan, Stiles, & Smith, 1999; Patrick, 1989).
6. Prepare for possible symptoms of secondary post-traumatic stress when crisis intervention is the predominant mode of service and take full advantage of support services. Professionals should be especially careful to avoid emotional isolation and social withdrawal from others when undertaking this form of practice.
7. Work to develop quality assurance programs in your work setting to reduce errors and thereby improved the overall effectiveness of service. As Donohue and Engle (2013) note, a number of errors in practice occur because of systemic issues and barriers rather than an individual's misjudgment or dysfunction. Put another way, the systemic problems set the stage for less than competent service by practitioners. Such programs are becoming the norm in medicine and are viewed as crucial to all health care under the Patient Protection and Affordable Care Act.

LEGAL RAMIFICATIONS OF INCOMPETENT PRACTICE

Counselors and therapists who perform incompetently are vulnerable to legal action as well as discipline by their professional association or licensing board. Incompetent service is often negligent service, and mental health professionals can be sued for negligence in civil court. Malpractice is often used synonymously with professional negligence, and it refers to a "negligent act committed by a professional that harms another" (Packman & Harris, 1998, p. 153). Professional negligence is usually identified as an unintentional tort, an injury for which a person can seek redress. Sometimes a tort claim is asserted to be intentional. This may happen, for example, when a client claims that unwanted physical contact was an assault and deliberate (Wheeler & Bertram, 2012). If the facts of the case merit a judgment against a mental health professional, damages can be awarded to the person(s) who have brought the suit (the plaintiff). The thought of being sued frightens most professionals, and with some justification. Litigation against mental health professionals has increased in recent years. As Voltaire once wrote, "I was never ruined but twice: once when I lost a lawsuit and once when I won one." However, practitioners should not be immobilized by such fears. They ought to take comfort in the relative infrequency of civil suits even for those who are guilty of incompetent practice.

Many responsible practitioners who worry about lawsuits fail to understand the distinction between ordinary mistakes, to which every professional is sometimes vulnerable, and negligence, for which one can be held liable. Four criteria must be met for a court to rule in favor of the plaintiff in a negligence action. (For a fuller explanation of these concepts, see Bennett et al., 2006.) The first criterion is that *the professional's duty to the client must be established*. To establish this duty, a practitioner needs to be in a professional relationship with that client. When clients enter into a professional relationship, they implicitly cede to the professional some control over their concerns, and the duty to the client is thus created. A professional does not have a duty to the person sitting next to her on the bus or to a person encountered in a social event. Moreover, one cannot be found negligent for any harm another person may inflict on other bus riders or partygoers. Nor does a professional have a duty to a prospective client with whom he or she has a five-minute phone call, the content of which results in an acceptable referral to another therapist (Smith, Pomerantz, Pettibone, & Segrist, 2012). The next logical question is, How long does it take to establish a relationship so that a duty can be defined? Courts have varied somewhat in their judgments, but in some jurisdictions as little as a single session has been found sufficient.

The second criterion for negligence is that *the professional must have breached a duty to the client*. Specifically, this means that the care provided fell below the accepted standard of care for the profession. The standard of care is defined as the quality of care that other competent professionals would provide in this kind of situation. The standard of care is *not* the best possible care, but rather, adequate care. Formerly, the standard of care was judged largely according to local standards, but since the onset of electronic communication and easy access to professional literature, the standard of care has become more uniform across jurisdictions. It is important to emphasize that this standard allows for mistakes and errors in judgment, and the errors one makes constitute negligence only if they are errors that other professionals, acting competently, would be unlikely to make. For example, a clinical counselor, exasperated with a client's frequent threats of suicide, makes the highly incompetent suggestion that a client "put up or shut up" about suicide. Later that day, after taking an overdose of sleeping pills, the client is rushed to the hospital. If a suit is brought against that professional, the central issues would be whether the suggestion made by the counselor is an error, and whether this error was one that other competent professionals would not make under the same circumstances. To answer these questions, the attorneys would look to the professional literature and the experts in suicide. If both evidence of error and substandard practice exist, then the counselor's behavior would have met the second criterion for negligence. However, the suit can be successful only if two additional criteria are met.

To meet the third criterion, *an injury or damage to the client must be established*. A professional's mistake, no matter how wrongheaded or incompetent, is not legally meaningful unless some injury results. (By the way, this criterion need not apply for an ethics complaint to be upheld.) If the suicidal client described in the last paragraph ignored the counselor's advice and immediately sought assistance from another more competent professional, that client would have difficulty demonstrating injury. Even an irresponsible blunder does not result in legal liability in the absence of a negative effect on the client.

Finally, if injury or damage does happen to the client, *the harm must be caused by the therapist's mistake*, or in legal terms, the therapist must be shown to be the proximate cause of the injury (Bennett et al., 2006). If the harm would have happened to the client regardless of the therapist's action, then negligence cannot be proved. (In this situation, the case that the counselor acted negligently and caused harm is quite strong).

In short, the standard for liability for negligence is a rigorous one, and its very rigor should reassure professionals about the minimal risk of frivolous or unjustified lawsuits. However, the best protection against lawsuits is, in compliance with the codes of ethics, practicing within the boundaries of one's competence and focusing on ethical ideals. Civil suits for practice beyond the limits of one's competence are unlikely to decrease in the decade ahead.

SUMMARY

Competence has three primary components: knowledge, skill, and diligence. Competence means that a professional works as effectively as other skilled professionals and according to accepted criteria. Competence is distinguished from perfection, because universal competence is unattainable. Rather, competence should be thought of as spanning a continuum from incompetent to exceptionally competent. A professional should always aim for higher levels of competence. Because of the evolving nature of knowledge and practice, competencies must be maintained through continuing education and consultation, or they will erode.

The ethics codes demand that to avoid harm to clients, professionals must practice within the limits of their competence. When seeking to develop new competencies or to determine whether a particular activity is within their existing skills, mental health professionals must evaluate their level of formal training and supervised practice in the area. Both formal training and supervised practice are prerequisites for competence. Those who judge their skills to be inadequate for a client's needs should refer the client to a competent colleague. Counselors and therapists in rural areas or in other small and specialized communities have special concerns about the limits of competence, because referral sources are scarce, and the pressures on them to act as generalists are great. The central ethical issue is the capacity to assist the client and avoid risk of harm. Professionals need to take developmental and cultural issues into account when evaluating their competencies, because no intervention has been demonstrated effective across all ages or cultures.

At times the stress of this occupation becomes overwhelming. When this happens, competent performance is threatened, and a formerly competent practitioner may provide inadequate service. The codes place the responsibility for self-monitoring stress on the individual professional, and they mandate that the professional limit or interrupt his or her practice if necessary to avoid harm to clients. Burnout caused by occupational stress and distress caused by emotional, relationship, or substance abuse problems are the most common reasons for this kind of incompetent service.

When professionals practice outside the boundaries of their competence or provide incompetent service, they are at risk for a civil suit filed against them in addition to an ethics complaint. Lawsuits are still relatively uncommon, and no diligent counselor or therapist needs to worry excessively about this eventuality. Professionals need to understand that negligence is not identical with professional error and that a lawsuit for professional negligence can be won only if (1) a demonstrable professional relationship with the client has been established; (2) the practitioner made a mistake that showed substandard care; (3) the client suffered an injury; and (4) the injury was directly caused by the professional's actions.

Discussion Questions*

1. There is debate in the mental health professions about the value of professional credentials such as licenses and certifications. Some argue that such credentials do more to protect the professions than to protect the public. What is your view on this issue?
2. Some say that the standards for practicing within the limits of one's competence are unfair to practitioners from small communities, who must try to help an extraordinarily wide range of people if they are to have any practice at all. They contend that the standard has a bias in favor of urban and suburban practitioners. What do you think of this argument?
3. Practicing within the boundaries of one's competence can also be challenging for professionals who serve unique populations because of a special language skill or an extensive knowledge of a particular population. Sometimes these professionals argue that the needs of the population for service should take precedence over traditional interpretations of competence. What do you think of this viewpoint?
4. Third-party payment presents new dilemmas for mental health professionals, who see competence as a combination of knowledge, skill, and diligence. What do you see as the dilemmas in third-party payment (as they relate to competence)?
5. How well do the workshops and continuing education programs you have seen advertised meet the criteria set forth here for evidence of scientific value?
6. A number of people enter the mental health professions because of their own histories of recovery from emotional pain. They want to help others live full lives, as they have learned to do. How might this history affect their risk for distress and dysfunction? Is such a history an advantage or a disadvantage in this regard?
7. Sometimes professionals find it very difficult to confront a colleague who is practicing outside the boundaries of his or her competence. What suggestions would you have for these professionals?

Cases for Discussion

Kim is a successful career counselor with more than 30 years of experience in the field. Her special interest is in helping "workaholics" learn to live more a balanced life without significantly compromising their work performance. She has developed an innovative counseling intervention for helping workaholics and has begun to offer seminars to teach other professionals her method.

*Note to course instructors: The *Instructor's Guide* for this book includes other discussion questions, class exercises, cases, and multiple-choice and essay test items for this chapter.

Enrollment in the six-hour seminar costs $475. During the seminar, she lectures on her approach, shows videos of her techniques with client-actors, and asks participants to role-play counseling sessions as practice. She also distributes a list of recommended readings and cautions participants about circumstances in which the procedure is contraindicated. After the question-and-answer period is completed, Kim wishes the audience success in their work with this population. One month later, Kim sends a questionnaire to participants, seeking feedback about their experience with the treatment procedures. Are graduates of this seminar competent to implement the intervention technique Kim has designed? Is Kim acting ethically in structuring the seminar in this way? If a dissatisfied client of one of Kim's students filed an ethics complaint against both Kim and the counselor who provided the service for incompetent and harmful treatment of her workaholic tendencies, would that claim have any merit?

Jonas finished his doctoral program in forensic psychology several years ago but is now dissatisfied with his profession and is looking into other avenues for psychological practice. He has been reading about personal coaching and executive coaching and decides that focus is a better match for his skills. He believes his training as a forensic psychologist—along with more reading on coaching—is sufficient to begin practice in this area. If Jonas told you of his plans, what do you think your ethical obligations are in talking with him? What are his ethical obligations before beginning this new type of work?

Recommended Readings

Baker, E. K. (2003). *Caring for ourselves: A therapist's guide to personal and professional well-being.* Washington, D.C.: American Psychological Association.

Barnett, J. E., Baker, E. K., Elman, N. S., & Schoener, G. R. (2007). In pursuit of wellness: The self-care imperative. *Professional Psychology: Research and Practice, 38*, 603–612.

Barnett, J. E., Doll, B., Younggren, J. N., & Rubin, N. J. (2007). Clinical competence for practicing psychologists: Clearly a work in progress. *Professional Psychology: Research and Practice, 38*, 510–517.

Bennett, B. E., Bricklin, P. M., Harris, E., Knapp, S., VandeCreek, L., & Younggren, J. N. (2006). *Assessing and managing risk in psychological practice.* Rockville, MD: The Trust.

Brems, C. (2000). The challenge of preventing burnout and assuring growth: Self-care. In C. Brems (Ed.). *Dealing with challenges in psychotherapy and counseling* (pp. 262–296). Pacific Grove, CA: Brooks/Cole.

Figley, C. R. (Ed.). (1995). *Compassion fatigue: Coping with secondary traumatic stress disorder in those who treat the traumatized.* New York, NY: Brunner/Mazel.

Gaubatz, M. D., & Vera, E. M. (2006). Trainee competence in master's level counseling programs: A comparison of counselor educators' and students' views. *Counselor Education and Supervision, 46*, 32–43.

Hatcher, R. L., Fouad, N. A., Campbell, L. F., McCutcheon, S. R., Grus, C. L., & Leahy, K. L. (2013). Competency-based education for professional psychology: Moving from concept to practice. *Training and Education in Professional Psychology, 7*, 225–234.

Helbok, C. M. (2006). National survey of ethical practices across rural and urban communities. *Professional Psychology: Research and Practice, 37*, 35–44.

Johnson, W. B., Barnett, J. E., Elman, N. S., Forrest, L., & Kaslow, N. J. (2012). The competent community: Toward a vital reformulation of professional ethics. *American Psychologist, 67*, 557–569.

Schank, J. A., Helbok, C. M., Haldeman, D. C., & Gallardo, M. E. (2010). Challenges and benefits of ethical small-community practice. *Professional Psychology: Research and Practice, 41*, 502–510.

Skovholt, T. M. (2001). *The resilient practitioner: Burnout prevention and self-care strategies for counselors, therapists, teachers, and health professionals.* Boston, MA: Allyn & Bacon.

Skovholt, T. M., & Starkey, M. T. (2010). The three legs of the practitioner's learning stool: Practice, research/theory, and personal life. *Journal of Contemporary Psychotherapy, 40*, 125–130.

Smith, P. L., & Moss, S. B. (2009). Psychologist impairment: What is it, how can it be prevented, and what can be done to address it? *Clinical Psychology: Science and Practice*, *16*, 1–15.

Wise, E. H., Hersh, M.A., & Gibson, C. M. (2012). Ethics, self care and well being for psychologists: Re-envisioning the stress-distress continuum. *Professional Psychology: Research and Practice*, *43*, 487–494.

Additional Online Resources

American Board of Professional Psychology: http://www.abpp.org/i4a/pages/index.cfm?pageid=3285.

American Counseling Association: http://www.counseling.org/publications/a.

American Counseling Association: Taskforce on Counselor Wellness and Impairment: http://www.counseling.org/wellness_taskforce/tf_resources.htm.

American Mental Health Association: Why Use a Clinical Mental Health Counselor? http://www.amhca.org/public_resources/why_use_a_mental_health_counselor.aspx.

American Psychological Association: APA's Advisory Committee on Colleague Assistance (ACCA): http://www.apa.org/practice/resources/assistance/acca-toolkit.pdf.

Colleague Assistance and Self-care: http://www.apa.org/practice/resources/assistance/index.aspx.

Association of State and Provincial Psychology Boards: Handbook on Licensure and Certification: http://www.asppb.org/HandbookPublic/HandbookReview.aspx.

Association of State and Provincial Psychology Boards: Earliest Time the EPPP (licensing exam) Can Be Taken by Jurisdiction & License Type: http://www.asppb.org/HandbookPublic/Reports/default.aspx?ReportType=EPPPEarliestTimeTaken.

National Career Development Association Career Counseling Competencies: http://www.ncda.org/aws/NCDA/pt/sd/news_article/37798/_self/layout_ccmsearch/true.

Ohio Psychological Association: Resources for Colleague Assistance: http://www.ohpsych.org/about/governance/committees-task-force-and-affiliates/colleague-assistance-program/.

Finding Help: How to Choose a Psychotherapist: http://www.apa.org/helpcenter/choose-therapist.aspx.

National Board for Certified Counselors: http://www.nbcc.org/OurCertifications.

Psychology Today's Therapy Directory of Credentials: http://therapists.psychologytoday.com/rms/content/therapy_credentials.html.

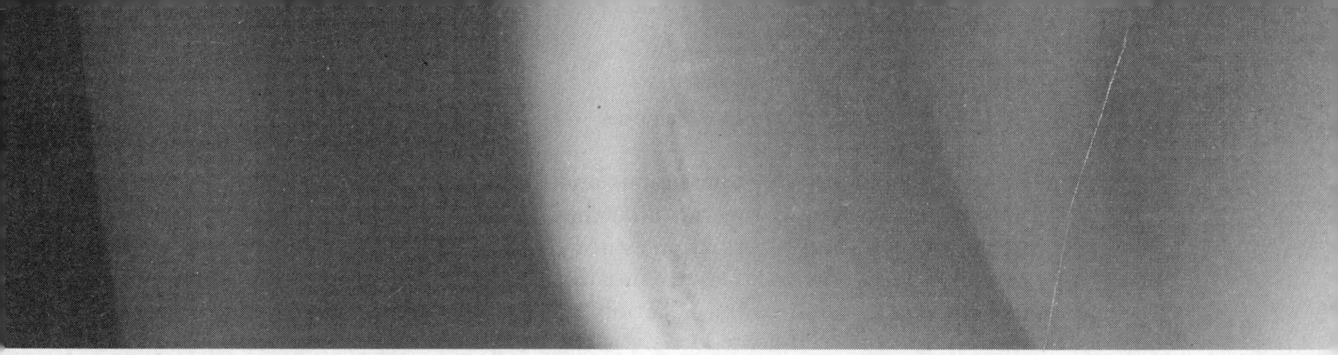

Confidentiality

CHAPTER 5

Supporting the Client's Dignity and Right to Privacy

This chapter discusses the scope of confidentiality, the distinction between its legal and ethical dimensions, the legal limits on confidentiality in counseling and psychotherapy, and the need to balance confidentiality against other ethical obligations, such as the professional's legitimate need to consult with colleagues. The chapter also examines the special considerations regarding confidentiality when working with minors, clients with contagious and life-threatening disorders, and clients in group and family services. The final section explores emerging issues in confidentiality, including dilemmas in managed care, clients at risk for homicide-suicide, and electronic communications between mental health professionals and the public.

"Can I tell you something in confidence?" is a question most people have been asked by friends and family. The questioner is seeking support or advice while hoping for control over private information. If the receiver of a secret promises confidentiality but fails to honor that promise, the other person feels betrayed, and the relationship is ruptured or compromised.

There are parallels between this experience and the expectations clients have when they enter counseling or psychotherapy. Typically, clients expect that the private material they reveal to a professional will not be shared without their consent. If clients discover that their trust has been misplaced, they feel betrayed, and their capacity to trust mental health professionals diminishes. Even in the best of circumstances, clients usually have conflicting feelings about revealing sensitive information to professionals. On the one hand, they feel a need for support and direction; on the other hand, they worry that they will be judged negatively for private thoughts and feelings. Thus, both clients and friends reveal secrets when they believe the receiver is worthy of their confidence and will not berate them for their faults and failings (Cullari, 2001). Moreover, confidence in confidentiality is not limited to those who seek services for themselves—it is as important in parents' willingness to permit their children to obtain therapeutic services as it is in adults' decisions to engage in the process (Jensen, McNamara, & Gustafson, 1991).

Of course the confidentiality of the professional relationship differs in many respects from that of friendship. First, nearly every portion of the conversations between mental health professionals and their clients is confidential, no matter how mundane. Clients may mention that they dislike Chinese food, play the harmonica, or lift weights. This information is not especially private or embarrassing, and it is probably easily shared in social situations without any expectation of confidentiality. However, if that communication takes place within a therapeutic relationship, it must be kept confidential. Why is this so? As Bok (1989) suggests, by guarding the privacy of even inconsequential disclosures, the professional is reassuring the client that more personal material will also be kept safe. After all, much of the material clients disclose in counseling is sensitive information to which no one else in their lives, not even their closest friends or partners, is privy. For example, a college student may admit that she has abused cocaine to a counselor before she tells anyone else, or a professional dancer may reveal that he uses self-induced vomiting to control his weight, even though he has hidden this information from all others.

The next distinction between confidences in friendships and in professional settings relates to clients' assumptions about therapy. Clients usually assume they can trust mental health professionals, so they omit the step of asking for reassurance of confidentiality. In fact, research suggests that most clients expect that *virtually everything* disclosed in counseling will be held in strict confidence (Miller & Thelen, 1986; VandeCreek, Miars, & Herzog, 1987). This frame of mind heightens a client's sense of betrayal if confidentiality is violated. Of course, not all clients assume clinicians are trustworthy, but most give them the benefit of the doubt. Unless the professional engages in an informed consent process about confidentiality and its limits, clients are likely to hold on to this misperception of the absolute nature of therapeutic privacy. (A full explanation of informed consent is provided in Chapter 6.)

The fourth contrast deals with the difference in consequences for the violator of the confidence. If friends violate a confidence, their major risk is a rupture in the friendship. If a professional violates a confidence, that individual's reputation, job, and license may be at stake, and he or she may be vulnerable to civil action for malpractice or breach of contract.

The last major distinction is in the scope of confidentiality. Confidentiality in counseling and psychotherapy encompasses not only the words spoken between professionals and their clients but also all records related to those interactions, and the identity of the clients. A professional is obligated not to disclose even the names of clients without their permission. Scholars have named this form of confidentiality *contact confidentiality* (Wheeler & Bertram, 2012). Mental health professionals are expected to provide a therapeutic environment in which client words cannot be overheard; their records are kept secure from unauthorized people; and their presence at the office is protected to the fullest extent possible.

Moreover, the death of a client does not automatically release a provider from his or her ethical obligation to maintain confidentiality. A notorious example of a violation of this imperative occurred after the murder of Nicole Brown Simpson (the ex-wife of O. J. Simpson), when her therapist, Susan Forward, spoke with the press about matters her client had revealed to her in therapy. As a result of those unauthorized disclosures, the Board of Behavioral Science Examiners of California took disciplinary action against Ms. Forward (Simpson case, 1994). Similarly, when Martin Orne, the psychoanalyst who treated Anne Sexton, the acclaimed American poet who had died by her own hand some years before, released hundreds of tapes of her therapy sessions to Sexton's biographer, there was a public outcry. Many called it a betrayal of Sexton (Burke, 1995). Orne broke no law because he complied with the statutory requirement to acquire a release from the deceased person's legal representative, but many professionals believe that the ethical obligation to confidentiality to the former client must sometimes take precedence over the rights of the next of kin. There is also the question of the ethics of retaining audiotapes of therapy sessions for years after the termination of services (and after the death of the client). Current advice recommends declining to release confidential records, even to legal representatives, in situations in which the professional has a reasonable basis upon which to believe that release would be inconsistent with the deceased client's wishes or best interest (Werth, Burke, & Bardash, 2002). Of course, should the professional receive a court order for such release, compliance with the order or appeal to a higher court is permissible.

In short, even though confidentiality in counseling and psychotherapy is built on the same foundation as confidentiality in social relationships, it holds unique obligations for the mental health professional. Driscoll (1992) calls the profession's duty to confidentiality a "sacred covenant." Research also supports the prominence of confidentiality in the day-to-day ethical issues practitioners face. For example, when surveyed, psychologists from nine different countries across the world named dilemmas involving confidentiality most frequently (Pettifor, 2004; Pope & Vetter, 1992). Most of these dilemmas involved the management of confidentiality when clients appeared to endanger others, but others dealt with the relationship between confidentiality and child abuse reporting and with clients with life-threatening communicable diseases. Two studies of college counselors revealed the same pattern (Hayman & Covert, 1986; Malley, Gallagher, & Brown, 1992). In recent years, confidentiality complaints were the fourth most common topic brought before psychology boards for investigation (Peterson, 1996) and the fifth most common for counseling boards (Neukrug et al., 2001), but they still represent a minority (approximately 5%) of such complaints.

ETHICAL PRINCIPLES AND VIRTUES UNDERLYING CONFIDENTIALITY

The importance of confidentiality derives primarily from the ethical principles of autonomy and fidelity, and secondarily from the principles of beneficence and nonmaleficence. Respect for autonomy affirms that each person has the power to decide who may access private information. Newton (1989) argues that privacy is an essential component of individuality and selfhood. If the individual loses the power to decide who knows his or her secrets, then in many respects no true self remains. Violations of confidentiality are fundamentally disrespectful to the dignity of the person. Confidentiality is also based on the principle of fidelity because counselors implicitly and explicitly promise not to disclose what clients reveal to them.

The principles of beneficence and nonmaleficence come into play when confidentiality is breached, because clients cannot benefit from an enterprise in which they have lost faith. Violations of confidentiality can also place clients at psychological and physical risk. For example, clients whose disclosures about their sexual orientation are betrayed can be ostracized from their families, victimized by gay bashing, and discriminated against at work. In a less dramatic example, a client who hears an embarrassing anecdote he shared with a mental health professional repeated at a social gathering can feel stripped of dignity and may remove himself from clinical and social supports important for his emotional stability. Moreover, violations of confidentiality undermine the public trust in the profession, diminishing its capacity to help people who may benefit from counseling and psychotherapy but who have come to distrust mental health professionals. Bok (1989) refers to this as a threat to the utility of counseling.

From a virtues perspective, when professionals honor confidentiality, they are demonstrating the virtues of integrity, trustworthiness, and respectfulness. Zealously guarding client privacy also indicates a true compassion for the courage it takes for clients to enter treatment and for the suffering that violations of trust cause. Honoring confidentiality requires integrity precisely because it can be difficult—the human tendency to want to share experiences does not bypass mental health professionals simply because they have a credential, nor does the desire to discuss important or difficult issues that arise at work end with entrance into this profession. Remember what Mark Twain quipped: "Three people can keep a secret if two of them are dead."

CODES OF ETHICS ON CONFIDENTIALITY

The ethics codes of both the ACA and APA refer extensively to confidentiality, emphasizing its place at the foundation of professional behavior. The ACA Code section on privacy and confidentiality (Section B) is the lengthiest in the document. See Appendix A, pp. 498–502, and Appendix B, pp. 544–545, to review this section before continuing with the chapter.

CONFIDENTIALITY AND COMMUNICATION WITH OTHER MENTAL HEALTH PROFESSIONALS

Both the APA and the ACA ethics codes allow profesionals to share relevant case information in order to consult for guidance about a case. The presumption is that the other professionals understand the need for confidentiality and carry the same obligation to keep client disclosures private. Whenever possible, however, the consultation should be conducted without revealing client-identifying information. Such a procedure avoids unnecessary risk to the client's privacy, especially since inadvertent disclosures of client data are acknowledged to be a rather frequent occurrence among clinicians (Pope & Vetter, 1992). When working in treatment teams that routinely discuss all cases by name, the codes recommend that the client be informed that team discussions will occur and give consent to that arrangement (see ACA Code Section B.3.b. and APA Code Standard 4.06). Clients who feel confident that the treatment team is working in their best interest typically agree to this arrangement.

Consultation to maximize the helpfulness of professional services must be distinguished from idle discussion of client material among co-workers. Professionals have a normal human impulse to share events from their workday with colleagues. Communicating such anecdotes can add a little humor to a stressful day or elicit peer support after stressful day. How do practitioners ethically meet this need? The first consideration must be for the dignity and welfare of the client. The best standard for determining whether informal information sharing with colleagues is ethical is to ask whether the client would understand the comment to be a professional consultation if he or she heard it. If the answer is no, the disclosure is likely to be ill advised. Second, even if the identity of the particular client is not revealed, the client may feel humiliated by a nonprofessional disclosure and be less willing to disclose personal information in future sessions. Thus, client information should be shared only within a formal consultation environment, and all sharing should respect the dignity of the individual. When unsure of whether a particular situation fits that criterion, one should use a variation of Kant's universalization principle (Newton, 1989): If the roles were reversed, and the professional were in the client's position, would the disclosure seem necessary and appropriate? If the answer is yes, the disclosure is probably acceptable. It is important to note that anonymously sharing a client anecdote is not always a violation of the code—rather, it represents a deviation from positive ethics and the lack of appreciation of the trust that the client has placed in us.

As discussed in greater detail in Chapter 14, when a worker is not yet licensed or is still in training, his or her supervisor also has access to confidential information from sessions. In fact, someone in training may not accept a client unless that client is willing to have the supervisor receive identifying information and know about the course of treatment. Whenever a mental health professional is being supervised for training or licensing purposes, that training status must be disclosed to the client at the initiation of services (see APA Code, Standard 10.01c and ACA Code Sections A.2.b and F.1.c).

Professionals in school, military, and business settings are working in cultures that are unaccustomed to or unreceptive to the level of confidentiality necessary in counseling (Lowman, 2006; McCauley, Hughes, & Liebling-Kalifani, 2008; Orme & Doerman, 2001; Tompkins & Mehring, 1993). For example, psychologists in the military indicate that dilemmas involving confidentiality of client disclosures is the second most common ethical conflict they face (Kennedy & Johnson, 2009; McCauley et al., 2008; Orme & Doerman, 2001). Teachers, administrators, and other school personnel often share student information and expect counselors to do the same (Lazovsky, 2008). Managers and senior officers are accustomed to discussing employee performance with human resource personnel or other supervisors and are unlikely to understand the reluctance of mental health professionals to do likewise (Lowman, 2012). In these environments, practitioners have a responsibility to educate their co-workers about their unique professional responsibilities, negotiate compromises with administrators when possible, and resist the ever-present temptation to trade client confidentiality for a perception of being a team player.

When mental health professionals employ assistants to work in their offices, those assistants sometimes need access to client data to carry out their responsibilities. In some states, office assistants are covered under privileged communication statutes, but regardless of their legal status, professionals are responsible for any breach of confidentiality by someone who works for them, as is expressed in Section B.3.a of the ACA Code and indirectly in Standard 2.05, Delegation of Work to Others, in the APA Code. Also see Fisher (2012) for helpful suggestions for supervising nonclinical staff in the management of patient privacy. Privacy regulations promulgated under the Health Insurance Portability and Accountability Act (HIPAA) (U.S. Department of Health and Human Services, 1996) and the Health

Information Technology for Economic and Clinical Health Act (HITECH) (2009) also stipulate that professionals are obliged to thoroughly train and monitor their employees' handling of client files and inform clients of the access that assistants may have to those files. (HIPAA and HITECH regulations will be discussed in greater detail in Chapter 12.)

CONFIDENTIALITY AND COMMUNICATION WITH SIGNIFICANT OTHERS OF THE PROFESSIONAL

Counselors and therapists have committed relationships with other adults. The norms of committed relationships suggest that adult partners share information about their daily lives with each other. This sharing not only helps the partners feel supported and revitalized for the next day, it also is a symbol of closeness between them (Baker & Patterson, 1990). Similar communications occur in close friendships. This relationship norm conflicts with the rules on professional confidentiality, however. Nowhere in those rules is an exception to confidentiality written for families or friends of mental health professionals. Baker and Patterson (1990) suggest that this standard is routinely violated, that mental health professionals frequently share information about client sessions with their partners. Woody (1999) refers to sharing of private client information with friends and family members as "the Achilles heel of the profession" (p. 608). Evidence from Pope et al. (1987) and Dudley (1988) offers some support for this interpretation. Research by Boudreaux (2001) offers stronger evidence that clinicians share client information with significant others. Boudreaux reported that 96% of his national sample of psychologists admitted sharing client data with partners. Participants characterized a majority of these disclosures (70%) as anonymous at least sometimes. This means, though, that 30% of the sample could not claim any level of anonymity for their clients in these conversations. The findings further suggest that client names were rarely shared with significant others, but other personal information that rendered the clients identifiable was more commonly disclosed. When queried about the reasons they discussed client information with partners, the psychologists indicated that they did so to reduce stress, help clients, and gain self-understanding. They believed that these disclosures benefited them but had a neutral effect on their relationship with their partners. The professionals who tended to withhold client information from partners did so to protect confidentiality, comply with regulations, and separate work from home life. Woody (1999) points out that family and friends are under no obligation to protect private client information, and in the event of divorce or other deterioration in the relationship, client information may even be used in vengeful ways that result in harm to both the clinician and the client. Even in normal circumstances, a friend or partner may inadvertently share client information or may encounter a person they are able to identify as the client about whom the counselor was speaking.

Is there an alternative way to resolve this conflict between family loyalty and professional responsibilities? Yes. The best solution is to develop a regular supervision or consultation relationship with another professional to deal with the inevitable emotional reactions to client cases. In that way, the professional gets the benefit needed to continue effective work without compromising confidentiality. Some practitioners also keep a private journal about their own feelings about their work. This journal is not a record of counseling and does not include any identifying client information, but is a reflection of the professional's experience of his or her day-to-day work life and can serve as an outlet for emotion. If this journal is kept secure, it may provide the kind of release and opportunity for reflection that is needed. Next, professionals should explain to their partners the standards governing confidentiality and the ethical principles underlying this rule, and should establish clear limits about the material that can be disclosed at home. An acceptable boundary allows a therapist to discuss broad outlines of problems he or she is experiencing at work. In this way, professionals can still feel connected to their partner by discussing important aspects of their work, but not breach ethical standards. This guideline means the following statement would be acceptable: "I'm saddened by news of a client's life-threatening illness, which is adding further pain to an already difficult situation"; however, the following wording would be problematic: "I'm working with a 35-year-old woman with two small children who is not responding to treatments for her HIV infection. She may have to leave her restaurant job; she has no health insurance; and her ex-husband, who is a lawyer, often misses child support payments and is not committed to caring for their children." (Notice that the first option omits age, occupation, gender, and details of the client's individual experience of the problem. It does not even identify the medical problem specifically.) A partner or close friend who has been informed about the professional's obligations in advance will likely understand the clinician's reactions and offer support without seeking further disclosure. In any case, the burden of maintaining confidentiality always rests with the professional.

Mental health professionals who use smartphones, fax machines, home computers, tablets, or handheld computers to store client information or communicate with clients, or who bring client records home from work, are vulnerable to inadvertent breaches of client confidentiality to family members. In these circumstances, the onus for avoiding such breaches falls squarely with the professional. Those who store client data on portable devices must take extra care to keep these items secure while in transport or away from their secure office location.

CONFIDENTIALITY AND PRIVILEGED COMMUNICATION

The terms *confidentiality* and *privileged communication* are frequently misunderstood by mental health professionals (Shuman & Foote, 1999). These terms are often used interchangeably, but there are important differences in their meanings. Confidentiality refers both to an ethical duty to keep client identity and disclosures secret and a legal duty to honor the fiduciary relationship with the client. It is primarily a moral obligation rooted in the ethics code, the ethical principles, and the virtues that the profession attempts to foster. The legal term *privileged communication* refers to the client's right to prevent a court from demanding that a mental health professional reveal material disclosed in a confidential professional relationship (Younggren & Harris, 2008) as part of evidence in a legal proceeding. Whereas the term *confidentiality* deals with the prevention of voluntary disclosure of inappropriate material by mental health professionals, the term *privilege* refers to the rules for preventing involuntary disclosures requested by parties in a legal action (Roback, Ochoa, Bloch, & Purdon, 1992). In other words, confidentiality binds the professional not to reveal client material even if he or she feels inclined to do so, and privilege protects client information from inappropriate disclosure pressed for by legal authorities, rather than entertained by the professional. Privilege, formally termed *testimonial privilege*, is established by law. Because common law requires all citizens to testify when called by the court, exceptions must be established by statute (Knapp & VandeCreek, 1986). Federal courts may interpret privilege differently from state courts. In the course of identifying relevant evidence to prepare for a trial, attorneys go through a process they call *discovery*, in which they seek out information to support their case. Materials obtained through discovery are typically available to both sides in any action coming before a court.

It is important to emphasize that the privilege is the client's, not the professional's; it is the client's right to refuse to reveal counseling or psychotherapy information to the court. Thus, a professional asserts privilege on behalf of a client and does not have the option to disclose privileged client information even if so inclined. The laws of all 50 states include some form of patient–psychotherapist privilege, though the specific definitions of what is privileged and what is not vary considerably from state to state (Younggren & Harris, 2008). In addition, the mental health disciplines whose clients can assert privilege vary considerably from state to state. Clients of psychiatrists and psychologists are routinely included; licensed social workers and counselors are also frequently named. Glosoff, Herlihy, and Spence (2000) found that licensed counselors are included in the privileged communication statutes of 44 states. In 16 states, the clients of school counselors are also covered by privileged communication statutes, and privilege sometimes extends to paraprofessionals and office assistants of mental health professionals (Fischer & Sorenson, 1996; Stone, 2009).

Subpoenas and Court Orders

Officers of the court can make demands for client information in three ways. First, they can issue a *subpoena*, a legal demand to appear to give testimony. Second, they can issue a *subpoena duces tecum*, a command to appear in court and bring along specific documents. Subpoenas are typically issued by a clerk of the court upon the request of an attorney without review of the legal merits of the demand for information. Finally, a court can issue a *court order* for a mental health professional to provide either documents or testimony, or both. In contrast to a subpoena, a court order is issued by a judge who has evaluated the legal merits of the demand for information and has ruled that it is properly executed and consistent with current law. In states where privileged communication statutes have been passed, counselors, social workers, and psychologists may not disclose material *even if subpoenaed by an attorney* unless they have client authorization to release that information. However, this does not mean that mental health professionals may ignore subpoenas! Instead, with the assistance of their own attorneys, they should respond by informing the court of their legal and ethical obligation to keep communication privileged, seek further guidance from a judge, and work toward limiting disclosure as much as legally permissible. To resolve the matter, the judge typically holds a hearing and then rules on the applicability of privilege in the case. A judge may also ask to view the disputed materials or speak with the professional about the contested testimony in his or her chambers. This is called an *in camera review*, and professionals may reveal confidential information to a judge for such a review because the purpose is to resolve whether the legal privilege holds in the case. Moreover, the judge is bound to protect the privacy of such information received in camera (Filaccio, 2005). If the judge rules that privilege is not applicable, he or she is likely to order the professional to comply with the attorney's request. In that event, the professional may testify or produce records from the counseling interaction, or do both. Clinicians who relinquish records and testimony without first seeking a judge's ruling about privilege are at risk for violating both legal and ethical standards.

Huber and Baruth (1987) make an important point about subpoenas: "Subpoenas should be viewed as the formal commencement, not the conclusion, of any disclosure controversy" (p. 20). Mental health professionals practicing in states that grant privilege to their clients are also at risk for a civil legal action against them if they disclose therapeutic information to a court without first seeking client consent or asserting privilege. In this situation, clients can sue the professional for violating their fiduciary relationship by an unwarranted breach of confidentiality. Professionals are ethically and legally protected, however, if a court refuses to acknowledge the client's right to confidentiality. The alternatives are to file an appeal of the ruling to a higher court or to endure the legal penalties imposed for refusing to testify or produce documents. Often this means being found in contempt of court. The Committee on Legal Issues of the APA has published a document that mental health professionals may find useful in sorting out these legal requirements, entitled *Strategies for Private Practitioners Coping with Subpoenas or Compelled Testimony for Client Records or Test Data* (APA, Committee on Legal Issues, 2006). The ACA Code indicates that counselors should seek client's permission for a disclosure to a court or seek a court order for such disclosure if consent is not forthcoming (Appendix A, Section B.2.d, p. 409).

The concept of privilege derived from one-on-one conversations such as those between priest and penitent, and attorney and client. Thus, when clients make disclosures to mental health professionals when others who are not co-participants in family or group therapy are present, their comments may not be viewed as privileged because the client had no reasonable expectation of privacy. A case that recently came before the Michigan Court of Appeals is a good example of this interpretation of privilege (Galley & Walsh, 2002). The Michigan court held that a student who disclosed information to a school counselor in the presence of other students and an administrative assistant was not protected by the privilege that typically covers school counselors in Michigan because the student had no reasonable expectation of privacy when he made the initial disclosure to this counselor. A similar finding was obtained in *U.S. v. Romo* (Mitrevski & Chamberlain, 2006), when privilege was denied because the disclosures to the therapist occurred outside of diagnosis or treatment of the inmate.

THE LIMITS OF CONFIDENTIALITY

Newton (1989) notes that our society is ambivalent about confidentiality. On the one hand, we value it and admire those who are loyal to their friends. Children ridicule tattletales, and nations reserve their most severe punishments for traitors. Most democracies have enacted laws to ensure that people can trust their lawyers with their confidences, their physicians with their illnesses, and their priests with their confessions. As indicated earlier, state laws also govern confidentiality between mental health professionals and their clients, requiring them to keep therapeutic disclosures private. It is important to note, however, that therapists and counselors are relative latecomers to this protection, and these laws are generally less complete and more weakly supported than for lawyers, physicians, or priests. This unwillingness to grant mental health professions the same degree of confidentiality as other professionals is a reflection of our society's ambivalence about confidentiality for mental health clients.

These reactions emerge from the antisocial nature of confidentiality, according to Newton (1989), because confidentiality frequently acts in opposition to some other public interest. To return to an earlier example, even though there is no public interest in a client's preferences for Chinese food or harmonica skills, there is a strong public interest in a client who tells a counselor about fantasies of violence against a boss. In the latter situation, the antisocial nature of confidentiality is clear because maintaining the confidence is in direct opposition to the society's desire to protect a citizen against harm. The stronger the likelihood this client will act on the fantasy, the greater is the public interest in disclosure. Prosecutors in criminal cases have also claimed a public interest in obtaining evidence from mental health professionals who have been providing services to an accused person. Society's discomfort with confidentiality has led to numerous limits on professional confidentiality. Some ethical and legal scholars argue that the ways in which the courts have eroded confidentiality are counterproductive to the client, the profession, and the public's need for access to the mental health system (e.g., see Baumoel, 1992; Bersoff, 2014; Bollas & Sundelson, 1995). These scholars wonder whether people will seek mental health services if they are not assured of confidentiality. On the other hand, Shuman and Foote (1999) contend that there is no convincing evidence that any of the legal limits imposed on confidentiality have negatively affected clients' willingness to seek help. Clearly, more systematic study of this question is needed.

However, the public also has an interest in the continuation of professional confidentiality insofar as professionals can help those who have antisocial tendencies to change their behavior. If no confidentiality existed, people might be less willing to disclose such tendencies and feelings. In a study of commuters at Union Station in Washington, D.C., Marsh (2003) found evidence to support that view. Her sample reported that they would be significantly less likely to disclose information that would put them at risk for involuntary commitment or criminal prosecution during therapy if their communications were not covered by state and federal privilege statutes. Without disclosure of antisocial tendencies, the professional's opportunity to prevent such acts in the future is lost. For these reasons, the legal system and professional organizations have sought to limit exceptions to confidentiality. Both systems have affirmed the fundamental value of confidentiality even as exceptions and limitations are codified. The tension between the public interest in the content of counseling and therapy sessions and its acceptance of confidentiality as a client's right has not been resolved. Thus, counselors and psychologists should keep current with changes in statutes, case law, and ethical mandates.

Currently there are nine major categories of exceptions to confidentiality in counseling and psychotherapy, described in the following section. (Some jurisdictions may have even more legal limits; California, for example, has 17 different limits to psychotherapist–client privilege [Donner, VandeCreek, Gonsiorek, & Fisher, 2008]). It is crucial to keep in mind, though, as Donner et al. (2008) comment so eloquently, "confidentiality must be first" (p. 371) and must be guarded. The existence of these legal exceptions should not cloud the professional's thinking about the sacredness of confidentiality.

1. Client Request for Release of Information

The first limit to confidentiality is based on the client's autonomy. Because clients have control over personal information, clients who are competent and wish to release information for communication elsewhere have the right to do so. The ACA Code addresses this provision in Section B.6.g, which requires written permission to disclose information or transfer records. It goes on to stipulate that counselors are responsible for taking steps to ensure that the confidentiality of those records is not compromised. The APA Code (Standard 4.05) simply indicates that client permission is required for disclosure of confidential information. Clients frequently waive their right to confidentiality when moving to a new community, obtaining medical care, or when they are seeking a consultation with another professional and wish the new clinician to see their records or speak with their former provider. Many people waive the right to confidentiality in order to have insurers cover the costs of their mental health services. (The impact of federal regulations from the Health Insurance Portability and Accountability Act [HIPAA, Public Law 104-191, 2003] and the Family Educational Rights and Privacy Act [FERPA] on client releases will be discussed fully in Chapters 12 and 13, respectively.) Professionals are also obligated to make arrangements so that the confidentiality of records is maintained when they end their practices or for situations in which they become incapacitated from illness or injury (Section B.6.h–i of the ACA Code and Standard 10.09 of the APA Code).

A release from a client does not give a counselor blanket permission to release confidential information to any party the client has named on a release form unless the professional has informed the client about the likely implications of such releases. If a client insists on a release to a party that the professional believes will not be in his or her best interest, that discussion should be documented in the client record, and a signed release of information should be obtained. Before the advent of legislation that so thoroughly protects consumer access to client records, ethical standards used to insist that counselors release client information only to qualified professionals. Such broad provisions have been eliminated because they are inconsistent with many state laws. The current wording is more consistent with most, but not all, state statutes. Ohio, for example, offers virtually unlimited client and patient access to health records and provides legal remedies for patients to sue professionals who fail to comply with the law (Ohio Revised Code, Section 3701.74, 2011). The ACA Code (Section B.5.c) also addresses this issue when the client is a minor, allowing the counselor to seek authorization from an appropriate person but advising that the minor client be informed about the release.

The ACA Code also requires that clients be allowed access to their own counseling records unless such access would not be in their best interests. The mandate also derives from the principles of autonomy and beneficence. The APA Code specifies client consent to release confidential information in Standard 4.05 and makes a more general comment on records, again focusing on the relationship between access and the best interests of the client in Standards 6.01 and 6.02.

As will be discussed in Chapter 12, this right to access means that records should be written with the assumption that the client may be reading them. Releases are not needed when a mental health professional has judged it necessary to begin involuntary commitment proceedings or when a mental health client has signed the HIPAA notice of privacy practices document to allow for communications to other mental health professionals, to third-party payers, or to staff involved in processing client records, appointments, and the like. Once the client has signed the notice of privacy practices, clinicians are allowed to discuss relevant aspects of the client's history and treatment with professionals involved in the hospitalization and to share client records with them as appropriate. The crucial word here is *relevant*—even HIPAA does not free a mental health provider from his or her obligation to limit such disclosures to content that is essential to treatment and to restrict disclosures to individuals responsible for care, payment, and operation of the professional service. In addition, the signature on the notice of privacy practices must indicate client understanding of its content and agreement. All too often, these documents are handled in such a way that clients sign them without attending to the content, or even worse, they are written in a style that makes reading comprehension difficult for most clients.

2. Court Orders for Confidential Information

The second major limitation to confidentiality occurs when the courts demand access to records and counselor testimony. There are several circumstances under which this may occur and under which privileged communication statutes usually do not apply. Confidentiality is generally not protected when a professional acts as an expert witness or as a consultant for the court to evaluate a person involved in a legal proceeding. Mental health professionals may be employed to assess whether a person is mentally competent to stand trial, is a fit parent, was mentally ill at the time of a crime, or has suffered psychological distress subsequent to an injury or accident. Mental health professionals have been increasingly involved in such activities over the last several decades. The person being evaluated has either waived confidentiality, or the court never recognized any such right in the first place. In these circumstances, the entire professional relationship is based on the assumption that information disclosed will be shared with the court.

As mentioned previously in the discussion of privileged communication, sometimes attorneys seek to obtain records from mental health professionals who have a preexisting therapeutic relationship with someone accused of a crime or whose fitness as a custodial parent is being challenged. Attorneys have also sought this information in civil suits and in federal courts adjudicating civil rights cases. In criminal courts, prosecutors often want to use, as evidence of guilt, the material the accused has revealed in counseling. In a significant federal case that came before the U.S. Supreme Court after conflicting holdings from lower courts (*Jaffee v. Redmond*, 1996), the family of a person killed by a police officer filed a wrongful death action and then sought counseling information from Karen Beyer, the licensed clinical social worker who counseled the officer after the shooting. The Illinois court considered that information privileged, but no such privilege for social workers had been established in federal courts. The federal district court ruled that the social worker should testify (thereby refusing to recognize the privilege), but the federal appeals court overturned that ruling. In its response to the final appeal, the U.S. Supreme Court determined in a 7–2 vote that the privilege should be honored and the social worker could not be forced to testify about her client's disclosures. Here is the language that Justice John Paul Stevens used in his opinion:

> Significant private interests support recognition of a psychotherapist privilege. Effective psychotherapy depends upon an atmosphere of confidence and trust, and therefore the mere possibility of disclosure of confidential communications may impede development of the relationship necessary for successful treatment. The privilege also serves the public interest, since the mental health of the Nation's citizenry, no less than its physical health, is a public good of transcendent importance. (*Jaffee v. Redmond*, p. 10)

Professional mental health organizations were relieved that the Court took such a strong stance in favor of the value of confidentiality. Whether a mental health professional has a legal right to refuse to give testimony in a particular court is not fully resolved, however. The Supreme Court ruling in *Jaffee v. Redmond* applies most directly to social workers, psychologists, and psychiatrists and does not address the privilege of other kinds of mental health professionals. However, a case that came before the Federal Appeals Court for the Ninth Circuit in 2001 ruled that the privilege applied to the client of an unlicensed counselor at an employee assistance program, thereby implying that *Jaffee* would apply to clients of licensed mental health professionals (*Oleszko v. State Compensation Insurance Fund*, 2001). Shuman and Foote (1999) point out that most courts still used the relevance of the professional's testimony to the case at hand as the primary criterion for compelling testimony and that privilege considerations often "take a back seat" when the information the professional has to share is crucial to establishing the facts of the case (p. 481). Eight years later, Simon and Shuman (2007) reported that federal judges have carved out federal exceptions to privilege very similar to the exceptions in state statutes, and Appelbaum (2008) notes that the legal questions regarding the confidentiality of disclosures of threats of harm are far from fully resolved. Thus, mental health professionals need to be informed about current regulations and case law governing privileged communication in their states and how those regulations apply to their profession.

Interestingly, Shuman and Foote indicate that the effectiveness of an argument in favor of privilege has depended partially on the number of other disclosures of confidential information to third parties that the professional and/or client have made. These authors go on to suggest that even routine disclosures to third-party payers, referral sources, or consultations with colleagues, have, in some circumstances, limited privilege. Clients' voluntary disclosures of psychotherapy content to other hospital patients have also compromised privilege. They recommend that clinicians use caution, even when making disclosures for which the client has signed a release, in situations in which the threat of court action is a substantial risk. Shuman and Foote also advise professionals to discuss with clients the implications of voluntary disclosures of psychotherapy content to other people.

3. Client Complaints and Litigation Against Mental Health Professionals

The third limit to confidentiality occurs when clients bring a legal action against their counselors or therapists. If a client wishes to sue a professional for negligence or breach of contract, the client must waive the right to confidentiality. Therefore, once he or she has seen a copy of the release, the professional may discuss the treatment in court without threat of legal sanction because all mental health professionals have a right to defend themselves against malpractice claims. Similarly, if a client files an ethics complaint against a mental health professional, the client must waive the right to confidentiality if the claim is to be pursued. Thus, when accused of misconduct, one can respond with case information and records to an ethics committee without worry about an unethical or illegal release of private information. (However, it seems prudent to verify that the committee has received a signed release from the client.) Some states have designated the filing of a malpractice claim as an exception to privilege, in which case a release would not be required, but is certainly not prohibited (Koocher & Keith-Spiegel, 2008).

4. Other Client Litigation

The fourth limit comes into play when clients initiate against another party a civil legal action that includes claims of psychological harm or emotional distress (Association of Trial Lawyers of America, 2001; Shuman & Foote, 1999; Swenson, 1997). The claim of psychological injury makes any relevant counseling material potentially available to the court. Access to that information is important for a fair hearing of the complaint and can be made available if the defendant seeks it. If the client reasserts a right to confidentiality of that information, the case may not be able to go forward. For example, when someone alleges that the anxiety disorder for which she is in treatment originated in the car accident for which another driver was at fault, she must release the counselor from confidentiality if she wishes testimony about her psychological distress to come before the court. It is important to note that confidentiality in such situations does not hold precisely because the client is voluntarily bringing legal action against someone else and has the freedom not to go forward with these claims if he or she does not wish to do so. A defendant in a criminal case is not there voluntarily; hence, the legal system more scrupulously guards his or her confidentiality.

5. Limitations Based in State and Federal Statutes

Child Abuse Reporting Some material has been excluded from professional confidentiality by statute. Every state has statutes mandating that counselors, psychologists, educators, and other mental health professionals report child abuse and neglect to the proper authorities. The Federal Child Abuse Prevention and Treatment

Act (1987) also demands such reporting. Similar federal legislation has been passed in Canada. See Mathews and Kenny (2008) for a comparison of child protection statutes in the United States, Canada, and Australia. The details of the statutes vary somewhat by state, but the central message is consistent: Mental health professionals, educators, medical personnel, and child care workers who learn of child abuse or neglect are legally obligated to report this information to social service or police agencies, usually within 24 hours. The penalties for failing to report usually include criminal sanctions. The reporting of abuse and neglect takes precedence over any legal privilege or ethical obligation to confidentiality. The APA Committee on Professional Practice has published a helpful document on the legal and professional issues in child abuse (APA, 1995). This publication summarizes the professional's role in assessing, reporting, and intervening when abuse or neglect occurs, and lists national resources available to assist mental health professionals in these processes.

The legislatures have reasoned that the public interest in protecting those who cannot protect themselves from abuse outweighs the obligation to confidentiality. However, even in mandated reporting situations, the law typically limits disclosure of confidential information to content relevant to the abuse or neglect. Other aspects of counseling disclosures that have no bearing on this matter can and should be kept confidential. Because the statutes vary from state to state, professionals must be aware of changes to and wording of statutes in their states or provinces.

Research shows that mandated reporting of child abuse and neglect occurs commonly in mental health practice; in 2012, for example, nearly 1.2 million mental health professionals and educators made reports about possible abuse or neglect (U.S. Department of Health and Human Services, 2012). According to Melton et al. (1995), 90% of child psychiatrists, 63% of clinical psychologists, and 70% of social workers have filed one or more reports of child abuse. Hermann (2002) reported that 89% of school counselors she sampled had reported child maltreatment to authorities. Bryant (2009) found that the mean number of reports by school counselors in the prior year was 6.1, with suspicion of physical abuse as the most common reason for reporting. Only a few studies have examined the impact of a report on the therapeutic relationship, and they have found mixed results (Steinberg, 1994; Watson & Levine, 1989). Not surprisingly, the most negative result seems to occur when the client is reported as the perpetrator (Levine & Doueck, 1995).

Brosig and Kalichman (1992) also describe a substantial amount of noncompliance with the reporting law. Their analysis of the literature concludes that almost one-third of clinicians have declined to report suspected child abuse or neglect. This trend in the findings has been supported by more recent studies of family therapists (Strozier, Brown, Fennell, Hardee, & Vogel, 2005) and psychologists (Cavett, 2002). Research suggests professionals experience a conflict between the desire to keep the client involved in counseling and maintain confidentiality, on the one hand, and recognition of legal mandates and potential harm to the child, on the other. Kennel and Agresti (1995) contend that "many professionals appear to place child abuse on a continuum of severity that separates *suspected* abuse from *reportable* abuse" (p. 612). The vagueness of some states' reporting laws also contributes to this noncompliance (Melton et al., 1995). Those who sometimes decline to report seem to want to be sure about the existence of abuse given the implications of a breach of confidentiality, but their hesitancy can cause them legal and ethical problems. Many statutes mandate reporting *suspicions* of abuse, not *incidences* of abuse. Thus, the professional bears the burden of determining whether the suspicion is reasonable, even though making this determination can be difficult. The ultimate criteria are avoiding harm to the child and protecting the child's best interests. For an excellent clarification of state laws in the United States on child abuse reporting, see Foreman and Bernet (2000) or NASW General Counsel (2013).

A number of other variables seem to influence this reluctance to report. When therapists fail to report, they often believe that reporting will not be in their client's best interest (Kalichman, 1999) and view child protective services as ineffective (Levine et al., 1991; Strozier et al., 2005). They worry that reporting will sever the counseling relationship or otherwise damage therapeutic progress or family functioning (Haas, Malouf, & Mayerson, 1988; Strozier et al., 2005). Rokop (2003) offers possible avenues for reducing the damage. Rokop's findings suggest that the damage to the therapeutic relationship from a mandated report can be substantially reduced if the therapist has developed a strong working alliance with these clients, communicated clearly about the mandate to report, expressed empathy with the client's distress over the report, and offered support subsequent to reporting.

A few mental health professionals attribute their failure to report to a personal conviction that confidentiality is absolute and should not be violated even in cases of child abuse or neglect. In essence, they are engaging in civil disobedience and opposition to the ethical standards of the profession. These individuals should understand that they are at risk for ethical and legal sanctions against them. Moreover, if their failure to report results in greater harm to a child, they must bear moral and legal responsibility for that harm. In other words, refusing to report child abuse has serious and long-lasting consequences for all involved. Practitioners who find themselves declining to report should examine their motivation and seek consultation with peers about this issue. They should apply the "well-lit room standard" and ask themselves whether they would be proud to communicate such a decision to a group of professional peers and whether they could expect that audience to respect their position. If not, failing to report is not really a matter of principles or civil disobedience; it is a matter of personal needs or lack of objectivity. It is also important to keep in mind that mandatory reporting applies not only to abuse but also to neglect and to actions of caretakers that put children at serious risk for abuse or neglect. The tendency to refer to this legal requirement as the mandated reporting of abuse should not lead professionals to lose sight of the responsibility to act when they have suspicions of neglect.

Professionals who are unsure about whether a particular situation meets the criteria for reporting have several options: They may call children's services and ask about a hypothetical situation; they may consult with another colleague; or they may seek a legal opinion. Online training in child abuse reporting has shown some effectiveness to helping professionals make responsible decisions about reporting (Kenny, 2007). According to research by Renninger, Veach, and Bagdade (2002), some professionals overreport abuse and neglect, that is, report instances that fall substantially short of the criterion for reporting, perhaps as a result of misunderstandings of their legal obligations and concern about the risks of nonreporting. Once again, these findings underscore the importance of careful consideration of both statutes and client privacy rights.

Elder Abuse Reporting All states also have statutes related to elder abuse, and 45 of them mandate that mental health professionals report neglect or abuse of dependent elders by those responsible for their care (Daly, Jogerst, Brinig, & Dawson, 2003; Welfel, Danzinger, & Santoro, 2000). In states that have such statutes, mental health professionals are mandated to report elder abuse or neglect to human service agencies if clients or family members disclose this information in session. As with child protection, state legislatures have reasoned that the duty to protect a dependent elder from harm is stronger than the professional's obligation to confidentiality. Thirty-eight states impose penalties on mandated reporters who fail to report. Because the wording of these statutes varies substantially by state, counselors need to be familiar with the law in states where they practice. For instance, even the definition of elder abuse can vary substantially by jurisdiction (Scheiderer, 2011). See Daly et al. (2004) for a state-by-state analysis of legal requirements, and Zeranski and Halgin (2011) for a thoughtful discussion of the application of the reporting laws to three complex cases.)

6. Dangerous Clients and the Duty to Protect

Having a client disclose an intent to harm someone else or a history of harming someone else is a very distressing circumstance for a mental health professional (Walfish, Barnett, Marlyere, & Zielke, 2010). In addition, this situation is far more common that novice professionals expect it to be. For example, Walfish et al. (2010) found that 13% of their sample of psychologists had experienced a client disclosure of unprosecuted murder, and 27% of the sample reported that at least one client had revealed a history of physical assault that had not been prosecuted. An even higher percentage (33%) had at least one client who told them about a history of sexual assault for which they had never been charged. Moreover, therapists encounter a client intending to harm or considering harming another person at least as frequently. Pabian, Welfel, and Beebe (2009) found that psychologists in their sample have encountered an average of three potentially violent clients in the last two years of practice.

Clearly then, it is crucial for mental health professionals to understand what such disclosures imply for confidentiality. In their study, Pabian et al. (2009) also reported the lack of such understanding. They reported that 76% of the 300 psychologists surveyed misinterpreted their legal duty when a client appears to be dangerous to others, a startling finding consistent with prior research. Why does this level of confusion exist? It exists partly because the ethical and legal standards frequently differ; partly because the landmark *Tarasoff* case was decided twice; partly because the law has been dynamic, not static; and finally because *duty to warn* has become the shorthand terminology for this responsibility, even though it does not consistently reflect the legal obligation. As will become evident in the paragraphs to follow, in many jurisdictions, no legal or ethical ethical mandate exists to break confidentiality, even when a client is at high risk of violence.

Clearly, however, communications from clients who are dangerous to themselves or other people are not always protected by the same level of confidentiality as other material. When the mental health professional judges a client to pose an immediate threat to others, the ethics codes permit disclosure of confidential information. This permission extends to some circumstances when the client is a danger to him or herself. The wording in the codes is as follows:

ACA Code Section B.2.a Serious and Foreseeable Harm and Legal Requirements

The general requirement that counselors keep information confidential does not apply when disclosure is required to protect clients or identified others from serious and foreseeable harm or when legal requirements demand that confidential information must be revealed. Counselors consult with other professionals when in doubt as to the validity of an exception. Additional considerations apply when addressing end-of-life issues.

Source: Reprinted with permission from American Counseling Association.

APA Code Standard 4.05 Disclosures

(b) Psychologists disclose confidential information without the consent of the individual only as mandated by law, or where permitted by law for a valid purpose such as to (1) provide needed professional services; (2) obtain appropriate professional consultations; (3) protect the client or patient, psychologist, or others from harm; or (4) obtain payment for services from a client or patient in which instance disclosure is limited to the minimum that is necessary to achieve the purpose.

Source: Copyright © 2010 by the American Psychological Association. Reproduced with permission.

The current codes are written to allow mental health professionals to breach confidentiality when they believe clients are dangerous; that is, they permit but do not mandate a breach. This permission can be traced back to a 1974 California case in which the family of a woman sued her killer's psychologist, his supervisor, and the University of California at Berkeley, where the psychologist worked because the psychologist failed to tell the woman at risk about the client's threat to kill her. The rulings of the lower state courts on this now famous *Tarasoff* case were appealed to the California Supreme Court, which ruled twice on the issue (*Tarasoff v. Regents of the University of California*, 1974, 1976). The result of these rulings imposed on California mental health professionals a *duty to protect* victims of violent clients. Currently, 23 states impose either a duty to protect or a duty to warn by statute, and 9 states have a common law duty as a result of court cases; 10 other states permit the breach of confidentiality to warn potential victims but do not mandate it, and 10 states have not definitively ruled on the issue (Benjamin, Kent, & Sirikantraporn, 2009). (These figures include Puerto Rico and the District of Columbia.) (For a fascinating review of the often misunderstood facts of the *Tarasoff* case, see Bersoff [2014]).

Prior to the *Tarasoff* case, professional standards advised or required *notifying* legal authorities about dangerous clients but contained no requirement to breach confidentiality otherwise. Prior legal standards endorsed hospitalization or other actions but had fallen short of requiring mental health professionals to break confidentiality to third parties not involved in the treatment. In *Tarasoff* and in many court cases and statutes since, the authorities have determined that mental health professionals have a duty to the public as well as to their clients (Werth, Welfel,

& Benjamin, 2009). The California court reasoned that if someone's life or health is at risk from a client, the benefit from a breach of confidentiality significantly outweighs the cost of that breach and should be undertaken if that is the best way to protect the third party from harm. The court ruled that "the privilege ends where the public peril begins" (*Tarasoff*, 1976, p. 347).

However, the crucial obligation identified by most courts and the legislatures is to use reasonable care to *protect* the one at risk (Benjamin et al., 2009). A breach of confidentiality to the victim is frequently a means to that end (and is mandated in 10 states), but it is not always an end in itself. In some states (e.g., Ohio), the duty can be carried out by hospitalizing the client (either voluntarily or involuntarily) or by intensifying outpatient treatment (Ohio Rev. Code § 2305.51, 1999). In Texas, if warning is permitted, it is the police who get warned, not the potential victim (Texas Health & Safety Code § 611.004(a)(2) [1995]).

When a mental health professional elects or is mandated to carry out this duty by breaching confidentiality to an intended victim, the responsibility does not end with the action of warning the victim. If it did, a telephone conversation with an intended victim might go something like this:

COUNSELOR: Are you Mr. X?

MR. X: Yes.

COUNSELOR: I am the counselor for Ms. Y, who has made a threat to kill you. I strongly believe she intends to carry out this threat as soon as she can. I do not know of Ms. Y's whereabouts since she left my office one hour ago. The police have been informed as well. Ms. Y stated that she had access to a gun. I believe she was going to get that gun when she left my office. Do you understand what I have told you?

MR. X: Yes, I understand.

COUNSELOR: Goodbye, then.

Such a scenario is ludicrous. The counselor in this situation has technically warned the intended victim but has done little to protect the victim. The person receiving the phone call might disbelieve the counselor and do nothing to protect himself; might be so traumatized from the news that he does not take steps to protect himself; or might get angry and decide to get his own gun and kill Ms. Y first. And these are just the obvious possibilities. It is noteworthy that Binder and McNiel (1996) found that when psychiatric residents were surveyed on their experiences with warning intended victims, two reactions dominated—the victims either already knew of the risk or denied that the client would ever hurt them. The point is that even the California court's 1976 ruling did not limit the responsibility to warning. They focused more on protection than on warning. In the *Tarasoff* case, warning the victim was viewed as a necessary part of protection because of the facts of that case, but the court did not see warning as essential in every situation. Put another way, the legal duty of the professional is to take steps to help protect the person from foreseeable harm from the client; warning the victim is a common way to discharge that duty but is not the only possible way to protect the third party in most jurisdictions (Benjamin et al., 2009).

If the professional does warn a victim, the mental health professional is expected to take reasonable steps to help that person get protection from the client. That assistance may take the form of assisting the person to connect with loved ones or obtaining police protection. A common way of protecting the victim is to restrain the freedom of the client so that access to the victim is blocked, an outcome usually achieved through hospitalization or involuntary commitment to a psychiatric unit. That option is not always available because many jurisdictions require that a person be diagnosed as *both* mentally ill and dangerous in order to authorize involuntary commitment (Simon & Shuman, 2007). Another option that is sometimes permitted is to intensify outpatient treatment in order to decrease the client's intent to harm. This option carries more risk because the freedom of the client is not restricted, but it also offers more protection to the privacy of the client. If intensifying outpatient treatment is the option chosen to protect the potential victim, the professional should take extra steps to ensure that this is the best alternative. Consultation with a knowledgeable colleague about the client's care is essential to making a responsible choice for this option. Of course, consultation is advisable in virtually all situations in which a professional is working with a client who is at significant risk for violence. Reviewing the case with a peer consultation group or individual helps a professional better assess both the level of risk and the best strategy for protecting the client from taking this disastrous action as well as protecting the person at risk of harm.

If all this sounds as if counselors and therapists must put themselves in jeopardy to protect victims, that impression is wrong. We are not expected to risk our personal safety, but rather to intervene with the client, the victim, or both, to prevent the violence as fully as reasonable.

Some subsequent court cases have clarified and extended the *Tarasoff* ruling in a number of ways. Some cases have limited the duty to situations of *imminent* danger, usually interpreted to mean situations in which an explicit threat of immediate action has been made or implied. If this threat is judged by the clinician as foreseeable and likely to be carried out in the near future, the duty is more likely to be imposed (Wheeler & Bertram, 2012). The great variety of interpretations of the duty to protect is well documented in the legal analyses of these cases, and all mental health professionals ought to keep current on the developments in case law and statutory law in their jurisdiction (Benjamin et al., 2009).

The duty does not extend to every situation in which a client may express a violent feeling toward another person. When people are angry, they often use violent language to express their anger. Many people in the midst of divorce have threatened to do bodily harm to their partners, and many people have said they would rather commit suicide than deal with Alzheimer's disease or AIDS. Few clients who utter these words will carry out a homicide or suicide. The responsibility of the professional is to sift through these angry and desperate words and identify those clients whose intent is truly violent. As Truscott and Evans (2001) point out, when clinicians develop strong therapeutic bonds with their clients, they are more likely to have sufficient influence to accurately assess the risk, diffuse violent impulses, and reduce the risk of acting out.

Violence Risk Assessment This process is called *risk assessment*. The literature indicates that although mental health professionals cannot predict dangerousness with a high degree of accuracy, their predictions are measurably better than chance (e.g., Otto & Douglas, 2010), especially in the short term. If they err, they are more likely to overpredict violence. In other words, they tend to predict danger in cases where no violent action ends up occurring (Smith & Meyer, 1987). In spite of the difficulties in reliably assessing future violence, the courts often impose on mental health professionals the duty to act to protect victims in cases of foreseeable danger. For this reason, professionals are well advised to become familiar with the literature on risk management with dangerous clients and to become as skilled as possible in assessing the risk of violence. The assessment always includes a history of the client's violent behavior, the current social conditions that may exacerbate or diminish the likelihood for violence, and the client's current psychological functioning (Borum & Verhaagen, 2006; Monahan, 2008; Werth, Welfel, & Benjamin, 2009). Borum and Reddy (2001) note six major topics for clinicians to evaluate: (1) the presence of attitudes that support or facilitate violence, (2) the client's capacity or means to carry out violence; (3) the crossing of a threshold toward violence, such as purchasing a gun or breaking a law; (4) the presence of an intent to carry out a violent action (in contrast to the idea of acting violently); (5) the responses of others to the client's plan; and (6) the degree of client compliance with professional recommendations to reduce risk.

A methodical assessment of dangerousness is also important because of the emotion that a violent client evokes in any practitioner and the frequency with which this happens. In one study of Pennsylvania psychologists, 14% of the participants had a client who committed suicide the previous year, and 18% reported having a client who had assaulted a third party (Knapp & Keller, 2004). Working with a client whom one thinks may cause injury is very stressful. Professionals can be overwhelmed by their sense of responsibility for the client's actions and may be concerned about their own safety under such circumstances (Walfish, Barnett, et al., 2010). If not balanced by a careful evaluation of the real risk, these fears and worries can compromise clear thinking and ethical action. For a more detailed discussion of risk management, see Borum and Verhaagen (2006), Monahan (1993), and Otto and Douglas (2010). Yang, Wong, and Coid (2010) provide evidence of the accuracy of nine risk assessment tools that professionals may use to assess a client's risk of violence. None of these tools offers a perfect prediction of violence (Truscott, 2009), but they do provide the clinician with a more reliable basis upon which to predict violence than individual judgment alone.

Court rulings in California (Leong, Eth, & Silva, 1992) suggest another reason for careful risk assessment before breaching confidentiality. In at least three cases, once a warning was issued to a third party, psychotherapists were required to give court testimony that went well beyond the *Tarasoff* warning. This testimony was used in all three cases to help establish the guilt of the defendants (clients) in criminal trials. According to Meyers (1991), "There is no way to tell whether psychotherapists, following *Tarasoff*, have ever saved a potential victim from injury, but it is clear that at least two psychotherapists, ordered to testify over objections and claims of privilege, helped prosecutors convict an ex-patient of first-degree murder and contributed to sentencing him to the penalty of death" (p. 27). A more recent case (*United States v. Chase*, 2003) suggests that a *Tarasoff* warning need not vacate all confidentiality. In this case, the federal court ruled that even though the psychologist issued a *Tarasoff* warning to protect FBI agents against a risk from Mr. Chase, her client, the fact of the warning did not eliminate the privilege. The court argued that the purpose of a *Tarasoff* warning is to protect a third party, and once its protective function has been served, the client's communications remained privileged if the client is no longer dangerous.

When attempting to determine the predictability of danger, a professional should consult with colleagues and possibly an attorney, both because of the risk of injury and because the exception to confidentiality typically applies to imminent danger, not potential danger. In other words, breaching confidentiality without imminent danger can result in legal and ethical complaints against the professional by the person whose privacy was not protected. Counselors, in particular, may need legal assistance in deciphering the meaning of the phrase "serious and foreseeable harm" in the section of the ACA Code that allows for disclosure without client consent. Even though many states, such as California and Ohio, have offered mental health professionals protection from liability claims stemming from good-faith breaches of confidentiality under this duty, not every state has addressed this matter either in case law or statutory law (Benjamin et al., 2009; Glosoff et al., 2000).

When warning is appropriate, the courts have also clarified who should be told about violent clients. Typically, law enforcement officers and/or the potential victims should be informed. Professionals should disclose only information relevant to the danger, not other confidential communications. In cases where the threat is against a senior official in the U.S. government, notifying the Secret Service is another option (Randazzo & Keeney, 2009). Professionals should also warn those so close to the possible victim (or their caretakers) that they too are in danger. For example, a dependent child of a custodial parent who is the object of the threat also is seen by the legal system as a person whom the professional has a duty to protect. Most state courts have rejected the notion that therapists have a duty to warn and protect in situations in which clients make broad or vague threats, or situations in which the victim is not identifiable. In that situation, the professional's duty shifts somewhat. If the risk assessment leads to the conclusion that the client is truly dangerous, but no way exists to identify a victim, the professional should consider initiating involuntary commitment proceedings against the client. (In a number of states, only psychiatrists and psychologists have the authority to initiate such proceedings on their own.) If a client is detained in a hospital setting as an emergency procedure, he or she endangers no one during the period of hospitalization.

The states vary in their interpretation of the duty to protect. In other words, there is substantial variation in the factors that must be present to trigger the duty. In a few states, a *history* of violent action coupled with a reasonably identifiable victim may be enough to require a breach of confidentiality, even in the absence of any specific threat (Benjamin et al., 2009). In other words, in those states an explicit threat of harm is not a necessary component for the duty to be imposed. These wide variations in state statutes are confusing and demonstrate the critical importance of becoming informed about local laws. Complicating matters even further is the rapid rate at which case law and statutory law on this subject change. For instance, Ohio law changed three times between 1991 and 1997. And California, a state that had long operated under a duty to protect standard, reverted to a duty to warn and protect standard in 2004 (*Ewing v. Goldstein*, 2004).

One final note about the duty to protect is in order. Courts interpret this duty to apply not only to situations in which a professional knows about a serious risk of danger but also to situations in which the professional *should have known* about the danger. This means that if the ignorance about a danger stems from incompetent or negligent practice, or from a refusal to explore issues for fear of what the client might say, then that professional has also violated this duty. The courts simply do not view incompetence or negligence as an adequate defense against a claim of failure to protect.

Given this history of legal challenges to the confidentiality of client communications, one may mistakenly conclude that confidentiality does not apply to violent clients. Such an interpretation is not only wrong, it is also inconsistent with court rulings that tend to support the need for confidentiality as a general principle in counseling and psychotherapy. Even in situations of imminent danger, confidentiality is not entirely eliminated. Any communications about the client must be limited to information relevant to the threat that may help prevent harm to the victim. No relevant information to prevent the harm should be withheld, but no peripheral information unrelated to the threat should be disclosed.

Duty to Protect When a Client Is Suicidal When adult clients are at immediate risk of suicide, the practitioner's primary obligation is to protect the adult client from the self-destructive impulse (Jobes & O'Connor, 2009). Whether there is a legal duty to breach confidentiality to inform significant others in the client's life is uncertain (Bongar, 2013). The legal and ethical responsibility to protect the client from harm is unequivocal, however. To achieve this goal, the most valuable tool is the strength of the therapeutic relationship with the client (Jobes & O'Connor, 2009) and the power of the trusted therapist to deescalate the situation. Thus, the first option to consider is intensifying treatment. In situations where a breach of confidentiality is unavoidable, professionals should act prudently in communications with family members or authorities and should reveal only material necessary to help the client. In an ideal situation, such disclosures are made with the client's consent and involvement so that they are not truly breaches of confidentiality, but rather the result of a joint decision to act toward a therapeutic goal. If a therapist judges that the client would not be safe with significant others or that intensifying the current treatment would be insufficient, then hospitalization may be wise. Careful risk assessment is important for the welfare of the therapist as well. Working with suicidal clients has been termed the most stressful aspect of clinical work (Hendin, Lipschitz, Maltsberger, Haas, & Wynecoop, 2000; Webb, 2011). Gaining competency in suicide assessment is crucial because of the likelihood that mental health professionals will confront this issue frequently in their careers. Rogers, Gueulette, Abbey-Hines, Carney, and Werth (2001) reported that 71% of the counselors they sampled had experienced at least one client suicide attempt, and McAdams and Foster (2000) found that 20% of counseling psychology trainees had parallel experiences. Bongar (2013), Capuzzi (2004), and Jobes and O'Connor (2009) are excellent sources of information on assessing suicidal risk. The special concerns in responding to situations when children and adolescents may be suicidal are thoroughly discussed in Berman, Jobes, and Silverman (2006).

7. Clients Planning Future Crimes

In most cases, clinicians are not required to disclose a client's past crime. However, according to Glosoff et al. (2000), when clients disclose that they are planning criminal action in the future, counselors may be compelled to disclose those comments to investigating law enforcement officers in the 17 states in which privilege excludes this type of content. These states include Alaska, Arizona, the District of Columbia, Idaho, Illinois, Indiana, Kansas, Louisiana, Massachusetts, Montana, New Mexico, Oklahoma, Oregon, South Carolina, South Dakota, Tennessee, and Washington. Examples of criminal activity to which this restriction might apply would be the selling of stolen goods, the purchase or sale of controlled substances, or involvement in schemes that defraud older adults of their money (Glosoff et al., 2000). Mental health professionals ought not to confuse this limit to privilege with the duty to protect that applies when a third party is in danger from a client. Even in those states listed above, the restriction of privilege for planned criminal activity is typically limited to situations in which a client is under investigation by law enforcement officials, and those officers seek information from the treating professional. In these states, professionals who know about a criminal act being planned may be forced to provide information over their own objections and the objections of their clients. Needless to say, anyone confronting such circumstances should research the particulars of his or her state law and consult with an attorney to determine the proper response to such requests.

8. Counseling Clients With Communicable and Life-Threatening Diseases

Many communicable diseases once thought to be fatal are either curable or can be treated as chronic diseases. HIV infection, once thought to be inevitably fatal, is now more appropriately considered a chronic disease. With proper care, people can live nearly normal lives for decades. Moreover, recent research has made some progress in developing a vaccine and topical applications to prevent HIV infection in women (National Institute of Allergy and Infectious Disease, 2013). Counseling people with HIV spectrum disorders and other communicable and life-threatening illnesses raises a number of ethical issues. Of greatest concern for mental health professionals are (1) the confidentiality of client disclosures, (2) the risk of discrimination against clients with these illnesses if information about their health status is not protected, and (3) the welfare of third parties at risk for infection because of their contact with the client. The most common behaviors that place others at high risk are the sharing of needles in intravenous drug use and unprotected sexual contact. (Of course, not all forms of unprotected sexual contact carry exactly the same degree of risk, but unprotected sex is the category under which some very high-risk behaviors fall.) The ethical dilemma for therapists lies in balancing their responsibility to the client who has such an illness and to people whom that client may be placing at risk for the infection. Given the restrictions on confidentiality when clients make threats of imminent homicide or suicide, scholars have vigorously debated whether the duty to protect applies in the case of these disorders (e.g., see Anderson & Barret, 2001). Only the ACA Code makes special reference to the limits of confidentiality for people with life-threatening communicable diseases, indicating in Section B.2.c. that disclosure may be justified when clients have a life-threatening and communicable disease that puts another at risk. The code specifies that the risk must be both serious and foreseeable. The standard also indicates that counselors must assess the client's intent to disclose his or her health status to the other(s) and must review state law relevant to confidentiality in this circumstance. It is crucial to reiterate that the ACA Code does not mandate disclosure; it merely indicates that it may be allowed in limited circumstances.

The APA Code does not specifically mention exceptions to confidentiality regarding communicable diseases, although in Standard 4.05.b it does indirectly address this issue when it allows psychologists to disclose confidential information without consent in order to protect someone from harm. In 1991, the APA published a resolution on applying duty-to-warn issues to people with HIV spectrum disorders. In this document, the APA opposed the establishment of a legal duty to warn provision for HIV-positive clients whose behavior increases the risk of transmitting the virus. As of this writing, except in the state of Utah (Glosoff et al., 2000), no legal duty to warn and protect people at risk for HIV exposure has been imposed on mental health professionals. The APA resolution describes the wording the association would find acceptable if such laws were written:

> If, however, specific legislation is considered, then it should permit disclosure only when (a) the provider knows of an identifiable third party who the provider has a compelling reason to believe is at significant risk for infection; (b) the provider has a reasonable belief that the third party has no reason to suspect that he or she is at risk; and (c) the client/patient has been urged to inform the third party and has either refused or is considered unreliable in his/her willingness to notify the third party. (APA, 1991)

The welfare of the client cannot be ignored—even when a professional decides he or she must breach confidentiality to protect a person at risk. That action should be carried out with prior notice to the client, and it should be implemented in a way that minimizes harm to the client. Hasty breaches of confidentiality based on emotion or intuition, rather than on careful assessment of the risks to clients and third parties, are inherently problematic. This message is underscored by research suggesting that the ability of mental health professionals to make objective decisions about breaches of confidentiality in the case of HIV can be compromised by their attitudes toward homosexuality (McGuire, Nieri, Abbott, Sheridan, & Fisher, 1995). McGuire et al. found that psychotherapists who scored higher on a measure of homophobia were more likely to breach confidentiality than those who scored lower in homophobic attitudes. Several other scholars have also found evidence of prejudiced attitudes toward people with HIV disorders among counselors, psychologists, and marriage and family therapists (Crawford, Humfleet, Ribordy, Ho, & Vickers, 1999; Pais, Piercy, & Miller, 1998; Palma & Iannelli, 2002). In these studies, uninformed male partners of gay men were significantly less likely to be identified as parties to warn than uninformed female partners of heterosexual men. Thus, the research demonstrates that mental health professionals from many disciplines need to be especially careful that any decision to disclose a client's health status to a third party is based on a rational consideration of the facts and on a balanced assessment of the rights of the client and of the person at risk.

Studies by Kozlowski (2004) and Nichols (2003) highlight that decision making on breaching confidentiality to protect a third party at risk for HIV infection is a complicated and contentious issue for practitioners even when heterosexist bias is not a major factor. For example, Kozlowski (2004) reported that 25% of his sample of psychologists were unwilling to breach confidentiality even when given a scenario in which a client with an HIV disorder persistently refused to disclose his or her status to an at-risk partner. Based on this preliminary research, the permission that the codes offer for professionals to break confidentiality to protect an at-risk person does not appear to have resulted in any uniform response to this dilemma. On a more positive note, Kozlowsky and Nichols also report that professionals frequently consult with colleagues when they are confronted with this difficult issue.

One factor that may contribute to the lack of consensus in practitioner response is the reality that laws governing communication about a client's HIV status to third parties are varied and confusing. Most laws refer to physicians and health care providers and their applicability to mental health professionals is either uncertain or untested. Some states mandate confidentiality; others permit disclosure in the event of risk to a third party (Melchert & Patterson, 1999), and according to Chenneville (2000), a few require disclosure. In jurisdictions that mandate confidentiality, breaches of confidentiality could lead the client to bring a civil suit against the clinician. In states that permit disclosure to partners and other people at risk of infection, immunity from liability for professionals is often part of the law. Needless to say, in this uncertain and rapidly changing environment, mental health professionals need to obtain competent legal advice about the regulations that govern practice in their state and to regularly update their knowledge.

Another option to direct breach of confidentiality to a person at risk for HIV infection may be disclosure to a partner identification program. These programs exist to inform people at risk of their vulnerability to exposure to the HIV virus when clients are hesitant or unable to notify partners themselves. In some states, submitting information to a partner notification program may substitute for an ethical or legal obligation to breach confidentiality (Chenneville, 2000). In 26 states, physicians and other health care professionals are required to make confidential notification of all who test positive for HIV to an appropriate public health department (Melchert & Patterson, 1999).

Clinicians should also become informed about interventions that increase the likelihood that a person with an HIV spectrum disorder or other life-threatening communicable illness will use methods that reduce risks to others (Kelly & Kalichman, 2002). If a client uses such methods consistently, then the issue of warning others becomes less salient.

9. Counseling Individuals at the End of Their Lives

Clinicians who work with clients at the end of their lives may sometimes encounter clients whose pain and suffering lead them to consider hastening their own deaths. Professionals faced with this circumstance are coping with one of the most complex and troubling ethical dilemmas in practice: Are they obligated to intervene to prevent the client's actions in the same way they would be obligated to prevent a suicide at a different point in an individual's life span? Does the proximity of a painful and difficult death of a competent person change in any way the clinician's duty to prevent suicide? Does the consideration of suicide in itself indicate the presence of a depressive disorder in a person nearing death from illness or injury? In other words, is there such a thing as *rational suicide*? If hastening the end of one's life can be rational in some circumstances, is it ethically acceptable for a mental health professional to assist or support the client in completing this action? What confidentiality obligations are imposed on a professional working with a client who has decided to hasten the end of life? Interestingly, the section in the 2005 ACA Code on end-of-life issues was substantially revised in the 2014 revision, giving counselors the option to maintain confidentiality, depending on law and the particular circumstances. In this situation, the code also obliges counselors to seek consultation.

In its documents on end-of-life issues, the APA takes a similar view—that no psychologist is mandated to breach confidentiality when a client is considering the hastening of death. However, this position has not been integrated into the APA Code (APA, 2010a). NASW issued its statement on hastened death situations in 1994, determining that social workers were allowed to assist clients with decisions involving the hastening of death (NASW, 1994/2003). In other words, the codes and guidelines give permission (after critical evaluation of the case and consideration of relevant laws), but they do not mandate disclosure. The literature on this topic (e.g., the APA's Working Group on Assisted Suicide and End-of-Life Decisions, 2000; Werth & Blevins, 2008; Werth & Richmond, 2009) offers a list of issues for professionals to consider:

- The competence and capacity of the client to give an informed consent, that is, the judgment to understand the meaning and implications of the decision
- The influence of co-morbid psychological conditions, pain and suffering, overall quality of life, cultural factors, financial concerns, and fears of loss of autonomy
- The availability of a social support system for the client
- The availability of other interventions that might reduce suffering and improve the quality of life (Gibson, Brietbart, Tomarken, Kosinski, & Nelson, 2006)
- The possible influence of coercion to hasten the end of life—either direct or indirect pressures

In a situation where a client is suffering from a serious depression or where the client's competence to give consent appears compromised by his or her medical condition, it seems clear that a mental health professional may break confidentiality to prevent that person from hastening death or may take other measures to keep that person safe. A professional may also defer a decision about breaking confidentiality until an assessment of the factors listed above is complete. In some jurisdictions, it may be possible for the professional to maintain confidentiality if the individual appears to be making a decision that is rational, uncoerced, uncomplicated by psychological problems, and undertaken after all reasonable alternatives to improve quality of life have been explored. Needless to say, however, the public policy debate now underway about assisted suicide may lead states to pass legislation that requires mental health professionals to take a different stance, so clinicians must keep abreast of changes in state statutes and case law that may affect the legality of their actions. Currently five states allow for aid in dying: Montana, New Mexico, Oregon, Vermont, and Washington (Eckholm, 2014). See Werth and Richmond (2009) for extensive discussions of the debate on the ethical issues embedded in these cases and guidance for professionals when such cases emerge. The case below exemplifies the dilemma of a professional working with a person who is planning to hasten her death.

The Case of Mildred

Mildred is a 59-year-old executive with an international sporting goods company who has lived a very full and rewarding life. She won medals in track in three Olympic competitions, established a foundation to help educate children who are refugees from war-torn countries, adopted and raised four children from Rwanda, and steered her company to great financial success. She was recently diagnosed with an advanced cancer for which treatment is rarely successful. Therefore, she has decided to forego treatment and live the fullest quality of life possible in the few months she has left. She has come to counseling to help her grown children and other family members adjust to her prognosis and to help prepare herself for her death. In the course of the conversation, she reveals to her counselor that when the pain becomes unbearable and she is near death anyway, she plans to take her own life to spare herself and her family the grief of watching her die a slow and painful death. Her counselor agrees to treat her and her family and not to interfere with her plan about her death as long as Mildred agrees not to tell the counselor exactly when she plans to cause her own death.

CONFIDENTIALITY WITH SPECIAL POPULATIONS

Much of the prior discussion assumes that counseling and psychotherapy are one-on-one activities with competent adult clients. When treatment varies from that framework, different considerations regarding the ethics of confidentiality emerge. The following paragraphs discuss the interpretation of confidentiality when providing services to children, groups, families, and people with diminished capacity.

Children and Adolescents

Any clinician working with minors is required to honor confidentiality in most of the same ways as with adults. No professional may gossip about a minor client, nor may he or she share client information with people other than parents or guardians without proper consent. The treatment records of children and adolescents must be kept secure from unauthorized access, and the identity of minor clients should also be protected. The rationale for this position is the same as for adult confidentiality. Without it, client autonomy is diminished, and the trusting counseling relationship is jeopardized. In short, respect for the client's dignity and welfare is not a concept limited to any age group. (Of course, the limits on confidentiality with adults described in the previous section of this chapter also apply to minors.)

The distinction in applying confidentiality to young clients stems from their legal status as minors. Minors are not granted the same privacy rights as adults. In fact, until 1967, U.S. law did not recognize that minors were "persons" with any privacy rights in constitutional terms. In that year, a U.S. Supreme Court ruling concluded, "neither the Fourteenth Amendment nor the Bill of Rights is for adults alone" (*In re Gault*, 1967). (That case involved Gerald Gault, a 15-year-old who was sentenced to detention until the age of 21 for making an obscene phone call. He was given this sentence without specific charges except for delinquency, and no records of the hearing were kept. An adult charged with the same offense would have been given a $50 fine and a maximum of two months in jail.) Since 1967, some foothold has been gained to view children and adolescents as persons; however, minors are generally not allowed to have secrets from their parents or guardians (Koocher & Keith-Spiegel, 1990). Thus, in the absence of state or federal statutes or court cases to the contrary, parents have a legal right to information disclosed in any educational or health care setting unless they give permission for it to be kept from them. In legal terms, this means parents have the "right of control" over their children.

As mentioned in Chapter 2, the ethics codes give only broad-brush attention to confidentiality with children and adolescents. The ACA Code requires counselors to try to get the assent of minors and to attend to the rights of their parents. (Please reread Section A.2.d of the ACA Code in Appendix A, pp. 492–493).

The APA Code is even less specific in Standards 4.01, 4.02, and 10.01, simply stating that psychologists protect the confidentiality of information they obtain and that they discuss with clients or the person legally capable of giving informed consent the nature and limits of confidentiality. Thus, the codes leave to the judgment of the individual professional the burden of applying these broad ethical standards to particular client situations.

Fortunately, a number of ethics scholars have examined the issue of confidentiality in counseling minors and have offered guidelines for determining how much confidentiality a child can be granted (Gustafson & McNamara, 1987; Rozovsky, 2011; Taylor & Adelman, 1989). A common thread is that the degree to which confidentiality can be honored is directly related to the age and maturity of the minor. The closer to the age of maturity, the greater the likelihood that the young person can be granted a fuller measure of confidentiality. This judgment is based on research that has found that adolescents 15 years or older seem capable of making judgments as competently as most adults (Mann, Harmoni, & Power, 1989; Weithorn, 1983). In other words, they seem to understand the nature, risks, and benefits of services sufficiently to give informed consent (Gustafson & McNamara, 1987). In contrast, children under 11 have not shown the necessary level of understanding to give informed consent. Moreover, younger children tend to be less assertive and to defer to authority rather than express their own wishes.

The capacity of children between 11 and 14 to understand counseling varies according to their level of cognitive development, particularly their attainment of formal operations thinking (Weithorn, 1983). When children have attained this level of thinking, they can conceptualize abstract possibilities and reason hypothetically, capacities that seem crucial for effective participation in counseling. Thus, when working with youngsters in this age range, scholars suggest assessing the client's cognitive maturity to determine his or her capacity to participate independently in counseling. Of course, not all children over 15 have attained the level of formal operations. Thus, a careful judgment about intellectual maturity is appropriate whenever counseling a minor. Arguing that cognitive maturity alone is not sufficient for judging a minor's capacity to understand and agree to treatment, Fundudis (2003) recommends taking into account four factors to determine a minor's competence:

- Chronological age (including developmental history and maturational progress)

- Cognitive level (including language, memory, reasoning ability, and logic)
- Emotional maturity (including temperament, stability of mood, attachment, educational adjustment, and attitudinal style)
- Sociocultural factors such as family values and religious beliefs

The law has also defined four general exceptions to parental consent for mental health services for minors (Gustafson & McNamara, 1987). The first exception is for the mature minor, a minor capable of understanding treatment and its consequences. Minors nearing the age of majority are most likely to be ruled mature by a court. According to Rozovsky (2011), the courts also take the complexity and risks of the therapy into account when deciding on maturity. The second exception is for a minor who is "legally emancipated" from parents and guardians. These adolescents operate with independence in virtually all aspects of their daily lives. The criteria for emancipation vary from state to state and are applied in a case-by-case basis, but they generally include factors such as the minor's status as the head of a household, employment, service in the armed forces, or marriage (Rozovsky, 2011). The third exception is for emergencies. Any minor can be treated if immediate treatment is urgently needed. Parents should be informed about treatment as soon as possible after the emergency is resolved (Lawrence & Kurpius, 2000). Finally, parental consent can be waived by a court order.

A number of states have enacted legislation that allows minors to receive medical and psychological treatment without parental consent when the requirement for parental consent would interfere with a youngster's willingness to seek treatment. For example, teenagers may often obtain care for substance abuse, pregnancy, sexually transmitted diseases, and contraception without parental knowledge. (See http://www.guttmacher.org/pubs/tgr/03/4/gr030404.html for a review of minors' rights to health care.) Federal law also stipulates that minors receiving substance abuse evaluation or treatment services must consent before information can be released (Gudeman, 2003). Thirty-one states allow minors to consent to outpatient mental health treatment, though the age of consent and the particulars of treatment allowable under these statutes vary substantially (American Academy of Pediatrics, n.d.). Ohio, for example, permits adolescents at age 14 or older to seek mental health services without parental knowledge for a limited number of sessions, after which parents must be informed or treatment ended. California affords the same rights to minors at 12 years or older, and the California attorney general recently clarified that the right to confidential care for minors prohibits school districts from informing parents they are releasing the student from school if the student is seeking services that the minor has the right to receive without parental knowledge (Lockyer & Duncan, 2004).

Some authors suggest that focusing on ways to keep counseling information from parents and guardians is misguided. Instead, they maintain that because parents have so much power in their children's lives, they should be welcomed into the process rather than excluded from it (Taylor & Adelman, 1989, 2001). This belief is consistent with the language in the ACA Code that advises counselors to work collaboratively with parents to best serve clients (B.5.b). These authors argue that, at times, keeping information confidential from parents "can seriously hamper an intervener's efforts to help a client" (Taylor & Adelman, 1989, p. 80). Enlisting parents' cooperation as an initial phase of services not only encourages them to cooperate with treatment but also provides an opportunity to educate them about the value of confidentiality with minors. Taylor and Adelman suggest a preliminary session in which parents are given information about the counseling process, are reassured that vital information that affects their child's well-being will be shared, and are instructed about the importance of trust and privacy for all clients. After such an orientation, parents are not only more likely to consent to services, but they are also more willing to support the professional's efforts and to respect their child's right to privacy about session content. Research by Nevas and Farber (2001) demonstrates that parents need not be viewed as adversaries to child therapy. Their research found that parents generally have very positive attitudes toward their children's experiences in therapy, that parents respect the skills of the clinician and appreciate the work he or she is doing with their child. Not surprisingly, if highly positive change is occurring in the child's symptoms, parents' attitudes toward the therapist are even more supportive.

Nevas and Farber (2001) describe several therapist actions that can foster continued positive attitudes of parents and children in therapy. They recommend that parents be explicitly informed that setbacks in progress are normal and that if a minor entered therapy with some ambivalence, a brief period in which the child acts in protest to therapy may ensue before services can be helpful. They also advise that ongoing communication with parents is essential, even if therapy is progressing satisfactorily, to keep therapy attendance steady. In regard to confidentiality, they recommend that parents directly communicate to their child that they understand the child's desire for confidentiality and that they will honor it as much as possible. The value of such steps takes on added importance when minors' and parents' perspectives on treatment goals differ, a very common occurrence according to Hawley and Weisz (2003). They reported that parents and children had nonoverlapping goals for therapy in 76% of the cases and that they disagreed on even the general domain of the problem (e.g., aggression vs. anxiety) almost half the time.

Needless to say, not all parents are willing to engage in such a process, and all too often a child's difficulties stem from the parents' problems. Adolescents caught in an alcoholic family may have parents who deny their substance abuse. Such parents often object to the teenagers' attempts to get counseling, but the adolescents still need a forum in which they can discuss their concerns and learn coping skills. Similarly, an adolescent struggling with sexual identity issues often may not be free to broach these matters with family. Some adolescents who do so are turned away from their homes and are also at risk for violence, even from family members, according to Hetrick and Martin (1987). In their study, 49% of the gay and lesbian adolescents who sought services to help them deal with violence against them indicated that they were assaulted by family members. A more recent study (Ryan, Huebner, Diaz, & Sanchez, 2009) not only shows a high rate of incidents of family rejection of LGB adolescents across three ethnicities, it also shows a substantially greater risk of negative health outcomes in early adulthood. Ryan et al. found that those with higher levels of family rejection were 8.4 times more likely to report attempted suicide, 5.9 times more likely to report high levels of depression, and 3 times more likely to report drug use and unprotected sexual activity (p. 349).

When parents are negative influences on their children, the clinician needs to weigh the legal rights of the parents or guardians against the child's emotional well-being and decide on a course of action that serves the child's best interests. The ultimate goal should be to find a way to get the family involved, because the best resolution to the youngster's difficulty may be family treatment. In the absence of family cooperation, promoting the welfare of the child and protecting him or her from harm always prevails. Even HIPAA specifies that parents' right to access their children's mental health records may be denied if it is "not in the best interests of the child to treat the parent as the child's legal representative" (U.S. Department of Health and Human Services, 1996, p. 693). (For a discussion of confidentiality and parents' rights in school settings, see Chapter 13.)

Group and Family Counseling

The fundamental ethical responsibility to respect the client's right to confidentiality does not change in group or family counseling. The professional must not disclose the identity of clients or information revealed in session to those who do not have a right to it. The presence of other people in the room when an individual client reveals personal information complicates confidentiality from both an ethical and legal perspective. First, as the codes indicate, the professional cannot guarantee that the other people hearing these disclosures will also respect the client's privacy. Of course, the practitioner emphasizes the importance of confidentiality in any multiple-client situation and asks all participants to honor confidentiality, but has limited power to enforce that request. Thus, all participants in group and family services need to understand this as another possible limit on confidentiality (see the ACA Code Sections B.4.a and B.4.b).

Second, whether information disclosed in group or family counseling can be regarded as legally privileged information is an open question in most jurisdictions. The privilege concept is based on one individual communicating privately to a lawyer, physician, or priest. When a person communicates information to a mental health professional in front of third parties, the claim that that information is privileged has not been universally honored in the legal system. This is called the *third-party rule*: Any information disclosed in front of third parties is generally ruled by the courts not to be privileged (Swenson, 1997). Thus, clients in multiple-person counseling also need to understand the uncertainty of whether privilege really applies, even in states that may grant the mental health professional privilege for individual counseling (Corey, Williams, & Moline, 1995). Some states, such as Minnesota, have privilege statutes protecting communications in group and family therapy, but most do not (Myers, 1991; Sales, DeKraai, Hall, & Duvall, 2008). *The Best Practice Guidelines of the Association for Specialists in Group Work* (ASGW, 2007) and the American Association for Marriage and Family Therapy *Code of Ethics* (AAMFT, 2001) extensively discuss confidentiality issues in multiple-person therapies and should be thoroughly read by all who conduct these therapies (see ACA Code Sections B.4.a and B.4.b).

It is important to distinguish between family counseling in which the family is seen as the client and situations in which family members attend sessions from time to time for therapeutic reasons. In these situations, the other family members are referred to as "collaterals," and they do not have the same confidentiality rights as clients (Ellis, 2012). Therefore, mental health professionals have a duty to clarify how confidentiality does and does not apply in these circumstances (more on this topic in Chapter 9).

CONFIDENTIALITY IN A MULTICULTURAL CONTEXT

Confidentiality is based on the belief that the individual has the right of autonomy, the freedom to make decisions for him- or herself, including in this case decisions about entering therapy and controlling the release of information about participation in therapy. Autonomy is an ethical principle with roots in Western philosophy—nowhere else on the planet is this principle given such an elevated status. In fact, in some cultural traditions, freedom to self-govern clearly takes second place to loyalty to family or deference to the wishes of elders, even with fully competent adults. The notion that family members can be excluded from information about a loved one's mental health is fundamentally inconsistent with some cultural values, just as incompatible in those cultures as the belief that a person who wants acceptance from the family can defy the wishes of elders to satisfy a personal desire or goal.

In such a context, confidentiality of communications in counseling can become complicated, as Meer and VandeCreek (2002) illustrate so well in their description of three cases of adult clients from South Asia receiving therapy in the United States. Upon learning that these adults were in treatment, the clients' families demanded disclosure about the content and progress of therapy. They also expressed great distrust of the therapist and high levels of hostility at the idea that a family member had discussed private family matters to a stranger in the first place. Complicating the matter even further was the reluctance of the clients to voice any disagreement with their parents' demands, a behavior that violated cultural standards of respect. How can a professional comply with the ethical mandate to honor confidentiality in such a situation? One obvious way is to ask the client to sign a release of information; however, that is only a partial solution to the dilemma because clients may feel little freedom to assert themselves. The more ideal ethical response is to anticipate the ethical implication of working with clients whose value systems are likely to differ from the value system underlying the profession's ethical principles and to discuss an approach to family communications at the initiation of service. Indeed, family treatment, if possible, may be the preferable mode of service in such a situation. Schwebel and Hodari (2005) present a case example of using family therapy responsibly with culturally diverse clients.

The ACA lists its provision regarding confidentiality and diverse populations as the initial standard under confidentiality, highlighting the importance of cultural considerations and the potential influence of cultural differences on views of confidentiality and privacy (Section B.1.a Appendix A, p. 498).

EMERGING CHALLENGES TO CONFIDENTIALITY: MANAGED CARE, TECHNOLOGY, AND INSTITUTIONAL VIOLENCE

When counseling and psychotherapy originated a hundred years ago, the only people involved were clients and their counselors (Heppner, 1990; Whiteley, 1984). All services took place in a face-to-face meeting, and all financial matters were handled directly by the individuals involved. Records were kept on paper if they were kept at all, and the professional and the client were the ones who decided the length and nature of treatment. The advent of third-party reimbursement, computerization of records, and access to mental health professionals through telephone, text, and online media have revolutionized the mental health care and compounded confidentiality dilemmas. For example, when insurers began to reimburse people for mental health expenses in the 1960s, they sought information regarding the nature of the problem and its treatment. If they were to pay for services, insurers had a right to know that appropriate services were being rendered. So clients signed a release so that their therapists could communicate with the insurers. When managed care came into being in the 1980s, the insurers' demands for information about diagnosis intensified, and their involvement in recommending both the length and type of treatment expanded. Currently, preauthorization of services is frequently required, a process in which a mental health professional contacts the insurer, describes the diagnosis and treatment plan, and asks for approval to offer services. If approval is given, a specific number of outpatient sessions is authorized. Managed care providers also claim the right to audit records to ascertain that billing and reimbursement was proper. Mental health professionals sometimes have to provide detailed information to justify additional sessions beyond the preauthorization level, a process called *utilization review or quality assurance*. Moreover, in an effort to make services cost effective, third-party payers have been increasingly insistent that clinicians use what they define as evidence-based treatments. Each of these demands risks compromising the privacy of the client.

In light of the increased role of managed care in mental health care and the computerization of client data, the United States Congress passed the Health Insurance Portability and Accountability Act (HIPAA) in 1996 to safeguard client data communicated via electronic networks. This legislation is designed to protect patients receiving health care (including mental health services) from unwarranted disclosures of personal health information and to provide patients some level of control over release of that information. It also mandates that providers that handle health information follow privacy guidelines or be subject to liability claims from patients and even federal criminal prosecution in some situations. Both the ACA and APA address this topic in their codes. In Section B.3.d, the ACA Code states, "Counselors disclose confidential information to third-party payers only when clients have authorized such disclosure." In parallel fashion, the APA Code specifies in Standard 10.01 that clients must give informed consent to the involvement of third-party payers in therapy. Thankfully, HIPAA has appeared to reduce some of the more egregious violations of client privacy that occurred before its existence. This legislation offers some assurance that unauthorized breaches of confidential information in the insurer's control will be reduced. However, because information communicated to third-party payers typically becomes part of the patient's health record in the database, clients ought to be informed about the risks to confidentiality and privacy that have not been fully eliminated by HIPAA. Chapter 12 includes additional discussion of the ethical implications of managed care.

Reports of Technology Breaches of Client Data In November 2011, backup computer tapes were stolen from TRICARE, the organization that handles health insurance for the military, risking private health information for nearly 5 million people. Other news reports of laptops being stolen from mental health professionals appear regularly in the media. For example, the laptop of an Oregon psychologist, containing thousands of patient records with identifying and diagnostic information, was stolen when his laptop was unsecured.

A computer's ability to store large amounts of data makes records vulnerable to theft, duplication, or loss on a level unrivaled by old-fashioned paper records. Conceivably, a professional's entire set of case records could be stored on one laptop or flash drive and thus easily stolen, lost, or ruined. Those who use electronic media for client records must be alert to this potential for misuse and make extra efforts to protect the client's confidentiality (Pope & Vasquez, 2011). Research on psychologists' use of technology shows substantial reliance on computers although this trend appears less dominant among psychologists in independent practice (McMinn, Bearse, Heyne, Smithberger, & Erb, 2011; Welfel & Bunce, 2003). Even 19 years ago, in the 1996 Rosen and Weil study, for example, 52% of clinicians reported storing client financial records on a computer, and 15% reported keeping case notes on a computer. Welfel and Bunce (2003) found that 44% of the psychologists they surveyed had exchanged emails with current or prospective clients on at least one occasion and that one-quarter of those email contacts included communication about therapeutic issues. It is also reasonable to assume that in the years since these studies were conducted, the rate of usage of electronic data storage has rapidly increased. Recent federal legislation, the Health Information Technology for Economic and Clinical Health Act (HITECH) (2009) that encourages the use of electronic health records, underscores the critical importance of privacy protections (see http://www.apapracticecentral.org/advocacy/technology/hitech-act.aspx for a summary of the provisions of the act). The ACA Code notes that counselors are obliged to take precautions when transmitting confidential data (Section B.3.e). The APA makes a general statement of applicability of the provisions of its code to all electronic forms of communication in the Introduction and includes the following statement in Standard 3.10(c): "Psychologists who offer services, products, or information via electronic transmission inform clients/patients of the risks to privacy and limits of confidentiality."

In light of these issues the following recommendations are sensible:

- Ensure that all computers and other devices are protected with strong passwords, in other words, passwords not obvious to others.
- Use encryption for any records stored on a hard drive (Pope & Vasquez, 2011).
- Use code numbers or pseudonyms to identify files, CDs, and other storage devices.
- Update virus protection compulsively.
- Be cautious about computers that are networked, and utilize all appropriate steps to protect data from viewing by others in the network.

- Because tablets, netbooks, and laptop computers are especially vulnerable to loss, theft, and breakage, professionals ought not to store identifiable client information on these devices if extra security, such as password protection and/or encryption, is not available.
- Use of smartphones should also be carefully monitored as these devices are even more vulnerable to loss. Because data stored on these devices may easily be accessed by unauthorized users, professionals must be particularly vigilent about using all available options for security. This holds true for text messaging and for storing client contact information on a smartphone or cell phone. When disposing of these devices, professionals must ensure that all clinical data has been fully erased (Sude, 2013).
- Mental health professionals should consider installing intrusion detection software, use a firewall, and be careful about where and how they store backup data (Ragusea, 2012) and ethical considerations in storing client data in the "cloud" (Devereaux and Gottlieb, 2012).

When using facsimile machines, caution should also be taken when transmitting client materials and client release forms. Fax machines may be located in an open, public space to which access is not restricted. Transmissions may occur when the receiving office is not open, so the documents may be unprotected for many hours. Consequently, a telephone, email, or text contact before sending a fax is prudent. The call can ensure that a qualified person is available to retrieve the confidential material. In parallel fashion, a follow-up contact is desirable to ensure that all materials were received as transmitted. In addition, the cover sheet on the facsimile should include a clear and easily readable statement about the confidentiality of material on the following pages. Highly sensitive client records, such as data that reveal a client's HIV status or history of incest, may not be appropriate for facsimile transmission under any circumstances.

The Ethics of Telemental Health and Other Online Services The Internet has become major avenue for interpersonal communication, and an increasing number of people are looking for friends and romantic partners online. For example, according to the Pew Internet Research Project, 38% of those who indicate that they are single and dating have used online dating sites or mobile dating apps (Smith & Duggan, 2013). Not surprisingly, then, a small but growing percentage of mental health professionals and clients have begun to use this medium for communication with clients. Most who take advantage of it use it to advertise their office practices or to maintain contact with clients between sessions (Maheu, Whitten, & Allen, 2001; Welfel & Bunce, 2003), but some offer online counseling, therapy, and coaching as an exclusive mode of treatment (Chester & Glass, 2006; Heinlen, Welfel, Richmond, & O'Donnell, 2003; Heinlen, Welfel, Richmond, & Rak, 2003). This use of the Internet for therapeutic purposes has attracted wide public and professional interest (e.g., Hsiung, 2002; Kraus, Zack, & Stricker, 2004; Maheu & Gordon, 2000) and, for a time, generated significant controversy. Some argued that telemental health has the potential to reach people reluctant or unable to attend face-to-face sessions, that it may facilitate self-disclosure about embarrassing content, that it may have unique appeal to young people, and that it is a necessary convenience in a time-pressured culture (Nelson, Bui, & Velasquez, 2011; Yuen, Goetter, Herbert, & Forman, 2012). Others have cautioned that exclusively text-based communications do not provide clinicians with sufficient information to accurately diagnose or effectively treat the problems which cyberclients present (Alleman, 2002; Childress, 1998; Rabasca, 2000). Two recent surveys (Neukrug & Milliken, 2011; Taylor, McMinn, Bufford, & Chang, 2010) indicated that both counselors and psychologists in the United States are still quite divided in their views of the ethics of online contact with clients. Some psychologists are simply unsure about the ethics of the activity (McMinn et al, 2011). However, a study of psychologists in Norway found very different results, with only 3% of respondents judging online contact with clients as unacceptable (Wangberg, Gammon, & Spitznogle, 2007).

Accurate estimates of the number of telemental health providers are nearly impossible to obtain. One large-scale study that used common search engines to identify sites claiming to offer online counseling or psychotherapy for emotional or relationship issues found 136 sites offering such services on the Web, typically for a fee (Heinlen, Welfel, Richmond, & Rak, 2003). A parallel study that focused on doctoral level e-therapists who self-identified as psychologists located 50 psychotherapy websites offered by this subset of professionals. Virtually nothing is known about the quality or competence of most exclusively online counseling (Maheu & Gordon, 2000). Of particular concern are the risks of breaches of confidentiality. The use of encryption methods reduces but does not entirely eliminate the possibility of unauthorized access to email communications. As Ragusea (2012) points out, the risk to these communications is less likely to come from a random hacker than from someone deliberately seeking access to the therapeutic communications of a particular client or therapist. Any email that comes into a workplace computer is the legal property of the employer, who may access it at will. Sections H.2.b–d of the ACA Code highlight the responsibility of the counselor to be aware of limitations to confidentiality in online communications, to communicate these limits to clients, and to use encryption for communications and websites and generally take all appropriate precautions for this medium.

Unfortunately, early research indicated that compliance with these standards is low. Heinlen, Welfel, Richmond, and Rak (2003) found that only 22% of the counselors in their sample indicated that they used any encryption method for client communications, and only 27% of psychologists in the parallel study employed encryption (Heinlen, Welfel, Richmond, & O'Donnell, 2003). Studies conducted even more recently do not show significant improvement. Shaw and Shaw (2006) reported that 27% of their sample of online counseling sites used encryption or other methods to make a site secure, and Recupero and Rainey (2006) found a nearly identical level of use of encryption or other security protections (29%). Yazvac (2009) reported that counselors were more likely to comply with ACA standards for online service than psychologists, but compliance in both groups was low. The pattern of compliance with NASW ethical standards is also uneven for social workers using online therapy sites (Santhiveeran, 2009). In Heinlen, Welfel, Richmond, and Rak (2003), a majority of websites offered potential clients reassurance about how seriously they took confidentiality, but only 30% of counselors and 39% of psychologists discussed any of the limits of confidentiality, such as the duty to warn and protect or the mandate for reporting child abuse.

In light of the risks to confidentiality, professionals entertaining the use of the Internet as a means of telemental health services need to be cautious about this venture and to keep abreast of research and policies related to this issue. (See Rummell and Joyce [2010] for a balanced analysis of ethical issues in online communication with clients.) Not only is careful attention to compliance with all ethics codes crucial, but consultation with an attorney about the legal risks of telemental health is also essential if clients are dissatisfied with or harmed by services, or their confidentiality is violated. Liability insurers should also be notified if such a professional activity is entertained. See Baker and Bufka (2011) for a discussion of risk management issues in this form of service. In 2013, the APA, in collaboration with the APA Insurance Trust and the Association of State and Provincial Psychology Boards, issued the *Guidelines for the Practice of Telepsychology*. This document contains eight guidelines that overlap substantially with the provisions in Section H of the ACA Code. The guidelines address the psychologist's responsibility to be competent with technology, to implement appropriate consent and confidentiality procedures, to abide by legal, ethical, and jurisdictional standards, and to attend to the security of communications. In addition, the guidelines exhort psychologists to use reasonable security measures, provide for proper disposal of records, and be sensitive to the issues related to using psychological tests in this medium. The ACA Code delves into even more specifics regarding online activities, indicating in Section H.5.c, for example, that counselors are responsible to ensure that any links on their websites are operational.

Professional-to-Professional Communication Caution is also needed when communicating client information via professional listservs or in email for professional consultation. Such communications should be undertaken only with appropriate client consent, using encryption when possible, and when the listserv participation is limited to professionals. Professionals should be especially cautious because the contents of an email communication can easily be copied into another document or email and transmitted to others. For more recommendations regarding responsible listserv use for mental health professionals, see Collins (2007).

Ethics and Social Media According to Taylor et al. (2010), 77% of the psychologists they surveyed have a page on a social networking site for personal use. The vast majority of these professionals (85%) used privacy settings. When asked about issues related to their profession that have emerged from their social networking use, some mentioned that they discovered that they shared mutual friends with clients, and others emphasized that they used the strongest possible privacy settings to avoid such complications (Taylor et al., 2010). Some indicated less stringent policies for students than for clients. Other complications mentioned in this survey included coming into contact with clients or their family members while using online dating services, receiving unsolicited client attempts to contact the psychologist on a social networking site, and seeing clients' comments about suicide or homicide on blogs or websites.

Sometimes, mental health professionals seek out clients' social networking pages (Dillio & Gale, 2011; Harris & Kurpius, 2014; Kaslow, Patterson, & Gottlieb, 2011). Consider the following situation:

The Case of Bruce and Lydia

Bruce is a mental health counselor whose practice includes many clients with substance abuse issues. From time to time he has doubts about the honesty of a client's remarks about his or her behavior and substance use. When Lydia, the client whom he has seen for several sessions, mentions that she has pages on two social networking sites, Bruce decides to check out the content on these sites but does not discuss this action with the client. Since Lydia has not set any privacy controls, Bruce is able to freely peruse the content she has posted. After he has done so, Bruce wonders whether he acted ethically.

In this situation, Bruce did not violate the confidentiality of Lydia's records, nor did he disclose information about her to unauthorized persons. Moreover, if the client placed no limits on access to her social networking page, she had no reasonable expectation of privacy from public viewing of whatever she posted there. Nevertheless, his actions appear inconsistent with the ethical values of the profession and may well be counterproductive clinically. As Kaslow et al. (2011) note, investigating clients' social networking sites without their knowledge or consent violates client trust and conflicts with a professional's obligation to the principle of fidelity. It is also inconsistent with the Principles of Beneficence and Nonmaleficence in the APA Code. Clients have no reason to suspect that their therapists will be searching for information about them online. The search may represent a boundary violation as well, depending on the nature of the content the client has included on the site. Even if Lydia has been inattentive to the privacy protections for her pages, that does not necessarily imply that she wishes open access to those with whom she has a professional, not personal, relationship. The activity also leaves the professional in a quandary about how to handle future sessions if the content of the site includes disclosures inconsistent with statements in therapy. If Bruce reveals that he searched her pages, he risks a rupture in the therapeutic alliance; if he withholds that information, he risks a secret that may inhibit progress or even an inadvertent slip of the tongue that accidentally reveals what he has learned from the search. Clinically, if a professional has doubts about the veracity or completeness of a client's disclosures, he or she has other options for exploring these doubts in session that do not risk client trust, professional boundaries, or client engagement in therapy.

Recent research reveals that Bruce's investigation of Lydia is not a rare or isolated event. Lehavot, Barnett, and Powers (2010) reported that 27% of the student psychotherapists they surveyed had looked for client information on the Internet. Dillio and Gale (2011) found that student therapists had searched either Google or social networking sites for information about 16.5% of the clients they had seen in the last year. In the Kaslow et al. study, some indicated acting out of curiosity, and others wanted to verify client statements or activities. Some had obtained prior client consent to the search, but most had not. Many wondered after the fact whether their actions had been ethical. More than three-quarters (76.8%) of Dillio and Gale's 854 participants believed such activities to be unacceptable at least, usually in spite of the frequency of their occurrence. The percentages of online searches without client consent appeared slightly lower in the more recent study by Harris and Kurpius (2014), but a majority still disclosed this activity. The only circumstance that renders such a search ethical is prior consent of the client (Dillio & Gale, 2011; Kaslow et al., 2011; Lehavot et al., 2010).

For the first time, the 2014 ACA Code addresses ethical responsibilities for counselors involved in social media in Section H.6. The code stipulates that if counselors use social media for professional purposes, they should have a presence separate from their personal pages, that any use of social media for therapeutic purposes should be included in the informed consent, and that counselors should seek client permission to review their social media presence. Finally this section emphasizes that counselors should protect client confidentiality in this medium, as in any other. See Appendix A, p. 531, for the exact language.

Kolmes and Taube (2014) remind mental health professionals to be alert to unexpected boundary complications when they use social media. In their survey, they note that finding client information online and through social media is not always the result of a deliberate search by the professional. Twenty-eight percent of the psychologists they surveyed reporting accidentally coming across client data online while using social media or a search engine such as Google. If this occurs, it may be wise to discuss this accidental finding in the next session to explore its possible implications for the therapeutic alliance and for treatment.

CONFIDENTIALITY AND THREATS OF HOMICIDE-SUICIDE

In the wake of the homicide-suicides such as the one that killed 32 people and injured 17 others at Virginia Tech in April 2007; the Newtown, Connecticut, shootings that left 27 dead, including 20 children; the incident at Fort Hood in 2014 that left 4 dead and 16 injured; and the countless other examples of homicides followed by suicides, mental health professionals are beginning to rethink their prior conceptualizations of the risk factors that point to danger to others simultaneous with danger to self. Even though these school and workplace killings garner extensive media attention whenever they occur, they are the least frequent type of homicide-suicide. (See Flynn and Heitzman [2008] for a detailed description of the impact of the Virginia Tech shootings on that campus and on college counseling centers across the nation.) Actually, of the 800 homicide-suicides that occur in the United States annually, the most common type involves the shooting of a female relative by a male perpetrator and appears to be motivated by a frustrated long-term intimate relationship and a combination of self-blame and other blame (Joiner, 2014). More than 80% of the homicide-suicides involve this combination of participants, either related to domestic violence or to declining health in aging partners (Malphurs, Eisdorfer, & Cohen, 2001). The pattern in Canada is remarkably similar (Gillespie, Hearn, & Silverman, 1998). Unfortunately, few of those with this potential for violence seek out mental health services, but if they do and they disclose any violent urges in treatment, these urges are much more likely to be focused on self-harm than harm to others. They tend to demonstrate risk factors that resemble those for suicide—such as depression, prior suicide attempts, substance abuse, and paranoia—but fail to show common risk factors for violence to others, such as impulsivity and a history of prior violent and aggressive acts (Hillbrand, 2001). Consequently, mental health professionals may not be as alert as they ought to be to the additional risk to others.

Joiner (2014), based on his extensive review of the literature and his own research, postulates that suicide is *always* the primary motive in homicide-suicide and that the person committing this act not only has planned it but sees it as virtuous. He clearly labels this view as a perversion of virtue, but it is helpful to understand that from the perspective of the perpetrator the act is grounded either in mercy, justice, duty, or glory. For example, the parent who kills a child and then kills herself can't envision a good life for her child without her, and so, because suicide seems like the only option for her, she must be merciful and spare the child a dismal life without her.

What does this mean for counselors and therapists who encounter individuals who are at high risk for suicide? It means that they should entertain the possibility, rare as it will turn out to be, that the client may pose a risk to others and assess for this potential (Welfel, 2009). The notion that suicide and homicide are nonoverlapping risks is clearly false in some situations. The ethical and legal obligation of the professional in this circumstance is to protect the client and others at risk from harm. Typically, that protection will take the form of notifying law enforcement and seeking hospitalization for the client, though the particular interventions may vary.

SUMMARY

Confidentiality is the cornerstone of effective counseling and psychotherapy because it allows the client to freely share experiences without fear of unwarranted disclosure to others. The ethics codes devote considerable attention to this topic, emphasizing its importance and the situations in which professionals may have permission to communicate client disclosures to others. Confidentiality in mental health and educational services covers both the content of disclosures and contact with clients, so the identity of those who seek services is also kept secret from public knowledge. This ethical standard is rooted in the principles of respect for client autonomy and fidelity to promises made.

Confidentiality is often also protected by legal statutes. In many states and the U.S. federal system, the clients of mental health professionals can prevent those counselors from testifying in court about material revealed in counseling. Such material is called *privileged communication*.

There are nine major exceptions to confidentiality, although some of these are quite limited in scope and applicability. Not all jurisdictions include all of these limits. These include (1) a client's request for release of confidential information; (2) a court order for confidential information; (3) an ethics complaint or lawsuit against a counselor or therapist; (4) other client litigation in which the client raises the issues of treatment as part of the client's civil suit against another party; (5) limitations to confidentiality based on statutes, such as reporting child and elder abuse; (6) dangerous clients who are putting themselves or others at imminent risk for injury or death; (7) clients with intent to commit criminal acts in the future (in some states); (8) clients with contagious life-threatening diseases, such as HIV disorders, whose behavior puts others at imminent risk of infection; and (9) some clients considering hastening their deaths.

Confidentiality issues also arise when professionals work with children, families, and groups. With children and adolescents, the issue is the degree to which the child client can keep disclosures secret from parents and guardians. The law tends to give minors few rights to privacy; the ethical guidelines tend to see confidentiality for minors increasing with age and maturity. Generally, the more mature the minor, the greater the measure of confidentiality that young person is given. When working with groups and families, practitioners need to be aware that they cannot guarantee clients the same degree of privacy as in individual counseling. When clients reveal personal information in front of third parties, the professional cannot prevent those third parties from breaching confidentiality. The professional should contract with all participants to honor confidentiality as a condition for inclusion in the group or family counseling, but clients need to understand that these contracts are voluntary, and counselors have little power to prevent other members from violating their promise if they decide to do so.

Confidentiality has also been threatened by several new developments. Managed care's persistent and extensive demands for sensitive client information, coupled with the uncertain protection of that data once it is released are major concerns for professionals. The advent of federal legislation offers several protections, but it is not foolproof. Second, the convenience and ease of electronic communications technology, such as the facsimile machine and the Internet, make them attractive vehicles for client communication. However, professionals must be fully cognizant of the risks of these technologies and take precautions to protect client data.

CONFIDENTIALITY CASE FOR ANALYSIS USING THE 10-STEP MODEL

Using the decision-making model presented in Chapter 2, consider the following case:

The Case of Raymond

Raymond is an 18-year-old college freshman living in a residence hall. He is the eldest of five children, and his parents live in a nearby state. Raymond is HIV positive, the result of an infected blood transfusion he received in childhood while living abroad with his family. He has been asymptomatic since then. Only his parents know of his HIV status; they have not even told his younger siblings or either set of grandparents. Raymond goes to see a college counselor because he is confused and worried. He has met a young woman and has gone on a few dates with her. He wants to become sexually intimate with her, but has not told her about his HIV status. Raymond is afraid that disclosure would end her interest in him or the interest of any young woman with whom he wants a serious relationship. He has some brochures about safer sex practices and believes that if he did become intimate with this woman, he would use a condom and follow other guidelines for safer sex. He is currently resistant to the idea of disclosing his HIV status to anyone. After a lengthy session, the counselor concludes that Raymond is likely to practice safe sex if he does become intimate with this woman. Moreover, intimacy is not imminent, because he will not see the girl again for a week. The counselor determines that there is no ethical basis for breaching confidentiality to this woman in the near future. Do you agree with that professional judgment?

Step 1: Develop ethical sensitivity.

- Do you agree that there is an ethical dilemma here? Why or why not?
- Whose welfare is affected by the actions of the counselor, and how?
- What was your immediate emotional and intellectual response to this case?
- How would you feel if you were in this counselor's position?

Step 2: Clarify facts, stakeholders, and sociocultural context.

- What facts of the case cause you to define it in this way? What is the context?
- Are there any other facts you should be considering? Who are the stakeholders?
- When you brainstorm about this case, what options can you identify?

Step 3: Define the central issues and options.

- What ethical issues appear in the case and the options you have identified?
- What other options might a colleague see in this situation?

Step 4: Refer to professional standards, guidelines, and regulations.

- What do the codes of ethics state regarding this issue? Have you identified all relevant sections of the code?
- What other guidelines have professional associations published on the topic?
- Are there laws in your jurisdiction that are relevant to this dilemma?
- Is there case law or other regulation governing this situation?
- Do the ethical standards or rules governing your license speak to the issue?

Step 5: Review ethics scholarship.

- What do scholars on this subject say about responsible resolutions of the dilemma?
- If scholars disagree, which arguments seem most compelling, and why?

Step 6: Apply ethical principles.

- What ethical principles underlie this dilemma?
- Does consideration of the principles lead to a single response or to different responses? If different, which principle do you think should take priority? Why?

Step 7: Consult with supervisors and other professionals.

- What are the views of your supervisor and colleagues on ethical resolutions of this dilemma?
- Do those views coincide with the recommendations of the codes, the scholars, and the ethical principles? In what ways do they differ?

Step 8: Deliberate and decide.

- Is your list of options still adequate? Should it be revised in any way? How?
- Now that you have accumulated all this information and heard others' perspectives, what have you decided?
- What is your rationale for that decision?

Step 9: Inform supervisors and document process and actions.

- How should you go about informing your supervisor, implementing the actions, and documenting your decision?

Step 10: Reflect on the experience.

- Now that you have been through this process, what has it meant to you?
- What have you learned?
- How will this experience change your response to similar ethical dilemmas?
- Do you have any knowledge that you ought to share with colleagues? If so, how can you do that most effectively?

Resolutions of Raymond's Dilemma

First, the choice the counselor makes is clearly a matter of ethics because the welfare of several people is at stake. Raymond may be harmed if his HIV status is disclosed to a third party. He may withdraw from counseling or may suffer harm in the residence hall where he lives if that information becomes widely known and communicated across the campus. After all, the third party to whom counseling information is disclosed has no legal or ethical obligation to keep that information secret. Other students may assume that Raymond is gay and make him the victim of "gay bashing." Raymond may drop out of college or feel the need to transfer elsewhere and lose credit for the term in the process. The disclosure of Raymond's HIV status at the college would also be painful for Raymond's family, whose capacity to cope with his illness seems already diminished. Raymond may decide that his family's secretiveness about his health status is the best course and never reveal his HIV infection to anyone again, even to other sexual partners. Other negative consequences for Raymond are possible: He may even become suicidal or self-destructive.

In addition, the welfare of the young woman Raymond is dating is at stake. If they become sexually active, and if the couple fails to take appropriate precautions, the sexual contact puts her at some risk for being infected with the virus. Currently, there is no known cure for HIV infection, although new therapies have substantially extended the life expectancy of people with HIV.

Given what's at stake here, the ethical dilemma can be defined as balancing Raymond's right to privacy and need for further counseling against the potential duty to warn and protect the young woman from HIV infection.

The relevant facts of the case are that Raymond is an adult who is so concerned about how his HIV status will affect his emerging romantic relationship that he sought the assistance of a professional counselor. He is, at this point, resistant to revealing his medical condition to anyone else, but is willing to consider precautions that reduce the risk of transmitting the virus. Several other facts are less clear. First, the counselor does not have independent confirmation of Raymond's HIV status. Even though it is unlikely that the client would purposely deceive the counselor, it is possible he is delusional or does not really understand the medical information he received eight years ago when he was only 10 years old. Moreover, it appears that his family has not talked much to him about his health, a circumstance that increases the possibility that Raymond may be misinformed about his medical status. A single session with Raymond may not be sufficient to judge his rationality, veracity, or sophistication of knowledge.

Second, the counselor has no verification that the young woman returns Raymond's affections, or that if she does, she is ready to advance the relationship to the level of sexual intimacy Raymond wants. Raymond's lack of dating experience makes such a misinterpretation of her interest even more likely than it might be for a college freshman with dating experience. Or the young woman's personal values may cause her to refrain from sexual intimacy until engaged or married.

Third, the counselor has no certain information about Raymond's commitment to using safer sex practices should he become sexually involved with this woman. He may or may not act responsibly. This fact is crucial because it has such important implications for the degree of danger to which the woman is exposed. Fourth, regardless of the use of safer sex practices, the exact risk of transmitting the virus in a single sexual encounter is unknown (Keeling, 1993). Many cases of repeated heterosexual intercourse have resulted in no transmission of the virus, but in some cases, transmission has occurred after a single contact. Fifth, the counselor has no knowledge of the woman's understanding of sexually transmitted diseases or her commitment to practices that minimize her risk of such infections. She may be fully prepared to insist on safe sex regardless of Raymond's inclinations on the matter. Sixth, the woman herself may be HIV positive. The rate of infection in heterosexual adolescents is rising, and she may have already contracted the virus. This is a statistically unlikely scenario, but not impossible. Taken together, these uncertainties show how little this counselor really knows about the degree of risk Raymond represents to this particular young woman.

The counselor's options are as follows:

- To inform the young woman immediately, even if Raymond does not agree to disclose the information himself immediately
- To keep the information confidential for the duration of counseling and to educate the client about safer sex practices
- To set disclosure of his HIV status to the woman as a counseling goal for Raymond
- To postpone a decision until the facts of the case are clearer.

The ACA Code allows disclosure of information about clients' life-threatening contagious diseases to third parties if necessary. It is important to note that the code *permits* such disclosure; the code does not mandate or even recommend disclosure. The exact wording is "A counselor ... may be justified in disclosing" (Section B.2.c). This wording means that the codes do not prescribe a certain behavior. Instead, they give permission for disclosing or for maintaining confidentiality. As in many other situations, then, the codes provide general guidelines, not specific mandates.

Applying these guidelines to this case, it is clear that there is not urgency to disclosure as the counselor could schedule additional sessions with the client in the intervening time period. Thus, it seems that the code does not endorse disclosure at this juncture but that future events may make it justifiable. The other professional documents on this topic also echo the message that counselors should carefully consider breaches of confidentiality in this situation and should avoid rushing to disclose because of the risk of harming the client. The state laws on the issue of disclosure vary considerably. For example, states such as Massachusetts forbid any disclosure of HIV status to third parties (Chenneville, 2000), whereas other states allow such breaches. Thus, depending on the jurisdiction, one would respond in very different ways to this dilemma.

Scholars' views generally echo the arguments in the documents of the professional associations. They suggest weighing the implications of disclosure for the client as carefully as weighing the risk to the third party. The decision-making model of Melchert and Patterson (1999) is a representative example of this perspective. These authors also remind counselors that disclosure may rupture the counseling relationship and thereby eliminate the counselor's potential to help a client learn how to disclose HIV status or use safer sex practices. It is this argument that swayed the counselor in the case and that appears particularly compelling given the young man's initial voluntary entry into counseling. After all, he could have continued developing the physical relationship with this young woman, never sought counseling, and never informed her of his medical condition. The counselor in this case has a valuable opportunity to help Raymond and to prevent his ever infecting anyone with the virus.

The ethical principles underlying this dilemma relate to respecting the autonomy of this man and avoiding harm to him and those in contact with him. There is also the issue of fidelity to promises made, unless the counselor explicitly explained the limitations of confidentiality at the outset of counseling. The principle of nonmalficence is most important to consider, especially the potential harm to the client and the woman. There is little doubt that disclosure without his consent will harm this young man, although his injuries are likely to be psychological rather than physical. Her potential injury is physical, but the psychological ramifications of exposure to HIV infection are also crucially important. Still, the probability of infection for her is lower than the risk of harm to him from disclosure. How should one balance an improbable but potentially fatal harm against a fairly certain (but not life-threatening) harm?

Given this information and the results of consultations with colleagues and supervisors, here is the revised list of options:

- Focus on safer sex practices and on getting Raymond to agree to a "no sex" contract for the immediate future. If the client agrees to these conditions, then no disclosure should be made at this juncture.
- Review with Raymond the limits of confidentiality again, and seek his permission to bring the young woman into a session to discuss the issue together. If he continues to

refuse such an approach in the subsequent sessions as well, reveal the client's information to her.
- Decide that if Raymond commits to practicing safer sex, then the danger is so low that there really is no justification for a breach of confidentiality.

The option that seems most ethically sound at this point is the first one. Raymond needs counseling, is willing to participate now, and seems prepared to accept some responsibility for his behavior insofar as he seems positively disposed to practice safer sex. Moreover, the risk to the young woman is not imminent, and the counselor has at least one week in which to work with the client before sexual contact is even possible. Given all this information, disclosure seems premature at this point. As events unfold, that decision may change, depending on Raymond's attitude and behavior and the degree of risk to the woman.

Discussion Questions*

1. Do you agree with the California court that "privilege should end where the public peril begins"? Why or why not?
2. Do you think that the fact that a child protection services agency is ineffective or overworked is a rationale for not reporting suspected child abuse? Why or why not?
3. Why do you think violations of confidentiality happen so frequently among practicing mental health professionals?
4. Do you think that "rational suicide" is possible? Should a duty to protect apply in this situation? (Explain.)
5. Some scholars are very concerned about the erosion of confidentiality in the courts and the managed care arena. How do you think counselors should approach the discussion of confidentiality with clients who want to submit claims to managed care companies or who may be facing court involvement?
6. Do you think children have the right to keep material confidential from their parents?

Cases for Discussion

Freda is a licensed mental health professional in private practice. Freda's former client, Maximillian, was killed in a boating accident. Several weeks later Maximillian's wife, Dora, makes an appointment with Freda to find out more about what her husband had been discussing in counseling sessions. Dora's grief about the sudden loss of her husband is still quite strong, yet she also seems to be learning how to cope without him and how to handle that grief. Freda remembers that in his last session Max expressed how much he loved his wife and how fortunate he felt to have such a strong marriage. Freda discloses this information to Dora, judging that Max probably would have wanted it revealed, and believing that, as his widow, Dora has a right to this information. Freda probably did not violate any law in telling Dora what Max talked about in counseling. Were her actions also consistent with the ethical standards of the profession? If the content of the sessions had been focused on Max's frustrations with his marriage, how would that affect your judgment about disclosing session content to Dora? What do you see as the ideal ethical solution here?

Abigail, a counselor in a community mental health agency, carries a caseload of clients with

*Note to course instructors: The *Instructor's Guide* for this book includes other discussion questions, class exercises, cases, and multiple-choice and essay test items for this chapter.

severe and persistent mental illness. To help her cope with the stress of such a demanding work life, Abigail frequently discusses cases with her spouse, Martin, who is also a licensed counselor (although he works at another agency across town). In her conversations with her husband, Abigail does not use clients' last names, but she does describe their problems and her therapeutic interventions in some detail. She is confident that this practice is ethical and that it has been useful to help her cope with the stresses of her work. She is convinced that she would be less effective as a therapist without them and that they have benefited her marriage as well. Abigail believes these disclosures of client information are ethical because she uses no client names and because Martin is also a mental health professional who honors confidentiality and understands its importance in therapy. Do you agree with Abigail's judgment that she is acting within the ethical boundaries of the profession?

Recommended Readings

American Psychological Association (APA). (2001b). *Council resolution on assisted suicide*. Retrieved from http://www.apa.org/ppo/issues/asreolu.html

American Psychological Association, Committee on Legal Issues. (2006). Strategies for private practitioners coping with subpoenas or compelled testimony for client records or test data. *Professional Psychology: Research and Practice*, *37*, 215–222.

American Psychological Association, Committee on Professional Practice and Standards. (1995). Twenty-four questions (and answers) about professional practice in the area of child abuse. *Professional Psychology: Research and Practice*, *26*, 377–383.

Baker, D. C., & Bufka, L. F. (2011). Preparing for the telehealth world: Navigating legal, regulatory, reimbursement, and ethical issues in an electronic age. *Professional Psychology: Research and Practice*, *42*, 405–411.

Bersoff, D. N. (2014). Protecting victims of violent patients while protecting confidentiality. *American Psychologist*, *69*, 461–467.

Bongar, B. (2013). *The suicidal patient: Clinical and legal standards of care* (2nd ed.). Washington, D.C.: American Psychological Association.

Canadian Psychological Association. (2006). Draft ethical guidelines for psychologists providing psychological services via electronic media. Retrieved from http://www.cpa.ca/docs/File/Ethics/Draft_Guidelines_EServices_31Oct2013.pdf

Donner, M. B., VandeCreek, L., Gonsiorek, J. C., & Fisher, C. B. (2008). Balancing confidentiality: Protecting privacy and protecting the public. *Professional Psychology: Research and Practice*, *39*, 369–376.

Foreman, T., & Bernet, W. (2000). A misunderstanding regarding the duty to report suspected child abuse. *Child Maltreatment*, *5*, 190–196.

Gustafson, K. E., & McNamara, J. R. (1987). Confidentiality with minor clients: Issues and guidelines for therapists. *Professional Psychology: Research and Practice*, *18*, 503–508.

Isaacs, M. L., & Stone, C. (2001). Confidentiality with minors: Mental health counselors' attitudes towards breaching or preserving confidentiality. *Journal of Mental Health Counseling*, *23*, 342–356.

Joiner, T. (2014). *The Perversion of virtue: Understanding murder-suicide*. New York: Oxford.

Joint Task Force for the Development of Telepsychology Guidelines for Psychologists. (2013). Guidelines for the practice of telepsychology. *American Psychologist*, *68*, 791–800.

Kalichman, S. C. (1999). *Mandated reporting of suspected child abuse: Ethics, law and policy*. (2nd ed.). Washington, D.C.: American Psychological Association.

McMinn, M. R., Bearse, J., Heyne, L. K., Smithberger, A., & Erb, A. (2011). Technology and independent practice: Survey findings and implications. *Professional Psychology: Research and Practice*, *42*, 176–184.

Monahan, J. (1993). Limiting therapist exposure to *Tarasoff* liability: Guidelines for risk management. *American Psychologist*, *48*, 242–250.

Remley, T. P., Jr., Herlihy, B., & Herlihy, S. B. (1997). The U.S. Supreme Court decision in *Jaffee v. Redmond*: Implications for counselors. *Journal of Counseling and Development*, *75*, 213–218.

Rummell, C. M., & Joyce, N. R. (2010). "So wat do u want to wrk on 2day?": The ethical implications of online counseling. *Ethics & Behavior*, *20*, 482–296.

Schank, J. A., & Skovholt, T. M. (2006). *Ethical practice in small communities: Challenges and rewards for psychologists*. Washington, D.C.: American Psychological Association.

Shuman, D. W., & Foote, W. (1999). *Jaffee v. Redmond's* impact: Life after the Supreme Court's recognition of a psychotherapist–patient privilege. *Professional Psychology: Research and Practice*, *30*, 479–487.

Sude, M. E. (2013). Text messaging and private practice: Ethical challenges and guidelines for developing personal best practices. *Journal of Mental Health Counseling*, *25*, 211–227.

Taylor, L., McMinn, M. R., Bufford, R. K., & Chang, K. B. T. (2010). Psychologists' attitudes and ethical concerns regarding the use of social networking web sites. *Professional Psychology: Research and Practice*, *41*, 153–159.

Truscott, D., & Evans, J. (2009). Protecting others from homicide and serious harm. In J. L. Werth, E. R. Welfel, & G. A. H. Benjamin (Eds.), *The duty to protect: Ethical, legal, and professional responsibilities of mental health professionals* (pp. 61–77). Washington, D.C.: American Psychological Association.

Truscott, D., Evans, J., & Mansell, S. (1995). Outpatient psychotherapy with dangerous clients: A model for clinical decision making. *Professional Psychology: Research and Practice*, *26*, 484–490.

Walfish, S., Barnett, J. E., Marlyere, K., & Zielke, R. (2010). "Doc, there's something I have to tell you": Patient disclosure to their psychotherapist of unprosecuted murder and other violence. Ethics & *Behavior*, *20*, 311–323.

Werth, J. L., & Blevins, D. (2008). *Decision-making near the end of life: Recent developments and future directions*. Philadelphia, PA: Routledge.

Werth, J. L., Welfel, E. R., Benjamin, G. A. H. (Eds). (2009). *The duty to protect: Ethical, legal, and professional considerations in risk assessment and intervention*. Washington, D.C.: American Psychological Association Press.

Younggren, J. N., & Harris, E. A. (2008). Can you keep a secret? Confidentiality in psychotherapy. *Journal of Clinical Psychology*, *64*, 589–600.

Additional Online Resources

The 'Lectric Law Library's definition of privileged communication: http://www.lectlaw.com/def2/p084.htm.

Ken Pope's Resources for Violence Risk Assessment: http://kspope.com/assess/violence.php.

HIPAA Privacy Rule and Public Health: http://www.cdc.gov/mmwr/preview/mmwrhtml/m2e411a1.htm.

Summary of the HITECH Act: http://www.healthit.gov/policy-researchers-implementers/hitech-act.

Informed Consent

CHAPTER 6

Affirming the Client's Freedom of Choice

Counseling and psychotherapy clients purchase professional services, either directly or indirectly. Even when a client does not write a check to the providerœ, he or she pays for services through taxes, tuition, or health insurance fees. As consumers, all clients have ethical and legal rights to information about the nature, risks, and potential benefits of those services. Because most people have no other way to gain reliable "product information," mental health professionals are obliged to provide it. Behnke, Perlin, and Bernstein (2004) refer to this responsibility to inform clients as the *law of no surprises.* The need for information is heightened by the fact that people's presuppositions about counseling and psychotherapy are often erroneous. For example, people may believe mental health professionals dispense advice or medication or that a single visit will be sufficient to relieve their distress. (Note how many people do not understand the difference between a psychiatrist and a psychologist.) Also, therapeutic service significantly affects the client's mental, emotional, and social functioning. Research demonstrates that counseling and psychotherapy are effective interventions for many human problems (e.g., see Kazdin, 2008; Lambert; 2013; Seligman, 1995; Wampold, 2001), but clients still may experience negative as well as positive results. Even in successful interventions, clients often encounter unsettling interruptions in normal patterns, feelings, and social relationships. They have a right to understand the potential for such occurrences, even if temporary. Finally, the most fundamental reason for providing information about counseling is that it shows respect for the client as a person with rights and responsibilities in a free society. A competent informed consent process demonstrates that the professional is seeing the client as a person—not a problem or diagnosis. Its central message is that counseling and psychotherapy are not activities done to a passive client by an all-knowing expert, but rather a collaboration of two fully engaged people, both of whom have talents and energies to commit to the process. Pomerantz (2012) refers to this approach to informed consent as *empowered collaboration.*

Informed consent has two central aspects. The first is *disclosure* of relevant information the client needs to make a reasoned decision about whether to initiate services, and the second is *free consent*. Free consent means that the decision to engage in an activity is made without coercion or undue pressure. Providing full information empowers the client to determine his or her level of involvement in treatment. Underlying the requirement of informed consent is a view of the client as an autonomous human being capable of directing his or her own life and of collaborating with a professional to make necessary changes. The call for informed consent rests on a model of counseling and psychotherapy as a partnership in which mental health professionals use their expertise to help clients achieve their own goals. In other words, as Knapp and VandeCreek (2011) note, the informed consent process is, at its essence, a process of shared decision making about care. Clients, in turn, use their understanding of themselves and their personal circumstances to help the professional identify useful interventions and to inform the practitioner about their progress.

This chapter seeks to provide a well-rounded overview of informed consent, beginning with a history of how this practice developed, and to dispel several myths about informed consent, including these misinterpretations:

- It is completed at the initial counseling session by having a client sign some forms.
- It is restricted to a discussion of the limits of confidentiality and little more.
- It is a distraction from the real business of treatment.
- It is undertaken primarily as a risk management strategy to protect the practitioner from legal liability.
- It is quickly understood and easily retained by clients at the initiation of service.

This chapter also describes the stance of the ethics codes on informed consent, the ethical principles and virtues undergirding those guidelines, the research on practitioners' and clients' interpretations of informed consent, and the interplay between ethical and clinical considerations. In its later sections, the chapter also explores the application of informed consent with minors, in assessment, emergencies, court situations, and with adults with diminished mental capacity. Finally, it concludes with cases for analysis. (Informed consent in research is discussed in Chapter 15.)

THE HISTORY OF INFORMED CONSENT

The requirement of informed consent in mental health service evolved from medical case law. Although the first case can be traced to England in 1767 (Smith & Meyer, 1987), before the twentieth century physicians had no duty to explain medical procedures to their patients or to obtain their express consent. A paternalistic attitude that doctor knew best reigned supreme. This attitude sprang from a society in which consumer rights was an unknown concept, and most citizens were poorly educated and ignorant about anatomy and physiology. This perspective began to change in 1914 when the judge in the *Schloendorff v. Society of New York Hospital* (1914) ruled that "every human being of adult years and sound mind has a right to determine what shall be done with his own body" (p. 93). Unfortunately, vestiges of paternalism persist in the medical and human service professions. As Haas and Malouf (2005) point out, this attitude toward recipients of care is problematic for two major reasons. First, it prevents people from becoming actively involved in their own care. In a doctor-knows-best system, patients do not feel responsible for their own health and recovery. Second, it is vulnerable to abuse. Uninformed patients can be exploited more easily, and unethical practitioners can avoid accountability more readily. Third, it simply insults the dignity of competent adults.

The spark for change ignited when patients won medical malpractice suits showing that physicians harmed them by failing to communicate the nature and risks of medical treatment. Other factors also encouraged the trend away from paternalism. Outrageous violations of patient rights in Nazi Germany and in the infamous Tuskegee experiments in the United States were the most striking of these influences (Jones, 1981). (In the Tuskegee experiments, African American men with syphilis were "studied" for 40 years to observe the progression of the disease. These men were told they would receive free medical care in exchange for their cooperation in the project. They were never informed of their diagnosis, were required to undergo painful procedures, and for decades were denied the penicillin that could cure them. Many died unnecessarily from this cruel and inhumane treatment.)

By the 1970s, U.S. case law had unequivocally established that patients had the right to knowledge that would equip them to make informed decisions about their own treatment. Because physicians were typically the ones who possessed the requisite knowledge, the courts ruled that physicians had an affirmative duty to provide such information. The court in *Canterbury v. Spence* (1972, p. 783) concluded that "[t]he duty to disclose is more than a call to speak merely on the patient's request, or merely to answer the patient's questions; it is the duty to volunteer, if necessary, information a patient needs for an intelligent decision." The standard used to determine whether consent is appropriately informed is the "reasonable person standard" defined as the information a reasonable person would need to make an informed decision (Knapp & VandeCreek, 2011).

In 1980, a California court expanded the physician's duty to include *informed refusal*; the term means that physicians have an obligation to explain the medical consequences if patients refuse a treatment. This reasoning is based on the notion that ordinary citizens are not likely to have sufficient medical knowledge to accurately evaluate the implications of rejecting treatment. Because physicians do understand, they are bound to communicate that information as well (*Truman v. Thomas*, 1980).

The importance of providing the client with reasonably complete information about treatment emerged from a medical malpractice case, *Natanson v. Kline* (1960). The court in *Natanson* specified that disclosure should include the nature of the illness, the treatment(s) available, the risks, and the probability of success as well as alternatives to treatment and their risks. Another case from 1979, *Osheroff v. Chestnut Lodge* (Klerman, 1990), was also influential in clarifying the specific components of informed consent. This case involved the failure of a psychiatric facility to inform a patient of the option of medication and outpatient care as an alternative to hospitalization for depression. The case was ultimately settled out of court, but it became well known in the psychiatric community for demonstrating the importance of informing patients about alternative forms of care. These types of information are still major components of informed consent in medicine and mental health today. At least four states (Colorado, Louisiana, Ohio, and Washington) have passed laws mandating disclosure of relevant information to psychotherapy clients (Handelsman, 2001), and of course HIPAA also mandates disclosure of information to all in the United States who seek any type of health care. Canadian provinces and the federal government of Canada have also passed legislation to require informed consent for all medical treatments (Truscott & Crook, 2013).

The mental health professions quickly applied these mandates to their work, and the ethics codes began to include requirements for practitioners to develop an informed consent process with their clients. It is important to note, though, that not all jurisdictions assert a legal duty for mental health professionals to engage in the type of informed consent required in medicine. However, the professions affirmed the connection between these legal rulings and the client's inherent right to self-determination, and endorsed the precedent in their codes of ethics. Although some have cautioned against applying medical methods of developing informed consent to the counseling process without considering the needs of the individual client (e.g., see Pope & Vasquez, 2011), scholars agree with the general trend.

UNDERLYING ETHICAL PRINCIPLES AND VIRTUES

The fundamental ethical principle underlying the precepts of informed consent is that of respect for autonomy, the right of the client to self-determination. A competent client should not be treated paternalistically or have his or her right to self-determination usurped by a mental health professional, regardless of the professional's rationale in doing so. As mentioned, the effects of counseling rest on the client, who thus ought to have the data needed to freely choose whether to proceed. This precept is also based on the virtue of respectfulness, the attitude that recognizes others' concerns and honors their dignity, and the principles of nonmaleficence and justice.

The virtue of trustworthiness is also at the foundation of informed consent. When clients understand the procedures, risks, and potential benefits of service, they are probably somewhat insulated from unanticipated unpleasant consequences of that service. For example, clients who are instructed about the emotional pain that can accompany exploration of family issues may better cope with that pain. Justice demands informed consent because justice implies treating other competent adults as equals. By developing informed consent with each client, professionals confirm that all people have the right to manage their own lives and have the potential to assist in their own care. Obviously, some people do not have that capacity, but justice requires that professionals assume competence until contrary information is available. Justice also means that clients should be treated as professionals themselves would wish to be treated. A failure to honor that right implies that we are treating our clients as unequal or less human than we are. Nagy (2005) recommends that clinicians "consider telling [clients] what you would want a good friend to know … if he or she were consulting a psychologist for the first time" (p. 89). Research also suggests that people want information about their prospective counselors (Hendrick, 1988), and that they may view professionals who provide information about informed consent as more expert and trustworthy (Wagner, Davis, & Handelsman, 1998; Walter & Handelsman, 1996).

Effective informed consent has also been demonstrated to have therapeutic benefits encouraging clients to initiate treatment, to reduce the anxiety associated with the initial sessions, and to become more fully engaged in it (Beahrs & Gutheil, 2001; Kerby, 2010). Unfortunately, some psychotherapists mistakenly believe that informed consent discourages client participation in psychotherapy (Croarkin, Berg, & Spira, 2003). That outcome seems likely only when the informed consent process is mishandled or incomplete.

CODES OF ETHICS ON INFORMED CONSENT

The ACA and APA ethics codes contain similar standards for informed consent. The ACA Code (2014) contains more detailed instructions about informed consent. In all it identifies more than 20 different pieces of information to be disclosed to the client, clarifying that informed consent is not necessarily limited to these items (see Section A.2.b, Appendix A, p. 492).

The APA Code discusses the topic in several different standards, but most of the information relevant to counseling and psychotherapy is contained in Standards 3.10 and 10.01.

APA Code of Ethics

Standard 3.10 Informed Consent

When psychologists conduct research or provide assessment, therapy, counseling, or consulting services in person or via electronic transmission or other forms of communication, they obtain the informed consent of the individual or individuals using language that is reasonably understandable to that person or persons except when conducting such activities without consent is mandated by law or governmental regulation or as otherwise provided in this Ethics Code.

Source: Copyright © 2010 by the American Psychological Association. Reproduced with permission.

Standard 10.01 Informed Consent to Therapy

a. When obtaining informed consent to therapy as required in Standard 3.10 Informed Consent, psychologists inform clients/patients as early as is feasible in the therapeutic relationship about the nature and anticipated course of therapy, fees, involvement of third parties, and limits of confidentiality and provide sufficient opportunity for the client/patient to ask questions and receive answers (see also Standard 4.02 Discussing the Limits of Confidentiality and Standard 6.04 Fees and Financial Arrangements.)

Source: Copyright © 2010 by the American Psychological Association. Reproduced with permission.

Taken together, these codes designate the components to an ethical approach to informed consent, though the 2014 ACA standards present other requirements for informed consent in Section A.2.a, such as the requirement that the rights and responsibilities of both parties be clarified both verbally and in writing. Scholars further recommend that several other topics be added to this list. First, scholars suggest that many of the *logistics* of counseling be disclosed, not just the fees and billing procedures (Haas & Malouf, 2005). Clients should understand procedures for making and rescheduling appointments, for reaching the therapist in an emergency, and for handling interruptions in service such as a therapist illness or vacation. If there is a standard length of appointment, such as the "50-minute hour," the client should be told about that practice. In addition, the likely length of treatment should be shared (Fisher & Oransky, 2008). Third, for *insurance reimbursement*, clients who wish to submit the costs of service to insurers, and who thus must release records, need explicit information about the implications for the confidentiality of their counseling records. Because managed care plans may limit reimbursement to certain evidence-based treatments, clients should be told about these restrictions.

Hare-Mustin, Marecek, Kaplan, and Liss-Levinson (1979) advise that when discussing the benefits and risks of therapy, professionals should attend to the *indirect effects* of therapy: consequences that are secondary to the changes the client seeks and agrees to. For example, a client who seeks treatment for agoraphobia (the fear of leaving familiar places) should understand that when his agoraphobia diminishes and he returns to his normal activities, this change may indirectly affect aspects of his life he did not expect to be affected. His aging parent may be uncomfortable with his son's absence from the home. Similarly, a spouse who is accustomed to always having her husband at home may have difficulty dealing with his mobility. Family members who prefer the client's old behavior may even sabotage the treatment. Of course, positive indirect effects of successful counseling are just as common. This client may experience new intimacy in his marriage, or a less strained relationship with his parent. Practitioners who know from experience and the professional literature that a therapeutic intervention is likely to affect additional aspects of a client's functioning need to tell the client as a part of the informed consent process.

Alternatives to counseling or psychotherapy that may be available for the client's problems should also be disclosed (Fisher & Oransky, 2008). The range of potential alternatives is wide; some examples include joining Alcoholics Anonymous for substance abuse problems, family or group therapy instead of individual counseling, psychotropic drugs for mental and emotional disorders, and self-help groups and books or coaching for less severe life stresses. Underlying this recommendation is the belief that a choice to enter counseling or psychotherapy can be freely made only if the client knows the other options. It is important to note here that if practitioners' professional judgment leads them to believe that counseling is the most desirable alternative, they can share that view with the client if the communication is noncoercive and objective. In addition, professionals are free to recommend alternative interventions as adjuncts to counseling or psychotherapy.

When psychologists are planning to use an innovative or untested intervention, clients need to be told, and consent for treatment must explicitly include an understanding of the nature of the proposed intervention, its risks, and available alternatives (APA Code, Standard 10.01b). Fisher and Oransky (2008) argue that consent ought to be highlighted in this circumstance because clients are likely to assume that any intervention a professional recommends rests on a sound research and theoretical base. How does one determine which interventions qualify as innovative or experimental? The most basic criterion is the absence of research and clinical evidence of the technique's effectiveness. In this section, the APA Code defines experimental treatments as "treatment for which generally recognized techniques and procedures have not been established."

Finally, professionals should include in their informed consent procedures an indication of how the client can address *grievances* should any arise (Handelsman & Galvin, 1988). Some state licensing laws require similar disclosures about methods for filing ethics complaints. Ohio, for example, requires all counselors, marriage and family therapists, and social workers to post or give to clients copies of a disclosure statement, one part of which must include the address of the state licensing board in the event that a client has a grievance against a professional. Practitioners who work in agencies would be well advised to also include internal agency grievance procedures. The most practical way to communicate this information is in a document that the client may keep and refer to later. It may also be placed on the agency's or practitioner's website.

Additional requirements for informed consent can be found in Section B.6.c and B.6.d of the ACA Code, which mandate informed consent for recording and observation of counseling sessions. Standard 4.03 of the APA Code has a similar message, although it omits the requirement related to observation and adds a mandate to get permission before recording the image as well as the voice of a person receiving services.

A client who does not wish to be electronically recorded has the right to refuse. Similarly, a client should understand that he or she can withdraw consent to record at any time without penalty. If the professional believes that electronic recording is essential for competent service, as may happen with a trainee, then the client who refuses recording or observation ought to be referred to someone for whom supervision is not required.

In the current editions of the ethics codes, both professions specify that the provisions related to informed consent apply not only to face-to-face meetings but also to forms of service that involve electronic communications. Thus, when counselors or psychologists are providing Internet-based service, telephone consultation, or facsimile transmissions to their clients, they need to abide by the informed consent standards. See ACA Code, Section H.2 (Appendix A, pp. 528–529), for a detailed description of additional informed consent provisions for electronic communications. For example, counselors are obliged to inform clients of the risks of technology failure, their training in online counseling, and the counselor's response time to an online communication, among other obligations. They must use means to verify client identity as well, since many online communications do not have visual or auditory components. Section H.2.d requires that counselors engaged in online interactions with clients use encryption and take precautions to ensure security. (The American Psychological Association Insurance Trust offers a sample document to explain a professional's policy on electronic communication with clients at http://www.apait.org/apait/applications/SampleElectronicCommunicationPolicy.doc.pdf.)

It is important to differentiate between *informed consent* and *notice* (Jacob & Hartshorne, 1991). Notice means informing people involved about impending events, but it does not assume a prior agreement to those events. Informed consent, therefore, is quite distinct from the mere practice of telling people what will be happening to them. Notice alone is ethically insufficient. Similarly, professionals who attempt to deal with informed consent through a blanket consent form are not complying with ethical or legal standards. In other words, those who use a single, general verbal or written consent procedure that is nonspecific and all-purpose are vulnerable to charges that they failed to develop proper consent (Jacob & Hartshorne, 1991). The 2010 version of the APA Code specifically requires psychologists to provide clients with sufficient opportunity to ask questions about professional services (and receive answers) in language they can understand.

INFORMED CONSENT AND THE HEALTH INSURANCE PORTABILITY AND ACCOUNTABILITY ACT (HIPAA)

The U.S. Congress passed the legislation that created HIPAA requirements in 1996, but regulations for the statute did not become effective for another seven years. This legislation has two major components: the protection of personal health (and mental health) information that may be shared for treatment or payment purposes, and the protection of the systems of electronic communication from unauthorized access. Technically, HIPAA requirements apply narrowly to electronic communication of personal client/patient information, but the wording in the legislation makes its provisions applicable to any professional who uses a fax, a text, or an email for any client. The legislation has two major goals—to give the patient/client control over release of personal health information while facilitating the most common types of communication about client/patient records without explicit permission for each and every release. In other words, HIPAA allows health care professionals to obtain a single signature on a *notice of privacy practices* document to allow for transmission of information to obtain payment from third parties, to provide treatment, and to keep the ordinary operations of the practice, agency, or institution proceeding in an orderly fashion. Along with other requirements for protecting client/patient data, this federal law requires all community-based mental health professionals to have clients read and sign the notice of privacy practices so that clients understand what information will be released without explicit consent and what recourse they have if personal health information is disclosed in ways that violate the law. If mental health professionals fail to follow the regulations outlined in HIPAA, the law allows for a client to bring a civil suit against the provider; the law also allows for criminal prosecution for extreme and willful violations of HIPAA provisions. Additional provisions regarding legal requirements for informed consent using electronic forms of communication are included in HITECH (2009).

It is important to note that compliance with HIPAA or HITECH is not in itself sufficient to meet most of the ethical standards for informed consent. For example, nothing in HIPAA touches on the benefits and limitations of service or alternatives to counseling or psychotherapy. Therefore, mental health professionals must supplement HIPAA procedures if they are to be compliant with other ethical (and legal) standards for informed consent. The U.S. Department of Health and Human Services provides a useful website with frequently asked questions, to assist mental health professionals with concerns about implementing HIPAA regulations, at http://www.hhs.gov/ocr/privacy/hipaa/faq/index.html.

APPROACHES TO INFORMED CONSENT

Two primary methods are commonly used to obtain informed consent—a discussion of the issues with no written forms (except for the HIPAA notice of privacy practices) or a discussion accompanied by additional documents, copies of which are given to the client. The most recent revision of the ACA Code specifies in Section A.2.a that informed consent should include *both* written and verbal components, and the APA standard requires that informed consent be documented (APA Code, Standard 3.10.d). Ethical standards of licensing boards frequently specify written consent for all mental health professionals. Research (Croarkin, Berg, & Spira, 2003; Handelsman, Kemper, Kesson-Craig, McLain, & Johnsrud, 1986; Somberg, Stone, & Claiborn, 1993) suggests that historically, a majority of psychotherapists have relied exclusively on oral discussion of informed consent. Those who do not supplement discussion with written consent forms or who fail to document consent are in violation of current ethical standards. In addition, informed consent is not completed when the initial discussion is over and the forms signed; all professionals need to have an ongoing discussion with clients about informed consent as necessitated by the services provided and to document in the client record each such discussion.

As the ACA Code indicates, verbal discussion should always be a part of informed consent. It allows the professional to adapt the wording of informed consent to the unique individual and to personalize the process. In addition, a verbal format encourages the client to ask questions and become more involved in the conversation. However, exclusive reliance on verbal discussion has several drawbacks. Most important, clients can be overwhelmed with information and may not absorb much of what they hear. Research suggests that forgetfulness is a significant problem even when written materials are used (e.g., see Cassileth, Zupkis, Sutton-Smith, & March, 1980). The risk of forgetfulness increases with the level of distress the client is experiencing. The distress may be so predominant that cognitive processing is compromised, but without a document to take home, clients have no way to review the information or to be sure that they really understood it. By the same token, the practitioner who uses an exclusively verbal format must guess at how much the client understood and remembered. Also, much of the specific information most useful to the client, such as options for addressing a grievance or procedures for contacting the therapist in an emergency, is especially vulnerable to forgetfulness. A final disadvantage is that this practice is at odds with the recommendations of legal scholars. Bennett et al. (2006) contend that written documents are rapidly becoming the "community standard," and they caution professionals that failing to use them may have adverse consequences for them in any legal challenge or ethics complaint. It is important to emphasize, however, that written consent forms offer the professional no protection against legal claims if the forms are unreadable or the client was manipulated into signing them (Appelbaum, Lidz, & Meisel, 1987).

Informed consent documents take various forms, but Zuckerman (2008) describes five distinct alternative formats. The first of these is the *client information brochure*. This multiple-page document provides a detailed description of the benefits, risks, goals, and methods of therapy as well as information about its costs, length, and logistics. It serves as an invitation to participation, an implied contract between the parties, and a communication about the standard of care the client has a right to expect (Woody, 1988).

The second format is the *question list*, devised as a guide to discussion and first recommended by Handelsman and Galvin (1988), and updated in 2004 (Pomerantz & Handelsman). It provides a structure for the client to interview the professional about therapy and reinforces the power and active role the client has in an effective therapeutic relationship. Sample questions include the following:

- What is the name of your kind of therapy?
- How will I notice if I am getting better?
- How will I reach you in an emergency?
- If I do not pay my bill, what will you do?
- How would therapy be different if I chose to pay without using insurance?

The third format is a *declaration of client rights*. Bennett et al. (1990) provide a recommended model. This form tends to be brief and formal. There are also several models available on the Web. The California document can be found at http://www.psychology.ca.gov/forms_pubs/consumer_guide.pdf

A *psychotherapy or counseling contract* is the next option for written informed consent. This contract delineates the rights and responsibilities of the participants and may be especially useful with reluctant clients, but it must be supplemented with extensive discussion and signed by both parties. Finally, a *consent-to-treatment form* is an option that is best used when other formats seem too detailed for the particular counseling relationship being initiated, but its brevity means that it also needs supplementation. The APA Insurance Trust has sample consent forms at http://www.apait.org/apait/download.aspx.

None of these forms is designed to be used exclusively. In fact, Zuckerman and other scholars encourage professionals to use multiple formats. All also urge that clients sign consent forms and keep copies of them, and that professionals retain copies for the client file. The strengths of these forms are that they become a permanent part of the record. If there is a grievance or misunderstanding about treatment, the forms can support the professional's claim that he or she explained that aspect of treatment in the consent process. Client forms can also speed up a time-consuming process. A verbal discussion of all the relevant aspects of consent might consume a good deal of the initial session, leaving inadequate time to hear the client's concerns. Finally, they can hold the attention of the client to the topic and reduce the amount of material that is missed or forgotten.

The problems with the written materials lie primarily in their vulnerability to misuse and misinterpretation by clients. The most obvious disadvantage of such forms is the tendency for professionals to rely too heavily on them. Clinicians can (and often do) erroneously assume that a document in the hands of a client substitutes for a discussion. When this happens, informed consent becomes pro forma, and the client's rights are not really protected (Pope & Vasquez, 2011; Zuckerman, 2008). In some settings, informed consent is (mis)handled by having a clerical staff member hand the document to a client and request a signature before an appointment. Or the setting assumes that the HIPAA notice of privacy practices substitutes for informed consent documentations. This approach violates both the spirit and the letter of the professional guidelines. Perhaps it is this tendency to misuse that has led some psychotherapists to mistakenly conclude that complying with informed consent guidelines discourages clients from participating (Croarkin et al., 2003).

Another major disadvantage is that the client may not have the necessary level of literacy. In fact, the research in mental health settings has found that the average informed consent form requires more than a 12th-grade reading ability (Handelsman et al., 1986; Handelsman & Martin, 1992). In fact, 63% of the forms used for informed consent in a study by Handelsman et al. (1995) were rated at the graduate school reading level, and the lowest rating was a seventh-grade reading level. The same problem exists in the HIPAA documents, as reported by Walfish and Ducey (2007), who noted that 82% of the notice of privacy practices documents in their research were written at a 12th-grade reading level. Because the average reading level of a U.S. citizen is lower than high school (ninth grade), many clients cannot understand the vast majority of such forms. (According to the National Assessment of Adult Literacy (2003), 1 in 20 Americans cannot read English at all.) Particularly troublesome is that the reading levels of psychotherapy consent forms are significantly higher than those used in medicine (e.g., see Feldman, Vanarthos, & Fleisher, 1994). In other words, our medical colleagues have made complex medical information more accessible to patients than we have made therapeutic information. One practical suggestion from Handelsman (2001) to increase readability is to decrease the number of words per sentence and the number of syllables per word. Improving readability has also been made easier by the sophistication of word processing programs—most have readability formulas built into them.

The final significant problem is that these forms can distance the client from the professional in the crucial early moments of counseling, when trust needs to develop. This situation occurs when professionals treat the documents as bureaucratic procedures to be rushed through and handled identically with every client. They see the process as an empty ritual devised as a risk management technique (Pope & Vasquez, 2011) rather than as a process of collaboration and open invitation for the client to actively participate in therapy. Approaching consent in this way can give clients the message that their individual needs are being ignored, that the paperwork is of more importance than their concerns, and that the professional does not care whether they really understand what they are being asked to sign. Pope and Vasquez remark, "Nothing blocks a patient's access to help with such cruel efficiency as a bungled attempt at informed consent" (1998, p. 126). As Beahrs and Gutheil (2001) note, unless informed consent procedures are carried out sensitively and adapted to individual client circumstances and cultural and social contexts (Bennett et al., 2006), they can inadvertently replace a positive expectancy of help with a suggestion of a negative outcome. Martindale, Chambers, and Thompson (2009) reported that the clients in their study sometimes found the consent documents overwhelming either because of their sheer volume or because of the emotional difficulty of reading and responding to them.

Some professionals rely on electronic recordings or online videos to inform clients about services. These recordings may be sent home with clients to view at their leisure, or they may be viewed in a private area in the office. These approaches seem underused and have good potential to help clients absorb a great deal of information in an efficient and familiar format. Moreover, clients are becoming accustomed to them as teaching tools as well as sources of entertainment. Many physicians use patient education recordings to help patients understand medical procedures. They can be replayed at will, can be made available in different languages, and are a livelier and more human format than written materials. These formats may reduce the client's anxiety, because they can provide a preview of the professional before sessions begin. An increasing number of mental health professionals are including information relevant to informed consent on their websites or social media sites—information related to the logistics of services, the credentials and areas of competence of the professional, and the policies and procedures related to insurance payment. All of these are helpful in preparing the client for services and reducing the burden related to consent in the early sessions.

Any method of developing informed consent requires a professional who can communicate a lot of information in an efficient and interesting way so that the process doesn't become tedious and overwhelming. Debunking the myth that informed consent is completed at the initial session lets the client comfortably accept all this information. Informed consent is a process, not an event. Marzillier (1993) captures this notion well when he states that the aspects of consent attended to initially represent a discussion of "the client's willingness to explore therapeutic prospects, not therapy itself" (p. 36). The process must be underway at the first contact, but it is not really finished until services end. For instance, as treatment options emerge during the course of counseling, professionals need to obtain the client's consent to each new treatment. When conducted skillfully and respectfully, informed consent is not an obstacle to trust and therapeutic progress, but rather a symbol of respect for the client's dignity and an invitation to actively collaborate with the professional.

THE INTERPLAY OF ETHICAL, CLINICAL, AND DIVERSITY CONSIDERATIONS

As with all other ethical dimensions of counseling, responsible development of informed consent requires good clinical judgment. Sound judgment about applying informed consent procedures is especially important when clients are in crisis or under very great stress. A client in crisis, for example, may be prepared to hear only about the nature and limits of confidentiality before discussing the crisis. A lengthy explanation of all aspects of informed consent could be counterproductive to a client whose mental health and well-being are at stake. It is important to note, however, that the crisis may require postponing the full discussion, not eliminating it.

In rare circumstances, no time is available for informed consent. Consider the following situation:

The Case of Jerry

A 36-year-old man knocks on the psychologist's door. When she opens it, the man blurts out, "Please help me! I have a loaded shotgun in the trunk of my car, and I think I'm going to kill myself." The man appears frightened, poorly groomed, sleep deprived, and desperate for help. The car is only 30 feet away, and the man still holds the keys in his hand. The psychologist immediately invites the man inside and asks him to tell her more about his distress. Within 45 minutes, the man has surrendered his car keys, agreed to be hospitalized, and wants to be saved from his own suicidal impulses. In another half-hour, transportation to the hospital arrives, and the man leaves in the ambulance. No informed consent procedure of any kind ever took place.

Was the psychologist acting unethically by omitting discussion of informed consent? The answer is negative if her professional judgment told her that to delay attention to the man's suicidal impulse would heighten his already high risk for self-destruction. Her primary obligation was to protect his best interests and his safety. If she believed she would be putting him at jeopardy by diverting his attention to any other matter, and if other competent professionals in a similar situation would make the same judgment, then her decision was fully justified and fully ethical. Legal scholars may suggest that the man gave *apparent consent* insofar as his behavior implied agreement to talk with the psychologist (Bray, Shepherd, & Hays, 1985). Should others question the psychologist's decision to defer informed consent content in such a circumstance, it is important to remember that the legal standard for evaluating whether informed consent was adequate is whether the professional provided what a reasonable person would want to know in that circumstance (Knapp & VandeCreek, 2011) and what another competent professional would have done if confronted with the same set of facts.

Judgment is also necessary in discussing the diagnosis, length of therapy, and potential benefits and risks. Learning that there is a psychiatric name for one's distress can be unsettling, so the requirement to inform the client needs to be balanced against the discomfort it may cause. For example, parents who learn that their child is being diagnosed with attention deficit disorder may be highly distressed by this information. Similarly, combat veterans who are informed that they have post-traumatic stress disorder may be overwhelmed with the news. Discomfort should be a signal to be tactful and compassionate in disclosure, *not* for complete omission of that information. Similarly, when providing information about the risks and benefits of counseling, mental health professionals need to take into account the client's need for hope of change and for optimism about the future, as well as available research evidence about therapeutic success rates. Clients often enter services feeling fearful and pessimistic, and a professional who is overly insistent about explaining risks and negative outcomes can cause a client to give up hope that counseling can help before the process even begins. Practitioners must gauge clients' interpretation of this material and help them see both sides of the equation. The goal is to provide accurate information to maximize client understanding without dimming client interest in or commitment to counseling. This process approach fits with the contention of Johnson-Greene (2007) that too often informed consent focuses so much on the checklist of topics to cover that there is comparatively little attention paid to what the client needs to know to engage in the professional relationship at the moment.

Another clinical consideration about informed consent is that some information required in developing informed consent simply cannot be determined accurately in the first session. A valid diagnosis may take several sessions to develop, and reliable estimates of the length and intensity of treatment can seldom be reached at intake. Similarly, the techniques and procedures that may address the presenting problems sometimes do not become clear immediately. The ethics codes acknowledge this reality and encourage the mental health professional to use professional judgment in determining how intensively and how frequently to discuss informed consent.

A final clinical consideration that interacts with the ethics of informed consent is that some clients tend to be reluctant to ask questions and unwilling to disagree with a professional. Clients often view mental health professionals as authorities and experts to whom an ordinary person should defer. Moreover, clients often hope their therapists approve of them. So it is not surprising that clients may not ask about aspects of informed consent that they do not understand and may censor their inclinations to refuse a suggested intervention. Professionals must be alert to nonverbal signs of confusion or resistance and must establish trust and acceptance so that genuine agreement to services can be secured. Settling for anything less undermines the chance of clinical success and compromises truly informed consent. When clients and professionals come from different ethnic, cultural, or social class backgrounds, the importance of ensuring that clients feel comfortable asking questions and that information is communicated in a way that makes sense to clients is heightened. The ACA Code emphasizes this responsibility in Section A.2.c (Appendix A, p. 492).

APPLICATIONS TO MINORS AND TO SPECIAL POPULATIONS

As with the issue of confidentiality, informed consent becomes more complex in working with certain populations. Children, teenagers, and people with impaired cognitive capacity are the most obvious of these populations because they are legally and ethically incapable of giving consent. They do not have the capacity to fully understand the meaning and implications of their choices about counseling. The wording in the ACA Code (Section A.2.d, Appendix A, pp. 492–493) obliges counselors to "seek assent" from anyone who does not have the capacity to give formal consent for services but does not make assent a prerequisite—notice the use of the word *seek*. This section also highlights the family's rights and responsibilities. Standard 3.10.b of the APA Code also advises psychologists to seek assent and to act in the best interests of anyone unable to offer independent consent (Appendix B, p. 543)

Minors

By law, minors usually cannot give informed consent for community-based treatment; at least one parent or guardian must give consent instead. (See Chapter 13 for additional discussion of informed consent in school counseling.) Unless one parent has been stripped of his or her parental rights, consent of both parents is advisable. As discussed in Chapter 5, under some circumstances adolescents may be allowed to consent to treatment. Minors can also receive treatment without parental consent in an emergency, if they are legally emancipated from family, or if a statute gives them that right.

Ethical requirements are more flexible than legal standards because the ethical standard for consent is based on the capacity of the client to understand the information presented and freely choose the course of action in response to that knowledge. The closer adolescents are to an age of maturity, the more likely they are to exhibit such comprehension and capacity to choose. Younger children are unlikely to have the cognitive maturity or ability to make a free choice. Given the interaction among these developmental factors, ethical guidelines, and legal requirements, most ethics scholars agree with the advice in the ACA and APA codes to obtain the *assent* of minors to counseling. As the adolescent matures, assent procedures should more closely approximate informed consent procedures. Assent to counseling means that counselors need to involve children in decisions about their own care and, to the greatest extent possible, obtain the child's agreement to engage in counseling (DeKraai et al., 1998; Koocher & Keith-Spiegel, 1990; Melton, 1981). The wording in the codes means that acquiring assent is not mandatory, although the good-faith effort to secure assent is; however, scholars clearly argue that it is sound practice, with both clinical and ethical value. The ethical ideal embedded in this practice is the communication of respect for the inherent dignity of the person, regardless of age or circumstance. As a practical matter, children and adolescents who do not understand counseling, and whose commitment to the enterprise is unknown, are unlikely to be cooperative clients who can work toward therapeutic goals. Without assent, they have little ownership of the goals that have been established. It is important to remember that assent is a supplement—not a substitute—for parental consent. The goal of the codes here is to instruct child therapists to honor the rights and preferences of both parties to the fullest extent possible. Ultimately, the best interests of the child are the highest priority in circumstances where parental preferences and minors' interests conflict.

The Case of Samantha

Samantha is a 12-year-old middle school student whose parents are seeking counseling for her at the community mental health center. Her parents are concerned because there is a great deal of gang activity in the neighborhood, and Samantha seems to be spending time with kids who are in one of the gangs. Samantha has a boyfriend, and her parents have overheard bits of their daughter's conversations that suggest that she is becoming sexually active. Samantha earns average grades, even though her test scores show she has considerable academic promise. She has had some conflict with parents, teachers, and peers, but no legal trouble. The parents want the counselor to evaluate Samantha and provide counseling. Her parents are eager to consent. Samantha, however, has no interest in counseling. She sees herself as a normal kid with boring teachers who don't understand kids and with overprotective parents. She refuses to give assent to therapy in the initial appointment; although she says she will "show up" to keep her parents off her back, she does not want to change. The counselor believes Samantha is at risk for several significant behavior problems.

If a child refuses to give immediate assent, going forward with services is not unethical, although its clinical value needs to be determined. In such a situation, a practitioner would be well advised to work closely with the family to help them appreciate the importance of the child's willing involvement in services. In the meantime, the professional should continue to attempt to build trust with the child so that assent can be gained as soon as possible. The ultimate criterion, of course, is the course of action most fitting with the best interests of the child. No therapist should keep a child in treatment if participation is not helping that child.

Research on professional practices regarding consent with minors focuses primarily on adolescents and has found that a growing percentage of psychologists seek to secure an adolescent's agreement to participate in psychotherapy (Beeman & Scott, 1991; Taylor, Adelman, & Kaser-Boyd, 1984). By 1991, 70% of child psychologists indicated that they regularly obtained the adolescent's agreement along with the parents' consent (Beeman & Scott, 1991). Gustafson, McNamara, and Jensen (1994) found that parents also readily agreed to services for their children when they perceived the problem as severe and when they believed they had a good understanding of the potential benefits and risks of treatment for their children.

Assent to services with minors (and consent by parents) is made even more important by the findings of research of the differences between children's and parents' expectations for mental health services. For example, Hawley & Weisz (2003) reported that 76% of the minors entering treatment had completely different goals for therapy than their parents, and more than half the sample did not even agree on the broad domain of problem for which they were seeking help.

People With Diminished Capacity

In most legal systems, adults are assumed to be competent to consent until evidence exists to the contrary. At times, professionals encounter clients with significant developmental disabilities, advanced dementia, or acute psychosis who are clearly not competent. Others fade in and out of competence, as may happen at the early stages of dementia. Such clients are said to have *diminished capacity*, meaning they cannot currently comprehend events that affect them. Without comprehension, they are unable to make an informed choice; others must make that choice for them in proxy consent. Usually, a family member or a court-appointed guardian fills this role. Regardless of the specific person providing the proxy consent, the professional must go through the consent procedure with the substitute as though he or she were the client. In addition, the professional is responsible for giving the client as much involvement in the decision making as he or she can manage.

When a client's capacity to give consent is in question, a prudent practice is to give the client the benefit of the doubt and go forward to the greatest extent possible, carefully monitoring the degree of the client's understanding of what is being communicated. In addition, professionals ought to consult with a colleague who is competent to objectively assess the client's capacity. The goal is to avoid treating clients paternalistically and to carefully evaluate the client's intellectual functioning. (See Moye, Karel, and Armesto [2007] for a useful review of strategies to evaluate competence to consent to treatment.) Taking away a client's freedom to choose is a serious step that should not be taken lightly. If the client's competence to consent is temporarily compromised (by intoxication or acute physical illness, e.g.), professionals should attempt to delay consent until the client's mental functioning is back to normal (Kitchener & Anderson, 2011). Adams and Boyd (2010) wisely note that individuals with intellectual disabilities still need and can benefit from service, and therefore counselors and therapists should not hesitate to work with this population.

COURT-MANDATED COUNSELING

Over the last 50 years, mental health professionals have become more involved with the courts (Brodsky, 2011; Stokes & Remley, 2001). Judges have learned of the value of mental health care for citizens who come before them, and they frequently mandate counseling for people whose legal difficulties seem to stem from emotional, relationship, or substance abuse problems. Shearer (2003) has referred to court-mandated treatment as an "ethical minefield," but others (e.g., Rooney, 2001) are more optimistic about finding a way to conduct this treatment ethically. Usually defendants are given a choice between a criminal or civil penalty and counseling. Many defendants in juvenile and adult courts thus choose counseling. Brodsky (2011) refers to this as a "Hobson's choice," a choice made only because the alternative is unacceptable. The histories and current predicaments of these people point to a strong need for intervention to help them cope with pain, learn alternative behaviors, and build healthier relationships. However, the circumstances under which they enter counseling raise questions about the degree to which their selection of counseling really represents a free choice. Consider the following questions:

- If jail is the only alternative, is the selection of counseling really voluntary?
- If losing custody of children seems imminent, will a parent feel coerced into treatment?
- After a third or fourth arrest for driving under the influence, would anyone choose permanent loss of driving privileges over temporary loss of license and counseling? If not, is there really any choice?
- Can a client who opts for therapy over the alternatives in any of the preceding situations be considered a willing and motivated client, ready to actively participate in the process?
- How does a mental health professional establish trust and measure therapeutic progress with a client who sees treatment as the "least worst" alternative?

These questions probe the contradiction between the usual definition of informed consent and its use in court settings. Ordinarily, informed consent is based on *capacity* (the ability to understand what they hear), *comprehension* (the understanding of the specifics of the information), and *voluntariness* (a free, unforced choice). Voluntariness is at risk when the alternative is illusory, when it is an option no rational person would choose. This practice seems to fall within Warwick and Kelman's (1973) definition of manipulation: the "structuring of options in such a way that one is more likely to be selected than others while preserving the appearance of free choice" (p. 403). Thus, in this setting, the clinician has a dilemma: Should he or she accept the client regardless of the lack of voluntariness, or should the contradiction be pointed out immediately and the service delayed until the client is in a better position to decide his or her own fate?

There is no absolute rule for this situation. The ACA Code comes the closest in Section A.2.e, indicating that the limits of confidentiality must be explained along with the nature of the information to be shared with the mandating party. It goes on to clarify that the mandated person has the right to refuse services, but that if refused, the counselor is obliged to explain whatever consequences may ensue from that refusal. Once again, the professional's judgment comes into play because the client does not always feel free to refuse. The task is to weigh the deficiency in consent against the possible good that counseling might do for a particular person. In essence, one engages in a kind of risk–benefit analysis, asking oneself, "Would service without free consent be likely to do harm? Would the failure to provide treatment, even under these compromised circumstances, be likely to cause more harm than providing it? Do I have the skills, compassion, and attitude to help the client overcome the distrust inherent in mandated services?" The answers to these questions should guide the decision. It is also important for the mental health professional to approach the prospective client with an attitude of openness—all too often these individuals become "the clients that no one wants" (Brodsky, 2011, p. 9), setting up a scenario in which a difficult process becomes virtually impossible because of the negative frame of reference of the professional.

In any case, the professional needs to proceed through an informed consent process with such clients, to disclose appropriate information, and to make sure the client understands it. The level of disclosure of counseling content to the party mandating the service must be made clear to the client. The ultimate objective of the mental health professional is to find a way to facilitate the court's interest in mental health services for citizens who would benefit from them without violating the rights and dignity of those citizens. Professionals should be encouraged by evidence that people can and do benefit from intervention even when they are mandated to participate and that they are often significantly better off than others in the same circumstance who are not getting services (Keaton & Yamatani, 1993; Peters & Murrin, 2000). Some research also suggests that mandated clients are aware that they have serious mental health issues that need changing and that they agree with the directive to get service (Rooney, 2001). Consequently, clinicians should not assume that mandated clients are hostile to service or unwilling to participate. They are clearly at greater risk for feeling coerced and being unmotivated, but they are not hopeless cases. Rooney (2001) emphasizes the value of honest and direct communication during the informed consent process so that mandated clients are knowledgeable about the treatment and the implications of their participation in it. Brodsky (2011) serves as a valuable resource for working with both mandated and otherwise reluctant clients.

The APA Code, Standard 3.10.c, specifics that when clients are legally mandated, the professional is responsible for informing them of the services to be provided, the court order for services, and the attendant limits on confidentiality in this situation.

INFORMED CONSENT IN ASSESSMENT

All counseling and psychotherapy includes some form of assessment, evaluation of client needs, or diagnosis of client problems—after all, a professional can treat only those concerns that have been identified. As will be described in greater detail in Chapter 10, the assessment process has been fraught with ethical problems for practitioners. Therefore, professional standards provide extensive description of the ethics of assessment, both in relation to informed consent and other aspects. See ACA Code, Section E.3, in Appendix A, p. 511, for all of the ACA provisions. Standard 9.03 of the APA Code also provides extensive guidance for consent in assessment. See Appendix B, pp. 532–533.

Paralleling the ethical mandates for consent in counseling and therapy, these standards emphasize the right of clients to full information about the purposes and uses of assessments prior to their implementation. Unless a court or other legal body has ordered testing, for example, to determine a person's fitness to stand trial, the client also has the right to refuse testing or release of data to any other parties. These standards have their most obvious application when standardized educational and psychological tests are used or when a formal diagnosis of an emotional or mental disorder is given, but also apply whenever the professional is making an evaluation of a client and placing that evaluation in a client record or communicating it to other parties.

RESEARCH FINDINGS ON INFORMED CONSENT

Research on informed consent in psychotherapy is both encouraging and discouraging. On the one hand, researchers have found that informed consent can benefit clients and therapists. Clients who have experienced a responsible informed consent process seem to view self-disclosure more positively and have more optimistic expectations for counseling outcome (Goodyear, Coleman, & Brunson, 1986). Also, some evidence suggests that adult clients view therapists who carefully develop informed consent as more trustworthy and expert than those who do not (Sullivan, Martin, & Handelsman, 1993). Similarly, parents of children appreciate informed consent information (Jensen, McNamara, & Gustafson, 1991) and expect that mental health professionals will provide that information to them. From the professional perspective, many psychologists appear to some extent to agree with the professional standards that define informed consent as an ongoing process, not an activity completed at the initiation of service (Pomerantz, 2005). Professionals in this study tended to expect that all aspects of informed consent take at least three sessions to complete.

On the other hand, research also suggests that compliance with informed consent mandates, both ethical and legal, is inconsistent. Moreover, some of the informed consent procedures in use seem to meet only the letter and not the spirit of the guidelines. In one study of the practices and attitudes of psychologists toward informed consent, Somberg et al. (1993) found that a majority of those sampled omitted several required components with most clients. Only 59.5% indicated that they discuss the limits of confidentiality with every client, and less than a third of the sample discussed the risks of therapy, its length, or alternatives with every client. Moreover, 18% reported that they *never* discussed the risks of therapy with clients. The timing of informed consent discussions was also highly variable. Of those who discussed major components of informed consent, most tended to do so by the end of the first session. A disturbingly high percentage, however, indicated that they discussed informed consent matters only "as the issue arises" (Somberg et al., 1993, p. 156). That implies that these psychologists discuss duty-to-protect issues or mandated reporting of child abuse only when the client brings up the issue. Research on the consent practices of rehabilitation counselors reveals a similar problem—only 56% of those in this study discussed the limits of confidentiality relating to dangerousness at intake, and only 45% described limits relating to abuse and neglect of vulnerable persons at intake (Shaw, Chan, Lam, & McDougall, 2002). Waiting until the client discloses something that cannot be held confidential is rather like closing the proverbial barn door after the horse has escaped. Postponing informed consent in this way also violates the principle of fidelity and the virtue of respectfulness. The point of the ethical mandates is that clients should understand the implications of such disclosures *before* they make them. Swenson (1997) describes the explanation of the limits of confidentiality as a "psychological *Miranda* warning" that clients must have in order to judge the consequences of their disclosures (p. 72). (A Miranda warning is the list of rights law enforcement personnel must disclose to a person accused of a crime before questioning.) Because in some circumstances courts can demand testimony from mental health professionals about clients, failing to develop properly informed consent can sometimes make clients incriminate themselves. Other researchers also have found the same variability and insufficiency in informed consent procedures and documents (e.g., Claiborn, Berberoglu, Nerison, & Somberg, 1994; Croarkin, Berg, & Spira, 2003; Sherry, Teschendorf, Anderson, & Guzman, 1991; Talbert & Pipes, 1988). In a study that compared psychiatrists with psychologists and social workers, Croarkin et al. (2003) found that psychologists had the highest level of endorsement of the importance of informed consent, and psychiatrists the lowest. Research on informed consent procedures with adolescent clients reveals better compliance with ethical guidelines. For example, Beeman and Scott (1991) found that 93% of the psychologists in their sample secured the informed consent of parents for treating their teenagers. As mentioned earlier, 70% also obtain the adolescent's agreement to participate.

Are professionals who are providing e-therapy, also called online counseling, doing a better job of compliance with informed consent? Unfortunately, no evidence supports that conclusion. In fact, research by Heinlen, Welfel, Richmond, and Rak (2003) and Heinlen, Welfel, Richmond, and O'Donnell (2003) suggests that more than half the professionals with online clinical services are largely noncompliant with informed consent provisions of the codes. Many consumers who are interested in online counseling or therapy must first pay for services before obtaining complete consent information, if they ever obtain it. Other studies come to similar conclusions about the incomplete nature of consent for online services (Recupero & Raimey, 2006; Santhiveeran, 2009; Shaw & Shaw, 2006). Recent research has indicated that some student therapists use social networking media to gain information about clients without their permission. Lehavot, Barnett, and Powers (2010) reported that 27% of their sample of psychology trainees had looked up clients on social networking media without clients' knowledge or consent. Some participants indicated that they took this action out of curiosity; others wanted to clarify the truth of clients' statements to them. Such actions are clearly inconsistent with ethical standards.

Surprisingly, according to Remley and Herlihy (2013), no malpractice cases have arisen from claims of negligent informed consent in outpatient psychotherapy or counseling despite evidence of inconsistent compliance with standards. Similarly, relatively few ethics complaints have dealt with this violation. Whether this low level of complaints will continue in an increasingly consumer-oriented and litigious society is an open question. In summary, despite client interest in informed consent information, and evidence that there may be both ethical and therapeutic value to communicating such information, the compliance of practitioners with this standard is incomplete at best and nonexistent at worst.

SUMMARY

Informed consent means that the client understands the counseling process and willingly agrees to it. Informed consent is required by the ethical codes and is based primarily in the ethical principle of respect for the client's human autonomy. Also, because counseling is a service that clients purchase and because that service has powerful effects on their lives, both during and after the process, clients have a right to understand its implications and to make a free choice about participating. The central ingredients in informed consent are understanding of the procedures, risks, benefits, and alternatives to counseling; the limits of confidentiality; the logistics of counseling; the counselor's qualifications; the use of counseling records and tests; and the indirect effects of counseling. In addition, clients have a right to know about any electronic recording, supervision of the counselor, or how to file grievances against their counselor. The need to discuss all aspects of informed consent as soon as feasible in the counseling process is superseded by considerations of the client's welfare. Particularly in a crisis, some aspects of informed consent may need to be deferred until the crisis is past.

In some situations, obtaining informed consent directly from the client is not always possible. Most notable among these are when the client is a minor or a person with diminished intellectual capacity. Scholars recommend securing the assent of a minor child to counseling, along with the informed consent of the parent or guardian. When a client does not seem to have the capacity to process information about informed consent in order to make a free choice about participating, then proxy consent should be obtained from someone acting on the client's behalf. Usually that substitute is a family member or a court-appointed guardian.

Even though some practitioners believe informed consent is a bureaucratic procedure to be dispensed with as soon as possible at the onset of counseling, both research evidence and ethics scholarship show that proper informed consent does not hinder, but potentially enhances, outcomes. Moreover, developing informed consent is more appropriately thought of as a continuous process, not a finite procedure. This process symbolizes cooperation and collaboration between partners pursuing a common goal. The research highlights the need for greater attention to compliance with ethical guidelines by practitioners.

Discussion Questions*

1. What do you think accounts for the inconsistency in informed consent procedures used by practitioners?
2. Does a client have a right to be ignorant of the risks of counseling or psychotherapy if that person does not want to know? Explain.
3. What methods of structuring the review of informed consent information do you think are best? Why?
4. Can there ever be truly informed consent in court-mandated situations? If you think not, can a professional ethically conduct such counseling? Explain.
5. In many mental health settings, people with severe mental disorders, such as schizophrenia, have the legal right to refuse treatment, including medications. If their disorder is not in remission and it clouds their thinking, is their refusal really an informed refusal? How can their rights to control over their own body be balanced against their need for treatment?
6. What do you think about using social networking media in professional practice? What actions would you consider ethical?

Cases for Discussion

The Case of Dr. Doolittle

Dr. Doolittle is a rehabilitation counselor who works with adults with spinal cord injuries. His clients have all their intellectual capacities intact but have mobility problems. The informed consent materials he uses make no reference to the risks or alternatives to counseling. He contends that his clients have experienced enough trauma and do not need to worry about the negative effects counseling may have. They have little to lose and everything to gain by counseling. He also believes there are no good alternatives to counseling for people with spinal cord injuries because they need emotional support, vocational counseling, and guidance in practical living issues. Is Dr. Doolittle justified in omitting these topics?

The Case of Ms. Berens

Ms. Berens is a high school counselor. One of her clients is a 15-year-old sophomore who has been truant from school for the last nine weeks. Marianna has refused to attend school since she had a tonsillectomy. Now, she stays at home reading, watching television, and doing household chores. If Marianna does not return to school soon, legal action will be taken. Homeschooling is not an option. Marianna has refused to assent to counseling, but her mother gave consent and insists that her daughter attend counseling anyway. Her mother has agreed to schedule counseling after students have been dismissed from school, to make her daughter's presence in the school less difficult. Ms. Berens has outlined the aspects of informed consent with Marianna, and she believes the young woman understands the concepts. Marianna indicates that she does not want to discuss her private life with a counselor. How can Ms. Berens balance the girl's refusal to give assent against her mother's consent to counseling?

*Note to course instructors: The *Instructor's Guide* for this book includes other discussion questions, class exercises, cases, and multiple-choice and essay test items for this chapter.

The Case of Dr. Marcus

Dr. Marcus is a skilled therapist with a full schedule of clients. To manage his busy schedule, he delegates responsibility for informed consent procedures to his office assistant, Mr. Williams. New clients meet with Mr. Williams for 30 minutes prior to their first appointment to complete patient questionnaires, insurance forms, and informed consent documents. (They are mailed a patient information brochure in advance of the appointment.) Mr. Williams has no professional education in counseling but has been trained by Dr. Marcus to conduct these meetings. Mr. Williams is careful to follow the protocol established by his boss and is diligent about checking to ensure that patients understand the contents of the documents they sign. Using this approach, Dr. Marcus believes the counseling sessions are more focused and that his obligation to informed consent is substantially fulfilled, although he does recognize that additional consent issues may arise in the course of counseling. Is Dr. Marcus's practice consistent with current standards for informed consent?

The Case of Mr. Zimmer

Mr. Zimmer is a family therapist who has begun working with a 37-year-old father of two teenagers who has been convicted of drunk driving. As part of his sentence, the father has agreed to attend family sessions to work with his wife and children on issues related to his recent abuse of alcohol. After the first few sessions, Mr. Zimmer realizes that this father is "going through the motions" and is saying what he thinks he should say rather than what he feels. The client is aware that a summary of sessions is being provided to the judge and that the therapist may have to speak with the judge or appear in court to talk about him. Mr. Zimmer confronts the father in a family session, but the father denies holding back his real thoughts and feelings, even after his wife states that she agrees with Mr. Zimmer. Ultimately, Mr. Zimmer decides to tell the father that he will report to the judge what occurs in counseling and will respond truthfully if the judge asks whether the father fully participated in family treatment. All agree to this resolution. Is it ethical?

Recommended Readings

Barnett, J. E., Wise, E. H., Johnson-Greene, D., & Bucky, S. F. (2007). Informed consent: Too much of a good thing or not enough? *Professional Psychology: Research and Practice*, *38*, 179–186.

Bennett, B. E., Bricklin, P. M., Harris, E., Knapp, S., VandeCreek, L., & Younggren, J. N. (2006). *Assessing and managing risk in psychological practice*. Rockville, MD: The Trust.

Brodsky, S. L. (2011). *Therapy with coerced and reluctant clients*. Washington, D.C.: American Psychological Association.

Cook, D. A. (2009). Thorough informed consent: A developing clinical intervention. *Psychotherapy: Theory/Research/Practice/Training*, *46*, 471–472.

Fisher, C. B., & Oransky, M. (2008). Informed consent in psychotherapy: Protecting the dignity and respecting the autonomy of patients. *Journal of Clinical Psychology*, *64*, 576–588.

Handelsman, M. M., & Galvin, M. D. (1988). Facilitating informed consent for outpatient psychotherapy: A suggested written format. *Professional Psychology: Research and Practice*, *19*, 223–225.

Moye, J., Karel, M. J., & Armesto, J. C. (2007). In A. M. Goldstein (Ed.), *Forensic psychology: Emerging topics and expanding roles* (pp. 260–293). Hoboken, NJ: Wiley.

Pomerantz, A. M. (2012). Informed consent to psychotherapy (Empowered collaboration). In S. J. Knapp, M. C. Gottlieb, & L. D. VandeCreek, (Eds.), *APA handbook of ethics in psychology* (Vol.1) (pp. 311–332).

Washington, D.C.: American Psychological Association.

Pomerantz, A. M., & Handelsman, M. M. (2004). Informed consent revisited: An updated written question format. *Professional Psychology: Research and Practice*, *35*, 201–205.

Sales, B. D., DeKraai, M. D., Hall, S. R., & Duvall, J. C. (2008). Child therapy and the law. In R. J. Morris & T. R. Kratochwill (Eds.), *The practice of child therapy* (pp. 519–542). New York, NY: Lawrence Erlbaum.

Somberg, D. R., Stone, G. L., & Claiborn, C. D. (1993). Informed consent: Therapists' beliefs and practices. *Professional Psychology: Research and Practice*, *24*, 153–159.

Weithorn, L. A. (1983). Involving children in decisions affecting their own welfare: Guidelines for professionals. In G. B. Melton, G. P. Koocher, & M. J. Saks (Eds.), *Children's competence to consent* (pp. 235–260). New York, NY: Plenum.

Wiger, D. (2005). *The clinical documentation sourcebook: The complete paperwork resource for your mental health practice* (3rd ed.). Hoboken, NJ: Wiley.

Zuckerman, E. L. (2008). *The paper office: Forms, guidelines, resources* (4th ed.). New York, NY: Guilford.

Additional Online Resources

Informed Consent in Psychotherapy & Counseling: Forms, Standards & Guidelines, & References: http://kspope.com/consent/index.php.

The Center for Ethical Practice: Sample adolescent informed consent form: http://www.centerforethicalpractice.org/Form-AdolescentConsent.

APA Insurance Trust: Sample psychotherapist–patient contract: http://www.apait.org/apait/resources/riskmanagement/inf.aspx.

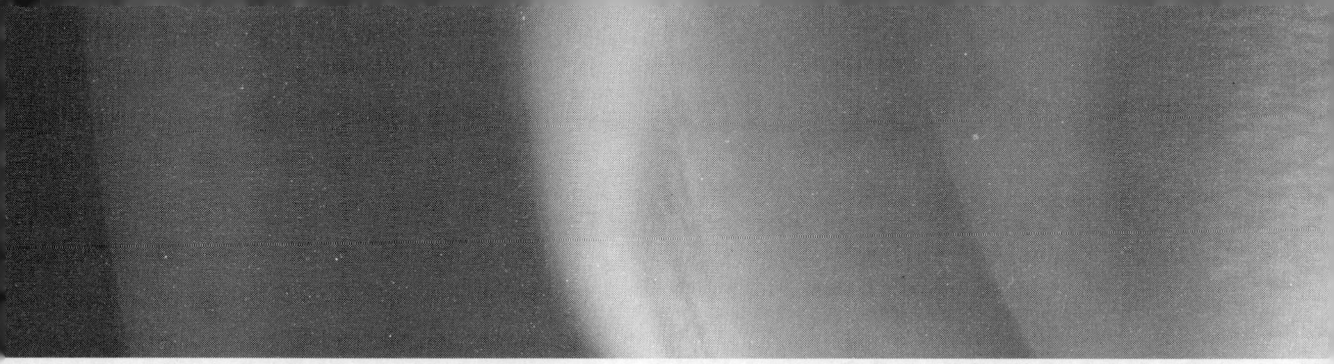

Sexualized Relationships With Clients, Students, Supervisees, and Research Participants

CHAPTER 7

Violations of Power and Trust

There are two unmistakable facts about sexual contact with clients. First, all mental health and human service professions expressly prohibit such contact during and immediately after a therapeutic relationship. The wording of the codes is unequivocal:

> **ACA Code of Ethics**
>
> **A.5.a. Sexual or Romantic Relationships Prohibited**
>
> Sexual or romantic counselor-client interactions or relationships with current clients, their romantic partners, or their family members are prohibited.
>
> Source: Reprinted with permission from American Counseling Association.
>
> **APA Code, Standard 10.05, Sexual Intimacies With Current Therapy Clients/Patients**
>
> Psychologists do not engage in sexual intimacies with current therapy patients/clients.
>
> Source: Copyright © 2010 by the American Psychological Association. Reproduced with permission.

(continues)

American Association for Marriage and Family Therapy (AAMFT) Code of Ethics 1.4

Sexual activity with clients is prohibited.

National Association of Social Workers (NASW) 1.09 Sexual Relationships

(a) Social workers should under no circumstances engage in sexual activities or sexual contact with current clients, whether such contact is consensual or forced.

The prohibition against sex with clients is grounded in empirical evidence of harm to clients and in the fundamental values of the professions.

In recent years, the codes have also clearly prohibited sexual contact between professionals and the family members of current clients, as is noted in Section A.5.a of the ACA Code, Section1.09b of the NASW Code, and in Standards 10.06 and 10.07 of the APA Code. In parallel fashion, psychologists and counselors are prohibited from initiating a professional relationship with prior sexual partners. Some state regulations also prohibit sexual contact with any client of the agency at which the professional is employed (see the Ohio Administrative Code for an example: http://codes.ohio.gov/oac/4757-5-04).

The second unmistakable fact that emerges from the evidence is that sexual misconduct by mental health professionals has not been eradicated despite the prohibition. Moreover, violators are not confined to those who are poorly trained, mentally unstable, and at the margins of the professions, but have included leaders in their fields (see, e.g., Noel & Watterson, 1992). Pope (1990a) cites examples of sexually exploitive therapists who have served as presidents of state professional associations, chairs of state licensing boards and ethics committees, and faculty in prestigious universities. This chapter examines the rationale behind the absolute proscription against sexual activity, the scope of the problem, and the characteristics correlated with sexual misconduct. The stance of the ethics codes on sexual contact with former therapy clients is described, along with the debate about its wisdom. The next focus is the ethics of sexual contact between professionals and those whom they teach, supervise, employ, consult, or conduct research with. The chapter presents strategies to help practitioners deal responsibly with sexual feelings that emerge during sessions and discusses the place of nonerotic touch in counseling and psychotherapy. Finally, it offers guidelines for practitioners working with clients who have been sexually exploited by former therapists.

RATIONALE FOR THE PROHIBITION

The reasons for the prohibition against sex with a client derive from the client's vulnerability to exploitation and the harm that exploitation causes for the client, the professional, and the reputation of the profession. Even though it would be gratifying to suggest that the professional associations have led the way in seeking to eradicate this problem, the truth is that the professions' early history on this issue is blemished. In the 1960s and 1970s, some mental health professionals even argued that sex with clients could be therapeutically valuable (e.g., see McCartney, 1966; Shepard, 1972), and scholars who tried to publish evidence of sexual misconduct had difficulty getting their research accepted in professional journals (Dahlberg, 1970; Gechtman, 1989). Until the landmark case of *Roy v. Hartogs* (1975), the courts were not interested in malpractice cases claiming sexual misconduct, because the legal system accepted professionals' claims that such accusations arose from the sexual fantasies of mentally unbalanced women (Pope, 1994; Sonne, 2012). The initial response of the therapist and police to Barbara Noel's claim that her psychiatrist sexually exploited her was, "You must be dreaming" (Noel & Watterson, 1992). However, the courage of many victims in pursuing claims, coupled with the perseverance of scholars researching this topic, has led all mental health professions to endorse the ban on sexual contact with clients and to take active roles in both discipline and prevention activities.

FACTORS THAT AFFECT CLIENT VULNERABILITY TO EXPLOITATION

Despite public awareness of the ethical and legal problems with sexual contact between client or patients and professional helpers, consumers of mental health services are sometimes ignorant about the ethics of sexual contact between therapists and clients. To complicate matters further, people typically enter treatment when their emotional distress is high, their interpersonal relationships are at risk, and their self-esteem is compromised. In this condition, people are more vulnerable to harm from irresponsible professionals than they would otherwise be. In addition, scholars suggest that a history of emotional and/or sexual abuse may increase vulnerability to sexual exploitation and heighten the damage inflicted (Pope, 1994). Somer and Saadon (1999) found that the majority of clients who experienced sexual contact with their therapists had histories of childhood sexual trauma or incest. However, Pope and Vetter (1992) found that such victimization histories existed in one-third of the cases (32%). Vulnerability increases when the professional labels such activity as "therapeutic"—an event that took place in 11% of the cases examined by Somer and Saadon. Still, it is important to note that the single best predictor of sexual exploitation of a client is the *therapist's history* of prior boundary violations (Pope & Vasquez, 2011).

Further complicating this vulnerability is the social stigma often associated with seeking mental health services. When belief in the stereotypes about people who see "shrinks" interacts with the self-doubt inherent in emotional distress, the possibility exists that clients will be overly deferential to a professional's recommendation. In this context, clients may ignore their own intuitions about appropriate and inappropriate professional behavior. Carolyn Bates captures her feelings thus: "I remember walking into Dr. X's office feeling absolutely humiliated that I needed psychological help and at the same time, feeling out of control emotionally" (Bates & Brodsky, 1989, p. 21).

The status of expert helper also encourages the client to give the professional "the benefit of the doubt" about what may be therapeutic. When she researched his background at the library, Barbara Noel remembers being impressed by the list of accomplishments of the psychiatrist to whom she had been referred (Noel & Watterson, 1992). Her skepticism about the wisdom of his recommended therapeutic approach was outweighed by her confidence in the judgment of such a renowned professional. Thus, a client may take at face value a professional's suggestions of an embrace at the end of a session or a dinner together after a session "to get a sense of your behavior in a social environment," and may not see these suggestions as overtures to start a social relationship. Even clients who wonder about the real meaning of such comments may resist making that interpretation. Sometimes clients lack the assertiveness to refuse a professional's request, even if they recognize its inappropriateness. They may also worry about the effect of refusal on future treatment, wondering if they will be abandoned or punished if they fail to comply. Professionals intent on pursuing a sexual relationship have sometimes suggested that the client's resistance to sexual contact stems from their emotional problems, and they suggest that physical contact would be a symbol of therapeutic progress. Carolyn Bates's therapist interpreted her denial of sexual interest in him as a sign of her problems relating to men (Bates & Brodsky, 1989). Clients sometimes acquiesce to social or physical contact because they trust the professional to have a therapeutic intention, or believe they have too much to lose if they fail to cooperate. Carolyn Bates describes the experience: "I could not doubt his interpretations of my resistance without doubting the doctor himself, and our entire therapeutic relationship. So I remained, unwilling to discount the trust I had spent 8 months building. I did not challenge him. I did not dare assert myself and state that I wasn't sexually attracted to him" (Bates & Brodsky, 1989, p. 32).

On occasion, clients experience sexual attraction to their therapists and fantasize about sex with them, but such fantasies are not common (Sonne & Jochai, 2014). Rarely, clients may be responsive to the idea of a sexual relationship with a therapist, but this responsiveness is rooted either in misunderstandings of the therapeutic process or in the mistaken belief that the feelings they have toward the professional are indications of true romantic love. Somer and Saadon (1999) found that 82% of the former clients they surveyed conceived of their sexual contacts with therapists as a romantic relationship at the time it was initiated. On rare occasions, clients' misinterpretation of the professional relationship is so extreme or their sexual boundaries so confused that they attempt to encourage a professional to be sexually interested. In their review of the literature, Hartl et al. (2007) reported that most mental health professionals have experienced one or more incidents of such sexual overtures, some unintentional, others deliberate. Some people who have been sexually exploited before by others in power may believe that sexual favors are the price they must pay for help. For others, the responsiveness stems from a misperception of the professional's concern and from unfamiliarity with the normal roles and behaviors associated with the therapeutic relationship. From the start of services, mental health professionals show concern through attentive listening, expressions of empathy, and attitudes of respect and warmth toward a client. Unless clients are informed about the nature of the counseling process, they may misinterpret these behaviors as expressions of personal interest and be unaware that the professional is not singling them out for special treatment.

Two other factors may put clients at risk for sexual exploitation. First, in daily life, most clients rarely experience such warm, attentive interest in their thoughts and feelings as they receive in counseling and psychotherapy, and they are drawn toward people who provide such attention. The professional's behavior may also represent exactly what the client has found desirable but often lacking in prior relationships. Second, the practitioner's professional status adds further attractiveness because people are often flattered by the attention of a person they see as having high social status. None of these motivations is a solid foundation for a meaningful personal relationship, and it is the responsibility of the professional to help the client understand the boundaries of the professional relationship. Consequently, even if the client appears willing or makes sexual overtures, sexual contact is still prohibited because it violates the autonomy of the client. The client's choice to enter into this sexual relationship is based at least in part on erroneous assumptions and dysfunctional experiences; hence, it is not an informed choice at all. For these reasons, ethics committees, disciplinary boards, and courts have dismissed all claims that clients consented to these sexual contacts. These bodies have consistently judged that the consent of the client in this situation is neither informed nor freely given. No client behavior, however provocative, justifies this misconduct.

Professionals who endorse the concept of transference see an even deeper problem with sexual intimacies with clients. They envision the therapeutic relationship as a relationship in which the client transfers onto the therapist feelings from prior significant relationships that have not been resolved. Often this means that the therapist is seen, at least on an unconscious level, as a parent figure, not just as another adult. A sexual contact with a client in such a framework takes on an incestuous character (Gabbard, 1989). Bates saw her relationship with Dr. X from this perspective: "I have no doubt that much of the trust and love I had for my father was directed toward Dr. X, for I perceived him as having both wisdom and an unconditional concern for my well-being" (Bates & Brodsky, 1989, p. 24). Parish and Eagle (2003) eschew the term transference, arguing that the term *attachment* is preferable, as it encompasses a broader range of client perceptions of the emotional connection to the therapist. They highlight that the attachment a client feels for the therapist can easily be confused with love.

Still other dimensions of sexual contact make it inherently exploitive. For one thing, sexual contact is contradictory to the principle of beneficence, the responsibility of a professional to do good. Clients rarely understand that they are relinquishing the possibility of further therapeutic progress in exchange for a sexual relationship. However, researchers point out that meaningful therapeutic progress stops when sexual contact begins (Kitchener, 1988). The professional has lost objectivity about the client and now has a personal interest in the client's present and future that inevitably affects professional functioning. For example, a clinician who is sexually involved with a client may refrain from making a necessary confrontation because of worry about interfering with a romantic evening later. At a deeper level, the clinician may no longer be inclined to facilitate client exploration of issues that threaten the future of their relationship. In parallel fashion, once clients begin intimate contact, they may censor their disclosures in counseling for fear of the effect such comments might have on the personal relationship.

Sexual contact with clients not only stops therapeutic progress but also inflicts significant psychological damage on the client (Bouhoutsos et al., 1983; Brown, 1988; Pope, 1988). Sexual contact thereby constitutes a flagrant violation of the ethical principle of nonmaleficence, the duty of the counselor to avoid harm. Pope (1988) and others (e.g., Gabbard, 1989) liken the psychological devastation of the syndrome to rape or incest, and identify parallels to battered-spouse syndrome and post-traumatic stress disorder. The psychological damage may appear immediately, or it may remain latent and emerge later. Specifically, Pope and Vasquez (2011, pp. 211–212) list 10 categories of distress:

- Ambivalence
- Guilt
- A sense of emptiness and isolation
- Sexual confusion
- Impaired ability to trust
- Confused roles and boundaries
- Emotional liability
- Suppressed rage
- Increased suicidal risk
- Cognitive dysfunction

It is clear that the mental health problems that victims of sexual exploitation incur are neither mild nor transitory, and are widespread (Somer & Saadon, 1999; Stake & Oliver, 1991). Through survey research and case studies, researchers have documented depression, substance abuse, suicides, hospitalizations, and prolonged psychological and interpersonal difficulties traceable to the sexual contact with the therapist (Bates & Brodsky, 1989; Bouhoutsos et al., 1983; Coleman & Schaefer, 1986; Feldman-Summers & Jones, 1984; Rutter, 1989; Somer & Nachamani, 2005; Sonne, Meyer, Borys, & Marshall, 1985). Pope and Vetter (1991) report that 11% of their sample needed psychiatric hospitalization, and 14% attempted suicide. Another important negative effect is that clients feel reluctant to reenter therapy, even though their presenting difficulty has not been resolved and the problems spawned by the therapist misconduct need attention. Carolyn Bates's eloquent words capture this pain: "Within 2 months [of ending therapy] the combined effects of the sexual abuse and the unresolved problems that had originally prompted me to enter psychotherapy made life seem unbearable. I was burdened with an unending depression, and my thoughts progressed from occasional ideas about suicide to a studied contemplation of it" (Bates & Brodsky, 1989, p. 40). Family and friends of those who have been sexually exploited also suffer negative effects (Schoener, Milgrom, & Gonsiorek, 1989) and become secondary victims of the abuse. Similarly, colleagues of a professional found guilty of such behavior are significantly disturbed by the event, according to Regehr and Glancy (1995). Unfortunately, research suggests that violators fail to appreciate the harm they have done. Some rationalize their behavior (Gartrell, Herman, Olarte, Feldstein, & Localio, 1989) as having positive effects for the client.

Professionals who engage in sexual misconduct sometimes do not limit their misconduct to the sexual arena. As Simon (1991, 1992) points out, sexual contact seldom arises in isolation. Instead, it usually occurs in a context of numerous ethical violations, such as omitting necessary treatments, including risky or counterproductive interventions, and diverting the sessions to focus on the therapist's problems. The therapists cited by Bates and Brodsky (1989), Jones (2010), and Noel and Watterson (1992) also engaged in many other practices that were unethical and substandard. Other research continues to support this conclusion. Somer and Saadon (1999) and Lamb and Catanzaro (1998) reported that other forms of boundary violations typically preceded sexual overtures, including inappropriate self-disclosures by the therapists, social contacts outside of sessions, unusually frequent physical contacts, and inappropriate discussions of the therapist–client relationship. A review of the disciplinary actions taken by licensing boards also reveals the slippery slope toward sexual misconduct for some professionals.

Amazingly, some offending professionals have continued to charge the client for the sessions, even if sex was the only activity. This happened to 19% of the clients in the Somer and Saadon study. One psychologist who admitted to having sex with his client argued that his continuing charges to the client were for the therapeutic minutes, not for the sexual minutes, during their sessions (Bates & Brodsky, 1989). Because there is absolutely no evidence that sex can be therapeutically useful, or that clients or therapists can make such artificial separations between sex minutes and therapy minutes, charging for that time is absurd. If bills are submitted to third-party payers, they too are being deceived about the professional's activities.

EFFECTS ON THE PROFESSIONAL AND THE PROFESSION

The effects on the professional judged guilty of the offense of sexual activity with a client are relatively minor compared to the harm caused to clients. Still, they are not insignificant. First, because the professional taboo against sexual contact with clients has become quite strong, other therapists are likely to view this practice with serious concern (see, e.g., Pope et al., 1987; Stake & Oliver, 1991). They probably have counseled clients who have been victimized by former therapists (Aviv, Levine, Shelef, Speiser, & Elizur, 2006; Stake & Oliver, 1991; Wincze, Richards, Parsons, & Bailey, 1996), have seen media reports about the problem, and have watched the cost of their liability premiums increase, due at least partly to substantial cash awards in sexual exploitation cases (Reaves & Ogloff, 1996; Smith, 1996; Zane, 1990). The professions have also taken an active role to educate their members about the implications of sexual misconduct. Those who violate this standard in such a climate risk loss of referrals from colleagues and vulnerability to complaints to ethics committees or licensing boards. Even colleagues who are reluctant to take active steps to report an irresponsible professional may stop referring clients to the offender and may end any collegial contact. There are emotional and personal consequences to therapists as well. They tend to experience guilt and loss of self-esteem, and their personal relationships get disrupted (Bouhoutsos, 1985; Herman et al., 1987).

Statistics on the number of ethics complaints lodged annually suggest that many instances of sexual misconduct go undetected and that not all professional colleagues act with the level of professionalism just implied. Noel (2008) surveyed clinical psychologists and reported that even though 84% of the respondents had knowledge of sexual misconduct by another professional, only 35% had ever encouraged a client to file a complaint, and only 10% had assisted clients in the complaint process. And, not surprisingly, the 10 psychologists in Noel's sample who reported a history of sexual intimacies with clients were less likely to encourage the client to report the offense than other psychologists. Research suggests that only 5% of victims take formal action against the therapist (Bouhoutsos, 1984; Pope & Bouhoutsos, 1986). However, when a complaint alleging sexual misconduct does go forward, most adjudicating bodies tend to respond with careful consideration and penalize violators. Because the professional standard is so unequivocal, professionals do not have the option of finding a loophole or of claiming extenuating circumstances to justify their behavior. If the practitioner is found guilty, the probability of disciplinary action is substantial, as is the risk of a malpractice suit, with damages amounting to the hundreds of thousands of dollars (Reaves & Ogloff, 1996). Those employed by agencies may lose their jobs. Licenses are often suspended or revoked, or restrictions are placed on future practice. Moreover, the professional liability insurers write policies to exclude or limit the amount they will cover for such claims, so the burden of that huge payment falls largely on the individual. In 24 states, criminal penalties for sexual misconduct have been added to the civil and professional liability risks (Celenza, 2007; Haspel, Jorgenson, Wincze, & Parsons, 1997). In all of them, sexual misconduct is considered a felony. Five states have determined that this is such an important public health issue that they have enacted reporting statutes that ask subsequent therapists to disclose client reports of sexual exploitation by prior therapists (Haspel et al., 1997). This kind of legislation is controversial and restricts client confidentiality, but its existence highlights how seriously legislative bodies have come to regard this problem.

All of this information may cause a professional to worry about the frequency and impact of false claims by clients. It may be reassuring to note that false claims against mental health professionals are rare. Their paucity may be attributable, in part, to the extensive information that claimants need to provide, coupled with the lengthy investigation process. The investigative process by licensing boards and ethics committees also severely limits the likelihood that a false claim will be adjudicated. See Chapter 11 for a detailed discussion of the process of examining claims of unethical practice.

Effects on the Reputation of the Profession

Data about the impact of sexual misconduct on the reputation of the profession are more difficult to obtain. Publicity about such misconduct probably makes people less likely to seek out professional services, and the profession cannot easily gather data about people who never become clients. Nevertheless, it is reasonable to assume some impact exists, especially in a culture that already exhibits such deeply rooted skepticism about the wisdom of seeking professional help for mental health problems. An online search for sites that discuss this issue yields sites that describe very painful client experiences with sexual overtures by therapists and other helping professionals, for example.

Worry about this problem may affect those who are brave enough to begin counseling. Clients who have learned of sexual exploitation through the media or through experiences of friends and family may have difficulty trusting a professional and may misunderstand legitimate inquiries into personal and sexual issues directly related to the presenting problem. Publicity about such unscrupulous behavior certainly does not simplify the task of convincing legislatures, government regulators, and insurers of the value of the professional services we provide.

CAUSES AND SCOPE OF THE PROBLEM

Who engages in sexual misconduct, and how frequently does it occur? This is the single most studied question in the area of ethical misconduct (Pope, 1994). Our knowledge about perpetrators comes largely from surveys of mental health professionals who have volunteered information about their sexual practices, along with data from ethics committees, disciplinary actions of licensing boards, and malpractice suits. A few studies have explored the reports of clients about sexual exploitation by former therapists (such as Brown, 1988; Somer & Nachmani, 2005; Somer & Saadon, 1999; Wohlberg, 2000), and some case studies have been published (Bates & Brodsky, 1989; Jones, 2010; Noel & Watterson, 1992). None of these sources of knowledge is an ideal gauge of the true scope of the problem. Disciplinary committees and the courts deal only with the accused; those not yet accused are not counted. Similarly, national surveys obtain data only from those willing to complete and return them to researchers—usually less than half of those to whom the form is mailed. Are those who have violated the codes as willing to complete the surveys as those who have not? There is no way to judge. Moreover, given the professional taboo against sex with clients, it is not unreasonable to wonder if all those who report no history of misconduct are answering sincerely. Still other flaws in the research exist. Client reports of exploitation by former therapists tell us nothing about people who have been exploited but who have not sought professional help again. Case studies give us a sense of the depth of the injury to individual clients but do not address the breadth of the problem. For these reasons, it is important to evaluate with some caution research about the scope of the problem. At the same time, the evidence can lead to some tentative conclusions:

- The majority of offenders are male, and the majority of victims are female (Pope, 1994). Male therapists have shown from 1.5 to 9 times the frequency of sexual misconduct of female therapists. This trend holds true for Great Britain, Israel, and Australia as well as the United States (Bisbing, Jorgenson, & Sutherland, 1995; Garrett, 1998; Somer & Saadon, 1999, 2005; Wincze et al., 1996).
- Sexual contact is not limited to adult clients. Reported victims include girls as young as three and boys as young as seven. The mean age for female minors was 13; for male minors, 12 (Bajt & Pope, 1989). In one report of therapist misconduct (Pope & Vetter, 1991), 5% of the victims were minors.
- Therapists who violate this standard tend to be older than the clients with whom they get involved. The average age of psychiatrists was 43, and of clients, 33 (Gartrell et al., 1989). For psychologists, the mean age was 42, and for their clients, 30 (Bouhoutsos et al., 1983). In the report of Somer and Saadon, therapists' ages ranged from 30 to 70, and clients' ages from 19 to 46.
- Data from the 1970s and 1980s show an aggregate rate of misconduct of 8.3% of those surveyed, but the percentage varies from study to study (Pope, 1990. In these studies, psychiatrists admitted this practice more than other professionals. However, once cohort effects are taken into account, differences in rates among the professions disappear (Pope & Vasquez, 2011).
- Surveys conducted since the 1990s generally show smaller percentages, with studies of counselor misconduct showing rates ranging from 1.7% (Thoreson, Shaughnessy, Heppner, & Cook, 1993) to 0.7% (Thoreson, Shaughnessy, & Frazier, 1995). Nerison (1992) reported rates from 3% for sexual contact with a current therapist. Social work data show an average rate of 2% (Bernsen, Tabachnick, & Pope, 1994). One study of family therapists yielded zero admissions of sexual contact with clients (Nickell, Hecker, Ray, & Bercik, 1995). Pope and Vasquez (2011) report that the rate of admission of sexual contact with client has decreased by approximately 10% per year. The change may represent a real decrease in incidence, a greater reluctance of professionals

to admit such behavior even in anonymous surveys, an increased focus on mental health professionals other than psychiatrists or psychologists, or a combination of these factors.

- Demographic characteristics other than gender have not been reliable predictors of sexual misconduct. Type of degree, experience, or theoretical orientation has not been consistently associated with this problem (Pope, 1994, 2000). Some evidence suggests that higher levels of education and higher levels of professional accomplishment are better predictors than more typical levels of professional achievement (Pope, 1990b), but neither of these variables is a strong predictor of sexual misconduct.
- The most reliable predictor of whether a client will experience sexual contact with a therapist is the therapist's history of such contact. Client variables, such as a history of past sexual abuse, do not reliably predict sexual contact with a therapist (Pope & Vasquez, 2011).
- Efforts to rehabilitate mental health professionals who have violated this standard have not shown much success (APA Insurance Trust, 1990; Pope, 1989). Others are less pessimistic about rehabilitation, however (Gonsiorek, 1997; Schoener & Gonsiorek, 1988), citing the variety of causes of therapist misconduct as a reason why such pessimism may be unwarranted.
- Clients are harmed by sexual contact with a therapist and the psychological effects are damaging even when the clients initially viewed the contact as romantic rather than exploitive (Somer & Nachmani, 2005).
- Some research suggests that most patient–therapist sexual contact occurs after therapy has ended (Pope & Vetter, 1991), but further research is needed to clarify this finding. And in some of these cases, the clients are former clients in name only; therapy was ended for the purpose of initiating a sexual relationship.

Having clues about who is vulnerable and how frequently this violation occurs is helpful but does not fully answer the question of why this happens. Barnett (2014) postulates three underlying reasons. The first is naiveté, not primarily about ethical standards, but about one's ability to handle sexual feelings toward a client without supervision, coupled with a lack of training in the issue. The second category of causes is broadly termed problems in professional competence stemming from distress, burnout, and difficulties in the clinician's personal life that spill over into therapeutic relationships. The final category of causes is problems with character, the individual's fundamental lack of concern for the welfare of the client and willingness to prey on those who come to seek help (pp. 176–177).

Data on Therapists' Sexual Attraction to Clients

Sexual attraction to clients is a widespread phenomenon among therapists; however, the vast majority do not act on that attraction and work to handle their reactions in a responsible manner. Research shows that 80% to 90% of the psychologists sampled admitted at least one experience of sexual attraction to a client, but only a tiny percentage acted on those feelings (Blanchard & Lichtenberg, 1998; Giovazolias & Davis, 2001; Pope et al., 1986; Rodolfa et al., 1994; Stake & Oliver, 1991). Data from social workers and family therapists reveal that sexual attraction to clients is a frequent occurrence in these professions also (Bernsen et al., 1994, Nickell et al.,

1995). In their review of the research, Pope and Vasquez (2011) note that sexual fantasies about clients are common. They report that nearly one-third of male psychologists (27%) and male social workers (30%) admit engaging in sexual fantasies about at least one client while engaged in sexual activity with another person, though the frequency of such fantasies appears to be quite low. Rodolfa et al. (1994) reported that 88% of their sample of psychologists admitted sexual attraction, but only 4% had acted in any way on the attraction. Sixty percent of these who experienced attraction sought consultation regarding the attraction (Rodolfa et al., 1994). When queried about why therapists refrain from acting on sexual attractions, a wide variety of reasons appeared, ranging from awareness of ethical and legal standards, to belief that such actions would be clinical counterproductive, to concern about being disciplined or sued. Others indicated that they would not pursue a sexual involvement because they were already in a committed relationship or because they view refraining from sexual overtures as a matter of common sense (Pope & Vetter, 1991).

Pope, Sonne, and Greene (2006) note that mental health professionals may mistakenly repress feelings of attraction out of worry that acknowledging attraction even to themselves would make them vulnerable to acting on the attraction. However, the opposite seems true; repressing the feelings and not dealing with them may actually make professionals more vulnerable to misconduct.

SEXUAL CONTACT WITH FORMER CLIENTS: CONTROVERSY AND CONFLICTING RULES

Consider the following case:

The Case of Olga and Manuel

The first step in answering this question is to evaluate the facts of the situation as written. Manuel was not diagnosed with a mental or emotional disorder at the time of counseling, and the majority of his problems were attributable to medical rather than psychological issues. Three sessions were held in which the counselor first ruled out the existence of a depressive disorder and then focused attention on bolstering the client's coping skills for work stress and responsibilities for aging parents. By the third session, the client reported improvement in coping skills, happiness that his other problems were relieved by changes in his medical treatment, and gratitude to the counselor for her assistance. Counseling terminated, the counselor reported the case as closed, and no contact occurred for five years. The initial meeting after those three years was accidental, at a community event, and the client, not the counselor, asked for the date. The client reports good functioning in the intervening period.

The incidence of therapist sex with former clients is higher than the rate with current clients. In reports published between 1977 and 1998, the incidence ranged from 3.9% to 11% (Akamatsu, 1988; Borys & Pope, 1989; Holroyd & Brodsky, 1977; Lamb et al., 1994; Lamb & Catanzaro, 1998; Salisbury & Kinnier, 1996; Thoreson et al., 1995; Thoreson et al., 1993). In some cases, the victims were former clients in name only. Somer and Saadon found that 33% of the offending professionals in their study ended therapy abruptly in order to begin a sexual relationship. Akamatsu (1988) reported a mean interval of 15.6 months between the end of therapy and the beginning of a sexual relationship, but Gartrell et al. (1986) indicated a shorter interval for most such contacts—less than 6 months. A majority of practitioners believe post-termination sexual relationships are unethical, but their disapproval of this practice is not as strong or unanimous as their condemnation of sex with current clients. Akamatsu found that 23% of his sample viewed this practice as "neither ethical or unethical" (1988, p. 455), and Lamb and his associates (1994) reported that the interval since termination affected psychologists' judgments of appropriateness. In other words, the longer the time elapsed since therapy, the fewer the number of respondents who condemned the practice. (When the time elapsed was a month or less, the practice was judged highly unethical.) In their survey of counselors, Salisbury and Kinnier (1996) indicated that a third of their sample viewed sexual contact with former clients as acceptable, at least under some circumstances, while Gibson and Pope (1993) found that 23% of counselors rated this behavior as ethical. In their survey of rehabilitation counselors and nationally certified counselors, Tarvydas, Leahy, and Saunders (2004) reported that nearly half the sample (45%) viewed becoming social friends with a former client as ethical, but unfortunately, the authors did not survey participants on their attitudes toward sexual contact with former clients. The most recent survey of counselor attitudes toward this practice showed that most professionals viewed this practice as unethical (57%) even after the five-year interval indicated in the ACA Code (Neukrug & Milliken, 2011).

This lack of consensus on the ethics of sexual contact with former clients stems partly from the early history of silence of the ethics codes on this issue. The codes of the APA, NASW, and ACA were mute on the subject until the 1990s. Currently, only the Code of the American Psychiatric Association and some psychiatric associations in other countries explicitly prohibit sexual contact with former patients (2008), though the current NASW Code strongly discourages it in 1.09c. The current U.S. standards allow sexual/romantic contact in very limited circumstances. For example, in the ACA Code, the stipulation is that no contact can occur with the former client or his or her family members for at least five years after the end of services (either face-to-face or distance). If, after that interval, the counselor is contemplating such contact, he or she must document that the contact is not exploitive and will not cause harm, to be acceptable. APA Standard 10.08 mandates an interval of at least two years, but also stipulates that even after two years, this practice is only rarely permissible. It also places the responsibility to demonstrate that this contact will not be exploitive. It also forbids such relationships if any thought of this possibility occurred during therapy.

The NASW Code appears to set an "in perpetuity" standard, but it does not offer a clear definition of the term *former client* (Mattison, Jayaratne, & Croxton, 2002). In their commentary on the APA Code, Canter et al. (1994) refer to this standard as an "almost never rule" (p. 98). The codes place a heavy burden of proof on the mental health professional to demonstrate that the situation with a former client is sufficiently extraordinary to qualify as an exception to the general rule. The professional bodies seem to want to allow for the circumstance in which the initial professional interaction between a client and a professional was brief and uncomplicated by severe dysfunction, not deeply transferential, properly terminated, and entirely ethical while it endured.

The professions seem to be alluding to a scenario, for example, in which a client seeks help to stop smoking, makes a decision about a career change, or seeks support during a normal grieving process. Strong emotional ties and deep attachments do not necessarily develop under such circumstances. The argument seems to be that if the professional relationship is truly terminated and the issues effectively resolved, then the rights of consenting adults to determine the people with whom they associate should take precedence over what may be a low risk of harm to the former client. The professional associations seem to have aimed to protect the professional who completes a therapeutic relationship in good faith from being forever barred from an intimate relationship with all former clients. The codes also suggest that any professional who entertains the idea of a sexual relationship with a client at any point before termination does not meet the criterion for the exception. The implication is that when professionals and former clients meet two years or more after therapy, their meeting must have been "accidental" and not anticipated by the therapist during their professional contact.

The two-year time period has also been recommended by Gonsiorek and Brown (1989) as the minimum interval before a sexual relationship with a former client. These authors have elaborated a set of rules for decision making about this matter that, when applied to the codes, make clearer the motive for the time limit in codes. Gonsiorek and Brown suggest that mental health professionals must differentiate between therapy in which transference is a central feature (Type A), and short-term therapy that gives limited opportunity for transference to become a major aspect of the interaction (Type B). These authors propose that sexual contact with Type A clients is never appropriate, regardless of the interval between the end of service and the subsequent contact. They also classify any therapy with severely disturbed clients as Type A, regardless of its duration. Post-termination contact with Type B clients is permitted only if the following conditions are met: (1) The initiation for the contact does not come from the therapist; (2) at least two years have elapsed since therapy; (3) no social contact has occurred in that two-year interval; and (4) therapy was completely terminated, and no recommendation for follow-up treatment was given. They suggest that if there is any doubt about whether a therapy falls into the Type B category, then it ought to be considered as Type A and be prohibited. Herlihy and Corey (1992, 1997) also refer to the length and type of counseling as factors that influence the ethics of a post-termination relationship. They contend that contact should be allowable if the counseling has been brief and not deeply personal.

The work of Gottlieb (1993) is also helpful in clarifying the professions' reasoning on this issue. Gottlieb identifies three aspects of the therapist–client interaction that should be considered in evaluating the ethics of multiple relationships. The first is the *power* of the therapist, and Gottlieb argues that in traditional psychotherapy relationships, the power of the therapist is high. The second dimension is *duration* of the relationship. Duration is really a subset of power. The longer the relationship endures, the greater the power the mental health professional has over the client, and the deeper the attachment. The third dimension is *clarity of termination*, referring to the likelihood that the client will ever contact the professional for additional services at a future point. He suggests that the professional must assume that the "professional relationship continues as long as the consumer assumes that it does, regardless of the amount of time elapsed or the contact in the interim" (p. 44). The higher the relationship is positioned on the continuum of power, duration, and clarity of termination, the more clearly prohibited the sexual contact.

Arguments Against the Time Limits As mentioned in Chapter 1, this provision was not originally proposed by the APA Ethics Committee when it was developing drafts of the 1992 code. (Earlier drafts had included a blanket prohibition against sexual contact with former clients.) Nor was it included in the first 15 drafts of the 1992 revision, many of which were published for member comment (Gabbard, 1994). In fact, it was added in the final debate by the APA governing body on the request of delegates who had not been part of the code-writing process. Many scholars believe this policy runs counter to the public interest and the profession's reputation. Gabbard (1994, 2002) summarizes these scholars' disagreement with the policy:

- The two-year designation is arbitrary and not based on any empirical evidence that transference is resolved in any particular time period. The suggestion that two years is sufficient is speculative, and the profession should not place former clients at risk based on speculation alone.
- Professionals do not have good measures of a successful resolution of transference. Moreover, it seems imprudent to leave the judgment of whether transference has been successfully resolved in the hands of a professional who is now entertaining a sexual relationship with a former client (Hartlaub, Martin, & Rhine, 1986). As Gottlieb (1993) notes, only the client can determine that the professional relationship has ended.
- The suggestion that one's professional responsibilities to a client are completed within two years after termination conflicts with other professional standards. For example, client records must be maintained for significantly longer than two years, and confidentiality must be maintained in perpetuity. If asked to testify in a legal proceeding, mental health professionals have no two-year limit on privilege.
- The unequal power relationship is never leveled off, and information obtained for therapeutic purposes is at risk for misuse in a later personal relationship. The professional cannot simply "forget" all the information shared in counseling, and the client cannot ignore the unequal power levels that existed during their professional encounter. Moreover, if a former client later feels exploited by a therapist, he or she may be reluctant to file a complaint.
- Allowing post-termination relationships may change the nature of therapy. Clients who experience sexual feelings for a therapist may know that there is the possibility in the future that the therapist can have a sexual relationship with them. Clients with powerful attractions may resist delving into issues that must be explored for their recovery but that may interfere with acting on their attraction. In similar fashion, therapists may deliberately or unintentionally shift the focus of the sessions because of the potential, however distant, of after-therapy contact with the client.
- There is no evidence that sexual contact with clients after two years of therapy is without risk to clients. In fact, research suggests that post-termination relationships can cause harm (Brown, 1988; Pope & Vetter, 1991). Clients have filed claims of psychological damage for relationships that began as long as four years after termination (Gottlieb, Sell, & Schoenfeld, 1988).
- The codes should not include an exception to the rule for a highly atypical case. The criteria set forth for a sexual relationship with a former client

disallow all but the most unusual situation from consideration for sexual contact. The professions' interest in protecting the autonomy rights of the professional in this rare instance seem to be overriding their commitment to protect the public from harm. Given the evidence of significant harm to clients exploited by therapists, the profession should not give the impression that this atypical case happens more commonly than it really does.

Koocher and Keith-Spiegel (2008) raise an interesting question related to the power differential and the influence of the past relationship on current relationships. They ask, "If after many years you ran into Sam Mendez, the high school teacher you respected above all others, would you say, 'Hey, Sam,' or 'Hello, Mr. Mendez?'" (p. 330). The reluctance most people experience to call a teacher by a first name is probably related to a continuing perception of the status of the teacher and the internalized nature of the relationship between a person and a well-respected professional from the past. Why would it be any different for a client and a former therapist?

It is also worth noting that several courts have determined that sexual intimacies with former clients still constituted professional negligence (*Cranford v. Allwest*, 1986; *Doe v. Samaritan Counseling Center*, 1990). A few states, including Massachusetts and Minnesota, do not specify any time period after which sexual contact with a former client would be permissible (Gorman, 2009). Thus, even 10 or 20 years after therapy, a professional may be putting his or her license at risk in these states.

Rationale Supporting the Current Standard What is the other side of the argument? One statement that can be made in defense of the standard is that it addresses a gap in the former codes. Prior to 1992, practitioners, ethics committees, and licensing boards had no guidance from the professions about how to address complaints against therapists who engaged in post-termination sexual relationships. Sell, Gottlieb, and Schoenfeld (1986) found that these bodies held widely divergent opinions about whether such relationships were ethical and about the appropriate length of time between therapy and the personal relationship. (At the same time, they point out that not a single psychologist charged with sexual exploitation was exonerated on the grounds that the disciplinary body believed an appropriate interval had elapsed since termination.) Thus, this part of the Code is an improvement over past codes, and it provides some guidance about how to evaluate the claims of therapists who tried to defend themselves against ethics' charges by arguing that the sexual activity began after therapy ended.

Canter et al. (1994) contend that this provision is more practical than the broader prohibition and easier to defend from constitutional challenges. They seem to be referring here to legal claims that such a rule would violate a professional's right of free association. Finally, some forms of therapeutic contact do involve minimal transference and are better characterized as *consultations* than as counseling or psychotherapy. These consultations parallel what Gonsiorek and Brown (1989) refer to as Type B therapy. For example, a single parent may meet with a mental health professional about her child's night terrors and receive the needed information and reassurance in a single session. The professional relationship between this parent and the professional is of a different character from the interaction in which a client attends multiple sessions to help him cope with a child's substance abuse problem. If the client in the first case has no intention of contacting the professional again for assistance and her life proceeds smoothly for the next several years, and she then wishes to initiate a personal relationship, this standard allows the professional to respond if the situation meets the other criteria laid out in the codes.

The debate on this issue will continue. Counselors and therapists who consider such a relationship with a former client should be extraordinarily cautious about acting on the idea. Careful consideration of all the aspects mentioned in the Code, along with consultation with trusted colleagues, are essential to a truly ethical result in this situation.

It is important to note that individual state laws may differ from the ethics codes on this issue. For example, Florida views the therapist–client relationship as existing "in perpetuity" and thus allows clients to sue for damages regardless of time elapsed since termination (Lamb et al., 1994). A therapist in that state who uses the Code to guide behavior may still be vulnerable to legal sanctions for sexual contact after termination. Thus, mental health professionals should understand the laws and regulations that may govern this issue in their states. See Gorman (2009) for a more detailed discussion of the variations in state laws regarding this topic.

SEXUAL CONTACT IN ONLINE, EDUCATIONAL, CONSULTATION, AND EMPLOYMENT SETTINGS

The most recent version of the ACA Code is the first to explicitly address sexual contact with clients/consumers with whom the professional interactions are in cyberspace. In Section A.5.e, ACA prohibits virtual sexual relationships with those with whom they have a current counseling relationship.

The codes also address other more conventional professional relationships. Consider the following case:

The Case of Isabelle and Yoritomo

Isabelle, a graduate student in counseling psychology, enrolls in a course in substance abuse counseling as an elective. The course is taught by Yoritomo, an adjunct faculty member with an active private practice in the community. About 10 weeks into the semester, Isabelle approaches Yoritomo after class, seeking additional readings on substance abuse educational programs for teenagers. They discuss the topic at length, and they meet a few times after that in Yoritomo's office to talk over the readings. When Isabelle is turning in her final examination, Yoritomo asks her to come to his office in a few minutes. At that time, he suggests that they continue to meet to discuss this issue and to get to know each other better. In an offhand way, he suggests that perhaps they could have dinner together sometime. Isabelle hears in his comments an invitation to a dating relationship. If her assessment of the professor's interest is correct, did Yoritomo act unethically? (After you have analyzed the issue independently, turn to the case analysis at the end of the chapter.)

The ACA and APA standards extend the prohibition of sexual intimacies with current clients to people in other kinds of professional relationships including students, supervisees and indicate that exploitation of anyone over whom the professional has authority is prohibited. The rationale for this prohibition parallels the rationale for excluding sex with clients—the power of the professional, the extended nature of the professional contact, and the frequent lack of clarity in termination. Supervisors and faculty determine whether a student will be allowed to graduate and practice his or her chosen profession. Graduate training in counseling and psychology typically lasts for several years, and new graduates rely on faculty and supervisors for references for a number of additional years. Employers have similar influence and determine whether their employees can succeed at their jobs. Participants in research projects rely on the good faith of researchers to interact with them appropriately. A person in any of these subordinate roles has significantly less power and may feel vulnerable to the potential misuse of the power by the superior. He or she may worry about the risks of refusing an overture and may become uncomfortable in the professional relationship thereafter, even if the person in power imposes no penalty for the refusal. An anonymous article, "Sexual Harassment" (1991), captures these strong feelings in the author's description of attempted sexual exploitation by a counseling faculty member. Even students and supervisees who agreed to a sexual relationship, and believed at the time that they were making free and uncoerced choices about sexual contact with faculty and supervisors, later come to label those relationships as coercive and a hindrance to their professional development (Ahlstrand, Crumlin, Korinek, Lasky, & Kitchener, 2003; Barnett-Queen & Larrabee, 1998; Glaser & Thorpe, 1986; Lamb & Catanzaro, 1998; Lamb, Catanzaro, & Moorman, 2003; Miller & Larrabee, 1995; Robinson & Reid, 1985). In other words, in retrospect, they tend to view the relationship as one in which the faculty members took advantage of their higher status and power. Other students and supervisees who learn that a fellow trainee is in a sexual relationship with a superior wonder whether they will receive fair consideration if they are competing with that person for professional rewards. When students and supervisees wish to end the sexual relationship before the superior does, they may be anxious about the implications of terminating the affair. Conversely, if superiors end the sexual contact before the termination of the professional contact, trainees may feel uncomfortable for the duration of their interaction.

Incidence of Violation of This Standard

Researchers have gathered data on this topic from two sources—from surveys of professionals who admit engaging in this practice, and from surveys of mental health professionals who experienced sexual overtures from faculty or supervisors while they were in training. More psychologists have been canvassed on this issue than counselors, social workers, or psychiatrists, but some data are available about each profession. Most studies have found a higher rate of sexual contact with trainees than with clients. The prevalence rate for faculty–student sexual contact ranges from 0% for female counseling faculty describing their actions as professors (Thoreson et al., 1995) to 17% of female psychologists reporting on their

TABLE 7.1 RATES OF SEXUAL CONTACT BETWEEN FACULTY, SUPERVISORS, AND STUDENTS IN THE PUBLISHED LITERATURE

Researchers	Research Population	Rate for Faculty	Rate for Supervisors
Pope, Levenson, & Schover, 1979	Psychology educators	12%	4%
Robinson & Reid, 1985	Psychologists' remembrances of training	13.6%	NR
Glaser & Thorpe, 1986	Female psychologists' remembrances	17%	NR
Pope, Tabachnick, & Keith-Spiegel, 1987	Psychologists	NR	3.3%
Thoreson et al., 1993	Male counselors	1.7%	2.5%
Miller & Larrabee, 1995	Female counselor educators' remembrances	6%	2.5%
Thoreson et al., 1995	Female counselors	0%	0.2%
Hammel, Olkin, & Taube, 1996	Psychologists' remembrances of training	11%	
Lamb & Catanzaro, 1998	Clinical and counseling psychologists	1.7%	1.5%
Barnett-Queen & Larrabee, 2000	Counselors and social workers	0.02% contact 0.07% advances made	
Caldwell, 2003	Counselor educators' remembrances	1% male 99.8% female	NR
Lamb, Catanzaro, & Moorman, 2003	Psychologists	1–2%	
Ahlstrand et al., 2003	Psychologists' remembrances	10% harassment Contact: 6% females, 1% males	
Zakrzewski, 2006	Psychologists' remembrances	2% contact 8.5% advances	

NR = not reported

© Cengage Learning 2013

own experiences during their student years (Glaser & Thorpe, 1986). The mean percentage for faculty–student sex across these studies is 8.8%. Fewer studies have examined sexual contact between clinical supervisors and supervisees, but the range of findings is from 0.2% (Thoreson et al., 1995) to 4% (Pope, Levenson, & Schover, 1979), and the mean is 2.5%. Table 7.1 provides the specific findings for each study. Most of the contact has been reported to occur between male faculty in their forties and female students in their late twenties and early thirties. In addition, the majority of relationships began while the supervisory relationship was in place. For example, Hammel et al. (1996) reported that 86% of the contacts in their study happened either during or prior to the professional relationship.

This literature also identifies a related problem. In the studies that asked mental health professionals about their experiences of sexual exploitation in graduate school, respondents described an even larger number of incidents in which faculty and/or supervisors made unwanted sexual advances. Unwanted sexual advances constitute sexual harassment. For example, Miller and Larrabee (1995) found that 18.7% of their sample of counselors experienced unwanted sexual advances. Robinson and Reid (1985) and Glaser and Thorpe (1986) indicated even higher percentages for female psychology students: 48% and 33%, respectively. The percentages of female students reporting sexual harassment by faculty or supervisors fell slightly to 17.8% in two more recent studies (Ahlstrand et al., 2003; Mintz, Rideout, & Bartells, 1994) and even more sharply (to 0.07%) in another (Barnett-Queen & Larrabee, 2000). The codes of ethics also clearly forbid sexual harassment (see APA Code 3.02 and ACA Code C.6.a).

DISTINGUISHING BETWEEN SEXUAL FEELINGS AND SEXUAL MISCONDUCT

As mentioned previously, research suggests that nearly all mental health professionals experience times when they have felt sexually attracted to a client and that they sometimes feel guilty, confused, and anxious when this happens (Pope, Keith-Spiegel, & Tabachnick, 1986; Rodolfa et al., 1994; Sonne & Jochai, 2014; Stake & Oliver, 1991). Other more positive reactions to these feelings have also been documented in the literature, including an experience of curiosity about the attraction and an interest in using it as a catalyst to make therapy more effective (Ladany, Hill, Corbett, & Nutt, 1996; Rogers, 2011). Others seem to view it as a normal human response and accept the feelings without undue emotional distress (Giovazolias & Davis, 2001). Unfortunately, the literature also indicates that training programs give insufficient attention to this issue (Hamilton & Spruill, 1999; Pope & Tabachnick, 1993), although some modest improvements have been achieved in recent years (Housman & Stake, 1998). Pope, Sonne, and Holroyd (1993) refer to it as "the topic that isn't there" (p. 23). Given the gravity of the problem of sexual misconduct by counselors and therapists, how should sexual attraction to clients or others under one's professional authority be viewed? Is attraction an ethical violation in itself? Occasional experiences of sexual arousal toward a client are normal and need not produce guilt or worry. They do not constitute misconduct. After all, professionals cannot leave their sexuality outside the consulting room door. Such feelings can be stirred by events in the clinician's personal life or by comments or behaviors of the client. If these feelings are handled responsibly, professionals can work effectively in the future with that client. An experience of sexual arousal must be distinguished from sexualizing of the therapy relationship. A momentary feeling that is not acted on nor disclosed to the client, and that does not prevent one from attending to the issues the client wishes to discuss, is not necessarily ethically problematic (Pope et al., 1993). Interestingly, professionals are almost equally divided about whether an experience of attraction helps or harms the effectiveness of therapy (Sonne & Jochai, 2014). Naturally, the professional has a duty to self-monitor and carefully scrutinize the quality of his or her service in that session. If the arousal significantly compromises the competence of service, then the professional should consider referring the client to another practitioner or, at a minimum, provide additional time to the client without charge, to compensate for the inadequate service.

Sexual feelings that occur more frequently, that are more prolonged, or that evolve into sexual fantasies about a client must be dealt with more deliberately. To help resolve the sexual attraction, a professional in this situation should consult a colleague or supervisor about what is occurring. In the Rodolfa et al. (1994) study, 60% of the sample took this action when attracted to a client. These psychologists reported that they used consultation to ensure that they were objective, that they were attending to the welfare of the client, and that they understood the motivation behind their attraction. If such consultation fails to keep the professional's attention on the client's needs, a referral is in order. Whenever sexual arousal is frequent or persistent, a counselor/therapist is well advised to seek therapy him- or herself to understand the source of this feeling. In the meantime, the counselor/therapist should accept only those clients with whom sexual arousal is unlikely to occur. Again, Rodolfa's findings highlight the importance of this recommendation: Of the psychologists sampled, 43% believed that their sexual attraction to a client had negatively affected therapy.

Other research indicates that trainees can be reluctant to discuss sexual feelings with supervisors and that they frequently misinterpret sexual attraction to clients as unethical in its own right (Housman & Stake, 1998; Ladany et al., 1996; Mehr, Ladany, & Caskie, 2010). A positive supervisory relationship can facilitate such communication (Ladany et al., 1997), but even then some trainees' misconceptions about sexual contact with clients are not remedied.

Epstein and Simon (1990) have published an exploitation index that can help mental health professionals identify early signals that they may be at risk for engaging in exploitive activities with clients or trainees. One section of this index asks the following questions:

- Do you find yourself comparing the gratifying qualities you observe in a patient with less gratifying qualities in your spouse or significant other?
- Do you feel that your patient's problem would be immeasurably helped if only he or she had a positive romantic involvement with you?
- Do you feel a sense of excitement or longing when you think of a patient or anticipate his or her visit?
- Do you take pleasure in romantic daydreams about a patient?
- When a patient has behaved seductively with you, do you experience this as a gratifying sign of your own sex appeal?
- Do you touch your patients? (Exclude handshakes.)
- Have you engaged in a personal relationship with a patient after treatment? (p. 459)

If sexual attraction prompts a professional to seek consultation or therapy, or to refer a client to another counselor, that professional may wonder whether the attraction ought to be disclosed to the client. After all, the client may notice that something is different or may wonder about what motivated the recommendation to refer. The professional in this situation must weigh the client's interest in disclosure against the potential for that information to cause harm or impede therapeutic progress. The nature of the transference, the client's distress, and the power of the professional make such a disclosure risky and potentially quite harmful. This revelation would probably draw attention away from the client's concerns. Only 5% to 10% of those who have experienced a sexual attraction have disclosed this feeling to the client, and most professionals refrained not only for personal reasons but also because they believed this type of therapist self disclosure to be inherently unethical (Fisher, 2004). Pope et al. (1993) have published a very useful book to help counselors and therapists understand their sexual feelings and manage them appropriately in professional settings.

What should professionals who have experienced sexual feelings for a client do when that client discloses a sexual attraction to them? Generally, the literature cautions against revealing the feeling, even if there is no intention to act on it (Pope et al., 1993). Almost 80% of psychologists and 83% of counselors view such a disclosure as unethical in itself (Gibson & Pope, 1993; Neukrug & Milliken, 2011; Pope et al., 1987). Some research supports this position. Using an analogue study with taped, scripted counseling simulations, Goodyear and Shumate (1996) found that mental health professionals judged therapists who disclosed their sexual attraction to a client as less therapeutic and less expert than those who held their reactions to themselves. This negative evaluation occurred even though the therapist in the simulation made it clear that he or she would not act on the felt attraction. Goodyear and Shumate seem to capture the sentiment of most professionals when they state that client expressions of attraction ought to be handled as manifestations of the client's distress rather than true romantic interest (p. 614). Of course, refraining from such disclosures does not mean that a client's expression of attraction should be ignored; rather, it should be addressed as a representation of the problem that provoked him or her to enter counseling. Clients should also be told that such feelings happen sometimes in the course of an intense therapeutic relationship. Hartl et al. (2007) present an excellent set of recommendations for handling clients' transference feelings and unintentional and intentional sexual overtures.

THE PLACE OF NONEROTIC TOUCH IN THIS CONTEXT

The issue of whether counselors should ever touch adult clients in counseling and therapy, even if the touch is meant to be nonerotic, has always been controversial (Durana, 1998; Phelan, 2009). Nonerotic touch includes such things as a handshake; a touch on the hand, arm, or shoulder; a hug; or other brief physical contact. In most cultures, a kiss does not seem to fit in this category (Stake & Oliver, 1991). On one side of the issue are those who view touch as a forbidden behavior that interferes with therapeutic progress, confuses clients, and risks the generation of overtly sexual feelings in both parties (Menninger, 1958; Wolberg, 1967). Wolberg called physical contact "an absolute taboo" (1967, p. 606). Interestingly, though, Freud used touch with his patients for some time but then came to reject its use quite vehemently (Kertay & Reviere, 1993). This strong rejection of touch has been based on the concepts of transference and clear boundaries between the roles of the client and the therapist. Touching a client, some argue, can blur the boundaries and encourage the participants to view the relationship more as a personal than a professional contact (e.g., Guntheil & Gabbard, 1993). Other therapists have taken the opposite view, believing that touch is valuable in engaging clients in the therapeutic process and promoting therapeutic change (e.g., see Levy, 1973; Smith, Clance, & Imes, 1998; Hunter & Struve, 1998). These professionals point to the evidence that human touch is essential to development in children (e.g., see Bowlby, 1951; Harlow, 1971) and to the common belief that a judicious use of touch may reassure or console a client in a way that verbal communication cannot. In fact, most therapists do have nonerotic physical contact with clients though handshakes and other socially accepted actions at least on occasion, and few evaluate that practice as unethical or untherapeutic (Nigro, 2004a; Neukrug & Milliken, 2011; Pope et al., 1987; Stake & Oliver, 1991; Stenzel & Rupert, 2004). Surveys by Pope et al. (1987) and Tirnauer, Smith, and Foster (1996) found that at least 85% of therapists used touch with clients. Some research suggests that the highest frequency of physical contact occurs between male professionals and female clients, with the male professionals initiating the contact (Holub & Lee, 1990). This finding, coupled with the evidence of higher levels of sexual contact by male therapists, has led some writers to be concerned about a *slippery slope* phenomenon, in which nonerotic touch can be a first step toward sexual contact (Guntheil & Gabbard, 1993; Holroyd & Brodsky, 1980). Recent research, however, suggests that same-gender touch is more frequent than cross-gender touch except when the touch is an expression of the relationship (Stenzel & Rupert, 2004). It is important to note that therapists who use touch are not more vulnerable to sexual misconduct than those who do not use touch (Pope, 1990b). Still, whenever professionals feel sexually attracted toward their clients, they should at that time avoid even nonerotic touch (Kertay & Reviere, 1993).

None of the ethics codes prohibit nonerotic contact with clients—in fact none except for the NASW Code (Section 1.10) mention it in any way. This section prohibits physical contact if there is a possibility of psychological harm.

What are the criteria for nonerotic contact with an adult client? How does a professional evaluate the benefit or harm from such contact? A definitive answer to this question awaits rigorous research on the subject, but several reasonable recommendations can be made. First, a professional must be clear about his or her motivation for touch. Professionals who explain their approach with comments such as "I'm just a touchy-feely sort of person" have not sufficiently examined their motivation or the need to modify personal habits to meet client needs and achieve therapeutic goals. In making such comments, professionals are implying that their own need to touch is more important than their clients' needs. Bacorn and Dixon (1984) hypothesized that counselors may sometimes touch clients to relieve their own anxiety in the face of the emotions clients express. Psychoanalytic therapists wonder if the urge to touch is based in unresolved personal issues or a need to be seen as an expert or loved person by the client. When practitioners are feeling strong countertransference, they ought to be especially cautious about touch, as those feelings may signal a risk of attending more to the counselors' personal needs than to the client's welfare. Such feelings can blur professional boundaries even when touch does not occur, but touching may accelerate that process. Minter and Struve (1998) also suggest that touch should also be avoided when the content of the session has focused on sexual matters, when a client has poor impulse control, and when the touch appears to function as a replacement for talk therapy. Other authors, such as Corey, Corey, and Callahan (2015), suggest that counselors should avoid touch if the behavior is not congruent with their feelings or they feel uncomfortable with it. Of course, genuineness of feeling is not the only criterion that should be used. After all, professionals can be sincerely wrong or misguided in their feelings.

Those who find they have a pattern of differentially touching male and female clients must also examine their motivation for touching. A differential pattern based on gender alone has been called sexist (Holroyd & Brodsky, 1980) and may signal that the counselor is not as attuned as required to the client's needs. Alyn (1988) argued that even if touch is not interpreted in sexual terms by females touched by male therapists, its use by these men can contribute to feelings of disempowerment in female clients.

The decision about whether to touch an adult client must also be grounded in an understanding of cultural and social issues. Touching has highly variable meanings in different cultures, and it is easy for an uninformed counselor to violate cultural norms. For example, Orthodox Jews would likely see any touch by a person of the opposite gender as inappropriate. Among other cultural groups, kissing on both cheeks is as universal and nonerotic a greeting as a handshake. Any decision to touch a client must therefore take into account the client's cultural definitions of touch. Social psychology also teaches us that the privilege of touching is based on socioeconomic status. A higher-status person has greater freedom to touch than does a person of lower status. Thus, a professional has more liberty to touch a client than a client has to touch the professional. Similarly, a professor has greater privilege than a student. Consequently, touching without regard for its roots in the counselor's power can be an abuse of that power.

Geib (1982) hypothesizes about the factors associated with a positive interpretation of touching. Geib identifies five factors:

- Clarity regarding touch, sexual feelings, and boundaries of therapy
- Client control in initiating and sustaining contact
- Congruence between the closeness in the relationship and the use of touch
- Client belief that the touch is for his or her benefit rather than the therapist's
- A match between the client's expectations for therapy and his or her experience of the therapist

In their research, Horton, Clance, Sterk-Elifson, and Emshoff (1995) also found that the strength of the therapeutic alliance is related to a positive interpretation of touch in therapy.

Client characteristics and experiences ought to weigh heavily in the decision about whether touch is therapeutically appropriate. Willison and Masson (1986) recommend avoiding touch if it creates discomfort in the client. Research shows that some clients have had prior experiences of sexual abuse and harassment, and these people may have difficulty with a therapist's use of touch. They may misinterpret it or be distracted from their therapeutic issues by it (Vasquez, 1988). Other clients dislike touch, either because of family history, individual experience, or the psychological issues that prompted them to enter counseling. For example, a client who has an obsessive-compulsive fear of germs may be overwhelmed by a clinician's touch. Physical contact early in the process may even cause such a client to drop out rather than risk another touch. Even for clients whose backgrounds and experiences do not rule out touch, professionals must accurately assess their readiness for touch (Durana, 1998). Readiness is related, of course, to the strength of the therapeutic alliance. Kertay and Reviere (1993) recommend discussing with a client the role of nonerotic touch in counseling. As a general guideline, they suggest asking permission before physical contact occurs, though Stenzel and Rupert (2004) found that few professionals discussed the contact prior to its occurrence. This recommendation seems especially prudent before the first time a counselor believes that physical contact may be therapeutic. Scholars who take a risk management perspective recommend analyzing the risk a client with long-standing psychopathology and relationship difficulties represents—the risk of misunderstanding the motivation of a therapist touch that results in a therapeutic rupture or punitive action against the professional (Bennett et al., 2006).

In short, all these factors should lead a mental health professional to be cautious about the use of touch. Some writers suggest completely abstaining from touch except for handshakes, but most agree to a judicious use of touch. Under the right circumstances, touch can be reassuring and therapeutically useful. In their study, Horton et al. (1995) found that clients were very positive about nonerotic touch, and many viewed the physical contact as especially important in resolving their problems. One study does not lead to any definitive conclusions, of course, but wisely and prudently used, touch may be therapeutic. At the same time, counselors and therapists ought to learn a whole repertoire of behaviors for demonstrating emotional connections with clients so that they can adapt their response to the needs of the individual client. If they decide to touch clients, the burden is on them to demonstrate that the touch served the needs of the client, not their own.

The topic of nonerotic touch is more complicated when providing counseling or psychotherapy for children because touch is normative in young children (McNeil-Haber, 2004). They initiate it for both appropriate reasons and ways (such as showing pleasure with another's actions by hugging) and inappropriate reasons (such as showing anger by hitting). Indeed, the few studies that have been conducted show that nonerotic touch is common during child counseling (Cowen, Weissberg, & Lotyczewski, 1983; Rae & Worchel, 1991), with approximately 40% of the therapists in these studies indicating that they hug child clients frequently. At other times, professionals must touch clients to keep them safe from injury or to prevent injury to themselves from hitting. Obviously, in those situations touching is entirely within ethical bounds—indeed the failure to hold a child's arm back before he or she hits another or strikes at a glass partition could be viewed as inherently unethical. When deciding whether touch is appropriate with children in less extreme circumstances, child therapists must take into account the child's age and maturity, cultural background, diagnosis and history, parental preferences, and the capacity of the child to verbalize his or her needs and preferences. Some institutions and schools have instituted "no touch" policies that must also be considered. Restraint from touch and consultation are prudent approaches when in doubt. (For an excellent discussion of the ethical issues related to touching children, see McNeil-Haber, 2004.)

PROVIDING EFFECTIVE SUBSEQUENT THERAPY FOR VICTIMS

Research shows that between 22 and 65% of professionals will see clients who report that former therapists sexualized their relationship (Pope & Vetter, 1991; Stake & Oliver, 1991; Wincze et al., 1996). Effective treatment for such clients requires expert and diligent treatment (Pope, 1994; Sonne, 1987). Therapists who seek to provide competent service to these clients should familiarize themselves with the research on the topic, get qualified supervision, and be prepared to have an emotional reaction to the information the client is disclosing. Sonne and Pope (1991) caution therapists that when they first hear of this exploitation, they may experience disbelief, denial, or minimization of the harm done. They may even be tempted to blame the victim or may experience sexual reactions to the material being revealed. Wohlberg (2000) reported that clients seeking therapy after sexual involvement with a prior therapist often feel revictimized by professionals who discount, minimize, blame, or react with inappropriate emotion. It is difficult to hear that fellow professionals have behaved in such destructive, self-serving ways. The kind of open, compassionate, empathic response that a mental health professional would give in any other highly personal disclosure is essential here, too. If a professional doubts that he or she is competent to provide this service, then a referral is appropriate. The article published by the APA Committee on Women in Psychology (1989), *If Sex Enters into the Psychotherapy Relationship,* is an important document to share with clients who reveal such a history. It is written for consumers to help them understand why the profession regards sexual contact as unethical and provides them with options to address their reactions, including ways to file a claim against the offender. If a client wishes to pursue a complaint against a former therapist, the current clinician should provide information about the process and to give the client the option to discuss, in subsequent sessions, feelings and reactions to pursuing a complaint. This document also has obvious use as part of an informed consent process for all clients. Both consumers and therapists support its value in that application (Thorn, Shealy, & Briggs, 1993). The California Board of Psychology has written its own brochure on sexual contact with a therapist and its regulations require that any psychologist whose client discloses sexual contact with a prior therapist provide that brochure to the client (see http://www.dca.ca.gov/publications/proftherapy.shtml).

Wohlberg (2000) cautions professionals not to pressure clients into taking action against the offending therapist, because clients may feel interrogated and unsupported. Remley & Herlihy (2013) name this overzealous effort to get the client to file a complaint as *intrusive advocacy*. Clients should also be informed about the Therapist Exploitation Link Line (TELL) as another resource for support for them in their recovery (http://www.therapyabuse.org/about_us.htm).

CASES REEXAMINED

The Case of Olga and Manuel

The first step in answering this question is to evaluate the facts of the situation as written. Manuel was not diagnosed with a mental or emotional disorder at the time of counseling, and the majority of his problems were attributable to medical rather than psychological issues. Three sessions were held in which the counselor first ruled out the existence of a depressive disorder and then focused attention on bolstering the client's coping skills for work stress and responsibilities for aging parents. By the third session, the client reported improvement in coping skills, happiness that his other problems were relieved by changes in his medical treatment, and gratitude to the counselor for her assistance. Counseling terminated, the counselor reported the case as closed, and no contact occurred for five years. The initial meeting after those three years was accidental, at a community event, and the client, not the counselor, asked for the date. The client reports good functioning in the intervening period.

The case description presents no information about the nature of the emotional ties or transference that occurred during the three sessions, nor does it indicate whether either party felt sexually attracted to the other while counseling was taking place.

When the standards in the ACA Code are applied, the following conclusions seem valid:

- More than five years have elapsed since termination.
- Counseling was of short duration.
- Termination seemed to be desirable to both parties and appropriate insofar as the client did not again seek counseling from Olga or anyone else.
- The client did not suffer from significant psychological problems at the time of counseling and did not admit any current psychological issues in his accidental meeting with the counselor, although when he made the counseling appointment, he was worried that he suffered from a serious mental illness.
- There is no evidence that the counselor initiated this personal contact with her former client.

Thus far, the contact seems to fit within the boundaries allowed by the rule. However, some important questions remain unanswered:

- What is the risk of an adverse impact of a dating relationship on the client?
- What was the nature of the emotional connection or transference between Manuel and Olga at the time of counseling?
- Did either party fantasize about a personal or sexual relationship while counseling was ongoing? If so, to what degree might this experience have affected the material disclosed by the client or the diagnosis assigned by the counselor?
- Does Olga practice in a state that has regulations that ban post-termination relationships under all circumstances?

In the absence of answers to these questions, one cannot decide if this contact would be permissible. Moreover, even if these questions were resolved in the most positive way possible, a prudent counselor would agree to a social relationship only after clear and frank discussions of the possible problems that might arise in a post-termination relationship. The first such conversation should take place with a supervisor or trusted colleague who can more objectively evaluate Olga's motivation. If colleagues fail to agree that this contact fits the criteria, Olga would be wise to refuse the invitation, at least for some time. The counselor should also consult with experts in the field who have differing views about the advisability of post-termination contact by reading their writings and judging the merit of their arguments in her case. If colleagues conclude that the situation meets the criteria set forth in the Code, and Olga believes she has satisfactory responses to criticisms of this kind of contact, she should give herself a little more time to be clear about her decision. After all, there is no time limit to decision making in this case. (Given the possibility of a messy ending to a personal relationship in this circumstance, Olga may want to consult her attorney as well.)

If at that point she still wishes to go forward, her second discussion should be with Manuel, before accepting or rejecting the invitation. At the end of that discussion, both the client and the counselor should understand that any future professional relationship between them would be completely ruled out. Even with this understanding, both should realize that their history will likely impose other complications on their personal relationship, with which they will need to cope. Moreover, as the relationship continues, Olga should meet regularly with a colleague to discuss any issues that develop relative to her professional history with Manuel. Manuel may be well served by a referral to another mental health professional for the same kind of discussion if he wishes it.

This case highlights both the burden that is placed on a mental health professional when trying to decide what is ethical and the crucial importance of continuing to place the welfare of the client over one's personal needs or desires.

The Case of Isabelle and Yoritomo

Isabelle, a graduate student in counseling psychology, enrolls in a course in substance abuse counseling as an elective. The course is taught by Yoritomo, an adjunct faculty member with an active private practice in the community. About 10 weeks into the semester, Isabelle approaches Yoritomo after class, seeking additional readings on substance abuse educational programs for teenagers. They discuss the topic at length, and they meet a few times after that in Yoritomo's office to talk over the readings. When Isabelle is turning in her final examination, Yoritomo asks her to come to his office in a few minutes. At that time, he suggests that they continue to meet to discuss this issue and to get to know each other better. In an offhand way, he suggests that perhaps they could have dinner together sometime. Isabelle hears in his comments an invitation to a dating relationship. If her assessment of the professor's interest is correct, did Yoritomo act unethically?

A review of the facts of the situation reveals that:

- An adjunct faculty member has asked a counseling student enrolled in his course to have dinner with him sometime.
- The invitation comes as the student is submitting her final examination and subsequent to several professional conversations related to the content of the course.
- The student's interest in pursuing a dating relationship with the instructor is unknown, as is her emotional reaction to his suggestion, but her interest in the subject matter he teaches is substantial.

The ACA ethics code prohibits sexual relationships with students, sexual harassment of students, and exploitive relationships with students (see Sections F.10.a and F.10.c in Appendix A, pp. 521, 522). If Yoritomo was asking Isabelle for a date before completing his instructional control, then he was violating this standard. He had not yet graded that final exam, nor had he determined the course grade. Did he ask at this time because he knew (at least unconsciously) that he had more power and that Isabelle might be more agreeable to a dinner together while he was still her instructor? If so, that means he attempted to exploit his professional position to get what he wanted from this student. Even if he intended to keep the grading completely separate from her answer to his question, his objectivity in evaluating this student's work is also likely to be compromised. Is that fair to her or to the other students in the course?

From Isabelle's perspective, she may feel trapped and be worrying about the implications of a refusal on her grade in the course. She also may have wished to continue her professional contacts with Yoritomo as she began to apply the content from his course to her work in the schools. She may wonder if the date is the "quid pro quo" for that continuing professional advice. If so, this behavior fits the definition of exploitation and sexual harassment. Similarly, she may have been considering asking him for a recommendation for doctoral programs if she did well on her final, an option that would be eliminated if she agreed to a date. She may also feel uncomfortable discussing a romantic relationship with a faculty member with friends who are also students in the program. In short, Isabelle is not in a position to make a free consent or refusal to his request.

Even if Yoritomo's intentions were entirely honorable, his request was unethical because he insensitively placed the student in an embarrassing and stressful position in which the lines between a professional and personal relationship were blurred. If he wanted to communicate to Isabelle a willingness to continue his assistance to her in her work at school, he had other options. He might have called her or sent her a note after course grades were submitted.

If Yoritomo had waited one month after the termination of the course to invite Isabelle to dinner, the ethics codes give less clear guidelines. They do not prohibit post-termination sex with students. The judgment in this case is based on the likelihood that his evaluative role will continue in some way, so that Isabelle's freedom to consent or refuse is jeopardized. Full-time faculty are likely to continue in some sort of evaluative role, whether to teach other courses to the same students, to be involved in placement or scholarship decisions, or to decide whether students are admitted to advanced graduate study. Yoritomo's status as an adjunct faculty member makes it possible that he could have no further evaluative role with students after they finish his course. That may remove one aspect of the ethics problem. However, if Yoritomo uses his course as a way to fill his social calendar, then his intent is exploitive and waiting a short time until grades are submitted does not eliminate the ethics problem with dating former students. In this as in all cases, the welfare of the population served must be the first consideration.

Ironically, the language in the ACA Code, Section F.10.c, does not actually caution against a faculty–former student relationship in any way. It cautions faculty to be aware of the power differential and discuss risks with former students prior to any such intimate relationship. However, its intent appears to be to avoid exploitation, harm, and misunderstandings with former students.

SUMMARY

Sexual exploitation of clients by therapists is a blatantly unethical practice, as is sexual contact with students, employees, supervisees, research participants, and others for whom the professional has responsibility. Sexual contact with former clients is always prohibited for at least two years after the termination of therapy. Even after two years, sexual contact is permitted only in the most unusual circumstances and only in some professions. The codes do not directly address the issue of sexual contact after teaching or supervision responsibilities have ended, but in these cases professionals must demonstrate that the supervisory responsibilities have truly ceased. Moreover, they must be able to show that the sexual contact is nonexploitive.

Sexualized relationships with clients have been widely studied, and the results show clear evidence of sexual exploitation by professionals. Up to 12% of therapists have admitted sexual contact with current and former clients, and some have acknowledged multiple contacts. Since this research relies on the willingness of professionals and clients to disclose such events in therapy, the reliability of that figure is probably not high. In any case, surveys of mental health professionals have found that approximately half of those sampled have seen at least one client who reports an experience of sexual exploitation by a former therapist. A similar percentage of faculty and supervisors have admitted the same misconduct. The only demographic variables associated with this violation are gender and, to a lesser degree, age. Older male therapists and faculty are more likely to engage in this behavior than younger or female therapists. Victims, on the other hand, are more likely to be female and younger than the therapist. Children as well as adults have become victims of sexual exploitation by therapists. Research has shown that sexual misconduct inflicts serious and long-lasting psychological damage on victims. In fact, that damage has been compared to the effects of rape or incest.

Sexual misconduct needs to be distinguished from experiences of sexual arousal. A great majority of counselors and therapists report having been sexually attracted to a client on occasion. The experience of attraction is not unethical in itself as long as it is handled responsibly. The counselor has the duty to monitor his or her behavior so that the attraction does not distract the client from the therapeutic focus of the session and does not prevent the counselor from providing competent service. Consultation and supervision are also advised when an attraction occurs.

Given this context, it is not surprising that the use of nonerotic touch as a therapeutic approach is controversial. Some call it taboo; others view it as an appropriate tool if used wisely. All professionals regard nonerotic touch as inappropriate if it serves the professional's needs over the client's or is insensitive to cultural, social, or gender considerations.

Discussion Questions*

1. Given the contents of the codes of ethics, how would you evaluate the ethics of a sexual relationship between a child counselor and the parent of one of her clients? Would sexual contact several months after termination be considered ethical?
2. What is your analysis of the debate on the two-year or five-year rule for post-termination sexual contact with clients? Which approach seems more prudent? If you sat on the committee assigned to write the next revision of the Code, what position would you take? Would you advise the APA to take this stance as well?
3. Professional associations seem caught between their commitment to protect the public from exploitive therapists and their obligation to promote the good image of the profession. Some criticize these organizations for being too passive about the dangers and lenient with offenders, and others argue that so much attention paid to the problems of a small number of practitioners gives the misimpression that all members act exploitively. What do you think the proper role of the professional association is in dealing with a serious ethical problem such as sexual misconduct?

---

*Note to course instructors: The *Instructor's Guide* for this book includes other discussion questions, class exercises, cases, and multiple-choice and essay test items for this chapter.

4. Do you think the codes of ethics ought to address sexual relationships with former students, supervisees, employees, or research participants? Why or why not?

Cases for Discussion

Benjamin, a clinical counselor in an outpatient unit of a general hospital, is about to meet a new client for an intake interview. He does not recognize the name of the person written on his calendar, but when he goes to the reception room to greet the new client, he sees a familiar face. Marcia is a woman whom he dated 20 years ago. Two years after their relationship ended, Marcia married someone else, and Benjamin started graduate school. Marcia has now been divorced for several years. She chose Benjamin for therapy for her depression because others recommended him and because she believed she could trust him with her problems. Benjamin tells Marcia that he is flattered that she still thinks so highly of him, but he must decline to accept her as a client. He goes on to explain that he does not believe he should provide counseling to someone with whom he once had a close relationship, even if it was many years ago. Marcia is upset by his refusal to see her and calls Benjamin's interpretation of ethics insensitive, legalistic, and uncaring. She storms out of his office, determined to try and cope with her problems on her own. Benjamin sends Marcia a letter in which he apologizes for upsetting her and tries to explain his views more fully. In that letter, he also gives her the names of three other clinicians whom he recommends. Did Benjamin act ethically? How do you respond to Marcia's comment that his view is "legalistic"? At this stage, is there anything else he ought to do about the situation?

Recommended Readings

Anonymous. (1991). Sexual harassment: A female counseling student's experience. *Journal of Counseling & Development*, *69*, 502–506.

Bartell, P. A., & Rubin, L. J. (1990). Dangerous liaisons: Sexual intimacies in supervision. *Professional Psychology: Research and Practice*, *21*, 442–450.

Bates, C. M., & Brodsky, A. M. (1989). *Sex in the therapy hour: A case of professional incest*. New York, NY: Guilford.

Gabbard, G. O. (Ed.). (1989). *Sexual exploitation in professional relationships*. Washington, D.C.: American Psychiatric Press.

Gutheil, T. G., & Brodsky, A. (2008). *Preventing boundary violations in clinical practice*. New York, NY: Guilford.

Hartl, T. L., Zeiss, R. A., Marino, C. M., Zeiss, A. M., Regey, L. G., & Leontis, C. (2007). Clients' sexually inappropriate behaviors directed towards clinicians: Conceptualization and management. *Professional Psychology: Research and Practice*, *38*, 674–681.

McNeil-Haber, F. M. (2004). Ethical considerations in the use of nonerotic touch in psychotherapy with children. *Ethics & Behavior*, *14*, 123–140.

Phelan, J. E. (2009). Exploring the use of touch in the psychotherapeutic setting: A phenomenological review. *Psychotherapy: Theory, Research, Practice, Training*, *46*, 97–111.

Pope, K. S. (1994). *Sexual involvement with therapists: Patient assessment, subsequent therapy, forensics*. Washington, D.C.: American Psychological Association.

Pope, K. S., Sonne, J. L., & Holroyd, J. (1993). *Sexual feelings in psychotherapy: Explorations for therapists and therapists-in-training*. Washington, D.C.: American Psychological Association.

Shavit, N. (2005). Sexual contact between psychologists and patients. *Journal of Aggression, Maltreatment, and Trauma*, *11*, 205–239.

Sonne, J. L., & Jochai, D. (2014). The "vissicitudes of love" between therapist and patient: A review of the research on romantic and sexual feelings, thoughts, and behaviors in psychotherapy. *Journal of Clinical Psychology*, 70, 182–195.

Zur, O. (2007). *Boundaries in psychotherapy: Clinical and ethical explorations*. Washington, D.C.: American Psychological Association.

Additional Online Resources

Advocate Web: http://www.advocateweb.org.

Sexual Issues in Psychology Training & Practice: http://kspope.com/sexiss/index.php.

Therapist Exploitation Link Line: http://www.therapyabuse.org/.

CHAPTER 8 Nonsexual Multiple Relationships and Boundary Issues

Risking Objectivity and Client Welfare

Consider whether the professionals acted ethically in the following situations:

Alberto and Peter

Alberto, a psychologist, is married to Sandra, a software engineer for a small company. Peter is Sandra's boss. Peter asks Sandra if Alberto can counsel his 16-year-old son, who has been suffering from panic attacks. Alberto is well known in the community for his skill in counseling people with anxiety disorders. Alberto phones Peter and suggests that the family come in for a consultation the next day.

Dominique and Roberta

Roberta, a neurosurgeon and client of Dominique, a grief counselor, comes to the final session of their counseling relationship with a gift for Dominique. Roberta says she wants to show her appreciation for all the help and support Dominique provided while Roberta was coping with the sudden death of her child in a car accident. The gift—a subscription to the next season of the most prominent theater company in the region—is valued at several hundred dollars. Dominique decides to accept the gift, even though she usually refuses expensive gifts from her clients. Dominique has reasoned that for someone in Roberta's position, a gift of a few hundred dollars represents a token, such as a flower or paperback book may represent a token from a college student client.

Roxanne and Li Qing

Li Qing, who has been going to counseling for shyness and social withdrawal, decides to take action to become more social, so she attends a church service one morning. Soon thereafter, she decides to join the congregation. Because her counselor, Roxanne, was out of town the weekends her client attends services, Li Qing does not know that Roxanne belongs to that church. When the client tells Roxanne that she has decided to join a church, the counselor discloses the coincidence of church membership and asks Li Qing to describe her feelings about it. The counselor decides to continue seeing the client, even though they will be members of the same church.

Olive and Dave

Olive is a psychologist in private practice. Olive's husband, Dave, is considering opening a fast-food restaurant. As they discuss the business opportunity, she learns that the regional representative from the fast-food chain is a former client who terminated therapy eight months ago. The client had received treatment for a major depressive episode. If Olive's husband goes forward with this restaurant, he will have ongoing contact with this former client of his wife. Olive asks Dave to investigate other franchise opportunities, saying that her past professional connections with the representative could make the arrangement awkward for everyone. Reluctantly, her husband agrees.

Theodore and Mr. Goodheart

Theodore is attending an open house at his child's elementary school. The child's teacher, Mr. Goodheart, approaches Theodore because he knows that Theodore is a licensed mental health counselor. Mr. Goodheart asks if Theodore has room in his schedule for a good friend of his who is anxious and depressed. The counselor gives Mr. Goodheart his card and tells the teacher to have his friend call to arrange an appointment.

Wilma and Keisha

Wilma is a licensed clinical social worker. Wilma's former client, Keisha, operates a private college admissions advising service. This client works with high school students and their families to help them with the college application process and with securing financial aid. Wilma has twins in their senior year of high school. When the two accidentally meet one Saturday at the post office, Wilma wonders whether Keisha could help her sort through the maze of college applications for her daughters. The next day, Wilma telephones Keisha and asks for an appointment for herself and the twins. In all, they have three meetings, for which Wilma pays the standard fee. At termination, Wilma and her daughters express satisfaction with the services they received.

Nadine and Gerhard

Gerhard, a stock broker and former client who terminated therapy with Nadine three years ago, calls Nadine to ask if she is interested in an investment opportunity. Nadine, a counseling psychologist nearing retirement, does some research and learns that it is a legitimate investment opportunity with potential for a substantial return. Nadine also knows from her therapeutic contact with Gerhard that he is scrupulously honest and probably highly competent in his work. Nadine suggests a meeting to discuss specifics. After several more meetings, she invests $10,000 in the business.

Oscar and Janine

Each week Oscar, a family therapist, goes to the local bakery for bread. He establishes a friendly relationship with Janine, the young person behind the counter. On various occasions, Janine has seen Oscar with his spouse, his children, and his parents. One day, Janine's name appears on Oscar's appointment calendar for a counseling session for relationship problems. The doctor learns from the secretary that when Janine made the appointment, she asked to see him in particular. Oscar is pleased that the person sought him out, and looks forward to a productive professional relationship.

Robin and Jon

Robin is a counseling psychologist with a private practice. Jon, a therapist in town with whom Robin has been acquainted for 10 years, requests that Robin see him as a client. The two have served together on the ethics committee of the state psychological association. Jon's sister was killed in a terrorist bombing, and he believes he is now suffering from post-traumatic stress. He is adamant that he wants to see Robin and not another therapist because he trusts her clinical judgment more than anyone else locally. Robin schedules an initial appointment that afternoon.

Benny and Jefferson

Benny has been Jefferson's therapist for eight months. Jefferson began therapy after his partner died in a fire at their home. Jefferson's family refused all contact with him years ago, when Jefferson told them he is gay. Since Jefferson has no family with whom he can spend the holidays, and since he has worked so hard to deal effectively with his grief and loneliness, Benny decides to invite Jefferson to share Christmas dinner with him and his wife at his home. Jefferson accepts.

What are your intuitions about the ethics of each situation? Do some seem more problematic than others? Do some seem acceptable, with no clear ethical dimensions at all? Are some difficult to evaluate without more information? The focus of this chapter is the issue of secondary connections with those with whom we have a professional role (sexual relationships with current and former clients were discussed in Chapter 7). The chapter begins by defining terms and proceeds to review the ethical standards and the rationale for those standards, including research on practitioners' beliefs and practices about this topic. Next it presents a set of questions practitioners should ask themselves when considering whether to become involved in a secondary relationship with a current or former client or whether to begin a professional relationship with someone with whom they have a personal connection. The chapter concludes by discussing the ethics of receiving gifts from clients, managing secondary contacts with clients in rural and small community settings, and engaging in barter with clients—the practice of trading goods and services instead of money for counseling.

DEFINITION OF TERMS

Whenever mental health professionals have connections with a client in addition to the therapist–client relationship, a secondary relationship exists. A number of different terms exist for this situation. For many years, the term *dual relationship* was used to explain such overlapping connections, but that term has fallen out of favor and is no longer contained in current ethics codes, at least partly because of its lack of explanatory value (Cottone, 2005). The counseling and psychology professions now use the term *boundary extension* or the designation *multiple relationship* for such an occurrence. In each of the cases just described, some level of additional professional–client relationship has been established or has the potential to exist.

Three other terms appear frequently in the mental health lexicon: *boundary crossings*, *boundary extensions* and *boundary violations* (Gutheil & Gabbard, 1993). These are grounded in the notion that there should be a division, a boundary, between the professional and personal lives of professional and client. This division fosters a more productive therapeutic process by increasing the likelihood that the professional has the objectivity needed to understand and treat the client's concerns and that the client has sufficient trust in the good will and altruistic motives of the therapist to share personal information and work through uncomfortable issues (Gabbard, 1994; Sommers-Flanagan, 2012; Sommers-Flanagan, Elliott, & Sommers-Flanagan, 1998). In other words, boundaries provide structure for the process, safety for the client, and the required emotional distance for effective therapeutic work (Gabbard, 1994; Sommers-Flanagan et al., 1998). Remley and Herlihy (2013) use the term *boundary crossing* to describe the kind of additional connection with a client that is grounded in the intent to help and has some credible evidence that benefit is likely to result. Sommers-Flanagan et al. (1998) also underscore the importance of evidence of benefit to the client and the risk inherent in any such extension, stating "[T]he fact that a therapist believes a boundary extension is therapeutically justified or nonharmful to the client does not make it so" (p. 40). The term *extension* seems preferable to *crossing* since it acknowledges that a clear boundary still exists, just in a different place. It is important to note, though, that a professional's ability to accurately predict whether an extension will really result in a good outcome is limited (Koocher & Keith-Spiegel, 2008).

A *boundary violation* or *boundary break* is a departure from accepted practice that causes the client harm or is very likely to cause harm. Implicit in this definition is the notion that the harm probably could (and should) have been anticipated if the professional either had more altruistic intent or was more rigorous in analyzing the risks and merits of the action before it was undertaken. Boundary violations often occur when professionals are too compromised to function competently, too impulsive, or too self-interested to attend to the effects of violations on clients. Boundary violations are never ethical. A recent court case in Minnesota illustrates an extreme nonsexual boundary violation in which a psychotherapist borrowed more than $100,000 from her client (Stodghill, 2011).

None of these terms represents a perfect description of the complexity of the relationships between clients and mental health professionals. As Austin, Bergum, Nuttgens, and Peternelj-Taylor (2006) point out, the metaphor of a boundary seems to suggest a clear line in the sand that cannot always be drawn or applied rigidly to each situation. The reality is that boundaries may be permeable in some circumstances—the challenge for the professional is to make responsible decisions about which circumstances merit relaxation of the usual parameters of the contact.

Sonne (1994) clarifies that multiple relationships can be either concurrent with the professional relationship or consecutive. If consecutive, the therapeutic role may precede or follow the other role. Because counselors and therapists function in a variety of roles in their professional and personal lives, the possibility of a multiple relationship is always present. The following list shows examples of multiple relationships.

Concurrent	Consecutive
Professional and personal (researcher and friend)	Professional, then personal (therapist, 2004–2005; business partner, 2007–2009)
Professional and professional (supervisor and counselor)	Professional, then professional (professor, 2000–2004; therapist, 2008–2009)
Multiple professional (employer, clinical supervisor, and clinician)	Co-worker, 2008; clinical supervisor, 2010–2011; therapist, 2014
Personal, then professional	Friend since college, 15 years; marriage counselor in 16th year

The debate about the conditions under which boundary extensions may be ethical has been one of the most energetic in the profession in recent years. Even ethics scholars who concur on the risks inherent in many kinds of boundary extensions do not advocate a universal ban on them and acknowledge the complexity of the issue (such as Kitchener, 1988; Koocher & Keith-Spiegel, 2008; Younggren & Gottlieb, 2004). Others argue that the professional associations and licensing boards have encouraged an unproductive interpretation of ethical standards that at times has prevented professionals from extending boundaries in ways likely to be helpful to clients (Campbell & Gordon, 2003; Lazarus & Zur, 2002; Moleski & Kiselica, 2005). All sources recognize that some extensions result from accidental contacts, and others are extremely difficult to avoid without denying clients access to services. Essentially, the major risks of concurrent or consecutive multiple relationships are that the existence of the connection outside of therapy will compromise both the judgment of the professional and the response of the client to treatment. The relaxation of boundaries on one dimension also has the potential to loosen other boundaries along a "slippery slope" to unethical conduct, although few boundary extensions lead to boundary violations. Still, the majority of egregious boundary violations involving exploitation addressed by licensing boards and ethics committees also include other boundary extensions, usually initiated prior to the serious violations. For example, a professional may precede hiring a current client to work for him or her with discussing office management practices during sessions. Indeed, it is the loosening of the boundary to tap into the client's expertise in office management that leads the professional to seek to hire the client in the first place.

Kitchener (1988) and Jennings (1992) refer to the multiple-relationship problem as one of conflict in social roles because of the often incompatible claims of each role on the professional. The greater the divergence between roles, the greater is the risk of an unsatisfactory therapeutic outcome. Role differences entail different expectations for self, other, and the relationship, along with varying obligations for each party. Role differences exist along a continuum, and the risk of problems with role differences varies directly with the degree of disparity in expectations and obligations. For example, the role expectations and obligations of a spouse and a professor diverge significantly. A spouse is expected to support, assist, and be especially attentive to the partner's needs, but a professor is obliged to be objective and fair to all students, singling no one out for special treatment. Moreover, the professor's duty is to evaluate students and to give negative evaluations to those whose performance is substandard. Thus, the roles of spouse and professor are so highly contrasting that the risk of misconduct by the professional and misunderstanding by the student rises significantly if they are merged.

The case of Alberto and Peter at the beginning of the chapter is a good illustration of diverging role expectations and obligations. Examining each person's role in the scenario reveals that the roles Alberto is considering are highly incompatible. The term boundary violation applies to this scenario because Alberto's intent cannot be focused on benefitting the client to the exclusion of other concerns. The risk of harm to the son is clear and predictable on the basis of a rational analysis of the facts of the situation. It would be extremely difficult for Alberto to put aside all his loyalty obligations to his partner and attend only to the welfare of the client.

Other role expectations and obligations are more similar and involve less vulnerability to negative outcomes. Combining the roles of therapist and shopper in a supermarket in which a client works illustrates a situation with almost no potential for harm. There is no conflict between the role obligations of shopper and therapist, except in the extraordinary unlikely event that the client's knowledge of the therapist's purchasing habits and food choices poses a problem for the client's experience in therapy. Because this situation has a minimal risk of harm, the worker in the supermarket ought not to be denied the mental health service she seeks because of her outside contact with the therapist. Boundary extensions at the low end of the role difference continuum carry very little chance that they will harm either party. This is the primary reason that the professions have never banned all such overlapping relationships. The permission for this type of boundary extension depends, of course, on the professional's capacity not to act on his or her self-interest and to respect the therapeutic boundaries when at the market.

Three other factors have influenced the profession's position on this issue. First, in some forms of boundary extensions the consumer stands to benefit substantially from the extension. Returning to the case of Oscar at the beginning of the chapter, the bakery clerk's personal life may be significantly improved if she enters counseling with him. She may gain the strength to end a problematic relationship or learn how to achieve the emotional intimacy with her partner that she has been seeking. Second, avoiding all boundary extensions would place a great burden on mental health professionals and those with whom they associate. Third, repudiating such actions is inconsistent with the right to free association of citizens in a democratic society.

Still another circumstance that may make a boundary extension more ethical is the cultural background of the client. Clients from non-Western collectivist cultures may be confused and offended by rigid boundaries that fail to flex in ways typical in the client culture (Barnett, Lazarus, Vasquez, Moorehead-Slaughter, & Johnson, 2007; Herlihy & Watson, 2003). For example, such a client may view a professional's refusal to accept a sibling as an additional individual client as a hurtful and rejecting event rather than the establishment of a therapeutic boundary aimed at maintaining professional objectivity. (See Ridley, Liddle, Hill, and Li [2001] for an excellent discussion of the role of culture in navigating multiple relationship issues.)

The current language in the standards of the ACA and APA attempts to take into account such complexity, but ultimately each applies a somewhat different standard for determining the conditions under which a multiple relationship may be acceptable. The APA Code emphasizes the evaluation of the psychologist's competence and objectivity, as well as the risk of exploitation in determining whether a multiple relationship is viable (Standard 3.05, Appendix B, p. 541).

The language in the 2014 ACA Code represents a substantial revision from the prior versions (ACA, 1995, 2005). Instead of advising counselors to "make every effort to avoid multiple relationships with clients that could impair their judgment or increase the risk of harm to clients," the language in the 1995 edition, or allowing them "when the interaction is potentially beneficial" as indicated in the 2005 version, the 2014 revision focuses on a risk–benefit analysis of the boundary extension. It clarifies when it may be acceptable for a counselor to begin a professional relationship with a person whom he or she knows from another context, and places restrictions on the initiation of personal relationships with former clients. It also identifies the documentation and consultation requirements when engaging in a boundary extension. (Please read ACA Code, Section A.6.a–e, in Appendix A, pp. 495–496).

These provisions suggest a more cautious approach to extending boundaries than the provisions included in the 2005 version of the Code. The implication is that boundary extensions should be approached carefully and with deliberation, and only in circumstances in which the additional contact with the current client is both brief and superficial. In parallel fashion, the Code appears to limit the circumstances in which a counselor may begin counseling with an already known person to those who would qualify as acquaintances rather than friends or colleagues. However, the Code does not specifically prohibit boundary extensions with individuals with whom a closer prior relationship existed, nor does it forbid additional contact with a current client that is more extended than attendance at a ceremony. In other words, the Code is silent about whether a counselor may accept as a client someone whom he or she knew 10 years ago in college and with whom they were friendly. Note the language—casual, distant, *or* past relationship. It does not say casual, distant, *and* past relationships. In similar fashion, the Code does not clearly restrict more extended outside contacts or connections with current clients. For example, accepting the mother-in-law of your next door neighbor as a client would not be expressly prohibited by this language. The Code does place the burden of proof on the counselor to justify that the benefit outweighs the risk and to document consent and precautions taken to prevent harm to the client. (The Code does not prohibit unrestricted bartering of services or products either, a topic to which we will return later in this chapter.) Clearly, however, the language in the Purpose section of the Code should be noted in making decisions in this arena. It states, "Counselors actions should be consistent with the spirit as well as the letter of these ethical standards." Unfortunately, the introductory material does not have the same enforcement strength as the numbered provisions.

"Potential harm" is the criterion in ACA Section A.6.e to determine whether a nonprofessional (nonsexual) relationship with a former client or those close to them is permissible. Almost any relationship or action has the potential for harm—I can cause a serious accident unintentionally just by driving to campus—so the term *potential harm* does not offer much guidance in itself. Despite the vagueness of this term, the implication is that counselors ought to be cautious about such connections, and although this section does not directly address it, the requirement for careful risk assessment, documentation, consent, and consultation would be crucial in such a situation. For example, in the case of Wilma and Keisha, she ought to have sought out consultation prior to approaching her former client and conducted a clear risk–benefit analysis and frank discussion with Keisha about the implications of this additional contact with her.

Sonne's (1994) advice to be risk preventive when it comes to boundary extensions is helpful. Koocher and Keith-Spiegel (2008) note that when there is a benefit to the professional from an outside contact, it is inherently a high-risk situation and should be avoided. In any event, prior to initiating a boundary extension, the professional should consult with knowledgeable, objective colleagues as noted in Section C.2.e of the ACA Code, which reads, "Counselors take reasonable steps to consult with other counselors, the ACA Ethics and Professional Standards Department, or related professionals when they have questions regarding their ethical obligations or professional practice."

Two additional cases related to this provision of the ACA Code are presented below for your consideration. Each in its own way illustrates the difficulty in applying this standard and the more fundamental complexity of boundary extensions for mental health professionals.

The Case of Mary Angela

Mary Angela, a counselor with a private practice, notices a man sitting in her waiting room. She finds this man attractive, and the book he is reading on the history of the American civil rights movement is one that she too is interested in. She learns that this man has accompanied her client to the office. At the end of the next session, Mary Angela asks the client about him; the client reveals that he is an old friend of her husband's from college who was widowed last year. He came with her to the office last week because her car had broken down that morning. He happened to be visiting her husband at the time and volunteered to drive her to the appointment. The client goes on to say that she rarely has any social contact with this man. The client volunteers to arrange a meeting between the man and Mary Angela by bringing him to the office. The counselor wonders whether she can agree to this arrangement and looks to the ACA Code for guidance.

The Case of Barney Johannes

A young adult client has been seeing Dr. Barney Johannes, a career counselor, for assistance in deciding on a career path after completing an undergraduate degree in psychology. As a result of counseling, the client decides to seek a graduate degree in mental health counseling and applies to several accredited programs. This client graduates with honors and has high scores on admissions examinations. Because the young man is so talented, Dr. Johannes encourages him to apply to the university at which he teaches and volunteers to be his advisor and help him obtain financial aid. Ultimately, the young man is accepted, awarded an assistantship, and enters that program. Both the counselor and this client are happy with the outcome; however, one of Dr. Johannes' colleagues expresses concern that he crossed a boundary inappropriately when he so actively advocated for this candidate over others. Dr. Johannes immediately reads the ACA Code to determine whether there is merit to the colleague's concern.

The 2010 APA Code also discourages multiple relationships, indicating that psychologists should "refrain from" such relationships if negative outcomes might reasonably be predicted. However, it places more emphasis on the impact of the multiple relationship on the psychologist in determining the ethics of the secondary contact. The standards require psychologists to evaluate whether the combination of roles being considered jeopardizes their professional judgment, the welfare of the client, or their capacity to function competently. The APA Code notes that multiple relationships not likely to cause impairment to the psychologist's judgment or harm to the client are not unethical. Still, neither code provides a blueprint for practice, so the burden of assessing the ethics of any given prospective boundary extension falls largely on the individual practitioner.

It is important to remember that the recommendation in the codes to be judicious about engaging in boundary extensions is not limited to the therapeutic setting. The care in the matter applies to the other professional roles counselors and psychologists take on—teacher, supervisor, consultant, researcher, or employer. The standards also clearly apply to individuals in close connection to the person in the professional relationship, so a client's partner, child, or close friend would also be subject to these provisions.

UNDERLYING DYNAMICS IN MULTIPLE RELATIONSHIPS

Ethics scholars have identified three underlying dynamics of the therapeutic relationship that can help practitioners evaluate the risk of any potential boundary extension. The professional has a duty to honor promises to the client, to be sensitive to their power over the client, and to be aware of the client's emotional vulnerability during treatment. These dynamics affect the potential for client benefit in such relationships.

The Fiduciary Obligation

Sonne (1994) focuses on the first dynamic, *fiduciary relationship* between a mental health professional and the client. The term derives from legal sources, and means that the professional's primary obligation is to promote the client's well-being. One who fails in this responsibility is violating the most fundamental covenant with the client. Boundary extensions imply that the professional is vulnerable to other interests that compete with promoting the welfare of the client and thus are typically contradictory to the fiduciary responsibility. To return to Alberto's case, he may have difficulty placing the well-being of the adolescent client above the wishes of the client's father, who is the boss of Alberto's partner. Or Alberto may wish so much to impress the boss with his therapeutic skill that the therapy becomes more of a display of Alberto's therapeutic talents than a treatment of the boy's panic attacks. In a particularly problematic scenario, Alberto's concern about his partner's future employment may cause him to neglect to report to authorities the father's physical abuse of the boy. In all three instances, Alberto is neglecting his fiduciary responsibility.

Simon (1992) describes this dynamic a little differently. He asserts that professionals have a *duty to abstinence* from gratifying self-interests in therapy. This duty means that the only acceptable profits from therapy are the fee paid and the satisfaction received from a client's therapeutic gains. This obligation to abstain is incompatible with many multiple relationships. The duty to abstinence is difficult to uphold when the temptations to serve self-interests are as strong as they will be for Alberto if he takes on the son of his wife's boss as a client. More is at stake for Alberto than the income from the therapeutic time or the client's welfare. One could even wonder whether Alberto is accepting this case with the specific goal of enhancing his wife's career.

The fiduciary obligation to the client is also connected to another responsibility cited by Simon (1992), *the duty to neutrality*. He postulates that a therapist is ethically bound to enhance the client's autonomy and independence. Simon also asserts that because autonomy and independence are so fundamental to the achievement of the client's therapeutic objectives, a professional should have no other agenda. If Alberto is committed to his wife and her welfare, he has little neutrality about this adolescent client. He may even attempt to interfere with this adolescent's appropriate developmental separation from parents if that separation displeases the parents. Another way to frame the duty to neutrality is to describe it as a duty to objectivity and disinterest in any particular aspect of the client's life other than attaining therapeutic aims. Disinterest and objectivity should not be confused with a cold or uncaring attitude (Pope & Vasquez, 2011), but rather are highly compatible with a warm, empathic approach.

Note that Alberto is at risk for violating his fiduciary duty to this client even if he enters the relationship *intending* to honor that obligation. For this multiple relationship to be problematic, he need not be self-interested or callous about his client. The intensity of his connection to his partner and the ramifications to them both if counseling does not proceed as the boss intends makes objectivity and exclusive devotion to the client's goals extremely difficult. In fact, counselors and therapists with good intentions to help people who need therapy are often especially vulnerable to boundary crossings that become boundary violations because they underestimate the limits their other role places on them and overestimate their capacity for objectivity in the face of strong personal interests. (The case of Benny and Jefferson is a good example of this circumstance.) In other words, they do not recognize the conflict of interest inherent in the situation.

The Client's Emotional Involvement

The second dynamic that makes multiple relationships risky is the client's *emotional attachment to the therapist*. The therapist becomes an important person in the life of the client, at least during their professional contact. Research shows that a substantial part of what makes treatment therapeutic is the human relationship between the people involved (e.g., see Duncan, 2010; Lambert, 2013; Wampold, 2010). Client trust, confidence in the therapist's expertise, clarity about the rules and boundaries of the relationship, and mutuality of expectations are all crucial features of successful therapy. When a professional has another role in a client's life, the client's emotional reaction is confused. Trust may be endangered, the rules for interaction may be obscured, and expectations may diverge. Exposure to the therapist's foibles in other settings may erode the client's confidence. In addition, sharing a very painful or embarrassing secret may be more difficult for a client who has multiple contacts with a professional. For fear of repercussions, a business executive may avoid disclosing her experiences of mania to a professional when the client views the therapist as a potential investor.

In a more practical vein, multiple roles may make the client unsure about when therapy begins and ends and what kinds of conversation are appropriate in which setting. A client who is also a neighbor may feel uncertain about when to bring up particular topics or may feel that *every* contact with the professional is appropriate for therapeutic dialogue. In the latter situation, a client could develop feelings of dependence; a professional, feelings of resentment. Of course, it is possible to work out a mutual understanding of what topics are appropriate for counseling and which are not prior to the initiation of the nonprofessional contact. A professional who serves on the community's board of United Way with a client can discuss with the client the parameters of their out-of-session contact and may be able to work out a mutually agreeable arrangement.

Theoretical orientation also plays a role in deciding whether nonprofessional contacts are advisable. Therapists who view transference as a central feature of counseling are particularly troubled by this dynamic. They contend that a client cannot work through a transference with a professional who plays another role in his or her life. Research shows that psychoanalytic therapists tend to view non-erotic multiple relationships as significantly less ethical than their cognitive or humanistic counterparts (Baer & Murdock, 1995).

The Power Imbalance

The third dynamic, the *power differential* between the professional and the client, was discussed at length as an important factor in sexual exploitation (Chapter 7). This imbalance may make clients acquiesce to the therapist's wishes even when doing so is at odds with their own desires. This can happen not only in session but also in the second relationship. A supervisee who is also a supervisor's client may defer any disagreement with the therapist/supervisor because the risk of negative fallout is so great. Clients can also fear emotional abandonment (Sonne, 1994) if they offend the therapist in his or her other role. If clients refuse the therapist/friend's social invitation, they may wonder if the therapist will retaliate by missing a session or even terminating therapy. The client's autonomy may be jeopardized by the secondary relationship (Kitchener, 1988).

The power difference also contributes to what has been called *role slippage* (Smith & Fitzpatrick, 1995). Role slippage means that the more powerful therapist may loosen the boundaries between the therapeutic relationship and the other relationship. A therapist might end a session with a conversation about a committee issue with a client who also serves on that body. Then, the therapist may suggest that they go out for a cup of coffee after a committee meeting to follow up on an unresolved issue. In this conversation, the therapist may disclose other information about himself to which the client does not know how to respond. Finally, the therapist may take even more time for the committee agenda in later sessions. Under these circumstances, a client may feel reluctant to divert the discussion to more relevant matters. After professionals disclose extensive information about their personal lives, clients may even come to see themselves as caretakers for the professional (Smith & Fitzpatrick, 1995). Eventually, both parties lose sight of the boundaries between the professional and personal relationships, and the focus on the client's therapeutic goal becomes secondary.

Still another aspect of boundary extensions is troublesome: The confidentiality of services may be endangered. The chances that a professional may inadvertently reveal information disclosed in counseling are increased by the outside contact. In the situation described in the last paragraph, the therapist might accidentally repeat to another committee member something the client said within session. Keeping track of what was said in which setting is burdensome. Intentional violations of confidentiality are also more likely when a professional's self-interest in a multiple relationship has not been met. The scenario of Wilma (the therapist who consulted a former client about her children's college applications) could lead to an intentional violation of confidentiality if Wilma were dissatisfied with the advice her former client gave her children. In anger she might disclose to her family something about the former client's reasons for seeking therapy.

THE VIEWS OF ETHICS SCHOLARS

Given the potential for problems, many ethics scholars take a stronger stance than the codes do against boundary extensions, especially those in which one role is therapeutic. Kitchener (1988) and Sonne (1994) argue that mental health professionals cannot accurately predict the degree to which their capacity to practice competently will be compromised, or the harm that may come to a client as their relationship progresses. In light of this reality, they contend that most multiple relationships represent "undue risks" that should not be undertaken. Pope and Vasquez (2011) assert that mental health professionals who engage in many kinds of boundary extensions are frequently justifying their behavior with reasons that do not stand the test of logic or true commitment to the client's well-being. Using Simon's terms (1991, 1992), close examination of these counselors' motives sometimes reveals that they are acting without neutrality or abstinence. These practitioners seem to underestimate the conflict of interest or to overestimate their own skill. Simon also argues that a multiple relationship places the therapist at risk for other boundary violations, in a slippery slope analogy. A therapist who takes on a former business partner as a client may then accept investment advice from another current client, suggest a business relationship with a supervisee, and so forth. When business relationships with clients become common and acceptable, the extension to social and romantic relationships is rather natural. Clear boundaries help keep the focus on the client's welfare and help avert many other problems as well.

Essentially, these writers are basing their arguments on the principle of nonmaleficence. Because preventing harm is such an important professional value and because that harm cannot always be foreseen, prudence and devotion to the client's welfare demand that counselors should regularly avoid multiple relationships.

Other scholars take a more liberal stand (e.g., see Cottone, 2005; Herlihy & Corey, 2014; Lazarus & Zur, 2002; Moleski & Kiselica, 2005), suggesting that the ethics of a multiple relationship need to be examined on a case-by-case basis and need to give more weight to potential client benefits. They contend that professionals can make reasonable assessments when they know about the facts of a particular situation. These scholars also view a rigid posture about boundaries as impractical, because mental health professionals live in communities and are bound to have contacts with people who may at some point be clients. They also point out the importance of the principle of beneficence and argue that prohibiting multiple relationships may diminish the professional's opportunity to do good. Finally, they stress the role of community and cultural variables in determining whether a multiple relationship is ethical. For instance, if at an agency with many Chinese immigrants, only one counselor speaks Mandarin, that counselor's special skill should be taken into account. That professional may be well advised to establish somewhat looser boundaries with those Chinese clients, because of the unique capacity to do good. Community variables also play a crucial role in a rural practitioner's decision making (see the fuller discussion later in this chapter). Lazarus and Zur (2002) contend that the current view of boundaries causes professionals to act with too much professional distance and results in less than ideal service to clients. Their views highlight the need to keep the focus in this debate on promoting the welfare of the client and not on protecting the professional from legal action or ethics complaints.

All scholars seem to agree on at least one point. Regardless of the stance a professional takes on any particular boundary extension, if he or she observes a pattern of extensions that is more frequent than colleagues working in similar communities, that person should step back and reevaluate the dynamics underlying the behavior. Along with that reassessment should come careful supervision and consultation to unearth the underlying dynamics of the practice.

Questions to Consider in Decision Making

Based on the codes, the literature, and the ethical standards, the following questions present important issues to address in determining whether a particular relationship is ethical:

- Are the role expectations and obligations so divergent as to be incompatible?
- Is promoting the client's welfare the professional's only motivation in initiating or accepting the professional relationship? Does the sociocultural context of the client make the boundary extension important to therapeutic process?
- Can the professional attain the same degree of objectivity about this person and competent practice as is achieved in other professional relationships?
- Is misuse of the professional's power a plausible occurrence?
- Is this a low-risk and high-benefit situation for the other person?
- Is the professional reasonably certain that the extension will not negatively affect the client's emotional involvement or capacity to achieve the therapeutic goal?
- Is the extension truly unavoidable? Have all other options really been considered?
- If a professional is embarking on a boundary extension, has an informed consent procedure been undertaken so that the client understands the situation, including its risks and the special arrangements that may be necessary?

- Have both parties evaluated the changes that may result in their other relationships because of the professional contact, and are they both comfortable with these changes?
- If the decision were presented to the practitioner's respected colleagues (using the clear-light-of-day standard), is it likely that they would support the decision to go forward with this extension?
- Is the professional willing to document the extension in case notes?
- Have provisions been made for continuing consultation and/or supervision to monitor the risks and benefits to the client as the relationship develops?
- Have the client and professional developed an alternative plan in the event that the relationship does not unfold as they expect so that harm can be remedied?
- Is the professional committed to diligently following up, so that if problems arise after the professional contact has ended, the professional will be able to provide assistance?

The length of this list of questions demonstrates the care a professional must take when considering initiating a boundary extension.

If the extension under consideration involves a former client, Anderson and Kitchener (1998) present a model of ethical decision making for post-counseling relationships. As part of that model, they recommend the following considerations as well:

- Was the relationship explicitly terminated; were the termination issues successfully processed; and has the length of time since termination been sufficient to allow both client and counselor to engage in new behaviors with each other?
- Can the confidentiality of disclosures from counseling be maintained in the post-counseling relationship, and is there a clear arrangement between parties for doing so?
- Does the client understand that by entering into this post-counseling relationship he or she may be relinquishing the opportunity to reenter a counseling relationship with this professional? Does the client understand the other possible ramifications?
- How serious were the former client's problems at the time he or she was receiving services; how strong was the transference; and how successfully were they resolved by the end of treatment? Have the problems resurfaced, or is the client's emotionally stable and self-sufficient? Anderson and Kitchener (1998) recommend avoidance of all post-therapy contacts when the client's problems were severe or characterological (p. 94).
- If this post-counseling relationship is avoidable, what is the professional's motivation for entering into it, and how seriously have the ramifications for the client been analyzed?

RESEARCH FINDINGS: PRACTITIONER AND CONSUMER VIEWS

The research on practitioners' attitudes toward boundary extensions is not as abundant as the literature on their views about sexual contact, but there is sufficient evidence to draw some reasonable conclusions. First, significant diversity appears in practitioners' opinions about the ethics of this practice. Some call it unquestionably unethical, but others show considerable tolerance for such multiple commitments. For example, in one study, 26% of psychologists labeled accepting a client's invitation to a party as unquestionably unethical, while 17.5% viewed the same practice as ethical under many circumstances (Pope et al., 1987). Responses to a related question in a recent study of Canadian counselors showed that 23% of the sample believed that it may be ethical to invite a client to a party or social event (Nigro, 2004a), while 77% responded that such an action is never ethical. Second, most studies reveal a greater tolerance for nonsexual boundary extensions than for sexual ones (Lamb, Catanzano, & Moorman, 2003; Neukrug & Milliken, 2011; Nigro, 2004a). More professionals view some extensions as ethical, and even when viewing them as unethical, do not see them as such egregious violations as sexual misconduct. For example, four different surveys found that many therapists viewed the practice of becoming friends with a former client as ethical at least sometimes. The percentages endorsing this view ranged from 44% (Borys & Pope, 1989) to 59% (Gibson & Pope, 1993) to 70% (Salisbury & Kinnier, 1996) to 83% (Nigro, 2004a). Even a survey conducted in 2011 found that some counselors found it ethical to have a counseling relationship with a current friend (4.6%), or a colleague (10.7%) (Neukrug & Milliken, 2011). Moreover, 26% of those surveyed by Borys and Pope admitted to becoming friends with a former client at least once. Pope et al. (1987) found that a much larger percentage admitted to this practice, a full two-thirds (67%) of their sample. Practitioners responding to surveys have also admitted engaging in several other kinds of multiple relationships. These include the following (Anderson & Kitchener, 1996; Borys & Pope, 1989; Pope et al., 1987; Lamb et al., 1994; Lamb & Catanzaro, 1998; Nigro, 2004b):

- Providing therapy to an employee
- Employing a client
- Going into business with current and former clients
- Providing therapy to students and/or supervisees
- Allowing a client to enroll in a course taught by the therapist
- Inviting clients to a party
- Selling goods to a client

The specific percentage acknowledging such activities varies from survey to survey, as does the form of the question asked, but each of the surveys found at least 2% of those responding endorsed these behaviors. The most common boundary extension reported was providing therapy to a student or supervisee (29%, Pope et al., 1987), and the least frequent was going into business with a current client (2%, Pope et al., 1987).

Some of the behaviors just listed are clearly prohibited by the ethics codes (such as providing therapy to a supervisee—ACA, 2014, Section F.6.c), but most others fit the category of avoidance unless client risk exceeds benefit. The available evidence does not reveal whether these activities met the criteria established by the codes or fell short of them. Nor does it reveal the outcomes of these relationships for the consumers or therapists involved, unfortunately. These data suggest that mental health professionals may not be acting as cautiously as they should when faced with a prospective boundary extension. To use a colloquial phrase—one need not be a rocket scientist to realize that providing therapy for a friend or employee has a high probability of clouding one's objectivity, impairing one's judgment, or impeding the progress of therapy—each of which harms the client.

Client and consumer attitudes toward boundary extensions are also ambivalent. Claiborn et al. (1994) found that former psychotherapy clients expressed more reluctance about this situation than about confidentiality or informed consent issues. Pulakos (1994) reported contradictory findings, with her small sample seeking more reaction from their therapists when they encountered their therapists outside of sessions. In a qualitative study of clients who become friends with their therapists during or after therapy, Gibb (2005) reported that clients who experienced negative outcomes also rated the harm they suffered as "devastating," and even those who did not regret establishing the friendship reported many negative reactions such as pain, confusion, awkwardness, and loss. Even this small and preliminary body of research underscores the need for professionals to use caution in entertaining boundary extensions; to consult extensively with clients and colleagues before their initiation; and to maintain those lines of communication during the nonprofessional contact.

ACCEPTING GIFTS FROM CLIENTS

Occasionally, clients bring presents to sessions. The urge to give gifts can be motivated by a number of different factors. Some clients are driven by a belief that gifts may gain them special status in their counselors' eyes or otherwise help maintain good service. For others, the action is connected to the very problems that sparked their decision to enter services. For instance, clients with low self-esteem may perceive gifts as the path to keep the professional interested in them, because they believe themselves to have little intrinsic value. A few clients may even attempt to use gifts as bribes for a positive report or a special favor. Still others wish to bestow a token of their appreciation for the gift that counseling has been to them or to ease the sadness of termination by leaving something from them with their counselor as they depart. Consequently, the ethics of accepting a gift from a client depends substantially on the circumstances under which it was offered and on the attitude of and impact on its recipient. The language in the current ACA Code captures this complexity in Section A.10.f. The APA Code does not explicitly mention this topic, but its standards prohibiting exploitation and avoiding conflicts of interest indirectly address this issue.

When gifts are a "quid pro quo" for better or special service, or are a manifestation of the client's dysfunction, the professional probably should not accept them. Taking them implies, in the first case, that the professional can be manipulated (and thus undermines trust and devotion to promoting client welfare), and in the second case, suggests that he or she agrees with the client's distorted self-assessment or view of relationships (and thereby inhibits therapeutic progress). However, when a present represents a token of appreciation for a successful therapeutic experience or a common cultural ritual (such as sharing holiday cookies in December), it may be ethical to receive it. Specifically, accepting a gift is more likely to be ethical if *all* the following criteria are met:

- It promotes rather than endangers the client's welfare.
- It does not compromise the therapist's objectivity or capacity to provide competent service in the future.

- It is a token of appreciation consistent with the client's cultural norms and with a small monetary value.
- It is a rare event.

The definition of what is expensive varies from person to person and from decade to decade. Research seems to indicate some consistency in the way mental health professionals define a token gift. Practicing psychologists, social workers, and counselors seem to believe that a value of approximately $25 or less is the limit for what is ethical (Borys & Pope, 1989; Neukrug & Milliken, 2011; Nigro, 2004a). When clients want to bestow more elaborate gifts on their therapists, that desire may be "grist for the therapeutic mill" that the two parties should discuss in session. (See Barnett [2011] for a fascinating discussion of what happened to him when a client attempted to offer him an expensive gift.) When a client seems insistent on giving a valuable gift as a symbol of the tremendously positive impact that treatment has had on his or her life, a compromise can sometimes be reached by having the client make an anonymous contribution to a charity in the name of the agency. The latter option seems prudent to consider only at the point of a successful termination and only after a full airing of the impact of the gift on the professional relationship and on the profession if the gift becomes known. An expensive present should not be accepted by an individual counselor because it poses such a high risk of reducing the counselor's objectivity. To expect counselors and therapists to be totally unaffected by an elaborate gift is to deny their humanity. It is for this reason that the counselor described in the opening section of this chapter should not accept Roberta's gift of a theater subscription. Even though a few hundred dollars represents little more than a token to this client, it probably carries more meaning to Dominique. She would be unlikely to be able to work objectively with Roberta in the future because of the past largesse. Moreover, if another wealthy client came her way, the counselor might be distracted by thoughts about the possibility of other such presents at termination. Instead of taking the tickets, Dominique could suggest that Roberta donate the tickets to a charity or to a school for the arts as an incentive for drama students. The counselor should simultaneously express to the client that the therapeutic change in her client is all the reward she needs, and should make sure that before she leaves, Roberta fully understands Dominique's rationale for refusing the gift.

Even token gifts, such as a loaf of homemade bread or flowers from a client's garden, should not become a recurrent event unless there is a compelling cultural influence. If gift giving is frequent, the practice ought to be discussed in the session. Perhaps the client brings presents because it is the only way she knows to express emotional connection. If so, helping the client learn alternative ways to express closeness can become an explicit therapeutic goal. A recurrent gift is also a distraction for the counselor. A professional might start to look forward to that loaf of fresh bread each week and then be disappointed when the client did not produce one. Such a motivation to see a client is inconsistent with the principles of neutrality and objectivity.

Those who are tempted to conclude that the simplest path is to refuse all client gifts should be cautious in taking such an absolute stance. In some cultural groups, gifts are important interpersonal rituals (as the ACA Code acknowledges). For these clients, an absolute refusal of all gifts might well be counterproductive. Similarly, for clients who wish to present a small token at termination of an intense and successful therapeutic relationship, the refusal to graciously receive a small present may interrupt a positive resolution of the relationship, especially if the client had no warning that gift giving might be inappropriate. In a study by Brown and Trangsrud (2008), psychologists appeared to take monetary, cultural, and relationship variables into account when deciding when to accept gifts. They also tended to examine the interaction of all these variables before deciding to accept or decline a gift, an approach consistent with ethical principles and recommendations of ethics scholars.

Herlihy and Corey (2014) recommend that the issue of gift giving be included in a professional disclosure statement or brought up during the informed consent process early in counseling so that no one ends up embarrassed, confused, or angry over an inappropriate present. They go on to suggest that a policy be written to discourage the practice. With such a policy, clients will then understand both the counselor's interpretation of the practice and the rationale underlying it long before they are likely to want to bring the counselor a present. Moreover, if the counselor's policy to dissuade clients from gift giving conflicts with the client's cultural tradition, the two can then discuss this discrepancy at an early stage. In short, clarifying policy at an early stage can prevent later misunderstandings. If Roberta had known that Dominique might not accept her gift, she might have saved herself both the cost of the tickets and the distress of their refusal at what was otherwise a very positive final counseling session.

On the other hand, discussing gift giving early in therapy may present problems. Adding one more item to the already long list of topics to discuss early in the informed consent process may make that process more cumbersome. The client may misinterpret the policy and assume that token gifts *ought* to be given. In some cultural contexts in which gifts are an important aspect of interpersonal relationships, this policy would be vulnerable to misinterpretation. Thus, professionals ought to consider the implications of such a policy before mandating it for all clients. With child clients, they may not be mature enough to understand such policies, and their confusion may interfere with therapeutic progress (Knox, 2008).

BOUNDARY EXTENSIONS AND MULTIPLE RELATIONSHIPS IN RURAL AND SMALL COMMUNITY PRACTICE

Mental health practitioners who work in large metropolitan areas can rather easily avoid many forms of boundary extensions. The pool of potential clients from whom they can build their practices is large, so there is little economic incentive to loosen boundaries. They can work in a different part of the city from their home to prevent contacts with clients, students, or supervisees in civic, religious, or social settings. In addition, urban practitioners have many referral sources for people whom they ought not to take on as clients, and they can be confident that the clients they decline to accept will still receive competent professional service. Urban and suburban counselors also have the benefit of the relative anonymity of the large city. Few people in the community know or care about their occupation. If they accidentally meet their clients in other settings, neither party has to worry that a brief conversation would reveal to the community their professional contact.

In contrast, rural practitioners have dramatically different experiences because of both the demographics of their communities and their cultural norms. Their pool of potential clients is smaller; their referral sources more limited; and the chances of preexisting, concurrent, or subsequent connections with clients, significantly greater. A smaller population base from which to draw clients can mean that turning away clients may be a financial hardship for these professionals and for consumers. Competent referral sources are often distant and inaccessible by public transportation, so clients' access to mental health care is more restricted when local practitioners decline to see them. Unless rural practitioners refrain from joining any social, religious, or civic organizations and commute long distances to the workplace, they cannot easily avoid additional contacts with clients (Schank & Skovholt, 2006). Pearson and Piazza (1997) refer to these as *circumstantial multiple relationships*. Moreover, in a small community many people know the professional's occupation and are acquainted with the people with whom the clinician may interact. As Jennings (1992) points out, "Life in the city is characterized by anonymity; whereas life in rural areas is characterized by an unusual degree of openness—one's behavior, and the behavior of one's family are not only open to public scrutiny, but become favorite topics of community discussion" (p. 94). Thus the avoidance of boundary extensions is more complex for rural practitioners. Rural practitioners often get requests to work with people with whom they are acquainted or whom they have seen at community, religious, or social functions. Even if one is unfamiliar with a particular person, he or she may know a family member and may be privy to information about the client from those other people (Gates & Speare, 1990; Hargrove, 1982). Sobel (1992) points out that complications also arise when the administrative assistant or others who work for the professional have connections with prospective clients. Rural practitioners also know that when professional contact ends, they are likely to have at least intermittent contact with the client afterward. Their children may have the same teacher; they may both volunteer for the United Way drive; or they may bump into each other waiting at the dentist's office. Since they drive the same streets all the time, they may even be involved in the same traffic accident at some point!

Research by Horst (1989) supports these claims. In her study of psychologists from urban and rural communities in Minnesota, she found significantly more overlapping relationships between rural practitioners and their clients. Rural psychologists had more out-of-session contact and experienced more after-termination contact. Most of the out-of-session contact was through involvement in joint large organizations or in accidental meetings in stores or other community settings. Rural practitioners were not significantly more likely to engage in boundary extensions that carried with them high risks of complications, however. For example, Horst found no difference between the rates at which urban and rural psychologists indicated they had accepted friends or employees as clients.

Public perception of the role of the professional also differs in rural places. People in cities expect that the professionals who serve them will be strangers; they seem to prefer that arrangement. Rural dwellers often take the opposite stance because they are so accustomed to interacting with familiar people and feel strong community ties. Thus they may be more likely to seek out a familiar therapist rather than a stranger (Helbok, 2003). The challenge for the rural practitioners, then, is to serve the mental health needs of the community without causing undue harm to clients with whom they have at least peripheral connections. In spite of stereotypes of idyllic rural life, research shows that residents of rural America experience the same levels of trauma, anxiety, and depression as their urban counterparts and are at greater risk from poverty and health problems (Roberts, Battaglia, & Epstein, 1999).

Of course, one must be careful not to characterize the contrasts among urban, suburban, and rural settings too extremely. Sometimes clients in suburbs and cities choose a particular therapist because he or she is part of a "shared community" with a client, participating in the same civic organization, social action group, or ethnic or cultural group (Adelman & Barrett, 1990). Mental health professionals in the military and university counseling centers, and those who work with individuals with particular issues or experiences such as counselors to the deaf or gay, lesbian, bisexual, or transgender communities, also experience many of the same problems with multiple relationships in communities with limited access to alternative services (Bleiberg & Baron, 2004; Guttman, 2005; Johnson, Ralph, & Johnson, 2005; Kessler & Waehler, 2005). Consequently, practitioners in these settings can be as familiar with the dilemma of overlapping connections as their rural counterparts. Two case illustrate the complexities of working while a member of a shared community. The first is Kessler and Waehler (2005), who present a case study of the ethical and clinical dilemmas a professional faced and worked to resolve when treating a client from a shared college community. The second is presented by Brown (2011). Still, professionals in larger population areas tend to have more referral sources and more opportunities for face-to-face consultation and supervision than those in small towns.

Along with the case of the bakery clerk presented in the opening section of this chapter, the following examples of ethical dilemmas derive from the author's brief experience as the only psychologist in a community of 8000 people (though client identity is carefully disguised). In each instance, the author had to assess whether the problems that might accrue from the multiple relationship or circumstantial contact might reasonably harm clients or otherwise prevent them from benefiting from therapy. At that time the nearest referral sources were at least 30 miles away and inaccessible by public transportation.

- A man who seeks counseling because of grief over his father's death works in the same office as the psychologist's partner. The partner is not the supervisor, but he does supervise this man's boss.
- A woman referred to the psychologist by her family physician for treatment of a panic disorder is the mother-in-law of the psychologist's neighbor. The psychologist sees this neighbor regularly, although they are acquaintances rather than friends. The prospective client does not drive a car.
- The psychologist is asked to give a deposition in a custody matter and finds when she goes to the hearing that the attorney doing the deposing is the estranged wife of a current client.
- The children of the psychologist and of her client attend the same day care center. In fact, on the day of the client's weekly appointment, both drive directly from the psychologist's office to pick up their children at day care. It is

the only day care center in town, and the client's work schedule does not permit changing the time of her counseling appointment.

- An accountant with whom the psychologist has done business on one occasion is referred to her for therapy after she is hospitalized for a brief psychotic break.

Jennings (1992) provides other vivid examples of recurring multiple-relationship problems in rural areas. In one instance, he was involved in a court case to give expert testimony and discovered when he entered the courtroom that the judge and three of the jurors had been clients in his private practice. In a second case, his teenage son had asked to the prom a girl whose parents were in therapy with Jennings. The boy, of course, had no knowledge of his father's connection to the family. All these cases highlight the close interconnections of people's lives in rural communities. They also illustrate the kind of harm an unscrupulous professional might inflict on clients. Participants in other research studies identify similar problems in rural practice (e.g., see Schank & Skovholt, 1997, 2006).

Jennings (1992) and Hargrove (1986) have argued that the professions have not paid enough attention to the special concerns of rural practitioners and that ethical standards derive too heavily from an urban culture. The most recent versions of the codes show more responsiveness to this criticism, with the clear statement that some kinds of multiple relationships are not unethical. Jennings offers additional guidelines to help the rural counselor act ethically. The first is to reject the notion that multiple relationships are avoidable in a rural setting. The price of rejecting all such contacts would be eliminating mental health services for many consumers. Traveling long distances to referral sources that the client is likely to distrust as "strangers" is not a viable option for most people. The decision about whether to accept a client must be made with the issue of accessibility of alternative services prominently in mind. Jennings recommends that those who work in rural settings make a real commitment to the fundamental ethical values of the profession and develop a generous capacity for tolerating ambiguity in their relationships. In his judgment, a mental health professional who is unequipped for such tolerance would be better suited to an urban climate. Research by Lear (1997) reveals that rural psychologists also tend to use the degree of emotional vulnerability of the client as additional consideration in their decision to enter or refuse a multiple relationship. Coyle (1999) recommends that the professional hypothesize about the worst-case scenario, and Campbell and Gordon (2003) advise consultation with colleagues prior to engaging in the professional relationship. Both activities can assist the professional in making an objective decision and changing any variables in his or her control to minimize the potential for a negative outcome.

Jennings also emphasizes the value of using extensive informed consent procedures when embarking on a therapeutic relationship with a client one knows from another interaction. Both parties should understand what the other expects when they meet in another setting. This aspect is especially important given the public awareness of the counselor's position. By merely addressing a person by name in the supermarket, a counselor could be perceived as signaling to other shoppers that the person is in counseling. Craig (quoted in Sleek, 1994) asserts that "When someone is parked in front of a psychologist's office, everybody in town knows it" (p. 27). Jennings also implies that ingenuity is an important asset for rural counselors in designing interventions to meet needs without putting clients at risk. His next recommendation is to use multiple relationship issues as "grist for the therapeutic mill." The client's feelings after encountering the therapist at a social function should be openly discussed, as should the client's interest in aspects of the therapist's life that are known in the community.

When the prospective multiple relationship is closer or more intense, Jennings suggests that "the psychological intervention is limited in direct proportion to the intensity of the interpersonal relationship" (p. 100). In other words, Jennings's view is that the rural mental health professional ought to offer only briefer, less intense services to those with stronger business, social, or community ties to the counselor and to reserve long-term counseling for people with whom outside connections are nonexistent or peripheral. A school psychologist in a rural community, for example, might go forward with an evaluation of a learning disorder in her physician's child, but would arrange for a referral for ongoing counseling services to help the child and the family cope with the disorder. Effant (quoted in Sleek, 1994) takes a different view of the problem of such multiple relationships, cautioning professionals about unanticipated complications. "Too many psychologists in smaller communities think they can handle multiple relationships, and that their clients can, too. It always complicates the relationship. The psychologist needs to be very humble about how different the process of therapy is going to be because of it" (p. 27).

In short, the rural or small community practitioner should be especially sensitive to the ethics of multiple relationships. Jennings calls this a more demanding standard than applies to urban professionals. Counselors and therapists need to continually balance the obligation to serve the public's mental health needs against the risk of harm and should seek out consultation to ensure that the difficult judgments necessitated by the environment are well founded.

THE ETHICS OF BARTER

The current professional codes allow bartering under some circumstances. The ACA Code permits bartering of both goods and services if it is not harmful, has been requested by the client, and is a regular community standard. The APA Code also identifies the risk of exploitation as a condition along with clinical considerations.

Bartering can jeopardize treatment in many of the same ways as a multiple relationship. The client's power to complain about working conditions or address problems in the service arrangement is limited. If the client voices discontent with the barter, will he or she then worry that the professional will terminate services? In addition, the emotional connections between the people get confused. For clients with some kinds of emotional problems, this confusion can stop or reverse therapeutic gains. Moreover, the progress of therapy may be endangered if the practitioner's neutrality is compromised by his or her investment in the service the client is providing. For instance, if a client is trading carpentry services for therapy and begins to recover from his depression before the counselor's deck is completed, the counselor may be tempted to prolong counseling to meet her own needs or simply fail to recognize the client's progress because it conflicts with her own agenda. The client may delay or hasten work on the deck, depending on his evaluation of therapeutic progress. Conversely, professional judgment may be impaired if the client has a major setback after the deck is completed. The counselor may provide less diligent care if no remuneration is possible or may be inclined to terminate therapy sooner than appropriate. One final problem is the difference in cost between the services. The services clients typically can provide have a lower monetary value than counseling or psychotherapy, so that when treatment is lengthy, the client may become like an indentured servant to the therapist, working long hours to pay off the accumulated debt (Kitchener & Harding, 1990; Koocher & Keith-Spiegel, 2008). In most economies, the hourly wage for a typist or house painter is considerably less than for a mental health professional.

Bartering goods is somewhat less complicated, because a market value for a good can be independently established, but even such arrangements can be complicated. As Koocher and Keith-Spiegel (2008) point out, if the thing the client wants to barter has true value, there is rarely any need to sell it to the therapist—other buyers can be found, and the profit can be used to pay for services the traditional way. In addition, a client who trades a piece of sculpture for sessions may believe the art has been undervalued and then feel cheated and resentful. Or the professional who gets salmonella poisoning from farm eggs bartered for treatment may feel poorly served by the arrangement. One final reason makes this practice risky. The legal recourse typically available to parties dissatisfied with a business transaction is not easily available to either client or clinician. A professional who brought a client to small claims court would be violating confidentiality, and a client taking the same action would be risking disclosure of counseling information.

The issues just presented seem to lead to the conclusion that barter is simply not worth the trouble it can cause for both professional and client. That generalization is mostly true. However, there are two important reasons not to eliminate the possibility of bartering altogether. Barter can have value in making professional services accessible to those whose financial resources are limited. Some people refuse to accept free services and see them as an affront to their dignity, but are willing to offer a barter arrangement. For clients who reject the argument that they have already paid for "free" services through their taxes, barter may be an important option (Canter et al., 1994). Others (Pope & Vasquez, 2011) argue that therapists should be careful about the frequency with which they claim that pro bono arrangements are not feasible as an alternative to barter, cautioning that self-interest and lack of ingenuity may be the real motivations for accepting barter in some situations. Second, in rural communities and some cultural groups, barter is a common practice and refusing to engage in it would run counter to cultural norms and restrict access to care (Canter et al., 1994; Helbok, 2003).

Sonne (1994) presents a divergent view, arguing that there is little evidence that barter is a common practice. Sleek (1994) echoes this view, suggesting that its prevalence has faded considerably even in rural environments in recent years. Fewer than 10% of psychologists have accepted goods or services for payment more than rarely in their practice (Borys & Pope, 1989; Pope et al., 1987). Sonne also points out the contradiction between the Code and some state regulations. California (California Department of Consumer Affairs, 2011) prohibits all forms of bartering in therapy, while Ohio declares it a multiple relationship that should be avoided (Ohio Administrative Code Section 4757-5-03). Some malpractice insurers exclude claims arising from a bartering arrangement (Bennett et al., 2006; Sonne, 1994). Sonne contends that these bodies are judging the problems more realistically. In any case, professionals who are considering barter with a client should assess not only their compliance with the Code but also the stance of their state licensing board and their liability insurer.

As with any other ethical issue, a practitioner should consult with other professionals and carefully scrutinize one's own motivation before proceeding with a bartering arrangement. One should also scrupulously document that process, the informed consent procedures, and the progress of therapy. That document should include the details of the barter and an alternative to the barter should either party become dissatisfied with the agreement at a later point. The designation of a mediator for any disputes should also be included in that document.

Interestingly, counselors and psychologists seem divided on the issue of whether barter can be ethical. Research shows that psychologists tend to view the practice as rarely ethical (e.g., see Baer & Murdock, 1995), but counselors view it more positively. In fact, Neukrug and Milliken (2011) found that slightly more than half (53%) of the counselors they surveyed rated barter for services or goods ethically acceptable. Canadian counselors hold similar views; Nigro (2004a) found that 61% rated bartering as ethical at least sometimes.

CASES REEXAMINED

Two of the cases from the opening section of the chapter are now analyzed using the codes and related literature.

Roxanne and Li Qing

In this case, the client, Li Qing, innocently began attending the same church that her counselor, Roxanne, frequents. When her counselor discovered the coincidence, she disclosed her membership to the client and initiated a discussion of the issue in a counseling session. Because Li Qing is a current client, the remarks in the codes clearly apply. Roxanne has a responsibility to avoid exploiting the client's trust and misusing her influence, or otherwise risking harm to the client. Now Roxanne must decide whether their attendance at the same church is likely to result in any of those negative outcomes. Too little information is given to determine whether bringing the topic up for discussion in session is a wise idea. Its wisdom depends largely on the client's emotional stability and particular problems, about which the case description doesn't give enough information. It also depends on the capacity of the counselor to respond in an appropriate way immediately after being surprised by this revelation. After all, there is no urgency to deal with this topic at this juncture. As long as the counselor can hold another session before the next church service, or refrain from church attendance until she analyzes the problem and decides whether to discuss it with her client, the topic can be postponed.

Several other factors should be considered before the counselor makes a judgment about the appropriateness of continued mutual participation in the church. The size and sense of community in the congregation is important. In a large congregation with multiple services, the two people could arrange not to attend functions simultaneously. A small congregation with one weekly service and strong sense of community would present more complications for both parties. In the latter circumstance, one option for the counselor would be to temporarily suspend her churchgoing until counseling with this client was terminated. Another alternative would be to attend services at a different church for the same period. One alternative seems clearly unethical—to ask the client to choose another church. Li Qing's choice of this congregation seemed to be driven by her therapeutic goals and made without knowledge of the counselor's affiliation. Suggesting that the client select another church might impede future progress and be especially difficult for a shy client to resist.

If, in the end, both parties decided that this multiple connection is appropriate and workable, they would need to follow the Code to be sure the client's best interests were protected, including the practical management of times when they met at church functions. Even if the multiple relationship is not judged problematic, Roxanne should avoid extensive personal contact with her client at church. For example, she ought not to co-chair a committee with her client or spend every social hour after church in conversation with Li Qing. The interactions at church should be cordial, brief, and infrequent, at least for the duration of the professional relationship. To answer questions from other church members who wonder how they became acquainted, they also should prepare a response that does not include divulging their professional relationship. These arrangements should be documented, and Roxanne should obtain ongoing case supervision to ensure the continuation of objective, competent care. The therapist has a responsibility to make a judgment about the advisability of this multiple relationship independent of her client's current expressions about the matter. The client may not foresee the potential problems, may have motives for desiring personal contact that would be counterproductive to real change, or may simply be mouthing words she believes the counselor wants to hear. The client's expressed feelings should be taken into account, of course, but they should not be the only factor considered. The burden to analyze all the considerations falls on the shoulders of the counselor, not the client.

Theodore and the Teacher's Request

Theodore, the parent of an elementary school child, is approached by his son's teacher (Mr. Goodheart) to provide counseling for a depressed friend of his. Theodore responds by giving the teacher his business card and suggesting he tell her friend to call to set up an appointment.

Does Theodore's connection through this prospective client's friend make this a multiple relationship to be avoided? Because the case deals with a prospective client, it undoubtedly falls within the purview of the codes. The crucial issue is whether his connection to the teacher will impair his judgment, impede the progress of therapy, or affect the client's capacity to relate to Theodore or to otherwise benefit from therapy. There is a relatively little chance that this distant a connection will cause such problems, but more information is needed to make a definitive judgment. At a minimum, Theodore ought to have asked Mr. Goodheart some questions about his relationship with this person and about his understanding of the rules of confidentiality should the friend accept a referral. The nature of the connection between the prospective client and the teacher is not clearly stated.

The term *friend* has a wide range of meanings. This man could be someone the teacher is simply acquainted with, or it could be his life partner. The latter circumstance would make the multiple relationship more problematic, as Mr. Goodheart would have a very big stake in the progress and outcome of therapy and may even need to be involved in joint sessions to resolve relationship difficulties. In that case, the multiple-relationship risks become much more likely. Even if the connection between the teacher and his friend is less intense, Theodore would have an obligation to clarify to all parties involved the boundaries between contacts and to reassure the client about the confidentiality of therapeutic material.

Next, a responsible resolution of this case also requires more information about the child and the family's frequency of contact with the teacher. If Theodore's son is an ordinary child whose parents need not be closely involved with his school, that circumstance would argue for the choice Theodore made, but if the child's characteristics require the family to have intense, frequent, or conflictual contact with school personnel, that would argue for a more cautious approach. In the latter circumstance, Theodore would be advised to go forward with the referral only if the relationship between the teacher and the prospective client is not especially close.

Finally, because of the potential complications, the prospective client may be reluctant to enter therapy with a person his friend knows or may simply wish to see a different mental health professional. Perhaps he knows he would wish to discuss therapy sessions with Mr. Goodheart but would hesitate if he chose Theodore as his therapist, or perhaps he would rather see a female professional or someone who is older. In other words, because Theodore cannot anticipate the client's preferences and because his ultimate commitment should be to the client's welfare rather than his own financial gain, Theodore's ideal action would be to give the teacher several other names of competent professionals, even if he also provides his own card.

SUMMARY

Effective, beneficial counseling and psychotherapy depend on the therapist's ability to provide objectivity and single-minded commitment to the client's welfare. It also depends on the client's ability to trust the professional. Implicit in that trust is confidence in the professional's selfless interest in the client and a sense of emotional closeness to the professional. When a practitioner has an additional personal or professional relationship with a client, objectivity, selfless commitment to the client, and client trust are all endangered to some degree. In other words, when a practitioner is both the friend and the researcher, or the therapist and the teacher, the professional is putting him- or herself in a conflict-of-interest situation. Both parties in the professional relationship may be hampered in reaching their therapeutic goals by the existence and demands of the other relationship. Having more than one relationship with a person with whom there is or has been a professional relationship is called a *multiple relationship* or *boundary extension*. The terms *boundary crossing* and *boundary violation* are also used, the former to designate multiple relationships at low risk for harm to clients, and the latter to identify high-risk relationships.

The ethical difficulties of multiple relationships are most apparent in therapeutic relationships, but they are often inappropriate in other forms of professional contact as well. Nonsexual multiple relationships with clients seem to occur more frequently than sexual relationships, according to researchers. The professions' ethics codes do not universally endorse multiple relationships, but their provisions have become less restrictive in recent years and thereby place a greater burden on the professional to use good ethical judgment. The criterion on which they base this judgment is the professional's duty to promote the client's welfare without undue risk of harm. Multiple connections with clients can impair objectivity, interfere with therapeutic progress, and affect the client's emotional connection to the clinician. They also can intensify the power difference between the professional and the client, and can result in exploitation of clients. Multiple relationships have these effects partly because the obligations and expectations from different roles are often inherently incompatible. The more divergent the obligations of two roles, the more likely the multiple relationship will be unethical.

Because not all multiple relationships can be avoided, especially in rural settings, professionals need to examine carefully whether to start a particular multiple relationship. Clients' access to alternative competent care ought to be considered, along with cultural variables and the potential for an individual to benefit from services despite the multiple connection. Generally, though, the attitude of the mental health professional should be to prevent risk (Sonne, 1994). High-risk relationships should not be initiated, even if they have the potential to do good. If the relationship cannot be avoided, the professional should discuss the implications and risks of the situation with the client and then carefully document both that discussion and the subsequent progress of counseling. The professional should seek expert supervision and develop an alternative plan in the event of unforeseen complications. If practitioners find themselves frequently engaging in multiple relationships, they need to examine their motivation and become more creative in finding alternative access to care for the clients involved.

Bartering—trading goods or services instead of money for counseling—is also a practice discouraged by the ethics codes, but not forbidden. A professional who is entertaining a bartering relationship with a mental health client should read the professions' codes carefully and should consult his or her state laws and regulations. Some states forbid the practice, and some professional liability insurers exclude claims resulting from a bartering arrangement.

Discussion Questions*

1. Research shows a great diversity in professionals' opinions about the ethics of nonsexual multiple relationships, in contrast to their views of sexual contact with clients. What do you think accounts for this diversity? Do you think it is healthy?
2. Do you agree with the standards written into the codes of ethics about nonsexual multiple relationships? Would you recommend stronger or more lenient wording? Why?
3. Friends, social acquaintances, and business associates frequently ask counselors to accept them as clients. Sometimes counselors do, taking the view that their preexisting knowledge of the client can facilitate therapeutic progress. They believe that in such relationships, trust occurs more easily and insight happens more quickly. Is their position justifiable based on the codes? How would you respond to a colleague who made such an argument?
4. Should bartering of services be distinguished from bartering for goods in the ethics codes? Is this a real distinction or a semantic one? What would you describe as an ideal standard on this issue?
5. What stance do you think you will take on accepting gifts from clients? Do you agree that this topic should be included in informed consent? How would you feel if your counselor initiated this kind of discussion at that point in the process?

*Note to course instructors: The *Instructor's Guide* for this book includes other discussion questions, class exercises, cases, and multiple-choice and essay test items for this chapter.

6. Given the literature on accepting gifts from clients, how would you evaluate the ethics of counselor gifts to clients, for example, at termination?
7. How would you evaluate the behavior of the other mental health professionals mentioned in the opening section of this chapter, but not reviewed yet?

Cases for Discussion

Portia is a counselor educator with a small private practice. A professor in the history department at the same university where Portia works calls Portia's practice to ask if she could schedule a counseling appointment. Portia knows this woman from campus and from serving together on the faculty senate. Portia suggests that the history professor make an appointment with her partner instead. In spite of receiving an explanation of the reasons why Portia would prefer to have the prospective client see her partner instead, the historian is angered by the action and refuses to make an appointment. Did Portia act appropriately or was she too legalistic in her interpretation of the multiple relationship provisions of the Code?

Six months after Deborah, a counseling psychologist, successfully terminated counseling with a musician client whom she treated for social anxiety, this client sends her a ticket to the orchestra's next performance, indicating that he remembers Deborah is fond of the pieces the orchestra will be playing that night. Deborah attends and approaches the musician after the concert to thank him for the ticket. He asks Deborah to attend a post-performance party with him and his wife. Deborah agrees. Within a few months, the three become friends who frequently attend music events together. In establishing a social relationship with a client six months after therapy, did Deborah violate the multiple relationship provision of the ACA Code? Did she violate any other provision? What do you see as the ethical risks and benefits, if any, of Deborah's actions?

Recommended Readings

Anderson, S. K., & Kitchener, K. S. (1996). Nonromantic, nonsexual posttherapy relationships between psychologists and former clients: An exploratory study of critical incidents. *Professional Psychology: Research and Practice*, *27*, 59–66.

Austin, W., Bergum, V., Nuttgens, S., Peternalj-Taylor, C. (2006). A re-visioning of boundaries in professional helping relationships: Exploring other metaphors. *Ethics & Behavior*, *16*, 77–94.

Barnett, J. E. (2011). But it's a really nice gift: Ethical challenges in responding to offers of gifts from clients. In W. B. Johnson & G. P. Koocher (Eds.), *Ethical conundrums, quandaries, and predicaments in mental health practice* (pp. 9–16.) New York, NY: Oxford.

Barnett, J. E., Lazarus, A. A., Vasquez, M. J. T., Moorehead-Slaughter, O., & Johnson, W. B. (2007). Boundary issues and multiple relationships: Fantasy and reality. *Professional Psychology: Research and Practice*, *38*, 401–410.

Borys, D. S., & Pope, K. S. (1989). Multiple relationships between therapist and client: A national study of psychologists, psychiatrists and social workers. *Professional Psychology: Research and Practice*, *20*, 283–293.

Gutheil, T. G., & Brodsky, A. (2008). *Preventing boundary violations in clinical practice*. New York, NY: Guilford.

Helbok, C. M. (2003). The practice of psychology in rural communities: Potential ethical dilemmas. *Ethics & Behavior*, *13*, 367–384.

Herlihy, B., & Corey, G. (1997). *Boundary issues in counseling*. Alexandria, VA: American Counseling Association.

Herlihy, B. & Watson, Z. E. (2003). Ethical issues and multicultural competence in counseling. In F. D. Harper & J. McFadden (Eds.), *Culture and counseling: New approaches* (pp. 363–378). Needham Heights, MA: Allyn & Bacon.

Johnson, W. B., Bacho, R., Helm, M., & Ralph, J. (2006). Multiple role dilemmas for military mental health care providers. *Military Medicine*, *17*, 311–315.

Pope, K. S., & Keith-Spiegel, P. (2008). A practical approach to boundaries in psychotherapy: Making decisions, bypassing blunders, and mending fences. *Journal of Clinical Psychology*, *64*, 638–652.

Schank, J. A., & Skovholt, T. M. (2006). *Ethical practice in small communities*. Washington, D.C.: American Psychological Association.

Simon, R. I. (1992). Treatment of boundary violations: Clinical, ethical and legal considerations. *Bulletin of the American Academy of Psychiatry and the Law*, *20*, 269–288.

Younggren, J. N., & Gottlieb, M. C. (2004). Managing risk when contemplating multiple relationships. *Professional Psychology: Research and Practice*, *35*, 255–260.

Additional Online Resources

Dual Relationships, Multiple Relationships, & Boundary Decisions: http://kspope.com/dual/index.php.

Dual Relationships, Multiple Relationships, Boundaries, Boundary Crossings & Boundary Violations in Psychotherapy, Counseling & Mental Health: http://www.zurinstitute.com/dualrelationships.html.

Multiple Relationships in Campus Counseling Centers: A Vignette: http://www.apa.org/monitor/2008/05/ethics.html.

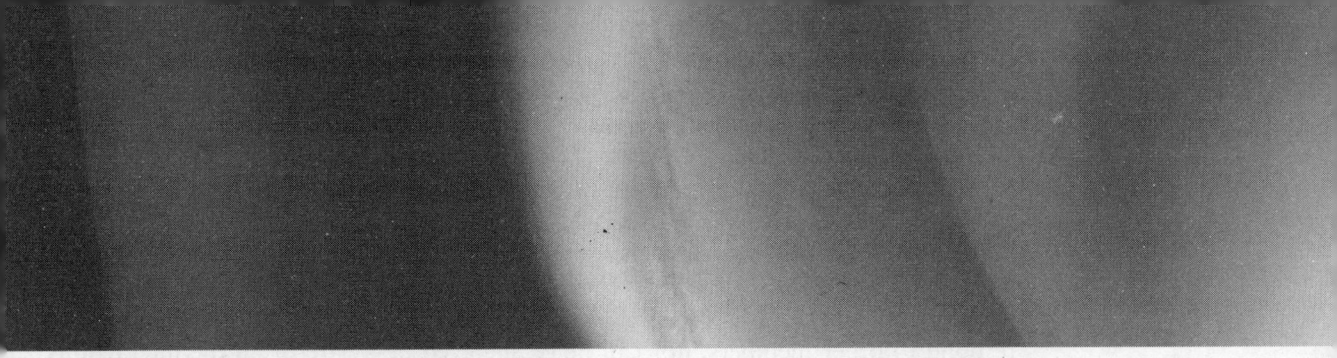

Interventions With Groups, Couples, and Families

CHAPTER 9

Unique Ethical Responsibilities

The fundamental ethical values and standards that guide individual counseling and psychotherapy are also at the core of group, couple, and family interventions. However, four features distinguish the ethical practice of these activities. First, the client is encouraged to disclose personal information not only to a professional but also to other participants who are not mental health professionals. Under these circumstances, admitting personal secrets feels (and is) riskier. The others to whom this personal information is revealed may be judgmental or may use that information in ways that are counterproductive to the client. Because only the professional can be held accountable for misusing personal disclosures, a client must rely on the good intentions of other participants to act responsibly. Both a high level of trust of others and a strong expectation of benefit from such disclosures are required for active engagement in multiple-person settings. In work with couples and families, the audience to whom a client discloses personal information is obviously quite familiar, but that familiarity does not necessarily reduce the risk for the participant. Indeed, family members have more opportunity to misuse that information than do strangers.

Second, the dynamics of therapeutic change are different in multiple-person settings. In individual counseling, the relationship between the two parties, coupled with the interventions used, results in therapeutic change. In group and family treatment, effectiveness is based largely on the interdependence that develops among all participants (Lakin, 1994; Knauss & Knauss, 2012; Yalom & Leszcz, 2005). Therapeutic change stems from the help and support members give each other as much as from the activities of the leader (Gladding, 2011; Morran, Stockton, & Bond, 1991). Typically, feedback from peers in a group has significant emotional impact on members (Corey & Corey, 2013; Klontz, 2004). Given this facet of therapy, group and family therapists have a duty to help clients develop an interdependence that empowers rather than weakens them. The skills and ethical sensitivities necessary for this task differ substantially from those required by individual counseling or psychotherapy.

Third, a therapist has less control over events that take place during or between sessions. The professional cannot always predict how participants will respond to other members, nor can he or she even be aware of all the interactions among members. The dynamics of this phenomenon are especially visible in family and couple counseling, where clients have continuous contact with each other, but are no less real in group therapy. For example, group members may continue a discussion initiated in a session over coffee afterward or may text or email each other between sessions. Or they may "friend" each other on a social networking site. Paradoxically, though, this lessening of control does not necessarily result in less power for the professional. Group clients can also become excessively dependent on the leader if that leader manipulates group process to foster such dependency. Family members may fall into the practice of deferring even minor decisions until the next session and may use the words and actions of the professional as the sole influence in arriving at a decision.

Finally, research shows that group and family interventions are powerful forms of care, with the capacity for greater good or greater harm than many forms of individual treatment (e.g., see Lambert, 2013; Yalom & Leszcz, 2005). Kottler (1994) maintains that the emotional intensity of the group in itself makes group treatment more powerful. Moreover, groups and families lend themselves to interventions that may be inherently riskier (Lakin, 1994). Because interpersonal issues can be resistant to traditional approaches, group and family therapists sometimes seek out innovative interventions to break through blocks to therapeutic gains. This drive to provide therapeutic benefit to these clients is well intentioned but must be balanced against the inherent risk in newer, riskier, and less proven techniques. In such situations, the principle of nonmaleficence should take precedence over beneficence.

This chapter examines the implications of these distinct features of group and family interventions on the ethics of practice. It also explores the applicability of the concepts discussed in previous chapters—competence, informed consent, confidentiality, and dual relationships—to multiple-person settings. Finally, the chapter ends with a brief discussion of the legal issues affecting these modalities.

GROUP COUNSELING AND PSYCHOTHERAPY

The APA Code makes relatively brief references to group psychotherapy, while the ACA Code refers to two responsibilities specific to work with groups. The first specific requirement is to screen prospective members for compatibility with the group (Section A.9.a); the second (A.9.b) is to protect clients from harm. It also identifies two responsibilities that apply to any multiple person situation. The first of these is the duty to explain confidentiality and its limits with this form of service (B.4.a.), and the second is to clarify which persons are clients and to ensure that all involved understand the limits of confidentiality (B.4.b). The APA Code discusses groups specifically in Standard 10.03 (Appendix B, p. 557), emphasizing the responsibility of the psychologist to explain confidentiality and it limits to all parties as soon as services begin. In Standard 7.07 the APA Code also specifies that if group or individual therapy is a program requirement, students must be free to find their therapists without program affiliation for the activity.

Ethics scholars have criticized the codes' failure to attend to the many other distinctive features of groups (e.g., see Lakin, 1994), but there are other sources of guidance for the practitioner beyond these codes. First, there are three useful documents published by the Association for Specialists in Group Work (ASGW), a division of the ACA. The first identifies a series of best practices for group leaders (ASGW, 2007). (See Appendix C for information to access this code on the Web.) The precepts presented in this document provide extensive advice about specific procedures group counselors should use from the orientation and screening stage of a group, to termination and follow-up. It also describes the practitioner's obligations regarding continuing education, referral of clients to other services, and the counselor's responsibility regarding the reporting of unethical behavior. The ASGW has also produced *Professional Standards for Training Group Workers* (2000) and *Multicultural and Social Justice Competence Principles for Group Workers* (2012). Both documents describe in detail the specific skills and knowledge base required for competent group leadership. Many years earlier, in 1973, the American Psychological Association published standards for therapists of growth groups, but that document is still useful to those who lead such groups today. A parallel professional association of group therapists, the American Group Therapy Association also publishes *Guidelines for Ethics* (2002) and *Practice Guidelines for Group Psychotherapy* (2007). See Leszcz and Kobos (2008) for a review of the application of the American Group Psychotherapy Association (AGPA) guidelines. (Links to these documents are also included in Appendix D.)

The second type of resource is the body of literature by ethics scholars that comments on how the codes view group treatment (e.g., see Corey et al., 1995; Forester-Miller, 2002; Klontz, 2004; Knauss & Knauss, 2012; Wilcoxon, Gladding & Remley, 2013; Williams, 1996; and the entire January 2007, issue of the *International Journal of Group Psychotherapy*). These and other scholars offer in-depth analysis of particular ethical concepts and elaborate on the application of group ethics to certain kinds of groups (also, see Aubrey & Dougher, 1990; Knauss, 2007; Krishna et al., 2011; Merta & Sisson, 1991; Ritchie & Huss, 2000). This growing body of research and theory offers the practitioner thoughtful analysis of some of the most complex issues in group work. Taken together, these resources compensate for the omissions in the codes and guide the practitioner to a solid understanding of his or her ethical duties in group settings.

Competence and Group Counseling

Obviously, competent group counseling requires knowledge of group theory, process, and research; successful supervised experience in leading groups; and a diligent attitude toward the work. Competent group leadership is not an automatic consequence of expertise in individual counseling. Effective leadership of a therapeutic group demands a background in this particular modality because of the power of the experience, the vulnerability of the client to harm from both the leader and other participants, and the potential for negative outcomes. The *Professional Standards for the Training of Group Workers* (ASGW, 2000) thoroughly delineates the knowledge base and skills essential for group leadership. It also identifies the special capacities required by the various kinds of therapeutic groups, ranging from task-oriented and psychoeducational groups to long-term psychotherapy groups. The ASGW standards focus on broad knowledge of research and theory as essential for competent practice. They proceed to elaborate details of essential skills and minimum levels of supervised experience. The message of these standards is that brief and cursory exposure to group theory and practice is insufficient for competent practice.

Unfortunately, some counselors and therapists fail to monitor their own competence as group leaders. Lakin (1994) decries the casual attitude of these professionals toward the complexities of group process. He labels involvement in group leadership without appropriate competence a serious ethical violation and argues that a group leader needs a comprehensive understanding of the role of group cohesion in fostering therapeutic progress. Helping the members develop enough cohesion to be beneficial without transforming group cohesion into pressure to conformity is a difficult task. Inadequately trained professionals either fail to foster enough cohesion or overemphasize it and make the group suffocating for some members. Lakin cites other unique aspects of groups, such as the encouragement of emotional expression or the formation of subgroups and scapegoating, which also require a skilled therapist with good judgment. Leszcz and Kobos (2008) note that leaders "have the responsibility for developing a climate of constructive emotional experience" (p. 1252). Otherwise, genuine emotional expression becomes false emotionality pressured by the group and has little therapeutic value.

Corey and Corey (2013) stress that no blanket group competence exists for all types of groups. A person qualified to lead a substance abuse group may not be competent to lead a long-term psychotherapy group or an assertiveness group. Counselors must always evaluate the match between the type of group under consideration and their prior training and experience.

The literature also suggests that not all clients can benefit from groups. In fact, some can be harmed by participation (Roback, 2000; Yalom & Leszcz, 2005; Leszcz & Kobos, 2008). Group leaders need the knowledge to identify such people and direct them to other types of service or to other kinds of groups. They must also be able to judge when a group is not helping a member and must take effective action to remedy the problem or refer the client to another source of assistance.

Finally, mental health professionals who lead groups are obligated to update their skills and knowledge lest they lose the competence they have established. The ASGW standards mandate participation in professional development activities, echoing the standards presented in the ACA and APA codes. The recent emergence of modalities such as Internet-based self-help groups (Barak, Boniel-Nissim, & Suler, 2008; Humphreys, Winzelberg, & Klaw, 2000) highlights the importance of continuing education. Knauss and Knauss (2012) note that when groups are focused on specific issues such as eating disorders, leaders must take care that they have sufficient competence in treating this problem and in group treatment.

Another competency requirement is for group leaders to attend to the after effects of a group meeting or a group experience. Klontz (2004) points out that in groups that encourage emotional expression, the transition from group to participants' ordinary lives may be difficult. He recommends that group leaders assist clients in aftercare by providing specific instructions for the transition, including recommendations for communication with family and friends outside the group about the group experience without compromising confidentiality or threatening or confusing loved ones. Clear guidelines for communication among group members outside of meetings must also be established (Leszcz & Kobos, 2008).

Informed Consent in Group Counseling and Psychotherapy

Because group treatment involves risks and responsibilities beyond those typically experienced in individual work, informed consent is crucially important. The informed consent process for groups begins with orienting the client to the group process and procedure before the beginning of the group sessions and also involves screening prospective group members. As with individual service, developing informed consent in groups should include describing the goals, techniques, procedures, limitations, risks, and benefits of the group. Professionals should make a special effort to ensure that prospective clients understand the roles of the therapist and other group members, as well as their personal responsibilities in group. Clients also need to know the characteristics of a typical group session and the expectations of members in those sessions. If the group is one in which emotional expression will be encouraged, clients should be told of this emphasis. Group sessions can be quite intense, and that intensity can be exhilarating or exhausting, or both. Clients who are prepared to expect an intense experience may not only make better choices about participation but may also better tolerate and learn from that climate.

Corey and Corey (2013) list risks specific to group counseling that should be explained to prospective group members, including scapegoating, group pressure to discuss private material, possible discomfort with confrontation and negative effects (even temporary) in the clients' lives stemming from the group experience.

The practical matters regarding fees, times and locations of meetings, duration of the group, and so forth should be addressed. If insurance is to be billed for group sessions, all aspects of informed consent relevant to third-party payers should be reviewed. If a co-leader is participating, explaining the co-leader's role and qualifications to clients is an obvious aspect of a fully informed consent. The client ought to be given an opportunity to meet the co-leader before the group begins, in order to ask him or her questions. In addition, clients should understand how co-leaders will communicate with each other about group members. Fallon (2006) offers additional specific suggestions for implementing effective consent for group treatment. The ASGW standards (2007) also elaborate careful attention to informed consent for group participation.

Because group cohesion is such an important feature of an effective group (Yalom & Leszcz, 2005), clients should also appreciate the degree of commitment asked of them when they join a group. Group members need to understand that their regular attendance and active involvement are necessary for the group's success. As the ASGW guidelines recommend, the delicate issue of dropping out of the group should be openly discussed. This is a delicate issue because all clients have the right to refuse to continue if they wish, but most group leaders want members to maintain participation at least until an individual has reached his or her goals for the group experience (Corey & Corey, 2013; Yalom & Leszcz, 2005). Part of what makes a group beneficial is its power to help clients work through difficult emotions and persevere with commitments to others. When people drop out, they may rob themselves of the opportunity for important personal learning, and they diminish group cohesiveness and effectiveness for other members. Most leaders, therefore, ask members to attend at least one final session to explain their decision to terminate to the other members (Corey et al., 1995). The goals of that session are to help the member reach some degree of closure to the group process, to limit the damage to group cohesiveness, and to improve the chances that the group will continue to have therapeutic power for remaining members. Its not-so-hidden agenda may be to encourage the person to change his or her mind and remain in the group (Kottler, 1982). When group leaders endorse this view about the importance of a "proper" termination process, they must disclose it to prospective clients and explain its rationale. With that knowledge, clients are then empowered to accept or reject the conditions of membership the leader has set forth. The legal concept of informed refusal (the right to reject offered services without penalty) also operates in groups. No group leader can ethically or legally coerce participation if an individual wishes to withdraw. Thus the goal is to enlighten without being biased and to encourage without pressuring. When dealing with culturally diverse groups, leaders bear the burden to take into account the role of cultural diversity in the client's reaction to both the group process and the policy on dropping out (ASGW, 2012).

Confidentiality and Privilege in Group Interventions

The professional's duty to maintain the confidentiality of client communications is unchanged in group work. However, the fact that nearly all of what is disclosed is communicated before other group members complicates both the ethics of confidentiality and the legal interpretation of privilege. As already discussed, other group members cannot be held accountable if they violate confidentiality. Group members who keep confidences do so out of a personal moral standard, a commitment to the group process, and/or some fear of group censure.

Even though group leaders cannot guarantee confidentiality, they are still obligated to do their utmost to encourage it. That responsibility entails thoroughly explaining of the role of confidentiality to each prospective group member, describing the specifics of its operations, and asking for a commitment to honor confidentiality at all times in the group. Unfortunately, research has found less than ideal levels of comprehension and compliance with these standards. Lasky and Riva (2006) reported that 36% of respondents to her survey of group counselors did not know whether privilege extended to group clients in their jurisdictions or what their responsibilities were if subpoenaed. Moreover, she found that 44% of those surveyed did not always review the limits of confidentiality with group members. (This confusion about a professional's duty when subpoenaed extends to all therapy situations, not just group therapy. In my experience conducting continuing education programs, nearly half of the practitioners attending misunderstand this responsibility.)

Most group scholars also recommend that leaders remind group members about confidentiality both at the first group session and periodically throughout the group process (ASGW, 2007; Corey & Corey, 2013). Reminders should be given immediately after particularly intense or risky sessions. Corey et al. (1995) emphasize that the issue of inadvertent disclosures should be addressed because even well-intentioned members may be vulnerable to accidental violations. Pepper (2003) advises group leaders to be clear about whether complete confidentiality is required or whether members can discuss general issues and feelings aroused by group, an issue that sometimes confuses group members.

A practical approach to ensuring that members have the skills and judgment to avoid breaks in confidentiality involves role-playing situations that may tempt members to violate confidentiality. In this simulation, one person might take the role of a friend who asks the group member about the identities of other group members, and another person role-plays a response. Group members themselves might develop scenarios they think could happen in their lives and act them out in group. Ideally, such simulations would take place fairly early in the group process and would give individual members confidence in their own abilities to honor confidentiality and in other members' commitment to secrecy. Group leaders may also opt to develop orientation videos that highlight confidentiality and show simulations of members successfully honoring confidentiality. Such measures can be especially useful with minor clients or others who may have difficulty managing confidentiality when peer pressure to disclose occurs.

Some group leaders use contracts for confidentiality that members must sign to join the group. These written contracts clarify expectations and highlight the importance of confidentiality to the therapeutic process. They are a visible representation of the value the leaders place on this facet of group behavior. The use of confidentiality contracts is supported by some ethics scholars (such as Corey et al., 1995), but preliminary research suggests that most practitioners do not favor them (Roback et al., 1992). These researchers found only 23% of group therapists in their survey actually used them. Bernstein and Hartsell (1998) point out that these contracts have symbolic rather than legal value and that no litigation related to group members' breach of confidentiality has ever occurred.

The limits of confidentiality that apply to individual counseling, elaborated in Chapter 5, are all transferable to group settings. The duty to warn and/or protect, to report child and elder abuse and neglect, to respond to a court order for confidential information, and to answer charges of unethical or illegal behavior made by clients all hold for group counseling. Therefore, all prospective members need to be informed about these limits to confidentiality. Special care should be taken in explaining that the professional's duty to confidentiality does not necessarily extend to other members of the group. Group leaders need to help clients understand the risks they are undertaking as well as the potential benefits of the group experience.

Unfortunately, there is a paucity of published research on compliance with this standard. The one published study that attended to this question found only 32% of group therapists who explicitly discussed the risks of disclosure of private information by other group members (Roback et al., 1992). Two other studies (Appelbaum & Greer, 1993; Lasky & Riva, 2006) also reported that a significant proportion of group therapists fail to discuss the limits of confidentiality with their clients. What accounts for this reluctance? No empirically based answer can be given yet, but Roback and colleagues (1992) hypothesize that group leaders are concerned that such information would discourage people from entering groups or from revealing personal material during sessions. However well intentioned the motivation for such a stance, it is inconsistent with existing ethical standards. Disregard of this standard could also spell legal trouble. Roback et al. point out that consciously deciding not to discuss the limits to confidentiality could be interpreted as deliberately misrepresenting the risks of the process, for which a group therapist could be held liable in the courts.

There is still another reason for informing clients about this limit. When violations or breaches of confidentiality do occur, the group often experiences at least a temporary setback in cohesion and productivity (Roback et al., 1992). In addition, after such a breach some members permanently retreat from active involvement in group process. Smokowski, Rose, and Bacallao (2001) refer to members who experienced distress after other members breached confidentiality as "group casualties." These negative outcomes argue strongly both for an emphasis on prevention by completely and explicitly discussing this issue with prospective group members and for a backup plan for recovery from such harm if prevention fails.

Legal considerations also argue for comprehensively discussing confidentiality. The degree to which privilege applies in group counseling varies considerably by state. Generally, state courts have held that any statement made in front of third parties is not covered by privilege (Paradise & Kirby, 1990; Swenson, 1997). In such jurisdictions, a group leader has no defense against disclosing client information to a court. In still other states, including California, Illinois, Kentucky, Minnesota, Colorado, Kansas, New Mexico, and the District of Columbia, a special kind of privilege for communications in group therapy has been established (Parker, Clevenger, & Sherman, 1997). Because of the changing nature of state statutes and the unique language in each state's revised code, professionals are well advised to stay current with laws in their state.

Privilege typically applies only to the licensed professional in the session, though Colorado, for example, extends it to unlicensed psychotherapists (Colo. Rev. Stat. Ann. Section 13-90-107). There is rarely any privilege for other group members who heard the same information as the leader, so they can be mandated to testify even if the mental health professional cannot. Explaining this reality to prospective members is essential. Failure to do so conflicts with members' right to make autonomous decisions about activities that affect them. Lest clients become overly concerned about some legal risks, it is important to balance this explanation of risk against the very low probability that it will occur. Court cases involving group counseling or therapy are relatively rare (Paradise & Kirby, 1990), and few group leaders or participants have actually had to testify against a group member. That should not foster complacency, but if history is any guide, the level of that risk is very small.

The Ethics of Group Work With Minors and in the Schools

Many scholars view group counseling as a useful and practical intervention for children and adolescents (e.g., Gladding, 2011; Greenberg, 2003; Knauss, 2007; Riester, 2002; Ritchie & Huss, 2000), although rigorous research on the effectiveness of group work with minors is still in its infancy (Shechtman, 2002). When professionals provide ongoing group counseling for young people, they face additional challenges to confidentiality. First, group leaders must consider how much information about a child's disclosures in group can or must be shared with parents. Unless operating under a statute or court ruling that grants an adolescent a right to confidentiality of disclosures made in counseling or psychotherapy, parents typically have the right to information about their children's comments in sessions. Of course, parents have the right to knowledge only of their own child's disclosures and not those of other participants. Therefore, group leaders are well advised to obtain parental consent to group participation at the initiation of a group and to seek parental waivers to their right to know everything their child communicates in order to encourage the child's trust and openness to the group experience. (See Chapters 5 and 6 for additional discussion of minors' and parental rights.)

In addition, group leaders must be sensitive to the developmental issues that may affect a young person's capacity to understand and maintain the confidentiality of disclosures made within the group. Young people may experience pressure from nonparticipating peers to discuss what has happened in group and may have limited skill in resisting such pressure (Ritchie & Huss, 2000). Therefore group leaders have a duty to be diligent in screening potential group members to assess their capacity to honor confidentiality, learn communication skills to resist peer pressure to breach confidentiality, and respond empathically to peer comments in group. When groups are conducted in schools, they can be a valuable tool to help promote student development and academic success (Greenberg, 2003; Riester, 2002; Ritchie & Huss, 2000; Shechtman, 2002). However, whenever group members are part of a closed system (such as a school), where they have ongoing out-of-group contact with other group participants and where nonparticipants may be aware of which students are leaving classes to attend group sessions, the task of maintaining confidentiality is quite demanding. To succeed in this task, not only should school counselors screen prospective members carefully, they should also orient students to expectations and regularly monitor compliance. Group leaders should also have a plan for responding should confidentiality be breached during an ongoing group experience.

Some evidence also suggests that inattention to group composition can negatively affect group effectiveness and even cause harm to children (Rhule, 2005). For example, Dishion, McCord, and Poulin (1999) found that groups that included only aggressive children and adolescents actually *increased* the risk of aggressive behavior in participants. The comments and actions of the more aggressive and delinquent youth in the groups actually taught the less aggressive youth new ways to act out. Other evidence indicates that group leaders must be especially careful about the use of their confrontation and negative feedback with youth members and about the structure of the feedback from peers, since harmful effects have been noted (Shechtman & Yanuv, 2001). These authors advise reliance on acceptance, empathy, and support as therapeutic approaches with a substantially greater likelihood of positive effects. The ASCA Ethical Standards for School Counselors (2010) note these responsibilities in Section A.6.

The Ethics of Multiple Relationships in Group Counseling and Psychotherapy

The prohibition against sexual contact with clients obviously extends to group work, as does the standard of avoiding other forms of multiple relationships that pose a risk to professional effectiveness. Although the dynamics of therapeutic change differ in groups, the therapist's power is not significantly reduced. Social, personal, business, or other connections with current clients can compromise the leader's professional judgment and objectivity and can affect the client's emotional response to the group. In addition, multiple relationships with group members can diminish group cohesion when other members suspect that one of their own has a special relationship with the leader. Such contacts can also engender more hostility toward the leader and distract the group from productive activities.

The Ethics of Concurrent Individual and Group Services

According to Taylor and Gazda (1991) and Lakin (1994), the practice of seeing the same clients in both group and individual counseling, or of gathering one's individual clients together into a group, happens rather frequently. A client may also start out in group and then be seen individually while the group continues. Professional codes do not address this behavior. Lakin (1994) reports that most practitioners see no ethical problem with it. However, Lakin (1994) has identified several important potential difficulties with concurrent individual and group interventions:

- Risks to confidentiality and privilege because of communications between co-leaders or difficulty remembering which disclosures were shared in which setting
- Interference with the client's emotional relationship with the professional and with transference, including "sibling rivalry" among group members and an increased risk of countertransference from the leader
- The creation of an overpowerful therapist and an overdependent client, resulting in a higher probability of misuse of therapeutic power
- The financial gain for referring to oneself that blinds a professional to the client's real needs (Fisher, 2003; Lakin, 1994; Taylor & Gazda, 1991)

Taylor and Gazda identify several ways to minimize these risks, the most central of which are informed consent to concurrent treatment, careful monitoring of the professional's power and the client's dependence, and scrupulous attention to the client's well-being. Supervision and consultation also seem crucial. Regardless of the precautions taken, the dangers of this practice should be acknowledged, and prudent counselors would be well advised to consider it as a last resort. If individual therapy is needed for a group member, a referral elsewhere should be considered. Similarly, when therapists are entertaining the idea of gathering their clients together into a group, especially an open-ended therapeutic group, those professionals ought to be clear about the rationale, get supervision or consultation, and be prepared to accept responsibility for problems that develop.

The Ethics of Involuntary Group Participation

Both the ASGW *Best Practice Guidelines* (2007) and ethics scholars discuss the complicated ethics related to involuntary group participation. Courts, treatment facilities, and other agencies often mandate group participation. The person involved theoretically has a choice, but the alternative is so unappealing that the person sees no other realistic course of action. A neglectful parent may be required to attend a parenting group as a condition of maintaining custody of his children, or a woman arrested for driving while intoxicated can "choose" between an alcohol education group and a criminal record. A person who enters a hospital for treatment of bipolar disorder (manic depression) may learn that participation in daily group therapy sessions is a condition of treatment. Without the group involvement, the person cannot receive the individual counseling or medication management that he or she really seeks. In each instance, the person agrees to group participation as the least worst alternative. The fundamental question underlying this practice, as noted in Chapter 6, is whether informed consent is really possible in the absence of free consent and whether it is ethical for mental health professionals to make such demands on clients. Neither the major codes nor the ASGW documents address this basic issue for group counseling, implying (but not explicitly stating) that the benefit the person and the society can receive from the group outweighs the temporary loss of autonomy about this decision. In one recent court decision, *Welch v. Kentucky* (Paul & Herbert, 2005), the court ruled that a patient's disclosures in group therapy could not be used against him in court since the patient's participation in group therapy was mandated by the legal system. In essence, the court argued that using his admissions of past criminal behavior in mandated group treatment would constitute a form of self-incrimination.

Corey and Corey (2013) also describe the practical dimensions of involuntary participation—the potential for the therapeutic work of the group to be advanced is severely limited if individuals do not have at least a basic level of commitment to the group. Involuntary clients who feel tricked and manipulated into group membership are unlikely to profit from the experience. Thus, most writers on the subject highlight the importance of dealing with the clients' feelings about involuntary participation both in screening sessions and early in the life of the group. They should be allowed to express their frustration about the loss of autonomy and their fears or reservations about the group. Corey et al. (1995) suggest that the chance to openly discuss these feelings may reduce resistance and increase cooperation. Brodsky (2011) advises that the *group conversation method* has shown value in encouraging group members' engagement in group treatment.

Developing informed consent is especially important with involuntary clients. If a client's activity in the group is to be reported to a court or public agency, the client should understand that fact and the implications of his or her behavior in the group for subsequent actions by those agencies. To return to the example of the parent who joins a group as a condition of retaining custody of his children, if the leader must report to the child protective agency that the man has been silent and uninvolved in group sessions, the man should be informed of that fact. If the counselor knows from experience that such a report is likely to reduce the chances that the client will keep his children, the counselor should also tell the client that.

In short, the central message in acting consistently with the ethical values of the profession while accepting nonvoluntary clients into groups is that the professional must zealously guard the client's remaining rights and work energetically to help the client make a free choice for participation. If that is not possible, at least the leader should aim for fully informed consent about the ramifications of the client's reaction to the mandate. If a professional believes that mandated group participation is unlikely to benefit the client and may bring harm, he or she then has an obligation to communicate that professional judgment to the parties demanding participation and to work toward an alternative therapeutic placement satisfactory to all involved.

Ethical Issues in Multicultural Groups

Few groups are homogeneous. Most include people of different religions, cultural backgrounds, ethnicities, genders, physical capabilities, sexual orientations, and ages. Sometimes the diagnostic label they share is all they have in common. According to Chen, Kakkad, and Balzano (2008), "cultural diversity expands the multiple perspectives that are already available in the group but also limits within-group communications, presenting an increased risk for misunderstanding and conflict" (p. 1264). Heterogeneous groups make group cohesion more difficult to achieve and the leader's skill even more crucial to its accomplishment. Ironically, in diverse groups there is sometimes greater pressure for cohesion, and professionals must be alert to pressures for cohesion that are insensitive to cultural values (Corey et al., 1995). Unfortunately, little research is available on how diverse cultural backgrounds affect group members' experiences (Chen et al., 2008). Similarly, group leaders need to recognize how their own cultural backgrounds affect their values and their approach to building a cohesive group. The APA's *Guidelines on Multicultural Education, Training, Research, Practice, and Organizational Change for Psychologists* (2003) is an especially useful resource for the mental health professional who seeks to develop these skills, as is the ASGW's *Multicultural and Social Justice Competence Principles for Group Workers* (2012).

Leader sensitivity to diversity issues also increases the likelihood that members will be treated fairly. Fairness implies that there is no conscious or unconscious discrimination against members because of differences. For example, a client whose cultural background discourages intense emotional expression or direct confrontation must be given flexibility in responding to the tasks of the group and must not be ridiculed or labeled as dysfunctional because of this cultural background. Because cultural differences are not always apparent to others, group leaders must work to protect the rights of all clients to dignified and fair treatment in the group. If leaders see other members scapegoating one participant because of cultural issues or otherwise behaving in insensitive ways, the professional has a responsibility to intervene to stop that behavior. Leaders whose own behavior models respect for each client go a long way toward achieving the goal of sensitivity. In addition to sensitive attitudes and knowledge of cultural differences, group counselors are obliged to learn strategies for leading multicultural groups that increase the likelihood of success. Resources such as DeLucia, Coleman, and Jenson-Scott (1992); Johnson, Santos-Torres, Coleman, and Smith (1995); and Merta (1995) discuss such strategies. Underlying some group tensions or professional insensitivity in diverse groups may be a conflict in values between participants. Remley and Herlihy (2013) point out, for example, that conceptions of the importance of autonomy for adults may vary by culture and that variability must be taken into account so that value conflicts do not inhibit group effectiveness.

COUNSELING AND PSYCHOTHERAPY WITH FAMILIES AND COUPLES

Because couples and family treatment is a separate discipline that demands significant expertise to practice effectively, its first tenet to be competent is sufficient training and supervised experience in the field (Wilcoxon et al., 2013). Professionals without dedicated training and supervision in this area would be well advised to remedy those deficiencies before involvement in this specialty to eliminate risks of ethical charges or malpractice claims for working beyond the boundaries of their competence (Wilcoxon et al., 2013). Two Canadian provinces and all 50 states (and the District of Columbia) license professionals to conduct marriage and family therapy, and the professional associations, the American Association for Marriage and Family Therapy (AAMFT), and the International Association for Marriage and Family Counseling (IAMFC) have developed standards for graduate training and practice in the discipline. (For a listing of state licensing boards, see http://www.aamft.org/iMIS15/AAMFT/Directories/MFT_Licensing_Boards/Content/Directories/MFT_Licensing_Boards.aspx?hkey=b1033df3-6882-491e-87fd-a75c2f7be070.)

Case Illustrations of Special Issues

The following scenarios represent fairly typical occurrences in the work of a professional who works with couples and families. The pages that follow examine the ethical issues embedded in each.

Scenario 1 One participant in couples counseling telephones and asks for an individual appointment to share some information he thinks the counselor should know but that he wishes to keep secret from his partner. He has been involved in an online relationship with someone for nearly a decade.

Scenario 2 A wife calls for an appointment for family therapy because of family conflict over a teenager's rebellious behavior. She cautions that her husband refuses to attend, although he has agreed to the attendance of the other four members of the family.

Scenario 3 A couple asks for marriage counseling to save their marriage at all costs to each partner personally. They say their individual happiness and emotional well-being are secondary to staying married and that their religion prohibits divorce. They have six children.

Scenario 4 A couple whose child was killed in a car accident 18 months ago recently separated. They begin couples counseling to see if there is any hope for their relationship. After a number of sessions, the counselor concludes that continuing the relationship would probably be destructive for one partner, but ending the relationship would probably be destructive for the other.

Scenario 5 After six individual therapy sessions, a client asks to begin couples therapy because she has realized that the crux of her problem is relational. Her partner is willing, and the counselor agrees with her assessment about the need to attend to relationship issues at this point. The therapist offers concurrent individual and couples counseling.

Scenario 6 A family with two parents and three children is experiencing significant conflict. The wife/mother started a business one year ago. It has been quite successful, and the demands on her time are extensive. Her efforts to get some household responsibilities reassigned to her partner or teenage children have not been successful. Two weeks ago, she got so upset that she went "on strike" from those chores. The whole family is now angry at her and frustrated with the chaos that has developed at home. The husband/father has requested the appointment "to straighten this mess out and get things back to normal."

Scenario 7 A same-sex couple makes an appointment with a heterosexual therapist. The partners are considering adopting a child and wish to discuss the implications of their decision on their relationship and the child. Their motivation is to ensure that the transition to parenthood goes as smoothly as possible for all members of the family.

Scenario 8 A minister refers a couple from her church to couples therapy because of domestic violence. The male partner has shoved, kicked, and verbally abused his female partner on numerous occasions during their 10-year relationship. The most recent occurrence took place five days ago. The woman approached the minister because she is worried about the effects of the violence on the children. The minister reveals that the man was defensive when queried about the violence, and tended to place a good part of the blame on his partner, but was willing to attend therapy sessions.

Analysis of the Scenarios

Scenario 1: Confidentiality of Disclosures to Couples Counselors in Individual Contacts The ethical standards of the American Counseling Association (2005a), the American Association of Marriage and Family Therapy (AAMFT, 2012), and the International Association of Marriage and Family Counseling (IAMFC, 2005) directly address this question. (See Appendix D for the websites that contain the complete AAMFT and IAMFC codes). In fact, the IAMFC Ethical Code is especially explicit in Section II.A.3, clarifying that all individual communications must be held confidential even if the individual disclosing the information is not a primary client, and it goes on to offer guidance about counselor options if an individual's confidential disclosure interferes with family treatment. Neither the ACA Code nor the APA Code explicitly attends to this issue, although the ACA Code does stipulate that the couple or family is the client unless otherwise specified (Section B.4.b). APA Standard 4.02 of the APA Code on confidentiality appears to support the view that individual communications are confidential unless the client waives confidentiality or some other legal duty is imposed. In her commentary on the Code, Fisher (2003) interprets it to mean that disclosures to psychologists in individual contacts may not be revealed in group or family sessions without permission of the client. Campbell et al. (2010) take a more conservative stance, advising therapists that the standard requires them to be clear with clients about their policy regarding family secrets at the initiation of services and periodically during treatment.

When these codes are applied to the first scenario, the ACA, AAMFT, and IAMFC standards indicate that if the counselor hears the "secret" from the individual family member in a one-to-one conversation, the counselor is obligated to keep that information confidential, even from other family members, unless the client waives that right. Needless to say, in this situation the family counselor has no duty to hear the secret communication in the first place and should decide how to respond to this client's request on the basis of clinical considerations and an assessment of what would be in the best interests of the couple. (See Fall and Lyons [2003] for a nuanced discussion of the ethical and clinical issues in responding to family secrets.) Most practicing therapists strongly endorse the confidentiality of individual disclosures and take the view that keeping the secret is likely to be unhelpful. They would not want to proceed with therapy under these conditions, but not all routinely make a clearly communicated policy at the initiation of services about their view of secrets (Butler, Rodriguez, Roper, & Feinhauer, 2010).

On a related point, as online communication between therapists and clients becomes more frequent, family counselors must be aware of the legal requirements related to these communications. Hecker and Edwards (2014) detail the legal duties of family therapists under HIPAA and the recent HITECH legislation.

Scenario 2: The Problem of Nonattending Family Members Many theories of family therapy are rooted in the view that real improvement in the functioning of family members is fundamentally tied to the treatment of the whole family system (see, e.g., Becvar & Becvar, 2006), and research evidence suggests that for some relational problems this claim has validity (Patten, Barnett, & Houlihan, 1991). According to this view, meaningful change in a dysfunctional family system requires the participation of all family members. If one member refuses to engage in therapy, systemic change becomes extremely difficult to achieve (Minuchin, 1974; Napier & Whitaker, 1978). For these reasons, some family therapists experience the nonattendance of one family member as both a clinical and an ethical dilemma. The codes of ethics are silent on this subject, but practitioners still wonder—should the members who want counseling be served, or should counseling be postponed until the reluctant member changes his or her view? How actively should the counselor work to involve the nonengaging person?

Scholars in family therapy have suggested a wide range of answers to these questions, but the recommendations of Teisman (1980); Wilcoxon and Fennel (1983); and Miller, Scott, and Searight (1990) are especially useful. All suggest efforts to remove the obstacles to the nonattender's participation without coercing involvement or interfering with that person's autonomy rights, which include the following:

- Taping a session with the other family members for the nonparticipating individual to review, with the goal of helping that person gain more knowledge of the process. (Consent of the other family members to taping is required, of course.) If misperceptions or fears are at the core of the refusal, this procedure might be effective (Teisman, 1980).

- Writing a letter to the nonattending person, explaining the family therapy process and describing the changes that may take place in the rest of the family as a consequence of counseling based on the research evidence. When a signed copy of this letter is returned, the therapist proceeds with family therapy even if the document is not persuasive to the nonattender (Miller et al., 1990; Wilcoxon & Fennell, 1983). Wilcoxon et al. (2013) include a sample letter to a nonattending member in their book.
- Offering a single individual session with the nonattender to help that person understand the concerns and allay fears and misperceptions of counseling (Teisman, 1980).
- Referring other family members for individual therapy until the whole unit is available (Negash & Hecker, 2010; Wilcoxon & Fennel, 1983).

The goal of each of these methods is to inform, demystify, and open the family counseling process to the reluctant person without any coercive tactics to change the nonattender's stance. The professional must approach this person with respect for his or her rights and with recognition that the resistance to therapy may serve an important function both for that individual and for the family. Huber (1994) cautions professionals to consider whether a refusal to treat because of one family member's unwillingness actually represents an alliance with the nonattender to keep the status quo in the family. Whittinghill (2002) echoes this view in his discussion of the role of family counseling in substance abuse treatment and also suggests that the definition of family should not be limited to blood relations—co-workers, friends, or community members may also function as family in some cases. Inviting such people into counseling may serve the same purpose for some clients as the inclusion of family members serves for others. Broadening the definition of family also makes this service more inclusive of diverse cultural traditions of kinship (Negash & Hecker, 2010). The current version of the ACA Code of Ethics echoes this theme in Section A.1.d: Support Network Involvement.

Scenarios 3 and 4: Conflicts Between Individual and Family Welfare As the stigma of divorce has faded, counselors hear pleas to save a marriage at all costs less frequently than they did 20 years ago. Yet the words are still voiced often enough to be of concern to ethics scholars and practitioners in this field. This request asks the professional to overlook the pain and dysfunction the relationship causes the partners and focus exclusively on continuing the marriage. Sometimes this desire is grounded in religious convictions or cultural background. At other times, it occurs because of fears of change, worries about the children, or a dysfunctional mutual dependency. At still other times, the narrow focus on continuing the marriage is the agenda of a professional who equates divorce with treatment failure (Margolin, 1982). In Scenario 4, the situation is somewhat different—the relationship is helping one partner and harming the other. Nevertheless, the ethical issue of how to respond to negative effects on the individuals involved is at the center of both cases.

Scholars in marriage and family counseling point out that the ideal interests of individuals frequently conflict somewhat with the best interests of the family (Margolin, 1982; Patten et al., 1991). Promoting individual and family development simultaneously is not always possible. Still, coping with minor compromises in individual functioning for the good of the family is a different order of problem from those presented in these scenarios.

The AAMFT Code enjoins professionals to aim for increased well-being of all involved in therapy, despite the practical problems and minor deviations already noted. Engaging in family counseling to save a marriage that is inherently harmful to at least one participant (Scenario 3) does not appear to be an appropriate use of the service. That is not to suggest, however, that it is the professional's role to advise the couple to divorce. This code is explicit on that point, noting that such decisions must be made autonomously by the clients.

Ethics scholars in family counseling generally concur on this point (e.g., see Gurman, 1985; Negash & Hecker, 2010). When caught in such dilemmas, professionals should carefully assess the degree of harm they believe will ensue from continuing the relationship. If it represents a serious and continuing harm for either member, counselors should discontinue work on that goal. Instead, counselors should frankly discuss their reservations with the clients. No practitioner should participate in an activity that seriously compromises a person's mental health, even if that person wants to continue. The principle of nonmaleficence takes precedence over other considerations.

Scenario 5: The Ethics of Consecutive Individual and Family Counseling
Consecutive individual and family counseling is not unethical as long as several conditions are met. First, the counselor has judged that such a sequence would be beneficial to the client and has the competence to engage in both activities. Second, an appropriate informed consent procedure has been conducted so that the client understands the different risks, benefits, procedures, and confidentiality issues of relationship counseling, especially the professional obligation to keep confidential information shared during individual counseling. Finally, a similarly careful informed consent procedure has been undertaken with the partner as well. As counseling progresses, the counselor must be alert for any issues that may arise because of the different histories of contact with the counselor. The partner needs time to develop the same level of trust as the original client, and the counselor should make a special effort to get a sound independent assessment of the partner's functioning in the relationship. Communications from the original client about the partner are not likely to convey a fully accurate picture of that person. In addition, the therapist should be alert for signs that either partner views the counselor as "taking sides" or for negative feelings the original client may develop in "sharing" the therapist with the partner.

It is important to note that the codes do *not* indicate that it is unethical to conduct *concurrent* individual and family therapy. Heitler (2001) presents several recommendations for ethical resolutions of the risks of dual treatment. But if a professional chooses to do so, a heavy burden to maintain the confidentiality of individual communications falls to the professional. Whatever the course of action taken, ethics scholars in family therapy advise a comprehensive approach to informed consent on issues of confidentiality (e.g., Lakin, 1994; Smith, 1999) and privilege (Bennett et al., 2006). Heitler (2001) presents other recommendations for ethical resolution of the risks of services that stem from dual roles and potential financial conflict of interest. A sensible stance on concurrent treatment is to avoid it when feasible and refer to others for the secondary treatment.

Scenarios 6 and 7: The Influence of the Counselor's Beliefs and Values About Gender Role Socialization and Sexual Orientation on Diagnosis and Treatment No helping process is value free. Family counselors have definitions of good and poor functioning, healthy and unhealthy communication, and normal and abnormal ways of relating. In fact, without these definitions, no therapeutic work could take place. As long as one distinguishes between desirable and undesirable change, one is invoking values. Sometimes family therapists have beliefs about healthy families that are too rigid and narrow and that fail to allow for individual differences and cultural influences (Melito, 2003). These beliefs often derive from our own cultural and social history and from the narrow exposure to other cultures and family patterns that happens so commonly in North American societies (McGoldrick, Giordano, & Garcia-Preto, 2005). As our society becomes increasingly diverse, families with mixed cultural backgrounds will also become more common, emphasizing the need for family counselors to possess cultural competency and self-awareness.

Gender bias is also a concern. Women who have been victimized in intimate relationships tend to view mental health professionals as insufficiently sensitive to their needs (Harway & O'Neil, 1999). Research by the APA (APA, Task Force, 1975; APA, 2007a) has also shown that mental health professionals tend to view behaviors that are nontraditional for women as less acceptable than traditional behavior. For example, they tend to assume that women will be better adjusted if they remain married than if they do not and that a woman's extramarital affair is more serious than a man's. Guterman (1991) and Sekaran (1986) also suggest that professionals are frequently less sensitive to the demands of a woman's career than to those of her partner's. In other words, evidence suggests that the way family therapists work with families has perpetuated existing norms (Lewis & Mellman, 1999). Some scholars have argued that family therapists have a responsibility to change sexist patterns in their clients (and themselves, of course) (Hare-Mustin, 1980), but others caution against a campaign to change client beliefs to those the therapist endorses (e.g., Negash & Heckler, 2010).

The goal of the responsible professional in dealing with family issues related to gender role is to respect the client's autonomy on the matter as much as possible, and to identify the ways in which the family's conceptualization of gender roles may be related to their dysfunction. In Scenario 6, the family therapist will need to help the family members communicate and renegotiate their mutual expectations. There are two pitfalls to be avoided: blaming the husband and children for not respecting the woman's right to change her responsibilities in the family, and assuming that the woman really should be taking responsibility for her household chores just because she is the wife. The therapist should help the family develop a response to the changing family circumstances that respects each member's human rights and recognizes each person's responsibilities to the family. One helpful document is APA's *Guidelines for Psychological Practice with Girls and Women* (2007a).

Professional values clearly come into play in Scenario 7 as well. The codes of ethics of the ACA, APA, and AAMFT all explicitly prohibit discrimination on the basis of sexual orientation. Thus, family therapists should be prepared to respond to the request of this couple for preparenting counseling, as they would for any other couple. The decision to accept them as clients should be based on clinical considerations without regard to their sexual orientation. If the therapist has competence in the area and knowledge about the literature relevant to this particular couple's concerns (e.g., see Fitzgerald, 1999; Ritter & Terndrup, 2002; Rohrbaugh, 1992; Scrivner, 1997), the couple should not be turned away simply because they are not heterosexual. If the professional's personal beliefs about homosexuality prevent him or her from providing objective professional service, then the therapist is responsible for locating competent referral sources for this couple. A professional who accepted this couple with the intention of "getting them to change their minds" because he or she thinks lesbians should not be parents would be violating the codes and the fundamental values of autonomy and respect for human dignity at the core of the values of all helping professions. See Janson & Steigerwald, (2002); Janson (2002); and APA's *Guidelines for Psychotherapy with Lesbian, Gay, and Bisexual Clients* (APA, 2011b) for helpful recommendations for treatment.

Scenario 8: The Ethics of Couple Counseling Concurrent With Intimate Partner Violence Intimate partner violence is fairly common among those seeking couples and family therapy (Simpson, Doss, Wheeler, & Christensen, 2007). Nearly two-thirds of those entering treatment have some history of abuse, and 6% of clients identify violence as a current problem (Timmons, Bryant, Platt, & Netko, 2010). Effective family work requires that participants feel free to share their ideas and feelings in session and to enact behavior change between sessions. Honest, direct communication between family members is the cornerstone of this modality. When one family member is being abused by another, the foundation for successful therapy is uncertain at best. Fearing the consequences, the victim may not openly express thoughts or feelings or attempt behavior change without risk of revictimization. In addition, one defense that victimizers frequently use—that the other partner provoked the abuse—is not really challenged when the problem is framed as a family issue. In such a context, it is harder to get abusers to take responsibility for their actions. Thus, many scholars recommend avoiding family therapy while there is ongoing intimate partner violence (e.g., see Houskamp, 1994). In this view, family counselors should see partners individually so each can explore his or her own needs. Joint sessions can be initiated after the abuser takes responsibility for the abuse and begins to rehabilitate, and the victim begins to feel some power and control. Because families who are experiencing intimate partner violence do not often freely disclose it, counselors should stay alert for signs of abuse in the assessment and screening phase of family counseling. Other writers argue that conjoint therapy can be conducted when there is a recent history of violence as long as the professional is competent and takes special steps to monitor family dynamics and keep the victim safe (e.g., McCollum & Stith, 2011). However, those scholars who view couples counseling as useful in these circumstances condition that recommendation on specialized training for the therapist in procedures to appropriately screen couples, enhance safety, and monitor progress. No mental health professional without such competencies should attempt treatment when one partner is at risk for violence. And it is clear from the research that such competence is not common among clinicians (Timmons et al., 2010).

Legal Issues in Family Counseling

A common legal issue for professionals working with families relates to divorce and custody. Many couples who have attempted couples counseling decide to divorce, so it is not surprising that the professionals who have worked with them get drawn into the legal battles. For instance, one partner's attorney may attempt to get the counselor or therapist to testify about the other partner's mental health and stability or about what happened during treatment. Obviously, the ethical duty to confidentiality applies here as in other forms of service, and some states may protect communications in family counseling as privileged. Nevertheless, family therapists are advised to be explicit during informed consent about confidentiality and privilege. They should explain to clients, preferably in writing (Ramisch, 2010) that they regard the family unit as the client, not any individual members. They should elaborate further the implications of that view for any future legal actions. Needless to say, family counselors should consult with their attorneys about such requests for information or testimony about clients whenever they occur.

Divorcing couples in custody disagreements sometimes attempt to get the professional to take one side or the other in those battles. On other occasions, well-intentioned (but misguided) professionals providing individual services to one partner are quite willing to become involved in the court proceedings to advocate on behalf of the client. Professionals should use extreme caution under such circumstances. Evaluations of child custody arrangements require special competencies that many professionals have not developed, and even if the professional has such competencies, an independent evaluator better serves the purpose. The psychological evaluation of the children and the fitness of the parents often significantly influence the court's decision. In addition, the role of influencing the court's decision about child custody is a very different role from that of therapist for the couple. When a mental health professional who has been working with one partner testifies in court about his or her professional interactions with the client and professional judgments about the mental health of that individual client, the professional is acting as a *fact witness*, not an *expert witness* conducting an objective evaluation of both parents (APA Committee on Professional Practice and Standards, 2003). A professional who is acting as an expert witness is usually employed by the court to evaluate the parents and has had no prior contact with either person. A fact witness is in the court to describe what he or she has observed, and has been a therapist for one or both parties. Because of the nature of that prior contact, he or she is not in a position to provide an objective view of the child's best interests or the parenting skills of the adults, since objective assessment for a legal proceeding was never the cause of the counselor's involvement with the family. Consequently, counselors are well advised to discuss the counselor's role when treating couples or families whenever there is a reasonable possibility that the relationship will terminate. Both the ACA and AAMFT standards prohibit professionals from mixing evaluative and counseling roles. The APA statement is more general on this issue but suggests the same approach.

Increasingly, courts are also using counselors, family therapists, and psychologists to act as expert witnesses and to assist in divorce mediation and child custody evaluations. The obligation of the professional providing these services is to give competent, honest, objective advice to the court and to ensure that all people being evaluated understand that the counselor is assisting the court and is not in a therapeutic relationship with them. (See Folberg, Milne, and Salem [2004] for an overview of family mediation processes, procedures, and ethics.)

Recent years have seen an increase in the number of ethics complaints against mental health professionals serving in these roles (Kirkland & Kirkland, 2001; Ohio Board of Psychology, 2003), and much negative press has been written about counselors and therapists who act as "hired guns" for attorneys. Professional associations have published guidelines to help professionals act ethically in such activities (see APA, 1994, 2010b), and ethics scholars have written widely on the subject (e.g., Benjamin, Andrew, & Gollan, 2003; Woody, 2000). Professionals asked to act in these roles should become familiar with this literature in order to make responsible decisions. Some of the most helpful materials are listed in the recommended readings at the end of this chapter.

SUMMARY

Group and family counseling and psychotherapy entail special ethical and legal challenges. These challenges include the competent use of power in modalities that have significant potential for good or harm, depending on the counselor's professionalism and the wise management of confidentiality issues in a setting where client disclosures cannot be guaranteed privacy. The emotional intensity of the setting, the powerful interventions commonly used, and the pressure for group cohesion can all have negative effects on clients if the professional does not manage these aspects of these interventions skillfully and sensitively. Confidentiality is complicated because other clients may reveal material discussed in session, and not all courts recognize privilege for professionals when other people also hear client communications. These additional risks and benefits make a careful and thorough informed consent process even more imperative in group and family therapy than in individual therapy.

Professional values and biases significantly influence group and family therapy. Counselors and therapists therefore need to recognize how their personal values may interfere with productive work and should base their actions on the principles of respect for human dignity and individual differences. Personal beliefs about what constitutes a family, about gender roles, and about sexual orientation play especially central roles in family counseling. Counselors using group and family therapy should consult the standards of the Association for Specialists in Group Work (2007, 2012) and the American Association for Marriage and Family Therapy (2012) for additional guidance on ethical practice in these modalities.

Discussion Questions*

1. Research has shown that many practitioners choose not to use confidentiality contracts in group counseling or psychotherapy. What do you see as the advantages and disadvantages of such a choice?
2. What do you see as the dangers and values of the methods that have been recommended to encourage nonparticipating family members to attend counseling?

*Note to course instructors: The *Instructor's Guide* for this book includes other discussion questions, class exercises, cases, and multiple-choice and essay test items for this chapter.

3. Should a counselor conduct individual and couples counseling simultaneously with the same clients? Why or why not?
4. Many practitioners regularly seek out co-leaders for their groups because of the therapeutic value of dual leadership. Does co-leadership also have ethical value? In what way?
5. If a member drops out of a group and is unwilling to attend even one more session to obtain "closure," should a leader try to persuade that member to change his or her mind? How far can the leader go in doing so before violating ethical standards?
6. Sometimes families have problems because members have differing ideas about social role expectations. For example, a man may believe that his wife should take care of the home, whereas she believes that responsibility should be shared. How can a family counselor ethically assist a family with such a conflicts?

Cases for Discussion

A person who was a part of an online support group revealed in an electronic message to other members that he had murdered his daughter. Among those who received the communication were several psychologists. At least some of the psychologists-members elected not to disclose this information to legal authorities, but other members did report the admission. Eventually, the man was convicted of this crime. (This is based on a real occurrence.) Imagine that an ethics complaint was made regarding one of the psychologists who did not disclose the comment to the police. Do you think this person acted unethically? On what basis? If you think there was an ethics violation, what discipline do you think would be appropriate for this infraction? What about the ethics of any psychologists who would break confidentiality for this reason?

Jeffrey and Joanne are co-leading a 10-session group for people recovering from divorce. Both are divorced professionals who are competent and experienced group counselors. At the start of the group, they ask all members to sign an agreement that they will not get romantically involved with one another while the group is in progress. All members agree and have complied. Over the course of the first five weeks of the group, the co-leaders work closely together. They begin to develop a mutual attraction and start to date by the sixth week of the group. They do not reveal their personal relationship to any group members. Are their actions in violation of the codes of ethics, or are their personal lives entirely separate from their professional activities?

Martin's parents are insisting that he attend family therapy with them, even though he strongly opposes the idea. Martin is a 13-year-old boy who lives with his father and stepmother. Martin is angry because his father began a relationship with the woman who is now his stepmother before he divorced his mother. Martin has been told that if he does not attend family therapy sessions. he will lose weekend privileges. Because Martin enjoys his weekend social activities, he feels as though he has no choice other than to accompany the rest of the family to therapy. In the sessions, Martin says little and seems to spend much of the time daydreaming. The therapist's efforts to get Martin to become more involved have met with little success. Nevertheless, the therapist encourages the parents to bring all the children to family sessions. Are the actions of the therapist justifiable? What other information would be helpful to you in making this decision? Would your answer differ if Martin were 17 years old instead of 13?

Recommended Readings

American Association for Marriage and Family Therapy (AAMFT). (2012). Code of ethics. Retrieved from http://www.aamft.org/imis15/content/legal_ethics/code_of_ethics.aspx

American Psychological Association (APA). (2010b). Guidelines for child custody evaluations in family law proceedings. *American Psychologist*, *65*, 863–867.

Association for Specialists in Group Work (ASGW). (2000). Professional standards for the training of group workers. Retrieved September 3, 2008, from http://www.asgw.org/PDF/training_standards.pdf

Association for Specialists in Group Work (ASGW). (2007). Best practice guidelines. Retrieved September 3, 2008, from http://www.asgw.org/PDF/Best_Practices.pdf

Association for Specialists in Group Work (ASGW). (2012). Multicultural and social justice competence principles for group workers. Retrieved from http://www.asgw.org/pdf/ASGW_MC_SJ_Priniciples_Final_ASGW.pdf

Benjamin, G., Andrew, H., & Gollan, J. K. (2003). *Family evaluation in custody litigation: Reducing risks of ethical infractions and malpractice*. Washington, D.C.: American Psychological Association.

Corey, G., Williams, G. T., & Moline, M. E. (1995). Ethical and legal issues in group counseling. *Ethics & Behavior*, *5*, 161–183.

Dishion, T. J., McCord, J., & Poulin, F. (1999). When interventions harm: Peer groups and problem behavior. *American Psychologist*, *54*, 755–764.

Fall, K. A., & Lyons, C. (2003). Ethical considerations of family secret disclosure and post-session safety management. *The Family Journal*, *11*, 281–285.

Rohrbaugh, J. B. (2008). *A comprehensive guide to child custody evaluations: Mental health and legal perspectives*. New York, NY: Springer.

Wilcoxon, S. A., Gladding, S. T., & Remley, T. P., Jr. (2013). *Ethical, legal, and professional issues in the practice of marriage and family therapy* (5th ed. updated) Englewood Cliffs, NJ: Prentice Hall.

Woody, R. H. (2000). *Child custody: Practice standards, ethical issues, and legal safeguards for mental health professionals*. Sarasota, FL: Professional Resource Exchange.

Additional Online Resources

ASGW: What every counselor should know about group work: http://www.asgw.org/PDF/Group_Stds_Brochure.pdf.

FamilyTherapyResources.net: http://www.aamft.org/iMIS15/AAMFT/Content/Resources/Resources.aspx.

Family & Marriage Counseling Links: http://family-marriage-counseling.com/resources.htm.

AAMFT Consumer Update: Children and Divorce: http://www.aamft.org/iMIS15/AAMFT/Content/Consumer_Updates/Children_and_Divorce.aspx.

Online Group Psychotherapy Resources: http://www.group-psychotherapy.com/links.htm.

CHAPTER 10

The Ethics of Assessment

Using Fair Procedures in Responsible Ways

Clients seek the professional help of counselors and therapists with two major goals in mind—to find solutions to their problems and to gain a better understanding of themselves. (Finding solutions, of course, involves getting relief from the emotional distress and/or interpersonal problems they are experiencing.) The procedures that professionals use to achieve the first goal are collectively called *assessment*. A wide variety of assessment procedures has been developed, ranging from clinical interviews to standardized tests, behavioral observations, mental status exams, data collection from significant others, and analysis of case records. Ideally, assessment is conducted as a collaborative process between a professional and a client. Competent assessments include judgments about client prognosis, strengths, and social supports, along with determinations of the scope and severity of problems (Ridley, Li, & Hill, 1998). Assessments can be expressed in a variety of ways, depending on the clinician's theoretical orientation and use of formal classification systems. The more accurate the assessment of the problems (and the resources a client has to address them), the more likely it is that those problems will be successfully resolved. Assessment is not limited to individual and multiple-person psychotherapy. For example, consultants assess the strengths and weaknesses of organizations; forensic psychologists assess a defendant's competence to stand trial; career counselors evaluate blocks to career decision making; and educational psychologists assess the characteristics of effective learning environments. Whatever the setting, accurate, fair, and responsible assessment is the cornerstone of successful intervention.

Two aspects of assessment are especially vulnerable to abuse: the use of diagnostic categories to describe client problems and the use of psychological and educational tests. This chapter attends to the ethics of diagnosis and testing, elaborating on relevant comments in the ACA and APA codes, the views of ethics scholars, and related research evidence. The chapter also considers guidelines for ethical assessment in a multicultural society and the responsible use of technology in diagnosis and testing. Finally, I review the use of psychological tests in employment settings.

THE ETHICS OF DIAGNOSIS

To diagnose means to define in professional terms the nature, limits, and intensity of a problem a client brings to counseling (Welfel & Patterson, 2004). Differential diagnosis refers to the process of determining which of the possible diagnoses best fit a particular person's symptoms. For example, a professional tries to differentiate the normal inclination of a pre-school child to be physically active and inattentive from the early signs of attention deficit hyperactivity disorder. The professional terms used to designate problems are derived from scholarly research and practice and are found in classification systems such as the *International Statistical Classification of Diseases and Related Health Problems* (ICD-10) (World Health Organization [WHO], 2014) and the *Diagnostic and Statistical Manual of Mental Disorders*, 5th edition (DSM-V) (American Psychiatric Association, 2013). The DSM is the most commonly used (and probably the most controversial) resource for classifying psychological problems in the world. However, the term *diagnosis* encompasses more than the medical model expressed in the DSM and the ICD. *Diagnosis* refers to any organized system for defining client problems in common use by mental health professionals. For example, family therapists sometimes diagnose family system problems, using typologies different from the DSM, but they are still classification systems because other family therapists give the same problems the same names (Kaslow, 1996; Sporakowski, Prouty, & Habben, 2001). In addition, career counselors often rely on their own terminology for evaluating career problems that is distinct from DSM or other psychodiagnostic categories (e.g., Hardin & Leong, 2004). Whatever the classification system, diagnostic names provide a shared language for professionals and can guide them to appropriate interventions. Using common classification systems also makes the findings of researchers accessible to practitioners and allows them to better apply research findings to help clients.

Because of its association with naming and specifying problems, diagnosis has been called "labeling" by some professionals, a term that implies that diagnosis is inherently dehumanizing and harmful (Hohenshil, 1996). Other writers caution against allowing diagnosis to distract from the human needs of the individual (Gergen, Hoffman, & Anderson, 1996; Gladding, 2012). Even counselors who acknowledge the value of diagnosis are somewhat ambivalent about its application or about the use of the DSM as the classification system of choice (Eriksen & Kress, 2005; Ivey & Ivey, 1998). When diagnosis is incompetently done or the diagnostic system lacks validity, such characterizations are not far from the mark. The history of mental health is replete with examples of harmful effects when diagnosis is misused, but evidence also shows that when appropriately conducted, diagnosis serves a valid and beneficial function for clients. In fact, effective, evidence-based practice *demands* careful definition of problems. We cannot treat what we have not identified. The relationship between diagnosis and treatment is like that of a map for a road trip. One is more likely to reach the destination by following a map than by intuitively selecting roads to see where they lead. The diagnosis is a map, a picture of the terrain that leads to a goal (destination), and a plan for reaching that goal (a sequence of roads to be taken). Nevertheless, it is important to acknowledge both the debate on the validity of diagnosis as currently practiced and the evidence that mental health professionals have sometimes misused the diagnostic processes (e.g., see Pope & Vasquez, 2011; Valliant, 1984; Wakefield, 1992). Practitioners who are philosophically opposed to the term *diagnosis* are free to substitute another term. Central here is the recognition of the value of carefully assessed client strengths, resources, and problems, not the acceptance of any particular word used to describe that process.

A Rationale for Emphasizing Ethics in Diagnosis

Ethics should govern the diagnostic process for many reasons. The most important is that diagnosing is one of the most influential activities in which a professional engages (Behnke, 2004). Applying a diagnostic name to clients' problems can powerfully affect many aspects of their functioning—self-esteem, career opportunities, eligibility for insurance, vulnerability to rejection and ridicule by others, and educational placement. Some kinds of diagnoses also influence whether licenses to practice an occupation will be granted, whether the state will allow a person the right to drive a car or purchase a firearm, or whether a court will allow an adult to adopt a child. For instance, people who have been diagnosed as substance dependent are often required by law to reveal that diagnosis when they apply for a driver's license. A history of a DSM diagnosis can also limit a person's eligibility for health or life insurance.

Second, diagnosis has ethical dimensions because it is an inherently imperfect process. Even though behavioral science has advanced substantially over the last century, our knowledge of psychological processes is still limited, and our capacity to reliably assess the functioning of a given individual is also restricted. Practical problems with the implementation of diagnostic systems form one part of the difficulty. In the real world, neither clients nor third-party payers are usually willing to engage in truly thorough assessment. (The increasing pressure of insurers and managed care companies for "instant" diagnosis is in itself an ethical dilemma and is addressed in greater detail in Chapter 12.)

The imperfections in the diagnostic process are not solely the result of client or insurance impatience, however. Mental health professionals have often made procedural and judgment errors (e.g., Hill & Ridley, 2001; Rabinowitz & Efron, 1997; Smith & Dumont, 2000; Spengler et al., 2009). McLaughlin (2002) refers to these as *human information processing errors*. Humans use heuristics, experience-based techniques for streamlining problem solving, to assist with processing the vast amount of information that comes to us, and these heuristics can either be very helpful in separating important content from insignificant detail or can erroneously classify the insignificant as important or neglect the relevant. Information processing errors based on the timing and vividness of symptoms are especially common. For example, the human tendency to seek quick answers to dilemmas flaws the diagnostic process (Anastasi, 1992; Groopman, 2007), as does the inclination to emphasize information received early in the interview over data gathered later, called a *primacy effect* (Meehl, 1960). Especially vivid symptoms may be given more importance in the diagnosis than they deserve, with other important symptoms given less salience simply because they are less vivid (Spengler, 2000). In addition, research suggests that clinicians tend to use only the subset of the diagnostic criteria with which they are most familiar in arriving at a diagnosis, thereby drawing erroneous conclusions

(Rubinson, Asnis, Harkavy, & Friedman, 1988). Client likeability also plays a role; those who are pleasant and easy to work with appear to get more attention from professionals in the diagnostic interview. And those who are unpleasant are more likely to get rushed through the process (Groopman, 2007).

Unfortunately, client payment method exerts undue influence over the diagnosis in subtle ways that professionals do not recognize. Kielbasa, Pomerantz, Krohn, and Sullivan (2004) and Lowe, Pomerantz, and Pettibone (2007) reported that psychologists were significantly more likely to use a DSM diagnosis when payment came through managed care than when clients paid out of pocket, *even when presented with identical descriptions of client symptoms*. When evaluating anxiety symptoms, psychologists in the Kielbasa et al. study (2004) were 10 times more likely to apply a DSM diagnosis to managed care clients than self-pay clients. And in Lowe et al. (2007), psychologists were five times more likely to give a DSM diagnosis to a client with a managed care payment, even when the mild social anxiety described in the vignette did not meet the criteria for a DSM diagnosis.

The diagnostic systems currently used are also far from ideal. The research evidence supporting the categories is uneven, and the categories themselves are often overlapping, inconsistent, and vulnerable to gender, racial, and social class bias (Brodie, 2004; Campbell, 1999; Dougall, 2010; Eriksen & Kress, 2008; Maddux & Winstead, 2005). There are unresolved philosophical debates about what constitutes a dysfunction (Wakefield, 1992). These imperfections place a heavy burden on the practitioner trying to use the diagnostic system in a responsible way. Even well-trained professionals do not always arrive at the same diagnosis for identical symptoms when using the DSM, partly because of the overlapping categories (e.g., see Kirk & Kutchins, 1992; Kutchins & Kirk, 1997).

Third, the mere existence of diagnostic identifiers means that mental health professionals may be biased in favor of using them, even when a diagnosis is unjustified. Two classic studies illustrate this tendency. One was conducted by Langer and Abelson (1974), who found that therapists were more likely to diagnose as psychologically disturbed people identified as patients than people labeled job applicants. The other study, even more famous, is that of Rosenhan (1973), in which pseudopatients got themselves admitted to mental hospitals by stating that they had been hearing voices. Once admitted, they displayed no other symptoms and denied any recurrence of the voices. In fact, they were instructed to behave as normally as possible from admission forward. No pseudopatient was ever identified as normal by the staff despite some lengthy hospital stays, and all had psychiatric diagnoses on their charts at discharge, although some charts were marked "in remission." (Ironically, the regular patients often questioned the pseudopatients about the legitimacy of their problems, but the staff never voiced such concerns.) Although others have severely critiqued Rosenhan's research (e.g., Spitzer, 1975), the point is that whatever its flaws, Rosenhan's study demonstrates the tendency of mental health professionals to skew the information they receive to fit preexisting categories. This inclination to pathologize normal behavior can also be seen in less dramatic ways when professionals mistake normal feelings of bereavement for depression, or label ordinary adolescent rebellion as conduct disorder. The practitioner's first responsibility in assessment is to evaluate evidence objectively, without presupposing that a person in the client role must have a diagnosable disorder.

In fact, Section E.5.d of the ACA Code explicitly states that counselors may refrain from giving a diagnosis if, in their judgment, that would be harmful to the client or others.

Fourth, in societies where stigma attaches to mental and emotional disorders, assigning an official diagnostic name to the client's pain can have powerful psychological effects in itself. Clients may feel ashamed or resist such a designation, and their coping skills may be tested. Clients may become despondent and erroneously conclude that they are beyond help, or they may act out in self-destructive ways. Conversely, clients may also have a powerful positive reaction, at least at first. Some may be relieved that there is a name for the confusing pattern of thoughts, feelings, and behaviors that they have been experiencing. Instead of engendering hopelessness, the name for their previously overwhelming problem encourages them to believe that they can be helped. Regardless of the specific reaction, though, its power means that professionals must act responsibly in communicating their assessments and help clients deal productively with them.

Fifth, as Matarazzo (1986) points out, the process of arriving at the diagnosis, of prodding the client for details of his or her experience, is in many ways an invasion of privacy no less severe than a physical examination by a physician or an audit by the Internal Revenue Service. Whenever a professional invades the privacy of another, certain conditions should exist: good reason for the invasion, potential for benefit, competent engagement in the activity itself, and the client's consent.

Counselors and therapists often lose sight of the threat that diagnosis represents to clients. In a now classic publication, Raimy (1975) suggests that people who voluntarily enter counseling have two underlying worries in addition to their presenting problems. First, they fear that professionals will confirm their worst fear—that they are truly crazy. Second, clients worry that the problems they have are so unique and unintelligible that no one can understand or help them. The latter belief means that clients may expect to be misunderstood and to remain isolated. Coming to a clear definition of the problem evokes the first deep-seated fear: Clients fear the diagnosis will confirm and make even more real their belief that they are crazy. Clients' second underlying worry sometimes results in a resistance to diagnosis, a resistance to believe that others have indeed had similar problems. Eventually, a skilled and compassionate professional can help a client revise such assumptions, but in the meantime one must be sensitive to the invasion and threat that diagnosis and testing represent.

Sixth, knowledge of diagnostic language can lead to casual diagnosis, the application of diagnostic terms to people with whom one does not have a professional relationship. For example, mental health professionals may be tempted to use their diagnostic skills to interpret the behaviors of politicians, disfavored colleagues, troublesome students, or others in their personal lives. (On one occasion, a graduate student reported to me that a college instructor in a psychology class had wondered aloud to the class whether this student suffered from attention deficit disorder because she seemed distracted during lecture; the instructor then added insult to injury by suggesting in front of the group that this student needed to go to the counseling center to get an evaluation.) Those who engage in such practices damage the reputation of the profession and lead people who are considering professional help to wonder whether they will be judged in the same cavalier way.

When mental health professionals engage in casual diagnosis, they encourage the misimpression that diagnosis is simple, magical, or dehumanizing. Recent television shows that include celebrity doctors with unspecified professional credentials may also lead the public to the same erroneous conclusion about diagnosis. The APA Code is the most explicit on this point in Standards 9.01b and 9.01c.

The need for Standard 9.01b first became apparent in 1964, when Barry Goldwater was a candidate for the U.S. presidency. At that time, there were a number of mental health professionals who publicly questioned his mental stability and fitness for office but who had never interviewed or evaluated the candidate. Their willingness to make such bold statements in the absence of any direct professional contact led the American Psychiatric Association to initiate what came to be termed as the *Goldwater rule*, which prohibits diagnosis in the absence of an examination (Slovenko, 2000). In a partial reversal of the standard in the 1992 version of the Code, Standard 9.01c of the current APA Code does allow for assessment via review of records—that is, without a face-to-face evaluation—as long as the psychologist clarifies that the assessment is based on analysis of records rather than direct interaction with the clients. The psychologist is also required to explain the reasons that the face-to-face evaluation is difficult to obtain or unnecessary in the particular circumstance (Behnke, 2005). A review of records to assess a client's needs is an activity quite distinct from casual diagnosis as long as it is based on the evidence provided and is prudent in the conclusions drawn in the absence of a more customary face-to-face assessment.

Still another misuse of diagnosis is to employ it as a means to enhance insurance reimbursement for services rather than an accurate statement of client problems. Pope et al. (1987) found that 35% of their sample admitted to conscious use of this practice at least sometimes. Of these, 3.5% reported that they did so very often. When Tubbs and Pomerantz (2001) repeated this study 14 years later, they found that 40% of psychologists admitted to deliberately altering a diagnosis to meet insurance criteria, with 3.3% acknowledging that they engaged in this behavior very often. Research into diagnostic practices of mental health counselors reveals a similar pattern, with 44% of clinical counselors admitting that they changed a diagnosis to obtain insurance reimbursement at least once (Danzinger & Welfel, 2001). And it is important to note that almost all mental health counselors use the DSM to diagnose (Eriksen & Kress, 2006). Changing a diagnosis for this purpose is not only inconsistent with ethical standards, it is probably illegal, and would likely be identified as insurance fraud in most situations and be subject to criminal penalties (Braun & Cox, 2005). Peterson (1996) notes that this action is the most common type of financial misconduct to come before ethics committees, licensing boards, and the courts. Standard 6.06 of the APA standards and Section C.6.b of the ACA standards clearly identify such practices as unethical. Such misdiagnosis is especially troubling when clients are prescribed psychotropic medications that are unnecessary and potentially harmful (Gray-Little & Kaplan, 1998).

A related ethical issue that has taken the forefront in the psychiatric profession is the influence of the pharmaceutical industry on how psychiatric diagnoses are constructed (Moncrieff, 2009). Moncrieff notes the correlation between the development of new psychopharmacological medications and the creation of new diagnoses and/or the dramatic increase in the incidence of a disorder for which medication becomes available. Other mental health professionals need to be alert as well to unintentional influences of this industry on diagnoses. (Chapter 15 discusses the influence of the pharmaceutical industry on research.)

Diagnosis can also be used to discredit people who are already objects of discrimination and disfavor in the society. As Szasz (1971) noted, diagnosis can serve as a form of social control. He gives the example of labeling slaves who ran away from slaveholders as mentally disordered, with a diagnosis of *drapetomania*. Another problem with diagnosis is evident in the tendency for members of minorities to receive more severe diagnoses than their majority counterparts for the same symptoms. For example, African Americans and Latinos have been more likely to receive diagnoses of schizophrenia than their European American counterparts (e.g., see Garb, 1997; Manderscheid & Barrett, 1991; NIMH, 1980; Pavkov, Lewis, & Lyons, 1989). At other times, emotionally disordered behavior is underdiagnosed, perhaps because deviancy is viewed as more normal or more frequent in diverse groups (see Gray-Little & Kaplan, 1998). In schools, ethical and legal challenges have been raised to many forms of educational and psychological testing, using evidence that such measures tend to discriminate against African American and Latino children (Suzuki & Kugler, 2001; Walsh & Betz, 1995).

The now famous research by Broverman and her colleagues (Broverman, Broverman, Clarkson, Rosencrantz, & Vogel, 1970) first highlighted how professionals show gender bias in their professional judgments. They found that mental health professionals used discrepant definitions of a healthy male and a healthy female, but the same professionals used nearly identical adjectives to describe healthy males and healthy adults. Using this logic, a female adult could not be judged both a healthy adult and a healthy woman. Their research sparked a number of other studies that found similar conclusions. Even recent studies have shown that gender bias still affects some counselors' judgments (Danzinger & Welfel, 2000). Gender bias in assessment does not affect females alone, however. A study by Robertson and Fitzgerald (1990) illustrates bias against males. These authors found that counselors diagnosed males in nontraditional roles as more disturbed than males whose behavior aligned more closely with gender expectations. Other scholars suggest that the behaviors that are labeled as disorders or dysfunctions reflect the prejudices of society. Kaplan (1983) challenged the profession to explain why behaviors commonly found in women in Western society are labeled as pathological when parallel behaviors in men are not. She questioned why the official nosology for psychiatric disorders identifies nonassertiveness and loyalty to loved ones even when they are cruel as dysfunctional, but fails to categorize difficulty expressing feelings, resistance to emotional closeness, and aggressiveness in interpersonal relationship as disorders. The former characteristics are more common among women; the latter, among men. Herman (1992) argued that gender bias is present in the diagnosis of borderline personality disorder and recommended that the symptoms present in the disorder may be more accurately described as a complex form of PTSD. However, the DSM does not currently include such a diagnosis.

A final example is equally disturbing. Despite the fact that homosexuality has not been identified as a mental disorder since 1973, a national survey of psychologists (Pope et al., 1987) found that 5.3% of the respondents believed that treating homosexuality per se as pathological was *unquestionably ethical*. When counselors were asked to respond to the same item, 14% of them made the same endorsement (Gibson & Pope, 1993). More recent research shows a reduction in misdiagnosis of homosexual clients (e.g., Keffala & Stone, 1999; Neukrug & Milliken, 2011; Stokes, 1999), but not an elimination of the problem. As recently as 2011, 5.8% of the professional counselors in Neukrug and Milliken's study viewed treating homosexuality as pathological as ethical. Taken together, these findings demonstrate the vulnerability of misuse of diagnosis for people from oppressed and marginalized groups.

This research also shows that defining a behavior as functional or dysfunctional does not take place in a social or cultural vacuum. As Marecek (1993) notes, all definitions of abnormal behavior are rooted in a culture's conception of what an ideal life is. Behaviors that appear bizarre in one society are viewed as normal and desirable in another. The variability in bereavement responses across cultures illustrates this fact. In some cultures, uncensored emotionality is encouraged and seen as completely normal, while regarded in others as extreme and dysfunctional. Similarly, what one culture calls appropriate assertiveness, another may label disrespectful arrogance. Thus, professionals who fail to take into account the social and cultural context of current definitions of health and disorder may erroneously designate a normal behavior as pathological (Kress, Hoffman, & Eriksen, 2010). Marsella and Kaplan (2002) propose that assessment of client problems should include *culturalogical interviewing*, a procedure that systematically explores the client's life context and perceptions of health and abnormality. For an excellent review of the issues in the use of the DSM with culturally diverse populations, see Alarcón et al. (2009); Kress, Eriksen, Rayle, and Ford (2005); Eriksen and Kress (2008); and Lopez and Guarnaccia (2005).

Finally, a diagnosis can become a "self-fulfilling prophecy" for a client. For instance, a person with an erroneous diagnosis of major depression may begin to interpret his or her normal variations in mood as problematic and may overreact to them. Others may begin to treat that person differently. In time, the focus on low mood can change behavior and thinking, and that person's ordinary adjustment problems may grow into the depressive disorder they have been labeled. A boy erroneously diagnosed with an attention deficit may stop attempts to concentrate on school work since he believes that he is not capable of focus, given the diagnosis.

In summary, diagnosis is a powerful tool that professionals must learn to use responsibly so that it helps rather than harms the client. Its misuse stems from a variety of causes, but underlying them all is insensitivity to the implications of diagnosis, insufficient skill with diagnosis, inadequate informed consent, or ignorance of the scientific and practical limitations of current diagnostic systems. For all these reasons, the ACA Code obliges counselors to be especially careful to obtain a proper diagnosis, with explicit attention to cultural considerations and awareness of the profession's flawed history of misdiagnosis deriving from cultural bias (Sections E.5.a–c).

THE ETHICS OF TESTING

> It is probably true that no one in the United States has or will escape being evaluated by assessment devices constructed, administered, or interpreted by psychologists. (Bersoff, DeMatteo & Foster, 2012, p. 45)

This statement highlights the breadth and scope of influence of psychological and educational testing in the current context and thereby underscores the crucial importance of ethical practice in the design and use of these assessment tools. The central ethical obligations in testing can be divided into (a) responsibilities of those who construct, market, and score psychological or educational tests and (b) the responsibilities of professionals who use tests with clients. Not only do the ACA and APA codes include extensive comment on these issues, but other guidelines and statements are also available for counselors and therapists, including the following:

- *Standards for Educational and Psychological Testing* (2004), the outcome of a joint effort of the American Educational Research Association (AERA, APA, and the National Council on Measurement in Education (NCME)
- *Code of Fair Testing Practices in Education* (2004), issued by the APA Joint Committee on Testing Practices
- *Guidelines for Psychological Evaluation in Child Protection Matters* (APA, 2013a)
- *Guidelines for Child Custody Evaluations in Family Law Proceedings* (APA, 2010b)
- *Guidelines for Assessment of and Intervention With Persons With Disabilities* (APA, 2011a)
- *Statement on the Use of Secure Psychological Tests in the Education of Graduate and Undergraduate Psychology Students* (APA, 2005)
- *Rights and Responsibilities of Test Takers: Guidelines and Expectations* (APA, 1999b)
- *Guidelines for Test User Qualifications* (APA, 2001c)
- *Psychological Testing on the Internet: New Problems, Old Issues* (Naglieri et al., 2004)

Taken together, these documents give clear direction for responsible test construction and use. Familiarity with the terminology used in these standards facilitates their interpretation:

Test Developer	The person or organization that constructs and publishes a test
Test User	The professional who has decided to administer and/or interpret a test to a given population
Test Taker	The person, that is, client, who will be completing the measure

Ethics for Test Developers

The fundamental ethical directives for test developers are (a) to prepare instruments with sufficient evidence to support their validity and reliability, with appropriate test norms, and with a comprehensive (and up-to-date) test manual and (b) to keep the welfare of the consumer as a higher priority than profit. According to this standard, an acceptable test manual elaborates research evidence, describes appropriate applications, and honestly conveys strengths and weaknesses of the test. In addition, test manuals should offer detailed information about norms, and describe the appropriateness of the test for groups of different racial, ethnic, and linguistic backgrounds. Current standards also encourage developers to provide data that help users to avoid common misinterpretations of results. Tests suited only for research should be clearly distinguished from those with clinical and educational applications. Professionals interested in developing a test for clinical or educational application should consult the *Standards for Educational and Psychological Tests* (AERA, APA, & NCME, 2014) for a full description of the ethics of test construction. Those interested in international use of psychological tests should consult the International Testing Commission document entitled *Guidelines for Translating and Adapting Tests* (2005).

In their marketing activities, developers must truthfully represent the test and restrict sales to professionals who are qualified users. (See the APA's *Guidelines for Test User Qualifications* [2001] for more details on standards for test use.) In other words, their drive to profit must be superseded by their commitment to the welfare of the test's intended audience. Most test developers require that users disclose their degrees, licenses, graduate courses, and training in psychological testing. Graduate students seeking to use tests in thesis research must provide similar information about the qualifications of the responsible supervisor.

The research by Eyde, Moreland, and Robertson (1988) and the availability of many psychological tests on the Web to anyone with a credit card (Erard, 2004) suggest that compliance with these standards is far from universal, but professionals' obligation to limit their use of tests to those in which they have received training stands, regardless. That control has been eroded somewhat by the availability of tests at Internet auction sites such as eBay, and to date the publishers have not been able to prevent such occurrences (LoBello & Zachar, 2007). The ACA Code addresses these responsibilities in Section E.2.a (Appendix A, p. 510) and in the APA Code in Standard 9.05 (Appendix B, p. 555).

Another major responsibility of test developers is to revise test content and procedures as research and environmental circumstances dictate. Even a measure that is well designed, uses an appropriate norm group, and shows sufficient evidence of validity and reliability at its creation can devolve into a test that fails to provide meaningful results because of changing evidence and circumstances. The Minnesota Multiphasic Personality Inventory (MMPI) (Hathaway & McKinley, 1943), developed just before World War II, represents an example of a measure that needed revision over time because of changing demographics, outdated language, and content that became inappropriate by the 1990s; hence the publication of the MMPI-2 and the MMPI-A.

Ethics for Test Users

Those who administer tests (usually mental health professionals) for the purpose of assisting clients have two sets of people to whom they have ethical obligations: test developers and test takers. Our discussion begins with a description of the former. Because virtually all tests are copyrighted and dependent on the unfamiliarity of test takers with the items, test users have a duty to protect the security of a test from theft and unwarranted uses. This obligation means that test users must keep testing materials in their possession and refrain from copying or otherwise disseminating test items in inappropriate ways. Test developers have made a substantial investment to develop a valid and reliable measure. Thus they have a right to fair profit from that creation and a right to exert control over the dissemination of that material.

The test security standard also means that sending a standardized test home with clients is an irresponsible practice. Surprisingly, many professionals seem unaware of this prohibition. Pope et al. (1987) reported that 24.3% of the psychologists they sampled sent tests such as an MMPI home with clients, to be completed there. Counselors seem equally ignorant. In a later study, 26% of counselors also failed to see the ethical problem in sending a test home with a client (Gibson & Pope, 1993). As soon as clients leave the office with a printed test, the professional has lost control of it and has no guarantee that it will be properly used or returned. Sending a test home with a client is unsatisfactory for clinical reasons as well because the clinician has no knowledge of the conditions under which the client took the test. The client may have failed to follow instructions, violated time constraints, or consulted with others about test items. In fact, professionals cannot even be certain that the test results they receive are those of the client. Perhaps a roommate or family member answered the questions, or perhaps responding to the items became a group project, with extensive discussion of the answers. If any of these events occur, the test results have become useless. Consequently, professionals should be resourceful about finding ways to get clients to complete instruments under controlled conditions. Scientific accuracy also demands that the test be administered under conditions as close as possible to the conditions established in the standardization of the test so that results can be compared to the norm group scores. The ACA Code is quite explicit on this point in Section E.7.d (Appendix A, p. 512), emphasizing both the importance of standardized conditions and the need for disclosure of any variations from those conditions necessitated by client disabilities or related factors.

Sometimes practitioners entertain the possibility of modifying existing instruments to serve their purposes, or they consider appropriating existing items from other measures into their own assessments without the knowledge or consent of the test developers. Because tests are copyrighted, it is both unethical and illegal for mental health professionals to use test items to develop their own tests or otherwise plagiarize existing measures; test publishers may seek legal redress. The practice also violates a practitioner's obligation to respect the rights of professional colleagues. The reliability and validity of the resulting homemade tests are also unknown, rendering its scores meaningless as well. Such instruments seem to have proliferated on the Web in recent years, along with promises and claims that the website providers do not often substantiate with objective research evidence (Buchanan, 2002; Kier & Molinari, 2004; Naglieri et al., 2004). This use of technology appears inconsistent with ethical standards and is generally misleading to the public. Both the ACA and APA standards prohibit the use of unscientifically developed measures and improper use of copyrighted instruments.

In addition, in 2005, the International Testing Commission published its *Guidelines on Computer-Based and Internet-Delivered Testing*. These guidelines are another useful resource that informs responsible testing practice. Even when tests appear psychometrically sound, the provision of online testing raises serious security issues, and all who avail themselves of this medium must be ever vigilant about security threats that may compromise the validity of results (Foster, 2010). The most recent version of the ACA includes extensive comment on tests administered and scored using technology, highlighting the obligation of the counselor to ensure that the test is used and scored appropriately to produce reliable and valid results (Sections E.2.b and E.7.c, Appendix A, p. 512).

Test Security and Client Rights: Conflicting Legal Obligations

Changes in state and federal regulations have substantially changed the contents of the ethics codes in recent years regarding test security as it pertains to clients' rights to access their treatment records. For any professionals subject to HIPAA regulation (a category that includes virtually all who provide clinical mental health services), the regulations require that clients be allowed to view their treatment records, including test results that are part of the personal record (HIPAA Privacy Rule, U.S. Department of Health and Human Services [DHHS], 1996). In parallel fashion, some state legislatures have enacted open-records legislation that also affirms the right of clients to access all information about them in a medical or mental health record. Ohio, for example, passed a wide-reaching statute in 2003 that not only confers the rights of clients to view their records, but prohibits all mental health professionals except physicians and chiropractors from refusing access to the record (Ohio Revised Code, Section 3701.74). Such statutes provide clients with the right to obtain copies of their records, though they can be charged for the costs of copying. Consider the following situations:

The Case of Margaret and Dr. DeJulio

Margaret, a 19-year-old community college student who has been having difficulty completing her nursing courses, was evaluated by Dr. DeJulio, a psychologist, in an attempt to determine her capacity to complete college-level work. As part of the assessment, the psychologist administered the Wechsler Adult Intelligence Scale (WAIS-IV) (Wechsler, 2008). Soon after the assessment was completed, Margaret formally requested copies of all information in her mental health record, including test findings. This request troubled Dr. DeJulio because the standard WAIS-IV protocol sheet on which any test taker's responses are recorded also includes actual test items that seem to be covered by test security and copyright provisions. It seemed to the psychologist that to follow HIPAA and state law about client access to records meant that he could not comply with copyright laws or honor the test publisher's right to test security.

The Case of David and Ms. Richley

When David, a 32-year-old supermarket manager and new father, began to experience stress in coping with the stress of parenthood and a demanding job, he sought counseling from Ms. Richley, a predoctoral intern in counseling psychology. As part of the assessment of his difficulties, the counselor administered an MMPI-2 (Butcher, Dahlstrom, Graham, Tellegen, & Kaemmer, 1989) to David. His responses showed mild elevations on scales 2 and 4. Both David and Ms. Richley found the test findings useful in his care. After six weeks of treatment, counseling was terminated by mutual agreement. Several weeks later, Ms. Richley received a request from David for a copy of his complete record, a request that was quickly honored. She provided him with all notes and forms related to his treatment, the MMPI-2 report, the bubble sheet for his MMPI-2 responses, and the profile sheet on which his scores were plotted. Approximately one week later, David called to seek a copy of the test booklet with the test items. When Ms. Richley explained to David that she was not at liberty to release them, David said that he believed he was entitled to that information under Ohio's medical records law. The counselor replied that she would explore the issue and get back to him as soon as she had an answer.

In response to such questions, ethics committees of the professional associations have devoted much attention to strategies to address this conflict and provide professionals with better guidance. Ultimately, these issues may require legal resolution in the courts or legislatures, but the professional associations have offered the following standards and recommendations for professionals caught in similar situations. The APA has taken the lead on this matter and has helped professionals by clarifying what constitutes test data that are part of the client's record and what assessment information belongs exclusively to the publisher. In Standard 9.07, APA clarifies that clients have a right to all data about their performance (assuming of course, that data will not cause them harm), but they do not have a right to the test materials that belong to the publisher of the test (see Appendix B, p. 556).

Based on these provisions, Ms. Richley concludes that she is correct in not giving David the booklet with the MMPI-2 items because that is a copyrighted *test material* that contains no client data. According to Behnke (2003), it is not subject to release because it contains no information that is unique to a particular client. Providing the items to a client would be violating the professional's obligations to test security. The situation Dr. DeJulio faces is more complex because the protocol sheet that includes the individual client's answers also contains WAIS-IV items. Under HIPAA and the language in the code, that protocol sheet appears to fit the definition of *test data*; however, giving it to the client seems inconsistent with copyright laws and with the agreement Dr. DeJulio signed with the test publisher when he purchased the instrument. Therefore, the ideal solution would be to speak with the client to determine whether she would be amenable to a summary of the protocol that omits the copyrighted items, or to a redacted version of the protocol that blacks out the test items but retains all of Dr. DeJulio's notations about her responses (Behnke, 2003; Fisher, 2003; Erard, 2004). If the client were to insist on the entire protocol as it exists in the record, Dr. DeJulio would be well advised to speak with an attorney about the conflict between copyright law and HIPAA. It is important to note, though, that both HIPAA and the APA standard allow a psychologist to withhold test data when a release is likely to be a threat to the safety of the client or otherwise cause substantial harm to him or her (Behnke, 2003). Kaufman (2009) offers strategies for situations in which mental health professionals are subpoenaed to provide test items and the like, and readers who work extensively with clients involved with the courts may find this a helpful reference on both legal and ethical issues in releasing test data.

Of course, both the ACA Code (Section I.1.c) and the APA Code (Standard 1.02) allow professionals to follow the law in situations in which their ethical standards contradict provisions of the law or regulations.

Obligations of Test Users

The ethical responsibilities of mental health professionals to the people to whom they administer tests are extensive and deserve detailed discussion. The first duty is *competence*. Weiner (1989) has remarked, "it is possible in psychodiagnostic work to be competent without being ethical, it is not possible to be ethical without being competent" (p. 829). Testing procedures are deceptively simple to the untrained person. At first glance the interpretation of personality inventories, achievement test scores, or other measures appears straightforward and uncomplicated. However, the process of choosing the right test for the intended purpose and audience requires sound professional judgment and extensive training to understand test manuals and research data (Cates, 1999). Similarly, proper test administration is crucial to a meaningful outcome and requires more than the ability to follow test instructions; it also demands knowledge of how to adapt the testing conditions to unique client circumstances without jeopardizing the validity of the results. For instance, mental health professionals should know how to modify, without invalidating the results, the administration of an individual intelligence test to a person who stutters, and should then know how to account for this modification in a report of results. Finally, interpreting scores, writing reports, and communicating those findings to clients are often the most demanding tasks of all. The ethics codes and scholarly writings (e.g., Anastasi, 1992; Pope, 1992) devote extensive attention to this topic.

What are the determinants of competence in the use of psychological tests?

- Formal study of the measures, including careful review of research, test manuals, and other related materials
- A background in statistics and measurement sufficient to understand the reliability, validity, norms, and descriptive data provided by the test publishers
- A knowledge of the test's strengths and limitations and its proper application with diverse populations
- A period of supervised experience in its use, including interpretation of the results to clients, after which a competent supervisor judges the professional to be competent

The length of time for developing such competencies varies depending on the background of the professional and the particular instrument. Instruction in complex personality tests such as the MMPI-2 (Butcher, Dahlstrom, Graham, Tellegen, & Kaemmer, 1989) or the Rorschach (Rorschach, 1951) requires significant study over many months. Of course, not all tests require this kind of protracted study, but each requires a similarly systematic approach to developing competence. Walsh and Betz (1995) suggest that the greater the likelihood that a test can be misused, the more stringent the criteria for competency should be.

Possessing a particular graduate degree is not in itself proof of competence. Nor does competence in the use of one test imply competence in any other test. Competence must always be determined on the basis of the particular training and experience of a given individual with a graduate degree in a mental health field. Historically, psychology programs have offered stronger training in testing (and most testing is conducted by psychologists [Frauenhoffer, Ross, Gfeller, Searight, & Piotrowski, 1998]), but not all psychologists have graduated from programs with comprehensive training in testing. Similarly, curricula in counselor education have tended to be less thorough in this area, but particular programs may be exceptionally comprehensive in this domain. The judgment about competence, then, is always determined on the basis of the individual's experience and background with a particular measure. Smith and Dumont (1995) report findings that suggest that some professionals are not as diligent as they ought to be about the boundaries of their testing competence. The psychologists in their study readily offered interpretations of a poorly validated test with which they had little experience or training.

Professional standards not only mandate that practitioners act responsibly themselves but also that they intervene when tests and assessment procedures are used by those who are not qualified to employ them (see the APA Code, Standard 2.06, in Appendix B, pp. 540–541). This mandate stems from the risk of misuse and harm to clients. The APA standard also states that psychologists should not take any action that promotes the use of assessment procedures by incompetent individuals.

Currently, two-thirds of states have some restriction on the use of psychological tests by individuals without a psychology license (Dattilio, Tresco & Siegel, 2007). In some jurisdictions, the regulations are quite clear. In six states (Alabama, Alaska, Arkansas, California, Tennessee, and Texas), the law restricts counselors from using projective tests, and even more states prohibit counselors from administering intelligence tests (Peterson, Lomas, Neukrug, & Bomer, 2014). Other states set specific competency standards. The state of Louisiana, for example, permits only those counselors "privileged" to administer psychological tests to do so. In the absence of that privilege in Louisiana, a counselor can be liable for claims of practicing psychology without a license (Remley & Herlihy, 2013; Watson & Sheperis, 2010). In fact, one such case already exists (*Louisiana v. Atterberry*, 1995). In Ohio, however, the state attorney general ruled against the position that only psychologists could use procedures labeled as psychological (Montgomery, 1996), thereby supporting the rights of other competent mental health professionals to administer tests. In any case, at this time, the general *ethical* standard is competence, not type of license. Needless to say, counselors should follow legal developments in their states to ascertain the legal standard that affects them. Professional associations have been actively involved in this controversy. The American Psychological Association formed the Task Force on Test User Qualifications, partly out of concern about incompetent test use. The final document they produced, APA's *Guidelines for Test User Qualifications* (Turner, DeMers, Fox, & Reed, 2001), identifies minimum competencies for proper test usage and takes the position that test competence is behaviorally based and not defined by a license or credential.

In addition to competence, Urbina and Anastasi (1997) describe a second important aspect of the ethics of testing. They posit that tests should meet a standard of *relevance* to the needs of a particular client. Testing for its own sake, or because of an institutional mandate, is inappropriate. As long as tests are stressful to clients, invade privacy, and are subject to misuse, the criterion of relevance must be met. Tests used for research may be used only with explicit informed consent to that use.

A third important ethical mandate for test users is *multiple criteria for decision making*. This means that tests never serve as the sole criterion on which clinical or educational decisions are based. Anastasi (1992) calls this the "hazard of a single score" (1992, p. 611). Tests are limited in their predictive ability, and the occasions in which they present invalid or unreliable results are not always apparent to the test user. Thus, all decisions that will affect a client's future must be founded on multiple criteria. For example, depression should never be diagnosed on the basis of an elevated test score alone. Professionals must find independent corroborating evidence to make such a diagnosis. That evidence should come from personal interviews, behavioral manifestations, reports from significant others, and so on. Ibrahim and Arredondo (1986) cogently state this obligation, arguing that competent assessment should be "multisource, multilevel, and multimethod" (p. 350). In parallel fashion, no academic placement for a child should be completed on the basis of test scores alone. The likelihood of error and harm to the client from reliance on test data alone is simply too great.

Finally, professionals should understand their responsibilities when asked to make inferences on the basis of test results. In other words, they have a duty to acknowledge the limitations of tests in making inferences about behaviors not directly assessed by the test. A counselor or therapist may wish to know whether a score can help predict future violence or suicidality. Whenever asked to make such inferences, professionals recognize that they cannot be as confident of their judgments as they may be of their description of current functioning based on test results. For example, a therapist can be more certain that an elevation on a depression scale indicates current dysphoria than that the elevation is an indicator of future mood. Thus, the comments of test users related to such inferences must not go beyond the available evidence and must include material that acknowledges the limitations of tests (Weiner, 1989). Similarly, clinicians must use care in writing test reports so that they do not violate security provisions of tests; they should not label clients or include conclusions not based on evidence; and they should use language understandable to clients who may read them (Michaels, 2006).

The American Psychological Association has published a set of case studies of ethical issues in using tests, which can help professionals examine the application of these ethical standards to specific situations (Eyde, Robertson, & Krug, 2010). Readers who plan to conduct testing as part of their professional practice are urged to consult this and the other resources listed in the recommended readings for further guidance.

Client Rights in Testing

The Case of Josephine

Josephine is admitted to an inpatient unit for treatment for postpartum depression. As part of the intake procedure, she is asked to take an MMPI-2 and other measures. She wonders how these tests will be used and why she needs to take them right now, but does not ask any questions, and no additional information is volunteered to her. She completes the measures on the second day of her admission. During her eight-day stay in the unit, the tests or their results are not mentioned to her again.

Ethical standards delineate a number of rights for clients and accompanying responsibilities for professionals to ensure that client rights are protected. Foremost among these is the right to *informed consent* about tests. Clients should be informed about the purposes, tasks, uses, and implications of the proposed testing, including any risks and benefits that may result. If testing data will be used in any decision making, clients should know that. For example, if an MMPI-2 will be employed to help determine a client's eligibility for a special treatment program, that should be disclosed. Similarly, if an educational test will have a role in deciding the appropriateness of special services, that information should be communicated to the child and the parents. APA's document *Appropriate Use of High Stakes Testing in Our Nation's Schools* (2001a) is a good resource on ethical issues with this form of educational testing (found at http://www.apa.org/pubs/info/brochures/testing.aspx). Clients have a right to have their questions about a test answered, although test items and other data that might compromise test security or the validity of results should not be excerpted from this general guideline. If copies of test reports are to be kept in a client's file, that should be explained as well. Needless to say, clients should also understand that they have the right to refuse testing or to withdraw their consent at any time. The specific wording of the ACA Code is contained in Sections E.3.a and E.3.b and in Standard 9.04 of the APA Code. These standards obligate the professional to obtain consent for testing, to explain the use of test results, and to do so in language the client can understand, that is, not technical jargon. The APA Code also identifies several circumstances in which exceptions to consent can be made, including situations in which testing is routine, in which the purpose of the testing is to evaluate client competence, or when the legal issues prevent it. Clearly, then, in the case of Josephine the actions of the professional administering the test were inconsistent with the requirements of both codes.

The ACA Code also requires counselors to inform clients about the most favorable conditions for testing. For example, if research suggests that sufficient rest and a positive test-taking attitude are likely to improve performance on an achievement test, clients should be told about the influence of these factors before the testing.

The second client right is to *feedback* about the results of the testing. For many years, feedback was regarded as optional, left to the discretion of the professional. The consumer rights movement was one important factor in changing that view, but there are still places where this right is not honored. The current standard is clear, however—unless a person waives his or her right to feedback before testing or if a law prevents it, the professional is bound to provide an interpretation of the results.

Direct communication with the client about results has been mandated for several reasons. First, tests are fallible, and the client ought to have an opportunity to respond to erroneous or misleading conclusions. The opportunity to correct such errors is especially important if test data will influence decisions made about the client's future. Discussion of results also assists the counselor in evaluating the reliability and validity of findings and in accurately interpreting subtle or confusing findings from the test. For instance, a moderate elevation on the L (lie) scale of the MMPI-2 may mean that the test taker was attempting to create a good impression in an unsophisticated way, or it may mean that the person has had an unusually strict religious upbringing. A discussion with a client about historical or current life circumstances can help the professional determine the more accurate interpretation of such scales and state with greater confidence the meaning of test scores.

Clients are also owed feedback. As Matarazzo (1986) notes, testing is not always easy for a client. The process often raises anxiety, pushes clients to focus on uncomfortable topics, and is often tedious and intellectually demanding. Counselors and therapists, who have typically thrived in academic settings and testing situations, tend to overlook the onerous connotation of the task for clients whose academic experiences may have been less rewarding. For some clients, the effort expended just to read the words on the page is substantial. Even for clients who are comfortable with the intellectual aspects of testing, there are still costs. For example, a person suffering from depression or anxiety must work hard just to focus enough to answer the questions and stay on task. In short, clients are making a considerable investment when they agree to testing, and clear, accurate feedback in language they can understand is a fair return for that investment.

A final reason for conducting a feedback session is that there is research evidence that it has therapeutic value (Finn & Kamphuis, 2006). For example, in one study (Finn & Tonsager, 1997), clients who received feedback on their MMPI-2 results experienced significant reductions in symptoms and distress. They also reported no negative consequences from the feedback; instead, they were overwhelmingly positive about the experience. This finding is consistent with the views of other scholars that feedback benefits client–psychologist rapport, client cooperation, and good feelings about tests and about mental health professionals (e.g., see Dorr, 1981; Finn & Butcher, 1991; Fischer, 1986; Newman & Greenway, 1997). In the case of Josephine, the providers not only violated feedback requirements, they also missed an opportunity to use the testing process in a therapeutic way.

Why, then, aren't mental health professionals universally enthusiastic about giving feedback? Pope (1992) identifies three reasons for their reluctance: (1) because they find giving bad news uncomfortable, (2) because they find it difficult to translate technical jargon into language clients can understand, and (3) because test results do not contain the kind of clear and unambiguous findings the client has hoped for (p. 268). Although all of these reasons are understandable, none is an excuse for avoiding feedback. When experiencing such reactions, professionals should seek out supervision about how to proceed skillfully and responsibly. If such reactions recur, one's competence in using the test is probably less than adequate, because competence in testing necessarily includes the capacity to explain negative findings sensitively, translate jargon easily, and discuss the limitations of tests openly.

The professional standards are rather vague in describing precisely what is meant by feedback. Does it mean sharing every descriptor associated with every scale? Does it require both verbal and written feedback? Can it be limited to a few sentences of general comments? How can the obligation to give feedback be balanced against the publisher's right to security for the test? The general guideline that seems most prudent is to provide as full a description as time, interest, and test security allow, omitting or postponing review of results that the counselor judges would be harmful to the client's current well-being. It is important to note that the codes do not require feedback under all circumstances. If a professional chooses to omit discussion of particular aspects of a test, the decision must be based on an objective consideration of the client's welfare, not on a wish to avoid an uncomfortable undertaking. Such a judgment should stand up to the "clean, well-lit room standard" and be periodically reviewed so that if a client's state of mind changed to be receptive to those findings, the professional would be able to disclose them.

When presenting feedback to clients, counselors and therapists are obliged to remind clients about the fallibility of tests and to present results in the form of hypotheses rather than conclusions. Tests do not contain absolute truths; rather, they offer hypotheses that may be helpful in understanding their behavior and in suggesting treatment strategies. Practitioners should prepare carefully for feedback sessions, be alert to the ways people can misunderstand scores, and take extra care to be precise in their descriptions (Pope, 1992). Each feedback session should include a focus on the client's experience during the test and on his or her goals for the session. The importance of plain, clear language understandable to the client is crucial—jargon does not communicate, nor does it advance client trust in the results. Even when professionals meet this criterion, they can err in another way by overwhelming the client with lengthy descriptions that cannot be absorbed in one session. This error occurs when trying to cover the test rather than to enlighten the client about its findings. When this occurs, counselors end up talking at length, giving the client little opportunity to respond and generally defeating the purpose of feedback—that is, to work collaboratively with the client to determine the meaning and impact of the test results for future sessions.

The professional's responsibility to provide feedback in language the client can understand has been highlighted in the codes recently. The *Standards for Educational and Psychological Tests* (AERA, APA, & NCME, 2014) define an appropriate explanation of results most clearly: "[They] should describe in simple language what the test covers, what scores mean, the precision of the scores, common misinterpretations of the test scores, and how test scores will be used" (Standard 5.10, p. 65).

Statutes and case law may affect the provision of feedback in some states and some settings. For example, when courts mandate psychological testing to determine a person's competency to stand trial, there may be no legal obligation at all to provide the client with information about test results (APA, Committee on Psychological Testing and Assessment, 1996). The court may even prohibit feedback. In that circumstance, the professional may follow legal rulings without worrying about ethical penalties. If permissible within that setting, however, professionals should seek to give some information to test takers, in recognition of their basic human rights. (See Section E.13 of the ACA Code on counselor ethics related to forensic settings, Appendix A, p. 514.)

Sometimes test results provide information that must be acted on (Pope, 1992). For example, a test may suggest a high probability of suicide or a substance abuse problem in a 12-year-old. In such an event, a professional's duty to protect is triggered, at least insofar as he or she must explore whether the test finding is accurate. If additional investigation reveals that the test result is supported by other information, the professional should act to prevent the likely harm.

When mental health professionals are employed as consultants and evaluators for organizations, they often have no direct relationship with the test takers. In essence, the organization is the client. An organization may use tests to screen inappropriate job candidates, or a court may seek to gather data to make a custody determination. In such instances, test takers may be asked to waive their right to receive test results. A mental health professional may honor such a waiver, provided the person agreed to it *prior to the testing* and was given appropriate information for an informed consent.

The length of feedback sessions will vary from client to client and from test to test. Practical concerns about the pressures imposed by managed care and brief therapy have a place in the discussion. However, the central determinants to the decision about how much time should be devoted to this task should be:

- The client's satisfaction that he or she understands the meaning and implications of the test results
- The professional's assessment that the feedback has clarified any confusion in the test findings
- Their agreement about the ways in which test results should influence treatment planning
- The implications of the release of these findings to others if the client agreed to the release prior to the testing

The process of providing clients with feedback about test results should be documented in the case record, along with the client's comments about the feedback and any aspects of the testing that need additional follow-up.

Clients also have the right to protection against another form of misuse of test results, that is, the inappropriate use of outdated or obsolete test findings. This standard stems from the fact that tests sample behavior in a single time period (Anastasi, 1992), which cannot have perpetual validity. Both codes unambiguously refer to this topic. For example, in Section E.11 the ACA Code prohibits the use of obsolete and outdated scores and obliges counselors to act to prevent the use of such scores by others.

The point at which tests become outdated or obsolete varies with the individual measure, the construct being assessed, and the person being evaluated. Depressed mood, for example, may be highly changeable and scores of that construct rapidly outdated, but measures of extroversion or spatial relations may be stable for an extended period. Judgments about this issue must be made on an individual basis according to the state of the science of measuring the relevant construct. Any test used to predict a future behavior, such as performance in graduate courses, becomes obsolete as soon as actual performance is known. In other words, standardized test scores are a much less reliable predictor of probability of successful completion of graduate school than a person's grades in his or her first year of graduate study. These provisions also apply to the assessments that professionals sometimes receive from outside sources such as school systems, courts, or other organizations.

Responsible Use of Test Interpretation Services and Computer-Based Testing

Counselors and therapists often contract with computer-based scoring and interpretation services for the psychological tests they administer to clients. Practitioners view these services as timesavers that relieve them of the onerous task of scoring complex instruments. In one study by McMinn, Ellens, and Soref (1999), 85% of psychologists indicated that they had used computer-based services to score psychological tests. Use of scoring services is ethical and probably a wise decision, since it avoids the scoring errors to which humans are prone. Along with the scores, these services frequently furnish a typed interpretation of the results; it is the use of these interpretations that is controversial. Several important conditions must be met before the use of computerized test interpretations is ethically justified.

First, the computerized interpretations must be based on criteria that have been subject to validation, and these results should be made available to subscribers to the service. Matarazzo (1986) has criticized the scoring criteria employed by the services because they have not presented documentation that the criteria are supported by scientific evidence, nor have the criteria been offered for objective review by independent scholars. This omission is particularly important because the reports are packaged to appear so professional, complete, and carefully crafted that they seem scientific. Anastasi terms this "the hazard of illusory precision" (1992, p. 611). Second, according to Matarazzo, these reports do not generate multiple interpretations of results, even though for some combinations of scores multiple interpretations are indeed possible. Other criticisms have been made about computerized reports. Bersoff and Hofer (1991) contend that such reports fail to be individualized and cannot take into account the unique characteristics of the test taker. In addition, they argue that these reports are "bland, impersonal, and nonspecific" (p. 243). Garb (2000) contends that the validity of some interpretive packages is highly questionable and that use of the packages may produce reports that have differential validity for different ethnic groups.

The most crucial danger of interpretive services is that counselors and therapists not otherwise competent to interpret tests will employ these interpretations in their work and present these results to clients. *The Standards for Educational and Psychological Tests* (AERA, APA, & NCME, 2014) condemn this practice. Computerized test interpretations should only be used in conjunction with professional judgment. A national survey of psychologists found that practitioners voiced concern about unqualified people using these interpretations as one of the primary ethical issues in assessment (Pope & Vetter, 1992). The responsibility of the test user to ascertain the meaning of results for each client does not diminish just because an organization that appears credible (but has no firsthand knowledge of the client) has written a report. The only responsible way to use such material is as a "second opinion." These materials should serve as aids to accurate assessment of test results, not as substitutes for clinician deficiencies. Professionals who would not be judged competent to interpret an instrument in the absence of such a report must not use these reports. Bersoff and Hofer (1991) and Snyder (2000) point out that if there are legal challenges to the use of computer scoring and interpretations, both the test user and the organization that provides that service are likely to be listed as defendants. Test users unable to demonstrate their independent competence would be vulnerable to a malpractice claim.

The final risk of computerized test interpretation is that even professionals skilled enough to interpret test results may overrely on the computer reports or may fail to be as diligent as necessary in their interpretation of scores. McMinn and his associates reported that a small percentage of psychologists (6%) used the computer interpretation as a substitute for their own interpretation at least rarely, but a larger percentage (56%) "cut and pasted" segments from the computer report into their own summary of test findings at least rarely. The McMinn study does not provide sufficient information to determine whether the professionals who cut and pasted violated any ethical guidelines in so doing. However, the procedure can be ethical only if the professional has a sound clinical rationale for selecting the designated segments in each case and if appropriate acknowledgment of the source of the statements is made in the professional's report. (For an excellent review of the ethical issues in computerized assessment, see Schulenberg and Yutrzenka [2004].)

Diversity Issues in Psychological Testing

The codes of ethics exhort mental health professionals to be alert to the ways in which gender, age, race, ethnicity, national origin, religion, sexual orientation, disability, language, or socioeconomic status may affect the appropriate administration or interpretation of assessment tools (APA Standard 9.06). The ACA Code attends both to the ethics of selecting tests for diverse populations and to their appropriate administration and interpretation in Section E.8 (Appendix A, p. 512). These standards, along with the *Guidelines on Multicultural Training, Research, Practice, and Organizational Change for Psychologists* (APA, 2003), and the scholarship on multiculturalism underscore the importance of three particular issues. First, because there is no such thing as a culture-free test (Urbina & Anastasi, 1997; Walsh & Betz, 1995) or a completely unbiased professional (Roysircar, 2005), professionals must select assessment instruments and interpret them in light of the client's social and cultural background. This position is echoed by Constantine and Sue (2005), who elaborate extensively on the meaning of competent multicultural assessment. These authors contend that counselors need *knowledge* of how potential bias may affect the interpretation of test results and *skill* in using measures for the benefit of diverse clients. (See Chapter 3 for more discussion of these competencies.)

One important consideration in this area is the availability of normative data for the client's population. When tests do not have norms for particular cultural groups, alternative measures should be sought. If no alternatives exist, those results should be interpreted with great caution. Second, test users should also carefully examine tests for content bias (Herlihy & Watson, 2003; Roysircar, 2005; Walsh & Betz, 1995). Content bias occurs when the items in a test are differentially familiar to different cultural groups. It may be very difficult for Native Americans from the desert Southwest to respond to test items about deciduous trees because they have few such trees in their environment. Similarly, urban dwellers may be unable to give meaningful responses to items that require knowledge of rural or suburban settings. Sensitivity to the impact of such items on the conclusions drawn from a test is crucial to avoid misinterpretation of the results. A desire to eliminate content bias in items has been a factor in the recent revision of several well-known personality inventories (such as the MMPI-2). Content bias has been the focus of much debate in the literature on tests of cognitive abilities with culturally diverse populations. Scholars have presented cogent arguments that lower scores from diverse groups on such measures are at least partially caused by content bias (Lonner & Ibrahim, 1996).

Third, because of their duty to avoid discrimination and to intervene whenever possible to stop it, professionals should be alert to the ways their test reports are used with culturally diverse clients. The best known legal case involving discrimination on the basis of test results was *Larry P. v. Riles* in California (1979). In that case, the court found that school officials had misdiagnosed a student and misused intelligence test results in a way that resulted in significant, perhaps permanent, harm to that child. This case acted as the impetus for reexamination of the testing practices with diverse students in California and other states. That case is a blatant example of the problem, but there are many other less dramatic violations of client rights. Too often test reports are superficially understood and then used in a discriminatory fashion. School officials who expect Mexican American students to have lower scores on achievement tests will be less likely to carefully interpret such test results and to account for the impact of culture and linguistic variables. They may overinterpret slight differences favoring European American students, when an accurate analysis of the findings would reveal no meaningful difference in performance by ethnic group. In this situation, if many of the Mexican American students spoke English as a second language, their almost equal scores to the European American students might realistically be viewed as indicators of higher achievement potential, given their comparative language disadvantage. Counselors and therapists must work energetically both to develop the competence to see the influence of such factors and to communicate appropriate ways to interpret tests to other professionals. One especially helpful guide to competent and responsible assessment for diverse populations is *The Handbook of Multicultural Assessment*, written by Suzuki, Ponterotto, and Meller (2008). In essence, the standards and literature on this issue point to the importance of counselors' personal commitment to nondiscrimination and appreciation of cultural differences. The professional must be alert to both intended and unintended discrimination, as both have negative impact on clients. In this context, the virtue of commitment to social justice and fair treatment for all takes on special importance.

Tests in Employment Settings

Psychological tests have found increasing use in employment settings over the last 30 years (Hogan, Hogan, & Roberts, 1996). They have been used primarily to assist in hiring and promotion (Arthur, Woehr, & Graziano, 2001). Intelligence tests, measures of verbal and mathematical reasoning, vocational aptitude batteries, and personality inventories are most commonly chosen. One trend is the use of "integrity tests" aimed at predicting a job applicant's honesty and attitudes toward theft (Camera & Schneider, 1994). When any tests are used in employment settings, there are several ethical issues to be dealt with:

- Has performance on the instrument been demonstrated by scientific evidence to be related to the job performance it ought to predict? Legal rulings have emphasized that the standard for acceptability of such testing is a demonstrated relationship to the variables of interest in the employment setting.
- Has the publisher followed ethical and legal guidelines?
- Do the people who select, administer, score, and interpret the results have the necessary competencies, and do they restrain misuse by unqualified individuals?
- Do those who are asked to take such tests understand their rights, and are their dignity and confidentiality appropriately honored?
- Do the tests avoid discrimination against people for reasons unrelated to job performance?
- Have the test's limitations been taken into account in interpreting results?
- Are test results used in conjunction with other data so that they are not the sole criterion on which any decision is based? Does the test provide more accurate information than alternative selection procedures?
- Does the law allow the kind of testing under consideration? For example, Massachusetts prohibits integrity testing for job applicants (Camera & Schneider, 1994).

If all these questions can be answered affirmatively, the use of testing in such environments is more likely to be consistent with current ethical standards. However, recent research has called into question their use, citing substantial numbers of false positives and risks of faking and coaching that compromise validity (Karren & Zacharias, 2007).

Laws That Affect Testing

Counselors and psychologists who employ tests should be aware of several federal laws that affect their work. The implications of such laws are especially widespread in educational and employment settings.

- Family Educational Rights and Privacy Act of 1974, or FERPA (the Buckley Amendment). This law protects the rights of parents and guardians to view their child's academic records and to control who else may have access to them.
- The Education for All Handicapped Children Act (Public Law 94-142) (1975). This law was enacted to guarantee the rights of children with disabilities an equal education, and it specifies that parents' consent is required prior to testing their child. It also mandates a fully informed parental consent to testing and access of parents to test protocols when testing is completed. The law requires that tests be in the child's language and be appropriate for the intended use.

- Public Law 101-336 (the Americans with Disabilities Act of 1990). This legislation protects the rights of people with disabilities and mandates that testing be appropriate for the individual, that it not be used to discriminate in employment options for people with disabilities, and that reasonable accommodations be made in testing for such people.

Consider the following situations:

The Case of Lee

Lee, a 14-year-old eighth-grade student, is being considered for placement in advanced classes in high school. Lee's parents immigrated to the United States from Korea five years ago, and the whole family recently became U.S. citizens. Lee learned English quickly after his arrival in the United States, but he had no exposure to English in Korea. His test scores in mathematics and verbal reasoning place him at the 86th percentile for eighth-graders in his district. The district uses a cutoff score of the 90th percentile to assign students to advanced classes. Lee has earned As in both math and English classes. His teachers believe Lee is appropriate for advanced placement, but the guidance counselor is concerned about his test score. The counselor suggests a compromise: Enroll Lee in the advanced mathematics class only. She cites two reasons for her suggestion: Asian Americans do well in math and English is his second language. Is her suggestion consistent with the ethical guidelines for counselors?

The Case of Miranda

After several counseling sessions that included some psychological testing, Miranda's counselor, Mr. Edwards, believes that his client's problems fit the criteria for two different diagnostic categories. Miranda's insurance company will reimburse services for one of these categories; for the other she is likely to be denied such payment. Because Miranda is motivated for counseling and is experiencing real emotional discomfort from her problems, Mr. Edwards is leaning toward using the diagnosis that is acceptable to the insurance company. He reasons that because he can justify either diagnosis, he is acting in accordance with ethical standards. Do you agree?

A number of ethical considerations arise in the case of Lee. The central ethical principles involved are justice and beneficence, the obligation to treat this student fairly and to help him progress academically. The provisions in the codes raise a number of questions to be resolved.

1. Are there norms for Asian American students or for ESL (English as a second language) students for the achievement test? If not, was appropriate caution used in interpreting Lee's results?
2. Is the counselor interpreting the percentile score appropriately, taking into account the psychometric evidence on the test? In particular, does she

understand how the standard error of measurement affects the meaning of the 86th percentile in comparison to the 90th percentile?

3. Was the test appropriate in other ways for Lee? What level of content or selection bias was present in the items that might have distorted the young man's true score?
4. Is the counselor using the test score appropriately, as one factor among several criteria for placement? Has the counselor considered that for students with limited English proficiency, Lee's score may actually show greater potential than a native speaker's score that is just a few points higher?
5. To what degree does the counselor's compromise represent a stereotype about Asian students and a failure to see Lee as an individual? Is the counselor unintentionally racist in this instance?
6. What evidence supports her assumption that five years' experience with English is insufficient for placement in advanced classes or that the test is a better predictor of high school success than middle school grades or teacher recommendations?
7. To what degree have the school personnel involved Lee and his parents in the decision? Have they honored the family members' rights to autonomy?
8. Will more harm come to Lee if he attempts the advanced classes and does not succeed or if he is denied the opportunity to enroll in them? Conversely, which option has the potential to provide the most benefit to Lee?

Without answers to these questions, it is difficult to come to a definitive judgment on the ethics of the counselor, but the brief evidence presented is enough to instill doubt that the counselor is in compliance with the letter or the spirit of the codes. At the least, she seems unequal to the challenge of properly interpreting test scores and insufficiently in awe of the power she wields to help or harm.

The case of Miranda deals with Mr. Edwards's effort to meet a true need for counseling that he sees in Miranda without depriving her of insurance reimbursement for those services. He seems motivated by an interest in doing good for this individual. However, more information is also needed in this case before his behavior can be deemed ethical. Specifically, one should resolve the following questions:

1. Is his analysis that the two diagnostic categories are equally valid for this client supported by objective evidence? Would competent colleagues arrive at a similar conclusion?
2. Has he taken into account how cultural variables may influence the appropriate diagnostic category for Miranda?
3. To what degree does Mr. Edwards's interest in insurance reimbursement reflect a true commitment to the welfare of the client rather than an interest in reliable payment for his services? Recent research suggests that payment issues influence diagnostic decisions more than professional realize (e.g. Lowe et al., 2007).
4. What implications would the use of the reimbursable diagnosis have for the client, other than payment? Does this diagnosis indicate a more severe mental illness? Would the use of such a category have negative impact on the client's life?

5. To what degree is the client informed and involved in the decision-making process about the appropriate diagnostic category? Does she understand the implications of submitting for reimbursement? Because the effects all fall on Miranda, is she being given the freedom to make the final decision about this issue?

If Mr. Edwards's conclusion is supported by evidence, is supported by competent colleagues, is freely chosen by a fully informed client, and is not motivated by self-interest or a desire to trick the insurer, then he has probably not violated an ethical standard. However, providing adequate answers to all those conditions may be more difficult than it first appears.

SUMMARY

The ethical standards applicable to assessment activities are based on the significant power the professional wields in this role. The imperfections in diagnostic systems and testing instruments, coupled with their vulnerability to misinterpretation by unqualified persons, also add to their power. Counselors and therapists, however, cannot avoid the task of assessing client problems on the grounds that assessment tools can be misused. Without a clear definition of the client's issues, the professional's ability to provide effective treatment is significantly impaired. Thus, professionals must proceed carefully and diligently in assessment activities, mindful of the rights and responsibilities of all involved.

When engaged in diagnosis, professionals must be careful to act competently, without discrimination or unintentional racism, and give clients clear information about the meaning and implications of the diagnosis. They should fully recognize the strengths and weaknesses of current diagnostic systems and the impact of such identifiers on clients.

Similarly, when using psychological or educational tests, practitioners should have extensive skill and training in order to use the findings in suitable ways with a given individual. They must possess the knowledge and skill to discriminate between valid and invalid findings and to take into account the cultural and social background of the test taker. They must not encourage those unqualified for the activity to engage in it, nor should they use outdated test results in their work. In most instances, clients have a right to feedback about the test results. The exact nature of that feedback is not prescribed by either the APA or ACA code, but it must convey as accurate and full a picture of the results as circumstances allow. The history of the profession is replete with examples of counselors misinterpreting test results with diverse and oppressed populations, so counselors must be especially vigilant not to repeat those violations and to stay current with the literature on multicultural aspects of assessment. When tests are used in employment settings, their scores must be correlated with job characteristics, and test takers must understand their rights. Professionals would also be well advised to know how the current laws in their jurisdictions affect the assessment process, as state laws vary and change rapidly.

Not only are counselors and psychologists bound to protect the rights of clients, they also have a responsibility to honor the rights of test producers, acting in ways that recognize their legal rights to ownership of and fair profit from test materials. Therefore, they must guard against violations of test security, must not plagiarize test materials, and must seek the option to use such materials only when qualified to do so, if possible. In turn, test producers are obligated to provide scientific evidence of the reliability and validity of their tests and other related materials in test manuals. They should assist counselors in the responsible use of assessment tools as much as possible.

Discussion Questions*

1. Do you think the flaws in the current diagnostic system make it impossible to use it responsibly? Why or why not? If not, how would you improve the diagnostic system?
2. Do the benefits of employment testing outweigh its liabilities? Why or why not?
3. Research shows that some professionals do not give clients negative feedback from testing; they report only positive results. What do you think about the ethics of this practice?
4. Currently test producers are asked by professional associations to market their tests only to qualified users. Is that a fair request in a free-enterprise system? What would happen if that restriction did not exist?
5. Some have argued that testing should not be used at all in educational settings with culturally diverse students. They have contended that the risk of test results being misused is so great with this population that they should never be a part of educational decision making. What's your analysis of this argument?
6. Currently, screening measures for common psychological disorders such as depression, anxiety, and attention deficit disorder are available online. Most professionals believe this is an important form of outreach to the public that helps people who may need psychological support to seek it. Do you agree?

Cases for Discussion

Mittie counsels many adults whom she diagnoses with attention deficit disorder. She has searched for a standardized test to facilitate diagnosis of these clients but has not identified one that she finds suitable for adults. Consequently, Mittie has begun to extract items from other existing tests and to combine them into a homemade instrument that she produces on her personal computer. Mittie does not think she is violating any copyright laws or ethical directives because she limits the use of her instruments to her own clients, does not charge a fee for the testing, does not use it as her only criterion in making the diagnosis, and does not allow other therapists access to it. Are the steps Mittie has taken sufficient to make her conduct consistent with her ethical and legal responsibilities?

Andrea is a skilled clinical counselor in private practice who is well respected by her colleagues for her expertise in treating women with depressive and anxiety disorders. As part of their intake into counseling, she asks clients to take a battery of three tests—a measure of depression or anxiety, a personality inventory, and a measure of coping skills. Clients complete the tests in her office, but after scoring them, Andrea either mails or emails them a copy of the report of her finding prior to the next session. She finds this procedure facilitates discussion in their face-to-face meeting because clients almost always read the report with great care. She does not use this procedure if the results suggest high risk of suicide or another dangerous act, but calls clients in for a review in person. Because she screens out high-risk reports prior to sending them to clients, she believes she is acting responsibly and sees no ethical problem with her action. Do you agree?

Recommended Readings

Anastasi, A. (1992). What counselors should know about the use and interpretation of psychological tests. *Journal of Counseling & Development*, 70, 610–615.

---

*Note to course instructors: The *Instructor's Guide* for this book includes other discussion questions, class exercises, cases, and multiple-choice and essay test items for this chapter.

Braun, S. A., & Cox, J. A. (2005). Managed mental health care: Intentional misdiagnosis of mental disorders. *Journal of Counseling & Development, 83,* 425–433.

Camera, W. J., & Schneider, D. L. (1994). Integrity tests: Facts and unresolved issues. *American Psychologist, 49,* 112–119.

Constantine, M. G., & Sue, D. W. (Eds.). (2005). *Strategies for building multicultural competence in mental health and educational settings.* New York, NY: Wiley.

Eriksen, K., & Kress, V. E. (2008). Gender and diagnosis: Struggles and suggestions for counselors. *Journal of Counseling & Development, 86,* 152–162.

Eriksen, K., & Kress, V. E. (2005). *Beyond the DSM story: Ethical quandaries, challenges, and best practices.* Thousand Oaks, CA: Sage.

Eyde, L. D., Robertson, G. J., Krug, S. E. (2010). *Responsible test use: Case studies for assessing human behavior.* Washington, D.C.: American Psychological Association.

Moncrieff, J. (2009). The pharmaceutical industry and the construction of psychiatric diagnoses. *Journal of Ethics in Mental Health*, 4(1, Suppl.), 1–4.

Suzuki, L. A., Ponterotto, J. G., & Meller, P. J. (2008). *Handbook of multicultural assessment* (3rd ed.). San Francisco, CA: Jossey-Bass.

Additional Online Resources

American Psychological Association Testing Information Clearinghouse: http://www.apa.org/science/programs/testing/test-clearinghouse.aspx.

American Psychological Association Finding information about psychological tests: http://www.apa.org/science/programs/testing/find-tests.aspx.

PART 3

Prevention and Remediation of Misconduct: The Before and After of Ethics

CHAPTER 11

Maximizing the Opportunity to Prevent Misconduct and Minimizing the Damage When Prevention Fails

This chapter begins with discussion of ways in which professionals can reduce the risks and stress of ethical problems by having a primary prevention plan in place. Ethical and legal issues occur frequently in clinical work and should not be surprising to any professional. The chapter goes on to describe what happens when prevention fails, beginning with complaint procedures used by professional associations and licensing boards and identifying the criteria for filing a complaint. Next, this chapter discusses counseling interventions to help the client who wants to take action against an unethical mental health professional. Finally, the chapter discusses a fundamental, but often neglected, aspect of professional ethics, accountability for self, and examines how mental health professionals ought to respond when they (and they alone) recognize that they have violated ethical guidelines for professional practice.

PRIMARY PREVENTION

Consider the following situation:

Burke's Ethical Questions

Burke is a clinical mental health counselor who is the clinical director in a practice with three other clinicians. The small suburban community in which he works has recently experienced a tragedy: Four teens have died from accidental overdoses of a street drug. It appears that none of these teens were regular drug users and that this was an instance of adolescent experimentation gone horribly wrong. Soon thereafter, there is a

(continues)

Burke's Ethical Questions *(continued)*

substantial increase in the number of teens seeking services, nearly all of whom were entering counseling at the advice of their parents and were covered under their parents' insurance. Because of their worry about their kids, these parents are seeking much more information from their children's counselors about what is discussed in counseling than typically happens when adolescents participate in mental health services. However, the adolescents are seeking more privacy than their parents want to give them. In addition, the clinicians have been asked to give newspaper interviews and to appear on news broadcasts to educate the community about the risks of drug use and about coping with such a horrible loss of young life. Burke is wondering how to handle these diverse demands in a way that is responsible. He has a feeling that if the staff is not careful, they could end up doing the wrong thing, even though they have the best intentions. He also feels uncomfortable because he knows he and his colleagues will profit financially from this terrible tragedy because of an increase in clients to their previously struggling practice.

Although the particular facts presented in the case of Burke are fictional, the issues it presents are quite real. It highlights the ways in which both emotional and intellectual factors influence ethical decision making. Burke is probably *thinking* about how to effectively manage this new caseload of kids while meeting his responsibilities to them and their parents. He is probably also *considering* how he and his colleagues can best use the knowledge they have gained about mental health and trauma to inform the community. Finally, Burke is probably also trying to *discern* how to ensure that all employees of the practice keep professional boundaries and offer competent services, as everyone in this small community has been touched in some way by this tragedy. At the same time, he is undoubtedly *feeling* many emotions—grief about the tragedy; anger at its senselessness and at whoever supplied these teens with drugs; worry about offending either the parents, who seem to want more information than is probably beneficial to their children's experience, or the teen clients, who want confidentiality but who are not paying the bill. And the struggling practice simply can't afford to see the teens on a pro bono basis (i.e., under the legal provision that allows them to seek services without parental knowledge), even though the law allows that. He also is *anxious* because he knows that if they act improperly, the high visibility of the practice may make a complaint to the licensing board more likely. He also *feels* uncomfortable because he can't help but acknowledge that this event also presents an opportunity to build the practice, increase his income, and maintain the employment of his staff.

Clearly at this point, Burke is raising important questions and recognizing emotions that will affect his problem solving and that represent potential conflicts of interest. In Rest's terms (1984), he is showing ethical sensitivity. But what else does he need to do at this point to prevent misconduct? And perhaps just as important, what could he have done prior to this tragedy to strengthen the likelihood that he and his employees will act responsibly and reduce the stress that compounds the terrible reality? The obvious response to the first question is for Burke to use to an ethical decision-making model (as discussed in Chapter 2) for each of the dilemmas he is facing, identifying the ethical issues and identifying options, applicable sections of the ACA Code, the regulations governing counseling in his jurisdiction, and the available scholarship. He should also consult with experts, the licensing board, or his malpractice insurer to get more guidance, and document all decisions and the rationale for each. These steps will help him make critical evaluative decisions rather than intuitive decisions.

However, if Burke and his staff had developed what Crowley and Gottlieb (2012) refer to as a *primary risk-management model*, they would have had more resources at their disposal, less stress, and a higher probability of responsible action when this tragedy struck. As these authors suggest, the fundamental value of a model for primary prevention of ethical misconduct is that it attends to the practitioner and focuses on the ways in which the "nonrational" factors can affect ethical decision making. Most models of ethical decision making put the major focus on the client or the context. The Crowley and Gottlieb model uses findings from psychology to bolster the capacity of the professional to act responsibly. For example, it uses the knowledge from social psychology that people pay differential attention to losses versus gains, tending to be so loss aversive that they sometimes make unwise choices just to avoid the chance of loss (Kahneman & Tversky, 1979). Similarly, the heuristics (the mental shortcuts) that people use to facilitate decision making may act to short-circuit careful consideration of an issue. Heuristics may play an especially prominent role when there is time pressure and high stress, as is the case in Burke's situation. In addition, a proactive approach to the management of ethical risks may reduce the likelihood of a discrepancy between what a professional knows should be done and what he or she actually does in a situation. Crowley and Gottlieb assert that such an approach not only reduces the immediate stress but acts as a way of proactive coping. Put another way, a primary prevention plan can foster a person's resilience in the face of an ethical challenge such as Burke's. Resilience in such a situation drives from the specific skills we professionals have developed in dealing with clinical, ethical, and legal issues, the personal characteristics that help us deal with other stresses, and the social supports and relationships that we have cultivated (Tjelveit & Gottlieb, 2010).

The model posited by Crowley and Gottlieb (2012) contains five stages:

- **Stage 1:** Resource accumulation: time for decision making, ethics education, organization and planning, consultation networks, and social networks.
- **Stage 2:** Attention and detection of risk: awareness of externals that make a particular ethical issue likely. (In this case, it may have been the research on the increase in drug use among teens in rural communities or police reports that showed an increase in teen drug use.)
- **Stage 3:** Initial appraisal of potential risk. (This would have happened as soon as the deaths of the teens were reported.)
- **Stage 4:** Preliminary risk management efforts: the development of a plan for action, using the resources accumulated at the earlier stage.
- **Stage 5:** Elicitation and use of feedback. When the plan to manage the risk has been implemented, a process of continuous evaluation of its effectiveness is put into place.

Another scholar who offers a model for ethical decision making that has considerable usefulness in preventing misconduct is Derek Truscott (2013). He argues that because the intuitive way of making ethical decisions is simple and efficient—it takes less time, is more likely to be consistent with personal values, and takes immediate emotional reactions into account—it presents a compelling (but probably unwise) alternative. Unfortunately, this attractiveness often leads us down the wrong path. Truscott suggests that by incorporating the personal-social dimension into all ethical decision making, we have a better chance of acting responsibly.

What this literature suggests is that prevention encompasses more than considering the situation carefully once it arises; it includes a well-developed and regularly updated plan that takes into account the emotional, nonrational aspects of ethical decision making as well as the environmental circumstances that may make the emergence of any set of ethical issues more likely. Prevention systems also necessarily contain a structure for social and professional support so that when challenges arise, our ability to act responsibly increases.

The reality, of course, is that professionals are as fallible as other humans and that what prevention systems offer is the opportunity to minimize the likelihood of ethical misconduct, not eliminate it. Consequently, we must be informed about how to act when we fail.

WHEN PREVENTION FAILS

The Case of Jack and Martina

A 20-year-old college student named Martina makes an appointment at the university counseling center with a counselor recommended by a close friend. Martina tells the counselor, Dominic, that she has been feeling anxious and depressed for a long time, but that lately these feelings have worsened. She goes on to say that she tried counseling in her hometown last summer but had "a bad experience" and didn't want to see that counselor again. She says that counselor, Jack, kept suggesting that she have a more active social life and repeatedly volunteered to take her to the movies to distract her from her anxiety. She refused Jack's offers but kept attending sessions until he suggested that they start dating once counseling was over. At that same session, he also told her how attractive she was. Martina's friend told her that Jack was acting unprofessionally and that most counselors don't do such things. Martina now wants to take some action against Jack so that "he can't keep using his practice as a dating service." She asks Dominic for guidance in figuring out how to report Jack's behavior.

Research suggests that clients frequently tell their counselors and therapists about unethical behaviors by other mental health professionals. According to Pope (1994), approximately half of all American mental health professionals have had at least one client who revealed sexual involvement with a prior therapist; the percentage for British psychologists is 22.7% (Garrett, 1998). Clients also call state licensing boards with questions about the ethics of a mental health professional (Wierzbicki, Siderits, & Kuchan, 2012). Sometimes clients are not as aware as Martina of the inherent problems in sexual exploitation and other ethical violations, but they do mention them in subsequent counseling experiences with sufficient frequency to require that professionals should be prepared for such eventualities.

When this happens, the new counselors have an opportunity to model ethical behavior and to counteract some of the damage done to the client and the profession by the prior provider.

Information about ethics violations also may come from co-workers and from one's own observations of others' behavior in the workplace. Reports from practicing professionals show that between 15% and 28% of practicing psychologists had personal knowledge of an incompetent or unethical colleague (Floyd, Myszka, & Orr, 1999; Schwebel, Skorina, & Schoener, 1994; Wood, Klein, Cross, Lammers, & Elliott, 1985). In one study that used a looser definition of personal knowledge (Golden & Schmidt, 1998), the percentage was much higher—69% of those surveyed reported knowing of at least one unethical action by a professional in the prior two years. Golden and Schmidt found four types of misconduct predominated: financial exploitation (39%), practice by unqualified personnel (25%), sexual exploitation (19%), and breach of confidentiality (17%). Of course, knowledge of peers' competency problems is not limited to practicing clinicians; counseling students also demonstrate awareness of their peers' problems (e.g., Brown-Rice & Furr, 2013).

Unfortunately, even very recent studies do not appear to result in lower rates of psychologist knowledge of peers' sexual misconduct: Noel (2008) surveyed clinical psychologists and found that 84% of them had been told of a colleague who had engaged in sexual contact with a client. These data suggest that professionals should prepare themselves to respond to a violation by another and should be aware of the practical and emotional aspects of filing ethics complaints in order to help clients like Martina.

FORMAL DISCIPLINARY PROCEDURES

When professionals act unethically, they may be disciplined by their employers, the state or provincial licensing board, and all the national and state professional associations to which they belong. Conceivably, complaints for the same set of actions may be filed in each organization. Professional associations commonly forward complaints against their members to licensing boards in the jurisdictions where the member holds a license. Interstate communication among licensing boards and professional associations also occurs through the National Practitioner Data Bank, an office in the U.S. Department of Health and Human Services, so that disciplined professionals cannot fraudulently obtain licenses in other states as easily as they once were able to (Kirkland, Kirkland, & Reaves, 2004). As discussed repeatedly in this book, counselors and therapists who violate standards are accountable to the courts in civil lawsuits for negligence, malpractice, or breach of contract, or in criminal court for violations of criminal statutes. In 15 states, sexual contact with a client carries criminal penalties for psychologists (Haspel et al., 1997). Three other states—Alabama, Michigan, and Ohio—criminalize sexual misconduct if it occurs through therapeutic deception, that is, if the therapist represents that sexual contact has a therapeutic purpose for the client. Multiple accountability also means there are multiple choices for those who wish to seek redress against professional misconduct. Clients often profit by assistance from their new therapists in sorting through their options.

Procedures for Filing Ethics Complaints

The procedures for making an ethics complaint vary according to the seriousness of the misconduct, with formal complaints generally reserved for more egregious violations.

Informal Remedies Through Professional Associations The ethics codes of the APA and ACA both recommend informal remedies as a first step in addressing misconduct. Their rationale for this strategy is not explicitly stated, but it is reasonable to surmise that it is based on an interest in rehabilitation rather than punishment; an interest in a speedy, nonbureaucratic resolution of problems; and minimization of negative publicity damaging to the mental health professions and the practitioner. The wording for these standards can be found in Appendix A, Section I.2.a, p. 538, and Appendix B, Standard 1.05, p. 538.

Formal Remedies When an informal resolution is not appropriate or feasible, professionals take action such as reporting the suspected ethics violation to the state or national ethics committees, unless this action conflicts with confidentiality rights that cannot be resolved. It is important to note that the ethics committees of some states serve only an educational function and have no adjudication function. In those states, complaints are referred to the national association and/or to the state licensing board.

A careful reading shows that neither code mandates that an ethics complaint be made; they say only *action* must be taken if an informal approach to the problem is unsuccessful. The APA statement also suggests avenues for the professional to pursue to address the suspected violation and uses the seriousness of the suspected offense and its harm or potential to harm consumers as the major criteria for deciding whether to file a formal complaint.

Minor violations seem amenable to private interventions such as a one-on-one conversation between the offending and the concerned professional. Consider the individual who does not obtain a complete informed consent to counseling as advised in the ethics code. Instead, she discusses only the limits of confidentiality very briefly. If there is no known harm to clients thus far and she seems to be acting from ignorance of the codes rather than disdain for them, informal confrontation seems a prudent choice. In this conversation, she can be educated about the ethics of informed consent and be placed on notice that further noncompliance will be taken more seriously. This approach lets the colleague retain some dignity and probably achieves as much behavior change as would be gained from a full ethics committee investigation. In addition, there is a practical argument in favor of an informal approach—it's speedier. A formal complaint can take months, even years, to resolve. An intervention for a minor infraction can take place immediately, and the harm can be remedied almost as quickly.

Using the employing institution to help change practitioner behavior before moving into association or licensing board channels also makes sense, especially in minor or moderate offenses. An employer with policies for adjudicating complaints can respond in a reasonable time frame and with consideration for the rights of all involved. The employer has clout over the employee and is in the position to monitor future behavior. The disadvantages of complaining to employers are variability in enforcement procedures and lack of influence over the professional if he or she takes employment elsewhere. In addition, personal relationships among employees often hinder objective processing of a complaint. Consequently, reporting a problem to an employer is more likely to be beneficial if it is mildly or moderately serious and needs an objective investigation, if monitoring the individual's future behavior is desirable, and if the employee is not likely to change jobs in the immediate future.

Using the seriousness of the offense as a criterion to determine the level of intervention, let us return to Martina's case. Clearly, her former counselor (Jack) did not comply with the ethical standards of either the ACA or APA regarding multiple relationships. In addition, Jack's invitation to begin dating immediately after counseling was terminated showed he was probably interested in a physical relationship with Martina. As noted in Chapter 7, the latter is even more emphatically prohibited by the codes (see Section A.5.a of the ACA Code of Ethics and Standard 10.5 of the APA Code).

The harm from such behavior is also important to examine, to ascertain whether this offense was serious enough for a formal complaint. Research evidence suggests substantial and often long-lasting harm to clients whose counselors engage in sexual contact with them (e.g., Bouhoutsos et al., 1983; Luepker, 1999; Wohlberg, 1999). Martina herself reports feeling even worse after her encounter with Jack. Even though no sexual contact took place, Martina's functioning deteriorated after Jack expressed romantic interest in her. That is probably sufficient to constitute psychological injury to Martina. Is there also harm that extends beyond Martina? The research evidence also suggests that professionals who engage in sexual contact with one client are more likely to have had sex with other clients (Pope, 1994). The possibility exists, then, that Martina is not the first client who has suffered Jack's advances. In any case, unless something changes Jack's behavior, Martina may not be the last client injured by this man's irresponsibility. Taken together, then, the evidence suggests that a formal complaint to the licensing board and the professional association is warranted. This man hurt Martina, may have hurt other clients in the past, and may do so again.

The inability of Dominic, the current counselor, to help rehabilitate Jack comes into play in the decision about using a formal resolution in serious cases such as Martina's. Because Dominic does not work at the same agency and has no supervisory relationship with the offender, he has no effective way to monitor Jack's behavior on an ongoing basis. Moreover, Dominic probably does not have time to fully investigate the incident and objectively evaluate the evidence presented by both parties. If no wrongdoing occurred, a counselor accused of a serious violation by a client also deserves the opportunity to have his or her name cleared. An informal resolution does not really allow such an outcome. Thus, from several perspectives, it is wiser to report a potentially serious violation to a body empowered to carefully investigate and to assert authority over future behavior than to use a private intervention. It offers better protection both to the professional who may be falsely accused and to the client who may have been victimized.

Another option that has been recommended and used with clients who have been sexually exploited by their therapists is mediation (Hartsell & Bernstein, 2008). Its primary advantage is its speed and moderate structure. It is processed faster than a formal complaint and has more structure than a one-on-one intervention. Its disadvantage is that a formal complaint to an association or licensing board may not be forthcoming, which is a substantial limitation for a serious offense. Mediation may also function to favor the professional, who is usually the more powerful party in the dispute. See Bouhoutsos and Brodsky (1985) for a more detailed examination of the use of mediation for professional misconduct.

One caution is in order about reporting violations. The language in the codes about resolving ethical violations also establishes the priority of the client's right to confidentiality over the professional's duty to intervene when another professional acts irresponsibly (Fisher, 2003). One can approach a colleague or file a complaint to a board or committee that involves a client *only* if the client has consented and waived his or her preexisting right to confidentiality. The only exceptions are situations in which there may be a legal mandate to act otherwise. So if Martina wanted to do nothing about her former therapist and wanted no information disclosed, professional ethics demand honoring her decision. (In some jurisdictions, the professional is obliged to offer the client contact information for the licensing board even if he or she expresses no interest in reporting when the issue emerges.) When an adult client makes this choice, mental health professionals may worry about future clients of this man, but the duty to the current client takes precedence. Of course, with time and good care the client may change her mind about making a complaint against the former professional, but no client should be coerced into reporting.

American Counseling Association Complaint Procedures

The functions and goals of the ACA Ethics Committee are to educate members about ethical standards and deal with ethics questions and complaints (ACA, 2005). The committee has nine members, all of whom are professional counselors who serve three-year terms. This body aims at protecting the rights of the person who originated the action and the rights of the counselor to a fair hearing.

Complaints against ACA members can come from the public, other members, or the committee itself, acting *sua sponte*. A *sua sponte* action means that if the Ethics Committee has information suggesting a member violated the standards, the committee itself can initiate the complaint. The committee has established and periodically revises its rules and procedures for handling ethics complaints.

The first contact with ACA's Office of Ethics and Professional Standards from a person considering an ethics complaint usually comes by telephone, although the ACA website also offers information on the steps in the ethics complaint process, at http://www.counseling.org/ethics. The first step is to verify the membership of the individual in question, usually by a faxed or mailed request. Once membership is verified, the person complaining is sent an official ethics complaint form to complete. Only signed, written complaints are processed. Once that form is received, if sufficient reason exists to explore the matter further, the person named in the complaint is notified of the charges being made and is given copies of the complaint and all related materials. He or she is asked to respond in writing within 60 days. Accused members have the option of asking for a face-to-face hearing before the committee. When all material has been obtained within the stated time limits, the committee deliberates about the case. The committee has several options in its ruling. It can determine that no ethics violation took place, that there isn't enough information to determine whether a violation took place, or that the person accused is guilty of the ethics violation. If misconduct is found, the committee then determines the appropriate sanction. The sanctions can range from remedial requirements to permanent expulsion from the organization. The latter is a rare occurrence—from 2010 to 2013, only one counselor was expelled from the ACA for ethics violations (ACA Ethics Committee, 2011, 2012, 2013), and none were expelled in the four prior years (Glosoff & Freeman, 2007; Sanabria & Freeman, 2008). Needless to say, the ACA has outlined detailed procedures so that members can appeal unfavorable decisions. The appeal committee is composed of six members appointed by the president-elect and is subject to confirmation by the ACA Governing Council.

American Psychological Association Complaint Procedures

The APA Ethics Committee also has both educational and enforcement mandates from the association (APA, Ethics Committee, 2001). Currently, eight people serve on the committee as regular members for three-year terms. One is a public, nonpsychologist member, and the rest are psychologists. There are also four associate members who do not vote and who act as fact finders. The APA also hires professional and support staff to assist the committee. All procedures for handling ethics complaints are published at http://www.apa.org/ethics/code/committee.aspx and are designed to balance the rights of the person complaining against the rights of the psychologist, respecting the dignity of each party in the process. Their goal is to prevent harm to the public and to prevent harm to members from malicious or frivolous claims. The approach typically taken by both the APA's and ACA's ethics committees is rehabilitative, with as much emphasis on interventions that can rehabilitate the counselor or psychologist as on sanctions against him or her.

A complaint may come before the APA committee in one of three ways. A consumer or other citizen can file a complaint; another mental health professional can complain; or the Ethics Committee can initiate action against a member, *sua sponte*. Usually the initial inquiry about a potential violation comes by telephone to the Ethics Office. In this contact, the person learns that all complaints must be written and is sent an official complaint form. This form requests identifying information from the person accusing as well as the accused, along with a detailed description of the situation. When the APA Ethics Committee receives a complaint (by postal service), it conducts a preliminary review focused on three areas. The first review determines whether the complaint is within the committee's jurisdiction, which usually means whether the person named in the complaint is an APA member. Current instructions ask the person filing the complaint to check for membership status prior to submission, although APA will double-check. If the person named is not a member, the case is immediately closed, and that action is forwarded to the person who originated the complaint. Information is usually provided so that the person can file a complaint with a state licensing board or other professional association if appropriate. The second level of action examines whether the complaint has been filed within the appropriate time limits. If the time limit is exceeded, the person who complains is given an opportunity to ask for a waiver of the time limit. The third focus is on the sufficiency of the information furnished. In other words, the committee assesses whether there is adequate evidence to warrant further investigation. The APA Ethics Committee Reports (e.g., APA, 2012, 2013d, 2014b) indicate that many complaints fail to progress beyond the preliminary investigation. Most cases are closed for one of these three reasons.

When a claim remains open, the next step is an evaluation by the chair of the Ethics Committee and the Ethics Office staff. This involves a determination of whether a *cause for action* exists. According to APA, a "cause for action shall exist when the respondent's alleged actions and/or omissions, if proved, would in the judgment of the decision maker constitute a breach of ethics" (APA, Ethics Committee, 2001, Rules and Procedure, Section 5.1). If a cause for action has been found, the person named in the complaint is notified of the filing and receives copies of the complaint. The member is required to respond in writing to the complaint within 60 days and may submit additional information about the matter for the committee to consider. The committee may also seek out information from other sources that it deems potentially relevant. Once this information is gathered, the committee decides whether there is enough information to show a cause for action. If there is not, the case is closed at this point, but if there is reason to suspect an ethics violation, a formal case is opened.

The psychologist involved is then formally charged with an ethics violation. The member receives written notification of the nature of the charges and the section(s) of the ethics code he or she is alleged to have violated. The psychologist is required to respond in writing within 30 days. In some cases, the psychologist is asked to appear in person before the committee. The person filing the claim is also notified of the formal charge and can submit additional information relevant to the charges in the allotted time period. When the investigation is complete, the committee deliberates and issues its ruling. It may dismiss the charges, recommend a sanction less than formal charges, or issue formal charges against the member. A lesser sanction is recommended when the committee believes that the violation occurred but that it would be better resolved without formal charges. In this respect, the committee is given a good deal of discretion. Formal charges are issued when the misconduct represents a substantial harm to another person or the profession. In this event, the committee recommends to the board of directors that the individual be dropped from membership in the organization. Here, too, the committee has a good measure of flexibility because it can let a member resign, instead of being dropped, if it believes the severity of the misconduct does not warrant the full action. Between 2006 and 2010, 84 members either resigned or were dropped from APA membership subsequent to an ethics investigation (APA Ethics Committee, 2011). The APA Board of Directors may accept or reject the recommendations of the Ethics Committee. Of course, a member may appeal a decision of the Ethics Committee, and a rather elaborate description of the appeal process is presented in the published rules.

Licensing Board Procedures

The procedures for complaining about the activities of a licensed professional vary from state to state (or province to province) and profession to profession. Generally, licensing boards are authorized to discipline professionals who violate the written regulations. The type of discipline ranges from reprimands and limitations placed on one's practice to permanent loss of license. For some offenses, criminal sanctions may also exist, and the board will turn evidence over to the legal system. A person seeking to give information about an ethics violation to a licensing board begins the process with a telephone call or letter to the appropriate state agency. Some state licensing boards provide information about initiating complaints on their websites. Because licensing boards have more authority and power to regulate the future actions of a professional, some scholars advocate that aggrieved clients should file first with a licensing board (e.g., Siegel, 1991). Interstate reporting also occurs so that a licensing board in one state can know if an applicant has been judged guilty of an offense in another state. Such reporting is also an argument for including a state board in any ethics complaint.

Some licensing boards do not offer professionals the option of informal resolutions of minor violations. The Ohio Counselor, Social Worker, and Marriage and Family Therapy Board, for example, mandates that these professionals report all suspected violations of other professionals unless such reporting would violate client confidentiality. Therefore, practicing professionals should be aware of licensing board regulations. A similar broadly worded statement appears in the rules of the Board of Professional Counselors and Therapists in Maryland. Both the ACA and APA codes state that professionals attempt to resolve the conflict in a responsible way (ACA Code, Section I.1.c, in Appendix A, p. 532, and APA Code, Standard 1.02, in Appendix B, p. 538.)

Complaints to Employers

As already mentioned, people who believe a mental health professional has acted inappropriately might also notify employers or supervisors about the problem. If a practitioner has partners in a group practice, any or all partners can be contacted. Large employers, such as community mental health centers and psychiatric hospitals, are more likely to have procedures in place for investigating such complaints. Smaller employers and colleagues in a practice are more prone to handle matters on a case-by-case basis. Again, people who complain need to identify themselves and provide specific information and documentation, if possible, about the events they believe are problematic. Employers who know that such information is also being forwarded to the licensing board or professional association may give the matter more serious attention, even though they may postpone a decision about the matter until the other bodies have ruled. Obviously, professionals in individual private practices are self-employed, so complaints against them must be referred to a professional association and/or licensing board.

SUPPORTING THE CLIENT THROUGH THE COMPLAINT PROCESS

When a client such as Martina wants to complain to an authority about a mental health professional, the current practitioner can play an important role in helping a client make sound judgments based on accurate information about the practical and emotional aspects of the process. Most clients have little knowledge of professional rules and regulations, and professionals provide a valuable service when they give clients such information. They can also help clients sort out their emotions about the prior experience and about the complaint process. Clients should understand that their identity will be known to the committee and/or licensing board and that the accused professional will have access to all materials they submit to the committee. The client is also likely to feel victimized by the former professional and may not easily understand the committee's responsibility to protect the rights of the accused as well as the victim's. It may reduce the client's frustration to explain that the principle of "innocent until proven guilty" holds in this arena.

Clients (and/or their parents or legal guardians) need full autonomy in deciding whether to file or proceed with the complaint, especially because only a minority of complaints submitted to professional associations result in formal charges against the member. So far, there is limited empirical evidence that complaining will help the person heal from the wound (Vinson, 1987). Clients should appreciate that most realistic benefit for them is the knowledge that if the action is successful, future clients are at less risk for harm.

Some counselors and therapists may have difficulty acknowledging that fellow professionals behave irresponsibly. They may take a "head in the sand" approach and minimize client accounts of counselor misconduct or attribute such accounts to negative transference or psychopathology. They may feel uncomfortable helping a client take action against a colleague for whom they feel empathy (Floyd et al., 1999; Levenson, 1986). Despite these entirely human feelings, professionals are bound to explore evidence of unethical practice by colleagues when clients mention them. If additional discussion clarifies a potentially serious unethical practice, the new professional has a duty to inform the client about ethical standards for professionals and his or her options for action. The professional's goal in such discussion is to keep an open mind, respect the dignity of all involved, and help the client determine his or her next step.

False claims against mental health professionals are relatively rare. Pope and Vetter (1991) report that about 4% of claims of sexual contact between therapists and clients were not true. The elaborate, time-consuming, and often uncomfortable process of filing a complaint militates against the filing of large numbers of false complaints. A professional who believes a client is falsely accusing a prior therapist of misconduct should explore the matter extensively in session. Those who worry about such false claims can also take comfort in the careful analysis by the committees and boards involved that also militates against a false finding against an innocent professional. In a controversial article on false claims using anecdotal evidence, Williams (2000) hypothesizes that there are six major antecedents that motivate false claims: malingering and fraud, revenge, psychopathology, recovered memory, advice from a subsequent therapist, and escape from unwanted treatment.

The client needs extra support at several other crucial points in the therapeutic process. First, putting the information in writing to the committee may cause the client to revisit the pain of the experience itself. Counseling time devoted to those feelings is wisely spent, focusing on the reality of the pain and attributing responsibility to the mental health professional (not the client) for the misconduct. The second point at which support is crucial arises if the committee decides not to pursue the complaint and issue formal charges (an event that occurs in a substantial proportion of cases). According to California enforcement data for 2009–2014 show that 4380 complaints were received against the 22,000 psychologists in the state, and that 935 of these complaints were judged appropriate for investigation

(California Board of Psychology, 2014). Of these, 156 (or 16.7% of investigations) resulted in discipline by the board. Professionals should be prepared to help clients process feelings of anger and sadness and brainstorm about alternatives when this happens. A third crucial point comes if the committee issues a ruling against the member. The outcome may be less than the client hoped for and may evoke feelings of betrayal. However, even if the outcome seems to fit the offense, the client may feel guilty about the negative consequences for the violator. Again, the client may take on the responsibility for the professional's behavior, blaming him- or herself for the outcome. Clarifying the professional's duty to honor the profession's standards in all situations may help the client think more accurately about whose behavior was problematic. Finally, no matter what the outcome of the complaint, the counselor must help the client find ways to bring closure to this episode.

RESPONDING TO AN ETHICS COMPLAINT

As discussed in Chapter 1, the risk of an ethics complaint happening to a U.S. counselor or therapist is extremely low (Van Horne, 2004). The possibility appears higher elsewhere. For example, in Australia, 20 of 100 psychologists who practice for 30 years can expect an ethics complaint filed against them, although few of these are categorized as violations that would cost the psychologist his or her license (Greyner & Lewis, 2012). In 2013, APA received complaints for only 0.0004% of the membership (APA, 2014). Even when a complaint is filed with a licensing board, 74% of psychologists in one state found that it was resolved to their satisfaction (Montgomery et al., 1999). Professionals who worry excessively about a complaint are misdirecting their energies. However, realistic concern is appropriate since as much as 11% of licensing board claims in a given jurisdiction can result in disciplinary action (Montgomery et al., 1999; Schoenfeld, Hatch, &, Gonzalez, 2001; Thomas, 2005 Van Horne, 2004). If you are informed that an ethics complaint has been leveled against you, the ethics codes contain guidelines for your response, indicating that you are required to cooperate with an ethics committee investigation. The exact wording is contained in the ACA Code, Section I.3, p. 533, and in the APA Code, Standard 1.06, Appendix B, p. 539.

The central message is that ignoring an inquiry by an ethics committee or licensing board is the worst possible response because failing to cooperate is an ethics violation in itself. The professional may be especially tempted to ignore an inquiry that appears groundless, but even frivolous and false claims require a response (Wheeler & Bertram, 2012). Cooperation entails providing all relevant information in a timely fashion. Each professional organization has somewhat different timelines, so it is important to refer to the rules governing the process in the organization to which the claim is made. Cooperation also means that you do not try to resign from the organization to avoid an ethics inquiry. Once a proceeding has begun, a member is usually not allowed to resign until the investigation is complete. Even then, a resignation may be accepted only under certain conditions. Many people wisely hire attorneys to assist them in this process and ensure that their rights are protected.

Learning of an ethics claim arouses strong emotions (Schoenfeld et al., 2001; Thomas, 2005). (See Peterson [2001] for an example of the reaction of a professional who believes he was wrongly accused and convicted.) A wise professional gets appropriate emotional support in this situation (Chauvin & Remley, 1996). If you believe that you have been falsely accused, these emotions can be truly overwhelming. In that situation, some reality testing is in order. History shows that most claims are dismissed before formal charges are issued, so there is no need to panic about a preliminary investigation.

If you have committed the unethical action with which you are charged, but believe there are relevant extenuating circumstances, you should document the particulars to the committee or licensing board. Extenuating circumstances do not excuse such behaviors (and members who try to make excuses hardly ever win the favor of the committee), but they can put the misconduct in context. If you have subsequently taken steps on your own to prevent such actions in the future, your case may be strengthened by providing such information to the committee. Such an approach is consistent with the committee's interest in rehabilitating professionals rather than punishing them. It is important to note, however, that the primary mandate of licensing board is to protect public safety. Rehabilitation of the professional is a secondary consideration for licensing boards. Professionals who take responsibility for their mistakes, express remorse, and demonstrate a sincere commitment to rehabilitation go a long way in helping to save their careers.

Thomas (2005) recommends that the accused professional refrain from making any contact with the client who has filed the complaint. The only exception to this advice occurs when the professional's attorney advises such contact. She also agrees with the advice of Chauvin and Remley (1996) to refrain from disclosing detailed information about the complaint to family and friends. This is an understandable but misguided effort to relieve the stress of a complaint that represents a violation of confidentiality in itself. The client filing the complaint released information to the Board or Ethics Committee, not others.

One recent development in licensing board procedures should be noted. At least one state is now posting "Notice of the Opportunity for a Hearing" when formal charges are made against a professional as well as posting the outcomes of the disciplinary process. See http://www.psychology.ohio.gov/compl.stm for an example from Ohio.

SELF-MONITORING: TAKING RESPONSIBILITY IN THE ABSENCE OF A COMPLAINT

> Observing more senior physicians, students learn that their mentors and supervisors believe in, practice, and reward the concealment of errors ... they learn to talk about unanticipated outcomes until a "mistake: morphs into a "complication." Above all, they learn not to tell the patient anything. (Berlinger, 2007, p. 41)

The typical mental health professional probably spends 30 to 40 years in practice. Even those who undertake this profession as a second career are likely to work for two decades. In that span of time, ethical mistakes of varying seriousness will almost certainly occur. As discussed in Chapter 1, many mental health practitioners admit both intentional and unintentional violations of ethical standards (Pope et al., 1987; Sherry et al., 1991; Tubbs & Pomerantz, 2001), but few of those violations are reported to any disciplinary body (Pope & Vasquez, 2011; Williams, 2000).

Inadvertent disclosures of confidential information are especially common examples of these missteps (Pope et al., 1987). Very limited data are available about the frequency with which therapists disclose their minor ethical errors to their clients. One qualitative study indicates that some do, but little is known otherwise about the level of awareness of less egregious ethical errors or professionals' responses to them (Medau, Jox, & Reiter-Theil, 2013).

Awareness of vulnerabilities is the cornerstone of prevention. As Tjelveit and Gottlieb (2010) note, vulnerabilities may be *general*, the kind that affect all of us, such as making errors when stressed or distracted, or they may be *idiosyncratic*, unique to the individual based on their background, unique life circumstances, or character. Professionals who fail to acknowledge their vulnerability to misconduct are naive at best and frightening at worst. And a professional culture (such as the one in medicine that Berlinger describes at the opening of the chapter) that encourages secrecy and nondisclosure of ethical errors or treatment errors is fundamentally wrong and counterproductive. In its essence, ethical practice is not about expecting perfection; rather, it is about taking responsibility for one's actions (whether ethical or unethical) and keeping the welfare of one's clients as the central aim. In some ways, one of the truest tests of a professional's commitment to ethical practice is the way that person reacts when he or she deviates from that path and colleagues, clients, or disciplinary bodies are not likely to discover that deviation. This is the "ethics is what happens when no one else is looking" notion. This capacity to be alert for inevitable errors, to acknowledge them, and to act to ameliorate their negative effects in the absence of external reprimands is closely related to the virtue ethics about which Meara et al. (1996) write so eloquently. Ultimately, our errors may teach as much about the ethics of practice than our successes. (See Schulz [2010] for an insightful analysis of the origins of error in humans, the nature of the experience of being wrong, and the lessons individuals and societies can learn from attention to error.) Virtuous professionals believe so strongly in the ethical values of the profession that they hold themselves accountable even when others do not. The ethical principles underlying this personal accountability are beneficence and fidelity. The very definition of a profession includes the notion that its members are self-regulating individuals who have internalized the ethical values of the profession that they have voluntarily joined and who are committed to acting in the best interest of the communities they serve (Pryzwansky & Wendt, 1999).

Behnke (2009) makes an important point about the relationship between a psychologist's experience in practice and his or her approach to ethics that has usefulness in understanding the kinds of vulnerabilities to ethical mistakes that emerge at different stages of a professional's career. He posits that new professionals may be vulnerable to an over-anxious and rigid approach to ethics that risks problems since it takes an overly risk-avoidant stance. At mid-career, Behnke suggests that a psychologist may be vulnerable to the persistent stress of work and outside life demands and may experience emotional exhaustion from the work, leaving that individual especially vulnerable to boundary issues. At the end of a person's career, Behnke argues that the very wisdom professionals have accumulated over a long career puts them at risk for an overly flexible approach to ethics, a view that because of the wisdom accumulated, the rules do not apply to them.

With the exception of the professional's responsibility to self-monitor and limit practice (ACA Code, Section C.1.d, and APA Standard 2.06), the ethics codes do not address this issue directly. Instead, they deal with the professional's responsibility to know the codes, act in accordance with them, and consult with others when in doubt (ACA Code, Section I; APA Code, Standards 1.01-1.08). In the same sections, the codes also describe strategies for handling the questionable behaviors of colleagues but are largely silent on one's duty after recognizing one's own ethical misconduct as a professional. The ethics literature also addresses the issue of colleague misconduct (e.g., Levenson [1986] and response to others' accusations [Chauvin & Remley, 1996; Thomas, 2005]) but contains little reference to recovery from one's own misconduct. Principle B of the APA Code touches on the matter in its statement, "Psychologists uphold professional standards of conduct, clarify their professional roles and obligations, accept appropriate responsibility for their behavior, and seek to manage conflicts of interest that could lead to exploitation or harm."

The ethics codes emphasize prevention of misconduct, and this emphasis is both understandable and noble, but any discussion of professional ethics that attends only to prevention is ultimately insufficient, in the light of human nature, research evidence about misconduct, and the limitations of current reporting mechanisms. Not discussing the predictability of some instances of ethical errors and the remediation of those missteps leads to the mistaken impression that mistakes are rare or avoidable or always egregious. In this context, practitioners are more likely to view their less serious ethical violations as problems that ought to be kept secret and hidden away. This approach is fully consistent with the positive ethics approach of Handelsman et al. (2005) and represents the outcome of an effective ethics acculturation process.

A THREE-STEP MODEL OF RECOVERY

The focus of this section, then, is on frank and open attention to ethical violations and on recommendations for coping responsibly with one's own mistakes. Because these recommendations are not codified in any official document, they are advisory, not enforceable. Their aim is to encourage mental health professionals to understand accountability at its most fundamental level. The foundation for these recommendations derives partly from the literature on the rehabilitation of offending counselors and psychotherapists (Brown, 1997; Gonsiorek, 1997; Layman & McNamara, 1997; Schoener & Gonsiorek, 1988; Welfel, 2005). The three essential questions that professionals need to answer when confronting their own mistakes are as follows:

- Have I understood exactly what went wrong and the degree to which self-interest, heuristics (intellectual shortcuts), or inattention to the emotion and the nonrational parts of the situation affected my behavior? And have I really acknowledged that I have violated professional standards?
- What damage have I done, and how can I undo or ameliorate that damage?
- What steps should I take to ensure that I do not repeat this mistake?

Acknowledging the Violation

As professionals in human service professions, we like to think of ourselves as honorable people, motivated by altruism rather than self-interest. It can be hard to accept that we have ethical blind spots (Brazerman & Tenbrunsel, 2012), especially if those blind spots happened out of self-interest. Even when abundant evidence of serious misconduct exists, we seem to want to minimize or rationalize our actions (Pope & Vasquez, 2011). The tendency to minimize violations that do not cause substantial harm or that are hidden from public view is likely to be even greater. The first task in self-monitoring is to fully acknowledge the ethical lapse and understand its nature and scope without catastrophizing about it. This task requires careful reflection and tolerance for the emotional discomfort that accompanies such reflection and relates to the ethical sensitivity discussed in the ethical decision-making model in Chapter 2. Allowing awareness of the emotional distress can act as a motivator to address the negative effects of the actions and work toward prevention of a recurrence. It is important here to focus on the ethical dimensions of the conduct, not its legal ramifications. The legal standard for malpractice, for example, is evidence of harm to the client, but the ethical standard is *risk or threat of harm to the client*, derived from the ethical principle of nonmaleficence.

Assessing and Responding to the Damage

Once a professional has become aware of a problematic behavior, the next step is to determine how much harm has been caused. Assessing harm to the client is the top priority, followed by damage to colleagues, to others in the community, and to the reputation of the profession. Consulting with a trusted colleague who is objective, knowledgeable, and able to identify unconscious biases of which the individual is unaware is often helpful. Colleagues can sometimes act as intermediaries with disaffected clients or co-workers who resist additional contacts with the offender because of their negative experience. For example, a colleague might telephone a client to explore ways in which the client's needs can be met, assuming, of course, that such a contact would not breach confidentiality obligations to the client. Perhaps a client would be willing to make an appointment with a different professional or participate in a meeting with the counselor with other professionals present to find an acceptable solution to the difficulty.

Once the level of damage is determined, the third step is to develop a strategy that will ameliorate that harm. The more serious the infraction, the more complicated the remediation is likely to be. A practitioner who has for several weeks provided incompetent service because of alcohol abuse has a much greater task in this regard than a therapist who acted incompetently on a single day because of illness or personal crisis. In the latter case, providing a day's worth of sessions without cost to compensate for the day of poor service is probably all that is required as long as the incompetent sessions did not inflict significant damage on clients.

The therapist seeking to compensate for weeks of incompetent service faces a more daunting task. The length of the incompetent service also increases the likelihood of meaningful negative effects for clients. A depressed client who receives inadequate therapy for three weeks will probably suffer more than one who gets a single bungled session. Clients may have terminated counseling prematurely and may be unwilling to engage in counseling again because of their bad experience. The ill effects may extend not only to clients but also to the client's family members and friends, to whom the counselor has little or no access. Colleagues may have experienced some negative fallout during the period of incompetent practice. Some attention to remedying negative impact on them is also in order. Obviously, in this kind of situation the capacity to remedy the harm is limited. If the original victims of the misconduct are inaccessible, then professionals might perform the equivalent of the "community service" penalty that criminal courts often impose for minor offenses. The point of such actions is to act to compensate the community for misbehaviors. Community service activities serve two purposes. They balance the scales in a small way, and they remind those involved of their responsibilities to the broader community.

One cautionary note is in order here. Ethical ideals do not require a Herculean effort to ameliorate all ill effects. The crucial feature of all such efforts is one's good-faith commitment to help those he or she has harmed and to address the damage to the profession's reputation in the community. Brown (1997) uses the term *amends* in this regard, and it seems quite fitting to express the notion that some sort of compensation is in order. Consultation can assist here, too, in sorting out reasonable from unreasonable efforts and in devising a workable plan to remedy damage.

The impact of remedies on those who suffered the original ill effects must also be assessed. Put plainly, if the cure is worse than the disease, it's no cure at all. Because the most important ethical standard is the welfare of the client, remediation efforts that jeopardize that welfare have no place in recovery from an ethical misstep. For example, if a counselor reveals identifying client information to a close friend in a lunchtime chat, that counselor has violated the ethics code. The purpose of the discussion with the colleague was not professional, not in the client's best interest, and there was no client authorization for the disclosure. When the counselor recognizes the blunder, he or she needs to carefully examine the best way to remedy that mistake. Speaking with the friend again to acknowledge the error and asking that person to honor confidentiality is one remedy that injures no one. Whether the violation is best disclosed to the client depends on its effects on the client, especially because it is likely to be a nonegregious infraction with little likelihood of negative consequences for that client (except, of course, if the friend turns out to be untrustworthy). If an objective assessment of a remedy reveals that it risks additional harm to a client, the clinician should seek alternative remedies. Because the task of implementing a remedy is emotionally stressful, however, particularly when it involves disclosure to a client, professionals may be tempted to rationalize that all such disclosures will be harmful and should not be done. The criterion for judging the appropriateness of a remedy is the long-term welfare of the client rather than the immediate self-interest of the practitioner. Consultation is essential here, too, in sorting out reasonable and helpful interventions from unreasonable or self-serving ones.

Rehabilitating the Professional

A professional who has erred begins the process of recovery with an honest self-evaluation that unflinchingly recognizes the mistakes made and seeks out the causes so that they will be less likely to recur. This evaluation attends not only to the contribution of cognitive errors and emotional components of the violation but also to any gaps in social and professional support that led to the misconduct. The goal here is not to engender guilt or shame, but rather to gather energy for the process of change and to make that process as comprehensive as possible. The ultimate goal is to fortify a professional's resilience in the face of future ethical challenges.

The nature of the rehabilitative activities will vary significantly with the violation. For minor infractions, one may need simply to reread the ethics code and consult with colleagues for a period to verify that one is interpreting the code in an acceptable way. For more serious matters, a formal plan for rehabilitation is in order. That plan may include:

- Therapy if personal problems or character flaws are at the root of the misconduct, though this is no panacea for the problem.
- Reduction in the scope of one's practice to reduce risk. (A person who has engaged in risk boundary extensions, for instance, may wish to refrain from accepting clients similar to the client with whom the violation was committed, to lessen the risk of a recurrence.)
- A temporary moratorium on therapeutic work until stability is regained.
- An arrangement with another professional to closely supervise one's practice so that any problematic behaviors can be quickly identified and stopped.
- A rearrangement of professional and social support resources.
- A program of self-education or formal ethics education to gain a better understanding of the codes and the ethical values of the profession.
- Enrollment in training experiences that improve clinical competency.

This list is not comprehensive. Rehabilitation activities should be tailored to the individual violation and to the violator's characteristics. Similarly, the period of time devoted to rehabilitation will vary widely. Approaches to subsequent offenses in the same domain ought to be treated more aggressively than first offenses, but even first offenses ought not to be ignored. Tjeltveit and Gottlieb (2010) present some helpful suggestions for avoiding ethical disaster that can also be used to help one prevent future misconduct.

Finally, even when the rehabilitation period seems complete, because of human frailty the professional ought to periodically engage in consultation activities that ensure that no slippage has occurred. Unfortunately, there is no convincing evidence that rehabilitation efforts are effective when they have been imposed by licensing boards and ethics committees for egregious offenses (Gonsiorek, 1997; Layman & McNamara, 1997).

Compassion and Empathy

There is one additional value in personal accountability: compassion. It reminds professionals that we are all vulnerable to ethical missteps and deters us from adopting an attitude of moral superiority toward professionals who have been accused of misconduct. By recognizing our own mistakes, we gain compassion and empathy for others. As Jerome (1889) wrote more than a hundred years ago, "It is in our faults and failings, not in our virtues, that we touch each other and find sympathy ... It is in our follies that we are one." Thus, when others seek us out for consultation after an infraction, we are more likely to take an approach of seeking rehabilitation rather than punishment, of giving sympathy rather than harsh personal judgment. This compassion is not incompatible with full accountability for behavior; it is the fullest application of ethical ideals.

SUMMARY

Counselors and therapists learn of ethics violations by other professionals in several ways—from clients, from colleagues, and through their own experience. Hearing of colleagues' misbehavior from clients is not uncommon. Counselors are obliged to address these violations themselves or help clients who choose to address them to do so. However, when the desire to confront a colleague about an ethics violation conflicts with a client's right to confidentiality, confidentiality takes precedence.

The ethics codes recommend beginning with an attempt at an informal resolution of the problem. Usually, this starts with a conversation between the concerned and the offending professional. If the concerned colleague is convinced that the offense did not occur or that rehabilitation efforts will be effective, no further action is necessary. If the colleague doubts whether the public will be protected from further misconduct, a formal complaint is the next step. Individuals may submit ethics complaints to a variety of bodies, including licensing boards, professional associations, and employers. Procedures for handling such complaints are laid out in state regulations, ethics committee rules and procedures, or employee policy manuals. The central issue for the committees hearing such complaints is balancing the rights of the person making the complaint against the rights of the person accused. As in all other aspects of Western society, a professional is assumed innocent until proven guilty.

If a client has experienced unethical behavior by a former counselor, the current counselor should explain the client's options about reporting and help the client deal with the emotions during the process. The client should be free to decide autonomously about pursuing a complaint, because the complaint process is long and demanding and can result in some re-experiencing of the initial pain. If the client decides to proceed, he or she needs to recognize that its primary benefit will be to future clients of that therapist, although it's possible the client will find the experience a healing one.

No mental health professional is immune to unethical practice. Survey data suggest that violations of confidentiality, informed consent, and multiple relationships are rather common. Those studies also show that professionals express concern about their past misbehaviors and worry about future missteps. In this context, counselors and therapists ought to recognize their own vulnerability to ethical violations and take personal responsibility for acting to remedy them, even if outside disciplinary bodies fail to catch their misconduct. This obligation is not codified in any professional ethical standards, and thus is not enforceable, but is consistent with the ethical ideals of mental health professions to promote the welfare of others and place clients' needs ahead of one's own. Specifically, professionals ought to assess the damage their misconduct has caused, develop a plan for intervening to reduce or compensate for that damage, and then turn their attention to rehabilitation so that they are less vulnerable to that violation in the future.

Discussion Questions*

1. Do you agree with the author's resolution of the case of Martina? Would you argue for an informal resolution? Why or why not?
2. Reporting an unethical behavior to an employer has both benefits and disadvantages. Discuss the strengths and weaknesses of this strategy.
3. Should the ethics codes contain more explicit references to remedies and rehabilitation? If so, what wording would you find acceptable? If not, why not?

*Note to course instructors: The *Instructor's Guide* for this book includes other discussion questions, class exercises, cases, and multiple-choice and essay test items for this chapter.

4. Is commitment to the ethical ideal of minimizing damage to clients and others naive and unrealistic in a world of malpractice litigation and disciplinary action by licensing boards?
5. What feelings might affect a counselor trying to support a client who is filing an ethics complaint against another counselor?
6. Do you think the findings of ethics committees should be made known to the public? Currently, many organizations provide information about members who have been disciplined for ethics breaches. What might be gained or lost by more widespread communication of such findings?
7. Under what circumstances do you think implementing a remedy for a misstep might be as harmful as the misstep itself? If clients are ignorant of ethical violations, should they be informed?
8. What are the ethical dilemmas for the colleague who acts as a consultant to a professional who discloses a serious ethical violation?

Cases for Discussion

The following cases are representative examples of ethical missteps that others are unlikely to file complaints about (or even know about). They highlight both the need for remedies for misconduct and the difficulty in implementing them on occasion. They also raise interesting questions about rehabilitation. Reflect on each case, come to a conclusion about the ideal ethical remedy, and plan for rehabilitation.

Dr. Portrain and Hypnosis

Dr. Portrain, a psychologist, attended a one-day seminar on the use of clinical hypnosis for post-traumatic stress. This seminar was his first exposure to hypnosis and was taught by an expert in hypnosis who has received high ratings for the quality of her presentation. After the seminar, Dr. Portrain spent several hours reading about hypnosis and discussed that material with his colleagues. A few days after the seminar, a man who had barely escaped a serious fire in his apartment building came for counseling. An assessment indicated a moderate level of post-traumatic stress. Dr. Portrain recommended hypnosis as the treatment of choice, omitting any mention of other approaches that might help this client. The psychologist was eager and excited about the ability to employ this new treatment tool so soon after the workshop. The man agreed to hypnosis, and Dr. Portrain conducted three sessions using hypnosis. At the end of those sessions, the man showed no improvement in his symptoms. While watching the man weep over his disappointment about not improving, Dr. Portrain then realized that he had been practicing beyond the boundaries of his competence and had unfairly pushed his client into an experimental treatment without explaining other options.

Dr. MacDuff's Funny Story

Mr. Betts told his therapist, Dr. MacDuff, about a very embarrassing event that had occurred on his recent honeymoon. The client was relieved to be able to discuss the issue with his therapist, and by the end of the session, had begun to appreciate the humor as well as the pain in the situation. The next weekend, Dr. MacDuff attended a party at a neighbor's home. During that party, the host initiated a "Tell us your most embarrassing moment" game, and the partygoers agreed to participate. When it was Dr. MacDuff's turn, he had difficulty thinking of anything that would spark real laughter in the group. So, he told of Mr. Bett's incident without identifying his client.

In fact, he simply referred to the person as an acquaintance. The group enjoyed the anecdote immensely; it was the highlight of the game. The next day he encountered a partygoer in the supermarket who again expressed his enjoyment of Dr. MacDuff's anecdote. At this point, the doctor began to feel uneasy about his behavior and to regret having told the story.

Ms. Spend's Creative Problem Solving

Ms. Spend, a licensed clinical counselor in private practice, has become increasingly frustrated with the demands of third-party payers. Recently, when she was treating a woman with major depression, the insurance company authorized only five sessions and would not raise that limit. The client decided to pay out of pocket for the rest of her sessions, but this represented a hardship to her, even at reduced fees. The next time Ms. Spend encountered a client insured by the same company, she entered a diagnosis more severe than the client's true symptoms in order to obtain more reimbursement. In this case, the insurer agreed to 10 sessions, a number both the counselor and the client judged adequate for the problem. Two weeks after that client terminated, Ms. Spend attended a seminar on ethical and legal issues in counseling and realized that her behavior with this client was not only unethical but also probably illegal.

The Case of Ms. Monderly

Ms. Monderly is a licensed clinical social worker who has been in practice for 10 years. She has recently moved to a new community and feels lonely. One day, she encounters a client who seems to have all the characteristics she values in a friend. The client seems to be experiencing the same feelings about Ms. Monderly. Ms. Monderly decides to refer this client to another therapist after three sessions. The other therapist is an expert in the problem the client is experiencing, but Ms. Monderly's motivation is based primarily on her desire to begin a friendship with this client. Two months after the termination, Ms. Monderly telephones the client to invite her to a museum opening. They begin to attend cultural activities regularly. At one activity a few months later, Ms. Monderly sees a colleague from the practice. The colleague seems surprised when he recognizes the client. His expression of surprise changes to disapproval when the client reveals in their brief conversation that she and Ms. Monderly have become very close friends. Ms. Monderly wonders whether she should have resisted her personal interest in this client and made other efforts to find friends in her new community.

The Case of Bob and Ted

Bob is a licensed clinical counselor who has operated a small group practice in a suburban office building for 20 years. He is well recognized for his expertise in working with clients with complex problems that require long-term counseling. One day, he receives a telephone call from another counselor (Ted) working in the same neighborhood. Bob does not know Ted. Ted tells Bob that he is currently in the office with a woman named Nancy who has come to see him to discuss her depression. Ted proceeds to tell Bob that Nancy has just accused Bob of sexual misconduct and that Ted wants him to explain what happened when Nancy came to see Bob. Ted tells Bob that nothing he can say will dissuade him from reporting Bob to the licensing board but that he still wants to hear what he has to say. Ted goes on to tell Bob that Bob's actions have been totally unprofessional and that he has traumatized this woman. Bob is shocked. He first tries to ascertain that this is not a crank call and to clarify that Ted is indeed a licensed professional.

The information Ted shares clarifies that he is a licensed clinical social worker and that he has Nancy's permission to make this phone call. As he listens to Ted describe Nancy and the comments she has made to Ted, Bob realizes that he does not even recognize the woman to whom Ted is referring. Bob asks Nancy to describe his physical appearance, but her description could fit many men and is not very helpful. Next Bob asks if Nancy would be willing to speak with him on the phone because he still has no memory of seeing Nancy. As soon as they begin the conversation Nancy realizes that she does not recognize Bob's voice. After a few more exchanges, Nancy comes to seriously doubt whether she has identified the right counselor. Ted mumbles a few words about getting more information and calling back later and hangs up. Bob is so upset by this conversation that he cannot sleep that night and immediately consults with a colleague. Bob then tries to figure out how to follow up with Ted, who has falsely accused him of a serious violation. (Bob later learns that Nancy had seen another counselor in a nearby building with the first name of Robert.) Discuss the ethical issues involved in the actions of both Ted and Bob. Should Bob just forget the whole matter at this point?

Recommended Readings

American Counseling Association. (2005b). Policies and procedures for processing complaints of ethical violations. Retrieved from http://www.counseling.org/docs/ethics/policies_procedures.pdf?sfvrsn=2

American Psychological Association, Ethics Committee. (2001). Rules and procedures. Washington, D.C.: Author. Retrieved from http://www.apa.org/ethics/code/committee.aspx - overview

Berlinger, N. (2007). *After harm: Medical error and the ethics of forgiveness*. Baltimore, MD: Johns Hopkins University Press.

Chauvin, J. C., & Remley, T. P., Jr. (1996). Responding to allegations of unethical conduct. *Journal of Counseling & Development*, 74, 563–568.

Crowley, J. D., & Gottlieb, M. C. (2012). Objects in the mirror are closer than they appear: A primary prevention model for ethical decision making. *Professional Psychology: Research and Practice*, 43, 65–72.

Levenson, J. L. (1986). When a colleague acts unethically: Guidelines for intervention. *Journal of Counseling & Development*, 64, 315–317.

Meara, N. M., Schmidt, L. D., & Day, J. D. (1996). Principles and virtues: A foundation for ethical decisions, policies and character. *The Counseling Psychologist*, 24, 4–77.

Schulz, K. (2010). *Being wrong: Adventures in the margin of error*. New York, NY: HarperCollins.

Thomas, J. T. (2005). Licensing board complaints: Minimizing the impact on the psychologist's defense and clinical practice. *Professional Psychology: Research and Practice*, 36, 426–433.

Tjeltveit, A. C., & Gottlieb, M. C. (2010). Avoiding the road to ethical disaster: Overcoming vulnerabilities and developing resilience. *Psychotherapy: Theory, Research, Practice, Training*, 47, 98–110.

Van Horne, B. A. (2004). Psychology licensing board disciplinary actions: The realities. *Professional Psychology: Research and Practice*, 35, 170–178.

Additional Online Resources

Association of State and Provincial Psychology Boards: What Are Psychologists Not Supposed to Do?: http://www.asppb.net/i4a/pages/index.cfm?pageid=3497.

National Practitioner Data Banks Guidebook: http://www.npdb-hipdb.hrsa.gov/resources/NPDBGuidebook.pdf.

List of State Counselor Licensing Boards: http://www.aascb.org/aws/AASCB/pt/sp/stateboards.

PART 4

Ethical Issues in Special Settings

CHAPTER

12 Ethics in Community, College, Addiction, and Forensic Settings

Avoiding Conflicts of Interest

In the early history of mental health work, most practitioners were employed by large institutions—schools, hospitals, colleges, or government agencies. The advent of licensing for mental health professionals resulted in a whole host of new employment opportunities, including the option to "hang out a shingle" and practice independently. Even more options came with the enactment of federal and state community mental health legislation in the 1960s. Fifty years after these changes, a minority of counselors, psychologists, and social workers work for large institutions. Most are employed by public mental health agencies or group practices, or they function in solo practices. Even professionals who are employed by schools or hospitals now often operate part-time private practices. In addition to the ethical issues already enumerated in the previous chapters, there are also special ethical concerns for those who work in community and private practice settings. This chapter addresses those special issues, focusing on ethical standards for client contacts, relationships with other professionals, obligations to third parties (such as insurers), ethical considerations in coaching, and forensic activities.

RESPONSIBILITIES TO CLIENTS

Community-based counselors and psychotherapists have six major types of responsibilities to clients. These responsibilities are not unique to community and private practice, but are especially salient for practitioners in these settings.

1. Payment Issues

The amount of money a counselor or therapist in private practice earns depends on the number of sessions conducted for payment. Even Freud himself was well aware of this issue, complaining frequently about his money problems (Freud, 1954). The more sessions for which the practitioner is paid, the larger his or her paycheck (except, perhaps in managed care situations, where practitioners can be rewarded for minimizing the number of sessions for each client). Thus, the primary ethical issue for those in private practice is coping with the conflict of interest inherent in these arrangements. A secondary issue is the level of discomfort many mental health professionals feel when dealing with payment for services by people who are in need of help. In our society, talking about sexuality seems easier than talking about money (Koocher & Keith-Spiegel, 2008). Consider the following situations:

The Case of Ms. Amberside

Ms. Amberside, a mental health counselor in private practice, is planning an expensive wedding trip to the Caribbean, for which she is saving money. Mr. Klepper has been in her care for some time for treatment of panic disorder. He met his treatment goals two months ago but remains in therapy because he is reluctant to terminate. He says he enjoys his weekly session and worries that the panic attacks will recur if he ends therapy. Mr. Klepper writes a check for therapy each week and never misses a payment. Ms. Amberside decides that her client should be able to terminate when he is ready and that she is doing no harm by extending his time in therapy beyond necessity.

The Case of Dr. Wrankley

Dr. Wrankley is seeing a client who has been mandated for therapy by the court. The court reimburses the therapist for these sessions at his full rate. This woman agrees to the arrangement because she sees it as her "least worst option." She reluctantly attends counseling and spends most of her sessions in rather superficial discussion of her problems. She resists Dr. Wrankley's efforts to focus on the treatment goals she agreed to and is making minimal progress. Dr. Wrankley recently established his practice and is struggling to meet expenses. Because he needs the income from the court, he allows the client to continue her current pattern in sessions. His reports to the court focus on her dependable attendance and describe the small changes she has made thus far, deemphasizing her resistance to therapy. He does not lie to the court, but his correspondence does not completely reveal his true professional judgment about the client's therapeutic progress.

Both Dr. Wrankley and Ms. Amberside are engaging in what Cummings (1995) has called *unconscious fiscal convenience*, overlooking important therapeutic dimensions of effective care because attending to them conflicts with the practitioner's financial self-interest. Such professionals are not maliciously exploiting their clients, but they do fail to see that the underlying motivation for their therapeutic decisions stems from their need for the fees these clients provide. Thus both are acting unethically. Ms. Amberside should instead be helping Mr. Klepper cope with the stress of termination and develop alternative environmental supports. Similarly, Dr. Wrankley ought to stop colluding with his client to deceive the court and should begin to encourage his client's more active involvement in therapy. Moreover, he should immediately provide more complete reports of her therapeutic progress to the court, informing his client of this action before he does so.

Another aspect of unconscious fiscal convenience is the common belief that paying for psychotherapy is therapeutic. In this view, clients who do not make a financial commitment to counseling are less invested in it and work less hard. Science does not support this interpretation. In fact, research has found no clear relationship between payment and outcome (Drexler, 1996; Pope, 1988), even when a sliding scale is used (Aubry, Hunsley, Josephson, & Vito, 2000). Others suggest that a fee has value in communicating to the client that this relationship is a professional relationship, distinct from friendship and with clear boundaries (Treloar, 2010; Zur, 2007), but no empirical evidence is available to evaluate this claim.

To avoid such conflicts of interest, professionals in private practice ought to engage in regular peer consultation and supervision about the financial management of their cases. Making the criteria for therapeutic decision making known to trusted colleagues is, in effect, using *the clean, well-lit room standard* (Haas & Malouf, 2005). This procedure acknowledges the difficulty in viewing clients objectively when one's financial well-being is at stake and provides a potentially effective method to prevent significant abuses. Such consultation also assists professionals in dealing more effectively with their reluctance to frankly discuss money matters with clients.

Even professionals who are motivated by altruism and are insightful about the conflict-of-interest potential in private practice are often uncomfortable discussing money matters with their clients. Even when the discomfort is low, most mental health professionals are what Knapp and VandeCreek (2008) describe as "reluctant business people" (p. 613). They want to hurry past the financial details and focus on therapeutic issues. Although such an attitude is understandable, it is also fraught with risks. Clients who are unclear about the costs of professional services are not giving truly informed consent. Under these circumstances, clients may be more likely not to comply with payment conditions or may feel anger or resentment toward the practitioner. According to the ACA Code, Section A.2.b, clients must be informed about the financial aspects of therapy as part of informed consent. The Code goes on to specify other responsibilities in relation to fee setting. The language in the APA Standard 6.04 is similar, adding a prohibition against misrepresentation and a requirement to act in ways consistent with the law. The standard also emphasizes the importance of informed consent about payment when clients fail to honor their financial obligations. In that situation, sometimes professionals must decide whether to contract with collection agencies or pursue legal action to get paid. Because such methods compromise confidentiality, clients must fully understand the implications of nonpayment. Interestingly, almost 4% of the legal claims filed against psychologists involved countersuits over collection of fees (Peterson, 1996). Fee and insurance complaints also represent a small percentage of ethics investigations undertaken by the APA (APA, Ethics Committee, 2014), usually in combination with other violations (APA, Ethics Committee, 2014). Of course, professionals are not obligated to employ collection agencies to obtain delinquent payments, but they are not prevented from doing so, provided the client had prior warning that such methods might result from nonpayment. Even if a client has consented to collection or other legal means to recover payment, a prudent professional is well advised to remind the client of that agreement before taking that step, so the client has the option to provide payment and avoid such actions. As a matter of fact, the APA Code includes that stipulation. Knapp and VandeCreek (1993) provide other recommendations for responsible use of collection services, including oversight of the means by which these services attempt to collect payment.

When clients are delinquent in paying, professionals wonder whether it is ethical to withhold copies of their records from subsequent therapists until payment is rendered. As Standard 6.03 of the APA Code states, psychologists may withhold records for nonpayment if the situation is not emergent. If a client needs the records for emergency care, the psychologist must provide them. The ACA standards do not directly address the issue. However, the Health Insurance Portability and Accountability Act (HIPAA) (1996) gives clients the right of access to records of care except under highly unusual situations, so practitioners would be well advised to seek legal advice before withholding records for nonpayment.

It is also important to note that state rules for financial aspects of professional practice may be stricter than the codes of professional associations. In Ohio, for example, the rules of the Board of Psychology (OAC Section 4732-17-01) direct psychologists and counselors to clarify financial arrangements no later than the end of the second session unless there is a compelling therapeutic reason to delay.

In spite of the passage of the Mental Health and Addiction Equity Act of 2008 and the Patient Protection and Affordable Care Act of 2010, professionals are often aware that insurance benefits may not be sufficient to cover the full cost of the recommended course of counseling or psychotherapy. The Standard 6.04d requires psychologists to disclose and discuss this situation with clients as soon as they recognize it and to assist clients in deciding what course of action they wish to take. As discussed in Chapter 6, clients should be empowered through informed consent to decide on payment issues themselves.

All codes encourage professionals to provide some services on a *pro bono* basis—that is, without fee—as a way of keeping in focus one's commitment to public welfare. Many psychologists follow this guideline (Knapp, Bowers, & Metzler, 1992). All codes also note that in establishing fees, professionals ought to consider clients' financial circumstances. Many professionals use a sliding scale, adjusting the fee to a client's level of income, and this practice is generally viewed as an ethically responsible way to make services available to people with low incomes. However, Bennett et al. (2006) caution professionals about the legal ramifications of using a sliding scale or otherwise varying fees for individual circumstances. All states have laws that prohibit health care providers from charging higher fees to those who have insurance than to those without coverage. Some states even have criminal penalties for violating this statute. Fisher (2003) suggests that offering lower fees to those without insurance amounts to inflating (and misrepresenting) the typical fee to the third-party payer. These authors also advise against waiving the co-pay amount for a client with insurance, for the same reasons. A sliding scale arrangement may still be possible, but it must be devised to comply with individual state laws and must always be used in a uniform way with full disclosure to prospective clients and insurers.

2. Interruption or Termination of Services

In personal relationships, adults can discontinue a personal relationship whenever they wish. Counselors and therapists, however, have no such freedom once they have embarked on a professional relationship with a client. A failure to continue needed services without cause or appropriate referral is usually termed *abandonment* and is prohibited by the codes. Failure to properly end treatment may also carry liability risks (Younggren & Gottlieb, 2008).

These standards are rooted in the profession's devotion to client welfare and to the protection of its reputation. Professionals who stop services on a whim or out of dislike for clients or prejudice against particular groups of clients diminish public confidence in the profession and damage the clients involved. Shiles (2009) refers to the latter type of referral as a discriminatory referral. Of course, sometimes professionals must terminate service in the middle of treatment because they obtain new employment, retire, or get sick. In such circumstances, they must help clients find appropriate referrals and do all they reasonably can to smooth the transition to the new counselor (Vasquez, Bingham, & Barnett, 2008). This duty transfers to the parents or guardians of minor clients or others not competent to give consent. A similar approach is advised if a client fails to pay for services as agreed. The professional may refer the client to alternative services but must facilitate the transition. If other services are not immediately available, professionals may not abandon clients in need because of nonpayment of fees. When interruptions in service are foreseeable (such as an elective surgery), professionals plan for them by refraining from accepting new clients and referring current clients to other mental health professionals. In those rare situations in which a client or person connected to the client represents a danger to the counselor, the codes explicitly allow for termination of services.

In its 2002 revision of the Code, APA changed its broad wording of the prohibition against abandonment and replaced it with language that allows for termination of services based on professional judgment, appropriate planning prior to termination, or risk of harm to the therapist from the client or person connected to the client (see Appendix B, Standard 10.10, p. 559). The current APA Code (2010) retains this language.

Counselors and psychologists in a sole practice must also make provisions for another professional to handle their caseloads in the event of their sudden death or disability. Those in larger agencies should see that policies and procedures for referral in this circumstance are in place at their agency. Because clients become attached to specific counselors and are often in the midst of emotional stress and disruption, professionals have a special duty to take all reasonable steps to ensure that clients will be well served in their absence. Bram's (1995) review of the literature in psychology suggests that this standard is frequently violated when therapists underestimate their clients' needs for interim service in their absence. Therapists who had been disabled for several months tended to minimize the impact of their disability on clients and to make only haphazard arrangements for referral in the interval.

Pope and Vasquez (2011) have identified several issues to be addressed if a professional is incapacitated for a lengthy period:

- Who will provide both ongoing treatment and crisis intervention for clients?
- Who will notify clients about the therapist's absence?

- How can clients obtain information about the therapist's course of recovery?
- How will the therapist's records be handled, and who will have access to them?

These authors also caution practitioners in private practice to carefully think through a "worst-case scenario," to help protect the welfare of clients from negative effects of an interruption of service. A proactive approach to such eventualities is an ideal strategy. Ragusea (2002) offers practical suggestions, in the form of a professional will, to help the private practitioner prepare for the possibility of sudden unavailability. Bennett et al. (2006) also guide the professional through the essential tasks to prepare for retirement or for the closing of a practice.

3. Records

The Case of Dr. Dennis

Dr. Dennis has opened a small private practice. Because he sees only a few clients each week, he wonders whether he can simplify his record keeping by writing all his notes on his tablet computer. He is also considering storing them in "the cloud."

Counselors and psychologists are obliged to keep records of counseling and psychotherapy, both to benefit clients and to help other professionals provide effective service. Good records encourage a professional to be reflective and planful about therapeutic contacts. Records can also help researchers study therapeutic processes and outcomes. This obligation is codified in the ethical standards and further supported by state and federal statutes and case law. Moreover, the APA has issued *Record Keeping Guidelines* (2007c), providing detailed information about the content, construction, and retention of mental health records. These guidelines are particularly valuable for practitioners who use electronic records (Drogin, Connell, Foote, & Sturm, 2010). Although some disdain such guidelines as an intrusion of bureaucracy into therapeutic work, most find the current standards valuable for maintaining quality care and for protecting professionals whose work is challenged by disciplinary boards, lawsuits, or third-party payers (Bennett et al., 2006; Shapiro & Smith, 2011). According to Shapiro and Smith (2011), properly kept records can work in favor of mental health professionals during malpractice litigation. The APA guidelines for records specify the content that ought to be included:

- Information relevant to the nature, delivery, progress, or results of services
- Identifying data, dates and types of services, fees, assessment and testing data, plans for intervention, consultations, summaries, and any release of information obtained
- Data in sufficient detail for subsequent mental health professionals to plan adequately for future care

Piazza and Baruth (1990) recommend that six categories of information be included in counseling records: identifying information; assessment information; treatment plans; case notes; termination summary; and other data such as consent forms, copies of correspondence, and releases. Adding to this list, Moline, Williams, and Austin (1998) suggest inclusion of medication history, a component also listed in HIPAA definitions of information to be included in health records.

Oversight of Other Staff Professionals are legally and ethically responsible both for maintaining the confidentiality of the records and for overseeing other staff who have contact with records. Those who work in large agencies or practices must educate support personnel about confidentiality issues and guard against careless procedures for handling client records. Nonclinical personnel should read only those data from client files needed for billing and related purposes. It is important to note that this guideline applies to all workers at agencies and practices without clinical licenses. Administrative directors with business degrees have no more right to access therapy notes than do typists or receptionists. Moreover, clinicians have no right to read the records of other practitioners without a legitimate professional reason. HIPAA regulations (1996) clarify the duties of professionals to effectively train and monitor employees to protect the privacy of client and patient records; the regulations also specify that professionals can be held liable for failures to properly train and supervise employees in confidentiality protections.

Forms of Records Records may be maintained in more than one medium (written document, computer data, taped material), but the professional is responsible for the confidentiality of records regardless of the medium. Professionals who store client data on computer hard drives or external storage devices must be especially attuned to the security of those files and must prevent others from accessing confidential material. (See Chapter 5 for an additional discussion of the confidentiality risks to client data stored on computers and smartphones.)

Many agencies stipulate that client records (written or computer based) may never leave the building without a signed release from the client. Such a policy helps prevent inadvertently compromising confidentiality. Cars, briefcases, laptops, tablets, and smartphones get stolen all too frequently.

Retention of Records Some states and provinces have laws that mandate that therapeutic records be retained for a specified length of time. In Massachusetts, records can only be disposed of 30 years after care, and in California records must be kept for at least 7 years (Koocher & Keith-Speigel, 2008). HIPAA also includes regulations governing record retention, mandating that all health care records be maintained for at least six years. In the event of a client's death, records must be kept for at least two years after the date of death. If a state law specifies that records should be maintained for longer than six years, that law should be followed. Whenever the provisions of HIPAA and state statutes conflict, whichever provision is stricter takes precedence. Mental health records of minors should be kept at least until they reach the age of majority, but the APA guidelines recommend retention for three years after the age of majority (APA, 2007c).

Disposal of Records Because some information stored in client records can become outdated and invalid, the ethics codes stipulate that professionals attend to the time-limited validity of some material in client records and that they alert others who may seek such records to the existence of outdated data. (The results from standardized tests are one example of material in a client's record that may become outdated.) When any portion of a record is disposed of, professionals should shred all documents before disposing of them.

Value of Records for the Professional Obviously, the primary goals in keeping records of therapeutic contacts are to provide high-quality service for clients and to maintain continuity of service if different caregivers are involved. A secondary purpose is to document that good care was provided, if questions about that care are raised in court or in disciplinary hearings. Appelbaum and Gutheil (1991) have referred to documentation and consultation as the "twin pillars of liability protection" (p. 201). Regardless of one's personal feelings about the merits of detailed records, this level of record keeping is rapidly becoming a "legal standard of care" for counseling and psychotherapy. In fact, the failure to keep adequate records has been used as evidence of poor care in court proceedings (Soisson, VandeCreek, & Knapp, 1987). Some therapists have lost their licenses because they failed to keep appropriate records (Wheeler & Bertram, 2012). The courts, too, tend to conclude that if there is no record of good care, there is no good care (Soisson et al., 1987). Bennett et al. (2006) point out that careful documentation provides evidence to disciplinary and legal bodies that a professional is providing services "in accordance with a reasonable standard of care" (p. 45).

A good record also protects a therapist in high-risk situations, such as a threat of suicide or injury to others. In that circumstance, scholars recommend documenting not only the ultimate judgment reached, but also a review of the factors evaluated to reach that judgment and of sources consulted in the process (Werth, Welfel, & Benjamin, 2009). Zuckerman (2008) also suggests that therapists quote the client's answers to risk-assessment questions. Professionals who detail such information in the record are less likely to be judged negligent in court, even if their decision turned out to be wrong (Peterson, 1996; Shapiro & Smith, 2011).

Ownership of Records Records of mental health care are considered in most jurisdictions to be the property of the professional, but clients typically have access to copies of those records and control their dissemination (Soisson et al., 1987). Anderson (1996) explains this concept quite succinctly: "You own the records, but your clients own the information contained in them" (p. 94). Consequently, mental health professionals ought to write notes that they would be willing to have the client read. Emotional statements, summary judgments, and personal opinions have no place in the record. Some scholars suggest that practitioners write records collaboratively with clients, to increase their involvement in the process, reduce their worry about what the records may contain, and lessen the risk of a malpractice claim (Mitchell, 2007; Shapiro & Smith, 2011). Once again, though, because the legal requirements for record keeping vary from state to state, all mental health professionals should stay abreast of laws in their states related to this issue.

Ethics of Dual Records Some counselors and therapists keep dual records. One set is the official record of services, and the other is their personal notes on the case. The latter allows the professional to sort through feelings and reactions to the counseling process, or they may be working notes that are drafts of thoughts about assessment or treatment (Koocher & Keith-Spiegel, 2008). In states with laws allowing for very broad client access to records, professionals should be especially cautious about such notes and get a legal consultation regarding their status. Shapiro and Smith (2011) advise professionals that all such notes are potentially discoverable in a court action (p. 159).

HIPAA and Psychotherapy Notes When the federal government was writing this legislation, provisions were included to allow for communication between providers and others involved in the health care and payment for services, without separate client consents for each such contact, as long as the client signed a copy of the Notice of Privacy Practices. This wording meant that third-party payers could not be refused access to complete client records if they wished to view them. Ultimately, the professional associations negotiated a compromise to such open records, with an exception to such access for *psychotherapy notes*. What is a psychotherapy note? Essentially, a psychotherapy note refers to what are typically called *process notes*, comments that express the professional's impressions of a client or analyze the nature of a conversation between a client and a professional (Holloway, 2003). Psychotherapy notes can be excluded from release without explicit client authorization as long as they are kept physically separate from the official client record. The following information can never be considered a psychotherapy note: "medication prescription and monitoring, counseling session start and stop times, the modalities and frequencies of treatment furnished, results of clinical tests, and any summary of the following items: diagnosis, functional status, the treatment plan, symptoms, prognosis, and progress to date" (HIPAA Section 164.501). It is important to note that many counselors and therapists do not habitually keep psychotherapy notes and are not required to do so by any ethical or legal standard, so this exclusion probably has more symbolic than real protection of client privacy from third-party payers. In addition, in any legal action against a therapist, a court can probably require a professional to produce such notes.

The Case of Dr. Dennis Revisited

The answer to this question now seems rather obvious. The security risks of keeping client records on a tablet outweigh the benefits, even for a small number of clients. (And over time, if it was used as the exclusive medium for keeping client records, the total number of client records on the tablet would be substantial.) Moreover, the life of such devices may not extend for the full period in which records must be kept, even if they are not dropped, stolen, lost, or defective. It may be possible for the therapist to write in-session notes on such a device, but using it for permanent storage of client records is problematic. There are also risks to storing records in "the cloud" as discussed in Devereaux and Gottlieb, (2012). These risks center on security risks and access when clinicians store electronic records remotely. See Devereaux and Gottlieb for a detailed discussion of the ethical issues in such record storage.

4. Advertising Services and Soliciting Clients

All community-based practices and agencies depend on a steady flow of clients and "billable hours" to survive. Thus, professionals in the community are motivated to market their services to those who may benefit from them or to market themselves to the health insurers in order to be included on the list of providers eligible for reimbursement under their plans. For many years, the advertising of mental health services was severely curtailed by ethical standards—and limited to brief, descriptive entries in telephone and service directories. To advertise mental health services in a manner similar to other consumer products was judged unseemly and risky to the consumer. Even the use of boldface type in telephone directory listings was discouraged (Shead & Dobson, 2004). In the late 1980s, the Federal Trade Commission (FTC) challenged the legality of such restrictions and caused a dramatic change in the professions' standards for advertising. (For a fascinating account of the confrontation between the FTC, with its emphasis on free speech and free trade, and the APA, with its emphasis on protection of the public and the reputation of the profession, see Koocher, 1994a.) Currently the U.S. guidelines for advertising allow for almost unlimited freedom in advertising. In fact, they expressly prohibit only two activities—deceptive practices and direct inperson solicitations—and restrict only one, the use of testimonials.

The wording in the APA Code, Standard 5.01 (Appendix B, p. 545) makes it clear that professionals are free to market their services in any way that avoids exploiting current or former clients or deceiving potential clients. Professionals may even solicit testimonials from former clients, as long as those clients are not vulnerable to undue influence, although this is a practice not recommended by most ethics scholars (e.g., see Koocher, 1994b). The use of testimonials for both current and former clients is also evident on websites of several online therapy providers. The dangers inherent in such freedoms to advertise are clear, and the duty to maintain the boundaries between legitimate marketing and misleading advertising falls squarely on the shoulders of the individual professional. Practitioners considering advertising should ask themselves the following questions:

- Is the description of the service fair, honest, and as comprehensive as possible?
- Are my credentials and training presented accurately? (An example of a misleading presentation would be a claim about the national influence of one's research when that research has never appeared in any of the professional literature.)
- Does the advertisement help the public obtain services and bring credit to the profession?
- If a testimonial from a former client is included, was it received from someone not under undue influence from me, and have I developed a plan for helping the person deal with any unintended consequences from his or her involvement in the testimonial?
- Do I have assurance that any former client offering a testimonial is unlikely to need my services again in the foreseeable future?
- Would my peers agree that the advertisement complies with professional standards?

- Have I done all I can to guarantee that others involved in the advertising will abide by the ethical standards for advertising?
- Am I claiming only those degrees that are from a regionally accredited university?

Canadian psychologists Shead and Dobson (2004) caution against three types of advertising that they suggest are inconsistent with the ethical values of the profession, though none is prohibited by the standards: claims of unique abilities; claims of comparative desirability of one's own service over other comparable professional services; and appeals to client fears and anxieties as the reason to seek out service. They argue that these practices offer no real assistance to consumers seeking competent care and actually undermine public confidence in the profession.

Knapp and VandeCreek (2008) recommend that mental health professionals examine their proposed advertisements from the perspective of the average person who may read or hear it. Using the example of a psychologist who identified a number of practice *specialties* in his advertisement, they questioned whether this term really accurately described that professional's capabilities and cautioned that the average person might understand a specialty as an area of exceptional expertise. They advise that a more accurate term for the consumer may be *proficiencies*, indicating competence, but not necessarily extraordinary talent or training.

Sturdivant (1993) points out that advertising of professional services can be a way to do good and do well. She argues that marketing can act as an educational tool that acquaints the public with resources they would not otherwise learn about. She refers to research by the Ohio Psychological Association showing that consumers respond positively to marketing information about counseling and psychotherapy, and that marketing results in increased respect for the profession. Similarly, Palmiter (2012) affirms that there is no ethical problem with marketing services, paying for marketing, or encouraging interactions with the media for the purpose of public education. Nevertheless, mental health professionals must carefully evaluate whether the specific content of advertisements and other marketing efforts meet applicable standards.

The ACA Code devotes an entire section to the delineation of rules for advertising and soliciting clients in Section C.3 (Appendix A, pp. 504–505). The ACA standards overlap substantially with the APA Code, but they omit some of the language on involvement with the media and add a more specific statement prohibiting the use of an employer to solicit clients for outside professional activities.

Consider the following case:

The Case of Shaun's Creative Strategies

Shaun has recently become licensed as a mental health counselor, but he has nearly 20 years of experience in the mental health field and is well recognized in his community for his expertise in treating clients with post-traumatic stress. He has opened a practice and begun advertising his services in telephone directories, on his personal website, and on a social networking website. He has been listed in the referral resource of his state counseling association. In addition, Shaun offers a "free initial consultation" in his advertisements. So far, more than a dozen clients have taken up that offer, and all have decided to continue in counseling with Shaun.

Has Shaun violated any portion of the ACA standards in the way he has marketed his practice? As long as the information he presents in the directories and website is accurate and not misleading to potential clients, he is probably in compliance in those areas. His use of a social networking website is only ethical if he has separate personal and professional pages (Section H.6.a). The use of a free initial consultation is potentially problematic, however. Zuckerman (2008) urges practitioners to avoid this practice because clients may feel committed after the first hour and may have difficulty declining further treatment. He also suggests that this practice may be seen as taking advantage of clients and perhaps be viewed as what the code refers to as *undue influence*.

Increasing numbers of professionals such as Shaun are now taking advantage of the marketing potential of the World Wide Web and Internet, using websites to advertise their local practices. Such websites typically include information about the educational background and license(s) of the professional, the types of services offered, and the logistics of scheduling appointments (Palmiter & Renjilian, 2003). They also aim at allaying prospective clients' fears and misapprehensions about counseling and psychotherapy by explaining some basic aspects of confidentiality and informed consent. They sometimes include pictures of the practitioners, so people can put a face with the name they see on the screen, and options for email contact to ask additional questions of the professional prior to scheduling an appointment. All of these features are designed to make professionals' services more accessible and less uncomfortable, and consumers respond favorably to such content. Many mental health professionals also have personal social networking sites (Taylor et al., 2010; Lannin & Scott, 2013), and some agencies have a presence on social networking sites. The content of these sites and the level of public access need to be carefully considered and regularly monitored. Lannin and Scott (2013) advise mental health professionals to approach the "small world" of social networking sites in the same way that rural professionals approach practice in small communities. With the use of social networking sites, the professional is at risk not only for improper marketing but also for the kinds of boundary issues and self-disclosure dilemmas that occur in rural practice.

Mental health professionals who offer e-therapy (also called Internet counseling) without face-to-face contact also include extensive advertising of their services on their websites. Some of the advertising claims appear reasonable, but others seem overstated given the dearth of published research on the effectiveness of this medium. The following is an example of an advertising claim from a website obtained in two recent studies (Heinlen, Welfel, Richmond, & Rak, 2003; Heinlen, Welfel, Richmond, & O'Donnell, 2003) that is derived from the provider's past experience in offering the service: "Thus far, most who have decided to try it report that virtual therapy is very helpful. About 1 in 10 finds usually in the first couple of exchanges that virtual therapy is inappropriate for their needs." Other professionals make much broader claims, none of which have yet been substantiated by research. Examples include the following: "We have arrived at the ultimate solution for your concerns ... There is no problem too big or too small"; or "We know you'll be satisfied." And still others make statements that they cannot honor, such as: "By using this service, you maintain complete anonymity and privacy." There is no such thing as complete anonymity and privacy on the Web. Any communication routed though a major server such as America Online or Yahoo! can be traced, and those servers typically have policies that require they retain copies of email sent through them for a year. Moreover, if a client reveals child abuse or an imminent intent to harm self or others, the professional is legally and ethically obligated to act to prevent that harm. In short, our research has found that some Internet users do not understand the limitations of electronic communications, do not provide prospective clients with balanced statements about the potential benefits and risks of e-therapy, and generally appear to violate professional standards for advertising. Some professionals also use e-therapy sites to extensively market the books, audiotapes, and other products they have published (Heinlen, Welfel, Richmond, & Rak, 2003; Heinlen, Welfel, Richmond, & O'Donnell, 2003). One site, for example, includes box references to such products interspersed with information on services, fees, and confidentiality matters. Reading the claims and promises included on such websites raises questions about whether self-promotion has taken priority over protection of the public welfare. Others claim degrees from unaccredited universities and unspecified training in counseling and psychotherapy.

5. Public Statements and Other Interactions With the Media

As is evident from the APA and ACA Codes, counselors and therapists also come into the public eye by making statements about news events, discussing their research and writings, and giving interviews in print and broadcast media. For example, when a national news organization wishes to do a story on a psychological disorder (such as agoraphobia or attention deficit disorder), reporters often seek out experts in the field. Similarly, when analyzing the aftermath of a disaster, reporters often ask mental health professionals to comment on its psychological and social repercussions. Many such reports appeared in the media during the 10-year anniversary of the 9/11 terrorist attacks. The APA standards expressly allow professionals to describe professional services available in disaster situations; such a practice is not considered improper solicitation. Conducted ethically, such interactions educate the public and bring credit to the profession. However, professional standards are sometimes violated. The most common violations are failing to present one's credentials accurately, making claims not supported by evidence, drawing conclusions based on intuition or a cursory review of the situation, and attempting to do therapy rather than education. The following are case examples of some of these violations:

The Case of Dr. Doppert and the Television Talk Show

Dr. Doppert, a well-known marriage and family counselor, has agreed to participate in a local television talk show on the subject of how couples recover from an episode of infidelity. The format is for two such couples to appear before a live audience to describe their experiences. At the end of the show, Dr. Doppert is to come on stage and spend five minutes with each couple to "help them heal" from the wounds of infidelity. When the show is taped, the therapist takes the assigned part and works with each couple before a live audience, with the cameras running. Aside from introductions and watching the earlier portion of the show, she has had no contact with the couples. Because the segment ran behind schedule, the counselor had three minutes on the air to help each couple express their feelings about infidelity. At the end of taping, she said good-bye to each couple and gave them her business card. Dr. Doppert was not paid for the time, but her book and practice were both mentioned when she was introduced to the audience.

The Case of Dr. Bewinger and the Book Tour

Dr. Bewinger has written a book challenging the conventional understanding of obsessive-compulsive disorder, suggesting that it is largely caused by improper diet. His conclusions are based on his therapeutic practice treating clients with this disorder. He has conducted no formal research studies and provides only anecdotal evidence for his claims. When asked for specifics, Dr. Bewinger reluctantly reveals that he has treated 12 clients successfully with this method. In the introduction to the book, four of those clients offer testimonials to the value of the approach, and one tour with him to promote the book. Moreover, Dr. Bewinger does not dispute the public announcements that refer to him as a psychologist, although he is actually a licensed mental health counselor. (Please note that the hypothesis about the etiology of obsessive-compulsive disorder presented in this scenario has *no basis in fact* and was created solely for this case.)

The Case of Mertice Mentrison

Mertice Mentrison has a Ph.D. in American history and a master's degree in counseling. Nevertheless, all the public announcements about her work as a substance abuse counselor use the title "Doctor."

Both Ms. Mentrison and Dr. Bewinger are violating the ethical standards listed earlier. Dr. Doppert's practice of intervening therapeutically with talk-show guests is likely to be violating the standard of providing an assessment and recommendations only within a professional relationship (APA Code, Standard 9.01b). Through her participation, she is also giving the television audience a false impression of therapy and of acceptable practices for couples' therapists. In addition, she is placing the chance to promote her book and practice ahead of the rights or needs of the couples on the show. Dr. Doppert's most ethical role in the show would be to provide information to the audience about the kinds of psychological and relationship difficulties that research shows commonly occur after infidelity. She should not in any way give the impression that she is providing a diagnosis or therapy to the couples in a few minutes on television. If Dr. Doppert limits her role to providing "advice" to individuals deemed competent, then she may not be violating ethical standards (Fisher, 2003). However, the ability of the audience to discriminate between advice and therapy is likely to be limited and therefore, regardless of the technical definition of her actions, Dr. Doppert's actions seem inconsistent with the values and ethical ideals of the profession. DeTrude (2001) cautions professionals against thinking they can exert this level of control in a live talk show. The pressure of the host and audience to break down boundaries may be overwhelming, compromising both the dignity of the client and the professionalism of the counselor. Behnke advises psychologists to "Ask yourself, 'Who may get hurt if this project goes badly, and in whose interest does it lie to make sure that doesn't happen?'" (Behnke, 2008, p. 46).

Dr. Bewinger's claims about his new treatment for obsessive-compulsive disorder violate Section 2.04 of the APA's code because they are misleading and do not give any scientific basis for his conclusions. They also seem to be motivated more by his desire to sell books than by any commitment to science or good treatment. From the information provided, it is difficult to determine whether the testimonials he includes violate the standard of undue influence, although the fact that a former client accompanies him on the book tour is worrisome. His conduct also contradicts the standard about misrepresenting his credentials, because he is not actively trying to keep others from characterizing him as a psychologist. His conduct shows a disregard for client welfare, scientific findings, and impact on former clients. This counselor is discrediting the profession and encouraging people who may have a serious emotional disorder to seek an unproved treatment, thus delaying their access to treatments that may truly help them.

Ms. Mentrison is violating the ACA Code, Section C.4.d, which proscribes use of the title "Doctor" unless a person's degree is in counseling or a closely related field. Since historians have no training in counseling, psychology, or human development as part of their doctoral studies, there is no justification for using that title. Ms. Mentrison is attempting to deceive the public into believing she has a credential she does not possess. For comprehensive guidance about ways to avoid these pitfalls and interact responsibly with the media, Schwartz (1999) is an excellent resource.

Sometimes counselors and psychologists are asked to give public testimony about matters before the legislature or to comment about social problems. Their expertise can be valuable in helping governmental bodies devise socially beneficial legislation and policy and in advancing quality mental health care for citizens. Professionals who seek to undertake this activity in an effective and ethical manner should read Sorensen, Masson, Clark, and Morin (1998), who provide a useful guide for professionals asked to provide testimony or advice about public policy issues. For psychologists with extensive interests in responsible interactions with the media, membership in Division 46 (Media) of APA may be helpful.

Consider the following case:

The Case of Dr. Fit

Dr. Fit, a psychologist who is well respected for her research on effective behavioral interventions for depressive disorders, is approached for an endorsement by a company that sells exercise equipment. She is offered payment for her services. This psychologist has long recommended that treatments for depressive disorders include a graduated program of physical exercise. Because the company is a reputable one with reliable exercise equipment, she agrees to participate in print and television promotions.

Has this psychologist violated professional ethical standards? A review of the APA Code does not reveal any direct violation, but ethics scholars caution against such a paid product endorsement whenever the endorsement may be potentially misleading or deceptive (Koocher & Keith-Spiegel, 2008). In this case, that may mean that the content of the endorsement of the exercise equipment leads people to believe that exercise prevents or treats depression as a substitute for professional intervention.

6. Involuntary Commitment

Counselors in community agencies or private practice sometimes see clients who are unable to meet their basic human needs and keep themselves safe because they are experiencing severe mental illness. In this mental state, a person may refuse to agree to hospitalization because of delusions and/or hallucinations. In such situations, counselors and therapists sometimes ask the courts to place the person in a protected environment until stabilized. When the placement happens without the person's consent, it is called *involuntary or civil commitment* (Swenson, 1997). Needless to say, deciding to take away someone's freedom of movement, even temporarily, is a serious matter that has both legal and ethical dimensions. U.S. courts use the "clear and convincing evidence" standard for such actions (Shapiro & Smith, 2011). History is replete with examples of people who were sent to mental institutions because they held deviant or unconventional beliefs and behaviors, but who were not truly mentally ill. In the United States in the 1950s, for example, 1 of every 300 people was held involuntarily in a mental hospital (Grob, 1994). More recently, there has been public outcry about the placement of religious minorities in mental hospitals in China (Eckholm, 2001).

Currently, all states have elaborate procedures to ensure that the rights of the person are not violated any more than necessary and that the hospitalization is truly unavoidable. The specific criteria vary from state to state, but the general standard for such placement is to find "the least restrictive environment possible" while still protecting the safety of the individual (Shapiro & Smith, 2011). Usually a preliminary hearing is conducted so that a judge can determine whether the action is legally warranted. Counselors and therapists involved in involuntary commitment decisions must be trained to assess mental and emotional disorders, be familiar with applicable laws and regulations, and be respectful of the dignity of the person involved. Professionals may breach confidentiality and ignore informed consent only as necessary to transfer the person to a safe environment. In recent years the option of an *outpatient commitment* has emerged in which a person is not hospitalized, but is kept under supervision in the community (Shapiro & Smith, 2011). Any commitment procedure is not a license to throw aside all usual protections of client rights and privacy. For example, if police are called to transport a client to a hospital, the officers should be given only that information they need to safely complete the transportation. The fundamental criteria to guide counselors' decision making are respect for their clients' inherent worth and dignity, and promotion of their clients' welfare.

Practitioners deciding whether a given individual requires commitment are often facing complex and contradictory situations. As mentioned in Chapter 5, determining dangerousness is difficult. Sometimes even the best efforts of mental health professionals cannot guarantee the safety of clients and their families, but practitioners owe competent and diligent care to all involved. Those dealing with such complex situations should gather relevant information, carefully assess dangerousness according to accepted criteria, and work to identify the least restrictive environment possible that will protect both the client and others at risk (Werth et al., 2009). In the current funding environment, substantial obstacles often hinder committing even those who meet every professional criterion for hospitalization. The problems of hospitalizing a person without insurance can be daunting. If the person to be involuntarily hospitalized is a minor, parental consent may be all that is required, although in some states a court hearing is also mandated (Shapiro & Smith, 2011). Throughout this frustrating and confusing process, professionals should maintain a steadfast commitment to the client's welfare and to an outcome that benefits the client, compromises his or her rights as little as possible, and also helps protect others at risk.

RESPONSIBILITIES TO COLLEAGUES

Counselors and therapists have obligations to conduct their interactions with other professionals in a way that honors their dignity, brings credit to their own profession, and avoids exploiting clients.

Cooperation and Respect

The generous federal funding that sparked the community mental health movement in the 1960s has long since disappeared, and now agencies are rivals in the battle for limited resources. Private practitioners compete with agencies and with each other for the limited number of insured clients. Both compete with hospital-based outpatient services. Most seek to become preferred providers for managed care networks, to gain access to insured clients (Danzinger & Welfel, 2001). In such an environment, professionals may feel tempted to forget their shared purpose of public service and to attend instead to the race for funds and clients. On a more optimistic note, the Patient Protection and Affordable Care Act of 2010 offers patients more protection and greater accessibility to insurance, along with parity of mental health treatment with other medical treatment. (See http://www.apapracticecentral.org/advocacy/reform/patient-protection.aspx for a summary of the law's provision for mental health.) It also may reduce competition among different disciplines because it prohibits insurers from refusing provider status to a whole class of mental health professionals.

Disciplinary differences in models of training and epistemological assumptions about mental health and mental illness may also lead to tension among professions (Glosoff, 2001). The directives in the codes caution professionals against oppositional attitudes toward peers and encourage them to actively collaborate with other mental health professionals. Such a perspective not only benefits the public but also serves the long-term interest of the professions, enhancing both access and quality of services. Professionals who take a short-term perspective or who center their energies on this month's billable hours may feel tempted to accept clients already receiving service elsewhere, or even to try to lure clients away from other practitioners. Keith-Spiegel and Koocher (2008) label the latter practice *pirating*. The codes strongly prohibit such practices.

Of course, if clients are dissatisfied with their therapists or strongly believe that supplemental care is needed, counselors and therapists must respect their rights to seek other care. As consumers, clients are free to choose their therapists. When two or more mental health caregivers are involved simultaneously in the care of a client, frequent communication among them is desirable, provided the client agrees to such contacts (Glosoff, 2001). If a client is not willing to allow such communications, then the professional must make an independent judgment about whether good care can be provided within that restriction. If a professional concludes that such a restriction represents a potentially harmful situation for the client, he or she should disclose that conclusion to the client, attempt to renegotiate the arrangement, or, if the renegotiation is not successful, ask the client to see the other professional exclusively. Of course, termination and referral should not be done abruptly, and effort should be made not to cause the client additional distress. In essence, where supplemental or alternative service appears contrary to clients' therapeutic needs, practitioners must balance their obligations not to abandon clients against their duty to avoid harm to those clients. Supervision and consultation are important resources to help resolve such issues.

A second important aspect of cooperation and respect among colleagues relates to the interactions among the different mental health professions. Disagreements about what services individual professions are competent to provide have erupted during the recent history of psychiatry, psychology, counseling, marriage and family therapy, and social work. Professionals schooled in one discipline may view differing training models with suspicion and tend to limit referrals and professional contacts to those with the same degree. Depending on one's perspective, this tendency to disdain related professions may be rooted in financial self-interest or in legitimate concern about the quality of services available to the public. Thus, behaviors that disparage the competence of other professions, that suggest to clients that other professions are less worthy than one's own, are not only unseemly but also contradict the values and standards expressed in professional codes (ACA Code, Section A.3, and APA Standard 3.09). When, in the current competitive climate, practitioners experience frustrations with other professionals, they must guard against expressing those feelings to clients or colleagues whom they may influence. Counselors and therapists should aim at finding ways to work together to counteract some of the social and political realities that limit or deny citizens access to quality mental health care. In fact, according to Johnson, Stewart, Brabeck, Huber, and Rubin (2004), respectful and competent interprofessional collaboration is becoming a "best practice standard" in psychology.

The Patient Protection and Affordable Care Act of 2010 also emphasizes and rewards cooperation among health care and mental health professionals, using the term *integrated health care* (SAMHSA, 2014). As research ever more clearly indicates the relationship between health and mental health, as well as the mental health implications of many chronic diseases, it behooves all professionals to work collaboratively on behalf of the clients/patients we see (APA, 2008a).

Fee Splitting

The term *fee splitting* refers to the practice of paying a fee to someone who provides referrals or receiving a fee from a professional to whom one sends referrals. In colloquial terms, fee splitting is a kind of kickback. The codes of ethics of all mental health professions prohibit such arrangements unless the fee can be traced to a specific service provided. A fee for a referral in the absence of a service is unethical (see, e.g., Section 6.07 of the APA Code). The rationale for this prohibition is the risk to client welfare inherent in fee splitting. If counselors personally gain from a referral, they are vulnerable to making referral decisions based on their own gain rather than on the best interest of clients. Many other professions, such as law and medicine, carry similar wording in their codes of ethics. Unfortunately, some counselors seem unaware of this prohibition. Gibson and Pope (1993) found that 8% of their sample endorsed this activity as ethical.

The prohibition of fee splitting raises questions about several rather common practices in private practice. Sometimes one professional whose name is on a practice (e.g., Dr. Enterprising and Associates) receives a percentage of the income of the other professionals in the practice for each client they see. The associates are not employees of Dr. Enterprising, but they subcontract with her for space, support services, and the like. In light of the code, ethics scholars have expressed concern about this practice (Haas & Malouf, 2005; Koocher, 1994b; Peterson, 1996). In their analysis of the APA Code, Canter et al. (1994) suggest that such fees are acceptable if the professional to whom the fee is paid offers some services to the referring professional. For example, if Dr. Stern uses office space, secretarial services, and utilities in Dr. Enterprising's practice, Dr. Stern may pay a fee to Dr. Enterprising for referrals he receives from her. The fee should be reasonable in light of the expenses Dr. Enterprising undertakes for the work of Dr. Stern. Moreover, the nature of the financial arrangement between Dr. Enterprising and Dr. Stern should be disclosed to the clients involved. Keeping such arrangements hidden from clients or those who pay for services is inappropriate. However, if the two professionals had separate practices and Stern paid his counterpart for referrals, that arrangement would violate the code because Dr. Enterprising would be providing no service to the client directly or indirectly. It is important to note that many states have laws prohibiting fee splitting and other forms of kickbacks (Fisher, 2003).

Questions have also been raised about the ethics of participating in provider networks or referral services. The consensus of current opinion is that professionals may ethically participate in health maintenance organizations, preferred provider organizations, or referral services, such as those often operated by state or local psychological associations, if the circumstances meet two conditions. First, the relationship must be disclosed to clients and does not violate the client's best interests; and second, the fee paid is justified based on services or expenses involved (Fisher, 2004; Koocher, 1994b). Peterson (1996) suggests that open communication with clients about these issues also reduces the risk of the appearance of a conflict of interest.

As third-party payers figure ever more prominently in access to care, professionals need to be sensitive to the ethical dimensions of the financial agreements they reach with insurers and other providers. They must ensure that decisions about client care are based on the needs of clients irrespective of the financial implications for themselves. Professionals should always be open about fees and billing procedures and should inform clients about the costs of services as soon as information becomes available. Some regulations are even more specific; Ohio, for example, requires mental health professionals to notify clients about fees no later than the end of the second session.

RESPONSIBILITIES TO THIRD PARTIES

The era is rapidly ending in which the interactions between a professional and a client concerned no one other than the parties involved. Clients who are ordered into counseling or therapy as a result of a legal proceeding, as a condition of continued employment, or who elect to use insurance to pay for services all have third parties deeply interested in (and often knowledgeable about) the content and progress of therapy. This section discusses the professional's ethical responsibilities to these third parties.

Mandated and Nonvoluntary Counseling and Therapy

American courts have frequently mandated that people enter counseling and therapy as a condition of their sentence or as an alternative to prison or a conviction. Teens who shoplift, belong to gangs, run away, or engage in drug violations are frequently mandated to get mental health treatment. College students who act disruptively may be pushed into counseling if they want to maintain their student status (Amada, 1993). Adults who drive drunk, have neglected or abused their children, or have been found guilty of stalking often "choose" counseling over jail or loss of rights. Similarly, children with aggressive behavior patterns may be sent to counseling (or to the hospital) by the courts or parents. Licensing boards often add counseling to their rehabilitation procedures for professionals found guilty of misconduct. Even counselor educators sometimes mandate therapy for trainees who appear to have problems developing needed competencies for the profession (Ivey, 2014).

As mentioned in Chapter 6, there are important concerns about informed consent under such circumstances. First, the professional and mandated person must be clear about who the client is and to whom the professional owes allegiance. If an outside body has dictated the goals of service, then the professional must make an independent judgment about the appropriateness of those goals for this individual. The involvement of a third party in the decision to enter counseling does not diminish one's responsibility to do good and avoid harm. If mental health professionals believe that clients will be unable to profit from the type of service recommended by the courts, they must communicate their concerns to the mandating party. They should also present alternatives to the mandated treatment, if any are available.

Clients need to understand that they have some choice about participating, even though the alternative is not appealing. In addition, clients need to understand the limits of confidentiality. If professionals are to submit regular reports to a board or court, clients must comprehend the nature of the reports and the possible consequences of such reports. Next, not all professionals are competent to work with mandated clients. Competency in this realm requires knowledge, experience, and skill (Rooney, 2001; Brodsky, 2011). Finally, professionals must avoid viewing mandated clients as second-class clients because they are involuntary. They ought to be accorded the same level of respect as any person who engages voluntarily in the process.

Interactions With Insurers, Managed Care Providers, and Other Payers

Some of the most agonizing ethical dilemmas for those practicing in community settings have arisen because of interactions with outside payers. On the one hand, the availability of reimbursement for mental health care has dramatically increased access to care (at least for those with health insurance). On the other hand, it has diminished both the freedom of mental health professionals to treat clients independent of outside concerns, and the privacy of clients. Moreover, until the recent passage of parity legislation and health care reform legislation, the limits set on the type or duration of care eligible for reimbursement prompted many mental health professionals to view access to quality care, particularly under managed care, as a sham. Its severest critics refer to managed mental health care (also referred to as behavioral health care plans) as "the rape of psychotherapy" (Fox, 1995, p. 147) or as "invisible rationing" (Miller, 1996, p. 350). Even calmer voices note that it caused "an upheaval in the practice community" (Acuff et al., 1999, p. 563) and that most professionals find it a negative influence on their work (e.g., Danzinger & Welfel, 2001; Neill, 2001; Phelps, Eisman, & Kohut, 1998). Practitioners also view managed care as a challenge to compliance with professional ethics (Gottlieb & Cooper, 2000; Glosoff et al., 1999; Murphy, DeBernardo, & Shoemaker, 1998; Sanchez & Turner, 2003). Decisions about reimbursement for care are made by people who have no contact with the client and who sometimes use criteria that oversimplify research findings or have uncertain scientific validity. Payers' interpretations of evidence-based practice have been questioned (e.g., Wampold, 2001). When clients are denied reimbursement for care that the professionals judge as essential, the professionals are placed in a difficult position. They then must provide care at lower cost, without reimbursement, or ask clients to pay out of pocket. Until the passage of mental health parity legislation in 2008 and the Affordable Care Act of 2010, insurers allowed people to be reimbursed for services only when the professionals involved in the case met their standards. Often, that meant being listed on a network of preferred providers. Professionals who did not wish to contract with the insurer in that way were effectively prevented from working with clients insured by that company. The criteria for getting listed were variable. Some professionals with sterling credentials and proven records were denied, while others with unproven skills were accepted. Danzinger and Welfel (2001) found that nearly half (48%) the mental health counselors they surveyed had difficulty getting accepted on managed care panels. Even if accepted, professionals could be removed from such lists whenever the insurers wished, and usually had little recourse. Fear of being terminated as an approved provider placed decision making about clients' needs under a shadow of worry about reprisals for recommending expensive or prolonged care. The 2008 federal legislation prohibits insurers from charging different co-pays for out-of-network providers, and the 2010 Affordable Care Act offers parity with medical coverage for both mental health and addiction services (Garfield, Lave, & Donohue, 2010; Pear, 2008).

Clients, too, face tough decisions—even the new federal legislation and the state parity laws do not mandate coverage for all diagnoses in the DSM, and states may have the power to limit some portions of the federal regulations, and, of course, the fight to amend or repeal the Affordable Care Act has not ended. The *Mental Health Patient's Bill of Rights* (1997), a document that was the combined effort of 17 national mental health organizations, still has relevance to help clients deal with the gaps in coverage and access that have not been remedied. Its ultimate goal is to protect clients from substandard care. Community practitioners should make copies available to their clients.

Regardless of the dissatisfaction of the professional community with managed care or the new legislation, there are no signs that oversight from payers will disappear in the near future. The Kaiser Family Foundation (2008) reports that 78% of adults in the United States participate in a managed care or HMO type of service. How can counselors and therapists cope with this form of reimbursement and still abide by standards for care set by their professions, licensing boards, and the law? Following is a primer for ethical survival in this context. Readers are urged to consult the sources listed in the recommended readings for a fuller discussion of these issues. I begin with a clearer definition and brief history of managed care.

Definition, History, and Data on Managed Care Managed mental health care involves efforts by companies to control the costs of services and prevent payment for services that are ineffective, unnecessary, or counterproductive. It seeks to achieve this goal by regularly reviewing use of services and by preauthorizing care (Corcoran & Winslade, 1994; Frager, 2000). Managed care originated as a response to the escalating costs of health care and was superimposed on outpatient mental health care, a small piece of the overall cost of health care in the United States (Iglehart, 1996). The costs of some segments of mental health care were growing rapidly, such as substance abuse treatment and inpatient adolescent treatment (MacCluskie & Ingersoll, 2000), but most costs for outpatient psychotherapy were not increasing at the same high rate as other forms of health care (Iglehart, 1996). Critics charge that the current mode of operation of most managed care companies stems primarily from profit motives and not from any overriding commitment to efficient, quality care except where quality may be profitable (e.g., see Miller, 1995, 1996; Wrich, 1995). Others recognize that the old fee-for-service model of payment was not without its ethical challenges and abuses (MacCluskie & Ingersoll, 2000; Welfel, 2001). There is no doubt, however, that managed care has dramatically reduced expenditures for mental health care. Spending on mental health declined 54% between 1988 and 1997 and has decreased more than any other segment of the health care industry (McCarthy, 1998). In a report from the Substance Abuse and Mental Health Services Administration (SAMHSA) (2010), spending on mental health care in 2001 had decreased from 7.2% of expenditures to 6.1% of expenditures nationwide, with an increasing proportion of this money going for prescription drugs and much less spent in inpatient care.

There are several variants of managed health care companies—health maintenance organizations, preferred provider organizations, and point-of-service plans. A review of research on psychologists' experiences with managed care indicates that they view the impact of managed care negatively and have experienced many episodes when necessary care was denied or delayed (Miller, 1996; Phelps et al., 1998) (an outcome that many hope will indeed be remedied by the health reform legislation). A few studies that have compared the outcomes of depressed clients in traditional fee-for-service arrangements with client outcomes in managed care found that managed care clients were more frequently underdiagnosed and had significantly worse outcomes (Rogers et al., 1993; Wells et al., 1989).

Special Ethical Concerns in Managed Care When professionals are considering signing a contract with a managed care organization (MCO), they need answers to each of the following questions before they agree to participate:

- Does the financial arrangement minimize conflict-of-interest issues?
- Are the people who are conducting the preauthorization of care and the periodic review of services trained professionals capable of understanding diagnostic and treatment issues and able to use protocols for care responsibly? Are those protocols evidence-based? If so, what is that evidence?
- Are resources available to meet special client needs and take into consideration unique client variables? How well does the system respond to the needs of culturally diverse populations (Newman & Bricklin, 1991)?
- To what degree does the process of preauthorization of care and utilization review intrude into client privacy (Haas & Cummings, 1991)?
- Can one be confident that the organization is complying with HIPAA privacy standards?
- How accurate is advertising for enrollment in the plan?
- Does the plan respond positively, or at least neutrally, to professionals who take a comprehensive approach to informed consent?
- Does the managed care organization give a fair hearing to requests for exceptions to standard care based on individual client needs?

Mental health professionals should also be advised that the standard of care used to make judgments about malpractice claims do not vary because of the limits of insurance or managed care policies (Appelbaum, 1993). Decisions about mental health care cannot be based on insurance or other financial considerations but should focus more narrowly on the welfare of the clients. Similarly, there is some suggestion in the law that mental health professionals need to act assertively when insurers deny coverage for treatment that they believe is necessary. Appelbaum (1993) refers to this standard as *the duty to appeal adverse decisions* and recommends that counselors and therapists act as advocates on their clients' behalf when care has been refused. Appelbaum also points out that the ethical and legal standards about abandonment and interruption of services are not suspended in managed care settings. Clients, of course, may elect not to continue treatment after reimbursement ends, but the choice should be in their hands, and they should understand the implications of ending treatment prematurely.

In sum, practitioners must guard against shifting the responsibility for adequate client care to the managed care company. They must guide decisions by the principle of competent diagnosis and treatment and must energetically work toward that goal regardless of the funding source for services provided. Counselors and therapists should not relinquish all their power to insurers.

Evidence of Ethics Violations in Dealing with Third-Party Payers Professionals who feel frustrated by the power third-party payers exert over their clients' access to mental health care and their own access to income may use more severe diagnoses than warranted (called *upcoding*) or otherwise change diagnoses to meet reimbursement criteria. In fact, between 1990 and 1993, 15% of the ethics claims filed with the APA Ethics Committee dealt with this form of misrepresentation (Peterson, 1996). Similarly, most of those responding to Pope et al. (1987) reported that they had altered an insurance diagnosis to meet reimbursement criteria. As mentioned already, if there is no objective, clinically justifiable reason for a change in diagnosis, this practice violates ethical standards (ACA Code, Section E.5.a; APA Code, Standard 6.06). It is also fraudulent and subject to legal penalties. Remley and Herlihy (2013) point out that any misrepresentation to an insurer regarding the facts of services that is designed to increase the likelihood of payment is considered fraud. If fraud is discovered, mental health professionals can be subject to civil suits to recover costs, and prosecutors may file criminal charges because fraud is a crime. Unfortunately, counselors do not seem aware of the implications of changing diagnoses to gain additional reimbursement (Mayfield [1996], as cited in Remley & Herlihy [2013]). Other unethical practices that have been documented in research studies are listed here:

- Tailoring treatment to the parameters acceptable for reimbursement, even when the professional believes that alternative treatment protocols were preferable
- Failing to disclose to clients the full extent of information that will be communicated to the insurers for fear of losing clients
- Implementing counseling interventions in which the professional has little training or supervision, because they are defined as the acceptable protocol by the MCO
- Terminating treatment when reimbursement ends without a referral to a more affordable service, even when continued counseling is needed

Emerging Issues in Interactions with Third-Party Payers Because of the frustrations and controversies related to managed mental health care, some professionals are eschewing participation and seeking alternative methods of providing quality, cost-effective services (Bittner, Bialek, Nathiel, Ringwald, & Tupper, 1999). Others are challenging the actions of behavioral health plans in court with some success (Nessman & Hendron, 2000), and still others have suggested that mental health professionals employed by managed care should be held accountable for actions inconsistent with the codes of ethics (Sank, 1997). What remains clear, though, is that professionals who give substandard care or who fail to provide needed continuing care when benefits are exhausted are at risk for malpractice claims and that defenses based on reimbursement issues alone have been insufficient to deflect such claims.

Secondly, much public concern has developed over the vast amounts of personal information insurers have accumulated and about their progress in establishing computer data networks so that they can share information more efficiently (Jeffords, 1999). As a result, federal rules for the protection of the security of computer systems that include health records were put into place (HIPAA, 1996). HIPAA does not afford clients absolute protection of privacy, but it has reduced the risk of flagrant violations and imposed serious penalties for individual or systemic violations of patient privacy.

ETHICS IN COLLEGE COUNSELING

Thirty years ago, counselors and psychologists in campus counseling centers typically dealt with developmental stresses and adjustment issues. In that era, conflict with peers, career indecision, adjustments to separation from family, and questions about sexuality and drugs were common topics when students made appointments at the counseling center. Some students experienced serious psychological distress and crisis, and others were coping with chronic psychological disturbances, but such serious problems occurred less frequently then than in recent years. In its 2013 survey of 97,000 college students, American College Health Association found that 11% of students reported a depressive disorder; 12.9% reported anxiety problems; 1.8% identified a substance abuse problem; and 6% listed experiences of panic attacks. Nearly one-third (31.3%) reported feeling so depressed that it was difficult to function at times, and 7.4% indicated that they had seriously considered suicide in the last 12 months. In another study, Soet and Sevig (2006) found that 20% of their college sample reported having received counseling at some time in the past, and 20% indicated they were currently receiving counseling services. In 2010, the directors of college and university counseling centers reported a continued increase in the number of students receiving psychotropic medication, and having chronic and severe emotional problems. In fact, 73% of the directors responded that their center had experienced an increase in the number of students presenting with severe emotional disorders (Association of University and College Counseling Center Directors [AUCCCD] [2012]. This group also reported that 21% of the students they counseled were diagnosed with severe mental health problems and that 24.5% of their clients were taking psychotropic medications.

At the same time that college mental health professionals were dealing with such issues, they were also affected by increasing concerns about liability by college administrators for student suicides and student acts of violence (Cooper, Resnick, Rodolfa, & Douce, 2008). The tragedies at Virginia Tech in 2007 and Northern Illinois University in 2008 highlighted the problems campus faculty, administrators, and professional staff experience when distressed students act violently, as well as the increasing demands on counseling center staff to try to prevent such violence (Davenport, 2009). A parallel response has occurred in light of student suicides, such as MIT student Elizabeth Shin's suicide in 2000. The community rightly demands that universities take steps to prevent such acts, and many colleges and universities have initiated threat assessment protocols when students are at risk to themselves or others. One difficulty with threat assessment is its potential to target students with mental health issues as a form of profiling (Pavela, 2008). Another risk is that students who fear dismissal or other punitive actions may be less likely to seek the help they need to avert harm on a campus focused on threat assessment.

The ethical dilemma for college counselors and psychologists in this era is that they are still bound by confidentiality standards and privilege laws because they are providing mental health services to adults. They are also obliged to honor whatever regulations govern their duties with clients at risk for violence to others in their jurisdictions. Consequently, college mental health professionals need to keep abreast of laws and regulations in their state or province regarding privilege and the duty to protect and to fully explain the limits of confidentiality that apply to their clients. They also have a responsibility to collaborate with college administrators to develop policies regarding threat assessment that protect student privacy as much as possible and that inform other educators about appropriate responses to students they encounter who appear to pose a threat to others. Finally, professionals need to familiarize themselves with recent federal legislation, including clarification of FERPA/HIPAA applications to college student counseling, the application of the Americans with Disabilities Act, and the Clery Act. For example, HIPAA regulations do not apply if an individual's records are subject to FERPA (Doll, 2011). Some students who have been required to leave campus have filed claims of discrimination based on disability. See Paludi (2008) for a detailed review of these issues.

THE ETHICS OF ADDICTION COUNSELING

Addiction counseling requires counselors who are competent in this form of treatment, who use power responsibly, and who honor boundaries. Competence is crucial since abuse of substances is one of the most common problems clients experience and because it occurs in conjunction with other mental health, social, and employment problems. In fact, the Substance Abuse and Mental Health Services Administration (SAMHSA) has named it the number-one public health problem in the United States. Each year drugs and alcohol are identified as a major cause of death for 100,000 Americans. (Tobacco is linked to the deaths of 440,000 Americans annually.)

For a long time, substance abuse treatment was the domain of peer helpers who themselves were recovering from addiction, based on the Alcoholics Anonymous 12-step model of treatment. Many helpers had no formal training in counseling, and their contribution derived from the wisdom and street smarts they gained by experience. This model originally developed because the mental health professions were not offering interventions that the clientele found helpful. These interventions often minimized the power of the addiction. In recent years, credentialing of substance abuse treatment professionals has become more common. The National Association for Addiction Professionals (NAADAC) is the major professional association representing addiction counselors and advocating for appropriate services. It requires members to abide by its code of ethics (NAADAC, 2011). The number of states that now require licensing of addiction counselors is growing, although in many jurisdictions licenses are available at the paraprofessional level. All other mental health professionals also work with clients with substance issues to some extent. Unfortunately, the level of training in this specific disorder has been highly variable, and so each professional needs to take responsibility for developing the necessary competencies to assist those with substance use problems. However, training in the treatment of substance abuse problems still has not become fully integrated into the training of psychologists and clinical mental health counselors (Margolis & Zweben, 2011). There is evidence that psychologists would value more training and support in treating substance abuse disorders (Pabian, 2014).

When substance misuse is the reason for initiating service, clients are often pushed into counseling by others—courts, employers, families—and are ambivalent at best. Addiction has typically resulted in changes in the brain that make ending the use of the substance especially complicated (Hyman & Malenka, 2001) and generally mean that the client may not return to use at any level. Consequently, one set of ethical issues in working with these clients is the degree to which there is some voluntary component to their presence in treatment. The initial resistance needs to give way to a willingness to work on issues, if interventions are to be helpful. Since initial resistance is quite common, counselors have an ethical responsibility to use their power wisely and not manipulate or coerce clients, but to educate them about the consequences of their substance use that they are not aware of or acknowledging.

The third major ethical issue relates to the appropriate management of professional boundaries, since many of those who work with substance abusing clients have a history of abuse themselves. This history is undoubtedly an asset to understanding client dynamics and to establishing a working alliance. At the same time, that history can make keeping clear boundaries more complicated. Self-disclosure is typically an important tool in this work, and professionals need to appreciate what is a therapeutically valuable self-disclosure and what constitutes a boundary violation.

The final important ethical issue is the tendency for clinicians' to hold negative biases toward clients with substance use problems. All too often, clinicians view clients with these diagnoses as hopeless or difficult to treat, and so care is compromised even before it can begin. In addition, research suggests that clinicians may fail to accurately identify women and older adults with substance use problems, since they do not always present with a typical substance use profile (Weisner & Matzger, 2003). For more detailed information on ethical and legal issues in addiction counseling, see Capuzzi and Stauffer (2011) or Roberts and Geppert (2008).

THE ETHICS OF COACHING

Coaching as a practice activity for mental health professionals emerged fairly recently, but it has grown dramatically in this brief period. According to Whybrow (2008), it is an activity in which thousands of mental health practitioners now engage. But what does this term really mean? What constitutes competent and ethical coaching? And what is the evidence that it is an effective intervention? All these questions are at the heart of responsible work. One definition comes from the British Psychological Society: "Coaching psychology is for enhancing well-being and performance in personal life and work domains underpinned by models of coaching grounded in established learning theory or psychological approaches" (British Psychological Society, Special Group on Coaching Psychology, n.d.). When directed at managers, this activity is typically referred to as executive coaching. According to Williams and Anderson (2006), this intervention includes assisting individuals with career transitions, helping individuals develop leadership skills and work cooperatively in teams, life coaching, and the more established activity of helping executives be more effective and run their organizations more smoothly.

Coaching is distinct from psychotherapy insofar as its focus is exclusively on the present and future. Coaching is also centered on helping clients achieve their potential and does not represent therapy for mental health issues (Anderson, Williams, & Kramer, 2012). A coach assisting an adult with attention deficit disorder, for example, would not attend to the distress that disability causes the individual, but rather would center attention exclusively on strategies the client can use to perform to the fullest at work and in personal relationships.

The roots of coaching are in humanistic psychology, as its aim is the fuller self-actualization of the individual, and it is seen by some as a complement to the positive psychology movement (Whybrow, 2008). Although some trace the roots of coaching to the 1920s, there is still a limited research base for this form of practice, with few controlled studies and numerous case studies, although the research that does exist is encouraging (Anderson et al., 2012; Greif, 2007). Training programs in coaching appear more commonly in Europe than in North America, and the efforts to develop accreditation standards for those programs are strongest there, as are the efforts to produce standards for competent practice and credentialing of mental health professionals for coaching (Whybrow, 2008). Two major associations currently exist for mental health professionals working in this arena: The International Association of Coaching (IAC) and the International Society for Coaching Psychology (ISCP). The central ethical issues in coaching parallel in many ways the ethical issues in counseling—confidentiality, consent, conflict of interest, and boundaries (Brennan & Wildflower, 2010). For example, Anderson et al. (2012) highlight that because coaches frequently meet with clients outside of a consulting office, boundaries are less clear and must be carefully monitored. Similarly, since executive coaches are frequently hired by organizations (called sponsors), and not by the specific client, conflict-of-interest issues can emerge. Both of these characteristics of coaching make the management of confidentiality of client disclosures and records more complicated.

The International Society for Coaching Psychology (ISCP) published a Code of Ethics and a Guide to Coaching Psychology Practice in 2008 and the International Association of Coaches (IAC) produced its code in 2003. Both codes contain statements similar to those in other helping professions and a more detailed section on practice guidelines. To qualify for membership, applicants must not only agree to abide by the code, but they must also show evidence of qualifications in coaching (IAC, 2003; ISCP, 2008). (See the IAC certification process: http://www.certifiedcoach.org/index.php/get_certified/learn/certification_overview).

In spite of these advances and new opportunities to develop competencies in coaching, it is important to note that no state licenses individuals for the practice of coaching or has requirements for such practice in their jurisdictions. Consequently, if a person is offering services as a personal coach without reference to his or her credentials as a mental health professional, it is unclear whether a client who feels the coach acted negligently has any legal recourse. In addition, the lack of specific regulation of coaching opens the door for unscrupulous or untrained persons to operate with impunity. Training programs in counseling, social work, or psychology rarely offer any systematic training in coaching; those who seek it must typically look beyond traditional programs. Moreover, as mentioned above, because there is limited research evidence for its effectiveness, the determination of what is competent coaching or what is below the standard of care for this activity is not clearly defined at this juncture. Although the activity is centered on working with clients who do not have clinical mental health issues as the focus of intervention, the question of negative effects of coaching is still unanswered. Finally, the research has not yet incorporated significant attention to issues of diversity in relation to coaching, so it risks the cultural encapsulation that Wrenn (1962) described so many years ago.

If a mental health professional is interested in developing coaching as another dimension to practice, I suggest the following:

- Completion of a systematic program of study of coaching that occurs as a supplement to training as a mental health professional
- Membership in a reputable organization that credentials coaches and offers a code of ethics and guidelines for practice, in other words, the IAC or ISCP
- Disclosure to clients of one's license to practice as a mental health professional along with any coaching credentials
- Discussion with prospective clients of the limits of the research base for the effectiveness and efficacy of coaching, that is, discussion of coaching as an innovative service as identified in the codes of ethics
- Careful management of conflict-of-interest, confidentiality, and boundary issues,
- Careful management of financial issues since clients pay out of pocket for these services
- Careful screening of clients so that the focus can be on enhancing life and/or work satisfaction and performance and so that those with significant mental health needs are screened from coaching services as a substitute for mental health care

THE ETHICS OF FORENSIC ACTIVITIES

The term *forensic mental health work* refers to those professional activities of a psychologist, counselor, or social worker that involve courts of law. They can be researchers, therapists and evaluators, consultants, or witnesses in court (Gottlieb & Coleman, 2012). These include activities such as conducting child custody evaluations, assessing a person's competence to stand trial, providing therapy to patients in a forensic unit in a psychiatric hospital, or acting as an expert witness in a legal case. Some professionals also consult with attorneys about jury selection or provide the court with information about the psychological functioning of a convicted person prior to the penalty phase of a trial, including death-penalty competency evaluations.

In almost all of these situations, the court or an agent of the court employs the mental health professional to provide professional advice relevant to court business in civil or criminal cases. The ethics of forensic activities have received increasing attention in the literature over the last decade, for several reasons. First, the courts are seeking out such advice more often (Haas, 1993). For example, in recent years, courts have increasingly utilized clinical mental health counselors along with psychologists and social workers to conduct child custody evaluations. (See Patel and Choate [2014] for a description of the best practices for counselors engaged by the court for these evaluations.) Second, the roles and loyalties of professionals who participate in forensic work are often confusing and conflicting (Bush, Connell, & Denney, 2006; Stokes & Remley, 2001). The demands, cultures, and norms of the courtroom and the mental health center are very different (Hess, 1998; Melton, 1994), and to act ethically, professionals need knowledge of these differences (Roesch, Zapf, & Hart, 2010; Weikel & Hughes, 1993). Third, the professional sometimes has significant power in this role. A judge, for example, may rely heavily on a psychological evaluation of parents in making child custody decisions or in competency hearings for elderly people. Finally, the ethics of forensics have earned their prominent place partly through dishonor. The existence, even in small numbers, of "hired guns" and experts who will argue for any side that pays them for testimony has placed a cloud of suspicion over the matter (Huber, 1991; Pope & Vetter, 1992). Some critics have nothing but disdain for expert testimony. Szasz (1973) referred to testimony by psychiatrists as "mendacity masquerading as medicine." Sampson (1993) describes a mental health expert witness as "someone who wasn't there when it happened but who, for a fee, will gladly imagine what it must have been like" (p. 69). However, there is nothing inherently unethical in providing professional services to a court. In fact, when conducted with allegiance to high ethical standards, such activities can bring credit to the profession and can improve the likelihood that the court will make a fair and reasoned evaluation of the questions before it.

Psychologists, school psychologists, and psychiatrists have had more involvement in these roles than other professionals (Bersoff, 1996; Crespi & Dube, 2005). In fact, one-third of school psychologists will testify in court at some point regarding their assessments (Crespi & Dube, 2005). However, counselors and social workers are increasingly present in the courtroom (Foster, 1996). Child welfare cases may even include a larger proportion of counselors and social workers than psychologists. Thus, questions about the ethics of forensics are the proper domain of all mental health professionals.

The central ethical questions to consider when engaging in such activities derive from the writings of ethics scholars (e.g., Stahl, 1999), published specialty guidelines (APA, 2011a), and the ethics codes. (Psychologists should note that in 2002 APA deleted the specific sections on forensic activities that had been included in the last version of the Code. Instead, references to forensic activities have been integrated with other professional activities in appropriate sections of that Code.) Those who seek a complete discussion on the ethics of forensic practice should read Gottlieb and Coleman (2012) and see the recommended readings at the end of this chapter. Here are the central questions:

Competence in Forensic Activities

1. Do I have the requisite competence, including knowledge of the law as it applies to my involvement? Do I have enough time to act competently?
2. Will I be able to honor the boundaries of my competence?
3. Can I operate so that my personal values and beliefs do not compromise my capacity to provide good service?
4. Can I competently supervise my staff?
5. Do I know the codes and professional guidelines relevant to forensic work?

6. Do I have knowledgeable colleagues with whom I may consult if necessary?
7. Am I prepared to make available to the court the scientific data that support my conclusions or recommendations?
8. If an emergency arises, can I provide necessary care?

Informed Consent in Forensic Activities

1. Do all parties involved understand my role, my competence and its limits, the fees, duration of service, and other practical matters related to the activity?
2. Is there a written informed consent document for clients to sign and a written contract with court personnel?
3. Have I reviewed informed consent issues with clients myself, and not relegated that duty to others? Do clients understand how evaluative data will be used and how my role differs from the role of a therapist?
4. Have I respected the civil rights of all involved?

Boundaries in Forensic Activities

1. Have I avoided or minimized potential conflicts of interest? Have I made the court aware of any potential conflicts?
2. Have I avoided situations of undue influence?
3. Have I declined to act as an evaluator or expert witness for people who have been my clients (Greenberg & Shuman, 1997)? Conversely, have I declined to accept as clients individuals for whom I served as court evaluator?

Confidentiality in Forensic Activities

1. Do the parties involved understand confidentiality and its limits? Do clients know that court-mandated evaluations will be shared with the court?
2. Are the records I keep secure?
3. Do I maintain confidentiality of disclosures not relevant to the business of the court, unless released?

Fees

1. Are my fees fair?
2. Have I refused any contingency-based form of payment?

Communications with Clients

1. Have I ensured (as much as possible) that reports, testimony, and the like generated from my services are communicated accurately and without deception?
2. Have I acted to correct any misrepresentations of my work?

3. Do I advertise my services in a way that fairly represents my competencies?
4. Do I understand the implications of my role, especially as expert witness, for the reputation of the profession, and am I committed to acting in ways that bring credit to the profession?

Child Custody Evaluations

1. Do I have the specialized competence required to conduct such evaluations (APA, 2010b; Gould & Martindale, 2007)?
2. Do I keep the best interests of the child in the forefront of my considerations and know how to deal with the ambiguity inherent in that criterion (Oberlander, 1995)?
3. Do I interview all involved and fairly assess multiple sources of data in making my evaluation?
4. Do I know how to deal responsibly with children's preferences for one parent (Oberlander, 1995)?
5. Do I refrain from agreeing to conduct such an evaluation if I have a preexisting relationship with any party that may compromise my objectivity and effectiveness?
6. Do I understand the legal risks associated with child custody evaluations (Benjamin, Gollan, & Ally, 2007)?

In light of these questions, consider the following cases:

The Case of the Social Worker's Evaluation

A clinical social worker is asked to make a child custody assessment in a divorce action. He interviews both children and the father in person. The mother had needed emergency surgery and could not keep her scheduled interview. The interview was postponed by one day, and the social worker went to the mother's hospital room for the interview. The mother was in pain and still somewhat groggy from the medication and anesthesia. The social worker submitted her report and recommendations based on these interviews and other available data.

The Case of the Defendant and the Pregnant Psychologist

A psychologist is asked to evaluate the competence to stand trial of a woman who is charged with killing her twin infant sons as they slept in their cribs. The woman's mental health records show a history of paranoid schizophrenia, and she was noncompliant with medications for several weeks prior to the violence. The psychologist is in her third month of pregnancy with twins herself, and she finds herself repulsed and frightened by this woman's actions. She believes she cannot deal with this case at this time and declines to participate, referring the case to a colleague.

The Case of the Psychologist and Jury Selection

A social psychologist has become a sought-after consultant to defense lawyers regarding jury selection. He uses his considerable expertise in human social behavior to help defense lawyers obtain sympathetic jurors. He keeps records of his effectiveness, and those records show that his advice generally results in impaneling juries more sympathetic to the defendant.

The psychologist who recognizes the impact of her personal situation on her capacity to provide objective, professional service to this defendant is acting in compliance with the professional standards and is making a judgment consistent with the best interests of the client. The social worker who uses unreliable information on which to base a custody evaluation is violating guidelines, however. A bedside interview while a person is still under the influence of anesthesia and pain medication is an insufficient basis for making generalizations about that person's fitness as a parent. In this situation, other pressures seem to have overtaken responsible judgment and promotion of the client's welfare. Moreover, the error is serious because the stakes are so high in this case.

A judgment about the ethics of the social psychologist's behavior needs more careful consideration. The U.S. system of jurisprudence is built on the right of a person to a zealous defense against any charges against him or her. The expertise of the social psychologist can be appropriately used to help defendants obtain jurors who are not likely to be biased against the person on trial and who will otherwise attempt to keep an open mind about the legal proceedings. His work is more likely to be within the ethical boundaries of the profession if his judgment about what constitutes a "sympathetic jury" is based on scientific evidence, not on personal whim or other idiosyncratic criteria. However, it is important to note that there is limited science behind the psychology of jury selection in general (Gottlieb & Coleman, 2012). Similarly, if his judgments rely on stereotypes alone—for example, a European American defendant should have a European American jury—they deviate from the ethical standards of the profession and fail to bring credit to it.

SUMMARY

Counselors and therapists in community and private practice settings must wrestle with conflict-of-interest dilemmas. They must balance their own need for and right to a fair profit from their work against clients' rights to services and their roles as professional helpers. In addition, outside parties, especially those who provide payment for professional services, often affect the relationship between the counselor and the client. There are six central ethical mandates for community-based practitioners. The first is to recruit clients with fair, complete, and honest descriptions of their capabilities and credentials, and to avoid direct solicitation of potential clients. Second, the fees charged for services ought to be fair, clearly communicated, and sensitive to the financial status of the client. Professionals have a right to a fair income, but they are not allowed to place their own financial gain ahead of the welfare of clients. Third, if service must be interrupted, mental health professionals ought to have in place mechanisms for alternative care so that clients' therapeutic progress will be minimally disrupted by the interruption. Fourth, records of services ought to be up to date, accurate, and confidential so that competent service can be provided and privacy can be protected. Those records should be maintained for sufficient time for follow-up care to be provided, and disposed of in ways that guarantee client privacy. Fifth, if outside sources mandate therapy, the professional gives primary allegiance to the client, with due respect for the rights of the third parties and informed consent for all involved. Sixth, if clients need to be hospitalized against their wishes, the procedures used should be respectful to clients and minimally restrict their freedom.

Relationships with colleagues in the community are built on respect, honesty, and fairness. Turf wars, private judgments about competencies, and disagreements among professional disciplines ought not to be carried into the consulting room. Financial arrangements between colleagues should be open to client inspection and free from any hint of fee splitting or other forms of kickbacks.

When dealing with outside payers for counseling and psychotherapy, counselors must advocate for their clients for needed services and for limited intrusion into their clients' rights to privacy. Moreover, they must assess appropriate diagnosis and treatment separately from insurance and financial considerations. The frustrations with insurers that mental health professionals commonly experience do not excuse any misrepresentations in diagnosis and treatment to those payers.

Professionals who work with college students need to be sensitive to the risks students in severe distress may cause to others on campus, but they also need to comply with ethical standards regarding the confidentiality of client contact. This responsibility has been made more acute by the substantial increase in the number of college students with serious mental health issues. Similarly, those whose work focuses on treatment of substance abuse issues must develop appropriate competence to treat this problem and act responsibly in managing boundaries when their own histories include experiences with substance abuse.

Finally, when coaching or engaging in forensic activities, mental health professionals need to recognize that those specialties require professionals to have focused training and experience before they can assert competency. The tenets of good science, informed consent, confidentiality of records and disclosures, avoidance of dual relationships and exploitation, and sensitivity to individual differences and cultural background apply as strongly to these undertakings as they do to therapy relationships.

Discussion Questions*

1. As mental health professionals feel increasing competitive pressures for limited financial resources, how can they better manage the competition between disciplines and avoid some of the disagreements that have plagued mental health professions in recent decades?
2. Do you agree that fee splitting is wrong? Does the distinction between fee splitting between individual professionals and participation in "provider networks" or referral services seem meaningful to you? Why or why not?
3. Some mental health professionals have welcomed the changes in advertising ethics spurred by the Federal Trade Commission, but others have decried those changes. How do you view the current standards for advertising and soliciting clients, especially the freedom to use testimonials?

*Note to course instructors: The *Instructor's Guide* for this book includes other discussion questions, class exercises, cases, and multiple-choice and essay test items for this chapter.

4. Many have challenged the current standards for record keeping as bureaucratic and designed primarily to protect the mental health professional. Do you agree with this view?
5. Some mental health professionals have refused to deal with insurers and managed care companies, asking their clients to handle that paperwork. They argue that their role is to provide clients with information relevant to their treatment and diagnosis and then to empower clients to deal with their insurers. Discuss the merits and deficiencies in this approach to managed care.
6. In an era in which funding for counseling and therapy services is limited, activities such as coaching and forensic work seem especially enticing to underpaid mental health professionals. Should there be a special credentialing process or other gate-keeping mechanism to ensure that only competent professionals offer their services in these arenas? If so, what would you recommend?

Cases for Discussion

Jordan's community sponsors a picnic each summer to honor the founding of the city. Local merchants rent booths at the picnic to display their products or services. Many give away free pencils, mugs, and bumper stickers to advertise their services. Jordan, a licensed counseling psychologist, rents a booth and hangs a banner on it that says "The doctor is in." She also dresses up to resemble the cartoon character who made that statement famous. In addition, Jordan gives away free copies of popular self-help books to anyone who schedules an appointment with her. One of the other mental health professionals in the community, who sees her booth, contacts the licensing board and files an ethics complaint against her for unprofessional behavior. Based on what you know, do you think there is reason for the licensing board to conduct an investigation here? Why or why not? If Jordan had mentioned her plan for the booth to you prior to the community picnic, what would you have advised her to do?

AnnMarie is employed in a large private practice. In addition to the ongoing supervision she receives from the psychologist who supervises her, she meets biweekly for additional consultation with the psychiatrist who established the practice. A few months after she starts working there, AnnMarie learns that the psychiatrist is billing clients for services that he has not provided. For example, when AnnMarie mentions a client's name in her meetings with him, he writes it down and charges that client for case consultation time. When AnnMarie gets advice and supervision from the psychiatrist, she believes such a charge is justified, but usually, the psychiatrist gives no guidance at all. AnnMarie resigns from the practice as soon as she learns about the way the psychiatrist bills for that time. Before she leaves, she tells her clients to check the bills they receive to ensure that there are not mistakes or irregularities. She tells no one else at the practice the real reason for her departure, but she knows she cannot participate in any billing practice that is unfair. Has AnnMarie done enough to be considered an ethical professional in this situation? Why? If you think she should have done more, what exactly should that be?

Don is a family therapist in a public agency that serves economically disadvantaged children and their families. His position requires him to make home visits to observe children in their normal family interactions and to intervene to help the parents respond appropriately to their children's needs and behaviors. In this role, he believes that he gains tremendous insight into the families he serves and that he forms strong and productive therapeutic bonds with them. There are times, however, when providing services in the clients' home raises ethical questions for him. When other people visit the home during the session, sometimes parents continue talking with him as though no one else is there. Even if the client assures him that they can talk freely in front of this visitor, Don is unsure whether to respond therapeutically or not. At other times, he observes behaviors that are illegal, such as another member of the household "playing the numbers" or smoking a joint. He wonders about his ethical and legal responsibilities in such situations. What advice would you offer him?

Recommended Readings

Amada, G. (1993). Some ethical considerations: A commentary on "Between Cordelia and Guido: The consultant's role in urgent situations." *Journal of College Student Psychotherapy*, *7*, 23–34.

American Psychological Association. (1994). Guidelines for child custody evaluations in divorce proceedings. *American Psychologist*, *49*, 677–680.

American Psychological Association. (2007c). Record keeping guidelines. *American Psychologist*, *62*, 993–1004.

American Psychological Association. (2013e). Specialty guidelines for forensic psychology. Retrieved from http://www.apa.org/practice/guidelines/forensic-psychology.aspx

Appelbaum, P. S. (1993). Legal liability in managed care. *American Psychologist*, *48*, 251–257.

Duffy, M., & Passmore, J. (2010). Ethics in coaching: An ethical decision-making framework for coaching psychologists. *International Coaching Psychology Review*, *5*, 140–151.

Garfield, R. L., Lave, J. R., & Donohue, J. M. (2010). Health reform and the scope of benefits for mental health and substance use disorder services. *Psychiatric Services*, *61*, 1081–1086.

Gottlieb, M. C., & Coleman, A. (2012). Ethical challenges in forensic psychology practice. In S. J. Knapp, M. C. Gottlieb, M. M. Handelsman, & L. D. VandeCreek (Eds.), *APA handbook of ethics in psychology* (Vol. 2, pp. 91–123). Washington, D.C.: American Psychological Association.

Haas, L. J., & Cummings, N. A. (1991). Managed outpatient mental health plans: Clinical, ethical and practical guidelines for participation. *Professional Psychology: Research and Practice*, *22*, 45–51.

Hess, A. K., & Weiner, I. B (1999). *Handbook of forensic psychology*. New York, NY: Wiley.

Kilburg, R. R., & Diedrich, R. C. (Eds.). (2007). *The wisdom of coaching: Essential papers in consulting psychology for a world of change*. Washington, D.C.: American Psychological Association.

Knapp, S., & VandeCreek, L. (1993). Legal and ethical issues in billing patients and collecting fees. *Psychotherapy: Theory, Research, Practice and Training*, *30*, 25–31.

Mitchell, R. W. (2007). *Documentation in counseling records* (3rd ed.). Alexandria, VA: American Counseling Association.

Piazza, N. J., & Baruth, N. E. (1990). Client record guidelines. *Journal of Counseling & Development*, *68*, 313–316.

Pomerantz, A. M., & Segrist, J. (2006). The influence of payment method on psychologists' diagnostic decisions regarding minimally impaired clients. *Ethics & Behavior*, *16*, 253–263.

Schwartz, L. L. (Ed.). (1999). *Psychologists and the media: A second look*. Washington, D.C.: American Psychological Association.

Stahl, P. M. (1999). *Complex issues in child custody evaluations*. Thousand Oaks, CA: Sage.

Vasquez, M. J. T., Bingham, R. P., & Barnett, J. E. (2008). Psychotherapy termination: Clinical and ethical responsibilities. *Journal of Clinical Psychology*, *64*, 653–665.

Wrightsman, L. S. (2000). *Forensic psychology*. Belmont, CA: Wadsworth.

Whybrow, A. (2008). Coaching psychology: Coming of age? *International Coaching Psychology Review*, *3*, 227–240.

Younggren, J. N., & Gottlieb, M. C. (2008). Termination and abandonment: Risk and risk management. *Professional Psychology: Research and Practice*, *39*, 498–504.

Additional Online Resources

American Counseling Association. Private Practice Pointers Preview Page: http://www.counseling.org/Counselors/PrivatePracticePointers.aspx.

American Mental Health Counselors Association Practice Resources: http://www.amhca.org/professionals.aspx.

American Psychological Association. Update on the Affordable Care Act: http://www.apa.org/monitor/2012/09/affordable-care.aspx.

American Psychological Association Practice Directorate: Information and resources for practicing psychologists: http://www.apa.org/practice/prof.html.

American Psychological Association Practice Directorate: Guidelines for Psychological Practice in Health Care Delivery Systems: http://www.apa.org/practice/guidelines/delivery-systems.aspx.

Guttmacher Institute: The HIPAA Privacy Rule and Adolescents: Legal Questions and Clinical Challenges: http://www.guttmacher.org/pubs/journals/3608004.html.

Kaiser Family Foundation: Focus on Health Reform: Summary of new health reform law: http://www.kff.org/healthreform/upload/8061.pdf.

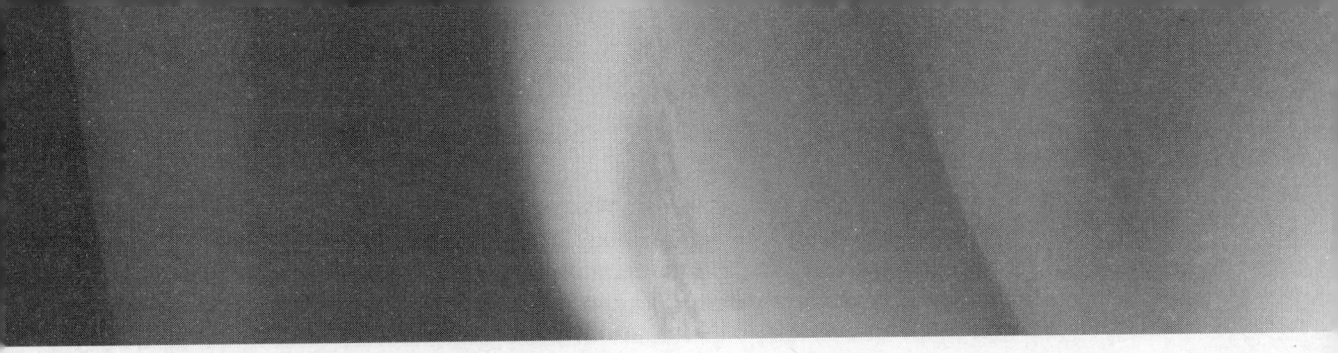

The Professional School Counselor

CHAPTER 13

Applying Professional Standards to the Educational Culture

Many of the ethical issues school counselors and school psychologists face are not unique to their setting. Consent and confidentiality issues are complicated whenever working with minors. All professionals who are part of large, public organizations deal with accountability to the public and delicate relationships with administrators. The duty to respond sensitively and competently with culturally diverse clients applies in all settings (Guzman, Calfa, Kerne, & McCarthy, 2013; Leong & Gupta, 2008; Lonborg & Bowen, 2004; Pedersen & Carey, 2003; Pedersen, Crethar, & Carlson, 2008). Laws governing work with minors frequently conflict with the ethical principles that govern professional practice (Stone, 2009; Stone & Zirkel, 2010). However, several issues are unique: (1) the conflict between the open communication norms among educators and the confidentiality norm of the counseling profession; (2) the obligation to assist students experiencing personal and social difficulties and the potential for parents' and community standards to conflict with students' needs; (3) the responsibility of the schools related to bullying, cyberbullying, and other harassing behaviors; (4) the confusing state and federal laws about parental rights to educational information about their children; (5) the obligations of school counselors with suicidal students; (6) the complications of group counseling in schools; (7) the ethical challenges in post-secondary planning; and (8) the ethics of peer counseling and peer mediation with minors.

Two other realities complicate the job of the school counselor. The first is the substantial number of school-age children diagnosed with behavior or mental health problems. According to the Institute of Medicine and National Research Council (2009) 14–20% of students meet criteria for these disorders, but only 20–30% of these are receiving the mental health services they need. Thus, the demand for school counselors to "fill the gap" can be great. However, the second reality limits their ability to assist students—the large number of students in their caseloads. According the ASCA (2011), the average student caseload in the United States is an incredible 471 students per school counselor. (Only two states meet ASCA's criteria of 250:1 for counselor caseloads: Wyoming and Vermont.) In California, the number is 811 students per professional school counselor. In these circumstances, it becomes impossible for a school counselor to be attentive to the educational, psychological, and social needs of those in his or her caseload. The ethical standards that guide this chapter's discussion of these issues are the Ethical Standards of the American School Counselor Association (ASCA) (2010), and the ACA Code of Ethics (2014). (The ASCA Code can be found in Appendix C, pp. 560–573).

THE COUNSELOR ROLE IN AN OPEN COMMUNICATION CULTURE

Many school counselors begin their careers as teachers, although only seven states require a teaching license as a prerequisite for licensing as a school counselor (ASCA, 2008b). (These states are Connecticut, Kansas, Louisiana, Nebraska, North Dakota, Oregon, and Texas.) As teachers, they appreciate the value of open communication with other school personnel about the students in their classes and know that effective teaching depends on adequate knowledge about psychosocial factors that affect student learning. A teacher who is concerned about a student's health or cleanliness, for example, would not hesitate to discuss those concerns with the school nurse. In fact, a failure to consult with other educators would be seen as shirking a responsibility of good teaching. Such consultation serves social purposes as well—it becomes an outlet for adult-to-adult conversation in a workday that is dominated by adult-to-child communications and helps maintain the web of social connections between co-workers (Ferris & Linville, 1985). The demands of open communication have become even greater with the explosion of technology and social media (Mullen, Griffith, Greene, & Lambie, 2014).

The norms of the counseling profession are significantly different. Counselors know that client communications are confidential and that disclosure is allowed only with client/parent knowledge and permission (and child assent in many cases) or with the best interests of the child in mind. Counselors are not permitted to use specific client matters as a means of fostering adult-to-adult social conversation. This clash of cultures not only makes the transition from the role of teacher to counselor more difficult for novices but also complicates the work of the experienced school counselor (Peterson, Goodman, Keller, & McCauley, 2004). Teachers and administrators often expect school counselors to communicate openly about students and see that expectation as grounded in concern for the best interests of students (Amatea & Clark, 2005; Reiner, Colbert, & Prusse, 2009). When counselors are not forthcoming about matters disclosed by students or parents, other educators may view counselors as less than team players and may feel reluctant to refer students for counseling. The institutional pressures on counselors to conform to school norms can be substantial (Schulte & Cochrane, 1995). Hermann's work (2002) supports this view; in her research, 51% of school counselors reported that they had felt pressure to reveal confidential student information during the preceding 12 months, and 19% had been asked to turn over student records of counseling.

School counselors often feel caught between these conflicting systems. On one hand, they want acceptance, respect, cooperation, and referrals from other school personnel, all of which seem to depend on open communication. They know that a collaborative relationship with other school personnel is ultimately helpful to the students they serve. On the other hand, they want to honor the confidentiality of student and parent disclosures and maintain their trust. At first glance, the two desires seem mutually exclusive, but there are responsible ways to resolve the conflict. Consider the following situations:

The Case of Reggie

Reggie is a fifth-grade student whose behavior has deteriorated over the last two months. He used to be an involved, conscientious student who wanted to learn. Now he spends most of his time in class with his head on his desk or his gaze out the window. He is not submitting homework and is failing. After consulting with other teachers, his math teacher, Mr. Kearns, learns that Reggie is behaving this way in all his classes, and so he refers the student to the school counselor, Dr. Jeffers. After a few counseling sessions and an explanation of confidentiality to Reggie and his mother, the child begins to reveal information about his personal life. His mother was recently diagnosed as HIV positive. Simultaneously, he learned that his mother had abused intravenous drugs until she became pregnant with him. Reggie feels sad, angry, and betrayed. Both Reggie and his mother do not want her illness or other aspects of their personal lives disclosed to anyone else at school. Mr. Kearns has felt frustrated by the counselor's lack of response to his questions about Reggie and has asked the principal for a meeting among all educational personnel involved with Reggie to discuss the child's deteriorating behavior. Dr. Jeffers is asked to attend. The teacher and principal are truly concerned for Reggie's well-being and want the counselor to help them help this student.

The Case of Gloria

The lunchtime conversation in the teacher's room focuses on a sophomore named Gloria, whose mother was shot while robbing a bank several years ago. The mother is incarcerated, and the father has been emotionally unstable since the robbery. The father frequently comes to school dressed in his pajamas and accuses staff of trying to poison his daughter. The father has refused psychological treatment. Gloria has become painfully shy and often skips school for several days after her father's visits there. Today's lunchroom conversation is recounting the father's most recent visit, and the emotions expressed around the table are a mixture of sympathy for the girl and shock at the father's wild accusations and outrageous behavior. The counselor takes a seat at the table and is asked what she thinks about all this.

In Reggie's case, the ethical and legal standards are clear. If both Reggie and his mother are adamant about keeping counseling disclosures confidential, the counselor must abide by their wishes. None of the exceptions to confidentiality apply here; there is no child abuse, no imminent danger to Reggie or threat to another, no court order, and no parental permission or request to disclose. The Preamble and Sections A.2, B.2, and C.2 of the ASCA Code emphasize the counselor's duty to respect the rights and privacy of students and their parents. See the ASCA Code, Appendix C, pp. 562–563, 567, 568).

Is the counselor's only choice to alienate colleagues and remain silent in the meeting? Fortunately, there are other options. The counselor can discuss with Reggie and his mother the teacher's concerns; give his mother information about the forthcoming meeting; seek guidance about exactly what information, if any, the counselor may reveal in that meeting; and ask permission from the principal to invite Reggie's mother and Reggie to the meeting. (The counselor may also wish to refer the family for family counseling in dealing with the difficult problem facing them. Such support may further assist Reggie to cope better with his mother's illness and history.) Before any conference about the student, the counselor ought to meet privately with the teacher and the principal to explain the confidentiality requirements and the limits they place on free and full discussion of counseling sessions. Description of any state and federal laws that seem relevant would also help other educators understand the dilemma posed by their request for counseling information. For example, the Health Insurance Portability and Accountability Act (HIPAA) (1996) and the Family Educational Rights and Privacy Act (FERPA) (1974) may be operative in this circumstance and may prohibit disclosure of the personal health information of the family.

The counselor can avoid a great deal of the aggravation in such situations by educating faculty, administrators, and school board members about the roles and responsibilities of school counselors *before a problem erupts* (Tompkins & Mehring, 1993; Watson, 1990). A straightforward staff education program would reassure colleagues that the goal of the counselor is to help teachers help students but that the legal and ethical parameters under which counselors work means they must, with appropriate permission, disclose private student/parent revelations. Ferris and Linville (1985) and Huss, Bryant, and Mulet (2008) advise written policies on confidentiality and written referral procedures that have school board approval. In addition, Tompkins and Mehring (1993) recommend that communication about confidentiality obligations begin at the time a professional is interviewing for a position. By initiating such a discussion, a counselor can get a clearer sense of the knowledge of and receptivity of the other educators to the confidentiality of student and parent disclosures. It is important to note that recent research suggests that other educators value the role of the professional school counselor in helping students deal with problems that interfere with educational achievement, so the foundation is present for counselors who make clear the implications of confidentiality for that role (e.g., Reiner et al, 2009).

In the second case, the lunchroom discussion about the sophomore's troubles and her father's unusual behavior seems more social than professional. Lunchroom discussions are not structured, professional interactions planned to benefit students. They can often deteriorate into gossip (Watson, 1990). Moreover, some teachers in the room may have no interaction with Gloria, and therefore have no need or right to know anything about her. For the counselor to participate in any such discussion would demean those individuals and would not bring credit to the counselor or to the profession. Therefore, the counselor should avoid comment on this topic even if Gloria were not a student in her assigned caseload. The refusal to discuss this issue need not be expressed in a morally superior or self-righteous way. When such events occur, it is natural for people to wish to talk about them later. For counselors, especially, that natural human desire must be superseded by their professional obligations. As with the last scenario, educating teachers to the unique responsibilities of counselors might have alleviated the pressure the counselor felt to participate. Perhaps, though, the only truly safe way to avoid such discussions is to refrain from sitting in the lunchroom or teacher's lounge when such events are likely to become the focus of conversation. Counselors should know that participation in such gossip might have legal as well as ethical consequences. Under such circumstances, all school personnel are vulnerable to claims of defamation of character (Alexander & Alexander, 2005; Fischer & Sorenson, 1996; Stone, 2009).

School counselors ought not to think of other educators in an adversarial way, however (see ASCA Code, Section C.2.d, Appendix C, p. 568). When students and parents are informed about the potential value of sharing information with relevant teachers and administrators and when they have control over the material that is revealed, they regularly agree to such releases. In the first case, Reggie and his mother may want to tell school officials something, and the counselor can help them articulate the kind of communication that would feel comfortable. For example, they may want to tell teachers that a member of Reggie's family is ill with a chronic disease and that Reggie is quite distracted and worried about that. Counselors must balance the value such disclosures would have for the student's education against the risk of other people incidentally or intentionally violating guidelines for the proper use of that information. The counselor can help all parties define the clients' views of appropriate and inappropriate uses of the disclosures, and thus help reduce the risk of violating the clients' wishes. The ASCA standards also speak to this point in Section B.2.

Research on the compliance of school counselors with these directives is limited. Two studies by Wagner (1978, 1981) suggested that approximately one-quarter of the counselors sampled admitted engaging in informal communications with others about clients. Most who engaged in this practice did not view it as ethical, though. Such frequent participation in a practice they acknowledged as unethical suggests that the open communication culture of the school powerfully influences counselor behavior.

Davis and Ritchie (1993) advise school counselors to inform administrators about any counselor activity that is likely to have legal repercussions for the school. If, for instance, a counselor decides to call an ambulance to bring a student in the midst of a psychotic episode to a psychiatric emergency room without parental consent (because the parents and the school nurse could not be reached), he or she should tell the principal about the action and its rationale, that is, the parents' unavailability and the safety risk to the student. This situation has potential legal ramifications, because the parents may claim that the action violated their right to consent and damaged the reputation of the family. At the same time, Davis and Ritchie caution counselors to use prudent judgment about such consultations, resisting the temptation to break confidentiality for any activity that has any potential for legal complications. However, in situations in which legal action is a significant possibility, administrators should be informed. After all, administrators will be in a better position to help and defend the school counseling program if they are aware of the situation. The ASCA Code deals with these questions in Section D.1 (Appendix C, pp. 568–569).

Determining whether a disclosure from a student should be kept confidential or disclosed to parents or school authorities is one of the most difficult issues facing school counselors and school psychologists. Jacob-Timm (1999) reported it to be the third most prominent ethical dilemma of school psychologists. Bodenhorn (2006) found it to be the most common ethical issue for practicing school counselors. Mitchell et al. (2003) note that school counselors "may feel as if they are walking a tightrope between being a professional helper and being an informant to parents" (p. 156). In a well-designed study of the factors that affect decisions about confidentiality among Florida school counselors, Isaacs and Stone (1999) found that counselors used the age of the student, level of the school, and dangerousness of the client situation as the primary criteria to decide whether to breach confidentiality. School counselors in that sample indicated that they would be likely to breach confidentiality under the following circumstances:

- Impending suicide with a firearm (97.6%) or information about possible suicide pact (88%)
- Retaliation for victimization (94.2%)
- Use of crack cocaine (83.7%)
- Sexual intercourse with multiple partners when HIV positive (80.7%)
- Imminent armed robbery plan (79.5%)
- Indications of depression (76.9%)
- Abortion (69.1%)
- Marijuana use (68.7%)

These percentages differ in some respects when the data are examined by level of school. Secondary school counselors are more likely to maintain confidentiality than elementary counselors about sexuality and drug use, but the responses of the entire sample are fairly consistent in regard to issues of dangerousness to self or others. For example, 82.2% of the elementary counselors would breach confidentiality if a student confided that he or she was smoking marijuana, but only 43.8% of high school counselors and 41.7% of middle school counselors would do so. More recent research generally supports the trend found by Isaacs and Stone (1999). For example, in their survey of school counselors' responses to student risk-taking behaviors, Moyer and Sullivan (2008) reported that as risk-taking behaviors increased in intensity and frequency, school counselors became more willing to break confidentiality to parents. They also found that the age of the student was a major influence on decisions about breaches of confidentiality, suggesting that age-inappropriate risk-taking behaviors, such as sexual activity at a young age, were more likely to result in parent notification. Lazovsky (2008) reported a very similar pattern of decision making regarding breaches of confidentiality among Israeli school counselors. School counselors seem to use school culture, level of trust and relationship with other school personnel, and their training in ethics, along with the best interests of the child, to decide how much information to share with other educators (Trice-Black, Riechel, & Shillingford (2013).

Anecdotal and research evidence suggests that students are deeply concerned about confidentiality. Recently, a 12-year-old wrote to Dear Abby, asking what to do about her frightening and persistent suicidal thoughts, mentioning that she could not tell her parents because they would react negatively, and that she could not disclose this to the school counselor because the counselor would inform the parents. Formal research suggests that this middle school student does not represent an isolated case. In three studies of the attitudes of high school students toward confidentiality, the overwhelming majority of students viewed it as important to their willingness to discuss their concerns with school counselors (Collins & Knowles, 1995; Helms, 2003; Lindsey & Kalafat, 1998). For example, Helms (2003) found that students were refusing professional assistance because they believed that counselors would tell their parents everything they said, that counselors would gossip about them, or that counselors would judge them negatively or berate them. In contrast to the feelings of the 12-year-old correspondent to Dear Abby, most students generally appear to acknowledge the need to contact parents in situations of imminent danger but recognize few other reasons as sufficient justification to disclose their confidences to parents (Collins & Knowles, 1995).

The ASCA Ethics Committee has produced three useful documents for school counselors to support them in their quest to manage confidentiality responsibly. The first, *Sharing Information with the School Principal* (1999), guides the school counselor to effective strategies to meeting the demands of administrators and needs of students. The second document, *Developing an Informed Consent Brochure for Secondary Students,* was published in 1996, and it identifies the necessary components of consent with high school students. The third document is ASCA's *Position Statement on Confidentiality* (2008a). All of these documents have value as tools to educate other school officials and parents about the school counseling role and function. Mitchell, Disque, and Robertson (2002) provide an additional set of practical guidelines for parents' requests for confidential information.

Stone (2009) points out that it may be legally permissible to share confidential student information with other educators if the purpose is to assist the student in getting the educational services needed. She cites the case of a student who is the topic of a meeting for planning services required because of the student's special needs. The counselor has learned that this student has a history of abuse, and elects to share this, without parent consent, with the other professionals in the meeting. Such an action is not likely to be considered a violation of FERPA or HIPAA or other parental rights because of the legitimate educational interest in the information (Stone, 2009, pp. 62–63). However, the ideal approach to this circumstance is to work to anticipate the potential value of this information for the meeting and proactively seek parental consent for disclosure. With that strategy, the counselor avoids the potential of a negative reaction from the parents when they learn of the disclosure and honors their desires to be in control of information that school personnel know about their child.

Privilege for Professional School Counselors

In this litigious era, courts are increasingly likely to ask school counselors and school psychologists to provide evidence about their work with parents or students (Jacob & Powers, 2009; James & DeVaney, 1995; Stone, 2009). They may subpoena a counselor to testify in a custody hearing for a child with whom the counselor has had extensive contact, or ask a counselor to produce a client's counseling records. If counselors or school psychologists violate confidentiality and reveal information that ought to have been kept private, they themselves can be brought to court to defend against charges of malpractice or defamation of character (Fischer & Sorenson, 1996; Jacob & Powers, 2009). For these reasons, school counselors need to become aware of the laws about privileged communication in their states. Fischer and Sorenson (1996) identify 18 states where the clients of school counselors can assert at least limited privilege in state courts. These states include Alabama, Arkansas, Idaho, Indiana, Iowa, Kansas, Maine, Michigan, Missouri, Montana, Nevada, North Carolina, North Dakota, Ohio, Oregon, Pennsylvania, South Dakota, and Virginia. Recently, the Attorney General in California clarified its statute on confidentiality for school counselors, affirming the general provision of confidentiality of student and parent disclosures and indicating several exceptions based on "clear and present danger" (California Education Code Section 49602, 2011). The interpretation of the statute also clarifies that school counselors cannot be held liable for actions consistent with the statute (Legal Opinions of the California State Attorney General, 2011).

In other states, no statutory privilege is established for school counselors. The 1996 U.S. Supreme Court decision in *Jaffee v. Redmond* has spurred further extensions of privilege (Jacob & Powers, 2009). According to Jacob and Powers, currently 75% of states have broadened the scope of their privilege laws to include non-doctoral-level professionals. Counselors in states with privilege for clients of school counselors have a responsibility to inform other school personnel about the implications of that privilege for their work. (See Chapter 5 for additional information about privileged communication).

SCHOOL POLICIES AND THE ROLE OF THE SCHOOL COUNSELOR

The ASCA National Model: A Framework for School Counseling Programs (2005), *The ASCA National Standards for Students* (2004), and ASCA's *The Role of the Professional School Counselor* (2009a) identify the educational, career, and personal/social development of students as the fundamental mission of the profession. They assert that the school counselor has a responsibility to collaborate with other educators and with the community to promote development in all these arenas. The ASCA Code also requires school counselors to advocate on behalf of students in Section D.1.a.

From time to time, however, promoting the educational, career, and personal/social development of students conflicts with the values of the community. For example, a predominant community value may support the belief that nonheterosexual orientations are morally wrong and/or are a lifestyle choice rather than a biological reality for the individual. Or a community may value athletic achievement so highly that it pressures educators to treat an athlete's academic work more leniently than that of other students. Coping with such community values is a significant challenge for the professional school counselor. How can the counselor support the development of LGBTQ (lesbian, gay, bisexual, transgender, and queer or questioning) students or athletes or any other favored or disfavored groups of students in these communities? Is it appropriate for the school counselor to ignore or challenge community values on these issues? What does it really mean when the code advises counselors to "work responsibly for change"?

Unfortunately, no easy answers exist for these questions. Several factors must be kept in mind, however. First, the students negatively affected by these values are not in a position to remove themselves from the family or school, nor is the counselor likely to immediately relinquish his or her job to avoid the conflict. Second, the young person's parents may well share the prevailing community view, and if so, the parents' values and wishes for their children must be taken into account. The school authorities may not wish to provoke any dispute with the community that they serve and that pays taxes to keep the school functioning. Prudent, deliberate, and well-planned responses to challenges to community values are essential. Counselors are more likely to get into difficulty with these constituencies if they take a highly confrontational stance or make public statements about the negative impact of the values. Working one-on-one, for example, with administrators to help them understand the long-term benefits of promoting the best interests of the students is a wise approach. In the case of LGBTQ students in an unsupportive community, the counselor may wish to remind authorities about the legal requirement to make the school a safe place for all students to learn (e.g., Title IX) or may wish to familiarize families with organizations that exist to help them understand their children, such as Parents and Friends of Lesbians and Gays (PFLAG). In similar fashion, school counselors might approach community leaders to acquaint them with the unintended negative implications of their views on LGBTQ individuals. The Gay Lesbian Straight Education Network (GLSEN) has many helpful materials for educators to use in this regard (http://www.glsen.org/). Few individuals with beliefs that LGBTQ sexual activity is morally wrong would endorse the kind of harassment that these teens experience at school and in the community. Therefore, school counselors have an opening to work with the community to make it clear that moral disagreement with homosexual activity does not give anyone permission to harass or harm LGBTQ students. In some situations, the school counselor may simply need to help students take a long-term view and learn coping strategies to survive. For example, connecting students with the resources available on the It Gets Better Project (http://www.itgetsbetter.org/) would be valuable.

Sometimes communities hold values that are inherently contradictory to the values of the counseling profession (Davis & Ritchie, 1993). Communities in which there is strong opposition to discussing sexuality or drug abuse in the schools can pose a problem for counselors whose students raise these issues. If the community frowns on providing contraceptive information, should a counselor refuse to provide a referral for contraceptive information to a student who seeks it? Should a counselor disclose to parents all student comments about drug experimentation in a community that expects such disclosures? In a community that has little tolerance or understanding of LGBTQ issues, should counselors help students who have questions about sexual identity? These are complicated questions, and the answers depend on a number of factors: the age and maturity of the student, the student's willingness to involve parents, the likelihood that the parents' response will not harm the child, the school policy on such matters, and the applicable laws and professional standards. No one benefits if counselors enrage a community and arouse its opposition to the counseling program. However, counselors cannot ignore the needs of students who seek information and service about sensitive issues. Indeed, gay, lesbian, and bisexual students are at substantial risk for suicide, conflicts with family, and violence from others (Byrd & Hays, 2013; McFarland, 1998; Remafedi, 1999). Strong parental and community values against sexual intimacy before marriage or drug experimentation will not guarantee that every student will act in accordance with those values. Ultimately, school counselors must make such decisions with the best interests of their students as the main priority.

In some situations, state and federal laws protect the rights of counselors to advise adolescents about sensitive issues. Fischer and Sorenson (1996) suggest that counselors who give adolescents competent advice and referrals to appropriate resources for birth control information are not likely to be successfully sued for malpractice. State laws often do not give counselors the same freedom about discussions of abortion, although there is great variability in state statutes on this matter. Counselors need to be cautious and alert to legal limitations on their comments when a pregnant student wants to discuss abortion. Stone (2009) advises counselors to be circumspect about sharing their personal views on this highly controversial matter. Stone (2002) also recommends attention to school board policy on discussing this issue. Once again, the ideal resolution is to help the teenager involve her parents in the decision making. The law is silent or unclear on other sensitive matters that do not involve abuse, neglect, or clear and imminent danger. The ASCA Code recognizes the rights of both students and parents, but it also affirms the appropriateness of a wide focus for school counseling on educational, personal, and social dimensions of development.

LEGAL ISSUES: STATE AND FEDERAL STATUTES

The legal issues that concern school counselors derive from state and federal statutes, case law, and sometimes from the opinions of a state's attorney general. One of the most important of the statutes is the Family Educational Rights and Privacy Act (FERPA) enacted in 1974 (sometimes referred to as the Buckley Amendment). This act contains four major sections designed to ensure that parent's rights to information about their children's education are honored. Part 1 ties the availability of federal funding to parental access to school records. Because federal money is crucial to the operation of most school districts, virtually all allow parents to inspect school records. Students who are 18 or older also have the same rights as parents, but parents' rights do not end when a student turns 18. Part 2 requires parental consent for medical, psychiatric, or psychological evaluations of a minor or for participation in "any school program designed to affect or change the personal behavior or values of a student" (Baker, 2007, p. 283). Part 3 prevents unauthorized people from viewing the educational records of children. Only school officials directly involved in the education of students may have access to their records. Directory information is exempt from this policy, and schools can release it without parental consent under certain conditions (McCarthy & Sorenson, 1993). Moreover, if a child is transferring from one school to another, schools can also transfer records without express parental consent, as long as they notify parents about the transfer. The No Child Left Behind Act of 2001 (NCLB, Public Law 107-110) builds on this stipulation by including the provision that schools must allow military recruiters the same access to students and student data that college admissions staff are offered. Finally, if subpoenaed by a court, schools may produce educational records if they are germane to the issue before the court. The final section empowers the U.S. Secretary of Education to develop regulations relevant to student privacy.

FERPA implies that students and/or their parents own the information in official school records, ought to have free access to that information, and have the right to control access to educational records. This law does not alter the confidentiality of communications otherwise protected by law and does not cover private records of school counselors or teachers, provided those private records are not shared with others. The latter stipulations provide some leeway for school counselors to have confidential communications with students and to keep separate records of such communications. In fact, given the stipulations of FERPA and related laws, school counselors would be well advised to keep all records of counseling completely separate from the official educational record of the student (Remley & Herlihy, 2013). However, they should note that if records of counseling are not truly private and are shared with other educators, then those documents are considered educational records (Doll, Strein, Jacob, & Prasse, 2011). According to Sorenson and Chapman (1985), noncompliance with this provision has been high, as 66% of school counselors did not grant parents access to files that were shared with other school personnel. In another study, Davis and Mickelson (1994) found that most school counselors did not understand parental rights to records. The 2010 revision of the ASCA Code (Section B.1.e) notes that compliance with FERPA confidentiality requirements is an ethical requirement for school counselors.

In this age of blended families and noncustodial parents, it is important to understand that FERPA gives the same rights to noncustodial parents that it extends to custodial parents (Stone, 2009). A parent becomes noncustodial when the court awards the rights to decision making about the children to the other parent in a sole custody arrangement, usually as a result of divorce (Wilcoxon & Magnuson, 1999). In a joint custody arrangement, both parents retain custody rights regardless of the place of residence of the child. Perhaps because the FERPA language is an exception to the exclusivity of the rights of custodial parents, Sorenson and Chapman (1985) found that 72% of the school counselors they surveyed reported school policies that denied noncustodial parents equal access to school records. If a counselor is dealing with sensitive information that may negatively affect a child if disclosed to either parent, the counselor needs to make a judgment about disclosure based on the best interests of the child. Careful consultation and supervision are in order under such circumstances. FERPA and other laws should not be interpreted to supersede the health and welfare of any child. Interestingly, according to Stone (2009), stepparents may also have some rights under FERPA, provided that the stepparent is present on a daily basis with one natural parent and the other natural parent is not in the home with the child. (However, this right of stepparents does not deny the noncustodial parent his or her FERPA rights.)

The Americans with Disabilities Act of 1990 also mandates parental access to student files. That law stipulates that if parents are disabled, the school must provide information in the records in a form they can understand (McCarthy & Sorenson, 1993). If parents do not speak or read English, the school must provide information in a language they can understand.

Two other federal laws are relevant to the responsible practice of school counselors: The Grassley Amendment (1994) to the Goals 2000: Educate America Act of 1994, and the Drug Abuse Office and Treatment Act (1976). The Grassley Amendment mandates that schools have parental consent prior to including their children in any survey, research, or evaluation of information relative to the personal and family lives of students. Examples of research that requires consent include studies of political affiliations, income, illegal or anti-social behavior, and evaluations of mental or psychological problems of students or other individuals connected to the student.

The Drug Abuse Office and Treatment Act (1976) guarantees the privacy of all records related to evaluation and treatment for substance abuse for any entity receiving federal funding. This law establishes strict guidelines for the release of such records and stipulates that minors receiving such treatment have privacy rights and must consent to release of their records, even to their parents. Exceptions include emergency treatment, court orders, and research that do not include any individually identifiable data on the student. The U.S. government publishes a useful resource for school personnel and parents that explains how to safeguard student privacy and updates personnel on recent and proposed changes in privacy laws: http://www2.ed.gov/policy/gen/guid/fpco/ferpa/safeguarding-student-privacy.pdf.

It is important to note that no comprehensive policy or practice on counseling records in the schools exists. Merlone (2005) surveyed a small sample of school counselors and found high levels of variability in the number and type of records they kept. Some kept formal files for each student; others kept a daily log of contacts or listed activities in regular reports. Several used multiple methods of record keeping. All were aware that their personal counseling records could be subject to subpoena if the state's privileged communication statute did not extend to school counselors and that there were exceptions to privilege even when such laws existed. All claimed to write notes with an awareness that others might gain access to them and that such notes are unlikely to be private from parents.

LIABILITY FOR SCHOOL COUNSELORS: AN EMERGING REALITY OR AN UNSUBSTANTIATED FEAR?

Not long ago, the common perception was that school counselors were insulated from malpractice liability unless they committed an egregious and willful act. The belief was that their peers in community agencies, hospitals, and private practice were targets for such actions, but that they were immune, either because of legal protections for educators or because of the relative invisibility of their counseling activities. Such beliefs have been called into question by recent court cases. School counselors can and do get sued sometimes (Fischer & Sorenson, 1996; Stone, 2009). Claims of malpractice are still less common for school counselors than for mental health counselors, because state laws usually indemnify schools from claims of negligence and malpractice (Stone, 2009). Fischer and Sorenson (1996) identify six activities that make school personnel vulnerable to malpractice claims. These include (1) administering drugs, (2) giving birth control advice, (3) giving abortion-related advice, (4) making statements that might be defamatory, (5) assisting in searches of student lockers, and (6) violating confidentiality and privacy of records. As already mentioned, counselors who stay informed about federal and state laws regarding contraceptive and abortion discussions with minors and who act competently are unlikely to be successfully sued for their activities in this domain. Similarly, close allegiance to confidentiality and privilege obligations dramatically reduces potential liability for defamation or other violations of privacy. When school counselors are involved in searches of student lockers, cars, or other possessions, they must take care that they abide by current policies and laws affecting such searches and that the privacy of the student is limited only to the degree necessary.

Liability for Student Suicides

One source of malpractice claims stems from student suicides. Until 1991, claims against school counselors related to student suicides resulted in little liability for counselors (Fischer & Sorenson, 1996). In that era, the courts generally ruled that a duty of care could not be imposed on school personnel who did not have sufficient training in diagnosing mental disorders. A Maryland court reversed that trend, finding that a school counselor could be held liable for a student suicide (*Eisel v. Board of Educ.*, 1991). In that case, a 13-year-old girl's friends reported her suicidal comments to a school counselor. That counselor, in turn, informed the counselor assigned to the girl to whom the statements had been attributed. The two counselors called the girl into their office and asked her about the matter. The girl denied making those statements. The counselors did nothing further, and later that day the girl was shot in a suicide pact with another student. The court ruled that the school counselor did indeed have a special relationship with the student and a duty of care to act to prevent this suicide. Specifically, they faulted the counselor for not notifying the parents about their daughter's suicidal comments. The court recognized that school counselors may not be able to control students to the same degree as mental health professionals in more restricted settings, but they asserted that counselors still have a duty to intervene to lessen foreseeable risks by informing the parents (Pate, 1992). This was the first time that a U.S. court had asserted that a school counselor had a duty to act to try to prevent a student suicide (Stone, 2009). Had the counselor in this case told the parents about the suicide threat, her liability probably would have ended at that point (Remley & Sparkman, 1993), unless the counselor had reason to expect that the parents would not respond appropriately. Sometimes adults deny or minimize the risk of suicide among young people (Wellman, 1984). In such circumstances, the counselor may need to act more energetically to ensure that the parents act to protect the child. A failure to respond to a serious suicide threat probably constitutes child neglect and should be treated as such.

In the *Eisel* case, the central issues were whether the risk to the student had been foreseeable and the counselor's very limited response to a life-threatening problem. It is important to note that Ms. Eisel was not an ongoing client of the school counselor, but rather a member of the student body assigned to that counselor's caseload. Once the counselor sought out Ms. Eisel to question her about her suicidal intentions, a special relationship was created. The obligation of the counselor is to take reasonable steps to prevent suicide among all students for whom he or she has responsibility. This case also underscores the value of attending to comments of other students. Counselors need to evaluate the veracity of remarks of other youngsters and to follow up when they believe the information conveyed may be true. The court cited the doctrine of *in loco parentis*, a doctrine that means that school personnel legally stand in the place of parents and therefore had an obligation to notify parents.

These events should not cause school counselors to overreact to potentially suicidal situations, however. Stone (2009) notes that even in the *Eisel* case, the court did not establish an absolute duty to act, but rather a duty to use reasonable care in the face of such a serious threat. Remley and Sparkman (1993), for example, caution counselors not to make hasty, emotional judgments about suicidal risk. Instead, school counselors ought to make reasoned assessments of risk, seek supervision and consultation, and act in an expeditious, but not rash, way when they judge risk to be high. It is important to note that not all such claims of counselor negligence after a student suicide have been supported by U.S. courts. In *Grant v. Board of Trustees of Valley View School District* (1997), the court did not hold school personnel responsible, although other court cases have agreed with *Eisel* (Stone, 2009). The ultimate reason, though, to take even vague threats of suicide seriously is the ethical obligation to act to protect the welfare of the student.

Although the rate of suicide in adolescents has been decreasing since 1994 (McKeown, Cuffe, & Schultz, 2006), suicide is still a leading cause of death in this age group. It results in death for 4400 young people each year in the United States (Centers for Disease Control and Prevention [CDC], 2009). Adolescent boys complete suicide at nearly four times the rate of adolescent girls, and that rate increases to nearly six times the rate of females in the early adult years (American Association of Suicidology [AAS], 2007). Moreover, 15% of high school students seriously consider suicide, and approximately 149,000 young people are treated from self-inflicted injuries (CDC, 2009). Consequently, legal scholars suggest that school counselors consider implementing suicide prevention programs at their schools (e.g., Hermann, 2002). Such programs alert adults and youngsters in the school to the warning signs for suicide and give them guidelines for responding. Prevention activities may help in reducing risk and in responding to serious mental health problems among adolescents, but they carry some risks, so they must be carefully designed and implemented (Gibbons & Studer, 2008; Reis & Cornell, 2008; Scott, Wilcox, Huo, Turner, Fisher, & Shaffer, 2010). The principle of beneficence should drive all such programs, though they may have some value in reducing legal liability of schools for student suicides (Corey et al., 2010).

When suicide does occur, counselors should provide support services for the student body to help students grieve and come to grips with the loss. The suggestion that adolescent peers are at risk for suicidal ideation after a student suicide adds merit to this recommendation (Feigelman & Gorman, 2008). Many schools have relationships with community mental health centers, and professionals from both settings collaborate to provide crisis intervention. Such interventions are consistent with the ethical and legal obligations of the profession. See Capuzzi (2002, 2004, 2009) for excellent guides to responsible practice in preventing and responding to student suicides.

D. H. Henderson (1987) reminds school counselors that the duty of care is not limited to issues of suicide or injury to others. School counselors bear a legal and ethical obligation to act in other types of foreseeable risks. For example, he suggests that counselors ought to refer students to appropriate care when they display evidence of severe mental and emotional dysfunction. Usually the best way to implement this duty is to get the youngster to agree to the parents' involvement. In the absence of that agreement, counselors must make their judgment on the basis of the child's best interests. Self-injury also falls within this category and is a problem that school counselors encounter frequently. According to Roberts-Dobie and Donatelle (2007), half the counselors they surveyed (51%) worked with students who self-injured in the prior school year, and 81% had worked with a student who self-injured during their careers. The ASCA Code covers this issue in Section A.7 (Appendix C, pp. 564–565) highlighting both the rights of parents, the requirement to act on behalf of the child at risk, and the importance of consultation in this circumstance.

Liability for Academic Negligence

In 2001, for the first time, a state supreme court allowed a charge of negligence related to the academic advice of a school counselor to go to trial. Prior to this time, virtually all state courts had rejected lawsuits against school counselors related to academic matters, largely because of the difficulties school counselors face in advising the large number of students in their caseloads about rapidly changing academic requirements (Stone, 2002). The case was *Sain v. Cedar Rapids Community School District*, 2001. In this case, a student sought out the advice of his school counselor about the English courses he would need to satisfy the NCAA (National Collegiate Athletic Association) academic requirements to maintain his eligibility for an athletic scholarship. According to the boy, the counselor misinformed the boy, resulting in the revocation of the boy's five-year athletic scholarship. In other words, the family asserted that the counselor's negligence in checking the facts, thereby failing to exercise due care, cost the young man's family thousands of dollars. The Iowa court found that the case could be tried as an issue of negligent misrepresentation, the type of error for which individuals in other professions such as accounting, law, and business have regularly been held accountable in civil court. By this ruling, the Iowa Supreme Court allowed the case to be considered; it did not rule on the outcome, but it set forth the notion that this kind of case of educational negligence against a counselor could have merit.

The ruling sparked much comment in the counseling literature, with some predicting disastrous effects on the willingness of school counselors to participate in academic advising (Reid, 2001). Calmer voices point to the unique factors about *Sain* that make future lawsuits related to academic advising unlikely (Stone, 2002). First, most academic misinformation does not result in the level of personal and financial harm caused in this case. Second, the standard for a successful malpractice suit remains high and difficult for claimants to meet. Third, *Sain* is a single case in one state and cannot necessarily be viewed as a portent of actions in other state courts. Finally, in my view, in an ironic way, *Sain* represents progress in the public view of the profession of school counseling. School counselors are now more likely to be viewed as professionals accountable for their actions. All other professions are subject to civil action when they commit major errors that harm those they serve—how can school counseling expect to be treated any differently and still be considered a legitimate profession?

Not all recent cases of academic negligence have met with the same fate as the Iowa case. Two cases (Wisconsin and California), both dealing with inaccurate advice that affected eligibility for an NCAA scholarship, were thrown out of court (Stone, 2009). So, for all these reasons, counselors should not hesitate to participate fully in academic advising; their liability risks for such actions are infinitesimally small, and their potential to help students meet their educational goals from competent advice is great. School counselors simply need to be diligent in certifying the accuracy of the information they have access to and informing students when information is uncertain or likely to change.

Professional school counselors also need to be responsible in the referrals they offer students and their parents. This means they should have reliable information about the competence of the professionals to whom they refer clients, and they should keep the list of referral sources up to date. Moreover, they should always offer more than a single referral if at all possible and should use the referral sources on the school's list of recommended referrals. If such a list does not exist, it would be prudent for school counselors to develop one. Recently, a counselor and school district in Florida were sued for offering a student just one referral to a person who was not on the school's approved list. When that outside counselor ended up abusing the student, the family went to court to hold the school personnel liable for the damages. The Florida court refused to hear the case, but it still serves as a message of caution for school counselors to make reasonable referrals to known professionals (Stone, 2009).

SCHOOL VIOLENCE: LEGAL AND ETHICAL DIMENSIONS

In recent years, tragic episodes of school violence have raised public awareness of the need for schools and communities to intervene to prevent students with destructive impulses from acting on them (Hermann & Finn, 2002; Sandhu & Aspy, 2000). Incidents in which the newborn infants of pregnant teenagers died soon after birth because of the neglect or other life-ending actions of their adolescent mothers have also caused a public outcry and demand for better support for girls facing unplanned pregnancies. In response to these events, some school districts have initiated policies that mandate that disclosures to counselors related to either destructive impulses or pregnancy be immediately reported to school authorities and parents. Such directives are motivated by a desire to save others from harm and to protect the students in trouble, and are consistent with the long-term goals of any school counselor. They are also consistent with ethical standards when the danger is clear and imminent. It is important to note, though, that California regulations clarify that school counselors are not obliged to disclose the pregnancy of a student to school officials (Legal opinions of the California State Attorney General, 2011).

At the same time, mandates clearly compromise the limited level of confidentiality that adolescents can be afforded when no imminent danger is anticipated. In that circumstance, such directives place school counselors and school psychologists in a difficult position. On the one hand, they can make clear to students this limit of confidentiality (in addition to the others) and thereby risk that the students will decide not to reveal that kind of information to them—clearly the more ethical option. Or they can explain it only after the disclosure has been made, in which case the individual student feels betrayed, and other students who learn of this disclosure to school authorities will quickly decide not to share such matters with anyone at school. In either case, the ultimate goal of the school officials—to prevent harm to students and their babies and get help for them—is thwarted. Counselors cannot be of assistance to students whose problems never get reported to them. Because such policies make students less likely to seek help, school counselors have an obligation to discuss the implications of these directives with administrators and to try to devise alternative approaches that do not impose a barrier to student access to counseling for those with such serious problems. Clearly, in the great majority of circumstances, the disclosure of nonimminent aggressive or illegal actions or pregnancies to family members and school authorities is a desirable outcome, but unless adolescents have some sense of control of that disclosure, and some sense of trust in adults at school, they will not reveal such feelings and will try to manage these situations on their own, with the help of peers, or through online sources. In that event, the opportunity to reduce the risk of violence is missed. Therefore, professional associations and school personnel need to take an active role to educate parents and administrators about the gains and losses inherent in the confidentiality policies they enact. School counselors must work with administrators and school boards to draft balanced policies that do not cut off student willingless to discuss personal and social problems with them.

Face-to-Face and Electronic Harassment

School counselors also have an ethical responsibility to act to prevent the day-to-day level of violence in schools that occurs when students are bullied and harassed. Physical intimidation and bullying are serious problems that affect substantial numbers of school-age children and can result in suicidal thinking for victims, violent forms of retaliation against bullies, and trauma responses (Carney, 2000; Hazler, 1996; Ross, 2003). Harassment at school because of gender, sexual orientation, and disability is an ongoing problem. Cyberbullying has emerged as a major issue for school personnel and a real threat to minors' safety. Between 12% and 43% of middle and high school students report that they have been victimized by cyberbullying, typically via email, chat rooms, social networking sites, and instant messaging (Dehue, Bolman, & Vollink, 2008; Hinduja & Patchin, 2010; Kowalski & Limber, 2007; Moessner, 2007). Social media has become a particular concern in this regard. It appears more common among females and seems to peak in early high school (Moessner, 2007). Increasing numbers of teen and preteen suicides have been linked to cyberbullying (Patterson, 2011). Media reports highlight the devastating effects cyberbullying can have. Consider the following case reported in the *New York Times* (Hoffman, 2010):

The Case of Cyberbullying by Identity Theft

Marie's ninth-grade son was withdrawn. He finally disclosed to her what had been happening over numerous weeks: he was being harassed at school because he was "saying nasty things about other kids on Facebook." However, the boy did not even have a presence on any social networking site; three other boys had stolen his identity and posted the comments. Why? They said it was because the boy was a "loser." Marie got the mystery of the harassers' identity solved only after contacting police. Two of the boys had also been harassing in face-to-face encounters, but one of the three had been the boy's friend since primary school. The school indicated it was unable to intervene because the activity did not happen on school property.

This incident highlights several features of cyberbullying: the ease with which it can happen, the devastating psychological and social effects on the victims, and the difficulty that parents and schools have in intervening to stop the harassment. Legal restrictions of the free speech rights of students who are not at school also complicate educators' ability to discipline offenders, but some actions are legal (Dooley, 2010). School counselors have a significant role in spite of the school's limited authority to intervene in such circumstances (Burrow-Sanchez, 2011). When messages sent through social networking sites contain sexual content in an effort to harass someone, the perpetrator can face serious legal consequences and, in some cases, has been listed as a sexual offender and become subject to all the same restrictions and public identification of convicted adult sexual offenders. (See Hoffman [2011] at http://www.nytimes.com/2011/03/27/us/27sexting.html?_r=1&scp=3&sq=sexting&st=cse for an example of the devastating consequences of sexting for a group of eighth graders in Washington.) School counselors can educate parents and children about the resources they can access and about the serious implications cyberbullying can have on those who perpetrate it. Given the predominance of the online bullying and its consequences, school counselors have an affirmative ethical responsibility to take on this educational role with parents, students, and other educators. The ASCA Code highlights this duty in Section A.10 and advises counselors to base prevention and intervention activities on the best available research.

Given the seriousness of bullying and cyberbullying, 49 states and three U.S. territories have developed both laws and public policy related to cyberbullying. Montana has policy statements, but no law (Stopbullying.gov, 2014). These regulations tend to address responsibilities of school districts to prevent and intercede when such harassment occurs. Some states also offer substantial guidance for school districts on the development and monitoring of prevention programs. (See the New York State *Dignity for All Students* website for an example of such guidance: http://schools.nyc.gov/RulesPolicies/RespectforAll/default.htm).

Gender violence and sexual harassment directed at female students begins in elementary school, peaks in the middle and early high school years, and continues into college experiences (Ponton, 1996; Young & Mendez, 2003). Few girls escape it. Relational aggression, usually girl-to-girl incidents of verbal, psychological, or physical abuse, has also risen dramatically in recent years (Archer & Coyne, 2005). Responses by school administrators have been uneven despite legal requirements that schools respond to claims of sexual harassment. For example, in their analysis of 27 sexual harassment cases, Sullivan and Zirkel (1999) found a consistent pattern in which the victims had notified multiple staff of the harassment, with no satisfactory resolution despite repeated attempts to tell authorities about the problem.

As mentioned earlier in the chapter, violence aimed at gay, lesbian, bisexual, transgender, and questioning students is also disturbingly common—more common and more invisible than other crimes against students (Gay, Lesbian, and Straight Education Network [GLSEN], 2009; McFarland & Dupuis, 2001). Nearly 90% of LGBTQ students in the GLSEN study reported harassment at school. The study found that the level of harassment had not decreased in 10 years, though the frequency of homophobic comments had lessened. Approximately 25% of gay and lesbian students are crime victims, compared to 9% of the general population (Comstock, 1991), and they experience high levels of verbal and physical assault. According to GLSEN's data, 40% of LGBTQ youth reported incidents of physical harassment, and 84% reported verbal harassment. Nearly one-fifth (19%) had been physically assaulted. Homosexual youth also miss school more frequently because of fears for their safety. They also experience lower high school grades because of absences and discomfort in school.

Some evidence suggests that school officials contribute to this problem. In a Massachusetts study, 97% of students reported homophobic comments from students, and 53% heard such comments from school staff (Massachusetts Governor's Commission on Gay and Lesbian Youth, 1993). A similar study in Iowa showed that teachers failed to respond to homophobic comments 97% of the time (Carter, 1997). Research on the attitudes of school counselors toward sexual minority students suggests that they recognize that these students are an underserved and invisible minority, but also indicates that many counselors may not be interested in working with such students. Price and Teljohann (1991) reported that 20% of the counselors they surveyed would not find working with gay and lesbian students "gratifying." Ruebensaal (2006) also found that school counselors were reluctant to work with gay or lesbian students on problems they felt comfortable addressing with heterosexual students.

Not only are such attitudes and behaviors inconsistent with the mandates in the codes of ethics to promote the welfare and dignity of clients and to act in nondiscriminatory ways, they may also be legally problematic. In 1999, the U.S. Supreme Court ruled that school officials who ignore student-on-student harassment may be held liable for violating Title IX when harassment is "so severe, pervasive, and objectively offensive that it denies the victim equal access to education" (*Davis v. Monroe County Board of Education*, 1999, p. 650). The literature on the experiences of LGBTQ youth in school suggests that the harassment they experience often meets that criterion. Other civil and federal cases that deal more directly with violence and intimidation based on sexual orientation have also held that schools are responsible when they fail to act to protect the safety and rights of gay and lesbian students. (See McFarland and Dupois [2001] for a detailed discussion of these cases.)

While all this sounds quite disheartening for educators, there are hopeful signs and evidence that supportive adults at school can and do protect LGBTQ students from such negative outcomes and that safe schools programs are having an impact on educators and the school community (e.g., Byrd & Hays, 2013).

Consequently, school counselors have both an ethical and legal responsibility to act to reduce the risk of harassment, intimidation, and violence against students. They need to use inclusive language themselves, challenge anti-gay and anti-female comments, make resources on homosexuality and gender bias visible to staff and students, take a leadership role in educating other staff about the relationship between harassment and school violence, and have appropriate referral sources available for students and parents who need them. The need for referral sources is especially crucial for gay, lesbian, and bisexual students whose invisibility in society makes it difficult for them to locate appropriate services on their own.

The ACA (1999), APA (1999a), and ASCA (2007) have produced materials to help school counselors and psychologists get the training they need to intervene to make schools safer. These materials clearly delineate the extent of the problem and offer strategies for helping, both in crisis situations and in the normal course of events. (See the recommended readings and online resources at the end of the chapter for information on obtaining these materials.) When school counselors use these resources and take conspicuous actions to make school a place where LGBTQ youth can thrive and not just survive, they will be implementing their full ethical responsibility to promote the welfare and dignity of students (Stone, 2009). And there is substantial evidence that when educators support LGBTQ students, these students are more likely to maintain high educational aspirations (Stone, 2009) and experience reduced risks to their mental health (Byrd & Hays, 2013).

ETHICAL ISSUES IN POST-SECONDARY PLANNING

One important responsibility of secondary counselors is to advise and assist students in making the transition from high school to post-secondary education or training. The era in which a high school diploma was sufficient to obtain a stable and rewarding job has long passed, and so counselors play a crucial role in helping students and parents make decisions about what type of post-secondary education is best for them. Many colleges, for example, give considerable weight to the letter of recommendation from an applicant's school counselor in deciding admissibility of a candidate; thus, the pressure on a counselor to support a student can lead to either inflated praise for the student's skills or disclosure of sensitive personal information about a student. Consider the following situation in light of that fact:

The Case of Mr. Bellasandro's Letter of Reference

Mr. Bellasandro has been Maria's counselor during her entire high school career. She has been an exceptional student, earning high grades, athletic honors, and awards for her participation in debate and chorus. Maria struggled the first semester of her junior year, a period in which she was sexually assaulted as she walked home from her part-time job one evening. She fought off her attacker but suffered a broken collarbone and other injuries. Maria also felt traumatized by the attack and had difficulty focusing on her school assignments for a few months. Her grades suffered that semester. Now that Maria is applying to highly competitive colleges, Mr. Bellasandro is worried that the weak semester will prevent her from being accepted to those colleges. To be sure that she is given full consideration, he discusses the sexual assault and its physical and emotional consequences for Maria in his letter of recommendation. Since Maria has signed a waiver for access to the letter, she has no idea that her counselor included information about the attack in his comments.

Mr. Bellasandro had both good intentions and a legal waiver supporting his decision to describe the reasons that Maria's grades had suffered that semester. His motives were altruistic, and the waiver Maria signed was virtually unconditional. However, his actions were still not entirely consistent with his ethical responsibilities to Maria. Why not? First, she had no reason to expect that the details of this violation would be included in his counselor's letter of reference, because her counselor did not discuss this issue with her or her parents prior to the submission of the letter. Second, since no professional can guarantee that the confidentiality of personal information will be maintained when released, students should be able to decide for themselves whether they wish to proceed with the release of such personal content. Maria may be at risk for additional emotional distress should she learn after she arrives at college that the admissions committee knew the details of the assault. Third, Mr. Bellasandro had no need to offer details of the attack to explain that medical problems detracted from Maria's ability to maintain her high academic performance that one semester. He could still have provided adequate information about the exceptional nature of this applicant without disclosing such sensitive information. Since high schools often publicize the acceptances of students into elite colleges as evidence of their own excellence, the question also arises about whether even a small degree of self-interest entered into this counselor's decision or his haste to act without consultation. Getting accepted at an Ivy League school not only advances Maria's future, it advances the school's reputation as well. For all these reasons, Mr. Bellasandro's actions serve as a caution for high school counselors to be sensitive to the implications of the comments they write in letters of recommendation. A study by Stone (2005) shows that the overwhelming majority of school counselors would not take the action Mr. Bellasandro did and would protect such sensitive information from disclosure without explicit permission.

As the *New York Times* (Winter, 2004) noted, another ethical issue has emerged for high school counselors in recent years as many students and parents become focused on admission to elite colleges and universities. Second- and third-tier institutions without such reputations must work hard to attract the most qualified applicants, and they look to school counselors to inform students about the quality of the education they too offer. Such schools have sometimes begun to invite high school counselors to their campuses for more than the typical facility tour, sometimes offering counselors free tickets to sporting events, concerts, skiing at major resorts, and complimentary meals at noteworthy local restaurants. They have been housed at the college's expense in deluxe hotels, as well. Such perks are intended to help the counselors have a good experience during their campus visit and to pass along their good experiences at these lesser-known colleges to students and parents when they advise them about college applications. Can counselors ethically accept such lavish treatment? The answer depends on the effect that accepting such perks would have on the students and parents who are relying on the objectivity of counselors in their recommendations of colleges. It is difficult to imagine that students and parents would not question the motives of the counselors and view their actions as conflicts of interest. It would also be difficult to imagine that school counselors, whose salaries are modest, would be completely immune to the effects of such lavish treatment during their college visits. Therefore, counselors must decline these extra benefits, although they certainly may participate in campus tours that better acquaint them with the merits of these colleges.

ETHICS OF GROUP COUNSELING IN SCHOOLS

According to Greenberg (2003), groups have been demonstrated to be an effective tool to help young people change and benefit from their education. Many of the problems that detract from young people's development relate to social skills and interpersonal relationships, two issues especially amenable to group work. They are also an efficient method for school counselors to reach many more students than they can work with individually. Psychoeducational and support groups that deal with the development of social skills, the management of emotions such as anger, and the response to losses such as divorce or the death of a sibling are most common. School counselors are well advised to refrain from offering groups that deal with clinical issues such as eating disorders or bipolar disorder (Kaffenberger & Seligman, 2003).

Since groups that take place in schools derive from a closed system—that is, only young people who attend the school are eligible to participate—confidentiality can be a concern. First, students who are uninvolved in group may learn who attends simply by virtue of their absence from class or by seeing them arrive at the counselor's office at group time. Second, helping young group members maintain the confidentiality of disclosures when they are likely to see other students outside of group and know them well can be difficult. The temptation to tell a friend is greater than when a group takes place in a location separate from school with individuals whose only contact with them is during group time. As mentioned in Chapters 5 and 6, clear informed consent procedures and extensive discussion of the importance of confidentiality assist in limiting the risk of violations, but they do not erase the possibility entirely. School counselors should also obtain the assent of children to participate and explain to them the extent to which their parents may be informed about their disclosures in group. School counselors should also be careful not to exceed the boundaries of their competence in conducting groups, taking care to focus on the issues for which the group was established and refraining from making the psychoeducational or support group a psychotherapy experience. School counselors should also be aware of a student's concurrent participation in counseling outside of school and should communicate with all involved (including the community counselor) about the advisability of inclusion in a group concurrent with individual treatment. With these precautions in place, group counseling can be a valuable tool for increasing the effectiveness of the school counselor. Section A.6 of the ASCA Code requires counselors to screen prospective group members, develop appropriate competence and use best practices, establish clear expectations for groups and for confidentiality, and monitor and follow up with members as needed.

ETHICS OF PEER HELPING PROGRAMS

Peer support programs exist under many names—peer counseling, peer support, peer intervention, peer facilitation, peer mediation, and peer conflict resolution. Their central feature involves training students to act as support people for other students who have problems or are at risk for developing problems. Peer helper programs have become more common over the last three decades as schools try to increase student access to support services without increasing costs (Ehly & Vazquez, 1998; Morey, Miller, Fulton, Rosen, & Daly, 1989). Low cost has not been the only factor in their expansion, however. They have been viewed as valuable gateways to attract reluctant students to counseling services they need. The original peer helping concept was construed as limited to developmental concerns and peer tutoring (Wheeler & Bertram, 2008). Peer intervention programs for such problems have expanded beyond the high school level. Many peer helping programs have been developed in elementary and middle schools (Myrick, Highland, & Sabella, 1995). For example, Bell, Coleman, Anderson, Whelan, and Wilder (2000) report on a peer mediation program for sixth through eighth graders that taught students conflict resolution and mediation skills and was successful in reducing aggressive behavior among participants.

Are all peer helping programs as effective as the one described in Bell et al. (2000) in meeting their goals, and what ethical problems arise from their use? According to Lewis and Lewis (1996), much of the evidence about the effectiveness and outcomes of peer helping programs that deal with substantive mental health issues is anecdotal rather than empirical. Research supporting the positive effects of peer mediation programs and programs that aim at improving school performance and attitudes is more prevalent (e.g., Tobias & Myrick, 1999). Lewis and Lewis urge more research, and they question the merit of using peer helping models for serious mental health problems in the absence of such outcome data. With some exceptions (e.g., Schellenberg & Parks-Savage, 2007), they note, "There is not yet a body of evidence documenting the effectiveness, or the safety, of using peer helping programs to address problems beyond the basic academic and developmental issues they were initially intended to address" (p. 312). To the degree, then, that counselors cannot demonstrate either the merit or the safety of such programs, there are serious questions about the ethics of their use.

In Section A.11, the ASCA Code takes note of the special responsibilities of counselors when using this form of helping when it emphasize the centrality of the counselor's role in such programs and his or her responsibility to guard student welfare. Peer helping programs require high levels of supervision. Helpers must be carefully chosen, well trained, and continuously monitored to ensure that they are skilled enough to provide services and that they do not exceed the limits of their competence. In their research, Lewis and Lewis (1996) found a disturbing pattern.

Many of the educators responsible for peer helping programs were not trained counselors. Thus, in those cases there were no professionals with the requisite training and experience to accomplish important supervisory tasks. In those circumstances, neither the helpers nor the supervisors have the competence to intervene appropriately.

The role demands on students who volunteer to be peer helpers are substantial. Professionals responsible for such programs see benefits to those volunteers, but some wonder whether they are overburdened for their developmental level (Lewis & Lewis, 1996; Morey et al., 1989). In Lewis and Lewis's study of 263 peer programs in Washington State, they found two cases in which peer counselors had completed suicides. Two incidents are not a sufficient basis for a sweeping conclusion about the risks of the helper role, but these events illustrate the need to screen candidates carefully, monitor stress, and supervise closely.

Even peer counseling programs that limit their focus to conflict resolution or developmental and educational issues must cope with ethical issues regarding confidentiality of student disclosures. Adolescent volunteers must, of course, be oriented to the importance of confidentiality and monitored for compliance, but their immaturity suggests that those precautions may still not prevent violations of confidentiality. Students using peer services ought to understand the limits of confidentiality, and supervisors should be prepared to respond when trust is broken. Volunteers should be ready to share student disclosures with supervisors, and users should be informed about such consultation. In addition, guidelines ought to be established to avoid dual-relationship problems and to explain the rules for assisting friends. In short, when school counselors initiate or take responsibility for existing peer counseling programs, they must be prepared to devote time and energy to the task of administering and supervising these programs. Moreover, they ought to systematically evaluate program impact on both those helped and volunteers, and modify ineffective or harmful programs.

SUMMARY

The ethical and legal issues confronting school counselors overlap significantly with those facing community counselors. Standards for competence to practice, informed consent, confidentiality, dual relationships, and fair assessment practices are applicable across all settings. However, five rather unique ethical challenges face school counselors. The first is the clash between the open communication patterns among educators and the limits of communication among professionals imposed by confidentiality standards and privilege laws. Counselors who understand such limits themselves and work to educate other school personnel about the impact of confidentiality on peer relationships are more likely to serve students, the school, and the profession effectively. On occasion, the open pattern of communication in school includes gossip and informal communications among educators. The ethics of school counseling clearly prohibit participation in such conversation. In fact, gossiping about students may leave counselors vulnerable to legal charges of defamation of character. Second, counselors must be prepared to work with parents and communities whose values differ from the fundamental values of the counseling profession. They must be respectful of parental rights, but also sensitive to the needs of the child. In many states, the right of school counselors to help children with matters relating to contraception, abortion, and other sensitive issues is legally protected, provided counselors work within the boundaries of their competence and do not insert their personal views into the counseling interaction. An active program of community education about counseling programs, coupled with evidence of program effectiveness, can reduce resistance to and suspicion of counselors. Third, counselors who develop and oversee peer counseling programs must ensure that the programs are helpful to student volunteers and to those they serve. Peer helping programs should be supervised by counselors and be limited to developmental and educational concerns because there is no clear evidence that such programs can responsibly assist young people with more serious mental health concerns.

Ethical school counselors should be familiar with the provisions of the Family Educational Rights and Privacy Act of 1974 and related laws dealing with special education and the rights of those with disabilities. Because state and federal laws affecting education change so rapidly, school counselors bear a responsibility to keep current with those changes and to ensure that school policies are consistent with statutes. Finally, school counselors are not immune to malpractice claims, although such claims occur somewhat less frequently for them than for other mental health professionals. Courts in recent years have tended to view school counselors as having a duty of care to prevent foreseeable danger to students by involving parents or other adults to help keep the students safe and secure the needed care. Recent legal rulings have also highlighted the duty of school counselors and other officials to be proactive in preventing harassment and intimidation of students that prevents them from equal participation in the educational activities of the school. Much of this harassment has been aimed at female students and at gay, lesbian, and bisexual students.

Counselors need also to be sensitive to the ethical dimensions of advising students about post-secondary planning, being accurate in their statements to colleges about a given student's talents as well as sensitive to the impact of the content of their disclosures about a student's personal life. They must also act in ways that do not jeopardize their objectivity or parents' and students' perception of their objectivity in accepting college tour activities. When conducting groups in the school, counselors who are aware of the complications of doing groups in a closed system and who stay within the boundaries of their own competence are likely to be most successful.

Discussion Questions*

1. Schools often have policies stating that all drug use information that comes to the attention of staff must be reported to administrators. Thinking of potential scenarios with students, at what point do you think it advisable for counselors to report drug use, and at what point should they honor confidentiality?
2. School counseling has endured substantial criticism in recent years for many of its activities. For example, self-esteem programs have been labeled as too humanistic, and drug and alcohol support groups have been called too intrusive into family matters. When such criticisms are made about school counseling, what do you see as the ethical obligations of the school counselor?
3. Do the confidentiality requirements for school counselors make it difficult for them to establish strong professional ties with other school personnel? Do those requirements make personal friendships with other staff more difficult?
4. How would you respond to the criticism that peer helping programs place helpers and those helped at risk when they attempt

*Note to course instructors: The *Instructor's Guide* for this book includes other discussion questions, class exercises, cases, and multiple-choice and essay test items for this chapter.

to deal with issues such as depression, suicide, drug use, and related problems? How would you balance the risks of such programs against their potential value to students?

5. What do you see as the ethical issues involved in suicide prevention and crisis intervention programs?
6. Should school counselors be immune from liability claims?

Cases for Discussion

Tito is a 16-year-old junior who has been in counseling with the school counselor, Miranda, intermittently since he began high school. Although he seems happy and easygoing most of the time at school, Tito has endured a great deal of family stress and disruption. Each of his parents has been married multiple times, and Tito has lived in 10 different houses during his life. He has had great difficulty getting along with his current stepfather, with whom he resides. They argue constantly, and Tito is punished severely each time he raises his voice. The counselor has been monitoring the situation and has observed no signs of abuse, although she clearly sees a mismatch between Tito's psychosocial needs at this time and his stepfather's style of parenting. One morning when Miranda enters her office, she has a voicemail message from Tito with a cell phone number to call as soon as possible. When she contacts Tito, she learns that he has run away following a huge argument with his stepfather. The argument frightened Tito because he thought he was in danger of hitting his stepfather. Tito tells Miranda that he is safe and off the streets. He then asks her if he should tell her where he is. Miranda replies that if he gives her that information he must understand that she may need to disclose it to his mother and stepfather. Tito pauses and decides not to reveal his location. Miranda then devises a plan for Tito that includes contacting his biological father to see if he can help mediate the situation. Tito agrees to call back before the end of school. Two hours later, Tito's stepfather calls Miranda and asks her if she knows where Tito is. When she says she does not, the stepfather remarks that he will call the police if he does not hear from the boy by dinnertime. Their conversation ends. Miranda plans to tell Tito of the stepfather's call when she hears from Tito and to ask him to contact his mother or stepfather immediately. Are Miranda's actions consistent with the ethical standards of the profession? Should she have maintained confidentiality about her telephone contact from Tito? What if the principal asked her if she knew where Tito was? Should she divulge what she knows to the principal?

Justin, a high school counselor, receives many reference forms for students applying for college, jobs, or other post-secondary experiences. Frequently these forms ask the counselor to rank the student in comparison to other students. Justin is uncomfortable with such forms, believing that they do not allow him much opportunity to describe the talents of individual students. However, he knows that refusing to complete the specified document may not be wise, so he regularly places students in the top 20% of rankings, even when he knows that ranking is inflated. He justifies his actions by attending to the inherent limitations of such ranking systems.

Nellie, a high school counselor, meets regularly with a sophomore named Michelle, who is struggling academically in spite of good test scores and good grades in middle school. The parents have been informed about the counseling sessions and have encouraged Nellie to discuss with their daughter any issues that will help her do better in school. As spring arrives and temperatures climb in the school, Nellie notices that Michelle still wears long sleeves. When asked about this, Michelle begins to cry and reveals to Nellie that she makes small cuts on her arms to help her numb the psychological pain she feels. Michelle shows Nellie the cuts, which are very small, superficial, and few in number. Nellie makes a contract with Michelle to stop cutting until they meet again. She also gets Michelle to agree to show the cuts to her pediatrician when she has her next appointment, in two weeks. In light of these events, the minor nature of the physical harm, and her worry about destroying the girl's trust in her, Nellie decides not to inform the parents.

Anaar is a 15-year-old first-year high school student who comes to the school counselor with a question: Is it illegal to sponsor an online contest to elect the "sluttiest" girl in the school? After Mrs. Jackson, her counselor, gets more information, Anaar reveals that she had a fight with a friend and organized this contest to get back at her friend for gossiping about her. Now the friend is threatening to tell her father, a lawyer, so that he can sue Anaar and her family. Anaar is very worried and also ashamed of her actions. How should the counselor handle this situation?

Recommended Readings

American Psychological Association. (1999). Warning signs: A youth anti-violence initiative. Washington, D.C. Retrieved from http://www.apahelpcenter.org/featuredtopics/feature.php?id=38

American School Counselor Association. (2007). Position statement: The professional school counselor and LGBTQ youth. Retrieved from http://www.safeschoolscoalition.org/RG-PositionStatement-asca.html

American School Counselor Association. (2008a). Position statements. Retrieved from http://www.schoolcounselor.org/school-counselors-members/about-asca-%281%29/position-statements

American School Counselor Association. (2010). Ethical standards for school counselors. Retrieved from http://www.schoolcounselor.org/asca/media/asca/Resource%20Center/Legal%20and%20Ethical%20Issues/Sample%20Documents/EthicalStandards2010.pdf

American School Counselor Association. (2011). The professional school counselor and the promotion of safe schools through conflict resolution and bullying/harassment prevention. Retrieved from http://www.schoolcounselor.org/asca/media/asca/home/positionstatements/PS_Bullying.pdf

Bauman, S. (2011). *Cyberbullying: What counselors need to know*. Alexandria, VA: American Counseling Association.

Crespi, T. D. (2009). Group counseling in the schools: Legal, ethical, and treatment issues in school practice. *Psychology in the Schools*, *46*, 273–280.

Fischer, L., & Sorenson, G. P. (1996). *School law for counselors, psychologists, and social workers* (3rd ed.). White Plains, NY: Longman.

Gay, Lesbian, Straight Education Network (GLSEN). (2008). National school climate survey. Retrieved from http://www.glsen.org/cgi-bin/iowa/all/home/index.html

Hermann, M. (2002). A study of legal issues encountered by school counselors and perceptions of their preparedness to respond to legal challenges. *Professional School Counseling*, *6*, 12–18.

Huss, S. N., Bryant, A., & Mulet, S. (2008). Managing the quagmire of counseling in a school: Bringing the parents onboard. *Professional School Counseling*, *11*, 362–367.

Jacob, S., & Powers, K. E. (2009). Privileged communication in the school psychologist client relationship. *Psychology in the Schools*, *46*(4), 307–318.

Kaffenberger, C. J., & O'Rourke-Trigiani, J. (2012). Addressing student mental health needs by providing direct and indirect services in the community. *Professional School Counseling*, *16*, 323–333.

Kaplan, L. S. (1996). Outrageous or legitimate concerns: What some parents are saying about school counseling. *The School Counselor*, *43*, 165–170.

Massachusetts Commission on Gay, Lesbian, Bisexual and Transgender Youth. (2008). Massachusetts high school students and sexual orientation: Results of the 2007 youth risk behavior survey. Retrieved from http://www.mass.gov/cgly/yrbs07.pdf

McFarland, W. P., & Dupuis, M. (2001). The legal duty to protect gay and lesbian students from violence in school. *Professional School Counseling*, *4*, 171–179.

Mullen, P. R., Griffith, C., Greene, J. H., & Lambie, G. W. (2001). Social media and professional school counselors: Ethical and legal considerations. *Journal of School Counseling*, *12*, 1–38.

Office of Special Education and Rehabilitation Services, U.S. Department of Health and Human Services. (1998). Early warning, timely response: A guide to safe schools. Retrieved from http://www.ed.gov/about/offices/list/osers/osep/gtss.html

Remley, T. P., Jr., & Sparkman, L. B. (1993). Student suicides: The counselor's limited legal liability. *The School Counselor*, *40*, 164–169.

Scott, M., Wilcox, H., Huo, Y., Turner, J. B., Fisher, P., & Shaffer, D. (2010). School-based screening for suicide risk: Balancing costs and benefits. *American Journal of Public Health*, *100*, 1648–1652.

Stone, C. (2009). *School counseling principles: Ethics and law* (2nd ed.). Alexandria, VA: American School Counselor Association.

Additional Online Resources

Advocates for Youth: Creating Safe Space for LGBTQ Youth: A Toolkit: http://www.advocatesforyouth.org/index.php?option=com_content&task=view&id=608&Itemid=177.

American Psychological Association: Healthy Lesbian, Gay, and Bisexual Students Project: http://www.apa.org/pi/lgbt/programs/hlgbsp/.

American School Counselor Association: The buzz on bullying: http://www.schoolcounselor.org/school-counselors-members/legal-ethical/legal-ethical-faq.

Cyberbullying Research Center: http://www.cyberbullying.us/.

Gay, Lesbian, and Straight Education Network (GLSEN) Anti-Bullying Resources: http://glsen.org/article/anti-bullying-resources.

It Gets Better Project: http://www.itgetsbetter.org/

Parents, Families and Friends of Lesbians and Gays (PFLAG): http://community.pflag.org/Page.aspx?pid=194&srcid=-2.

Stop cyberbullying: http://www.stopbullying.gov/cyberbullying/.

U.S. Department of Education: Safeguarding student privacy: www2.ed.gov/policy/gen/guid/fpco/ferpa/safeguarding-student-privacy.pdf.

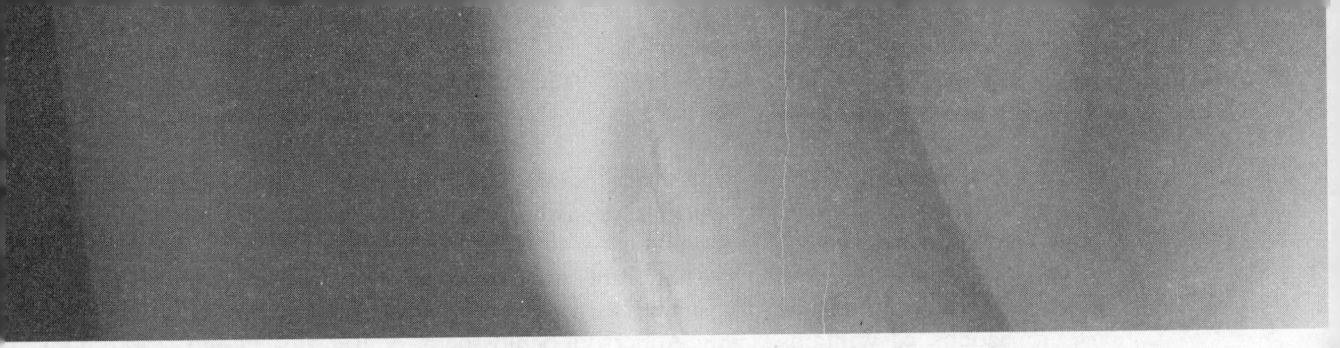

The Ethics of Supervision and Consultation

CHAPTER 14

Modeling Responsible Behavior

A common misperception about supervision is that it is an activity that occupies a small and insignificant proportion of a professional's time and priorities. The reality is that it is an integral part of effective practice for many professionals. Professional psychology has identified it as a core competency for practice (Kaslow, 2004). According to Osipow and Fitzgerald (1986), 64% of counseling psychologists regularly spend time supervising other professionals. In fact, supervision is a job requirement for many psychologists (Sutter, McPherson, & Geesman, 2002) and counselors, and is one of the top five activities in which psychologists engage (Norcross, Hedges, & Castle, 2002). Moreover, the scholarly literature emphasizes the crucial importance of supervision in developing and maintaining professional competence (e.g., see Bernard & Goodyear, 2013; Bradley & Ladany, 2010; Falender & Shafranske, 2004; Falender, Shafranske, & Falicov, 2014; Thomas, 2010). Both ethical and legal guidelines and the practitioners who oversee training clinics view supervised clinical experience as a prerequisite for competence and credentialing, but clinical competence alone is insufficient for supervisory competence (Barnett, Cornish, Goodyear, & Lichtenberg, 2007; Falendar & Shafranske, 2007; Rings, Genuchi, Hall, Angelo, & Cornish, 2009; Thomas, 2010).

Nevertheless, ethics complaints and malpractice claims relating to supervision have been rather common for many years. In 1985, VanHoose and Kottler concluded that negligent supervision was a leading cause in many malpractice suits. More than two decades later, Koocher and Keith-Spiegel (2008) noted that supervisor failure to identify and act on supervisee inadequacies remains the most common cause of ethics complaints against supervisors. Licensing board disciplinary actions frequently include misconduct in supervision along with other violations. In Ohio, approximately 30% of all disciplinary actions involve supervision violations as at least one component of the action (R. Ross, personal communication, June 22, 2011). In addition, some of the most famous malpractice cases in the history of mental health have stemmed at least partly from inadequacies in supervision (e.g., *Tarasoff*, 1974, 1976). In a fascinating argument, Slovenko (1980) proposes that had the supervising mental health professional in the *Tarasoff* case handled his supervisory duties responsibly, the plaintiffs might not have been able to show negligence.

Research also shows that some supervisors disregard their responsibilities to clients, show disdain for supervisee rights, and even exploit them (e.g., see Allen, Szollos, & Williams, 1986; Anderson, Schlossberg, & Rigazio-DiGilio, 2000). One study by Ladany, Lehman-Waterman, Molinaro, and Wolgart (1999) showed that one-third of counseling psychology trainees experienced supervisors who violated one or more guidelines in the standards of the Association for Counselor Education and Supervision (ACES) (1993). One-third of these supervisors failed to honor standards for evaluating and monitoring trainee competence and activities, and nearly one-fifth (17.9%) violated guidelines related to confidentiality, session boundaries, respectful treatment of trainees, and openness to alternative perspectives. Overall, more than half of the supervisors in this study failed to uphold at least one of the ethical standards during the time period examined. In research a decade later, Wall (2009) found a similarly discouraging level of ethical misconduct among supervisors, in many of the same categories. Using a qualitative research design to explore what they bluntly termed "lousy supervision," Magnuson, Wilcoxon, and Norem (2000) identified three broad forms of incompetent supervision. One stems from poor management and organization of supervision, the next from technical and cognitive deficits, and the last from relational or affective deficits. The specific lapses the participants identified ranged from humiliation and intimidation during supervisory sessions to boundary violations with other supervisees and clinical incompetence. Moreover, the negative effects of problematic supervision may linger, according to Ramos-Sanchez et al. (2002), who found a substantial negative impact of the skill development of trainees with negative supervision experiences. For example, trainees with supervisors who interact with them in problematic ways are more likely to avoid disclosing information about their work with clients in supervision (Gross, 2005; Hess et al., 2008) and unlikely to discuss their discomfort with supervision with their supervisors (Mehr, Ladany, & Caskie, 2010). Thus, those who experience deficits in supervision are at greater risk of providing less than optimal service to clients they counsel (Barnett et al., 2007). Supervisors who fail to demonstrate ethical practice are negative role models to trainees and risk "teaching" supervisees that unethical practice is tolerable (Goodyear & Rodolfa, 2012).

Three factors may explain the discrepancy between the desired and actual state of supervision. The first factor is the rather common practice of equating competence as a practitioner with competence as a supervisor. Both the ethics codes and the literature on supervision strongly belie this assumption (Bernard & Goodyear, 2013; Falendar & Shafranske, 2007; Thomas, 2010). Skill and experience as a practitioner is a necessary, but not sufficient, condition for competence in supervision. Later in this chapter, I examine the components of supervisor competency presented in the codes and the literature and identify some of the additional requirements for supervision enacted by state licensing boards.

Second, supervision is a process that involves multiple roles (Bernard & Goodyear, 2013; Johnson, 2007). The supervisor is a teacher, mentor, adviser, consultant, and evaluator to the supervisee, as well as a counselor (from a distance) to the clients of the supervisee. Successfully managing these diverse roles requires knowledge, self-awareness, and experience. Without these characteristics, ethical lapses occur. The following pages elaborate on this issue and provide recommendations for success in this task.

The third and final factor that relates to improper supervision is the inability of the supervisor to place the welfare of the supervisee and the supervisee's clients ahead of his or her own interests. When this happens, supervisees get exploited or neglected. This misconduct ranges from behaviors such as inattention to the supervisees' and clients' needs, to imposition of personal values, to sexual harassment, to financial exploitation. Whatever its particular form, such misbehavior limits the effectiveness of the supervisory experience, compromises the value of the counseling experience to the clients, and sometimes traumatizes the supervisee (Gray, Ladany, Walker, & Ancis, 2001; Nuttgens & Chang, 2013; Orlinsky & Rommestad, 2005; Ramos-Sanchez et al., 2002; Slimp & Burian, 1994). The following pages examine the forms such negligence and exploitation take and ways to minimize that risk. The content of this chapter is drawn not only from scholarly writings and the codes of ethics of the professions, including the *Standards for Counseling Supervisors,* published in 1990 by ACES; the *Approved Supervisor Model* (2007) from the American Association of State Counseling Boards (AASCB); and the Association of State and Provincial Psychology Boards (ASPPB) *Guidelines for the Supervision of Doctoral Level Candidates for Licensure* (2003a) (currently under revision). The chapter also refers to ACES *Best Practices in Counseling Supervision* (2011) and to the competencies identified by doctoral internship training directors (Rings, Genuchi, Hall, Angelo, & Cornish, 2009).

It is important to note that this chapter focuses first on clinical supervision, defined by Bernard and Goodyear (2013) as an evaluative process by which a senior clinician works with a junior clinician over an extended period of time to help the supervisee develop appropriate professional competence while simultaneously protecting the public from any harm that a novice clinician might inflict. Training supervision is the supervisory activity that occurs prior to licensing. Work supervision, the activity of supervising employees who do clinical work at any level, and mandated supervision of disciplined professionals, will be discussed separately since they deal with supervision of those who have already obtained a license and/or supervision of unlicensed individuals, such as psychometricians.

COMPETENCE TO SUPERVISE

To understand the ethical and legal dimensions of competence in supervision, we must retrace our steps to the components of competent practice. As you recall, clinical competence requires knowledge, skill, and diligence in work with clients. Novice professionals are deemed competent after they demonstrate to supervisors and to licensing authorities sufficient levels of these qualities in work with a variety of clients. Supervisors, then, are the final gatekeepers of the profession, who act as the last checkpoint against the admission of unskilled or untherapeutic people into the professional community. The process of determining which novices are competent demands careful and sustained attention to the activities of the supervisee.

Untrained supervisors are likely to have difficulty meeting those demands. When they fail in this ethical duty, they damage the profession, the public, and probably the person inappropriately admitted to the profession.

The ACES *Standards for Counseling Supervisors* (1990) elaborates in great detail the characteristics and competencies of effective supervisors. In this way, the standards provide a road map for professionals who want to assess their supervisory competence. Parallel competencies have been recommended by Falender and Shafranske (2004) for professional psychologists. The competencies are summarized as follows:

- Clinical competence, including skills in assessment and intervention, development of a therapeutic alliance, case conceptualization, record keeping, and evidence-based practice
- Attitudes and traits consistent with the role, such as sensitivity to individual differences, motivation and commitment to supervision, and comfort with the authority accompanying that role
- Familiarity with the ethical, legal, and regulatory dimensions of supervision
- Knowledge of the professional and personal facets of the supervisory relationship and the impact of supervision on the supervisee
- Understanding of the models and methods of supervision and the developmental process of supervisees
- Competence in multicultural supervision, including awareness of the research on the challenges and opportunities therein
- Capacity to evaluate a supervisee's performance fairly and accurately and to provide constructive feedback and plans for remediation of trainee deficits
- Grasp of the rapidly expanding body of theory and research on supervision

Both the length and complexity of this list demonstrate that competence as a practitioner is but a small part of responsible supervision. In light of these standards, the notion that supervisory skills are acquired through "on-the-job training" or by osmosis is misguided. As noted by Pope and Vasquez (2011), competence in this context means that it is as unprofessional to supervise without competence as it is to conduct a neuropsychological assessment or child custody evaluation without demonstrated skill. When researchers (Navin, Beamish, & Johanson, 1995) used the ACES Standards to ascertain the competence of counselors currently in the supervisory role, many fell short, especially of the standard relating to training in supervision. Other research also supports this conclusion (Hess & Hess, 1983; Scott, Ingram, Vitanza, & Smith, 2000). Even supervisees seem unsure of the supervisory training of those who oversee their work. A survey of psychologists by McCarthy, Kulakowski, and Kenfield (1994) found that 72% of the sample felt uncertain about whether their supervisors had training in supervision.

Of course, ethical standards deal with more than objective knowledge and observable skill. They also place considerable emphasis on the attitudes and values of the supervisor, requiring the same kind of diligence in supervisory responsibilities that is expected in direct service. Also embedded in the standards and the other literature on supervision (e.g., Ancis & Ladany, 2010; Falender, Shafranske, & Falicov, 2014; Leong & Wagner, 1994) is a mandate for sensitivity to individual differences and the concerns of culturally diverse supervisees. Research suggests that many counseling supervisors do not appear sensitive to multicultural issues in their interactions with supervisees (Fukuyama, 1994; Ladany et al., 1999) and tend to have less training in multicultural issues than their supervisees (Constantine, 1997). According to Jerrigan, Green, Helms, Perez-Gualdron, and Henze (2010), supervisees report self-doubt and feelings of powerlessness when supervisors fail to competently attend to multicultural issues in supervision. In one recent study, female psychologists and training directors showed significantly greater multicultural competence than staff psychologists and male training directors, but these authors also found a need for ongoing continuing education in multicultural supervision for all supervisors (Gloria, Hird, & Tao, 2008). Yabusaki (2010) recommends that the establishment of collaborative learning environments, appreciation of the supervisee's developmental status, and appropriate mentoring are all important factors to improve the supervision experience of diverse trainees. Falender, Shafranske, and Falicov (2014) have published an excellent resource identifying the specific competencies for multicultural supervision and the strategies to develop and implement competent supervision of diverse populations.

The ACA Code addresses the topic in Section F.2, emphasizing training and continuing education in supervision, and sensitivity to the cultural issues that arise in the supervisory relationship. The section goes on to specify that supervisors must be competent to provide online supervision if they use this medium—a topic that will be discussed in the next section of this chapter.

The APA Code requires competence in supervision (Standard 2.01) and addresses the need for the professional to assign responsibilities to supervisees in appropriate ways and to provide them with proper oversight in Standard 2.04. It is important to note that the Code specifies the responsibilities of supervisors, not just in therapeutic practice but also in teaching, assessment, research, and work with animals.

RESPONSIBLE USE OF SUPERVISORY POWER

Supervision is often an emotionally intense experience for supervisees. They are coping with the heavy emotional demands of clinical work and are in the midst of making important decisions about their professional futures (Falender & Shafranske, 2004; Slimp & Burian, 1994). Moreover, supervisees have limited ability to protect themselves when their supervisors act inappropriately. The supervisory relationship also involves a strong emotional connection between those involved and parallels therapy in some regards. Ladany, Ellis, and Friedlander (1999) emphasize the power of the alliance and the speed with which it is formed (or damaged). Reactions similar to transference and countertransference happen frequently, and supervisors often become aware of the ways in which the personal problems of supervisees affect their functioning with clients (Bernard & Goodyear, 2013). Supervisees also look to their supervisors as models of professional behavior (Vasquez, 1992). As a result, supervisors who act unethically may be "teaching" those under their influence to engage in those behaviors. At the very least, however, supervisors who misuse their influence are losing an opportunity to show less experienced colleagues the proper behavior of a professional. For all these reasons, the person in the supervisory role has substantial power and can use it to help or harm supervisees.

The codes of ethics and guidelines address issues of power and exploitation in broad terms, grouping together many classes of people over whom professionals may have authority. The codes' most specific comments deal with sexual exploitation (ACA Code, Sections F.3b–d, and APA Code, Standards 3.02 and 7.07). Their prohibition of sexual contact or sexual harassment of supervisees is as unequivocal as their prohibition of sexualization of the therapeutic relationship.

Legal prohibitions against sexual exploitation of supervisees are also common. According to Avery and Gressard (2000), 18 states have regulations that prohibit sexual contact between supervisors and trainees. Many other jurisdictions include prohibitions of exploitive relationships with supervisees in their licensing regulations.

Avoiding Unhealthy Dependency

Kurpius, Gibson, Lewis, and Corbet (1991) assert that supervisors who foster an unhealthy dependency on them are also misusing their power. The goal of supervision is not to have the supervisee deferring all judgment to the supervisor, but rather to help the supervisee develop the skills, judgment, and confidence to accurately discriminate when to work independently and when to seek assistance. At first, of course, novice professionals are rather dependent on their supervisors for guidance, reassurance, and practical strategies. This kind of dependence at this stage of development is not problematic. What is problematic is a supervisory style that fails to encourage independence, or worse, actively encourages dependency. Magnuson et al. (2000) found that supervisors who acted in rigid, authoritarian ways and demanded obedience and deference from trainees were often cited as examples of lousy supervisors. Supervisors who are uncertain whether their behavior meets this standard should evaluate it in light of the "clean, well-lit room standard" (Haas & Malouf, 1995) and seek consultation.

Limiting the Number of Supervisees

Responsible use of power in supervision encompasses more than avoiding exploitive behaviors. Four other dimensions exist. One is the responsibility to limit the number of supervisees to a manageable level so that the needs of supervisees and their clients are met. What number of supervisees is manageable? The answer depends on several factors: (1) the competence of the supervisor, (2) the experience and training of the supervisee, (3) the time available for supervision, (4) the client population, and (5) the laws and regulations governing supervision in one's jurisdiction.

In general, when the demands of the population served and the needs of the supervisee are high, and the experience or time availability of the supervisor is low, fewer people should be supervised. Regulatory bodies often set a maximum of three to five supervisees per licensed professional. The Association of State and Provincial Psychology Boards recommends no more than three supervisees per psychologist (ASPPB, 2003b). The model proposed by the American Association of State Counseling Boards (AASCB) (2007) indicates that five should be the maximum number of trainees at any given time. These limits are sensible, given the often intense demands of the supervisory process and the legal dimensions of supervision. (The latter topic will be discussed in subsequent sections of this chapter.) However, those regulations do not imply that it is ethical for all licensed professionals to take on that number of supervisees. Such a judgment should be based on the criteria listed earlier. In some cases, there is no ethical justification for even a single supervisee. Supervisors who tend to accept many supervisees need to examine the advisability of that practice. If supervision is being used as a method of increasing income or professional reputation, then the practice is misguided. The only supportable justifications for multiple supervisees are public need and interest in the development of the supervisees.

Three other aspects of supervision are important to understand the need for limitations on the number of supervisees. First, supervision is typically conducted as a face-to-face activity (ACES, 1993; AASCB, 2007; ASPPB, 2003a), and the supervisor should have the option of face-to-face interaction with clients if necessary. Supervision by mèmo or email is not a substitute for person-to-person contact, though it may be viable as a supplement to direct contact. Nor is a "review of case notes" a viable alternative, although the research by Navin et al. (1995) shows that such a practice has been rather common. The need to arrange meetings puts a practical limit on the number of supervisees. Second, not all states stipulate a maximum number of supervisees for all professions. When such regulatory gaps exist, the determination of a prudent and responsible number of supervisees is left to the individual practitioner. Third, a supervisee cannot shift all the responsibility for decision making about this matter to the supervisor. A supervisee is also responsible for knowing and abiding by the ethical and legal standards governing practice. Thus, any professional is obliged to refuse to accept supervision from someone who has an excessive load of supervisees. In this situation, the counselor needs to make alternative arrangements and, if possible, to tactfully inform the supervisor about the reason for that decision.

Videoconferencing (or any technology that closely approximates the face-to-face interaction) may be an option, provided that the technology is secure and the client/patient gives explicitly permission for the use of electronic communication (ACES, 2011). However, the use of such technology does not mean that additional supervisees would be acceptable. In fact, the use of technology in supervision, may actually be more demanding on supervisor time and attention than the face-to-face format. (More information on the use of technology in supervision follows in later sections of the chapter.)

Responsible use of power also demands that the supervisor respect the trainee's autonomy. One important way to honor this autonomy is through developing informed consent to supervision. It is the responsibility of the supervisor to ensure that the supervisee understands and freely consents to the conditions of supervision. McCarthy, Sugden, Koker, Lamendola, Maurer, and Renninger (1995) identify seven specific topics that the supervisor ought to address in the informed consent process. Supervisees should be instructed, first, about the *purposes of supervision*, that is, to foster their development as competent professionals and to protect the welfare of their clients. Second, they also have a right to know the *qualifications, credentials, style, and theoretical orientation of the supervisor* as consumers of a professional service. Third, they should be briefed about the *logistics* of supervision—times, frequency, emergency procedures, paperwork, and other demands imposed by licensing boards or internship requirements. Supervisors should also provide the name of at least one other professional whom the supervisee might contact in the event that the supervisor was unreachable in a crisis. Fourth, supervisees have a right to understand the *process and procedures* for supervision, including the roles, expectations, and responsibilities of each person. For example, if a supervisor expects a supervisee to prepare for his or her meetings in a particular way, such an expectation should be communicated. Frequently, supervision involves reviewing tape recordings of sessions with clients. In this event, developing informed consent with the client would include explanation of taping procedures and the ways the tapes will be used in supervision.

The fifth and perhaps most crucial of the guidelines suggested by McCarthy and her colleagues states that supervisees should be instructed about the *procedures for evaluating their performance*. This recommendation is supported by the ethics codes (APA, Standard 7.06, and ACA, Sections F.5.a and F.5.b). Evaluation procedures must include provisions for frequent, objective feedback sessions about performance and specific recommendations for remedying deficiencies. Supervisors' evaluation procedures should also aim at building the supervisees' skills in accurate self-evaluation (Bernard & Goodyear, 2013). Supervisees in danger of failing must be informed about this risk immediately. They should also be briefed about the particular areas of deficiency and the level of improvement necessary to remain in good standing (Bernard & Goodyear, 2013). To avoid confusion, written evaluations are essential. As discussed in the opening paragraph of this chapter, many ethics complaints regarding supervision involve violations of these evaluation guidelines. Too often, supervisees misunderstand the role of the supervisors and/or misjudge their progress in supervision. Supervisees have much at stake in the process and have often had little prior experience with individual supervision as a method of evaluation. Consequently, comprehensive attention to this issue is crucial. Allen et al. (1986) found that supervisors judged by psychology interns to be ideal were clear, thorough, and respectful in their evaluation procedures. As Goodyear and Rodolfa (2012) note, because supervisors often feel connected to those they supervise, providing negative evaluations can provoke feelings of dissonance. However, the discomfort associated with negative evaluations does not release the supervisor from this obligation.

The sixth component of informed supervision, according to McCarthy et al., is *instruction in the ethical and legal issues in supervision and practice*. Ethics education in graduate programs tends to focus more on direct service issues than on teaching and supervision concerns (Welfel & Hannigan-Farley, 1996), so supervisors cannot be confident that their supervisees are educated about these topics. Even if the material was discussed in ethics courses, prudent supervisors remind supervisees about ethical and legal standards, providing copies of the codes and guidelines for supervisees to refer to as needed. As mentioned, the ACA Code specifically charges supervisors with the duty to instruct supervisees about the boundaries of their relationship.

Finally (seventh), McCarthy et al. recommend that supervisors use a *written informed consent document* that contains information relevant to each of the six areas just described, for each person to sign as a contract for their work together. This practice protects the legal rights of both parties and also symbolizes the dignity and autonomy of each. It formalizes their mutual commitment to the learning process and the welfare of the clients. McCarthy et al. include a sample contract in the appendix to their article that can serve as a model for others to use. Thomas (2010) also delineates critical components of a supervision contract.

Other scholars recommend documenting each supervisory session, both to improve evaluation of supervisees and to monitor the care given to clients (Falender & Shafranske, 2004; Thomas, 2010). The content of these documents should include five items:

- Date and time for the meeting
- A list of cases discussed
- Notes about client progress
- Recommendations to the supervisee
- Issues for follow-up in future meetings

If the supervisee is having significant difficulty in meeting client needs or learning required concepts, documentation of the meeting should also contain a plan for remedying those deficiencies. These records should be kept in a confidential file, accessible to supervisor and supervisee. Bridge and Bascue (1988) have published a one-page form that efficiently meets these requirements. Thomas's *The Ethics of Supervision and Consultation* (2010) also contains forms for this purpose.

Online Supervision

Much discussion has emerged recently about the viability of online supervision, the circumstance in which the trainee and the supervisor are not meeting in person but via email, chat, or videoconferencing.

Consider the following scenario:

The Case of a Request for Dr. Slane

Dr. Slane is a mental health counselor with extensive experience and considerable training in supervision in counseling adolescents who are making the transition from American Indian reservations to college campuses. He was recently contacted by Ms. Simms, a counseling student in another state, who has the opportunity to begin a predoctoral internship with that population at a large university. However, the program is new and her designated site supervisor has little training or experience with this population. Ms. Simms asks Dr. Slane to act as her supervisor and proposes weekly telephone and email contact along with one in-person contact at the beginning of the semester, to meet supervisory requirements. Dr. Slane is pleased that Ms. Simms contacted him, and he believes he has the expertise she needs to serve this population, but he wonders about the ethics of this arrangement.

In this era of electronic communication and increased disciplinary emphasis on specific supervisor qualifications, such arrangements are likely to become more common. They certainly have advantages. They make a much larger potential pool of qualified supervisors available; they help students obtain the kinds of training experiences they most desire; and they allow more practicum and internship experiences in small agencies and underserved areas. But there are inherent problems. For example, the supervisor in this circumstance has no access to Ms. Simms's clients or their records, and his capacity to intervene in an emergency is limited. Also, as mentioned in Chapter 5, whenever communications via computer are involved, risks to client confidentiality increase, as do the risks of miscommunications in exclusively text-based interactions. For the first time, the 2014 revision of the ACA Code speaks directly to the issue of online supervision in Section E.2.c (Appendix A, p. 510), indicating that only those competent to use such technologies should consider online supervision and that they must be careful about protecting the confidentiality of all communications. The Code does not contain a specific standard for online supervision, though it states in its introduction and in its standards for confidentiality that the same criteria apply to all professional activities using technology. The scholarly literature has also commented on this mode of supervision. Mallen, Vogel, and Rochlen (2005) recommend that if online supervision is to be provided, it ought to continue to emphasize ethical guidelines in use for face-to-face services and those that relate to the unique challenges of online service. They also encourage trainees to be prepared to discuss both client concerns and their own reactions, and for both supervisor and supervisee to keep careful documentation of supervision. They also urge that online supervisors have access to full-length transcripts of supervisee sessions and that both parties be especially vigilant about diagnosis and ongoing assessment of client problems in light of the lack of access to nonverbal clues in some online formats (p. 791). The ethical dilemmas with online supervision arise because, with the exception of videoconferencing and careful review of complete tapes or transcripts of client sessions, the supervisor is completely dependent on the judgment and the accuracy of the trainee description of relevant content from client sessions. Of course, such reliance on supervisee judgment is not unique to online supervision—in-person supervisors often leave the topics of supervisory sessions to the discretion of the supervisee. However, in face-to-face supervision, the supervisor has more complete access to the trainee's nonverbal reactions, and the trainee is aware that the supervisor has access to client files and to meetings with the client as needed. Such direct access to client files and sessions is a major concern with online supervision, even if it includes videoconferencing. Consequently, my view is that online supervision that does not include video ought to be a supplement to face-to-face supervision, not a substitute for it. The ACES (2011) best practice guidelines are also consistent with this view. In Ms. Simms's case, she could develop a joint supervision arrangement in which Dr. Slane and her site supervisor collaborate in her training so that she gains access to the unique expertise of Dr. Slane and has the close supervision only her onsite supervisor can supply.

A few studies have been conducted comparing trainees' experiences in online and face-to-face supervision. Nelson, Nichter, and Henriksen (2010), for example, found in a small group qualitative study that both groups were satisfied with the supervision, and both were able to build trust in the process, though technology problems were a continuing frustration for the online supervision group. In another small group comparison of online and in-person supervision, Lenz, Oliver, and Nelson (2011) found that while students felt rapport and support and expressed some very positive feelings about the online experience, the authors also found that online supervision produced less focus on the cases that the supervisees were working with, a rather unsettling outcome. Obviously, more research is needed to identify the strengths, limitations, and ethical challenges of online supervision.

It is important to note that as states and provinces begin to regulate online counseling and therapy, they are also attending to online supervision. Most, but not all, state rules relating to the practice of telemental health also include reference to online supervision (McAdams & Wyatt, 2010). Here is the language for Ohio, "*Telepsychology* means the practice of psychology or school psychology as those terms are defined in divisions (B) and (E) of Section 4732.01of the Revised Code, including psychological and school psychological supervision, by distance communication technology such as but not necessarily limited to telephone, email, Internet-based communications, and videoconferencing" (Ohio Board of Psychology (2011).

Consider the following case:

The Case of Julian and the Smartphone

Julian is a "digital native" who sends and receives hundreds of texts each day on his smartphone. He is currently a doctoral intern in a community mental health center. He has started to text his clinical supervisor after sessions with clients whom he and his supervisor discussed in the last supervision meeting. Julian uses the texts to give his supervisor summaries of how the plans they developed worked in these sessions. Julian finds this activity very helpful, and he believes it makes the supervisory sessions more productive and the work with the clients more effective. His supervisor, Marla, is a bit uncomfortable with this mode of communication, even though Justin does not use full names in the content of the texts, and she wonders if it should continue.

There are several possible risks to Julian's practice. The first is that text messages tend to be less secure than other modes of electronic communication. These messages also stay on a person's phone until erased. Secondly, there is a question about whether any content related to client treatment is legally required to be in the formal record under HIPAA regulations. Third, a clinician in a health care setting may be at risk if he or she fails to follow the recommendations of the Joint Commission regarding texting about health care matters. General texts related to the degree of learning that Julian is experiencing, for example, "Just had a successful counseling session that I am eager to discuss with you," or were questions related to logistics, such as, "Can we meet at 10 instead of 11 tomorrow?" These texts are not legally or ethically problematic. Explicit informed consent is required for all such communications, whether regarding simple logistics or more substantive matters. In this digital era, all supervisors should anticipate the possibility of this kind of use of messaging and should develop policy about it, to be discussed with supervisees at the initiation of the supervisory relationship. An example of such a policy for client contact is found in the American Psychological Association Insurance Trust (APAIT) sample policy http://www.apait.org/apait/applications/SampleElectronicCommunicationPolicy.doc.pdf.

MULTICULTURAL SUPERVISION

It goes without saying that supervisors must be sensitive to issues of diversity. At the very least, the supervisor is obligated to avoid actions that reflect gender, ethnic, age, religious, or sexual orientation bias but they must go beyond that. The ACA Code succinctly states in Section F.2.b, "Counseling supervisors are aware of and address the role of multiculturalism/diversity in the supervisory relationship."*

Unfortunately, research shows that insensitivity about these issues is not unknown. The problem has existed for decades. In the Allen et al. (1986) study, such behaviors were a major factor in earning counselors the designation "worst supervisor." Even well-intentioned supervisors can exhibit inappropriate behaviors. Williams and Halgin (1995) point out that in the hope of fostering congenial relationships, European American supervisors of African American supervisees often avoid discussing their racial difference. That avoidance is likely to have the opposite impact. Similarly, these scholars suggest that supervisors sometimes show insensitivity to the impact of their power over African American supervisees. They fail to understand the supervisees' level of discomfort with the one-down position in a society that has so often discriminated against their race. It is interesting to note that in one of the few empirical studies of cross-cultural supervision, Vander Kolk (1974) found that at the start of the supervision experience, African American students anticipated less acceptance and empathy from their supervisors than did their European American counterparts. The research of Cook and Helms (1988) and of McRoy, Freeman, Logan, and Blackmon (1986) offers similar findings, suggesting that ethnically and culturally diverse supervisees begin the supervisory relationship with a more guarded and distant attitude toward European American supervisors.

In parallel fashion, supervisors can hold different objectives or behaviors unfairly based on the age, gender, religion, sexual orientation, or cultural background of supervisees. They may even discriminate on the basis of these factors in accepting students to supervise. Again, Allen et al. (1986) found that students who encountered supervisors who acted in these ways labeled those professionals as bad supervisors.

It is important to keep in mind that culturally insensitive behaviors can also be directed at ethnically diverse supervisors by trainees and other professionals. Murphy-Shigematsu (2010) identifies several sources of racial microaggressions against diverse supervisors and suggests that supervisors examine how those micro-aggressions may benefit or impede their approach to supervision.

Bernard and Goodyear (2013) offer some suggestions for minimizing these problems. First, supervisors must reject the "myth of sameness" and acknowledge the reality and contributions of cultural diversity. Second, they must understand that

*Source: Reprinted with permission from American Counseling Association.

their own views of the world may not be shared by their supervisees and that this difference does not represent a deficiency in anyone. Third, they encourage supervisors to devote the same energy to appreciating cultural diversity in supervision as they may use in understanding how cultural diversity affects therapy relationships. They must also be committed to self-monitoring their own behavior and to developing the knowledge and skills required for effective cross-cultural supervision. Vasquez (1992) offers another valuable recommendation: Supervisors of culturally diverse professionals ought to become familiar with the special challenges inherent in integrating ethnic identity with professional identity. See the January 2013 issue of *The Counseling Psychologist* for a series of articles offering additional recommendations for effective multicultural supervision based on competency benchmarks and on research with diverse supervisees.

Other Personal Values and Beliefs

Supervisors also need to be aware of the ways in which other personal beliefs and values may affect the supervisory process, as identified in Section A.4.b of the ACA Code, and in Standard 3.04 Avoiding Harm, and Standard 3.08 Exploitative Relationships in the APA Code. Because of the limited power of the supervisee, the person in authority must be able to separate professional from personal beliefs and values and to use only the former in teaching and evaluating the supervisee. Consider the following situation:

The Case of Dr. Ziblinsky's Dilemma

Dr. Ziblinsky supervises two predoctoral interns at a college counseling center. She also serves on the board of directors of the Planned Parenthood agency in her community. One of her interns, Mr. Appleton, is an active participant in the local right-to-life group. Dr. Ziblinsky learns of Mr. Appleton's involvement in that organization a few months into the internship. Soon thereafter, she begins assigning female clients to the other intern, in the belief that Mr. Appleton's personal values would prevent him from effectively counseling female students about reproductive issues. Dr. Ziblinsky also finds herself being more businesslike and task oriented with Mr. Appleton than with the other intern. When Mr. Appleton realizes what is happening, he asks for a meeting with her to discuss the matter. In that meeting, Dr. Ziblinsky defends her decision, arguing that it is in the best interests of the students who seek counseling at the center.

In this scenario, Dr. Ziblinsky has failed to distinguish personal from professional belief. She has allowed her own strong beliefs about reproductive issues to inappropriately influence her professional judgment about a supervisee. She is preventing Mr. Appleton from seeing female clients based on speculation rather than on any evidence that he intends to impose his beliefs on clients. Thus, this supervisor acted unethically. First, the frequency with which female clients seek counseling about an unexpected pregnancy is rather low. It certainly happens, but most female clients have other issues. To eliminate all female clients from his calendar is an overreaction to a relatively low-probability event. Second, even if a client does present with an unexpected pregnancy, Dr. Ziblinsky has no evidence that her intern will attempt to impose his personal beliefs on that client. Mr. Appleton may have already thought through this issue and decided on a strategy to refer the client to another counselor under this circumstance. In addition, Dr. Ziblinsky is violating professional standards insofar as she is allowing her disdain for this intern's personal beliefs to affect her behavior in supervision. She has begun a pattern of treating Mr. Appleton differently from the other intern. This is discrimination based on a characteristic that has not shown any relevance to his competence as a professional. The intern also needs to have broad training. Preventing him from counseling women limits his training and his competence. Such limits should be imposed only when justified by evidence of incompetence or misconduct. Then she further complicates her ethical error by failing to recognize the problem when her intern speaks to her about it. The supervisor has thereby missed an opportunity to change her behavior to comply with her duty to this student. In short, in the name of doing what she believes to be the right thing for women with unexpected pregnancies, she has failed to act responsibly. Her initial motivation was not self-interested because she did not personally profit in any way from her decision, but it was self-absorbed and inattentive to her duties to the intern. If she continues her current behavior, Dr. Ziblinsky will violate all five ethical principles—beneficence, nonmaleficence, justice, fidelity, and respect for autonomy.

When faced with such issues in supervision, supervisors ought to ask themselves the following questions:

- Is this belief or value truly relevant to professional behavior?
- Am I treating supervisees or their clients unfairly by my actions?
- Am I fostering the growth of the supervisee by this action?
- Would objective colleagues be likely to come to the same conclusion?
- What alternative courses of action may better comply with professional standards?
- Will consultation or therapy assist me in meeting my supervisory obligations?
- If I have already acted in inappropriate ways, how can I undo or minimize the harm that has been done?

Supervisors are also obliged to respect differences in theoretical orientation. Failure to respect theoretical differences implies that one already has "the truth" about effective therapy. Such an attitude is not only disrespectful of the autonomy of others; it is also inconsistent with scientific evidence. No research shows that one theoretical approach to counseling is superior to all the others. Thus supervisors ought not to criticize supervisees for using alternative approaches as long as the intern is competent and can show the relevance of the approach to a client's problem. If a supervisor has a strong investment in a particular theory or method, that investment should be made known to the supervisee before the relationship begins so that he or she can make an informed decision about whether to engage in this supervisory relationship. Of course, if a supervisee is using an approach that one believes will be counterproductive or ineffective, then the supervisor is obligated to suggest alternatives. The encouragement of alternative strategies should be based on objective analysis rather than on personal preferences or overidentification with a theory.

RESPONSIBILITIES FOR CLIENT WELFARE

Supervisors have ultimate legal and ethical responsibility for the welfare of their supervisees' clients. When supervisors have competent, diligent supervisees who foster the welfare of their clients, there is little conflict between their obligations to both parties. However, when supervisees act in ways that do not positively affect the well-being of clients, supervisors feel conflicting obligations. On the one hand, they must help supervisees overcome problems so that they can continue to develop as professionals. If a supervisor intervened with every mistake, supervisees would not be able to improve their skills, and if high levels of competence were established for novice professionals to work with clients, very few would attain the standard. On the other hand, supervisors must protect the welfare of the client from inept care. How can a supervisor meet both these obligations? The ACES guidelines are helpful in this regard. They establish that both are important duties, but that the supervisor's first responsibility is to the client. The duty to the supervisee's development as a professional is secondary. The ACA Code reiterates that message in its opening standard, A.1.a, placing client welfare as the highest priority.

The APA Code uses a wider lens in viewing the issue, grouping together the obligations of psychologists to act with concern for the welfare of all parties with whom they interact in its statements in Principle E: Respect for People's Rights and Dignity (Appendix B, p. 537).

The best remedy for the problem, of course, is prevention. Supervisors must thoroughly assess the skills of the supervisee at the beginning of the experience and must assiduously monitor changes. Trainees should be carefully supervised so that errors can be prevented or minimized when they occur. The complexity of cases they are given should match their prior training and experience, and the clients they serve should understand the nature of the counseling they are receiving and the recourse they have if dissatisfied. None of these responsibilities can be met with a laissez-faire style of supervision. Supervisors should be guided by the goal of maximizing student learning without risking client welfare.

Vasquez (1992) notes that interns and others under supervision sometimes suffer distress that impairs their functioning in the professional role. They are not immune from the problems that can afflict other professionals—substance abuse, major mental illness, grief, loneliness, or marital dissatisfaction. Thus she recommends that supervisors be alert for such difficulties and intervene as soon as such problems begin to compromise a supervisee's work. The ACA Code and the ACES document (1993) support this recommendation (ACA, Section F.3; ACES, Section 2.12). Lamb, Cochran, and Jackson (1991) have defined trainee competence problems more broadly, to encompass two other characteristics. One is an unwillingness to comply with professional ethical standards, and the second is an inability to meet minimum criteria for competence. Regardless of the scope of an individual supervisor's definition of problematic competence (formerly termed *impairment*), it is clear that supervisors are obliged to monitor supervisee progress and intervene when meaningful deficits occur to protect client welfare and to facilitate supervisee development. Lamb et al. (1991) have offered a comprehensive set of guidelines to aid in identifying and remedying intern impairment. These guidelines emphasize the importance of frequent communication among supervisors, regular feedback meetings with supervisees, and formal procedures for responding to impairment when other efforts are insufficient. When such interventions are unsuccessful, probation or dismissal may become necessary. (See McAdams, Foster, and Ward [2007] for a discussion of legal and ethical issues in dismissing students from academic programs for non-academic reasons.) The recent competency movement in professional psychology also offers a detailed set of recommendations for supervisors and training directors to promote competent professional practice and to intervene when problems arise (Kaslow, Rubin, Forrest, et al., 2007).

The responsibility of the supervisor to the client extends to two other areas. First, the supervisor is bound to oversee the confidentiality of client disclosures and records. This duty behooves supervisors to educate and monitor those they oversee regarding confidentiality standards and procedures. It also means that they make sure clients have been informed about and consented to the supervisee's communications with the supervisor. In Ohio, the standard is even stricter for psychologists in training. A disclosure statement is required to ensure that clients understand that they are being served by a trainee and may have access to the supervisor if they so request. This document must be signed by the trainee, the supervisor, and the client, and a copy given to the client (Ohio Administrative Code Section 4732-13-04).

Second, when sessions are to be recorded or observed, supervisors should ascertain that clients have agreed to the practice and understand how the recordings will be used. They also monitor the care supervisees take over the confidentiality of those recordings. If a client refuses consent, the supervisor must judge whether the supervisee is capable of providing competent service in the absence of such monitoring. If the supervisor concludes that recording is essential for competent service or is a requirement for the supervisee, he or she must help the supervisee communicate that to clients and obtain alternative care. Prudent supervisors guard the client's right to autonomy about recording and recognize the obligation of the institution to provide competent, beneficial service to that client. Clients should also understand that they may withdraw consent for recording at any time. If a person is not legally competent to give consent, a parent or guardian must provide consent for recording. Client assent is still essential, however.

BOUNDARY ISSUES

Sexual exploitation is not the only form of boundary violation to which supervisors are vulnerable. Because of the close, collegial nature of supervisory relationships, those in authority can lose track of the evaluative aspect of those relationships and begin to see supervisees as friends or fully qualified colleagues. If you recall the case of Yolanda from Chapter 2, she was at risk for entering a multiple relationship with her supervisee when she wanted to invite her to join her in social and community activities. Because the boundaries between supervisee and supervisor can get blurred even more easily than boundaries in other professional relationships, professionals must be vigilant about monitoring their behavior and should set clear limits. The codes do not absolutely forbid social or business relationships with supervisees, but they caution against them. The responsibility to place client welfare ahead of the supervisee's experience means that the supervisor must be able to clearly see what is happening with the client and have the energy to intervene when needed. Social or business relationships compromise that capacity. In a multiple relationship, professionals can come to prize their friendship or financial connection to the supervisee more than they value a client's welfare. When in doubt about the ethics of a particular relationship, the supervisor should consult with colleagues for guidance. Supervisors should also note that the ACA Code is clear on one point: multiple relationships that compromise the objectivity of the supervisor or that exploit the supervisee are unethical (ACA Code, F.3.a.). The 2014 revision of the ACA Code has written new language in regard to multiple relationships with supervisees, paralleling the revisions in the section on multiple relationships with clients. Here is the exact wording:

ACA Code of Ethics

F.3.a Extending Conventional Supervisory Relationships

Counseling supervisors clearly define and maintain ethical professional, personal, and social relationships with their supervisees. Supervisors consider the risks and benefits of extending current supervisory relationships in any form beyond conventional parameters. In extending these boundaries, supervisors take appropriate professional precautions to ensure that judgment is not impaired and that no harm occurs.

Source: Reprinted with permission from American Counseling Association.

This section makes clear that while boundary crossings are not prohibited, they must be carefully considered and monitored so that they do not have negative effects on the supervisee or supervisory experience. The section also requires counselor supervisors to clearly define the professional relationship, with the implication that the nature of the relationship between supervisor and supervisee should be clear to both parties. In section F.3.d, the Code goes on to indicate that counselors may not undertake supervisory relationships with their individuals with whom they have an inability to remain objective. Since this section is entitled "Friends or family members," the implication is that it would apply most directly to those individuals. Of course, the Code clearly prohibits sexual contact with supervisees and sexual harassment of them (Section F.3.b–c).

Unfortunately, research suggests that boundary violations occur rather frequently. For instance, Navin et al. (1995) reported that 25% of their sample of field supervisors was aware of social interactions between supervisors and trainees that they viewed as incompatible with the supervisors' duties.

Supervisors have sometimes taken on the role of counselor or therapist for those they supervise. In a survey of mental health professionals at college counseling centers, Sherry et al. (1991) found that 48% of respondents admitted such behavior at least on rare occasions. Of these, 3% acknowledged treating supervisees at least fairly often. The therapy-like nature of supervision makes this role slippage understandable, but rarely ethical (Goodyear & Rodolfa, 2012). Whiston and Emerson (1989) identify several specific problems with this practice. First, it can compromise a supervisor's objectivity about both the supervisee and the client and thereby interfere with one's duty to both. In addition, it diminishes the capacity of supervisors to carry out their responsibility to the profession and the public to act as gatekeeper against admitting ineffective individuals into the profession. Second, the client/supervisee is more vulnerable to a supervisor's misuse of power and is likely to be confused about which rules apply when. A supervisee might be reluctant to reveal personal information in counseling, fearing its impact on supervision. Moreover, Whiston and Emerson point out that when such a relationship is occurring, another violation must have preceded it—a failure of informed consent. Finally, if there are any group supervision activities occurring, a nonprofessional relationship with one supervisee complicates the process of group supervision. If other group members know of the counseling activity, they may be uncomfortable and fail to take full advantage of the experience. Similarly, the supervisee in the relationship may have worries about the confidentiality of counseling information and about the way he or she will be evaluated in the supervision.

The wording of the ACA Code suggests that the profession finds that reasoning cogent, prohibiting supervisors from providing counseling to current supervisees in Section F.6.c and clarifying that supervisee personal issues allowed to be covered in supervision only when they impact services to clients. The APA Code expresses a similar sentiment in Standard 3.05 Multiple Relationships and in Standard 7.04 Student Disclosure of Personal Information (Appendix B, p. 549).

Unfortunately, many practitioners seem oblivious to the ethical implications of counseling supervisees. In 1987, 13% of psychologists labeled this practice as ethical (Pope et al., 1987). Four years later, Gibson and Pope (1993) found that 44% of the counselors participating in their survey endorsed this view. However, a later survey indicated a shift in this view, with mental health professionals from a variety of professions ranking providing therapy to a student or supervisee as more unethical (Pomerantz, Ross, Gfeller, & Hughes, 1998).

At first glance, avoiding a counseling component of supervision seems inconsistent with the recommendation to monitor the effect of supervisees' personal problems on their work. However, ethics scholars provide a reasonable resolution of the dilemma. The bedrock of their scholarship is recognition of the limits on the depth and breadth of exploration of personal issues in supervision. Whiston and Emerson (1989) offer guidelines for distinguishing supervision from counseling. First, as the ACES guidelines also advise (Section 2.11), any discussion of personal issues should focus on their relationship to professional development. Personal issues that appear irrelevant to professional functioning have no place in a supervisory discussion. Second, the function of the supervisor is to *identify* personal problems that may be inhibiting the supervisee's performance, not to *resolve* those issues. The latter is the task of a counselor or therapist with no conflicting role obligations, to whom the supervisor may refer the supervisee. Third, when supervisees reveal personal matters in connection with a case discussion, supervisors should respond with basic empathy and understanding of the issue but should refrain from interpretations or comments that would make deep exploration of personal matters more likely. Supervisors ought not to act in a cold and unfeeling way in response to such supervisee disclosures, however. Supervisor warmth is a highly valued quality among interns and facilitates their development (Allen et al., 1986). Thus, supervisors should show compassion and concern but refrain from moving into deeper therapeutic territory. Moreover, supervisees who are informed about the distinction between therapy and supervision are better able to respect the boundaries between those two activities and to understand the meaning of supervisors' responses to personal issues. For example, if a supervisee reveals that he is distracted by news that his parent has been diagnosed with a stage IV cancer, a supervisor may discuss the matter with him, show sympathy, and ask whether there is any way in which she can be of assistance. None of those actions involves deep probing into personal issues. (See Neufeldt and Nelson [1999] for a fuller discussion of this issue.)

What if students do not request counseling or seem unaware of the need for it? Wise, Lowery, and Silverglade (1989) suggest that students' capacity to respond to a supervisor's recommendation to seek counseling may be related to their stage of professional development and trust of the supervisor. They suggest that students who have moved beyond their initial fears of incompetence and now focus on specific counseling techniques are more likely to be receptive to such advice.

Layered Supervision

To become a competent supervisor, one must have supervised experience in supervision as well as academic training. Graduate programs often provide clinical experience in supervision to advanced students by having them oversee the work of beginning students (Scott et al, 2000). Doctoral students commonly supervise master's-level students, for example. In the long run, this practice benefits the profession, the public, and the supervisees. However, it also raises difficulties. For example, when there are several layers of supervision, the professionals who have the ultimate responsibility for the client find more distance between them and the client. Their sense of the client's progress is obscured. They must develop careful and consistent data-gathering methods to overcome this weakness. Second, they have responsibilities for the learning of not one, but two supervisees, whose needs, skills, and attitudes may vary significantly. Third, supervisors must be especially alert for compromised confidentiality of client disclosures and violations of client autonomy rights. The more people who hold confidential information, the more likely those inadvertent breaches will occur. Fourth, when supervision is layered, the responsibility for client welfare may be diffused and problems may be missed because each professional assumes another was responsible. The supervisor at the top layer must guard against such a diffusion of responsibility. Finally, as Herlihy and Corey (2014) note, even when layered supervision is carried out within the boundaries of the ethical standards, the experience of being supervised by other students can be uncomfortable. Thus supervisors need to appreciate this discomfort and keep discussion lines open so that those who are ill at ease with the arrangement feel they may voice their concerns and get them resolved.

LEGAL ASPECTS OF SUPERVISION

Two kinds of legal issues are of special concern to mental health professionals involved in supervision: (1) the liability of supervisors for both their own actions and the actions of supervisees and (2) the legal rights of professionals under supervision.

Liability Issues

The most important legal issue in supervision relates to the degree of liability a supervisor bears for the actions of supervisees. To understand the liability issues, one must begin with the nature of the service a client has a right to expect when working with a supervisee. As Harrar et al. (1990) point out so perceptively, when a client agrees to such counseling, he or she is *not* consenting to substandard or harmful care. The contract implicit in that consent is for the service providers to give competent and helpful service. When that does not occur, clients have been wronged, and it is their right to seek redress. Thus, supervisors are liable for their own actions *and* for the negligent acts of those they supervise. Harrar et al. define the first kind of liability as *direct liability*. It parallels the liability any practicing mental health professional would have in relation to negligence in his or her work. In other words, this form of liability holds when the harm to the client occurred at least partly because the supervisor failed to conduct supervision in accordance with ethical and legal standards. Supervisors may be directly liable under a variety of circumstances, including, but not limited to, the following: failing to meet with supervisees, neglecting important client information that supervisees share with them, neglecting to keep records of supervision, or assigning clients to supervisees who are inadequately trained to deal with the clients' concerns. Since trainees often are unsure about what must be disclosed to supervisors, Thomas (2010) recommends that supervisors specify that all of the following be immediately communicated: (1) disputes with clients; (2) allegations of unethical behavior by supervisees; (3) threats of a lawsuit or complaint; (4) suicidal attempts, history, or threats, along with threats of violence toward others; and (5) deviations from standard practice.

Vicarious liability also exists for supervisors. The Latin term associated with this concept is *respondeat superior*, and it means, "Let the master respond." It means that supervisors may be held liable for the actions of their supervisees even when the supervisors have not been negligent in carrying out their supervisory duties. The rationale behind this principle is based on the influence supervisors have over trainees and their ability to know what is happening in sessions supervisees are conducting. Vicarious liability applies only to actions "within the course and scope of the supervisory relationship" (Disney & Stephens, 1994, p. 15) and is tempered by other factors such as the extent of the supervisor's power over the subordinate, the part of the service in which the negligence occurred, the circumstances of the actions, the motivation of the supervisee, and the likelihood that the supervisor could have reasonably predicted the supervisee's action. Vicarious liability also assumes that the subordinate has voluntarily chosen to be under the supervisor's guidance and direction (Harrar, VandeCreek, & Knapp, 1990). In short, even exemplary supervisory behavior does not entirely eliminate the risk of vicarious liability, though it certainly reduces the risk. Vicarious liability might occur if a supervisee provides incompetent service to a client but has withheld relevant information about the course of treatment from the supervisor. A supervisor might also be held liable, for example, if a supervisee disclosed confidential information to someone outside the workplace.

Given these facts, one may wonder why mental health professionals agree to take on the responsibilities of supervision in the first place. Are they ignorant of the liability issues? Do they value supervision so much that they willingly accept the risk? Do they act grudgingly, feeling there is little alternative? Based on the available evidence, ignorance of this legal standard probably is the most significant factor, but no definitive research exists on that issue. Regardless, supervision is vital to the future of the profession and the provision of quality services to the public. Competent professionals, then, must find ways to minimize their risk. Bernard and Goodyear (2013) recommend that supervisors establish an open, trusting relationship with supervisees so that supervisees are willing to discuss all aspects of their work with clients in supervisory sessions. I would add to that a requirement that supervisees record counseling sessions so that supervisors can hear or see exactly what has transpired in session. Even though supervisors may not have the time to review a complete recording of every supervisee session, as long as a recording exists, the option is available if needed. Moreover, recordings encourage supervisees to share more fully with supervisors in their discussions, as they recognize that supervisors may well learn about the events in counseling through the recording. A comprehensive orientation to the supervision experience that focuses on ethical and legal issues and allows the supervisor to carefully assess supervisee strengths and weaknesses may also reduce the likelihood of subordinate misconduct or client disservice. Finally, Bernard and Goodyear encourage professionals to stay current with legal developments that may affect them and to take special care in documenting supervision when supervisees are acting incompetently. A good record of supervision will at least minimize direct liability. Liability insurance for supervisors is also in order. It does not prevent problems, but it may reassure professionals that their financial resources are not vulnerable to a lawsuit.

Due Process Rights of Supervisees

When working in public institutions, supervisees have the same due process rights against unfair government action as do other citizens. These rights derive from the Fourteenth Amendment to the U.S. Constitution and prevent states from taking actions against individuals without giving them notice and opportunity to oppose such action. Those who work for private organizations have due process rights if the policies and procedures of the organization stipulate them. Many private universities, hospitals, and community agencies recognize this right. Applied to supervision, this means that the supervisee has a legal right to supervisory feedback, periodic evaluations, and opportunities to file grievances about actions they think have been unfair. Bernard and Goodyear (2013) argue that some of the most egregious violations of trainees' due process rights occur when they receive negative final evaluations without any prior warning that their performance is significantly substandard. To avoid such violations, they advise professionals to periodically communicate negative performance evaluations in specific terms that include the changes needed that would deem adequate performance. Such an action prevents misunderstanding about how much improvement is sufficient for success. Due process rights are meant to protect supervisees from arbitrary action based on incomplete, irrelevant, or untrue evidence. Such rights do not mean that all supervisees have the right to a passing grade or a positive evaluation; the duty of the supervisor is also to protect the public from incompetent professionals. Instead, due process suggests that supervisors must be sensitive to the implications of negative findings on those they oversee and must ensure that negative judgments are fair and appropriate.

Guest and Dooley (1999) discuss the issue of whether supervisors can be held liable for actions toward supervisees that do not directly harm clients. Can they be sued for malpractice if they failed a student without prior warning, made disrespectful statements about a student, or insisted upon doing therapy with a supervisee? These scholars argue that a duty of care probably exists and that a supervisee may be able to meet the other standards for a successful malpractice suit based on such actions. Bernard and Goodyear (2013) point out, however, that no such lawsuits have been brought to court to date.

RELATIONSHIPS WITH THIRD-PARTY PAYERS

Frequently, clients of unlicensed supervisees are submitting the costs of their care for reimbursement by insurers, who, before providing payment, typically require evidence that the supervisee is supervised by a licensed mental health professional. Some unscrupulous supervisors have used this mechanism to increase their incomes. The most egregious cases have involved supervisors overseeing the work of dozens of supervisees and submitting the claims as though they themselves had provided the service (Harrar et al., 1990). As already mentioned, supervision under these conditions fails to meet the standard for competent oversight and thereby violates ethical rules. If it also deceives the third-party payer about the nature of the service provided, the practice is likely to be illegal, too, as a form of insurance fraud. Neither private insurers nor government agencies allow this behavior. In fact, they have aggressively pursued legal action against serious violators. For all these reasons, supervisors are cautioned to be exceedingly cautious about practices that may be inconsistent with guidelines and contracts, and to educate those they oversee about the proper methods for submitting claims.

Work Supervision

In the course of their careers, mental health professionals from many disciplines take on the role of clinical supervisor of other licensed workers employed by the same agency or institution. They may also supervise employees who do not have any professional license, such as case managers or psychometricians. The ethical duties of professionals in these positions parallel those of training supervisors in many ways. They are responsible to ensure that clients receive competent care and employees are given appropriate rights and responsibilities. One of the challenges of work supervision is monitoring the work of those whom they oversee when the needs of the organization exert pressure to provide services. Another is managing boundaries effectively since co-workers can often become friends. In each of these circumstances, the supervisor must work diligently to understand the role, to advocate so that supervisees have appropriate work duties, and to honor the boundaries between supervisor and supervisee. The standards of the codes of ethics related to supervision apply to work supervision as much as to training supervision. It is important, as well, for work supervisors to be familiar with regulations of licensing boards, because boards frequently enact regulations governing supervision of unlicensed personnel.

Mandated Supervision

A third type of supervision exists. Mandated supervision occurs when a licensing board, employer, or ethics committee of a professional association requires professionals to have all or some portion of their work supervised because of a violation. Its goal is to ensure that the violation does not recur and to rehabilitate the professional so that he or she can again undertake independent practice (Thomas, 2010). In these situations, the supervisor is confronted with both clinical and ethical challenges, a few of which overlap with the challenges of court-mandated counseling. The supervisor not only has responsibilities to the clients of the disciplined professionals and to the professional but also to the board or organization that arranged for the supervision. Consequently, practicing responsibly in mandated supervision requires substantial skill as a supervisor in order to establish a productive supervisory alliance with the professional that also allows for communication with third parties; set reasonable goals and methods of evaluation of the professional's work; and be committed to the protection of clients, even if that means reporting continued problems to the mandating party. For a fuller discussion of mandated supervision, see Thomas (2010).

CONSULTATION

Consultation comes in many forms. Sometimes it refers to the meeting of two or more licensed counselors or therapists to get feedback on complicated cases or to simply ensure that the care they offer is fully competent. Such consultation is usually termed *clinical consultation*, and it is a voluntary process in nearly all cases. Clinical consultation can be an ongoing process in which the professionals meet regularly, or it can be an event that happens only when an urgent client issue emerges. The latter is common when a client may be at risk of harming others. At other times, it involves consultation with other professionals—teachers, administrators, faculty in higher education—regarding concerns they have about the individuals with whom they work. A teacher, for example, may ask for a consultation to help with managing the behaviors of children with ADHD, or a university faculty member may seek the advice of the counseling center staff about intervening with a disruptive student. Consultation in these circumstances is usually dyadic and often occurs between professionals employed in the same institution. In educational circles, it is sometimes referred to as *collaboration* rather than consultation. The task is to help the other professional identify the source of the problem or confusion, develop a strategy for intervention, and create ways to evaluate the outcomes of the strategy. Sometimes the consultation is a legal or ethical consultation. In that situation, the consultant helps the consultee go through an ethical or legal decision-making process. What distinguishes consultation from supervision in these cases is the equality of the participants in the process. Both are licensed to practice—one is seeking the specific expertise of the other. (See Thomas [2010] for an excellent review of ethical issues in clinical consultation.)

The other major type of consultation is organizational consultation. These consultation relationships are triadic rather than dyadic (Brown, Pryzwansky, & Schulte, 2011) and include the consultant, the consultee, and the client. For example, a business may hire a psychologist to help the president of the company understand why morale and productivity are low and develop a plan for improvement. In this case, the consultant is the psychologist, the consultee is the company executive, and the client is the group of employees. With this type of consulting, the client does not hire the consultant, shape the consultant's responsibilities, or sometimes even know a consultation is underway. Yet, ultimately, consultants influence the client system and are responsible for their effects on that system. Mental health professionals who are not attuned to the implications of their work in this type of consultation can violate the rights of the clients and impair the ways in which the system impacts them. For example, the director of a large mental health agency may contract with a consultant to help increase the staff's productivity and generate more revenue for the agency. The impact of the consultant's work will be felt not only by the staff but also by the clients whom the agency serves. In some ways, both staff and consumers are part of the client system, although they had no voice in deciding whether to hire a consultant or in setting the initial goals for the arrangement. Yet both groups may experience the greatest impact of any recommendations implemented after the consultation. Newman (1993) cautions consultants to stay aware of all three participant groups in consultation, to be sensitive to the effects of their work on all parties, and to avoid situations in which their work may be used to the detriment of the client system. A wise consultant seeks to involve all parties in designing a consultation agreement at the earliest possible stage. Such involvement not only shows respect for client rights, but it also improves the chances of the project's success and helps identify related goals or problems. By including all parties, the consultant may learn, for example, that a given problem is a bookkeeping or reimbursement matter rather than a client contact issue.

Newman (1993) also points out that managing confidentiality and informed consent is more complicated in organizational consultation situations, especially when the consultation is aimed at organizational change. How should a consultant handle one-on-one disclosures from employees? Are they confidential? Consultants need to be clear about their purpose and relationship with each employee with whom they interact and to forewarn any person when material cannot be kept confidential. A consultant hired to help smooth the merger of two mental health agencies should very directly tell the clients if he or she believes that keeping individual confidences conflicts with achieving broader institutional goals. What is less complicated, of course, is the consultant's obligation to keep information related to the organization or people involved confidential from those who have no right to that information. Such disclosures are simply wrong.

As discussed in Chapter 6, informed consent refers to the free and educated choices people make about matters that affect them. In organizations, senior executives often make decisions about hiring consultants and their assignments. Employees and clients have less involvement and less power, and as a result, employees who disagree with the process or goals of consultation may be reluctant to voice reservations for fear of repercussions. Consultants need to be sensitive to the hierarchical nature of organizations and work skillfully with all parties to approach informed consent as closely as possible. Counselors can educate executives, for example, about the value of not coercing employees, and they can respect employees and encourage them to relinquish unwarranted caution.

Finally, consultants must also be alert to multiple-relationship issues (Zur & Anderson, 2006). Not only must they avoid sexually exploiting people they serve, but they must also be sensitive to nonsexual multiple relationships that may compromise their objectivity. Consultants often work intensively with a few individuals, even in organizational consulting. Such intensive contact can lead to inappropriate blending of roles. Consultant and friend, or consultant and business partner, are two such contacts that probably present ethical problems. When a consultant develops a personal relationship with one partner in consultation, he or she is vulnerable to ignoring the interests of the other partner. Moreover, when one is a business partner of a psychologist in a group practice and simultaneously a consultant on productivity, it is easy to lose track of the needs and rights of the clients and the other employees.

Values and Consultation

The values of the consultant are important in two respects (Newman, 1993). First, because consultants cannot be value-free, they must become aware of the ways in which their values influence consultation process and outcome. Such awareness will help the professional avoid unconsciously imposing personal values in unproductive ways. Second, consultants should be prepared to respond to conflicting values in their work. Conflicts are not inherently destructive, but they can be harmful if ignored or improperly handled. For example, the consultant who is committed to collaboration to address problems may have significant conflict with directors who believe in a more authoritative and centralized approach to management, unless both parties can openly discuss and resolve the issue.

Competence for Consultation

Many mental health professionals provide consultation in the middle and late stages of their careers, but relatively few have formal academic training in consultation. Scholars decry this situation, both because of the risk to clients and because of lost opportunities for good outcomes (e.g., see Hellkamp, Zins, Ferguson, & Hodge, 1998; Lowman, 2006). Practitioners seem to make the same mistake in thinking about competence to do consultation that they make in thinking about competence to supervise—they embrace the myth that clinical skills are sufficient. However, there is a body of knowledge related to consultation to be learned, a set of skills that need to be practiced under supervision, and a capacity for judgment that is acquired with experience (e.g., see Dougherty, 2008). Lowman (2006) notes that most counselors and therapists would be appalled if people without any counseling training presented themselves as counselors, yet counselors sometimes offer themselves as consultants without having been trained to consult. The tendency to misjudge the knowledge required for consulting does not release any professional from the obligation to work within the boundaries of competence.

Finally, competence to consult in one setting does not imply competence in all settings or activities. A professional competent to provide case consultations may not be the best resource for organization issues. Similarly, personal problems or preexisting relationships may compromise competence with a given client. Those who represent themselves as skilled consultants must be prepared to demonstrate the sources of their knowledge and be ready to take responsibility for harm their interventions cause.

Ethical Issues in Intervention for Consultants

Because of the triadic relationships among consultant, consultee, and client system in mental health, consultants should keep the effects of their interventions on clients in the forefront of their thinking. Moreover, they need to be alert for ways in which others might misuse their findings, and work to prevent such misuse. Executives who seem to want to use a consultant report to dismiss older employees, for example, must be energetically dissuaded from such action. If persuasion fails, consultants should withdraw from the project. In other words, consultants cannot shift to others the responsibility for the ways those others use their recommendations.

Even well-designed interventions that are likely to do good may also carry some negative consequences. Consultants cannot ignore negative impacts because the cost–benefit ratio is positive. Instead, they must be cognizant of the power they exert and seek to prevent or minimize those side effects as much as possible.

Finally, consultants should base interventions and recommendations on empirical findings to the highest degree possible (Newman, 1993). They should distinguish experimental or untested recommendations from those well supported by prior research. Empirical data cannot always provide direct guidance for every consulting situation in cookbook fashion, but can act as a foundation for effective interventions (Newman, 1993; Newman, Robinson-Kurpius, & Fuqua, 2002).

Fees for Consulting

Why do many professionals become involved in consultation at some point during their careers? This involvement stems partly from the challenge of the activity, partly from the status inherent in it, and partly from the financial gain to be had, especially in organizational consulting. A well-reputed consultant can earn a handsome living. If one is competent, conscientious, and committed to the public good, that reimbursement is well deserved and not an ethical issue. However, at times, the opportunity for significant income may cloud a professional's judgment. Such a person may accept consulting contracts without true competence for the financial gain, or may ignore findings and interventions inconsistent with the hopes and expectations of whoever is writing the checks. In the latter situation, consultation becomes telling the executives what they want to hear and is a sham from which no one is likely to benefit, even the executives. This is a true conflict of interest and is obviously inconsistent with ethical standards. For example, a consultant who encourages a board of directors to replace its director and then maneuvers herself into the director's position is flagrantly violating ethical principles.

Records of Consultation

Just as records of counseling and psychotherapy improve service to clients and help protect professionals against claims of negligence, so too do records of consulting increase the likelihood of effective service. Consultants should have written contracts setting out the relationship, fees, goals, and practical aspects of the consultation. Issues of confidentiality and informed consent should be addressed in such contracts, along with any unique elements of the consultation. Similarly, consultants should keep progress notes and document any areas of concern or disagreement with special care. A copy of all reports to the consultee should be retained, along with copies of correspondence and telephone contacts. Consultants should protect the confidentiality of these records in the same way counseling records are protected.

Consultation with the Military in a Post–September 11 World

The United States Department of Defense has hired psychologists and psychiatrists as consultants for decades. As early as the 1920s, psychologists developed psychological tests to help the military identify soldiers at risk for battle fatigue (subsequently identified as post-traumatic stress disorder). During the wars in Iraq and Afghanistan, the Department of Defense employed psychologists to assist them in designing effective interrogation techniques to be used with detainees. (For a thoughtful analysis of the involvement of mental health professionals in this activity, see Kalbeitzer [2009]). When reports surfaced that several psychologists had been involved in advising interrogators on "how to use detainees' fears and longings to increase distress" (e.g., Lewis, 2005), the president of the APA organized a task force to evaluate the ethics of such consultation. The group issued its report; later that year, the association issued a resolution cautioning members against involvement in such activities and reaffirming its position that psychologists were not prohibited from acting as consultants to military in interrogation settings. The resolution denounces members' involvement in torture and any other cruel, inhuman, or degrading treatment or punishment of enemy combatants. The association's refusal to issue a blanket condemnation of all forms of consultation related to military interrogations of detainees resulted in a storm of controversy for the APA. Other psychologists argued that the APA should define such consultation activities with military interrogators as inherently unethical (Pope & Gutheil, 2008). A fall 2008 vote of the APA membership resulted in a major change in policy, prohibiting all members from working in settings where "persons are held outside of, or in violation of, either international law (e.g., the UN Convention Against Torture and the Geneva Conventions) or the U.S. Constitution (where appropriate), unless they are working directly for the persons being detained or for an independent third party working to protect human rights" (APA, 2008b, http://www.apa.org/news/press/releases/2008/07/interrogations.aspx). In 2010, the association revised Standards 1.02 and 1.03 of the Code to make its position clear.

SUMMARY

When people take on supervisory responsibilities, they must keep in mind a number of ethical obligations and legal duties. Not only must they demonstrate competence to supervise as well as competence to practice, they must also guard the rights of the supervisee to a beneficial learning experience with fair and appropriate feedback about performance. Even more important than the progress of the trainee, though, is the welfare of the clients served by the trainee. A supervisor holds both ethical and legal responsibility for clients' welfare, and when the needs of the supervisee conflict with those of the clients, the codes mandate that clients' concerns take precedence. The legal requirement to care for the client stems from the client's right to competent service regardless of the counselor's level of training.

Supervisors are also ethically bound not to engage in activities that exploit their supervisees. They are especially cautioned to avoid sexual contact, insensitivity to issues of diversity, and introjection of personal values into the professional relationship. Supervisors who fail to act responsibly themselves, or who have supervisees who act unethically, are held liable for the consequences. The latter principle is called *vicarious liability*. Similarly, those who violate the due process rights of trainees or clients' rights to confidentiality can be held legally responsible for those failures. Finally, supervisors need to be attuned to their legal and ethical obligations when working with third-party payers and to be scrupulously accurate about reporting services rendered by supervisees.

When consulting, mental health professionals need to recognize that this specialty requires professionals to have focused training and experience before they can assert competency as consultants. The tenets of good science; informed consent; confidentiality of records and disclosures; avoidance of multiple relationships, conflicts of interest, and exploitation; and sensitivity to diversity issues apply as strongly to these consultation and supervision relationships as they do to therapy relationships.

Discussion Questions*

1. Many current supervisors indicate that they have had little formal training in supervision. Given the standards you have read, how would you address this problem? Should such training be mandated? Should there be a test for supervision? What other ideas do you have?
2. A substantial minority of supervisors in one study referred to supervisees as "friends." Some strongly believed that their personal connection to the trainee enhanced rather than compromised their supervision. Is there any merit to that view? If you were consulting with them about this issue, how would you respond?
3. What do you believe is the ethically ideal way for a supervisor to respond to a sincere, well-motivated, but incompetent performance by an intern? How long should a supervisor allow an intern whose interactions with clients are unsatisfactory to continue to try to improve?

Cases for Discussion

Bart is widely regarded as the most talented supervisor and clinician in the community mental health center where he works. He typically supervises several interns who learn a great deal from him and express great satisfaction with the process and outcome of their experiences in supervision.

*Note to course instructors: The *Instructor's Guide* for this book includes other discussion questions, class exercises, cases, and multiple-choice and essay test items for this chapter.

Bart also has a part-time private practice. A number of former interns have sought Bart out for counseling when they needed support. In fact, former interns and their friends and loved ones have come to represent about 25% of Bart's caseload. He finds therapy with these clients a rewarding and productive endeavor. Consequently, after students successfully complete their internship, Bart distributes his business card to each intern in the event that he or she wants to contact him in the future. Are any of Bart's actions here in violation of the code of ethics of the ACA or the ACES guidelines? If you were in Bart's position, would you also hand out your card to graduating interns? If not, what would you do if a former intern asked to see you in counseling?

Philip is a school counseling intern at a middle school. One of his clients has a number of bruises on her arms and legs. When asked, the girl cannot account for the bruises—she just shrugs her shoulders and says, "I don't know." Philip reports this client's injuries to Vivian, his supervisor, and he tells her he plans to call the child abuse hotline. Vivian suggests that no report is necessary because her case is already under investigation for a different injury that was reported to them by the child's teacher two weeks ago. At first, Philip is surprised by his supervisor's advice, but then he decides that she must be correct and does not report this new incident. Should Philip have made a report anyway? Did Vivian meet her ethical and legal responsibilities as a supervisor? If a complaint were filed against Philip for his inaction here, could he defend himself by saying that he was an intern following his supervisor's recommendation?

Marsha is a doctoral student in counseling, who hopes to complete an internship in a shelter for survivors of domestic violence. This agency has no professional with the proper credential to supervise her, although there are several highly competent professionals from other disciplines who work at the shelter. Because she is committed to this population and site, Marsha devises an arrangement that she believes will allow her to complete her internship at the agency she wants and still meet all training and licensing requirement. She has set up a distance supervision contract with a highly competent supervisor in her field, who lives 100 miles away. Marsha will send audio and videotapes to him weekly, and they will conduct supervision by telephone and by email communication at regular times each week. In all, the supervisor has agreed to spend a minimum of two hours per week in supervision activities, for which Marsha will reimburse him $50 weekly. The director of the domestic violence shelter has been made aware of this arrangement, has accepted it, and has agreed to allow the supervisor to call her to discuss any clients that he feels Marsha is not serving competently. The state licensing board has also agreed to this arrangement as long as the agency and the supervisor put their arrangement in writing and send them a copy.

Recommended Readings

Association for Counselor Education and Supervision. (1990). Standards for counseling supervisors. *Journal of Counseling & Development*, *69*, 30–32.

Association for Counselor Education and Supervision. (1993). Ethical guidelines for counseling supervisors. *Counselor Education and Supervision*, *34*, 270–276.

Association for Counselor Education and Supervision. (2011). Best practices in counseling supervision. Retrieved from: http://www.acesonline.net/wp-content/uploads/2011/10/ACES-Best-Practices-in-clinical-supervision-document-FINAL.pdf

Association of State and Provincial Psychology Boards. (2003c). Supervision guidelines. (Under revision in 2011). Retrieved from https://c.ymcdn.com/sites/asppb.site-ym.com/resource/resmgr/guidelines/current_asppb_supervision_gu.pdf

Barnett, J. E., Cornish, J. A. E., Goodyear, R. K., & Lichtenberg, J. W. (2007). Commentaries on the ethical and effective practice of clinical supervision. *Professional Psychology: Research and Practice*, *38*, 268–275.

Bernard, J. M., & Goodyear, R. K. (2008). *Fundamentals of clinical supervision* (4th ed.). Boston, MA: Allyn & Bacon.

Brown, D., Pryzwansky, W. B., & Schulte, A. C. (2011). *Psychological consultation and collaboration* (7th ed.). Boston, MA: Pearson.

Cikanek, K., Veach, P. M., & Braun, C. (2004). Advanced doctoral students' knowledge and understanding of clinical supervisor ethical responsibilities: A brief report. *Clinical Supervisor, 23*, 191–196.

Disney, M. J., & Stephens, A. M. (1994). Legal issues in clinical supervision. In T. P. Remley (Ed.), *ACA legal series* (Vol. 8). Alexandria, VA: American Counseling Association.

Falender, C. A., Burnes, T. B., & Ellis, M. V. (2013). Multicultural clinical supervision and benchmarks: Empirical support informing practice and supervisor training. *The Counseling Psychologist, 41*, 8–27.

Gottlieb, M. C., Robinson, K., & Younggren, J. N. (2007). Multiple relations in supervision: Guidance for administrators, supervisors, and students. *Professional Psychology: Research and Practice, 38*, 241–247.

Ladany, N., Friedlander, M. L., & Smith, M. L. (2005). *Critical events in psychotherapy supervision: An interpersonal approach*. Washington, D.C.: American Psychological Association.

Ladany, N., Lehman-Waterman, D., Molinaro, M., & Wolgart, B. (1999). Psychotherapy supervisor ethical practices, working alliance and supervisee satisfaction. *The Counseling Psychologist, 27*, 443–475.

Thomas, J. T. (2010). *The ethics of supervision and consultation: Practical guidance for mental health professionals*. Washington, D.C.: American Psychological Association.

Additional Online Resources

American Association of State Counseling Boards: A Compilation of Supervisor Requirements by State: http://associationdatabase.com/aws/AASCB/asset_manager/get_file/37393?ver=19.

Counselors and Therapists as Teachers and Researchers

CHAPTER 15

Integrity, Science, and Care

Many counselors and psychologists are involved in training the next generation of professionals and in research to advance the science of the profession. The central ethical issues embedded in these activities mirror those of direct service: competence, responsible use of power, and promotion of the welfare of those in their care. This chapter discusses how each obligation is met when teaching and conducting research.

THE ETHICS OF TEACHING

Our society views teachers ambivalently. On the one hand, they are held in high regard: "What office is there which involves more responsibility, which requires more qualifications, and which ought, therefore, to be more honourable, than that of teaching?" (Martineau, 1837). On the other hand, they are viewed with disdain and distrust: "He who can, does. He who cannot, teaches" (Shaw, 1903). Even those who see some value in teaching are concerned about its potential for abuse: "A teacher should have maximal authority, and minimal power" (Szasz, 1973). This ambivalence stems partly from the high hopes that citizens have for education and partly from their occasional disappointments over unrealized hopes. The enterprise of teaching others to be effective counselors and therapists is also fraught with potential for good or ill. When good occurs, the next generation is entrusted with the wisdom of the past and provided the skills to extend it, and when bad happens, either incompetent people are admitted to the profession, or qualified people are discouraged from it. Szasz's wish to contain the power of the teacher cannot be realized, though. Instead, the task of the profession is to ensure that its teachers use their power responsibly.

Unfortunately, the literature on the ethics of training mental health professionals is not as abundant as the publications on ethics in counseling and psychotherapy or supervision, but there are still valuable resources available. Several experts have addressed the issue; the recent versions of the ethics codes speak to this activity; and some empirical studies have been conducted. The central ethical issues in this body of literature deal with competence to teach; the responsible use of power; the management of multiple and sometimes conflicting role obligations; and the duties to the profession, the students, and the public.

Competence to Teach

Faculty who teach counselors and therapists ought first to be competent practitioners. In addition, they must be knowledgeable about their subject matter, prepared for their work, and committed to facilitating student learning. In an era in which the mental health professions and their accrediting bodies are placing increasing emphasis on competency-based training for students, the responsibility for competent teaching and mentoring has never been greater (Hensley, Smith, & Thompson, 2003; Kaslow, Grus, Campbell, Fouad, Hatcher, & Rodolfa, 2009). Nearly all psychology faculty acknowledge occasional incidences of inadequate preparation for classes, but the number who admit sometimes teaching material they have not mastered is also surprisingly high—38% (Tabachnick et al., 1991). The percentage of counselor educators who report teaching material for which they are not competent is almost identical—36%, according to Schwab and Neukrug (1994). Faculty also have a responsibility to present information fairly and to distinguish between personal opinions and established theory and research. In the same survey, nearly 4% admitted bias in teaching is a frequent practice. The obligation to stay current in a rapidly changing discipline is especially important. Tabachnick et al. (1991) found uneven compliance with this standard. In that study, 36% of teaching psychologists admitted teaching a course without updating lecture notes.

When teaching content for which scientific support is scarce, that limitation needs to be clearly stated. Cutting-edge, speculative, or experimental material should be labeled as such. This recommendation does not mean that faculty must curtail their presentations to long-established constructs, but it does suggest that students should be informed about the distinction between concepts in the mainstream of professional thinking and those too new or speculative to be widely accepted. Professors who keep in mind the ultimate goal of teaching—to educate practitioners capable of making objective, informed, independent judgments about the merits of innovations—will be better equipped to make wise decisions about such matters. If there is substantial debate about the merits of a particular theory or method, both sides of the argument should be presented. This guideline does not imply that faculty need to hide their own perspectives from students. Showing students the rationale for one's personal assessments about unsettled issues in the profession can help students develop appropriate criteria for making similar judgments themselves. However, neither demeaning others who hold different views nor dismissing the valid positions of others is consistent with ethical standards. In Standard 7.03, the APA Code emphasizes accuracy in both syllabi and presentations, along with sufficient information for students to be informed about teaching and evaluation experiences. The ACA Code speaks to the issue by emphasizing that counselor educators must be competent in the courses they teach and competent in understanding multicultural issues in counseling (Section F.7.b–c). In some universities, faculty are asked to teach courses not directly related to their research and teaching expertise. When such requests are made, faculty must evaluate whether they can perform competently, just as practitioners need to judge whether a particular activity falls within their boundaries of competence. If a subject falls outside their areas of competence, they must decline to teach it unless they can obtain continuing education beforehand. The statement from the ethics codes on working within the boundaries of one's competence apply equally to teaching and therapy (see Section C.2.a of the ACA Code and Standard 2.01 of the APA Code).

Frequently, graduate students in counseling and psychology serve as teaching assistants or instructors in undergraduate or master's-level courses (Branstetter & Handelsman, 2000). These authors found that most had scant formal instruction in teaching effectiveness and little training in professional ethics prior to teaching, but still less than half of the teaching assistants they surveyed had ever received any supervision for their teaching. Not surprisingly, then, in one survey, 90% of undergraduates reported witnessing unethical behavior by psychology graduate assistants (Fly, van Bark, Weinman, Kitchener, & Long, 1997). The APA standards (Section 2.05) require professionals to train subordinates appropriately and oversee the work of those to whom they are delegating responsibility. Clearly, this evidence shows that compliance with these standards is low.

Responsible Use of Power

As discussed in Chapters 7 and 14, sexual harassment, sexual exploitation, and related abuse of the less powerful position of students happen rather frequently in graduate programs in counseling and psychology. In published research, the mean percentage of faculty who admit sexual contact with students is 8.8%. In one study, almost one-third of female psychology graduate students reported incidents of sexual harassment (Glaser & Thorpe, 1986). In another study, psychology internship directors singled out faculty–student sexual contact as a continuing blind spot for those who teach (Welfel, 1992), a finding echoed in a study of mental health counselors and social workers by Barnett-Queen and Larrabee (2000). These researchers reported that 1.8% of the sample had sexual contact with educators during their training. The attention sexual harassment has received in the media does not seem to have eliminated the problem. In the study by Barnett-Queen and Larrabee (2000), counseling students experienced sexual advances at approximately twice the rate of social work students—9.5% of counselors in comparison to 4% of social workers.

Blevins-Knabe (1992) offers some insights into the reasons sexual harassment occurs in higher education. She suggests that faculty are blind to the implications of their actions. They tend to perceive their behavior as friendly and supportive and are reluctant to admit its sexual motivation, but students find it harassing. Sometimes both faculty and students are willing participants in sexual relationships. When sexual relationships are consensual, Blevins-Knabe believes that shared professional interests, personal insecurities in the students, unresolved personal issues in faculty, and sex role socialization factors all are influential. Interestingly, though, when viewed in retrospect, neither faculty nor students perceive "consensual" relationships as freely chosen or beneficial to the personal or professional development of either party (Glaser & Thorpe, 1986; Miller & Larrabee, 1995; Pope et al., 1979; Robinson & Reid, 1985).

There are also effects on other students who hear discussion of sexual advances by faculty. Adams, Kottke, and Padgit (1983) reported that 13% of female students and 3% of male students tried to avoid working with faculty known or rumored to have made sexual advances to other students. Rubin, Hampton, and McManus (1997) found that women students were especially uncomfortable with sexually harassing behaviors. Of course, some faculty prey on vulnerable students and are exclusively motivated by self-interest, but others initiate sexual contact because of personal dissatisfactions, life crises, or neurotic tendencies. The current ethics codes explicitly forbid sexual contact with current students under any circumstances (ACA, Section F.3.b; APA, Standard 7.07). Thus, faculty must set clear boundaries in their relationships with students and seek out professional assistance when tempted to make sexual advances. (And sexual attraction for a student is rather common; Lamb, Catanzaro, and Moorman [2004] found that a majority of the psychologists they surveyed [54%] had that experience.)

Sexual contact is not the only abuse of faculty power, nor is it probably the most common. Faculty sometimes exploit students' needs for professional success and clinical or research experience as well. They also abuse their power when they discriminate on the basis of characteristics unrelated to academic performance and when they fail to be sensitive to the implications of their decisions on students' or colleagues' futures. Here are some examples of such abuses:

Professor Yelter's Grading Procedures

Professor Yelter assigns research topics to students in her course according to the content areas she needs to include in her book in progress. The topics for some of these papers are only peripherally related to course content, and students have no option to change topics. When the papers are submitted, she attends only to the quality of the reference list rather than the analysis of the topic. She grades according to the potential usefulness of the students' work to her book.

Dr. Marsher's Classroom Style

Dr. Marsher encourages discussion in his classes. When many students have raised their hands to respond to an issue he has offered for discussion, he almost always acknowledges male students first. In addition, he is more likely to give male students time to develop their thoughts and respond to differing perspectives. His typical interaction with female students is briefer and less patient.

Professor Pastione's Research Projects

Doctoral students assigned to Professor Pastione soon learn that if they wish to receive a positive letter of recommendation from her after they graduate, they should volunteer to help her with her research projects. If they are involved in other faculty research or do not have the time to volunteer for Professor Pastione, they ought to find another adviser because she will not support them, no matter what their other competencies or experiences.

In the first case, Professor Yelter is using students in the class as unpaid, unacknowledged research assistants. Moreover, she is placing her own interests ahead of their learning and providing them with no viable alternative to the plan she has established. Such an action is contrary to the ethical principles of beneficence and respect for autonomy. It is also inconsistent with the sections of the codes that require faculty to act as role models for ethical behavior (ACA Code, Section F.6.a), to give students credit for research contributions (ACA Code, Section G.5.f), and to avoid exploitive relationships (APA Code, Standard 3.08). Dr. Yelter's ethical problems do not end there. Her behavior also violates the stipulations in the codes dealing with objectivity in assessment (APA Code, Standard 7.06.b).

Needless to say, Professor Yelter ought to stop this practice, assign topics directly related to course content, and use fair and objective grading criteria. If she needs research assistance with her project, she should hire someone. If a student elects to volunteer for that job in order to gain experience, that arrangement would also be ethical, provided the student's efforts were acknowledged and other forms of exploitation were avoided. She also could benefit from remedial education about the power she holds over students who may not feel free to challenge her requirements or question their grades. Her current actions stand in direct opposition to acting as an appropriate professional role model.

Dr. Marsher is engaging in gender bias. This behavior is inappropriate because it gives unfair advantage to some students on the basis of a characteristic irrelevant to professional competence. It violates sections of the Code that proscribe discrimination. Dr. Marsher may be unaware of this bias, but his ignorance does not excuse it. Students taking his courses may feel unable to communicate their experience to him for fear of retribution. Once grades are submitted, though, those who will not be participating in additional courses with Dr. Marsher are ideal candidates to address the matter, through course evaluations, conversations with the professor, or discussions with other faculty in the program. Needless to say, if other faculty learn of this behavior, they too have an obligation to address it with Dr. Marsher, assuming that the student involved does not object to such an approach.

The essence of Professor Pastione's ethical problem is the way in which she has transformed a basic obligation of her position, the writing of letters of recommendation, into a "service for sale" in exchange for labor on her projects. Students willing to work "earn" a positive evaluation, apparently without regard for their actual capacities as counselors. This practice not only exploits students' vulnerabilities, it also violates a professor's obligation to ensure that only competent students are admitted into the profession. The ACA Code (Section F.6.d) is quite explicit on this issue, although it substitutes the term *endorsement* for recommendation.

Professor Pastione has also violated her duty to respect autonomy and avoid harm. Unless assisting this faculty member with her research is an explicit condition of admission or continuation in the doctoral program that is fully disclosed in writing at the time of application, her demand violates students' rights to informed consent to educational procedures. However, as long as Professor Pastione uses research assistance as the "quid pro quo" of evaluation, no degree of informed consent could transform her behavior into an ethically acceptable practice.

In addition, Professor Pastione harms students in several ways. Those who reject participation in her project, unaware of the consequences, are injured by the unexpected and unfair endorsement they receive. Other students may not have the luxury of working for free, needing to support themselves through graduate school. The professor's practice may even cause harm to those who get an undeserved positive reference. Students whose talents lie in another field are not necessarily better off for earning a credential they do not deserve. In the long run, these students may be better helped by learning during training that they are not sufficiently competent to practice. The pain in that event may be significantly less than the pain of a malpractice suit, termination from jobs, or other problems that stem from incompetence. Even more important, Professor Pastione may be harming the public served by these ineffective students. The solution? Obviously, Professor Pastione must stop this practice, recruit research assistants in a more appropriate fashion, and base comments in letters of evaluation on actual performance. She should also seek to redress the wrongs she has done in past letters of reference, sending revised copies to students for future use.

Neglect of Responsibilities: Another Misuse of Power

Keith-Spiegel (1994) makes a point about psychology educators that applies to faculty in related professions. The mandate to avoid harm is more complex to interpret in the teacher role than in the role of counselor or therapist. Clearly, a teacher wishes not to cause harm to students, but when students' work is substandard or their attitude irresponsible, a teacher's concern about harm to students must be balanced against his or her duty to the clients whom the student may serve and the reputation of the profession. As discussed in Chapter 4, admitting people who are unable or unwilling to abide by professional standards does not inspire public trust. Thus, faculty who fail to prevent unqualified people from practicing are overlooking one of their major responsibilities. The goal of faculty is, of course, to help all students meet the standards set for competence, but when that fails, they must not accept unqualified people. Again, the ACA Code speaks to this issue most directly, specifying procedures for dealing with student deficiencies in Section F.9.b (Appendix A, p. 521).

The following case exemplifies a common ethical failure to meet this standard:

The Case of Dr. Dorian's Dilemma

Dr. Dorian is an untenured faculty member who hopes to achieve tenure in a few years. In his university, competent teaching and good relationships with students figure prominently in tenure review. Dr. Dorian has a student in practicum whose performance is unsatisfactory. His substantial efforts to help this student to improve have been fruitless. Moreover, the student does not seem to understand the limits of his competence and tends to take on cases for which he is unqualified. Dr. Dorian believes this student ought not to pass practicum, but he also fears that this vocal and well-connected student will file a grievance over a failing grade and focus the attention of university administrators on his situation. In light of the complications a failing grade will cause for him, Dr. Dorian decides to pass this student.

To comply with the ethical standards, Dr. Dorian should record the grade he believes the student earned, in spite of the discomfort that may ensue. If Dr. Dorian has graded fairly, communicated the poor performance to the student, and documented his repeated interventions to help the student remediate his problems, responding to a grievance is not difficult. In most universities, students must demonstrate that grading procedures were arbitrary or discriminatory—a rather difficult standard to meet. It seems that Dr. Dorian's anxiety about tenure is overriding his judgment. At a deeper level, Dr. Dorian may think ethical behavior is a matter of convenience. When standards are easy to follow, he may willingly comply, but when compliance causes him personal discomfort, he breaks the rules. Such behavior is unprofessional.

Other violations of this standard are not so blatant. Some derive from a good-hearted desire on the part of faculty to help all students reach their full potential. This aim is admirable and ought to be a guidepost for faculty behavior. It becomes problematic, however, when students who do not perform competently are allowed to progress. Faculty cannot lose sight of their obligations to such students' potential clients. In this situation, faculty ought to focus on helping students redirect their career goals if remediation efforts fail. At other times, overcrowded classes make careful assessment of each student's competencies difficult. Faculty overwhelmed by their teaching load, research responsibilities, and administrative demands may succumb to giving all students "the benefit of the doubt" rather than engage in the difficult task before them. Neither overwork nor compassion for an individual student is a sufficient justification for actions that defy a professional standard, although 10% of psychology faculty admitted that the likeability of a student had influenced their grading (Tabachnick et al., 1991).

In one study exploring why psychology faculty sometimes ignore cheating, Keith-Spiegel, Tabachnick, Whitley, and Washburn (1998) found that most often faculty feel the evidence is insufficient to confirm the dishonesty, but several less rational reasons also play a part. For example, faculty say that sometimes reporting feels too stressful, takes more courage than they have, involves more effort than they want to expend, and results in retaliation or legal challenges they want to avoid. Others rationalized that cheating students would probably fail the course anyway and that only the inexperienced cheaters, not the chronic offenders, are likely to get caught. Needless to say, none of these reasons justifies failing to confront incidences of academic dishonesty by students in mental health disciplines. Those who cut corners by cheating may be at risk for taking other unethical actions with clients and colleagues when they complete their degrees. In a more recent study, Vacha-Hasse, Davenport, and Kerewsky (2004) reported that most psychology training programs (52%) in their sample do dismiss at least one student every three years, but an almost equal percent (54%) did not have written guidelines for intervening with problematic students.

The fear of a lawsuit challenging their judgment or right to fail or dismiss a student is a real concern of some faculty, and it appears as a substantial barrier to the initiation of dismissal procedures for problematic students (McAdams, Foster, & Ward, 2007; Vacha-Hasse et al., 2004). This anxiety usually proves unwarranted. As long as faculty have clear evidence of unsatisfactory performance in academic or clinical courses, the courts have been supportive of their judgments (Remley & Herlihy, 2013). Approximately 80% of students who experience dismissal do not contest the program's actions (Vacha-Hasse et al., 2004). When students do contest, the quality of the program's policies and procedures are crucial to deflecting legal challenges (McAdams et al., 2007). Many faculty prefer to counsel into alternative careers students who are unsuccessful in mastering the requisite content and skills (Forrest, Elman, Gizara, & Vacha-Haase, 1999). Such a course of action protects the student's privacy and saves him or her from embarrassment. Needless to say, when students are dismissed from a program, they have all the due process rights to a fair hearing of their concerns that they would have if dismissed from an internship site (Kaplin & Lee, 1995; Kerl, Garcia, McCullough, & Maxwell, 2002). (See Chapter 14 for a discussion of trainee due process rights in supervision.)

Conflicts Between Students' Religious or Moral Values and Program Requirements for Professional Competency

What are the ethical responsibilities of educators of future mental health professionals when students' religious beliefs conflict with the ability of the program to offer them training to be competent to serve a diverse population? What are the ethical responsibilities of students who seek to gain a license to function as mental health professionals? These are very important questions since all people have a right to religious freedom under the Constitution, and no training program should denigrate or challenge a student's religious beliefs because they seem inconsistent with the philosophy of the program. On the other hand, programs have a duty to ensure that the students they graduate are competent to serve the public, and the public includes individuals with diverse needs, backgrounds, and belief systems that do not always align with the values of the mental health professional. Graduates also have a responsibility to be sufficiently competent to serve the public.

The most common example of such a conflict is the situation in which students profess a religious belief that homosexuality is in opposition to their religion and that they cannot work with LGBTQ clients in any way that suggests acceptance of the client's sexual identity and behavior. In contrast, the view of the professional associations is that LGBTQ relationships are not immoral and that professionals should be competent to work with LGBTQ clients in the same way they work with heterosexual clients regarding issues that relate to their sexual orientation (APA, 2011b; Kaplan, 2014). Several legal cases have come before the courts in recent years as students have challenged training programs' right to ask them to become competent to serve the needs of LGBTQ clients related to their sexual orientation (e.g., *Keeton v. Anderson-Wiley*, 2011; *Ward v. Wilbanks*, 2010). In these cases, students in counselor education programs challenged the requirement that they develop competence to work with LGBTQ clients. In the Keeton case the court ruled that the university was not infringing on the student's religious freedom, holding that the training requirements were reasonable and that students could not refuse to develop competence in counseling a whole class of people. In the Ward case, the district court granted a summary judgment in favor of the university, determining that the facts of the case favored the university's position so convincingly that no reasonable jury would decide in favor or Ms. Ward (*Ward v. Wilbanks*, 2010). This summary judgment was overturned by the appeals court, which held that the case should be allowed to go to a jury (*Ward v. Polite*, 2012). The holding by the appeals court questioned both the clarity of the ACA Code on the issue of referrals based on counselor values and the transparency of the program's requirements for training. Ultimately, the case was settled out of court. (For an excellent summary of the specifics in these cases and others, see Behnke, 2012; Herlihy, Hermann, & Greden, 2014). The ACA's official position on this issue indicates four major points as detailed below. It is important to note, however, that the appeals court disputed that a referral because of a value conflict was explicitly prohibited either by the Code or in the counseling literature.

- Professional counselors may not deny counseling services to a homosexual person (or an individual belonging to any other protected class of clients) on the basis of the counselor's values.
- Referrals are to be made on the basis of skill-based competency, not values.
- To avoid abandonment, referral is an option of last resort.
- The counselor's ethical obligations to an individual start at first contact or assignment, not at the first session (Kaplan, 2014, p. 146).

In the interval since these cases were decided/settled, at least one state has enacted what is called "conscience clause legislation" stating:

> A university or community college shall not discipline or discriminate against a student in a counseling, social work, or psychology program because the student refuses to counsel a client about goals that conflict with the student's sincerely held religious belief if the student consults with the supervising instructor or professor to determine the proper course of action to avoid harm to the client. (Arizona HB 2565 "University Students' Religious Liberty Act," 2011)

Similar legislation has been introduced in other states, but to date these bills have not been enacted or were passed in a form that the state professional association negotiated. In light of the conflicting nature of the legal decisions and the concerns about religious freedom embedded in this issue, faculty and supervisors must keep current on legal developments.

Fortunately, both scholars and professional associations have offered guidance to programs and students to help them address this conflict responsibly. The APA Board of Educational Affairs has produced a statement to guide training programs to resolve the conflict (APA, 2013). The APA document clarifies that training programs must be respectful of trainees' religious beliefs and provide a supportive learning environment that fosters self-awareness and does not attempt to restrict or denigrate any personal beliefs. At the same time, the profession affirms that competence in treating diverse populations is a core competency, and therefore students cannot be allowed to pick and choose which core competencies they will learn because the core competencies have been identified based on benefit to the public. It goes on to state, "Thus trainees entering professional psychology training programs should have no reasonable expectation of being exempted from having any particular category of potential clients/patients assigned to them for the duration of training" (APA, 2013). This policy allows for referral in specific cases and assumes that the welfare of the client is the higher priority, but it stands firm on the need for training in core competencies. Given this requirement, the position statement also emphasizes the need for programs to be clear and transparent about what they require of students. The practical way to accomplish this is through content in student handbooks, program websites, syllabi, and related documents. Programs must also be equally committed to due process and to a well-documented policy and procedure for student development and remediation of deficiencies in competence.

Farnsworth and Callahan (2013) offer a five-step model for programs to address such conflicts. This model begins with an explicit recognition of the conflict, then proceeds to a process to assist the student in reflecting about the value conflict and a process to categorize the conflict. At this point in the model, recommendations for training can be developed and then implemented. The final step in this model includes recommendations for disposition of the case (p. 206). In a practical article that illustrates how stressful a lawsuit can be for faculty and students alike, Dugger and Francis (2014), two of the faculty involved in the Ward case, offer recommendations for training programs facing a similar legal challenge.

Distinguishing Mentoring From Problematic Boundary Crossings

Faculty and students often have several different kinds of professional contacts. A student may serve as a research assistant, pupil in a class, collaborator on a manuscript, and supervisee in a practicum seminar to the same faculty member simultaneously. Consecutive involvement in multiple roles is even more common with students and faculty. For example, one of my former graduate assistants was simultaneously a teaching intern under my supervision and a collaborator on a manuscript in preparation. Were either of us acting unethically? Many would see no ethical dimension to our multiple types of interaction. In fact, multifaceted and prolonged connections between faculty and students, usually termed *mentoring relationships*, are often viewed as desirable, both by scholars and by the parties involved (Bowman, Bowman, & DeLucia, 1990; Bowman, Hatley, & Bowman, 1995; Schweibert, 2000). Some scholars associate mentoring with higher student achievement, satisfaction, and persistence in academic programs (e.g., see Bean & Kuh, 1984). Mentoring relationships are very common in graduate study in psychology; research shows that 67% of graduate students in psychology report that they had mentors during their degree programs, and the overwhelming majority (91%) was satisfied with them (Clark, Harden, & Johnson, 2000).

Still, some ethics scholars have expressed caution about multiple connections with students, and their inherent risks (Johnson & Nelson, 1999; Kitchener, 1992; Warren, 2005. Clark et al. (2000) reported that 2% of mentors had sexualized their relationships with students. Mentoring can blur the objectivity of the professional, incur jealousy or misunderstanding in other students (Bowman et al., 1995), and make other boundaries that ought to be observed harder to maintain. For instance, faculty working closely with students may begin to use students as confidants about personal matters, socialize extensively with those students, or otherwise forget the distinction between professional and personal relationships. When students become more like friends than students, faculty may have difficulty honoring their responsibilities as gatekeepers to the profession. The power imbalance in the relationship cannot be ignored either, because it diminishes the reciprocity that characterizes ordinary friendships. In most cases, the faculty member probably feels freer than the student to express feelings, ask favors, or seek emotional support. At some level, the student is aware that the faculty member has tremendous influence over his or her future. For these reasons, the codes caution professionals to honor boundaries (ACA Code, Sections F.10.d and F.10.f; APA Code, Standard 3.05). The two criteria used in the APA Code to evaluate the advisability of a particular multiple relationship are worth reviewing here. A multiple relationship is inappropriate when it would impair the professional's objectivity or might harm or exploit the other person. The ACA allows for boundary crossings but provides extensive commentary on the type and length of such extensions:

ACA Code of Ethics

Section F.10.f Extending Educator–Student Boundaries

Counselor educators are aware of the power differential in the relationship between faculty and students. If they believe that a nonprofessional relationship with a student may be potentially beneficial to the student, they take precautions similar to those taken by counselors when working with clients. Examples of potentially beneficial interactions or relationships include, but are not limited to, attending a formal ceremony; conducting hospital visits; providing support during a stressful event; or maintaining mutual membership in a professional association, organization, or community. Counselor educators discuss with students the rationale for such interactions, the potential benefits and drawbacks, and the anticipated consequences for the student. Educators clarify the specific nature and limitations of the additional role(s) they will have with the student prior to engaging in a nonprofessional relationship. Nonprofessional relationships with students should be time limited and/or context specific and initiated with student consent.

Source: Reprinted with permission from American Counseling Association.

Honoring boundaries is a rather abstract term. In relation to faculty–student relationships, I believe it also means:

- Refraining from using the student as a confidant about personal matters or about matters of frustration with colleagues.
- Ensuring that the bulk of the time spent together focuses on professional issues. Friendly interactions are not to be avoided, but a preponderance of talk about social events is inadvisable. (One should keep in mind that the goal of the student is to learn from the faculty member.)
- Declining repeated one-on-one social engagements in favor of group events.
- Setting limits to discussions of personal stresses that the student is experiencing, or referring the student to counseling, just as one would do as a clinical supervisor.
- Refusing a mentoring relationship with relatives or with students with whom one has had a prior or ongoing personal relationship.
- Clarifying the parameters of the relationship and the roles at the onset so that both parties understand their roles and the relevant contents of the ethics codes.
- Making mentoring activities available to all qualified students, with awareness that students from diverse populations may have less access to mentors than other students.
- Consulting with colleagues periodically about mentoring issues so as to deal with minor problems and receive external feedback about the relationship.
- Allowing students who wish to withdraw from a mentoring relationship to do so with dignity and without retribution.

Using these criteria and the decision-making model from Chapter 2, consider the ethics of the following situations:

The Case of the Summer Job

A graduate student runs a house-painting service in the summer. She uses the earnings from this business to fund her education for a doctoral degree. A faculty member notices a flyer advertising her business on a bulletin board and contracts with the student to have his house painted next summer. The student will be enrolling in his group therapy course the following fall.

The Case of the Therapy Partner

A faculty member has a part-time psychotherapy practice. She asks an especially talented student, who has recently graduated, to join the practice.

The Case of the Generous Donation

A student's family has suffered a devastating house fire that has disabled her parents. Because her parents had been funding her education and are no longer in a position to do so, she fears she will not be able to continue enrollment next quarter. She has applied for financial aid but is unlikely to receive the aid in time for registration. Her advisor, on hearing of her situation, writes her a check for next quarter's tuition, telling her she can repay the loan when her financial aid gets straightened out.

The Case of the Request for a Ride

A professor's car is out of service. One of the students in his class lives nearby. The professor asks that student for a ride to campus the next day.

Bowman et al. (1995) surveyed students and faculty to ascertain their views on the ethics of several kinds of multiple relationships. They included vignettes dealing with social, monetary, mentoring, and sexual contacts. As expected, virtually all respondents found sexual contacts inappropriate, but there was little unanimity in other responses. No more than three-quarters of the sample came to agreement on the ethics of faculty who hire students to babysit; maintain a concurrent friendship with a student or have students as primary social contacts; or keep silent from other faculty a student's slur against homosexuals, made in a social setting. This disparity in response speaks to several issues, including the general lack of attention this topic has received in the professional literature, the abstractness of the codes on this matter, and the conflict in professional and personal obligations. In other words, both faculty and students seem to recognize the complexity of ethical decision making in this area and the degree to which a particular activity must be evaluated in its context. The survey by Tabachnick and her associates (1991) suggests similar uncertainty about the ethics of nonsexual faculty–student contacts. Nearly 49% labeled asking a student for a small favor (such as a ride home) as ethical under many or all circumstances, and 37% saw it as rarely or never ethical. Similarly, 29% of faculty viewed lending students money as ethical in most or all situations, but 50% held a contrary view.

Faculty who are tempted to take rigid stances in opposition to all forms of multiple connections with students are probably overreacting to the risks and sidestepping their ethical obligation to foster the development of their students. Lloyd (1992) has remarked that some faculty seem to have a "mentoring phobia." Although that characterization seems strongly worded (and inconsistent with research evidence), it does put a name to the discomfort and worry some faculty feel about their relationships with graduate students. Careful consideration of ethical guidelines, and the preceding criteria for managing multiple professional contacts, should reduce the risks of such relationships without compromising their potential benefits. (Those who seek examples of other hypothetical cases that have ethical dimensions should refer to Keith-Spiegel, Wittig, Perkins, Balogh, and Whitley [1993].)

Personal Growth Experiences for Students

The emotional stability of the mental health professional is crucial to the success of counseling. Many ethics complaints result from character flaws, neurotic tendencies, or other deficiencies in coping with personal stresses. Many students whom educators identify as distressed are emotionally unstable or unsuited for clinical work (Forrest et al., 1999). For these reasons, educators have a duty to ensure that students have the emotional stability and temperament for the profession and that the personal issues that may be impeding their effectiveness are identified and resolved. Accreditation and licensing standards also mandate that training programs ensure that graduates are emotionally stable enough to be competent to work with clients.

Experiences that increase empathy with clients, give students opportunities to "walk in clients' shoes," and involve students in experimental learning are all valued by mental health professions as crucial teaching tools. These same experiences also help students become aware of the ways in which their own emotions, defenses, and coping strategies affect their capacity to work effectively with clients. Thus, many programs interweave personal growth experiences in the curriculum (Merta, Wolfgang, & McNeil, 1993). In counseling labs, students frequently practice counseling skills on each other; in group classes they engage in group experiences; and in testing courses they often take the psychological tests they are studying. The inclusion of such personal growth experiences has been controversial, partly because it pits a student's right to privacy against the profession's responsibility to admit only competent professionals to the field (Corey et al., 2015). Counselor educators have divided viewpoints on the ethics of such experiences (Schwab & Neukrug, 1994). Students express both positive and negative attitudes toward such experiences, believing that they are important teaching tools but worrying that such experiences will push them into uncomfortable levels of personal disclosure (Anderson & Price, 2001). Section F.8.c of the ACA Code stipulates that faculty are responsible for explaining the nature of these experiences prior to their initiation and for clarifying that personal disclosures are at students' discretion.

In its most recent revision of the APA Code, Standard 7.04 specifies that programs are not allowed to require disclosure of highly sensitive personal information unless this requirement is documented in program materials so that prospective and current students are aware of it. The only exception allowed occurs when such information may be needed to address problems interfering with professional competence.

The APA Code uses similar language regarding required participation in individual or group therapy, indicating that students must be allowed to obtain such therapy outside of the program (Standard 7.05).

The appropriate use of personal growth experiences depends on adequate informed consent, on a boundary between materials subject to grading and the type or quality of self-disclosure in the experience, and on an agreement that the faculty member acts in all possible ways to respect the dignity of the student.

Because at times faculty are obligated to reveal or follow up on disclosures in growth experiences, students should clearly understand, prior to the experience, the circumstances that would require such action. For example, a student should be informed that comments about child abuse or neglect made in the presence of a mental health professional cannot be held in complete confidence. Similarly, if a student reveals a strong dislike for another racial group with whom she is likely to work, a faculty member must pursue that matter with the student. Because so much may be at stake for them, students ought to understand in advance the implications of disclosures. Faculty involved in growth experiences may find that written documents are helpful accompaniments to oral review of these issues with students.

When a course involves a significant amount of self-disclosure or involvement in personal growth activities, programs sometimes use part-time faculty. These faculty are less involved in other dimensions of the program and are less likely to have continuing student contact, so both students and faculty may approach the experience more comfortably and confidently. If the part-time faculty member is competent and the student is more open to disclose and participate, student growth may occur at a faster rate than with a regular faculty member. This option is not essential or always feasible, but it eases the ethical complications for all involved. Patrick (1989) also recommends avoiding placing the student in the client role in peer counseling whenever possible, suggesting instead that students from other programs in the university would be more appropriate.

Faculty overseeing such experiences have a demanding task. The codes provide guidance, but ultimately they must make difficult judgments. Student deficiencies are often on the border between competence and incompetence, and between outrageous and simply undesirable. Following a systematic strategy for ethical decision making is crucial in such ambiguous situations, as is consultation with colleagues. Rigorous admissions standards help reduce the problem but do not eliminate it.

Sometimes programs require students to obtain their own therapy as part of professional development. The APA Code does not speak directly to this issue, but it indicates that students must be allowed to obtain such therapy outside of the program and faculty must not be involved (Standard 7.05). The ACA Code does indicate that if students request counseling for themselves, faculty should assist them in finding appropriate services (Section F.9.c). As Prosek, Holm, and Daly (2013) and Ivey (2014) assert, there can be benefits to the use of mandatory counseling participation, among them a reduction in stress, anxiety, and depressive symptoms, all of which increase the likelihood that trainees will develop needed competencies for professional functioning.

An Ethics of Care

Kitchener (1992) highlights a fundamental ethical issue for faculty in mental health. Commitment to teaching is not the only reason mental health professionals become educators. Many find research, consultation, and community involvement at least as important. Indeed, universities often make rewards for faculty contingent on activities outside the classroom. Inadequacies with students or in instructional approach are regularly overlooked by institutions when faculty bring in research grants or consulting contracts to the university. One can invest in other activities, of course, not only because they can reflect positively on the training program and advance knowledge but also because of personal enjoyment. However, counseling and psychology educators ought not to sacrifice competent and caring teaching to attend to other responsibilities. Applying Nodding's concept of an ethics of care (1984), Kitchener points out that faculty who fail to care about the program, the courses, and the students are inadequate role models who are failing to promote the welfare of those they serve. Such an uncaring attitude is not a minor ethical deviation; it runs contrary to the profession's deepest ethical values.

Obligations to Colleagues

Of course, faculty have obligations to colleagues as well as to students. Principle B: Fidelity and Responsibility of the APA Code addresses this issue when it emphasizes the need for professional relationships of trust and personal responsibility for a psychologist's actions. The next case illustrates misconduct toward colleagues:

Professor Caste's Letter of Reference

Professor Caste agrees to review the promotion file of a counselor educator at another university because he is an expert in the same field as the candidate. His two-paragraph letter of review arrives several weeks later. It shows very little attention to the file of materials submitted to him. Not only does Professor Caste's letter show no evidence of having read the most important materials submitted for review, but it miscounts the total number of publications, misinterprets others, and makes inferences not supported by the evidence. Professor Caste ends his letter with a negative recommendation for promotion.

This behavior is inconsistent with the provisions of the codes that deal with avoiding harm and acting competently. Universities regularly rely on external evaluations of scholarship, and professionals asked to undertake this duty must carry it out diligently. Professor Caste's negligence may have cost a worthy teacher a promotion, or even a job, if a tenure decision was involved. The best way for Professor Caste to remedy his mistake (in the event that he recognizes the error of his ways) is to send a retraction of his initial letter, admitting the inadequacies in his first review, along with a replacement letter that fairly evaluates the candidate's work. If the promotion has been denied, he ought to encourage the university to reconsider its decision and share his communications with the candidate. He also owes an apology to the candidate. In the absence of such action, the candidate for promotion would be justified in filing an ethics complaint against him.

THE ETHICS OF RESEARCH

Most counselors and psychologists do not identify themselves as researchers. Instead, they perceive research as an activity for those in academia or in specialized research settings. Although much attention has been given to developing graduate curricula to train competent scientist-practitioners, in reality most graduates fit that definition only insofar as they are consumers of research.

Economic and societal changes seem to be fueling a challenge to this distinction between researchers and mental health practitioners. The demand for evidence-based practice in mental health and educational settings suggests that a much wider sampling of professionals needs to be involved in designing and implementing research and evaluation activities (Bradley, Sexton, & Smith, 2005; Eisen & Dickey, 1996; Lambert, 2010b; Sexton, Whiston, Bleuer, & Walz, 1997). For example, managed health care systems are seeking not only data on the effectiveness of given treatments with particular clients, but also information about the outcomes of a specific form of treatment or setting (Dimmitt, Carey, & Hatch, 2007; Reed & Eisman, 2007). Schools and community agencies are experiencing increased pressures for accountability. Consequently, the days have passed when practicing professionals could relinquish involvement in research and evaluation to academics. Third-party payers and clients alike are seeking more evidence that treatments are effective and produce expected outcomes (Goodheart, Kazdin, & Sternberg, 2007; Sexton & Liddle, 2001). This section highlights the major ethical issues practitioners confront and directs them to appropriate resources for future study. The essential ethical responsibilities of the researcher are (1) to develop scientifically acceptable research protocols that are worth participants' time and have a reasonable chance of yielding meaningful findings, (2) to protect the rights and safety of research participants (both human and animal), (3) to report results fairly and accurately, and (4) to cooperate with colleagues and share research data. Readers who seek more detailed information about ethical standards and regulations in research may find very helpful the section in Volume II of the *Handbook of Ethics in Psychology* (Knapp, Gottlieb, Handelsman, & VandeCreek, 2012).

Good Science and Good Ethics

Most research in our field requires the participation of human beings, and some of those research designs carry risks for those participants. A researcher who wants to examine the social and emotional effects on children whose parents have HIV spectrum disorders is exposing those children and their parents to a psychological risk. In revealing information that the researcher requests, participants may feel painful emotions or become aware of problems they had not yet recognized. The parents and children may encounter some difficulties in their interactions subsequent to the research. These risks are not insurmountable and may be worth enduring for the information gained. However, if the research design is not scientifically rigorous, the chance of making valid and meaningful conclusions is almost nonexistent. Substantial flaws in the design might even lead to results that contradict the actual state of affairs. In either event, it is unfair to subject people to the psychological risks of such research without the potential for scientific gain.

Rosenthal (1994) takes this analysis one step further. He contends that poorly designed and executed research is unethical even if the participants are not at risk for harm or discomfort. He argues that participants are donating valuable commodities, such as their time, attention, and cooperation. These commodities are no less valuable in low-risk research than in higher-risk research. In an interesting analogy, he encourages researchers to view participants as a kind of "granting source" to whom investigators have obligations. Poorly designed research not only wastes people's time but also makes people more skeptical about the value of research participation and makes it more difficult for other researchers with more meritorious projects to recruit participants. Inadequate research designs violate the duty to beneficence and to fidelity, even if they avoid risk of harm. Institutional review boards (IRBs) may reject even low risk studies if there is no evidence of scientific merit (Fisher & Vacanti-Shova, 2012). Gelso (1985) frames this question as one of rigor and relevance. Meritorious research attends to both the rigor of the research design and the potential of the research to be relevant to practice.

Good science also assumes sensitivity to issues of diversity (Fisher & Vacanti-Shova, 2012; Scott-Jones, 2000). Researchers, for example, who make generalizations to both genders on the basis of research with only one gender, or who fail to acknowledge limitations of their samples in cultural or ethnic diversity, are acting inappropriately. Their findings may cause harm and are vulnerable to misuse, particularly with populations not represented in their samples. Insensitive research can also do harm to diverse groups by "invalidating their life experience, defining their cultural values as different or deviant, or imposing the values of the dominant culture upon them" (Fisher & Vacanti-Shova, 2012, p. 364).

How can a practitioner ensure that a study is of sufficiently high quality to justify the risks? Obviously, good science requires researchers who are competent to conceptualize, design, and analyze data in their projects and to be knowledgeable about recent research on the same topic. Practitioners with weaknesses in any of these domains should seek training and consultation before embarking on research that involves human or animal subjects.

In recent years, the Internet has become a major medium for research, especially for recruiting participants who then complete research tasks online. Psychologists also use the Internet as a tool to study how the Internet is affecting people's lives and relationships. The ability to use the Internet to find participants and conduct research has opened up new opportunities for access to diverse populations and for examining different research questions. The Internet can often produce huge samples not obtainable in other methods of study. And as many doctoral students have discovered, collecting survey data via the Internet is much less expensive than the postal service. Many of the ethical issues in using the Internet for research overlap with the issues in mail, telephone, or face-to-face research, such as protecting participants' rights, managing risks to privacy, and ensuring merit of the work. However, there are unique concerns, such as verifying that the person who is participating is the person the research expects, managing informed consent through electronic means, and protecting the data collected from unauthorized users. For more information about the ethics of Internet research, see Hoerger and Currell (2012).

Protecting the Rights of Research Participants

Ensuring that a project has scientific merit is only one component of ethical research. Scientific gains cannot be made at the cost of the health or well-being of participants. History has taught many lessons about the devastation blind devotion to science can inflict when the rights of participants are ignored. The Tuskegee experiments, the injection of live cancer cells into chronically ill patients in the 1960s, and the electronic surveillance of jury rooms without jurors' knowledge are just three of the most notorious of such examples of harmful research (Katz, 1972). The mental health professions have attempted to prevent the recurrence of such misconduct by giving this topic extensive coverage in the ethics codes. In fact, protecting the rights of participants receives more attention in the codes than any other issue in research ethics. In essence, these documents require the following:

- Fair and noncoercive recruiting of participants that honors their dignity
- Responsible use of incentives to participate, avoiding incentives that are practically impossible to refuse
- Communicating informed consent in understandable ways
- Vigorously protecting the rights of those vulnerable to abuse (such as prisoners or institutionalized patients) or those incompetent to give consent
- Providing for children to "assent" to research, even though consent for such participation must come from parents and guardians (Kodish, 2005; Powell & Vache-Hasse, 1994)
- Avoiding deception about particulars of the research unless it is justified by the scientific merit of the study and no good alternatives exist (Kimmel, 2012; Pittinger, 2002)
- Describing of the results of research to participants if they wish, as soon as the data are ready for dissemination (Fernandez, Kodish, & Weijer, 2003) (a process also referred to as *debriefing*)
- Protecting the anonymity of research participants and the confidentiality of their disclosures unless they explicitly consent to release of personal information
- Overseeing others involved in the research, such as graduate students and technical staff, so that they do not violate participants' rights

Many of the ethical mandates just listed have also been codified into laws or regulations. Federal rules are spelled out in Title 45 of the Code of Federal Regulations (Office for Protection from Research Risks, Protection of Human Subjects, 1991) and are delineated in HIPAA regulations (HIPAA, 1996). Thus, penalties for their violation can extend beyond the discipline of a professional association. As part of regulations governing human research subjects, the federal government has mandated the creation of institutional review boards (IRBs) at research institutions to approve and oversee the conduct of any research that involves risk of harming human subjects. Much of the responsibility of institutional review boards is directed toward ensuring that researchers respect participants' rights and minimize risks. These committees have the power to approve, reject, or mandate changes in research proposals that come before them and to monitor ongoing research for compliance with legal mandates. A negative vote by an IRB prevents research from going forward, and an unfavorable review of research in progress can stop its continuance. In psychological or clinical research, IRB review panels are especially attentive to the completeness and comprehensibility of informed consent procedures, the voluntariness of participation, and the protection of the confidentiality of information received. They also examine research proposals to ensure that participants understand that they can withdraw from research at any point without penalty and that they can contact researchers with questions at any point in the process. All investigators connected with an institution must have their research approved by an IRB. This duty applies to students, faculty, volunteers, and to other paid employees. Any professional who is not affiliated with an institution that is subject to IRB regulations is still obliged to follow the law and the ethical mandates for responsible research (Fisher & Vacanti-Shova, 2012).

Mental health researchers rely on animal research less commonly than their counterparts in basic social science, but there have been important studies, particularly using primates, in which mental health researchers have been involved. The animal rights movement has severely criticized the use of animals in psychological and medical research as inherently cruel (Galvin & Herzog, 1992; Koocher & Keith-Spiegel, 2008). The philosophical debate about the morality of animal research is not resolved, but this movement has caused several changes, including more federal regulation, clearer ethical standards, and the emergence of institutional review boards at organizations that conduct animal research (Bersoff, 2008). Therefore, it behooves mental health professionals to be aware of the ethical guidelines for research with animals. In 1993, the APA published the *Guidelines for Ethical Conduct in the Care and Use of Nonhuman Animals* (2012b), which explains the circumstances under which animal research is justified, the responsibilities of those who care for the animals, the conditions for humanely housing animals, the appropriate experimental and field research procedures, and the responsible use of animals for educational purposes. These standards were designed to help prevent the abuses of animal welfare that helped fuel the protests by animal rights activists and to ensure that meritorious research can continue. See Perry and Dess (2012) for an extensive discussion of ethical care of research animals.

Fair and Objective Reporting of Results

Once data are collected and analyzed, researchers have several more ethical obligations. The most basic obligation is not to misrepresent the results in any publication or communication of them to participants or colleagues. Unfortunately, this form of research misconduct has occurred on more than one occasion. Miller and Hersen (1992) cite several notorious examples of such misconduct. Investigators have fabricated data, changed findings, selectively reported only supportive results, and engaged in a variety of efforts to mislead the public about the nature of their findings. Sales and Lavin (2000) also note that pressure on researchers to maintain funding by grant sources sometimes tempts researchers to engage in misconduct. Recent research by Martinson, Anderson, and de Vries (2005) reveals that research misconduct is more common than ever believed. In their study of thousands of research scientists in the United States, they found that one-third of the respondents had engaged in at least one type of research misconduct (either fabrication, falsification, or plagiarism) in the previous three years. Both the ACA Code (Section G.4.a) and the APA Code (Standards 8.10 and 8.11) are explicit on the requirement for research integrity. Perfect and Stark (2008) caution professionals to remember that not all plagiarism is deliberate. They refer to unconscious plagiarism, suggesting, for example, that it can occur when researchers erroneously think an idea is theirs when they actually came across it previously. And finally, it is possible to plagiarize oneself by republishing content that has already been published without acknowledging the prior publication.

Deliberate violations of this kind are classic examples of conflicts of interest. They seem to happen when researchers' self-interest overtakes their judgment and when research environments push hard for productivity, without regard for professional standards of conduct. It can also take place when outside commercial interests fund the research (Fisher & Vacanti-Shova, 2012). When professionals intercede to make the research misconduct of others known, they are clearly acting in accordance with ethical standards. When professionals act as "whistleblowers," in the long run they tend not to regret that they took this step, in spite of the discomfort that action can engender, especially when others or institutions try to retaliate against them. See Sprague (1993) for a fascinating history of his experience as a whistleblower regarding the research misconduct of Stephen E. Breuning.

One other cause of trimming or altering research data must be acknowledged. In small, single-authored studies and qualitative research designs, the principal investigator is often the only person who has access to the raw data. Investigators conducting this kind of research tend to have little supervision and little chance of being caught if they alter the data. When researchers have much riding on the outcome of a study, they can be vulnerable to altering data to fit their expectations. Consequently, the ethics of research depends on the integrity of the individual researcher and the commitment of research centers to properly oversee all projects at their institutions. Researchers tempted to turn a blind eye to the ethical standards in this matter and who cannot be swayed by an appeal to the ethical values of the profession are well advised to remember two things: Even a small misrepresentation of the data can ruin a career and a reputation, and enforcement of standards in this arena is improving.

Sometimes researchers obtain findings that are contrary to their expectations or to their current theory. In this situation, an investigator may be tempted not to publish these results. However, not publishing such findings also runs counter to the duty to accurately communicate results, and is inappropriate. Hiding such results may mean that other researchers pursue unproductive paths and that a more complete explanation of the phenomenon of interest is delayed. Once again, the professional's responsibility is to serve the greater good rather than his or her own personal preferences. This responsibility is codified in the ACA Code, Section G.4.b, along with the duty to correct errors found in research after dissemination (G.4.c).

The emergence of qualitative methods of research has been met with both enthusiasm and skepticism in the field of mental health. The paradigm upon which it operates is quite different from traditional quantitative methods, and it presents its own unique research challenges. The potential impact of the unconscious assumptions of the researcher on the results, the increased risks to participants who often reveal much more about themselves than they do in quantitative studies, and the issue of dual role relationships take on great importance in qualitative research. See Haverkamp (2005) and Rowan (2000) for a detailed discussion of these issues.

Cooperation With Research Colleagues

The ultimate goal of clinical research is to add to the profession's and the public's understanding of human behavior. Research serves a social good insofar as it informs professionals about matters that affect the efficacy of their work with clients. The aim of research is not to build the reputation of an investigator or to gain anyone job security or financial reward, although these outcomes may be secondary benefits of good research. Thus, research is, by definition, a cooperative endeavor in which research findings are shared with colleagues and peer criticism is conducted in an educative rather than punitive fashion. Withholding information from colleagues who are making good-faith requests for data is unethical precisely because it contradicts the fundamental purpose of research. Of course, it is important to acknowledge that researchers are often in competition with each other for funding, promotions, or public acclaim. To some degree, this competition can motivate researchers to conduct more rigorous research, but it can also spark hostile and uncooperative attitudes among those working in the same field.

Researchers are also advised to retain raw data for a number of years so that other qualified researchers may have access to it if they wish to reanalyze the data. The Code does not specify an exact interval for retaining such data, but it is prudent to keep data for at least 10 years. Now that a great deal of data can be stored on a portable computer disk, it may be feasible to keep raw data indefinitely. The only caution about such sharing of data relates to the rights of research participants.

Credit for Publishing Research

The same pressures that sometimes influence the willingness of professionals to share data also affect their attitudes toward research publications and cause them to accept undue credit in publications (Barnett & Campbell, 2012; Geelhoed, Phillips, Fischer, Shpungin, & Gong, 2007). Godlee (2009) published research that suggests that as many as 20% of articles in medical journals include an "honorary author" who did not contribute to the research. In a "publish or perish" environment, researchers may become overly concerned about the number of their publications and less attentive about the quality of these publications or their own actual contribution to the study. Some have been known to "trade authorships" in exchange for favors. Both codes speak directly to this issue, and their messages are clear. They dictate that professionals accept authorship on work in which they have made a significant contribution. The order of authorship ought to reflect the level of contribution to the research and writing. Second, no one may take credit for publications in which he or she was uninvolved. A role as director or department chair at the time a project was conducted, for example, does not constitute involvement. Faculty who take more credit than is due are misusing their power over students, a practice that results in considerable distress, as the study of Nguyen and Nguyen (2006) illustrates. Third, when student theses or dissertations are published, students have first authorship if the adviser's name also appears on the publication (APA Code, Standard 8.12c). Generally, advisers should consider a second authorship only if they were substantially involved in the research (APA Ethics Committee, 1983). In other faculty–student research collaborations, faculty are obliged to respect the contributions of students and give them appropriate credit for their work (Fine & Kurdek, 1993; Goodyear, Crego, & Johnston, 1992), a view that students strongly support (Tryon, Bishop, & Hatfield, 2007). Finally, when submitting a manuscript for publication, it should be sent to only one journal at a time (ACA, G.5.g). However, if one journal chooses not to publish the manuscript, of course the author may send the manuscript to another journal.

A corollary responsibility of faculty who supervise student research is to educate students regarding research integrity, an activity that does not seem to be occurring on any systematic level in master's-level courses (Wester, 2007). Wester offers several recommendations to remedy this omission, and the Office of Research Integrity of the U.S. Department of Health and Human Services has numerous resources on its website to assist both educators and researchers (http://ori.dhhs.gov/). Not surprisingly, doctoral students express great confidence in the training they have had to conduct research responsibly, though few of them undertake research studies with clinical or diverse populations (Fisher, Fried, & Feldman, 2009).

SPECIAL ETHICAL CONCERNS FOR COUNSELING AND THERAPY RESEARCHERS

There are four special concerns of researchers in counseling and psychotherapy process and outcome. The first relates to experimental design. Research that explores the usefulness of counseling interventions usually employs comparison groups. One or more groups receive the experimental treatment, and another receives either a standard treatment or a placebo. Because all participants might benefit from the new treatment for their problems, one must question whether it is ethical to withhold the experimental treatment. Several factors should be considered when designing such research. First, there is no assurance that the experimental treatment will be helpful; it may have no effect or may even be counterproductive. Second, without comparison groups, no one can be sure of the effects of the new treatment, and its real usefulness cannot be determined with confidence. Third, usually experimental treatments are not truly withheld, but rather delayed. When comparison groups are used, the standard of practice is to offer the new treatment to those groups once the initial round is complete. Researchers who are considering a research design that does not at least offer a delayed exposure to an experimental treatment found useful after a first round of experimentation are not acting consistently with current guidelines.

The second special concern deals with the impact of treatments on participants. Whenever research is being conducted on clinical populations, researchers have an obligation to be alert for deterioration effects and to intervene if the deterioration puts a participant at risk. In this situation, the scientific profit must be sacrificed to the well-being of the individual. An appropriate referral must be made. Those who volunteer for such research should also clearly understand this option at the time they give consent for participation. Additional ethical concerns emerge when conducting psychotherapy efficacy research with children or others unable to give legal consent (Kendall & Suveg, 2008).

The third special issue concerns the accessibility of written information about clients and the need for client consent to such activities. Research that reviews client records without the actual participation of the client is controversial. Since no one is put at risk or inconvenienced, in one sense no consent for this research seems necessary; however, a review of client records is probably not within the expectations clients had when they consented to counseling. A commitment by the researcher to honor the confidentiality of the documents lessens the ethical concerns somewhat, but the practice is still not fully consistent with respect for the client's dignity and privacy. Thus, when possible, it seems best to obtain client consent before review of any records or to include a provision for that consent in the general consent obtained at the onset of counseling or therapy so that HIPAA standards are met. If neither of these options is feasible, perhaps the clinicians involved with the clients can remove all identifying data from the records before researchers use them. (See DuBois [2008] and Fisher & Vacanti-Shova [2012]) for a detailed analysis of ethical issues in mental health research.)

Ethical questions also arise when clinicians publish clinical case material. The codes oblige professionals to take extra care with confidentiality and consent in this circumstance. See APA Code, Standard 4.07, for the specific language (Appendix B, p. 545).

Stoller (1988) cites examples of clients who found case material about them published without their knowledge or consent. They felt sad and betrayed. Even when consent is sought for such publication, Garvey and Braun (1997) caution that mental health professionals must be alert for clients who acquiesce rather than consent for fear of alienating the professional. Because dissemination of knowledge from case studies is an important mechanism to teaching new professionals and exploring the effects of complex treatments, professionals ought not to be discouraged from using them. Rather, they should be scrupulous that the rights of the client to consent, confidentiality, and anonymity are protected. The journal *Counseling and Values* published a special issue in 2010 on writing about clients that would be very valuable to anyone interested in such an activity.

The fourth special concern is the provision of feedback. The ethics codes mandate that participants be given feedback about the outcomes of research if they are interested in that information (ACA, Section G.2.h; APA, Standard 8.08). Some research suggests that feedback to participants about the results of a study is frequently neglected, however. McConnell and Kerbs (1993) found that more than 30% of the researchers in their study failed to provide the feedback they had agreed to provide when people were asked to participate in their studies. According to the authors, this happened largely because researchers gave feedback a low priority. To avoid this problem, researchers ought to realign their priorities and structure their time better to honor their duty to feedback. The failure to follow up may diminish participants' willingness to volunteer for future studies.

Because conducting research can be expensive, finding funding for research can provide ethical challenges for researchers, especially in an era in which pharmaceutical companies, insurers, and other for-profit entities are often interested in supporting research on therapeutic interventions (and are some of the few sources with the resources to fund studies). In situations in which a third party is offering financial support to research, the mental health professional must disclose this support, design the research as objectively and rigorously as possible, be free to publish results even if they contradict the interests of the funding sources, and be alert to possible misuses of the results. Reports of researchers or pharmaceutical companies withholding results that do not support the use of the medication under study or others falsifying data to align with the expectations of funding sources have occurred frequently in the literature. In fact, when physicians and psychologists are receiving funding from pharmaceutical companies, manufacturers of medical devices, and related third parties, many hospitals, professional journals, and professional associations require disclosure of such relationships in all public communications of research data.

SUMMARY

The ethical issues of teaching closely parallel supervision. The faculty member has obligations not only to students but also to the public whom those students will serve and to the profession. Faculty members violate ethical standards when they teach without proper knowledge, without proper sensitivity to individual differences, or with nonobjective techniques. They are also guilty of misconduct when they exploit their students' needs for positive evaluations, research experience, or clinical involvement. Faculty who act irresponsibly with colleagues are no less guilty of misconduct.

Because faculty are encouraged to act as mentors to students, they must be careful not to take mentoring past the boundary of an appropriate professional contact. Boundaries of faculty–student relationships need not be drawn as rigidly or as narrowly as boundaries between clients and therapists, but they still exist. An ethics of care and respect for student autonomy is one useful guide to effective, responsible teaching and advising.

Researchers have several important ethical obligations, including conducting research studies that are of sufficient quality to contribute to knowledge, protecting the rights of human and animal participants, communicating and sharing research results with the professional community, avoiding fraudulent or misleading publication of results, and claiming authorship only when justified. Researchers must give priority to their responsibilities to honor the dignity of participants and help advance science over their personal interests.

Discussion Questions*

1. Some counseling and psychotherapy training programs require students to obtain individual counseling during graduate school. Assuming counseling is not provided by the teaching faculty, what do you see as the ethical dimensions of this practice?
2. How should faculty members deal with insensitive and prejudiced comments they overhear students making outside the classroom?
3. Universities are strongly encouraging faculty to teach courses via distance learning and the Internet. Some entire programs in mental health are in a distance-learning format. What do you see as the ethical implications of such approaches to clinical training in light of the gatekeeper responsibilities of faculty?
4. Some doctoral programs strongly encourage doctoral students to do their dissertations in the same areas as faculty research. They are not prohibited from choosing other options, but they get little support for such choices. Is this an ethical violation? Why or why not?
5. Much research in our field involves "convenient samples," such as college or graduate

*Note to course instructors: *The Instructor's Guide* for this book includes other discussion questions, class exercises, cases, and multiple-choice and essay test items for this chapter.

students, rather than other, less accessible groups in society. What ethical issues does such a practice engender?

6. Complete objectivity in research is impossible. Researchers naturally "hope" for particular outcomes for their studies. How can those involved in research deal effectively with the ethical implications of their disappointment when research findings contradict their expectations?

Cases for Discussion

Jefferson teaches methods of counseling to mental health counselors. In the course, he illustrates concepts with examples from his own private practice and sometimes shows videotaped role-plays of techniques to the class. In one session, he asks for a volunteer from the class who is willing to reveal a personal concern before the group so that he can do a live demonstration of a counseling session in class. He sees such demonstrations as crucial to effective teaching of counseling methods. In 18 years of teaching, he has never been refused this request. The personal concerns students have discussed have ranged from test anxiety to suicidal depression. After the class, he refers volunteers who need further counseling to the university counseling center. Is Jefferson's practice consistent with ethical guidelines for mental health educators? If not, what can he do to make it more ethical?

Kara is conducting research on the ethics of Internet counseling. She is most interested in the quality of the counseling Internet counselors provide. She poses as a client with depressive feelings and gets online counseling from 35 different websites. She publishes her research in a major journal. One of the Internet counselors recognizes the question that Kara poses and files an ethics complaint against her. He charges that she violated the ethics code because she deceived him into believing she was a real client and that he did not consent to participate in research. If you were on the ethics committee, how would you respond to this complaint against Kara?

Recommended Readings

Association for Counselor Education and Supervision (ACES). (2009). Guidelines for research mentorship in counseling/counselor education. Retrieved from: http://www.acesonline.net/wp-content/uploads/2010/12/ACES-research-mentorship-guidelines.pdf

American Psychological Association (APA). (2012b). Guidelines for ethical conduct in the care and use of nonhuman animals in research. Retrieved from http://apa.org/science/leadership/care/guidelines.aspx?item=1

Barnett, J. E., & Campbell, L. F. (2012). Ethical issues in scholarship. In S. J. Knapp, M. C. Gottlieb, & L. D. VandeCreek (Eds.), *APA handbook of ethics in psychology* (Vol. 1, pp. 309–333). Washington, D.C.: American Psychological Association.

Behnke, S. H. (2012). Constitutional claims in the context of mental health training: Religion, sexual orientation, and tensions between the first amendment and professional ethics. *Training and Education in Professional Psychology*, 6, 189–195.

Fine, M. A., & Kurdek, L. A. (1993). Reflections on determining authorship credit and authorship order on faculty–student collaborations. *American Psychologist*, *48*, 1141–1147.

Fisher, C. B., & Vacanti-Shova, K. (2012). The responsible conduct of psychological research: Overview of ethical principles, APA code standards and federal regulations. In S. J. Knapp, M. C. Gottlieb, M. M. Handelsman, & L. D. VandeCreek (Eds.), *APA handbook of ethics in psychology* (Vol. 2, pp. 335–369). Washington, D.C.: American Psychological Association.

Haverkamp, B. E. (2005). Ethical perspectives on qualitative research in applied psychology. *Journal of Counseling Psychology*, 52, 146–155.

Herlihy, B. J., Hermann, M. A., & Greden, L. R. (2014). Legal and ethical implications of using religious beliefs as the basis for refusing to counsel certain clients. *Journal of Counseling & Development*, 92, 148–153.

Johnson, W. B., & Campbell, C. D. (2004). Character and fitness requirements for professional psychologists: Training directors' perspectives. *Professional Psychology: Research and Practice, 35*, 405–411.

Keith-Spiegel, P., Wittig, A. F., Perkins, D. V., Balogh, D. W., & Whitley, B. E., Jr. (1993). *The ethics of teaching: A casebook*. Muncie, IN: Ball State University.

Kodish, E. (2005). *Ethics and research with children: A case-based approach*. New York, NY: Oxford.

Rosenthal, R. (1994). Science and ethics in conducting, analyzing, and reporting psychological research. *Psychological Science, 5*, 127–134.

Sales, B. D., & Folkman, S. (Eds.). (2000). *Ethics in research with human participants*. Washington, D.C.: American Psychological Association.

Sieber, J. E., & Tolich, M. B. (2013). *Planning ethically responsible research: A guide for students and internal review boards* (2nd ed.). Newbury Park, CA: Sage.

Tabachnick, B. G., Keith-Spiegel, P. S., & Pope, K. S. (1991). Ethics of teaching: Beliefs and behaviors of psychologists as educators. *American Psychologist, 46*, 506–515.

Welfel, E. R. (2012). Teaching ethics: Models, methods, and challenges. In S. J. Knapp, M. C. Gottlieb, & M. M. Handelsman (Eds.), *APA handbook of ethics in psychology* (Vol. 2, pp. 277–305). Washington, D.C.: APA Press.

Additional Online Resources

Office of Research Integrity module on avoiding plagiarism: http://ori.dhhs.gov/education/products/plagiarism/.

Other guidelines from the Office of Research Integrity: http://ori.dhhs.gov/publications/handbooks.shtml.

References

Acuff, C., Bennett, B. E., Bricklin, P. M., Canter, M. B., Knapp, S. J., Moldawsky, S., & Phelps, R. (1999). Considerations for ethical practice in managed care. *Professional Psychology: Research and Practice, 30*, 563–575.

Adams, A., & Sharkin, B. S. (2012). Should continuing education be mandatory for re-licensure? Arguments for and against. In G. J. Neimeyer & J. M. Taylor (Eds.), *Continuing professional development and lifelong learning* (pp. 157–178). Hauppauge, NY: Nova Science Publications.

Adams, J., Kottke, J. L., & Padgit, J. S. (1983). Sexual harassment of university students. *Journal of College Student Personnel, 24*, 484–490.

Adams, Z. W., & Boyd, S. E. (2010). Ethical challenges in the treatment of individuals with intellectual disabilities. *Ethics & Behavior, 20*, 407–418.

Adelman, J., & Barrett, S. E. (1990). Overlapping relationships: Importance of a feminist ethical perspective. In H. Lerman & N. Porter (Eds.), *Feminist ethics in psychotherapy* (pp. 87–91). New York, NY: Springer.

Agency for Healthcare Research and Quality. (2005). National healthcare disparities report. Retrieved from http://www.ahrq.gov/qual/nhdr05/nhdr05.htm

Ahlstrand, K. R., Crumlin, J., Korinek, L. L., Lasky, G. B., & Kitchener, K. S. (2003, August). *Sexual contact between students and educators: Issues and ethics*. Paper presented at the annual meeting of the American Psychological Association, Toronto, Canada.

Akamatsu, T. J. (1988). Intimate relationships with former clients: National survey of attitudes and behavior among practitioners. *Professional Psychology: Research and Practice, 19*, 454–458.

Alarcón, R. D., Becker, A. E., Lewis-Fernandez, R., Like, R. C., Desai, P., Foulks, E., & Primm, A. (2009). Issues for DSM-V: The role of culture in psychiatric diagnosis. *Journal of Nervous and Mental Disease, 197*, 559–560.

Alexander, K., & Alexander, M. D. (2005). *American public school law* (6th ed.). Belmont, CA: Thompson West.

Alleman, J. R. (2002). Online counseling: The Internet and mental health treatment. *Psychotherapy: Theory/Research/Practice/Training, 39*, 199–215.

Allen, G. J., Szollos, S. J., & Williams, B. E. (1986). Doctoral students' comparative evaluations of best and worst psychotherapy supervision. *Professional Psychology: Research and Practice, 17*, 91–99.

Alyn, J. H. (1988). The politics of touch in therapy: A response to Willison and Masson. *Journal of Counseling & Development, 66*, 432–433.

Amada, G. (1993). Some ethical considerations: A commentary on "Between Cordelia and Guido: The consultant's role in urgent situations." *Journal of College Student Psychotherapy, 7*, 23–34.

Amatea, E. S., & Clark, M. A. (2005). Changing schools, changing counselors: A qualitative study of school administrators' conceptions of the school counselor role. *Professional School Counseling, 9*, 16–27.

American Academy of Clinical Neuropsychology (AACN). (2007). Practice guidelines for neuropsychological assessment and consultation. *The Clinical Neuropsychologist, 21*, 209–231.

American Association for Marriage and Family Therapy (AAMFT). (2012). Code of ethics. Retrieved from http://www.aamft.org/imis15/content/legal_ethics/code_of_ethics.aspx

American Association of Christian Counselors. (AACC). (2004). AACC Code of ethics. Retrieved from http://www.aacc.net/about-us/code-of-ethics/

American Association of Pastoral Counselors (AAPC). (2012). Code of ethics. Retrieved from http://www.aapc.org/about-us/code-of-ethics

American Academy of Pediatrics. (n.d.). Confidentiality laws tip sheet. Retrieved from http://www.aap.org/en-us/advocacy-and-policy/aap-health-initiatives/healthy-foster-care-america/Documents/Confidentiality_Laws.pdf

American Association of State Counseling Boards (AASCB). (2007). Approved supervisor model. Retrieved from http://www.aascb.org/associations/7905/files/AASCB_Supervision_Model-0607.pdf

American Association of Sexuality Educators, Counselors, and Therapists (AASECT). (2004). Code of ethics. Retrieved from http://www.aasect.org/sites/default/files/documents/Code%20of%20Ethics%20and%20Conduct.pdf

American Association of State Counseling Boards (AASCB). (2009). Listserv survey—CEU reporting. Retrieved from http://associationdatabase.com/aws/AASCB/asset_manager/get_file/37352

American Association of Suicidology (AAS). (2007). Youth suicide fact sheet. Retrieved from http://211bigbend.net/PDFs/YouthSuicideFactSheet.pdf

American College Personnel Association (ACPA). (2006). Statement of ethical principles and standards. Retrieved from http://www.acpa.nche.edu/sites/default/files/Ethical_Principles_Standards.pdf

American Counseling Association (ACA). (1995). Code of ethics and standards of practice. Retrieved from https://www.counseling.org/Resources/Library/ACA%20Archive/Code%20of%20Ethics%201995.pdf

American Counseling Association (ACA). (1998). Principles for identifying the early warning signs of school violence. Alexandria, VA: Author.

American Counseling Association (ACA). (1999). *The layperson's guide to professional ethics*. Washington, D.C.: Author.

American Counseling Association (ACA). (2005a). Code of ethics and standards of practice. Retrieved from http://www.ncblpc.org/Laws_and_Codes/ACA_Code_of_Ethics.pdf

American Counseling Association (ACA). (2005b). Policies and procedures for processing complaints of ethical violations. Retrieved from http://www.counseling.org/docs/ethics/policies_procedures.pdf?sfvrsn=2

American Counseling Association (ACA). (2009). Competencies for counseling transgender clients. Retrieved from http://www.counseling.org/Resources/Competencies/ALGBTIC_Competencies.pdf

American Counseling Association (ACA). (2011a). *Ethics Committee summary FY 2010*. Washington, D.C.: Author.

American Counseling Association (ACA). (2011b). United States student-to-counselor ratios. Retrieved from http://www.counseling.org/PublicPolicy/ACA_Ratio_Chart_2011_Overall.pdf

American Counseling Association (ACA) and the Association for Lesbian, Gay, Bisexual, and Transgender Issues in Counseling (ALGBTI). (2012). Competencies for counseling with lesbian, gay, bisexual, queer, questioning, intersex and ally individuals. Retrieved from http://www.counseling.org/docs/competencies/algbtic-competencies-for-counseling-lgbqqia-individuals.pdf?sfvrsn=6

American Counseling Association (ACA). (2013). Ethics Committee summary 2012–2013. Retrieved from http://www.counseling.org/docs/ethics/complaints_fy13_i.pdf?sfvrsn=2

American Counseling Association (ACA). (2014). Code of ethics. Retrieved from http://www.counseling.org/resources/aca-code-of-ethics.pdf

American Counseling Association (ACA) and the Association for Lesbian, Gay, Bisexual, and Transgender Issues in Counseling (ALGBTI). (2009). Competencies for counseling transgender clients. Retrieved from http://www.counseling.org/Resources/Competencies/ALGBTIC_Competencies.pdf

American Educational Research Association (AERA), American Psychological Association (APA), & National Council on Measurement in Education (NCME). (2014). *Standards for educational and psychological tests*. Washington, D.C.: Author.

American Group Psychotherapy Association (AGPA). (2002). AGPA and NRCGP guidelines for ethics. Retrieved from http://www.agpa.org/home/practice-resources/ethics-in-group-therapy

American Group Therapy Association. (2007). Practice guidelines for group psychotherapy. Retrieved from http://www.agpa.org/home/practice-resources/practice-guidelines-for-group-psychotherapy

American Medical Association (AMA). (2001). Principles of medical ethics. Retrieved from http://www.ama-assn.org/ama/pub/physician-resources/medical-ethics/code--medical-ethics/principles-medical-ethics.page

American Medical Informatics Association. (2006). Statement of ethical principles and standards. Retrieved from http://www.amia.org/about-amia/ethics

American Mental Health Counselors Association (AMHCA). (2010). Code of ethics for mental health counselors. Retrieved from http://www.amhca.org/assets/news/AMHCA_Code_of_Ethics_2010_w_pagination_cxd_51110.pdf

American Music Therapy Association (AMTA). (2008). Code of ethics. Retrieved from http://www.musictherapy.org/about/ethics/

American Psychiatric Association. (1999). Psychotherapy and managed care position statement. Retrieved from http://www.psychiatry.org/advocacy–newsroom/position-statements

American Psychiatric Association. (2009). Principles of medical ethics with annotations especially applicable to psychiatry. Retrieved from http://www.psychiatry.org/practice/ethics

American Psychiatric Association. (2013). *Diagnostic and statistical manual of mental disorders* (5th ed.) [DSM-V]. Washington, D.C.: Author.

American Psychoanalytic Association (APsaA). (2009). Principles and standards of ethics for psychoanalysts. Retrieved from http://www.apsa.org/About_APsaA/Ethics_Code.aspx

American Psychological Association (APA). (1973). *Guidelines for psychologists conducting growth groups*. Washington, D.C.: Author.

American Psychological Association (APA). (1981a). *Ethical principles*. Washington, D.C.: Author.

American Psychological Association (APA). (1981b). *Specialty guidelines for the delivery of services: Clinical psychologists, counseling psychologists, organizational/industrial psychologists, school psychologists*. Washington, D.C.: Author.

American Psychological Association (APA). (1982). *Ethical principles in the conduct of research with human participants*. Washington, D.C.: Author.

American Psychological Association (APA). (1991). *Legal liability related to confidentiality and the prevention of HIV transmission*. Washington, D.C.: Author.

American Psychological Association (APA). (1992). *Ethical principles of psychologists and code of conduct*. Washington, D.C.: Author.

American Psychological Association (APA). (1993). *Guidelines for ethical conduct in the care and use of animals*. Washington, D.C.: Author.

American Psychological Association (APA). (1994). Guidelines for child custody evaluations in divorce proceedings. *American Psychologist*, *49*, 677–680.

American Psychological Association (APA). (1997). What practitioners should know about working with older adults. Retrieved from http://www.apa.org/pi/aging/resources/guides/practitioners-should-know.aspx

American Psychological Association (APA). (1999a). Guidelines for psychological evaluations in child protection matters. *American Psychologist*, *54*, 586–593.

American Psychological Association (APA). (1999b). Rights and responsibilities of test takers: Guidelines and expectations. Retrieved from http://www.apa.org/science/ttrr.html

American Psychological Association (APA). (1999c). *Suggestions for psychologists working with the media*. Washington, D.C.: Author.

American Psychological Association (APA). (1999d). *Warning signs: A youth anti-violence initiative*. Washington, D.C.: Retrieved from http://www.apahelpcenter.org/.featuredtopics/feature.php?id=38

American Psychological Association (APA). (2001a). Appropriate use of high stakes testing in our nation's schools. Retrieved from http://www.apa.org/pubs/info/brochures/testing.aspx

American Psychological Association (APA). (2001b). APA's Council of Representatives passes resolution on assisted suicide. Retrieved from http://www.apa.org/monitor/apr01/council.aspx

American Psychological Association (APA). (2001c). Guidelines for test user qualifications: An executive summary. *American Psychologist*, *56*, 1099–1113.

American Psychological Association (APA). (2003). Guidelines on multicultural education, training, research, practice, and organizational change for psychologists. *American Psychologist*, *58*, 377–402.

American Psychological Association (APA). (2005). Statement on the use of secure psychological tests in the education of graduate and undergraduate psychology students. Retrieved from http://www.apa.org/science/leadership/tests/test-security.aspx

American Psychological Association (APA). (2007a). Guidelines for psychological practice with girls and women. Retrieved from http://www.apa.org/practice/guidelines/girls-and-women.aspx

American Psychological Association (APA). (2007b). Statement on third party observers in psychological testing and assessment: A framework for decision making. Retrieved from http://www.apa.org/science/programs/testing/third-party-observers.pdf

American Psychological Association (APA). (2007c). Record keeping guidelines. *American Psychologist*, *62*, 993–1004. Retrieved from http://www.apa.org/practice/recordkeeping.pdf

American Psychological Association (APA). (2007d). Reaffirmation of the American Psychological Association position against torture and other cruel, inhuman, or degrading treatment or punishment and its application to individuals defined in the United States code as "enemy combatants." Retrieved from http://www.apa.org/about/policy/torture.aspx

American Psychological Association. (2008a). Blueprint for change: Achieving integrated health care for an aging population. Retrieved from http://www.apa.org/pi/aging/programs/integrated/integrated-healthcare-report.pdf

American Psychological Association. (2008b). Summary of APA policy on psychologists' involvement in national security interrogations: Association's strict prohibition against torture and abuse tied to international standards for the protection of human rights. Retrieved from http://www.apa.org/news/press/releases/2008/07/interrogations.aspx

American Psychological Association. (2009a). Appropriate therapeutic responses to sexual orientation. Retrieved from http://www.apa.org/pi/lgbt/resources/therapeutic-response.pdf

American Psychological Association (APA). (2009b). A stronger vision for APA. Retrieved from http://www.apa.org/monitor/2009/04/vision-apa.aspx

American Psychological Association (APA). (2009c). Report of the Ethics Committee, 2009. *American Psychologist*, *64*, 464–475.

American Psychological Association (APA). (2010a). Ethical principles of psychologists and code of conduct. Retrieved from http://www.apa.org/ethics/code/index.aspx

American Psychological Association (APA). (2010b). Guidelines for child custody evaluations in family law proceedings. *American Psychologist*, *65*, 863–867.

American Psychological Association (APA). (2010c). Report of the Ethics Committee, 2009. *American Psychologist*, *65*, 483–492.

American Psychological Association (APA). (2010d). Survey findings emphasize the importance of self care for psychologists. Retrieved from http://www.apapracticecentral.org/update/2010/08-31/survey.aspx

American Psychological Association (APA). (2011a). Guidelines for assessment of and intervention with persons with disabilities. Retrieved from http://www.apa.org/pi/disability/resources/assessment-disabilities.aspx

American Psychological Association (APA). (2011b). Practice guidelines for LGB clients. Retrieved from http://www.apa.org/pi/lgbt/resources/guidelines.aspx

American Psychological Association (APA). (2011c). Practice guidelines regarding psychologists' involvement in pharmacological issues. *American Psychologist*, *66*, 835–849.

American Psychological Association (APA). (2012a). Report of the Ethics Committee, 2011. *American Psychologist*, *67*, 398–408.

American Psychological Association (APA). (2012b). Guidelines for ethical conduct in the care and use of nonhuman animals in research. Retrieved from http://apa.org/science/leadership/care/guidelines.aspx?item=1

American Psychological Association (APA). (2013a). Guidelines for psychological evaluation in child protection matters. *American Psychologist*, *68*, 20–31.

American Psychological Association. (2013b). Guidelines for the practice of telepsychology. Retrieved from http://www.apapracticecentral.org/ce/guidelines/telepsychology-guidelines.pdf

American Psychological Association. (2013c). Guidelines for the undergraduate psychology major. Retrieved from http://www.apa.org/ed/precollege/about/psymajor-guidelines.pdf

American Psychological Association (APA). (2013d). Report of the Ethics Committee, 2012. *American Psychologist*, *68*, 370–379.

American Psychological Association. (2013e). Specialty guidelines for forensic psychology. Retrieved from http://www.apa.org/practice/guidelines/forensic-psychology.pdf

American Psychological Association (APA). (2014a). Guidelines for psychological practice with older adults. *American Psychologist*, *69*, 34–65.

American Psychological Association (APA). (2014b). Report of the Ethics Committee, 2013. *American Psychologist*, *69*, 520–529.

American Psychological Association (APA), Advisory Committee on Colleague Assistance. (2009). Tools of engagement for colleague assistance. Retrieved from http://www.apa.org/practice/resources/assistance/acca-toolkit.pdf

American Psychological Association (APA), Committee for the Advancement of Professional Practice. (1995). *CAPP practitioner survey results*. Washington, D.C.: American Psychological Association.

American Psychological Association (APA), Committee on Legal Issues. (2006). Strategies for private practitioners coping with subpoenas or compelled testimony for client records or test data. *Professional Psychology: Research and Practice*, *37*, 215–222.

American Psychological Association (APA), Committee on Professional Practice and Standards. (1995). Twenty-four questions (and answers) about professional practice in the area of child abuse. *Professional Psychology: Research and Practice*, *26*, 377–383.

American Psychological Association (APA), Committee on Professional Practice and Standards. (2003). Legal issues in the professional practice of psychology. *Professional Psychology: Research and Practice*, *34*, 595–600.

American Psychological Association (APA), Committee on Psychological Testing and Assessment. (1996). Statement on the disclosure of test data. *American Psychologist*, *51*, 644–648.

American Psychological Association (APA), Committee on Women in Psychology. (1989). If sex enters into the psychotherapy relationship. *Professional Psychology: Research and Practice*, *20*, 112–115.

American Psychological Association (APA), Ethics Committee. (1983). *Authorship guidelines for dissertation supervision*. Washington, D.C.: Author.

American Psychological Association (APA), Ethics Committee. (2001). *Rules and procedures*. Washington, D.C.: Author. Retrieved from http://www.apa.org/ethics/code/committee.aspx#overview

American Psychological Association (APA), Insurance Trust. (1990). *Bulletin: Sexual misconduct and professional liability claims*. Washington, D.C.: Author.

American Psychological Association (APA), Joint Committee on Testing Practices. (2004). Code of fair testing practices in education. Retrieved from http://www.apa.org/science/fairtestcode.html

American Psychological Association (APA), Practice Directorate. (2006). Advancing colleague assistance in professional psychology. Retrieved from http://www.apa.org/practice/acca_monograph.html

American Psychological Association (APA), Task Force. (1975). Report of the task force on sex bias and sex role stereotyping in psychotherapeutic practice. *American Psychologist*, *30*, 1169–1175.

American Psychological Association (APA), Working Group on Assisted Suicide and End-of-Life Decisions. (2000). Report to the Board of Trustees. Retrieved from http://www.apa.org/pi/aseol/introduction.html

American Psychological Association Insurance Trust (APAIT). (n.d.). Sample electronic communication policy. Retrieved from http://www.apait.org/apait/applications/SampleElectronicCommunicationPolicy.doc.pdf

American School Counselor Association (ASCA). (1996). *Developing an informed consent brochure for secondary students*. Alexandria, VA: Author.

American School Counselor Association (ASCA). (1999). Sharing information with the school principal. Retrieved from http://www.schoolcounselor.org/Ethics/sharing.html

American School Counselor Association (ASCA). (2004). *The ASCA national standards for students*. Alexandria, VA: Author.

American School Counselor Association (ASCA). (2005). *The ASCA national model: A framework for school counseling programs* (2nd ed.). Alexandria, VA: Author.

American School Counselor Association (ASCA). (2007). A framework for safe and successful schools. Washington, D.C.: Author.

American School Counselor Association (ASCA). (2008a). Position statements. Retrieved from http://www.schoolcounselor.org/files/positions.pdf

American School Counselor Association (ASCA). (2008b). State certification requirements. Retrieved from http://www.schoolcounselor.org/school-counselors-members/careers-roles/state-certification-requirements

American School Counselor Association (ASCA). (2009a). The role of the professional school counselor. Retrieved from http://www.schoolcounselor.org/administrators/role-of-the-school-counselor

American School Counselor Association (ASCA). (2010). Ethical standards for school counselors. Retrieved from http://www.schoolcounselor.org/asca/media/asca/Resource%20Center/Legal%20and%20Ethical%20Issues/Sample%20Documents/EthicalStandards2010.pdf

American School Counselor Association (ASCA). (2011). Student-to-school counselor ratio: 2010–2011. Retrieved from http://www.schoolcounselor.org/asca/media/asca/home/ratios10-11.pdf

Americans with Disabilities Act (Public Law 101-336). (1990).

Anastasi, A. (1992). What counselors should know about the use and interpretation of psychological tests. *Journal of Counseling & Development*, *70*, 610–615.

Ancis, J. R., & Ladany, N. (2010). A multicultural framework for counselor supervision. In L. J. Bradley & N. Ladany (Eds.), *Counselor supervision: Principles process and practice* (3rd ed., pp. 53–96). Philadelphia, PA: Brunner-Routledge.

Anderson, J. R., & Barret, R. L. (Eds.). (2001). *Ethics in HIV-related psychotherapy: Clinical decision making in complex cases*. Washington, D.C.: American Psychological Association.

Anderson, R. D., & Price, G. E. (2001). Experiential groups in counselor education: Student attitudes and instructor participation. *Counselor Education and Supervision*, *41*, 111–119.

Anderson, S. A., Schlossberg, M., & Rigazio-DiGilio, R. (2000). Family therapy trainees' evaluations of their best and worst supervisors. *Journal of Marital and Family Therapy*, *26*, 79–91.

Anderson, S. K., & Handelsman, M. M. (2010). *Ethics for psychotherapists and counselors: A positive approach*. Malden, MA: Wiley-Blackwell.

Anderson, S. K., & Kitchener, K. S. (1996). Nonromantic, nonsexual posttherapy relationships between psychologists and former clients: An exploratory student of critical incidents. *Professional Psychology: Research and Practice*, *27*, 59–66.

Anderson, S. K., & Kitchener, K. S. (1998). Nonsexual posttherapy relationships: A conceptual framework to assess ethical risks. *Professional Psychology: Research and Practice*, *29*, 91–99.

Anderson, S. K., Williams, P., & Kramer, A. L. (2012). Life and executive coaching: Some ethical issues for consideration. In S. J. Knapp, M. C. Gottlieb, M. M. Handelsman, & L. D. VandeCreek, (Eds.), *APA handbook of ethics in psychology* (Vol. 2, pp. 169–181). Washington, D.C.: American Psychological Association.

Anonymous. (1991). Sexual harassment: A female counseling student's experience. *Journal of Counseling & Development*, *69*, 502–506.

Appelbaum, P. S. (1993). Legal liability in managed care. *American Psychologist*, *48*, 251–257.

Appelbaum, P. S. (2008). Privilege in the federal courts: Should there be a "dangerous patient exception"? *Psychiatric Services*, *59*, 714–716.

Appelbaum, P. S., & Greer, A. (1993). Confidentiality in group therapy. *Hospital and Community Psychology*, *44*, 311–313.

Appelbaum, P. S., & Gutheil, T. G. (1991). *Clinical handbook of psychiatry and the law* (2nd ed.). Baltimore: Williams & Wilkins.

Appelbaum, P. S., Lidz, C. W., & Meisel. A. (1987). *Informed consent: Legal theory and clinical practice*. New York, NY: Oxford.

Archer, J., & Coyne, M. (2005). An integrated review of indirect, relational, and social aggression. *Personality and Social Psychology Review*, *9*, 212–230.

Arizona HB 2565 "University Students' Religious Liberty Act." (2011). Retrieved from http://www.azleg.gov/legtext/50leg/1r/bills/hb2565s.pdf

Arredondo, P., Toporek, R., Brown, S. P., Jones, J., Locke, D., Sanchez, J., & Stadler, H. (1996). Operationalization of the multicultural counseling competencies. *Journal of Multicultural Counseling and Development*, *24*, 42–78.

Arthur, W., Woehr, D. J., & Graziano, W. G. (2001). Personality testing in employment settings: Problems and issues in the application of typical selection practices. *Personnel Review*, *30*, 657–676.

Artman, L. K., & Daniels, J. A. (2011). Disability and psychotherapy practice: Cultural competence and practical tips. *Professional Psychology: Research and Practice*, *41*, 442–448.

Association for Counselor Education and Supervision (ACES). (1990). Standards for counseling supervisors. *Journal of Counseling & Development*, *69*, 30–32.

Association for Counselor Education and Supervision (ACES). (1993). Ethical guidelines for counseling supervisors. *Counselor Education and Supervision*, *34*, 270–276.

Association for Counselor Education and Supervision (ACES). (1999). *Guidelines for online instruction in counselor education*. Alexandria, VA: Author.

Association for Counselor Education and Supervision (ACES). (2009). Guidelines for research mentorship in counseling/counselor education. Retrieved from http://www.acesonline.net/wp-content/uploads/2010/12/ACES-research-mentorship-guidelines.pdf

Association for Counselor Education and Supervision (ACES). (2011). Best practices in counseling supervision. Retrieved from http://www.acesonline.net/wp-content/uploads/2011/10/ACES-Best-Practices-in-clinical-supervision-document-FINAL.pdf

Association for Lesbian, Gay, Bisexual and Transgender Issues in Counseling (ALGBTIC). (2009). Competencies for counseling transgender clients. Retrieved from http://www.counseling.org/Resources/Competencies/ALGBTIC_Competencies.pdf

Association for Lesbian, Gay, Bisexual and Transgender Issues in Counseling (ALGBTIC). (2012).

Competencies for counseling with lesbian, gay, bisexual, queer, questioning, intersex and ally individuals. Retrieved from https://www.ceunits.com/trainings/pdf_download/182/

Association for Multicultural Counseling and Development. (1996). Multicultural counseling competencies. Retrieved from http://www.counseling.org/docs/competencies/multcultural_competencies.pdf?sfvrsn=5

Association for Specialists in Group Work (ASGW). (2000). Professional standards for the training of group workers. Retrieved from http://www.asgw.org/pdf/training_standards.pdf

Association for Specialists in Group Work (ASGW). (2007). Best practice guidelines. Retrieved from http://www.asgw.org/pdf/best_practices.pdf

Association for Specialists in Group Work (ASGW). (2012). Multicultural and social justice competence Principles for group workers. Retrieved from http://www.asgw.org/pdf/ASGW_MC_SJ_Priniciples_Final_ASGW.pdf

Association of State and Provincial Psychology Boards (ASPPB). (2003a). *Guidelines for the supervision of doctoral level candidates for licensure*. Peachtree, GA: Author.

Association of State and Provincial Psychology Boards (ASPPB). (2003b). *Guidelines for the supervision of uncredentialed personnel providing psychological services*. Peachtree, GA: Author.

Association of State and Provincial Psychology Boards (ASPPB). (2005). Code of conduct. Retrieved from http://www.asppb.org/publications/model/conduct.aspx

Association of State and Provincial Psychology Boards (ASPPB). (2009). Guidelines on practicum experience for licensure. Retrieved from https://c.ymcdn.com/sites/asppb.site-ym.com/resource/resmgr/guidelines/final_prac_guidelines_1_31_0.pdf

Association of State and Provincial Psychology Boards (ASPPB). (2012). ASPPB disciplinary data system report. Retrieved from c.ymcdn.com/sites/www.asppb.net/resource/resmgr/dds/dds_historical_report_2013.pdf

Association of Trial Lawyers of America. (2001). Psychotherapy records are discoverable in cases involving emotional distress. *Trial*, *37*, 106.

Association of University and College Counseling Center Directors, (AUCCCD). (2012). Annual survey. Retrieved from http://files.cmcglobal.com/Monograph_2012_AUCCCD_Public.pdf

Aubrey, M., & Dougher, M. J. (1990). Ethical issues in outpatient group therapy with sex offenders. *Journal for Specialists in Group Work*, *15*, 75–82.

Aubry, T. D., Hunsley, J., Josephson, G., & Vito, D. (2000). Quid pro quo: Fee for services delivered in a psychology training clinic. *Journal of Clinical Psychology*, *56*, 23–31.

Austin, W., Bergum, V., Nuttgens, S., Peternalj-Taylor, C. (2006). A re-visioning of boundaries in professional helping relationships: Exploring other metaphors. *Ethics & Behavior*, *16*, 77–94.

Australian Psychological Society. (2007). Code of ethics. Retrieved from http://www.psychology.org.au/about/ethics/

Avery, L., & Gressard, C. F. (2000). Counseling regulations regarding sexual misconduct: A comparison across states. *Counseling and Values*, *45*, 67–77.

Aviv, A., Levine, J., Shelef, A., Speiser, N., & Elizur, A. (2006). Therapist–patient sexual relations: Result of a national survey in Israel. *Israeli Journal of Psychiatry and Related Sciences*, *43*, 119–125.

Bacorn, D., & Dixon, D. (1984). The effects of touch on depressed and vocationally undecided clients. *Journal of Counseling Psychology*, *31*, 488–496.

Baer, B. E., & Murdock, N. L. (1995). Nonerlotic dual relationships between therapists and clients: The effects of sex, theoretical orientation and interpersonal boundaries. *Ethics & Behavior*, *5*, 131–145.

Baird, K. A., & Rupert, P. A. (1987). Clinical management of confidentiality: A survey of psychologists in seven states. *Professional Psychology: Research and Practice*, *18*, 347–352.

Bajt, T. R., & Pope, K. S. (1989). Therapist–patient sexual intimacy involving children and adolescents. *American Psychologist*, *44*, 455.

Baker, D. C., & Bufka, L. F. (2011). Preparing for the telehealth world: Navigating legal, regulatory, reimbursement, and ethical issues in an electronic age. *Professional Psychology: Research and Practice*, *42*, 405–411.

Baker, E. K. (2003). *Caring for ourselves: A therapist's guide to personal and professional well-being*. Washington, D.C.: American Psychological Association.

Baker, L. C., & Patterson, J. E. (1990). The first to know: A systematic analysis of confidentiality and the therapist's family. *American Journal of Family Therapy*, *18*, 295–300.

Baker, S. B. (2007). *School counseling for the twenty-first century* (3rd ed.). Englewood Cliffs, NJ: Prentice Hall.

Barak, A., Boniel-Nissim, M., & Suler, J. (2008). Fostering empowerment in online support groups. *Computers in Human Behavior*, *24*, 1867–1883.

Barkan, R., Ayal, S., Gino, F., & Ariely, D. (2012). The pot calling the kettle black: Distancing response to ethical dissonance. *Journal of Experimental Psychology: General*, *141*, 1–16.

Barnett, J. E. (2011). But it's a really nice gift: Ethical challenges in responding to offers of gifts from clients. In W. B. Johnson & G. P. Koocher (Eds.), *Ethical conundrums, quandaries, and predicaments in mental health practice* (pp. 9–16). New York, NY: Oxford.

Barnett, J. E. (2014). Sexual feelings and behaviors in the psychotherapy relationship: An ethics perspective. *Journal of Clinical Psychology*, *70*, 170–181.

Barnett, J. E., Baker, E. K., Elman, N. S., & Schoener, G. R. (2007). In pursuit of wellness: The self-care imperative. *Professional Psychology: Research and Practice*, *38*, 603–612.

Barnett, J. E., & Campbell, L. F. (2012). Ethical issues in scholarship. In S. J. Knapp, M. C. Gottlieb, M. M. Handelsman, & L. D. VandeCreek, (Eds.), *APA handbook of ethics in psychology* (Vol. 1, pp. 309–333). Washington, D.C.: American Psychological Association.

Barnett, J. E., Cornish, J. A. E., Goodyear, R. K., & Lichtenberg, J. W. (2007). Commentaries on the ethical and effective practice of clinical supervision. *Professional Psychology: Research and Practice, 38*, 268–275.

Barnett, J. E., Doll, B., Younggren, J. N., & Rubin, N. J. (2007). Clinical competence for practicing psychologists: Clearly a work in progress. *Professional Psychology: Research and Practice, 38*, 510–517.

Barnett, J. E., Lazarus, A. A., Vasquez, M. J. T., Moorehead-Slaughter, O., & Johnson, W. B. (2007). Boundary issues and multiple relationships: Fantasy and reality. *Professional Psychology: Research and Practice, 338*, 401–410.

Barnett, J. E., Wise, E. H., Johnson-Greene, D., & Bucky, S. F. (2007). Informed consent: Too much of a good thing or not enough? *Professional Psychology: Research and Practice, 38*, 179–186.

Barnett-Queen, T., & Larrabee, M. J. (2000). Sexually oriented relationships between educators and students in mental health education programs. *Journal of Mental Health Counseling, 22*, 68–84.

Bartell, P. A., & Rubin, L. J. (1990). Dangerous liaisons: Sexual intimacies in supervision. *Professional Psychology: Research and Practice, 21*, 442–450.

Bates, C. M., & Brodsky, A. M. (1989). *Sex in the therapy hour: A case of professional incest*. New York, NY: Guilford.

Bauman, S. (2011). *Cyberbullying: What counselors need to know*. Alexandria, VA: American Counseling Association.

Baumoel, J. (1992). The beginning of the end for the psychotherapist-patient privilege. *Cincinnati Law Review, 60*, 797–826.

Beahrs, J. O., & Gutheil, T. G. (2001). Informed consent in psychotherapy. *American Journal of Psychotherapy, 158*, 4–8.

Bean, J. P., & Kuh, G. (1984). The reciprocity between student–faculty informal contact and academic performance. *Research in Higher Education, 21*, 461–477.

Bearse, J. L., McMinn, M. M., Seegobin, W., & Free, K. (2013). Barriers to psychologists seeking mental health care. *Professional Psychology: Research and Practice, 44*, 150–157.

Beauchamp, T. L., & Childress, J. F. (1983). *Principles of biomedical ethics* (2nd ed.). Oxford, England: Oxford University Press.

Beauchamp, T. L., & Childress, J. F. (2001). *Principles of biomedical ethics* (4th ed.). Oxford, England: Oxford University Press.

Beauchamp, T. L., & Childress, J. F. (2012). *Principles of biomedical ethics* (6th ed.). Oxford, England: Oxford University Press.

Becvar, D. S., & Becvar, R. J. (2006). *Family therapy: A systemic integration* (6th ed.). Boston, MA: Allyn & Bacon.

Beeman, D. G., & Scott, N. A. (1991). Therapists' attitudes toward psychotherapy informed consent with adolescents. *Professional Psychology: Research and Practice, 22*, 230–234.

Behnke, S. H. (2003). Release of test data and APA's new ethics code. *APA Monitor, 34*, 70–71.

Behnke, S. H. (2004). Release of test data and the new ethics code. *APA Monitor, 35*, 90–91.

Behnke, S. H. (2005). Diagnoses, record reviews, and the new Ethics Code. *APA Monitor, 36*, 80–82.

Behnke, S. H. (2008). Reflections on media ethics for psychologists. *APA Monitor, 39*, 46.

Behnke, S. H. (2009). Ethics from a developmental perspective. *APA Monitor, 40*, 68.

Behnke, S. H. (2012). Constitutional claims in the context of mental health training: Religion, sexual orientation, and tensions between the first amendment and professional ethics. *Training and Education in Professional Psychology, 6*, 189–195.

Behnke, S. H. (2014). Talking about ethics. *APA Monitor, 45*, 64.

Behnke, S. H., Perlin, M. L., & Bernstein, M. (2004). *The essentials of New York mental health law: A straightforward guide for clinicians of all disciplines*. New York, NY: W. W. Norton.

Behnke, S. H., & Warner, E. (2002, March). Confidentiality in the treatment of adolescents. *APA Monitor, 33*, 44–45.

Bell, S. K., Coleman, J. K., Anderson, A., Whelan, J. P., & Wilder, C. (2000). The effectiveness of peer mediation in a low-SES rural community school. *Psychology in the Schools, 37*, 505–516.

Bennett, B. E., Bricklin, P. M., Harris, E., Knapp, S. J., VandeCreek, L. D., & Younggren, J. N. (2006). *Assessing and managing risk in psychological practice*. Rockville, MD: The Trust.

Benjamin, G. A. H., & Gollan, J. K. (2003). *Family evaluation in custody litigation: Reducing risks of ethical infractions and malpractice*. Washington, D.C.: American Psychological Association.

Benjamin, G. A. H., Gollan, J., & Ally, G. A. (2007). Family evaluation in custody litigation: Reducing risks of ethical and malpractice infractions. *Journal of Forensic Psychology Practice, 7*, 101–111.

Benjamin, G. A. H., Kent, L., & Sirikantraporn, S. (2009). A review of duty to protect statutes, cases, and procedures for positive practice. In J. L. Werth, E. R. Welfel, & G. A. H. Benjamin (Eds.), *The duty to protect: Ethical, legal, and professional responsibilities of mental health professionals* (pp. 9–28). Washington, D.C.: American Psychological Association.

Berlinger, N. (2007). *After harm: Medical error and the ethics of forgiveness*. Baltimore, MD: Johns Hopkins University Press.

Berman, A. L., Jobes, D. A., & Silverman, M. M. (2006). *Adolescent suicide: Assessment and intervention* (2nd ed.). Washington, D.C.: American Psychological Association.

Bernard, J. L., & Jara, C. S. (1986). The failure of clinical psychology graduate students to apply understood ethical principles. *Professional Psychology: Research and Practice, 17*, 313–315.

Bernard, J. L., Murphy, M., & Little, M. (1987). The failure of clinical psychologists to apply understood ethical principles. *Professional Psychology: Research and Practice, 18*, 489–491.

Bernard, J. M., & Goodyear, R. K. (2013). *Fundamentals of clinical supervision* (5th ed.). Boston, MA: Allyn & Bacon.

Bernsen, A., Tabachnick, B. G., & Pope, K. S. (1994). National survey of social workers' sexual attraction to their clients: Results, implications and comparison to psychologists. *Ethics & Behavior, 4*, 369–388.

Bernstein, B. E., & Hartsell, T. L., Jr. (1998). *The portable lawyer for mental health professionals*. New York, NY: Wiley.

Berry, J. W., & Sam, D. L. (1997). Acculturation and adaptation. In J. W. Berry, M. H. Segall, & C. Kagitibasi (Eds.), *Handbook of cross-cultural psychology* (pp. 291–326). Needham Heights, MA: Allyn & Bacon.

Bersoff, D. N. (1996). Education and training in psychology and law/criminal justice: Historical foundations, present structures, and future developments. *Criminal Justice and Behavior*, *23*, 200–235.

Bersoff, D. N. (Ed.). (2008). *Ethical conflicts in psychology* (4th ed.). Washington, D.C.: American Psychological Association.

Bersoff, D. N. (2014). Protecting victims of violent patients while protecting confidentiality. *American Psychologist*, *69*, 461–467.

Bersoff, D. N., DeMatteo, D., & Foster, E. E. (2012). Assessment and testing. In S. J. Knapp, M. C. Gottlieb, M. M. Handelsman, & L. D. VandeCreek (Eds.), *APA handbook of ethics in psychology* (Vol. 2, pp. 45–74). Washington, D.C.: American Psychological Association.

Bersoff, D. N., & Hofer, P. J. (1991). *Legal issues in computerized psychological testing*. Hillsdale, NJ: Erlbaum.

Betan, E. J., & Stanton, A. L. (1999). Fostering ethical willingness: Integrating emotional and contextual awareness with rational analysis. *Professional Psychology: Research and Practice*, *30*, 295–301.

Biaggio, M., Duffy, R., & Staffelbach, D. F. (1998). Obstacles to addressing professional misconduct. *Clinical Psychology Review*, *18*, 273–285.

Binder, R., & McNiel, D. (1996) Application of thę Tarasoff ruling and its effect on the victim and the therapeutic relationship. *Psychiatric Services*, *47*, 1212–1215.

Birrell, P. J. (2006). An ethic of possibility: Relationship, risk, and presence. *Ethics & Behavior*, *16*, 95–115.

Bisbing, S. B., Jorgenson, L. B., & Sutherland, P. K. (1995). *Sexual abuse by professionals: A legal guide*. Charlottesville, VA: Mitchie.

Bissell, L., & Haberman, P. (1984). *Alcoholism in the professions*. New York, NY: Oxford University Press.

Bittner, S., Bialek, E. D., Nathiel, S. Ringwald, J. & Tupper, M. (1999). An alternative to managed care: A "guild" model for the independent practice of psychotherapy. *Journal of Marital and Family Therapy*, *25*, 99–111.

Blanchard, C. A., & Lichtenberg, J. L. (1998). Counseling psychologists' training to deal with their sexual feelings in therapy. *The Counseling Psychologist*, *26*, 624–639.

Bleiberg, J. R., & Baron, J. (2004). Entanglement in dual relationships in a university counseling center. *Journal of College Student Psychotherapy*, *19*, 21–34.

Blevins-Knabe, B. (1992). The ethics of dual relationships in higher education. *Ethics & Behavior*, *2*, 151–163.

Bloom, P. (2013). *Just babies: The origin of good and evil*. New York, NY: Crown.

Bodenhorn, N. (2006). Exploratory study of common and challenging ethical dilemmas experienced by professional school counselors. *Professional School Counseling*, *10*, 195–202.

Bok, S. (1989). *Secrets: On the ethics of concealment and revelation*. New York, NY: Vintage Books.

Boland-Prom, K. W. (2009). Results from a national study of social workers sanctioned by state licensing boards. *Social Work*, *54*, 351–360.

Bollas, C., & Sundelson, D. (1995). *The new informants: The betrayal of confidentiality in psychoanalysis and psychotherapy*. Northvale, NJ: Aronson.

Bombara, M. J. (2002). Relationships among school counselors' level of moral reasoning, demographic characteristics, and their use of ethical decision making resources *Dissertation Abstracts International: Section A, Humanities and Social Sciences*, *62*(11A), 3687.

Bongar, B. (2013). *The suicidal patient: Clinical and legal standards of care* (3rd ed.). Washington, D.C.: American Psychological Association.

Borum, R., & Reddy, M. (2001). Assessing violence risk in *Tarasoff*-situations: A fact-based model of inquiry. *Behavioral Sciences and the Law*, *19*, 375–385.

Borum, R., & Verhaagen, D. (2006). *Assessing and managing violence risk in juveniles*. New York, NY: Guilford Press.

Borys, D. S., & Pope, K. S. (1989). Dual relationships between therapist and client: A national study of psychologists, psychiatrists and social workers. *Professional Psychology: Research and Practice*, *20*, 283–293.

Boudreaux, C. T. (2001). Psychologist disclosures of client information to significant others. *Dissertation Abstracts International: Section B, The Sciences and Engineering*, *62*(6), 1566.

Bouhoutsos, J. C. (1984). Sexual intimacy between psychotherapists and clients. In L. Walker (Ed.), *Women and mental health policy* (pp. 207–227). Beverly Hills, CA: Sage.

Bouhoutsos, J. C., & Brodsky, A. M. (1985). Mediation in therapist–client sex: A model. *Psychotherapy: Research and Practice*, *22*, 189–193.

Bouhoutsos, J. C., Holroyd, J., Lerman, J., Forer, B., & Greenberg, M. (1983). Sexual intimacy between psychotherapists and patients. *Professional Psychology: Research and Practice*, *14*, 185–196.

Bowlby, J. (1951). *Maternal care and mental health*. Geneva: World Health Organization.

Bowman, R. L., Bowman, V. E., & DeLucia, J. L. (1990). Mentoring in a graduate counseling program: Students helping students. *Counselor Education and Supervision*, *30*, 58–65.

Bowman, V. E., Hatley, L. D., & Bowman, R. L. (1995). Faculty-student relationships: The dual role controversy. *Counselor Education and Supervision*, *34*, 232–242.

Brabeck, M. M. (2000). *Practicing feminist ethics in psychology*. Washington, D.C.: American Psychological Association.

Bradley, L. J., & Ladany, N. (2010). *Counselor supervision: Principles, process and practice* (4th ed.). Philadelphia, PA: Brunner-Routledge.

Bradley, L. J., Sexton, T. L., & Smith, H. B. (2005). The American Counseling Association Practice Research Network (ACA-PRN): A new research tool. *Journal of Counseling & Development*, *83*, 488–491.

Brady, J. L., Guy, J. D., Poelstra, P. L., & Brokaw, B. F. (1997). Vicarious traumatization, spirituality, and the treatment of adult and child survivors of sexual abuse. In B. H. Stamm (Ed.), *Secondary traumatic stress: Self-care for clinicians, researchers, and educators* (pp. 29–36). Luthersville, MD: Sidran.

Bram, A. D. (1995). The physically ill or dying psychotherapist: A review of ethical and clinical considerations. *Psychotherapy Theory/Research/Practice/Training, 32*, 568–580.

Branstetter, S. A., & Handelsman, M. M. (2000). Graduate teaching assistants: Ethical training, beliefs, and practices, *Ethics & Behavior, 10*, 27–50.

Braun, S. A., & Cox, J. A. (2005). Managed mental health care: Intentional misdiagnosis of mental disorders. *Journal of Counseling & Development, 83*, 425–433.

Bray, J. H., Shepherd, J. N., & Hays, J. R. (1985). Legal and ethical issues in informed consent to psychotherapy. *American Journal of Family Therapy, 13*, 50–60.

Brazerman, M. H., & Tenbrunsel, A. E. (2012). *Blind spots: Why we fail to do what is right and what to do about it*. Princeton, NJ: Princeton University Press.

Brems, C. (2000). The challenge of preventing burnout and assuring growth: Self-care. In C. Brems (Ed.), *Dealing with challenges in psychotherapy and counseling* (pp. 262–296). Pacific Grove, CA: Brooks/Cole.

Brems, C., & Johnson, M. E. (2009). Self care in the context of threats of violence or self-harm from clients. In E. R. Welfel, J. M. Werth, & G. A. B. Benjamin (Eds.), *The duty to protect: Ethical, legal, and professional considerations in risk assessment and intervention* (pp. 211–228). Washington, D.C.: American Psychological Association.

Brennan, D., & Wildflower, L. (2010). Ethics in coaching. In E. Cox & T. Bachkirova. (Eds.), *The complete handbook on coaching* (pp. 369–380). London: Sage.

Bricklin, P., Bennett, B., & Carroll, W. (2003). *Understanding licensing board disciplinary procedures*. Washington, D.C.: American Psychological Association.

Bridge, P., & Bascue, L. (1988). A record form for psychotherapy supervision. In P. Keller & S. Heyman (Eds.), *Innovations in clinical practice* (Vol. 7, pp. 331–336). Sarasota, FL: Professional Resource Exchange.

British Association for Counselling and Psychotherapy. (2001). Ethical framework for good practice in counselling and psychotherapy. Retrieved from http://www.bacp.co.uk/ethical_framework/

British Psychological Society, Special Group in Coaching Psychology (n.d.). What is coaching psychology. Retrieved from http://www.sgcp.org.uk/sgcp/about-us/frequently-asked-questions.cfm

Brodie, R. E. (2004). Race, sex, and class bias in the diagnosis of DSM-IV disorders. *Dissertation Abstracts International: Section B, The Sciences and Engineering, 64*(11B), 5774.

Brodsky, S. L. (2011). *Therapy with coerced and reluctant clients*. Washington, D.C.: American Psychological Association.

Brosig, C. L., & Kalichman, S. C. (1992). Clinicians' reporting of suspected child abuse: A review of the empirical literature. *Clinical Psychology Review, 12*, 155–168.

Broverman, I. K., Broverman, D., Clarkson, F. E., Rosencrantz, P., & Vogel, S. (1970). Sex role stereotypes and clinical judgments of mental health. *Journal of Consulting and Clinical Psychology, 34*, 1–7.

Brown, C., & Trangsrud, H. B. (2008). Actors associated with acceptance and decline of client gift giving. *Professional Psychology: Research and Practice, 39*, 505–511.

Brown, D., Pryzwansky, W. B., & Schulte, A. C. (2011). *Psychological consultations: Introduction to theory and practice* (7th ed.). Boston, MA: Allyn & Bacon.

Brown, L. S. (1988). Harmful effects of posttermination sexual and romantic relationships between therapists and their former clients. *Psychotherapy: Theory/Research/Practice/Training, 25*, 249–255.

Brown, L. S. (1997). Remediation, amends or denial? *Professional Psychology: Research and Practice, 28*, 297–299.

Brown, L. S. (2011). Everyone I know knows everyone I know: Boundary overlap in the life on one lesbian psychotherapist. In W. B. Johnson & G. P. Koocher (Eds.), *Ethical Conundrums, Quandaries, and Predicaments in Mental Health Practice* (pp. 17–24). New York, NY: Oxford.

Brown-Rice, K. A., & Furr, S. (2013). Preservice counselors' knowledge of classmates' problems with professional competency. *Journal of Counseling & Development, 91*, 224–233.

Bruff v. North Mississippi Health Services, Inc. (2001). (5th Cir. 244 F. 3d 495).

Bryant, J. K. (2009). School counselors and child abuse reporting: A national survey. *Professional School Counseling, 12*, 333–342.

Buchanan, T. (2002). Online assessment: Desirable or dangerous? *Professional Psychology: Research and Practice, 33*, 148–154.

Buckard, A. W., & Ponterotto, J. G. (2008). Cultural identity, racial identity, and the multicultural personality. In L. A. Suzuki, J. G. Ponterotto, & P. J. Meller (Eds.), *Handbook of multicultural assessment: Clinical, psychological, and educational practice* (3rd ed., pp. 52–72). San Francisco, CA: Jossey-Bass.

Burke, A., Harper, M., Rudnick, H., & Kruger, G. (2007). Moving beyond statutory ethical codes: Practitioner ethics as a contextual, character-based enterprise. *South African Journal of Psychology, 37*, 107–120.

Burke, C. A. (1995). Until death do us part: An exploration into confidentiality following the death of a client. *Professional Psychology: Research and Practice, 26*, 278–280.

Burrow-Sanchez, J. J. (2011). How school counselors can help prevent online victimization. *Journal of Counseling & Development, 89*, 3–10.

Bush, S. S., Connell, M. A., Denney, R. L. (2006). *Ethical practice in forensic psychology: A systemic model for decision making*. Washington, D.C.: American Psychological Association.

Butcher, J. N., Dahlstrom, W. G., Graham, J. R., Tellegen, A., & Kaemmer, B. (1989). *Minnesota Multiphasic Personality Inventory-2 (MMPI-2): Manual for administration and scoring*.

Minneapolis: University of Minnesota Press.
Butler, M. H., Rodriguez, M. A., Roper, S. O., & Feinhauer, L. L. (2010). Infidelity secrets in couple therapy: Therapists' views on the collision of competing ethics around relationship-relevant secrets. *Sexual Addiction and Compulsivity*, *17*, 85–105.
Byrd, R., & Hays, D. G. (2013). Evaluating a safe space training for school counselor and trainees: A randomized control group design. *Professional School Counseling*, *17*, 31–46.
Caldwell, L. W. (2003). Sexual relationships between supervisors and supervisees during psychology graduate training. *Dissertation Abstracts International: Section B, The Sciences and Engineering*, *63*(10B), 4879.
California Board of Psychology. (2014). Enforcement program update. Retrieved from http://psychology.ca.gov/about_us/meetings/materials/20140821_7.pdf
California Department of Consumer Affairs. (2011). Professional therapy never includes sex. Retrieved from https://www.dca.ca.gov/dca/publications/proftherapy.shtml
California Education Code. (2011). CAL. EDC CODE § 49602. Retrieved from http://codes.lp.findlaw.com/cacode/EDC/2/d4/27/10/s49602
Camera, W. J., & Schneider, D. L. (1994). Integrity tests: Facts and unresolved issues. *American Psychologist*, *49*, 112–119.
Campbell, C. D., & Gordon, M. C. (2003). Acknowledging the inevitable: Understanding multiple relationships in rural practice. *Professional Psychology: Research and Practice*, *34*, 430–434.
Campbell, L. C., Vasquez, M., Behnke, S. H., & Kinscherff, R. (2010). *APA Ethics Code commentary and case illustrations*. Washington, D.C.: American Psychological Association.
Campbell, T. W. (1999). Challenging the evidentiary reliability of the DSM-IV. *American Journal of Forensic Psychology*, *17*, 47–68.
Canadian Counselling and Psychotherapy Association. (2007). Code of ethics. Retrieved from http://www.ccpa-accp.ca/_documents/CodeofEthics_en_new.pdf
Canadian Psychological Association. (2006). Draft ethical guidelines for psychologists providing psychological services via electronic media. Retrieved from http://www.cpa.ca/docs/File/Ethics/Draft_Guidelines_EServices_31Oct2013.pdf
Canadian Psychological Association. (2010). A resource guide for psychologists: Ethical supervision in teaching, research, practice and supervision. Retrieved from http://www.cpa.ca/docs/File/Ethics/COEresGuideSuperAppNov2010-Rev14June2011.pdf
Canter, M. B., Bennett, B. E., Jones, S. J., & Nagy, T. F. (1994). *Ethics in psychology: A commentary on the APA Ethics Code*. Washington, D.C.: American Psychological Association.
Canterbury v. Spence, 464 F. 2d 772 (DC Cir., 1972).
Capuzzi, D. C. (2002). Legal and ethical challenges in counseling suicidal students. *Professional School Counseling*, 6, 36–45.
Capuzzi, D. C. (Ed.). (2004). *Suicide across the lifespan*. Washington, D.C.: American Counseling Association.
Capuzzi, D. C. (2009). *Suicide prevention in the schools: Guidelines for middle and high school settings* (2nd ed.). Alexandria, VA: American Counseling Association.
Capuzzi, D. C., & Stauffer, M. D. (2011). *Foundations of addiction counseling* (2nd ed.). Upper Saddle River, NJ: Merrill.
Carey, J. C., Dimmitt, C., Hatch, T. A., Lapan, R. T., & Whiston, S. C. (2008). Report of the national panel for evidence-based school counseling: Outcome research coding protocol and evaluation of student success skills and second step. *Professional School Counseling*, *11*, 197–206.
Carney, J. V. (2000). Bullied to death: Perceptions of peer abuse and suicidal behavior during adolescence? *School Psychology International*, *21*, 44–54.
Carter, K. (1997, March 7). Gay slurs abound. *Des Moines Register*, p. 3.
Carter, R. T. (2007). Racism and psychological and emotional injury: Recognizing and assessing race-based traumatic stress. *The Counseling Psychologist*, *35*, 13–105.
Cartwright, B. Y., Daniels, J., & Zhang, S. (2008). Assessing multicultural competence: Perceived versus demonstrated performance. *Journal of Counseling & Development*, *86*, 318–329.
Cassileth, B. R., Zupkis, R. V., Sutton-Smith, K., & March, V. (1980). Informed consent? Why are its goals imperfectly realized? *New England Journal of Medicine*, *323*, 896–900.
Cates, J. A. (1999). The art of assessment in psychology: Ethics, expertise, and validity. *Journal of Clinical Psychology*, *55*, 631–641.
Cavett, A. M. (2002). *Mandatory child abuse reporting: behaviors, attitudes and beliefs among psychologists regarding current and proposed statutes* (Doctoral dissertation, University of North Dakota).
Celenza, A. (2007). *Sexual boundary violations: Therapeutic, supervisory, and academic contexts*. Northfield, NJ: Jason Aronson.
Centers for Disease Control and Prevention (CDC). (2009). Suicide prevention. Retrieved from http://www.cdc.gov/violenceprevention/pub/youth_suicide.html
Chauvin, J. C., & Remley, T. P., Jr. (1996). Responding to allegations of unethical conduct. *Journal of Counseling & Development*, *74*, 563–568.
Chen, E. C., Kakkad, D., & Balzano, J. (2008). Multicultural competence and evidence-based practice in group therapy. *Journal of Clinical Psychology*, *64*, 1261–1278.
Chenneville, T. (2000). HIV, confidentiality and duty to protect: A decision-making model. *Professional Psychology: Research and Practice*, *31*, 661–670.
Chester, A., & Glass, C. (2006). Online counselling: A descriptive analysis of therapy services on the Internet. *British Journal of Guidance and Counselling*, *34*, 145–160.
Cikanek, K., Veach, P. M., & Braun, C. (2004). Advanced doctoral students' knowledge and understanding of clinical supervisor ethical responsibilities: A brief report. *Clinical Supervisor*, *23*, 191–196.
Claiborn, C. D., Berberoglu, L. S., Nerison, R. M., & Somberg, D. R. (1994). The client's perspective: Ethical judgments and perceptions of therapist's practices. *Professional*

Psychology: Research and Practice, 25, 268–274.

Clark, R. A., Harden, S. L., & Johnson, B. W. (2000). Mentor relationships in clinical psychology doctoral programs: Results of a national survey. *Teaching of Psychology, 27*, 262–268.

Clayton, S., & Bongar, B. (1994). The use of consultation in psychological practice: Ethical, legal and clinical considerations. *Ethics & Behavior, 4*, 43–57.

Cohen, E. D., & Cohen, G. S. (1999). *The virtuous therapist: Ethical practice of counseling and psychotherapy*. Pacific Grove, CA: Brooks/Cole.

Coleman, E., & Schaefer, S. (1986). Boundaries of sex and intimacy between client and counselor. *Journal of Counseling & Development, 64*, 341–344.

Collins, L. H. (2007). Practicing safer listserv use: Ethical use of an invaluable resource. *Professional Psychology: Research and Practice, 38*, 590–698.

Collins, N., & Knowles, A. D. (1995). Adolescents' attitudes towards confidentiality between the school counselor and the adolescent client. *Australian Psychologist, 30*, 179–182.

Commission on Rehabilitation Counselor Certification (CRCC). (2010). Code of professional ethics for rehabilitation counselors. Retrieved from https://www.crccertification.com/filebin/pdf/CRCC_COE_1-1-10_Rev12-09.pdf

Committee on Ethical Guidelines for Forensic Psychologists. (1991). Specialty guidelines for forensic psychologists. *Law and Human Behavior, 15*, 655–665.

Comstock, G. D. (1991). *Violence against lesbians and gay men*. New York, NY: Columbia University.

Constantine, M. G. (1997). Facilitating multicultural competency in counseling supervision. In D. B. Pope-Davis & H. L. K. Coleman (Eds.), *Multicultural counseling competencies: Assessment, education and training, and supervision* (pp. 310–324). Thousand Oaks, CA: Sage.

Constantine, M. G., & Sue, D. W. (Eds.). (2005). *Strategies for building multicultural competence in mental health and educational settings*. New York, NY: Wiley.

Cook, D. A. (2009). Thorough informed consent: A developing clinical intervention. *Psychotherapy: Theory/Research/Practice/Training, 46*, 471–472.

Cook, D. A., & Helms, J. E. (1988). Visible racial/ethnic group supervisees' satisfaction with cross-cultural supervision as predicted by relationship characteristics. *Journal of Counseling Psychology, 35*, 268–273.

Cooper, S. E., Resnick, J. L., Rodolfa, E., & Douce, L. (2008). College counseling and mental health services. In B. W. Walsh (Ed.), *Biennial review of counseling psychology* (Vol. 1, pp. 209–230). New York, NY: Routledge.

Corcoran, K., & Winslade, W. J. (1994). Eavesdropping on the 50-minute hour: Managed mental health care and confidentiality. *Behavioral Sciences and the Law, 12*, 351–365.

Corey, G., Corey, M., & Callanan, P. (2015). *Issues and ethics in the helping professions* (8th ed.). Pacific Grove, CA: Brooks/Cole.

Corey, G., Williams, G. T., & Moline, M. E. (1995). Ethical and legal issues in group counseling. *Ethics & Behavior, 5*, 161–183.

Corey, M. S., & Corey, G. (2013). *Groups: Process and practice* (8th ed.). Pacific Grove, CA: Brooks/Cole.

Cornish, J. A. E., Gorgens, K. A., Monson, S. P., Olkin, R., Palombi, B. J., & Abels, A. V. (2008). Perspectives on ethical practice with people who have disabilities. *Professional Psychology: Research and Practice, 39*, 488–497.

Coster, J. S., & Schwebel, M. (1997). Well-functioning in professional psychologists. *Professional Psychology: Research and Practice, 28*, 5–13.

Cottone, R. (2012). Ethical decision making in mental health contexts: Representative models and an organizational framework. In S. J. Knapp, M. C. Gottlieb, M. M. Handelsman, & L. D. VandeCreek, (Eds.), *APA handbook of ethics in psychology* (Vol. 1, pp. 99–121). Washington, D.C.: American Psychological Association.

Cottone, R. R. (2001). A social constructivism model of ethical decision making in counseling. *Journal of Counseling & Development, 79*, 39–45.

Cottone, R. R., & Claus, R. E. (2000). Ethical decision making models: A review of the literature. *Journal of Counseling & Development, 78*, 275–283.

Cottone, R. R., Tarvydas, V., & House, G. (1994). The effect of number and type of consulted relationships on the ethical decision making of graduate students in counseling. *Counseling and Values, 39*, 56–68.

Cowen, E. L., Weissberg, R. P., & Lotyczewski, B. S. (1983). Physical contact in interactions between clinicians and young children. *Journal of Consulting and Clinical Psychology, 51*, 132–138.

Coyle, B. E. (1999). Practical tools for rural psychiatric practice. *Bulletin of the Menninger Clinic, 63*, 202–222.

Cranford Ins. Co. Inc. v. Allwest Ins. Co., 645 F Supp. 1440 (N.D. Cal. 1986).

Crawford, I., Humfleet, G., Ribordy, S., Ho, F., & Vickers, V. (1991). Stigmatization of AIDS patients by mental health professionals. *Professional Psychology: Research and Practice, 22*, 357–361.

Crawford, R. L. (1994). Avoiding counselor malpractice. In T. P. Remley (Ed.), *ACA Legal Series* (Vol. 10). Alexandria, VA: American Counseling Association.

Creamer, T. L., & Liddle, B. J. (2005). Secondary traumatic stress among disaster mental health professionals responding to the September 11 attacks. *Journal of Traumatic Stress, 18*, 89–96.

Crespi, T. D. (2009). Group counseling in the schools: Legal, ethical, and treatment issues in school practice. *Psychology in the Schools, 46*, 273–280.

Crespi, T. D., & Dube, J. M. B. (2005). Clinical supervision in school psychology: Challenges, considerations and legal and ethical issues for clinical supervisors. *Clinical Supervisor, 24*, 115–135.

Crethar, H. C., Rivera, E. T., & Nash, S. (2008). In search of common threads: Linking multicultural, feminist, and social justice counseling paradigms. *Journal of Counseling & Development, 86*, 269–278.

Croarkin, P., Berg, J., & Spira, J. (2003). Informed consent to psychotherapy: A look at therapists' understanding, opinions, and practices. *American Journal of Psychotherapy, 57*, 384–401.

Crowley, J. D., & Gottlieb, M. C. (2012). Objects in the mirror are closer than they appear: A primary prevention model for ethical decision making. *Professional Psychology: Research and Practice, 43*, 65–72.

Cruz, M. (2007). Ethical dilemmas faced by professional counselors in their working scenarios. *Dissertation Abstracts International: Section B, The Sciences and Engineering, 68*(11A), 3294.

Cullari, S. (2001). The client's perspective of psychotherapy. In S. Cullari (Ed.), *Counseling and psychotherapy* (pp. 92–116). Boston, MA: Allyn & Bacon.

Cummings, N. A. (1995). Unconscious fiscal convenience. *Psychotherapy in Private Practice, 14*, 23–28.

Curtin, L., & Hargrove, D. S. (2010). Opportunities and challenges of rural practice: Managing self amid ambiguity. *Journal of Clinical Psychology, 66*, 549–561.

Dahlberg, C. C. (1970). Sexual contact between patient and therapist. *Contemporary Psychoanalysis, 5*, 107–124.

Daly, J. M., Jogerst, G. J., Brinig, M. F., & Dawson, J. D. (2004). Mandatory reporting: Relationship of APS statute language on state reported elder abuse. *Journal of Elder Abuse and Neglect, 15*, 1–21.

Damasio, A. (2007). Neuroscience and ethics: Interactions. *American Journal of Bioethics, 7*, 3–7.

Danzinger, P. R., & Welfel, E. R. (2000). Age, gender, and health bias in counselors: An empirical analysis. *Journal of Mental Health Counseling, 22*, 135–149.

Danzinger, P. R., & Welfel, E. R. (2001). The impact of managed care on mental health counselors: A survey of perceptions, practices and compliance with ethical standards. *Journal of Mental Health Counseling, 23*, 137–150.

Dattilio, F. M., Tresco, K. E., Siegel, A. (2007). An empirical survey on psychological testing and the use of the term *psychological*: Turf battles or clinical necessity. *Professional Psychology: Research and Practice, 38*, 682–689.

Davenport, R. (2009). From college counselor to "risk manager": The evolving nature of college counseling on today's campuses. *Journal of American College Health, 58*, 181–183.

Davis v. Monroe County Board of Education, 526 U.S. 629. (1999).

Davis, J. L., & Mickelson, D. J. (1994). School counselors: Are you aware of ethical and legal aspects of counseling? *The School Counselor, 42*, 5–13.

Davis, T., & Ritchie, M. (1993). Confidentiality and the school counselor: A challenge for the 1990s. *The School Counselor, 41*, 23–29.

Dehue, F., Bolman, C., & Vollink, T. (2008). Cyberbullying: Youngsters' experiences and parental perception. *Cyber Psychology & Behavior, 11*, 217–223.

DeKraai, M. B., Sales B. D., & Hall, S. R. (1998). Informed consent, confidentiality, and duty to report laws in the conduct of child therapy. In R. J. Morris & T. R. Kratochwill (Eds.), *The practice of child therapy* (pp. 540–559). Needham Heights, MA: Allyn & Bacon.

DeLucia, J. L., Coleman, V. D., & Jenson-Scott, R. L. (1992). Cultural diversity in group counseling. *Journal for Specialists in Group Work, 17*, 194–195.

DeTrude, J. (2001). Counselors dealing with the media. In E. R. Welfel & R. E. Ingersoll (Eds.), *The mental health desk reference: A practice based guide to diagnosis, treatment, and professional ethics* (pp. 398–403). New York, NY: Wiley.

Deutsch, C. J. (1984). Self-reported sources of stress among psychotherapists. *Professional Psychology: Research and Practice, 15*, 833–845.

Deutsch, C. J. (1985). A survey of therapists' personal problems and treatment. *Professional Psychology: Research and Practice, 16*, 305–315.

Devereaux, R. L., & Gottlieb, M. C. (2012). Record keeping in the cloud: Ethical considerations. *Professional Psychology: Research and Practice, 43*, 627–632.

Dillio, D., & Gale, E. B. (2011). To Google or not to Google: Graduate students' use of the Internet to access personal information about clients. *Training and education in professional psychology, 5*, 160–166.

Dimmitt, C., Carey, J. C.; Hatch, T. (2007). *Evidence-based school counseling: Making a difference with data-driven practices*. Thousand Oaks, CA: Corwin Press.

Dinger, T. J. (1997). The relationship between two ethical decision making models and counselor trainees' responses to an ethical discrimination task and their perceptions of ethical therapeutic behavior. *Dissertation Abstracts International: Section A, Humanities and Social Sciences, 58*(3A), 0750.

Dishion, T. J., McCord, J., & Poulin, F. (1999). When interventions harm: Peer groups and problem behavior. *American Psychologist, 54*, 755–764.

Disney, M. J., & Stephens, A. M. (1994). Legal issues in clinical supervision. In T. P. Remley (Ed.), *ACA Legal Series* (Vol. 8). Alexandria, VA: American Counseling Association.

Doe v. Samaritan Counseling Center, 791 P.2d 344 (Alaska, 1990).

Doll, B. (2011). Youth privacy, school records, and the ethical practice of psychology in schools. *Professional Psychology: Research and Practice, 42*, 259–263.

Doll, B., Strein, W., Jacob, S., & Prasse, D. P. (2011). Youth privacy when educational records include psychological records. *Professional Psychology: Research and Practice, 42*, 259–268.

Donner, M. B., VandeCreek, L. D., Gonsiorek, J. C., & Fisher, C. B. (2008). Balancing confidentiality: Protecting privacy and protecting the public. *Professional Psychology: Research and Practice, 39*, 369–376.

Donohue, W. T., & Engle, J. L. (2013). Errors in psychological practice: Devising a system to improve client safety and well being. *Professional Psychology: Research and Practice, 44*, 314–323.

Dooley, J. J. (2010). Cyber-bullying: Legal implications and strategies for schools. *Journal of Cyber Therapy and Rehabilitation, 3*, 428–430.

Doromal, Q. S., & Creamer, D. G. (1988). An evaluation of the Ethical Judgment Scale. *Journal of College Student Development, 29*, 151–158.

Dorr, D. (1981). Conjoint psychological testing in marriage therapy: New wine in old skins. *Professional Psychology: Research and Practice, 12*, 549–555.

Dougall, J. L. (2010). The influence of client socioeconomic status on counselors' attributional biases and objective countertransference reactions. *Dissertation Abstracts International: Section B, The Sciences and Engineering, 71*(6), 3960.

Dougherty, A. M. (2008). *Psychological consultation and collaboration in school and community settings* (5th ed.). Pacific Grove, CA: Brooks/Cole.

Drane, J. F. (1982). Ethics and psychotherapy: A philosophical perspective. In M. Rosenbaum (Ed.), *Ethics and values in psychotherapy*. New York, NY: Free Press.

Drexler, L. P. (1996). Does money matter? The effect of fee structure on psychotherapy effort and outcome variables. *Dissertation Abstracts International: Section B, The Sciences and Engineering, 56*(12), 7042.

Driscoll, J. M. (1992). Keeping covenants and confidences sacred: One point of view. *Journal of Counseling & Development, 70*, 704–708.

Drogin, E. Y., Connell, M., Foote, W. E., & Sturm, C. A. (2010). The American Psychological Association's revised "record keeping guidelines": Implications for the practitioner. *Professional Psychology: Research and Practice, 41*, 236–243.

Drug Abuse Office and Treatment Act. (1976). 42 USC 290 Sections 3 & 42 C.F.R. Part 2.

Dubin, S. S. (1972). Obsolescence or lifelong education: A choice for the professional. *American Psychologist, 27*, 486–496.

DuBois, J. M. (2008). *Ethics in mental health research: Principles, guidance, and cases*. New York, NY: Oxford.

Dudley, E. (1988, October). *Ethical complaints against family therapists submitted to the AAMFT ethics committee*. Paper presented at the National Meeting of the American Association of Marriage and Family Therapists, New Orleans.

Duffy, M., & Passmore, J. (2010). Ethics in coaching: An ethical decision making framework for coaching psychologists. *International Coaching Psychology Review, 5*, 140–151.

Dugger, S. M. & Francis, P. C. (2014). Surviving a lawsuit against a counseling program: Lessons learned from *Ward v. Wilbanks*. *Journal of Counseling & Development, 92*, 135–141.

Duncan, B. L. (2010). *On becoming a better therapist*. Washington, D.C.: American Psychological Association.

Duncan, B. L., Miller, S. D., Wampold, B. E., & Hubble, M. A. (2010). *The heart and soul of change: Delivering what works in therapy* (2nd ed.). Washington, D.C.: American Psychological Association.

Durana, C. (1998). The use of touch in psychotherapy: Ethical and clinical guidelines. *Psychotherapy: Theory, Research, Practice, Training, 35*, 269–280.

Eberlein, L. (1987). Introducing ethics to beginning psychologists: A problem-solving approach. *Professional Psychology: Research and Practice, 18*, 353–359.

Eckholm, E. (2001, February 18). China's crackdown on sect stirs alarm over psychiatric abuse. *New York Times*, pp. 1, 6.

Eckholm, E. (2014, February 7). Aid in dying movement takes hold in some states. *New York Times*. Retrieved from http://www.nytimes.com/2014/02/08/us/easing-terminal-patients-path-to-death-legally.html

Education for All Handicapped Children Act (Public Law 94–142). (1975).

Ehly, S. W., & Vazquez, E. G. (1998). Peer counseling. In K. Topping & S. W. Ehly (Eds.), *Peer-assisted learning* (pp. 219–233). Mahwah, NJ: Lawrence Erlbaum.

Eisel v. Board of Educ., 597 A. 2d 447 (Md. Ct. App. 1991).

Eisen, S. V., & Dickey, B. (1996). Mental health outcome assessment: The new agenda. *Psychotherapy: Theory/Research/Practice/Training, 33*, 181–189.

Ellis, E. M. (2009). Should a psychotherapist be compelled to release an adolescent's treatment records to a parent in a contested custody case? *Professional Psychology: Research and Practice, 40*, 557–563.

Ellis, E. M. (2012). What are the confidentiality rights of collaterals in family therapy? *The American Journal of Family Therapy, 40*, 369–384.

Employee Assistance Professionals Association (EAPA). (2009). Code of ethics. Retrieved from http://www.eapassn.org/files/public/EAPACodeofEthics0809.pdf

Epstein, R. S., & Simon, R. I. (1990). The Exploitation Index: An early warning indicator of boundary violations in psychotherapy. *Bulletin of the Menninger Clinic, 54*, 450–465.

Erard, R. E. (2004). Release of test data under the 2002 Ethics Code and the HIPAA privacy rule: A raw deal or just a half-baked idea? *Journal of Personality Assessment, 82*, 23–30.

Eriksen, K., & Kress, V. E. (2005). *Beyond the DSM story: Ethical quandaries, challenges, and best practices*. Thousand Oaks, CA: Sage.

Eriksen, K., & Kress, V. E. (2006). The DSM and professional counseling identity: Bridging the gap. *Journal of Mental Health Counseling, 28*, 202–217.

Eriksen, K., & Kress, V. E. (2008). Gender and diagnosis: Struggles and suggestions for counselors. *Journal of Counseling & Development, 86*, 152–162.

Everett, C. A. (1990). The field of marriage and family therapy. *Journal of Counseling & Development, 68*, 498–502.

Ewing v. Goldstein, 120 Cal. App. 4th 807. (2004).

Eyde, L. D., Moreland, G. J., & Robertson, G. L. (1988). *Test-user qualifications: A data-based approach to promoting good test use*. Washington, D.C.: American Psychological Association.

Eyde, L. D., Robertson, G. J., & Krug, S. E. (2010). *Responsible test use: Case studies for assessing human behavior*. Washington, D.C.: American Psychological Association.

Falender, C. A., & Sharfranske, E. P. (2004). *Clinical supervision: A competency-based approach*. Washington, D.C.: American Psychological Association.

Falender, C. A., & Sharfranske, E. P. (2007). Competence in competency-based supervision practice: Construct and application.

Professional Psychology: Research and Practice, 38, 232–240.

Falender, C. A., & Sharfranske, E. P., & Falicov, C. J. (2014). *Multiculturalism and diversity in clinical supervision: A competency based approach*. Washington, D.C.: American Psychological Association.

Fall, K. A., & Lyons, C. (2003). Ethical considerations of family secret disclosure and post-session safety management. *The Family Journal, 11*, 281–285.

Fallon, A. (2006). Informed consent in the practice of group psychotherapy. *International Journal of Group Psychotherapy, 56*, 431–453.

Family Educational Rights and Privacy Act (FERPA). (1974). 20 U.S.C.A. 1232g; 34 CFR Part 99 (West, 1997).

Farah, M. J. (2012). Neuroethics: The Ethical, Legal, and Societal Impact of Neuroscience. *Annual Review of Psychology, 63*, 571–591.

Farnsworth, J. K., & Callahan, J. L. (2013). A model for addressing clinician-client value conflict. *Training and Education in Professional Psychology, 7*, 205–214.

Federal Child Abuse Prevention and Treatment Act, 42 U.S.C. 1510 (Supp. 1987).

Feigelman, W., & Gorman, B. S. (2008). Assessing the effects of peer suicide on youth suicide. *Suicide and Life Threatening Behavior, 38*, 181–194.

Feldman, S. R., Vanarthos, J., & Fleisher, A. B., Jr. (1994). The readability of patient education materials designed for patients with psoriasis. *Journal of the American Academy of Dermatology, 30*, 284–286.

Feldman-Summers, S., & Jones, G. (1984). Psychological impacts of sexual contacts between therapists or other health care professionals and their clients. *Journal of Consulting and Clinical Psychology, 52*, 1054–1061.

Fernandez, C. V., Kodish, E., & Weijer, C. (2003). Informing study participants of research results: An ethical imperative. *IRB, 25*, 12–19.

Ferris, P. A., & Linville, M. E. (1985). The child's rights: Whose responsibility? *Elementary School Guidance and Counseling, 19*, 172–180.

Figley, C. R. (1995). *Compassion fatigue: Coping with secondary traumatic stress disorder in those who treat the traumatized*. New York, NY: Bruner/Mazel.

Filaccio, M. (2005). Discovery, confidentiality, and in camera review: Is it possible to serve two masters? *The Family Journal: Counseling and Therapy for Couples and Families, 13*, 68–70.

Fine, M. A., & Kurdek, L. A. (1993). Reflections on determining authorship credit and authorship order on faculty-student collaborations. *American Psychologist, 48*, 1141–1147.

Finn, S. E., & Butcher, J. N. (1991). Clinical objective personality assessment. In M. Hersen, A. E. Kazdin, & A. S. Bellack (Eds.), *The clinical psychology handbook* (2nd ed., pp. 362–373). New York, NY: Pergamon.

Finn, S. E., & Kamphuis, J. H. (2006). Therapeutic assessment with the MMPI-2. In J. N. Butcher (Ed.), *MMPI-2: A practitioner's guide* (pp. 165–191). Washington, D.C.: American Psychological Association.

Finn, S. E., & Tonsager, M. E. (1997). Information gathering and therapeutic models of assessment: Complementary paradigms. *Psychological Assessment, 9*, 374–385.

Fischer, A. R., Jome, L. M., & Atkinson, D. R. (1998). Reconceptualizing multicultural counseling: Universal healing conditions in a culturally specific context. *The Counseling Psychologist, 26*, 525–588.

Fisher, C. B. (2012). *Decoding the ethics code: A practical guide for psychologists*. Washington, D.C.: American Psychological Association.

Fisher, C. B., Fried, A. L., & Feldman, L. G. (2009). Graduate socialization in the responsible conduct of research: A national survey on the research ethics training experiences of psychology doctoral students. *Ethics & Behavior, 19*, 496–518.

Fisher, C. B., & Oransky, M. (2008). Informed consent in psychotherapy: Protecting the dignity and respecting the autonomy of patients. *Journal of Clinical Psychology, 64*, 576–588.

Fisher, C. B., & Vacanti-Shova, K. (2012). The responsible conduct of psychological research: Overview of ethical principles, APA code standards and federal regulations. In S. J. Knapp, M. C. Gottlieb, M. M. Handelsman, & L. D. VandeCreek, (Eds.), *APA handbook of ethics in psychology* (Vol. 2, pp. 335–369). Washington, D.C.: American Psychological Association.

Fisher, C. D. (2004). Ethical issues in therapy: Therapist self-disclosure of sexual feelings. *Ethics & Behavior, 14*, 105–121.

Fischer, C. T. (1986). *Individualizing psychological assessment*. Pacific Grove, CA: Brooks/Cole.

Fischer, L., & Sorenson, G. P. (1996). *School law for counselors, psychologists, and social workers* (3rd ed.). White Plains, NY: Longman.

Fisher, M. A. (2008). Protecting confidentiality rights: The need for an ethical practice model. *American Psychologist, 63*, 1–13.

Fisher, M. A. (2009). Ethics-based training for nonclinical staff in mental health settings. *Professional Psychology: Research and Practice, 40*, 459–466.

Fitzgerald, B. (1999). Children of lesbian and gay parents: A review of the literature. *Marriage and Family Review, 29*, 57–75.

Fleck-Hendersen, A. (1995). Ethical sensitivity: A theoretical and empirical study. *Dissertation Abstracts International: Section B, The Sciences and Engineering, 56*(10), 2862.

Flower, J. T. (1992). A comparative study of how psychologist gender relates to moral sensitivity. *Dissertation Abstracts International: Section B, The Sciences and Engineering, 53*(11), 2527.

Floyd, M., Myszka, M. T., & Orr, P. (1999). Licensed psychologists' knowledge and utilization of a state association colleague assistance committee. *Professional Psychology: Research and Practice, 29*, 594–598.

Fly, B. J., van Bark, W. P., Weinman, L., Kitchener, K. S., & Long, P. R. (1997). Ethical transgressions of psychology graduate students: Critical incidents with implications for training. *Professional Psychology: Research and Practice, 28*, 492–495.

Flynn, C., & Heitzmann, D. (2008). Tragedy at Virginia Tech: Trauma and its aftermath. *The Counseling Psychologist, 36*, 479–489.

Folberg, J., Milne, A., & Salem, P. (2004). *Divorce and family mediation: Models, techniques and applications*. New York, NY: Guilford.

Foreman, T., & Bernet, W. (2000). A misunderstanding regarding the duty to report suspected child abuse. *Child Maltreatment*, *5*, 190–196.

Forester-Miller, H. (2002). Group counseling: Ethical considerations. In D. Capuzzi & D. R. Gross (Eds.), *Introduction to group counseling* (3rd ed., pp. 185–204). Denver: Love Publishing.

Forrest, L., Elman, N., Gizara, S., & Vacha-Haase, T. (1999). Trainee impairment: A review of identification, remediation, dismissal, and legal issues. *Counseling Psychologist*, *27*, 627–686.

Forstein, M. (2001). Overview of ethical and research issues in sexual orientation therapy. *Journal of Gay and Lesbian Psychotherapy*, *5*, 167–179.

Fortener, R. G. (2000). The relationship between work setting, client progress, suicide ideation, and burnout in psychologists and counselors. *Dissertation Abstracts International: Section B, The Sciences and Engineering*, *60*(11), 6404.

Foster, D., & Black, T. G. (2007). An integral approach to counseling ethics. *Counseling & Values*, *51*, 221–234.

Foster, D. F. (2010). Worldwide testing and test security issues: Ethical challenges and solutions. *Ethics & Behavior*, *20*, 207–228.

Foster, S. (1996, April). Taking the stand as an expert witness. *Counseling Today*, pp. 2, 26.

Fouad, N. A., Grus, C. L., Hatcher, R. L., Kaslow, N. J., Hutchings, P. S., Madson, M. B., & Crossman, R. E. (2009). Competency benchmarks: A model for understanding and measuring competence in professional psychology across training levels. *Training and Education in Professional Psychology*, *3*(4, Suppl.), S5–S26.

Fowers, B. J., & Davidov, J. (2006). The virtue of multiculturalism: Personal transformation, character, and openness to the other. *American Psychologist*, *61*, 581–594.

Fowers, B. J., & Richardson, F. C. (1996). Why is multiculturalism good? *American Psychologist*, *51*, 609–621.

Fox, P. J. (2003, August). *Walking the walk: Does moral judgment equal ethical behavior?* Paper presented at the annual meeting of the American Psychological Association, Toronto, Canada.

Fox, R. E. (1995). The rape of psychotherapy. *Professional Psychology: Research and Practice*, 26, 147–155.

Frager, S. (2000). *Managing managed care: Secrets of a former case manager*. New York, NY: Wiley.

Frauenhoffer, D., Ross, M. J., Gfeller, J., Searight, H. R., & Piotrowski, C. (1998). Psychological test usage among licensed mental health practitioners: A multidisciplinary survey. *Journal of Psychological Practice*, 4, 28–33.

Freeman, S. J. (2000). *Ethics: An introduction to philosophy and practice*. Belmont, CA: Wadsworth.

Freud, S. (1954). *The origins of psychoanalysis: Letters to Wilhelm Fleiss, drafts and notes (1887–1902)*. New York, NY: Basic Books.

Fundudis, T. (2003). Current issues in medico-legal procedures: How competent are children to make their own decisions? *Child and Adolescent Mental Health*, *8*, 18–22.

Fukuyama, M. A. (1994). Critical incidents in multicultural counseling supervision: A phenomenological approach in supervision research. *Counselor Education and Supervision*, *34*, 142–151.

Gabbard, G. O. (Ed.). (1989). *Sexual exploitation in professional relationships*. Washington, D.C.: American Psychiatric Press.

Gabbard, G. O. (1994). Reconsidering the American Psychological Association's policy on sex with former patients: Is it justifiable? *Professional Psychology: Research and Practice*, *25*, 329–335.

Gabbard, G. O. (2002). Post-termination sexual boundary violations. *Psychiatric Clinics of North America*, *25*, 593–603.

Gallardo, M. E., Johnson, J., Parham, T. A., & Carter, J. A. (2009). Ethics and multiculturalism: Advancing cultural and clinical responsiveness. *Professional Psychology: Research and Practice*, *40*, 425–435.

Galley, M., & Walsh, M. (2002, February 27). Statements to school counselors not protected Michigan court rule. *Education Week*, *21*, 9.

Galvin, S. L., & Herzog, H. A. (1992). The ethical judgment of animal research. *Ethics & Behavior*, *2*, 263–286.

Garb, H. N. (1997). Race bias, social class bias, and gender bias in clinical judgment. *Clinical Psychology: Science and Practice*, *4*, 99–120.

Garb, H. N. (2000). Introduction to the special section on the use of computers for making psychological judgments and decisions. *Psychological Assessment*, *12*, 3–5.

Garcia, J. G., Cartwright, B., Winston, S. M., & Borzuchowska, B. (2003). A transcultural integrative model for ethical decision making in counseling. *Journal of Counseling & Development*, *81*, 268–277.

Garfield, R. L., Lave, J. R., & Donohue, J. M. (2010). Health reform and the scope of benefits for mental health and substance use disorder services. *Psychiatric Services*, *61*, 1081–1086.

Garrett, T. (1998). Sexual contact between patients and psychologists. *Psychologist*, *11*, 227–230.

Gartrell, N., Herman, J., Olarte, S., Feldstein, M., & Localio, R. (1989). Prevalence of psychiatrist-patient sexual contact. In G. O. Gabbard (Ed.), *Sexual exploitation in professional relationships* (pp. 27–38). Washington, D.C.: American Psychiatric Press.

Garvey, N., & Braun, V. (1997). Ethics and the publication of clinical case material. *Professional Psychology: Research and Practice*, *28*, 399–404.

Gates, K. P., & Speare, K. H. (1990). Overlapping relationships in rural communities. In H. Lerman & N. Porter (Eds.), *Feminist ethics in psychotherapy* (pp. 97–101). New York, NY: Springer.

Gaubatz, M. D., & Vera, E. M. (2006). Trainee competence in master's level counseling programs: A comparison of counselor educators' and students' views. *Counselor Education and Supervision*, *46*, 32–43.

Gawande, A. (2007). *Better: A surgeon's notes on performance*. New York, NY: Metropolitan Books.

Gay, Lesbian, Straight Education Network (GLSEN). (2009). National

School Climate Survey. Retrieved from http://www.glsen.org/cgi-bin/iowa/all/library/record/2624.html?state=research&;type=antibullying

Gechtman, L. (1989). Sexual contact between social workers and their clients. In G. O. Gabbard (Ed.), *Sexual exploitation in professional relationships* (pp. 27–38). Washington, D.C.: American Psychiatric Press.

Geelhoed, R. J., Phillips, J. C., Fischer, A. R., Shpungin, E., & Gong, Y. (2007). Authorship decision making: An empirical investigation. *Ethics & Behavior*, *17*, 95–115.

Geib, P. G. (1982). The experience of nonerotic physical contacts in traditional psychotherapy: A critical investigation of the taboo against touch. *Dissertation Abstracts International: Section A, The Humanities and Social Sciences*, *43*(1), 0248.

Gelso, C. J. (1985). Rigor, relevance, and counseling research: On the need to maintain our course between Scylla and Charybdis. *Journal of Counseling & Development*, *63*, 551–553.

Gergen, K. J., Hoffman, L., & Anderson, H. (1996). Is diagnosis a disaster? A constructionist trialogue. In F. W. Kaslow (Ed.), *Handbook of relational diagnosis* (pp. 102–118). New York, NY: Wiley.

Gibb, J. J. (2005). Patients' experience of friendship with their therapists: A phenomenological study of non-sexual dual relationships. *Dissertation Abstracts International: Section B, The Sciences and Engineering*, *65*(3), 3707.

Gibbons, M. M., & Studer, J. R. (2008). Suicide awareness training for faculty and staff: A training model for school counselors. *Professional School Counseling*, *11*, 272–276.

Gibson, C. A., Breitbart, W., Tomarken, A., Kosinski, A., & Nelson, C. J. (2006). In J. L. Werth, Jr., & D. Blevins (Eds.), *Psychosocial issues near the end of life: A resource for professional care providers* (pp. 137–162). Washington, D.C.: American Psychological Association.

Gibson, W. T., & Pope, K. S. (1993). The ethics of counseling: A national survey of certified counselors. *Journal of Counseling & Development*, *71*, 330–336.

Gillespie, M., Hearn, V., & Silverman, R. A. (1998). Suicide following homicide in Canada. *Homicide Studies*, *2*, 40–63.

Gilligan, C. (1982). *In a different voice: Psychological theory and women's development*. Cambridge, MA: Harvard University Press.

Gilroy, P. J., Carroll, L., & Murra, J. (2002). A preliminary survey of counseling psychologists' personal experiences with depression and treatment. *Professional Psychology: Research and Practice*, *33*, 402–407.

Giovazolias, T., & Davis, P. (2001). How common is sexual attraction to clients? The experiences of sexual attraction of counseling psychologists toward their clients and the impact on the therapeutic process. *Counseling Psychology Quarterly*, *14*, 281–286.

Gizara, S. S., & Forrest, L. (2004). Supervisors' experiences of trainee impairment and incompetence at APA-accredited internship sites. *Professional Psychology: Research and Practice*, *35*, 131–140.

Gladding, S. T. (2011). *Group work: A counseling specialty* (6th ed.). Englewood Cliffs, NJ: Prentice Hall.

Gladding, S. T. (2012). *Counseling: A comprehensive profession* (6th ed.). New York, NY: Macmillan.

Gladding, S. T., Remley, T. P., & Huber, C. H. (2011). *Legal, ethical, and professional issues in the practice of marriage and family therapy* (3rd ed.). New York, NY: Prentice Hall.

Glaser, R., & Thorpe, J. (1986). Unethical intimacy. A survey of sexual contact and advances between psychology educators and female graduate students. *American Psychologist*, *41*, 43–51.

Gloria, A. M., Hird, J. S., & Tao, K. W. (2008). Self-reported multicultural supervision competence of White predoctoral intern supervisors. *Training and Education in Professional Psychology*, *2*, 129–136.

Glosoff, H. L. (2001). Ethical issues related to interprofessional communication. In E. R. Welfel & R. E. Ingersoll (Eds.), *The mental health desk reference: A practice-based guide to diagnosis, treatment, and professional ethics*. New York, NY: Wiley.

Glosoff, H. L., & Freeman, T. (2007). Report of the ACA Ethics Committee: 2005–2006. *Journal of Counseling & Development*, *85*, 251–254.

Glosoff, H. L., Herlihy, B. J., & Spence, E. B. (2000). Privileged communication in the counselor-client relationship. *Journal of Counseling & Development*, *78*, 454.

Glosoff, H. L., & Pate, R. H. (2002). Privacy and confidentiality in school counseling. *Professional School Counseling*, *6*, 20–27.

Godlee, F. (2009). More than 20% of articles have a guest author, study shows. *British Medical Journal*, *339*, b3783.

Golden, L., & Schmidt, S. J. (1998). Unethical practice as perceived by mental health professionals: The next generation. *Counseling and Values*, *42*, 166–170.

Gonsiorek, J. C. (1997). Suggested remediations to remediation. *Professional Psychology: Research and Practice*, *28*, 300–303.

Gonsiorek, J. C., & Brown, L. S. (1989). Post-therapy sexual relationships with clients. In G. R. Schoener, J. H. Milgron, J. C. Gonsiorek, E. T. Luepker, & R. M. Conroe (Eds.), *Psychotherapists' sexual involvement with clients* (pp. 289–301). Minneapolis, MN: Walk-in Counseling Center.

Good, G. E., Thoreson, P., & Shaughnessy, P. (1995). Substance use, confrontation of impaired colleagues, and psychological functioning among counseling psychologists: A national survey. *Counseling Psychologist*, *23*, 703–721.

Goodheart, C. D., Kazdin, A. E., & Sternberg, R. J. (Eds.). (2007). *Evidence-based psychotherapy: Where research and practice meet*. Washington, D.C.: American Psychological Association.

Goodyear, R. K., Coleman, T., & Brunson, B. I. (1986, August). *Informed consent for clients: Effects in two counseling settings*. Paper presented at the annual meeting of the American Psychological Association, Washington, D.C.

Goodyear, R. K., Crego, C. A., & Johnston, M. W. (1992). Ethical issues in the supervision of student research: A study of critical incidents. *Professional Psychology: Research and Practice, 23*, 203–210.

Goodyear, R. K., & Rodolfa, E. (2012). Negotiating the complex ethical terrain of clinical supervision. In S. J. Knapp, M. C. Gottlieb, M. M. Handelsman, & L. D. VandeCreek, (Eds.), *APA handbook of ethics in psychology* (Vol. 2, pp. 261–275). Washington, D.C.: American Psychological Association.

Goodyear, R. K., & Shumate, J. L. (1996). Perceived effects of therapist self-disclosure of attraction to clients. *Professional Psychology: Research and Practice, 27*, 613–616.

Gorman, S. W. (2009, April). Comment: Sex outside of the therapy hour: Practical and constitutional limits on therapist sexual misconduct regulations. *UCLA Law Review, 56*, 963.

Gottlieb, M. C. (1993). Avoiding exploitive dual relationships: A decision-making model. *Psychotherapy: Theory/Research/Practice/Training, 30*, 41–48.

Gottlieb, M. C., & Coleman, A. A. (2012). Ethical challenges in forensic psychology. In S. Knapp, M. C. Gottlieb, M. M. Handelsman, & L. D. VandeCreek (Eds.), *APA Handbook of Ethics in Psychology* (Vol. 2, pp. 91–124). Washington, D.C.: American Psychological Association.

Gottlieb. M. C., & Cooper, C. C. (2000). The future of health care: Ideals and realities. *The Counseling Psychologist, 28*, 263–266.

Gottlieb, M. C., Handelsman, M. M., & Knapp, S. J. (2013). A model for integrated ethics consultation. *Professional Psychology: Research and Practice, 44*, 307–313.

Gottlieb, M. C., Robinson, K., & Younggren, J. N. (2007). Multiple relations in supervision: Guidance for administrators, supervisors, and students. *Professional Psychology: Research and Practice, 38*, 241–247.

Gottlieb, M. C., Sell, J. M., & Schoenfeld, L. S. (1988). Social/romantic relationships with present and former clients: State licensing board actions. *Professional Psychology: Research and Practice, 19*, 459–462.

Gould, J. W., & Martindale, D. A. (2007). *The art and science of child custody evaluations*. New York, NY: Guilford.

Grant v. Board of Trustees of Valley View School District. (1997). No. 365-U, 676 N.E. 2nd 705 (Ill. App. Ct.).

Grassley Amendment. (1994). Sec. 1017 of GOALS 2000: The Educate America Act under the heading "Protection of Pupils": 20 U.S.C. Section 1232h.

Gray, L. A., Ladany, N., Walker, J. A., & Ancis, J. R. (2001). Psychotherapy trainees' experience of counterproductive events in supervision. *Journal of Counseling Psychology, 48*, 371–383.

Gray-Little, B., & Kaplan, D. A. (1998). Interpretation of psychological tests in clinical and forensic evaluations. In J. Sundoval, C. L. Frisby, K. L. Geisinger, J. D. Scheuneman, & J. R. Grenier (Eds.), *Test interpretation and diversity* (pp. 141–178). Washington, D.C.: American Psychological Association.

Greenberg, K. R. (2003). *Group counseling in K–12 schools: A handbook for counselors*. Needham Heights, MA: Allyn & Bacon.

Greenberg, S. A., & Shuman, D. W. (1997). Irreconcilable conflict between therapeutic and forensic roles. *Professional Psychology: Research and Practice, 28*, 50–57.

Greene, J. D. (2005a). Cognitive neuroscience and the structure of the moral mind. In S. Laurence, P. Carruthers, & S. Stich. (Eds.) *The Innate Mind: Structure and Contents* (pp. 338–352). New York, NY: Oxford University Press.

Greene, J. D. (2005b). From neural "is" to moral "ought": What are the moral implications of neuroscientific moral psychology? *Nature Reviews Neuroscience, 4*, 847–850.

Greene, J. D., & Paxton, J. M. (2009) Patterns of neural activity associated with honest and dishonest moral decisions. *Proceedings of the National Academy of Sciences USA, 106*(30), 12506–12511.

Greif, S. (2007). Advances in research on coaching outcomes. *International Coaching Psychology Review, 2*, 220–247.

Greyner, B. F. S., & Lewis, K. (2012). Prevalence, prediction, and prevention of psychologist misconduct. *Australian Psychologist, 47*, 68–76.

Grob, G. N. (1994). *The mad among us: A history of the care of America's mentally ill*. New York, NY: Free Press; 1994.

Groopman. J. (2007). *How doctors think*. Boston, MA: Houghton Mifflin.

Gross, S. (2005). Student perspectives on clinical and counseling psychology practica. *Professional Psychology: Research and Practice, 36*, 299–306.

Gudeman, R. (2003). Federal privacy protection for substance abuse treatment records: Protecting adolescents. *Youth Law News*. Retrieved from http://www.youthlaw.org/fileadmin/ncyl/youthlaw/publications/yln/2003/issue_3/03_yln_3_gudeman_substance.pdf

Guest, C. L., Jr., & Dooley, K. (1999). Supervisor malpractice: Liability to the supervisee in clinical supervision. *Counselor Education and Supervision, 38*, 269–279.

Guntheil, T., & Gabbard, G. (1993). The concept of boundaries in a clinical practice: Theoretical and risk management dimensions. *American Journal of Psychiatry, 150*, 188–196.

Gurman, A. (1985). On saving marriages. *Family Therapy Networker, 9*, 17–18.

Gustafson, K. E., & McNamara, J. R. (1987). Confidentiality with minor clients: Issues and guidelines for therapists. *Professional Psychology: Research and Practice, 18*, 503–508.

Gustafson, K. E., McNamara, J. R., & Jensen, J. A. (1994). Parents' informed consent decisions regarding psychotherapy for their children: Consideration of therapeutic risks and benefits. *Professional Psychology: Research and Practice, 25*, 16–22.

Guterman, J. T., & Rudes, J. (2008). Social constructionism and ethics: Implications for counseling. *Counseling and Values, 52*, 136–144.

Guterman, M. (1991). Working couples: Finding a balance between family and career. In J. M. Kummerow (Ed.), *New directions in career planning and the workplace* (pp. 167–193). Palo Alto, CA: Consulting Psychologists Press.

Gutheil, T. G., & Brodsky, A. (2008). *Preventing boundary violations in clinical practice*. New York, NY: Guilford.

Gutheil, T. G., & Gabbard, G. O. (1993). The concept of boundaries in clinical practice. *American Journal of Psychiatry*, *150*, 188–196.

Guttman, V. (2005). Ethical reasoning and mental health services with deaf clients. *Journal of Deaf Studies and Deaf Education*, *10*, 171–183.

Guy, J. D., Poelstra, P. L., & Stark, M. J. (1989). Personal distress and therapeutic effectiveness: National survey of psychologists practicing psychotherapy. *Professional Psychology: Research and Practice*, *20*, 48–50.

Guzmán, M. R., Calfa, N. A., Kerne, V. V. H., & McCarthy, C. (2013). Examination of multicultural counseling competencies in school counselors. *Journal of School Counseling*, *11*(7). Retrieved from http://jsc.montana.edu/articles/v11n7.pdf

Haas, L. J. (1993). Competence and quality in the performance of forensic psychologists. *Ethics & Behavior*, *3*, 251–266.

Haas, L. J., & Cummings, N. A. (1991). Managed outpatient mental health plans: Clinical, ethical and practical guidelines for participation. *Professional Psychology: Research and Practice*, *22*, 45–51.

Haas, L. J., & Malouf, J. L. (2005). *Keeping up the good work: A practitioner's guide to mental health ethics* (4th ed.). Sarasota, FL: Professional Resource Exchange.

Haas, L. J., Malouf, J. L., & Mayerson, N. H. (1988). Personal and professional characteristics as factors in psychologists' ethical decision making. *Professional Psychology: Research and Practice*, *19*, 35–42.

Hamilton, J. C. & Spruill, J. (1999). Identifying and reducing risk factors related to trainer–client sexual misconduct. *Professional Psychology: Research and Practice*, *30*, 318–327.

Hammel, G. A., Olkin, R., & Taube, D. O. (1996). Student-educator sex in clinical and counseling psychology doctoral training. *Professional Psychology: Research and Practice*, *27*, 93–97.

Handelsman, M. M. (2001). Accurate and effective informed consent. In E. R. Welfel & R. E. Ingersoll (Eds.), *The mental health desk reference: A practice-based guide to diagnosis, treatment, and professional ethics* (pp. 453–458). New York, NY: Wiley.

Handelsman, M. M., & Galvin, M. D. (1988). Facilitating informed consent for outpatient psychotherapy: A suggested written format. *Professional Psychology: Research and Practice*, *19*, 223–225.

Handelsman, M. M., Gottlieb, M. C., & Knapp, S. J. (2005). Training ethical psychologists: An acculturation model. *Professional Psychology: Research and Practice*, *26*, 59–65.

Handelsman, M. M., Kemper, M. B., Kesson-Craig, P., McLain, J., & Johnsrud, C. (1986). Use, content and readability of written informed consent forms for treatment. *Professional Psychology: Research and Practice*, *17*, 514–518.

Hansen, N. D., & Goldberg, S. G. (1999). Navigating the nuances: A matrix of considerations for ethical-legal dilemmas. *Professional Psychology: Research and Practice*, *30*, 495–503.

Hansen, N. D., Randazzo, K. V., Schwartz, A., Marshall, M., Kalis, D., Frazier, R., & Norvig, G. (2006). Do we practice what we preach? An exploratory survey of multicultural psychotherapy competencies. *Professional Psychology: Research and Practice*, *37*, 66–74.

Hardin, E. E., & Leong, F. T. L. (2004). Decision-making theories and career assessment: A psychometric evaluation of the Decision Making Inventory. *Journal of Career Assessment*, *12*, 51–64.

Hare-Mustin, R. T. (1980). Family therapy may be dangerous to your health. *Professional Psychology: Research and Practice*, *11*, 935–938.

Hare-Mustin, R. T., Marecek, J., Kaplan, A. G., & Liss-Levinson, N. (1979). Rights of clients, responsibilities of therapists. *American Psychologist*, *34*, 3–16.

Hargrove, D. S. (1982). An overview of professional considerations in the rural community. In P. A. Kelly & J. D. Murray (Eds.), *Handbook of rural community mental health* (pp. 169–182). New York, NY: Human Sciences Press.

Hargrove, D. S. (1986). Ethical issues in rural mental health practice. *Professional Psychology: Research and Practice*, *17*, 20–23.

Harlow, H. F. (1971). *Learning to love*. New York, NY: Albion.

Harper, F. D., & McFadden, J. J. (Eds.). *Culture and counseling: New approaches*. Needham Heights, MA: Allyn & Bacon.

Harrar, W. R., VandeCreek, L. D., & Knapp, S. J. (1990). Ethical and legal aspects of clinical supervision. *Professional Psychology: Research and Practice*, *21*, 37–41.

Harris, S. E., & Kurpius, S. E. (2014). Social networking and professional ethics: Client searches, informed consent, and disclosure. *Professional Psychology: Research and Practice*, *45*, 11–19

Hartl, T. L., Zeiss, R. A., Marino, C. M., Zeiss, A. M., Regey, L. G., & Leontis, C. (2007). Clients' sexually inappropriate behaviors directed towards clinicians: Conceptualization and management. *Professional Psychology: Research and Practice*, *38*, 674–681.

Hartlaub, G. H., Martin, G. C., & Rhine, M. W. (1986). Recontact with the analyst following termination: A survey of 71 cases. *Journal of the American Psychoanalytic Association*, *34*, 895–910.

Hartsell, T. L., Jr., & Bernstein, B. E. (2008). *The portable ethicist for mental health professionals* (2nd ed.). New York, NY: Wiley.

Harway, M., & O'Neil, J. M. (Eds.). (1999). *What causes men's violence against women?* Thousand Oaks, CA: Sage.

Haspel, K. C., Jorgenson, L. M., Wincze, J. P., & Parsons, J. P. (1997). Legislative intervention regarding therapist sexual misconduct: An overview. *Professional Psychology: Research and Practice*, *28*, 63–72.

Hatcher, R. L., Fouad, N. A., Campbell, L. F., McCutcheon, S. R., Grus, C. L., & Leahy, K. L. (2013). Competency-based education for professional psychology: Moving from concept to practice. *Training and Education in Professional Psychology*, *7*, 225–234.

Hathaway, S. R., & McKinley, J. C. (1943). *The Minnesota multiphasic personality schedule*. Minneapolis: University of Minnesota Press.

Haverkamp, B. E. (2005). Ethical perspectives on qualitative research in applied psychology. *Journal of*

Counseling Psychology, 52, 146–155.
Hawley, K. M., & Weisz, R. (2003). Child, parent and therapist (dis) agreement on target problems in outpatient therapy: The therapist's dilemma and its implications. *Journal of Consulting and Clinical Psychology*, *71*, 62–70.
Hayman, P. M., & Covert, J. A. (1986). Ethical dilemmas in college counseling centers. *Journal of Counseling & Development*, *64*, 318–319.
Hays, D. G. (2008). Assessing multicultural competence in counselor trainees: A review of instrumentation and future directions. *Journal of Counseling & Development*, *86*, 95–101.
Hazler, R. J. (1996). *Breaking the cycle of violence: Interventions for bullies and victims*. Washington, D.C.: Accelerated Development.
The Health Information Technology for Economic and Clinical Health Act (HITECH). Title XIII of Div. A and Title IV of Div. B of the American Recovery and Reinvestment Act of 2009. Pub L. No 111-5 (2009).
Health Insurance Portability and Accountability Act of 1996 (HIPAA). Pub. 1. No. 104-191, 110Stat. 1936 (1996).
Hecker, L. B., & Edwards, A. B. (2014). The Impact of HIPAA and HITECH: New standards for confidentiality, security, and documentation for marriage and family therapists. *American Journal of Family Therapy*, *42*, 95–113.
Heinlen, K. T., Welfel, E. R., Richmond, E. N., & O'Donnell, M. S. (2003). The nature, scope and ethics of psychologists' E-therapy websites: What consumers find when surfing the Web. *Psychotherapy: Theory, Research, Practice, Training*, *40*, 112–124.
Heinlen, K. T., Welfel, E. R., Richmond, E. N., & Rak, C. F. (2003). The scope of WebCounseling: A survey of services and compliance with NBCC's guidelines for Internet counseling. *Journal of Counseling & Development*, *81*, 61–69.
Heitler, S. (2001). Combined individual/marital therapy: A conflict resolution framework and ethical considerations. *Journal of Psychotherapy Integration*, *11*, 349–383.
Helbok, C. M. (2003). The practice of psychology in rural communities: Potential ethical dilemmas. *Ethics & Behavior*, *13*, 367–384.
Helbok, C. M. (2006). National survey of ethical practices across rural and urban communities. *Professional Psychology: Research and Practice*, *37*, 35–44.
Helbok, C. M., Marinelli, R. P., & Walls, R. T. (2006). National survey of ethical practices across rural and urban communities. *Professional Psychology: Research and Practice*, *37*, 36–44.
Hellkamp, D. T., Zins, J. E., Ferguson, K., & Hodge, M. (1998). Training practices in consultation: A national survey of clinical, counseling, industrial/organizational, and school psychology faculty. *Consulting Psychology Journal: Practice and Research*, *50*, 228–236.
Helms, J. E. (2003). A pragmatic view of social justice. *The Counseling Psychologist*, *31*, 305–313.
Henderson, D. H. (1987). Negligent liability and the foreseeability factor: A critical issue for school counselors. *Journal of Counseling & Development*, *66*, 86–89.
Hendin, H., Lipschitz, A., Maltsberger, J. T., Haas, A. P., & Wynecoop, S. (2000). Therapists' reactions to patients' suicides. *American Journal of Psychiatry*, *157*, 2022–2027.
Hendrick, S. S. (1988). Counselor self-disclosure. *Journal of Counseling & Development*, *66*, 419–424.
Hensley, L. G., Smith, S. L., & Thompson, R. W. (2003). Assessing competencies of counselors in training: Complexities in evaluating personal and professional development. *Counselor Education and Supervision*, *42*, 219–230.
Heppner, P. P. (Ed.). (1990). *Pioneers in counseling and development: Personal and professional perspectives*. Alexandria, VA: American Counseling Association.
Herlihy, B. J., & Corey, G. (1992). *Dual relationships in counseling*. Alexandria, VA: American Association for Counseling and Development.
Herlihy, B. J., & Corey, G. (1997). *Boundary issues in counseling*. Alexandria, VA: American Counseling Association.
Herlihy, B. J., & Corey, G. (2014). *ACA ethical standards casebook* (7th ed.). Alexandria, VA: American Counseling Association.
Herlihy, B. J., Hermann, M. A., & Greden, L. R. (2014). Legal and ethical implications of using religious beliefs as the basis for refusing to counsel certain clients. *Journal of Counseling & Development*, *92*, 148–153.
Herlihy, B. J., & Watson, Z. E. (2003). Ethical issues and multicultural competence in counseling. In F. D. Harper & J. McFadden (Eds.), *Culture and counseling: New approaches* (pp. 363–378). Needham Heights, MA: Allyn & Bacon.
Herman, J. L., Gartrell, N., Olarte, S., Feldstein, M., & Localio, R. (1987). Psychiatrist–patient sexual contact: Results of a national survey, II: Psychiatrists' attitudes. *American Journal of Psychiatry*, *144*, 164–169.
Herman, L. (1992). *Trauma and recovery*. New York, NY: Basic Books.
Hermann, M. A. (2002). A study of legal issues encountered by school counselors and perceptions of their preparedness to respond to legal challenges. *Professional School Counseling*, *6*, 12–18.
Hermann, M. A., & Finn, A. (2002). An ethical and legal perspective on the role of school counselors in preventing violence in schools. *Professional School Counseling*, *6*, 46–54.
Herrington, R. (1979). The impaired physician—Recognition, diagnosis and treatment. *Wisconsin Medical Journal*, *78*, 21–23.
Hersch, S. M. (2004, May 10). Torture at Abu Ghraib. *New Yorker*.
Hess, A. K., & Hess, K. A. (1983). Psychotherapy supervision: A survey of internship training practices. *Professional Psychology: Research and Practice*, *14*, 504–513.
Hess, A. K., & Weiner, I. B. (1999). *Handbook of forensic psychology*. New York, NY: Wiley.
Hess, S. A., Knox, S., Schultz, J. M., Hill, C. E., Sloan, L., Brandt, S., ... Hoffman, M. A. (2008). Predoctoral interns' nondisclosure in supervision. *Psychotherapy Research*, *18*, 400–411.
Hetrick, E. S., & Martin, A. D. (1987). Developmental issues and their resolutions for gay and lesbian

adolescents. *Journal of Homosexuality, 14*, 25–43.

Hill, A. L. (2004a). Ethics education: Recommendations for an evolving discipline. *Counseling and Values, 48*, 183–203.

Hill, A. L. (2004b). Ethical analysis in counseling: A case for narrative ethics, moral visions, and virtue ethics. *Counseling and Values, 48*, 131–148.

Hill, C. L., & Ridley, C. R. (2001). Diagnostic decision making: Do counselors delay final judgments? *Journal of Counseling & Development, 79*, 98–104.

Hill, M., Glaser, K., & Harden, J. (1998). A feminist model for ethical decision making. *Women and Therapy, 21*, 101–121.

Hillbrand, M. (2001). Homicide-suicide and other forms of co-occurring aggression against self and against others. *Professional Psychology: Research and Practice, 32*, 626–635.

Hinduja, S., & Patchin, J. W. (2010). Cyberbullying: Identification, prevention, and response. Retrieved from http://www.cyberbullying.us/Cyberbullying_Identification_Prevention_Response_Fact_Sheet.pdf

Hoerger, M., & Currell, C. (2012). Ethical issues in Internet research. In S. J. Knapp, M. C. Gottlieb, M. M. Handelsman, & L. D. VandeCreek, (Eds.), *APA handbook of ethics in psychology* (Vol. 2, pp. 385–400). Washington, D.C.: American Psychological Association.

Hoffman, J. (2010, December 4). As bullies go digital, parents play catch up. Retrieved from http://www.nytimes.com/2010/12/05/us/05bully.html?ref=cyberbullying

Hogan, R., Hogan, J., & Roberts, B. W. (1996). Personality measurement and employment decisions: Questions and answers. *American Psychologist, 51*, 469–477.

Hohenshil, T. H. (1996). Editorial: The role of assessment and diagnosis in counseling. *Journal of Counseling & Development, 75*, 64–67.

Holcomb-McCoy, C. C., & Myers, J. E. (1999). Multicultural competence and counselor training: A national survey. *Journal of Counseling & Development, 77*, 294–302.

Holland, T. P., & Kilpatrick, A. C. (1991). Ethical issues in social work: Toward a grounded theory of professional ethics. *Social Work, 36*, 138–144.

Holloway, J. D. (2003, February). More protections for patients and psychologists under HIPAA. *APA Monitor, 34*, 22.

Holroyd, J., & Brodsky, A. (1977). Psychologists' attitudes and practices regarding erotic and nonerotic physical contact with clients. *American Psychologist, 32*, 843–849.

Holroyd, J., & Brodsky, A. (1980). Does touching patients lead to sexual intercourse? *Professional Psychology, 11*, 807–811.

Holub, E. A., & Lee, S. S. (1990). Therapists' use of nonerotic physical contact: Ethical concerns. *Professional Psychology: Research and Practice, 21*, 115–117.

Horst, E. A. (1989). Dual relationships between psychologists and clients in rural and urban areas. *Journal of Rural Community Psychology, 10*, 15–24.

Horton, J. A., Clance, P. R., Sterk-Elifson, C., Emshoff, J. (1995). Touch in psychotherapy: A survey of patients' experiences. *Psychotherapy: Theory/Research/Practice/Training, 32*, 443–457.

Houser, R., Wilczenski, F. L., & Ham, M. (2006). *Culturally relevant ethical decision making*. Thousand Oaks, CA: Sage.

Houskamp, B. (1994). Assessing and treating battered women: A clinical review of issues and approaches. *New Directions for Mental Health Services, 64*, 79–89.

Housman, L. M., & Stake, J. E. (1999). The current state of sexual ethics training in clinical psychology: Issues of quantity, quality, and effectiveness. *Professional Psychology: Research and Practice, 30*, 302–311.

Hsiung, R. C. (Ed.). (2002). *E-therapy: Case studies, guiding principles, and the clinical potential of the Internet*. New York, NY: Norton.

Huber, C. H. (1994). *Ethical, legal, and professional issues in the practice of marriage and family therapy* (3rd ed.). New York, NY: Prentice Hall.

Huber, C. H., & Baruth, L. G. (1987). *Ethical, legal and professional issues in the practice of marriage and family therapy*. Columbus, OH: Merrill.

Huber, P. W. (1991). *Galileo's revenge: Junk science in the courtroom*. New York, NY: Basic Books.

Humphreys, K., Winzelberg, A., & Klaw, E. (2000). Psychologists' ethical responsibilities in Internet-based groups: Issues, strategies, and a call for dialogue. *Professional Psychology: Research and Practice, 31*, 493–496.

Hunter, M., & Struve, J. (1998). *The ethical use of touch In psychotherapy*. Thousand Oaks, CA: Sage Publications.

Huprich, S. K., & Rudd, M. D. (2004). National survey of trainee impairment in counseling, clinical, and school psychology programs and internship. *Journal of Clinical Psychology, 60*, 43–52.

Huss, S. N., Bryant, A., & Mulet, A. (2008). Managing the quagmire of counseling in a school: Bringing the parents on board. *Professional School Counseling, 11*, 362–366.

Hyman, S. E., & Malenka, R. C. (2001). Addiction and the brain: The neurobiology of compulsion and its persistence. *Neuroscience, 2*, 696–703.

Ibrahim, F. A., & Arrendondo, P. M. (1986). Ethical standards for cross-cultural counseling. *Journal of Counseling & Development, 64*, 349–352.

Iglehart, J. K. (1996). Managed care and mental health. *Health Policy Report, 334*, 131–135.

In re Gault, 387 U.S. I (1967).

Institute of Medicine and National Research Council. (2009). *Preventing Mental, Emotional, and Behavioral Disorders Among Young People: Progress and Possibilities*. Washington, D.C.: The National Academies Press, 2009.

International Association for Coaching Psychology (IACP). (2008) Code of ethics. Retrieved from http://www.isfcp.net/ethics.htm

International Association of Coaching (IAC). (2003). Code of ethics. Retrieved from http://www.certifiedcoach.org/index.php/about_iac/iac_code_of_ethics/

International Association of Marriage and Family Counseling (IAMFC). (2005). Ethical code for the International Association of Marriage and Family Counseling. *The Family Journal, 14*, 92–98.

International Coaches Association. (2003). Code of ethics. Retrieved from http://www.certifiedcoach.org/index.php/about_iac/iac_code_of_ethics/

International Society for Coaching Psychology. (2011). Ethics. Retrieved from http://www.isfcp.net/ethics.htm

International Testing Commission (ITC). (2005). Guidelines on computer-based and Internet-delivered testing. Retrieved from http://www.intestcom.org/Downloads/ITC Guidelines on Computer - version 2005 approved.pdf

International Union of Psychological Science. (2008). Universal declaration of ethical principles for psychologists. Retrieved from http://www.sagepub.com/cac6study/pdf/UniversalDeclaration.pdf

Isaacs, M. L., & Stone, C. (1999). School counselors and confidentiality: Factors affecting professional choices. *Professional School Counseling*, 2, 258–266.

Isaacs, M. L., & Stone, C. (2001). Confidentiality with minors: Mental health counselors' attitudes towards breaching or preserving confidentiality. *Journal of Mental Health Counseling*, *23*, 342–356.

Ivey, A. E., & Ivey, M. B. (1998). Reframing the DSM: Positive strategies from developmental counseling and therapy. *Journal of Counseling & Development*, *76*, 334–350.

Ivey, G. (2014). The ethics of mandatory personal psychotherapy for trainee psychotherapists. *Ethics & Behavior*, *28*, 91–108.

Jacob, S., Decker, D. M., & Hartshorne, T. S. (2010). *Ethics and law for school psychologists*. Hoboken, NJ: Wiley.

Jacob, S., & Powers, K. E. (2009). Privileged communication in the school psychologist—client relationship. *Psychology in the Schools*, *46*, 307–318.

Jacob-Timm, S. (1999). Ethically challenging situations encountered by school psychologists. *Psychology in the Schools*, *36*, 205–217.

Jaffee v. Redmond, 1996 WL 315841 (U.S. June 13, 1996).

James, S., & Foster, G. (2006). Reconciling rules with context: An ethical framework for cultural psychotherapy. *Theory & Psychology*, *16*, 803–823.

James, S. H., & DeVaney, S. B. (1995). Preparing to testify: The school counselor as court witness. *The School Counselor*, *43*, 97–102.

Janson, G. R. (2002). Family counseling and referral with gay, lesbian, bisexual, and transgendered clients: Ethical considerations. *The Family Journal*, *10*, 328–333.

Janson, G. R., & Steigerwald, F. J. (2002). Family counseling and ethical challenges with gay, lesbian, bisexual, and transgendered (GLBT) clients: More questions than answers. *The Family Journal*, *10*, 415–418.

Jeffords, J. M. (1999). Confidentiality of medical information: Protecting privacy in an electronic age. *Professional Psychology: Research and Practice*, *30*, 115–116.

Jenaro, C., Flores, N., & Arias, B. (2007). Burnout and coping in human service practitioners. *Professional Psychology: Research and Practice*, *38*, 80–97.

Jennings, F. L. (1992). Ethics of rural practice. *Psychotherapy in Private Practice*, *10*, 85–104.

Jensen, J. A., McNamara, J. R., & Gustafson, K. E. (1991). Parents' and clinicians' attitudes toward the risks and benefits of child psychotherapy: A study of informed consent content. *Professional Psychology: Research and Practice*, *22*, 161–170.

Jensen, R. E. (1979). Competent professional service in psychology: The real issue behind continuing education. *Professional Psychology: Research and Practice*, *10*, 381–389.

Jerome, J. K. (1889). *Idle thoughts of an idle fellow*. New York, NY: Dutton.

Jerrigan, M. M., Green, C. E., Helms, J. E., Perez-Gualdron, L., & Henze, K. (2010). An examination of people of color supervision dyads: Racial identity matters as much as race. *Training and Education in Professional Psychology*, *4*, 62–73.

Jevne, P., & Williams, D. R. (1998). *When dreams don't work: Professionals caregivers and burnout*. Amityville, NY: Baywood.

Jobes, D. A., & O'Connor, S. S. (2009). The duty to protect suicidal clients: Ethical, legal, and professional considerations. In J. L. Werth, E. R. Welfel, & G. A. H. Benjamin (Eds.), *The duty to protect: Ethical, legal, and professional responsibilities of mental health professionals* (pp. 163–180). Washington, D.C.: American Psychological Association.

Johnson, B. W., & Nelson, N. (1999). Mentor-protégé relationships in graduate training: Some ethical concerns. *Ethics & Behavior*, *9*, 189–210.

Johnson, C. E., Stewart, A. L., Brabeck, M. M., Huber, V. S., & Rubin, H. (2004). Interprofessional collaboration: Implications for combined-integral doctoral training in professional psychology. *Journal of Clinical Psychology*, *60*, 995–1010.

Johnson, I. H., Santos-Torres, J., Coleman, V. D., & Smith, M. C. (1995). Issues and strategies in leading culturally diverse counseling groups. *Journal for Specialists in Group Work*, *20*, 143–150.

Johnson, W. B. (2007). Transformational supervision: When supervisors mentor. *Professional Psychology: Research and Practice*, *38*, 259–267.

Johnson, W. B., Bacho, R., Helm, M., & Ralph, J. (2006). Multiple role dilemmas for military mental health care providers. *Military Medicine*, *17*, 311–315.

Johnson, W. B., Barnett, J. E., Elman, N. S., Forrest, L., & Kaslow, N. J. (2012). The competent community: Toward a vital reformulation of professional ethics. *American Psychologist*, *67*, 557–569.

Johnson, W. B., Barnett, J. E., Elman, N. S., Forrest, L., & Kaslow, N. J. (2013). The competence constellation model: A communitarian approach to support professional competence. *Professional Psychology: Research and Practice*, *44*, 343–354.

Johnson, W. B., Porter, K., Campbell, C. D., & Kupko, E. N. (2005). Character and fitness requirements for professional psychologists: An examination of state licensing application forms. *Professional Psychology: Research and Practice*, *36*, 654–662.

Johnson, W. B., Ralph, J., & Johnson, S. J. (2005). Managing multiple relationships in embedded environments: The case of aircraft carrier psychology. *Professional Psychology: Research and Practice*, *36*, 73–81.

Johnson-Greene, D. (2007). Evolving standards for informed consent: Is it time for an individualized and flexible approach? *Professional Psychology: Research and Practice*, *38*, 179–186.

Joiner, T. (2014). *The perversion of virtue: Understanding murder-suicide*. New York, NY: Oxford.

Joint Task Force for the Development of Telepsychology Guidelines for Psychologists. (2013). Guidelines for the practice of telepsychology. *American Psychologist*, *68*, 791–800.

Jones, J. H. (1981). *Bad blood: The Tuskegee syphilis experiment—A tragedy of race and medicine*. New York, NY: Free Press.

Jones, S. (2010). A survivor's account of sexual exploitation by a Jungian analyst. *Journal of Analytical Psychology*, *55*, 650–660.

Jordan, A. E., & Meara, N. M. (1990). Ethics and the professional practice of psychologists: The role of virtues and principles. *Professional Psychology: Research and Practice*, *21*, 107–114.

Kaffenberger, C. J., & O'Rourke-Trigiani, J. (2012). Addressing student mental health needs by providing direct and indirect services in the community. *Professional School Counseling*, *16*, 323–333.

Kaffenberger, C. J., & Seligman, L. (2003). *Helping students with mental and emotional disorders*. Upper Saddle River, NJ: Merrill Prentice-Hall.

Kahneman. D. (2011). *Thinking fast and slow*. New York, NY: Farrar, Straus & Giroux.

Kahneman, D., & Tversky, A. (1979). Prospect theory: An analysis of decisions under risk. *Econometrica*, *47*, 263–291.

Kaiser Family Foundation. (2008). Employer health benefits. Retrieved from http://ehbs.kff.org/images/abstract/7791.pdf

Kalbeitzer, R. (2009). Psychologists and interrogations: Ethical dilemmas in times of war. *Ethics & Behavior*, *20*, 156–168.

Kalichman, S. C. (1999). *Mandated reporting of suspected child abuse: Ethics, law and policy* (2nd ed.). Washington, D.C.: American Psychological Association.

Kant, I. (1964). *Groundwork of the metaphysics of morals* (H. J. Paton, Trans.). New York, NY: Harper & Row (original work published 1785).

Kaplan, D. M. (2014). Ethical implications of a critical legal case for the counseling profession: *Ward v. Willbanks*. *Journal of Counseling & Development*, *92*, 142–146.

Kaplan, L. S. (1996). Outrageous or legitimate concerns: What some parents are saying about school counseling. *The School Counselor*, *43*, 165–170.

Kaplan, M. (1983). A woman's view of the DSM-III. *American Psychologist*, *38*, 786–792.

Kaplin, W. A., & Lee, B. A. (1995). *The law of higher education* (3rd ed.). San Francisco, CA: Jossey-Bass.

Karren, R. J., & Zacharias, L. (2007). Integrity tests: Critical issues. *Human Resource Management Review*, *17*, 221–234.

Kaser-Boyd, N., Adelman, H. S., & Taylor, L. (1985). Minors' ability to identify risks and benefits of therapy. *Professional Psychology: Research and Practice*, *16*, 411–417.

Kaslow, F. W. (Ed.). (1996). *Handbook of relational diagnosis and dysfunctional family patterns*. New York, NY: Wiley.

Kaslow, F. W., Patterson, T., & Gottlieb, M. (2011). Ethical dilemmas in psychologists accessing Internet data: Is it justified? *Professional Psychology: Research and Practice*, *42*, 105–112.

Kaslow, N. J. (2004). Competencies in professional psychology. *American Psychologist*, *59*, 774–781.

Kaslow, N. J., Grus, C. L., Campbell, L. F., Fouad, N. A., Hatcher, R. L., & Rodolfa, E. R. (2009). Competency Assessment Toolkit for professional psychology. *Training and Education in Professional Psychology*, *3*(4, Suppl.), S27–S45.

Kaslow, N. J., Rubin, N. J., Bebeau, M. J., Leigh, I. W., Lichtenberg, J. W., Nelson, P. D., & Smith, I. L. (2007). Guiding principles and recommendations for the assessment of competence. *Professional Psychology: Research and Practice*, *38*, 441–451.

Kaslow, N. J., Rubin, N. J., Forrest, L., Elman, N. S., Van Horne, B. A., Jacobs, S. C., ... Thorn, B. E. (2007). Recognizing, assessing, and intervening with problems of professional competence. *Professional Psychology: Research and Practice*, *38*, 479–492.

Katz, J. (1972). *Experimentation with human beings*. New York, NY: Russell Sage Foundation.

Kaufman, P. M. (2009). Protecting raw data and psychological testing from wrongful disclosure: A primer on the law and other persuasive strategies. *The Clinical Neuropsychologist*, *23*, 1159–2009.

Kazdin, A. E. (2008). Evidence-based treatment and practice: New opportunities to bridge clinical research and practice, enhance the knowledge base, and improve patient care. *American Psychologist*, *63*, 146–159.

Keaton, B. & Yamatani, H. (1993). Benefits of mandatory EAP participation: A study of employees with last chance contracts. *Employee Assistance Quarterly*, *9*, 67–77.

Keeling, R. P. (1993). HIV disease: Current concepts. *Journal of Counseling & Development*, *71*, 261–274.

Keeton v. Anderson-Wiley, 664 F. 3d 865 (2011).

Keffala, V. J., & Stone, G. L. (1999). Role of HIV serostatus, relationship status of the patient, homophobia, and social desirability of the psychologist on decisions regarding confidentiality. *Psychology and Health*, *14*, 567–584.

Keith-Spiegel, P. (1994). Teaching psychologists and the new APA ethics code: Do we fit in? *Professional Psychology: Research and Practice*, *25*, 362–368.

Keith-Spiegel, P. (2014). *Red flags in psychotherapy. Stories of ethics complaints and resolutions*. New York, NY: Routledge.

Keith-Spiegel, P., Tabachnick, B. G., Whitley, B. E., Jr., & Washburn, J. (1998). Why professors ignore cheating: Opinions of a national sample of psychology instructors. *Ethics & Behavior*, *8*, 215–227.

Keith-Spiegel, P., Wittig, A. F., Perkins, D. V., Balogh, D. W., & Whitley, B. E., Jr. (1993). *The ethics of teaching: A casebook*. Muncie, IN: Ball State University.

Kelly, J. A., & Kalichman, S. C. (2002). Behavioral research in HIV/AIDS primary and secondary prevention: Recent advances and future directions. *Journal of Consulting and Clinical Psychology*, *70*, 626–639.

Kempwith, T. J. (2005). *Collaborative consultation in the schools* (3rd ed.). Saddle River, NJ: Pearson.

Kendall, P. C., & Suveg, C. (2008). Treatment outcome studies with children: Principles of proper practice. *Ethics & Behavior*, *18*(2/3), 215–233.

Kennedy, C. H., & Johnson, W. B. (2009). Mixed agency in military psychology: Applying the American Psychological Association ethics code. *Psychological Services*, *6*, 22–31.

Kennel, R. G., & Agresti, A. A. (1995). Effects of gender and age on psychologists' reporting of child sexual abuse. *Professional Psychology: Research and Practice*, *26*, 612–615.

Kenny, M. C. (2007). Web-based training in child maltreatment for future mandated reporters. *Child Abuse & Neglect*, *31*, 671–678.

Kerby, S. E. (2010). Informed consent as a predictor of working alliance and perception of counselor/psychotherapist. *Dissertation Abstracts International: Section B, The Sciences and Engineering*, *70*(9), 5826.

Kerl, S. B., Garcia, J. L., McCollough, C. S., & Maxwell, M. E. (2002). Systematic evaluation of professional performance: Legally supported procedure and process. *Counselor Education and Supervision*, *41*, 321–332.

Kertay, L., & Reviere, S. L. (1993). The use of touch in psychotherapy: Theoretical and ethical considerations. *Psychotherapy: Theory/Research/Practice/Training*, *30*, 32–40.

Kessler, L. E., & Waehler, C. A. (2005). Addressing multiple relationships between clients and therapists in lesbian, gay, bisexual and transgender communities. *Professional Psychology: Research and Practice*, *36*, 66–72.

Kielbasa, A. M., Pomerantz, A. M., Krohn, E. J., & Sullivan, B. F. (2004). How does clients' method of payment influence psychologists' diagnostic decisions? *Ethics & Behavior*, *14*, 187–195.

Kier, F. J., & Molinari, V. (2004). Do-it-yourself testing for mental illness: Ethical issues, concerns, and recommendations. *Professional Psychology: Research and Practice*, *35*, 261–267.

Kilburg, R. R., & Diedrich, R. C. (Eds.). (2007). *The wisdom of coaching: Essential papers in consulting psychology for a world of change*. Washington, D.C.: American Psychological Association.

Kimmel, A. J. (2012). Deception in research. In S. J. Knapp, M. C. Gottlieb, M. M. Handelsman, & L. D. VandeCreek, (Eds.), *APA handbook of ethics in psychology* (Vol. 2, pp. 401–421). Washington, D.C.: American Psychological Association.

Kirk, S. A., & Kutchins, H. (1992). *The selling of DSM: The rhetoric of science in psychiatry*. New York, NY: Aldine De Gruyter.

Kirkland, K., & Kirkland, K. L. (2001). Frequency of child custody evaluation complaints and related disciplinary action: A survey of the Association of State and Provincial Psychology Boards. *Professional Psychology: Research and Practice*, *32*, 171–174.

Kirkland, K., Kirkland, K. L., & Reeves, R. P. (2004). On the professional use of disciplinary data. *Professional Psychology: Research and Practice*, *35*, 179–184.

Kitchener, K. S. (1984). Intuition, critical evaluation and ethical principles: The foundation for ethical decisions in counseling psychology. *The Counseling Psychologist*, *12*, 43–55.

Kitchener, K. S. (1988). Dual role relationships? What makes them so problematic? *Journal of Counseling & Development*, *67*, 217–221.

Kitchener, K. S. (1992). Psychologist as teacher and mentor: Affirming ethical values throughout the curriculum. *Professional Psychology: Research and Practice*, *23*, 190–195.

Kitchener, K. S., & Anderson, S. K. (2011). *Foundations of ethical practice, research and teaching in psychology* (2nd ed.). Mahwah, NJ: Lawrence Erlbaum.

Kitchener, K. S., & Harding, S. S. (1990). Dual role relationships. In B. Herlihy & L. B. Golden (Eds.), *Ethical standards casebook*. Alexandria, VA: American Counseling Association.

Kitchener, R. F., & Kitchener, K. S. (2012). Ethical foundations of psychology. In S. J. Knapp, M. C. Gottlieb, M. M. Handelsman, & L. D. VandeCreek, (Eds.), *APA handbook of ethics in psychology* (Vol. 1, pp. 3–42). Washington, D.C.: American Psychological Association.

Kleespies, P. M., Van Orden, K. A., Bongar, B., Bridgeman, D., Bufka, L. F., Galper, D. I., ... Yufit, R. I. (2011). Psychologist suicide: Incidence, impact, and suggestions for prevention, intervention, and postvention. *Professional Psychology: Research and Practice*, *42*(3), 244–251.

Klerman, G. L. (1990). The psychiatric patient's right to effective treatment: Implications of *Osheroff v. Chestnut Lodge*. *American Journal of Psychiatry*, *147*, 419–427.

Klontz, B. T. (2004). Ethical practice of group experiential psychotherapy. *Psychotherapy: Theory, Research, Practice and Training*, *41*, 172–179.

Knapp, S. J., Bowers, T. G., & Metzler, B. (1992). A survey of Pennsylvania psychologists. *Psychotherapy in Private Practice*, *11*, 83–99.

Knapp, S. J., Gottlieb, M., Berman, J., & Handelsman, M. M. (2007). When laws and ethics collide: What should psychologists do? *Professional Psychology: Research and Practice*, *38*, 54–59.

Knapp, S. J., Gottlieb, M. C., Handelsman, M. M., & VandeCreek, L. D. (2012). *APA handbook of ethics in psychology* (Vol. 2). Washington, D.C.: American Psychological Association.

Knapp, S. J., & Keller, P. (2004, January). Survey reveals stressful events for psychologists. *The Pennsylvania Psychologist*, *64*, 6, 8.

Knapp, S. J., & VandeCreek, L. D. (1986). Privileged communication for psychotherapists: An overview. *Psychotherapy in Private Practice*, *4*, 13–22.

Knapp, S. J., & VandeCreek, L. D. (1993). Legal and ethical issues in billing patients and collecting fees.

Psychotherapy: Theory/Research/Practice/Training, 30, 25–31.

Knapp, S. J., & VandeCreek, L. D. (2007). When values of different cultures conflict: Ethical decision making in a multicultural context. *Professional Psychology: Research and Practice, 38*, 660–666.

Knapp, S. J., & VandeCreek, L. D. (2008). Ethics of advertising, billing, and finances in psychotherapy. *Journal of Clinical Psychology in Session, 64*, 613–625.

Knapp, S. J., & VandeCreek, L. D. (2011). *Practical ethics for psychologists* (2nd ed.). Washington, D.C.: American Psychological Association.

Knauss, L. K. (2007). Legal and ethical issues in providing group therapy to minors. In R. W. Christner, J. L. Stewart, & A. Freeman (Eds.), *Handbook of cognitive-behavior group therapy with children and adolescents: Specific settings and presenting problems* (pp. 65–85). New York, NY: Routledge.

Knauss, L. K. & Knauss, J. W. (2012). Ethical issues in multiperson therapy. In S. J. Knapp, M. C. Gottlieb, M. M. Handelsman, & L. D. VandeCreek (Eds.), *APA handbook of ethics in psychology* (Vol. 2, pp. 29–43). Washington, D.C.: American Psychological Association.

Knox, S. (2008). Gifts in psychotherapy: Practice review and recommendations. *Psychotherapy: Theory, Research, Practice, Training, 45*, 103–110.

Kodish, E. (2005). *Ethics and research with children: A case-based approach*. New York, NY: Oxford.

Kohlberg, L. (1984). *The psychology of moral development: The nature and validation of moral stages*. San Francisco, CA: Harper & Row.

Kolmes, K., & Taube, D. O. (2014). Seeking and finding our clients on the Internet: Boundary considerations in cyberspace. *Professional Psychology: Research and Practice, 45*, 3–10.

Koocher, G. P. (1979). Credentialing in psychology: Close encounters with competence? *American Psychologist, 34*, 696–702.

Koocher, G. P. (1994a). APA and the FTC: New adventures in consumer protection. *American Psychologist, 49*, 322–328.

Koocher, G. P. (1994b). The commerce of professional psychology and the new ethics code. *Professional Psychology: Research and Practice, 25*, 355–361.

Koocher, G. P. (2003). Ethical issues in psychotherapy with adolescents. *Journal of Clinical Psychology, 59*, 1247–1256.

Koocher, G., & Keith-Spiegel, P. S. (1990). *Children, ethics and the law*. Lincoln: University of Nebraska Press.

Koocher, G., & Keith-Spiegel, P. S. (2008). *Ethics in psychology and the mental health professions: Standards and cases*. New York, NY: Oxford.

Kottler, J. A. (1982). Unethical behaviors we all do and pretend we do not. *Journal for Specialists in Group Work, 7*, 182–186.

Kottler, J. A. (1994). *Advanced group leadership*. Pacific Grove, CA: Brooks/Cole.

Kowalski, R. M., & Limber, P. (2007). Electronic bullying among middle school students. *Journal of Adolescent Health, 41*(6, Suppl.), S22–S30.

Kozlowski, N. F. (2004). Management of confidentiality with HIV-positive male and female psychotherapy clients. *Dissertation Abstracts International: Section B, The Sciences and Engineering, 64*(9), 4045.

Kraus, R., Zack, J., & Stricker, G. (2004). *Online counseling: A handbook for mental health professionals*. New York, NY: Academic Press.

Kress, V. E., Eriksen, K. P., Rayle, A. D., & Ford, S. J. W. (2005). The DSM-IV-TR and culture: Considerations for counselors. *Journal of Counseling & Development, 83*, 97–104.

Kress, V. E., Hoffman, R. M., & Eriksen, K. (2010). Ethical dimensions of diagnosing: Considerations for clinical mental health counselors. *Counseling & Values, 55*, 101–112.

Krishna, M., Jauhari, A., Lepping, P., Turner, J., Crossley, D., & Krishnamoorthy, A. (2011). Is group psychotherapy effective in older adults with depression? A systematic review. *International Journal of Geriatric Psychiatry, 26*, 331–340.

Kurpius, D., Gibson, G., Lewis, J., & Corbet, M. (1991). Ethical issues in supervising counseling practitioners. *Counselor Education and Supervision, 31*, 48–57.

Kutchins, H., & Kirk, S. A. (1997). *Making us crazy: DSM: The psychiatric bible and the creation of mental disorders*. New York, NY: The Free Press.

Kuther, T. L. (2003). Promoting positive ethics: An interview with Mitchell M. Handelsman. *Teaching of Psychology, 30*, 339–343.

Ladany, N., Ellis, M. V., & Friedlander, M. L. (1999). The supervisory working alliance: Trainee self-efficacy and satisfaction. *Journal of Counseling & Development, 77*, 447–455.

Ladany, N., Friedlander, M. L. & Smith, M. L. (2005). *Critical events in psychotherapy supervision: An interpersonal approach*. Washington, D.C.: American Psychological Association.

Ladany, N., Hill, C. E., Corbett, M., & Nutt, L. (1996). Nature, extent, and importance of what therapy trainees do not disclose to their supervisors. *Journal of Counseling Psychology, 43*, 10–24.

Ladany, N., Lehrman-Waterman, D. E., Molinaro, M., & Wolgast, B. (1999). Psychotherapy supervisor ethical practices: Adherence to guidelines, the supervisory working alliance, and supervisor satisfaction. *The Counseling Psychologist, 27*, 443–475.

Ladany, N., O'Brien, K., Hill, C. E., Melincoff, D. S., Knox, S., & Peterson, D. (1997). Sexual attraction towards clients, use of supervision, and prior training: A qualitative study of psychology predoctoral interns. *Journal of Counseling Psychology, 44*, 413–424.

Ladd, J. (1991). The quest for a code of professional ethics: An intellectual and moral confusion. In D. G. Johnson (Ed.), *Ethical issues in engineering* (pp. 130–136). Englewood Cliffs, NJ: Prentice Hall.

LaFromboise, T. D., Foster, S., & James, A. (1996). Ethics in multicultural counseling. In P. B. Pederson, J. G. Draguns, W. J. Lonner, & J. E. Trimble (Eds.), *Counseling across cultures* (5th ed., pp. 47–72). Thousand Oaks, CA: Sage.

Lakin, M. (1994). Morality in group and family therapies: Multiperson therapies and the 1992 ethics code. *Professional Psychology: Research and Practice, 25*, 344–348.

Lamb, D. H., & Catanzaro, S. J. (1998). Sexual and nonsexual boundary violations involving psychologists, clients, supervisees, and students: Implications for professional practice. *Professional Psychology: Research and Practice, 29*, 498–503.

Lamb, D. H., & Catanzaro, S. J., & Moorman, A. S. (2003). Psychologists reflect on their sexual relationships with clients, supervisees, and students: Occurrence, impact, rationales, and collegial interventions. *Professional Psychology: Research and Practice, 34*, 102–107.

Lamb, D. H., & Catanzaro, S. J., & Moorman, A. S. (2004). A preliminary look at how psychologists identify, evaluate, and proceed when faced with possible multiple relationship dilemmas. *Professional Psychology: Research and Practice, 35*, 248–254.

Lamb, D. H., Cochran, D. J., & Jackson, V. R. (1991). Training and organizational issues associated with identifying and responding to intern impairment. *Professional Psychology: Research and Practice, 22*, 291–296.

Lamb, D. H., Strand, K. K., Woodburn, J. R., Buchko, K. J., Lewis, J. T., & Kang, J. B. (1994). Sexual and business relationships between therapists and former clients. *Psychotherapy: Theory/Research/Practice/Training, 31*, 270–278.

Lambert, M. J. (2010a). *Prevention of treatment failure: The use of measuring, monitoring, and feedback in clinical practice.* Washington, D.C.: American Psychological Association.

Lambert, M. J. (2010b). Yes, it is time for clinicians to routinely monitor treatment outcome. In B. L. Duncan, S. D. Miller, B. E. Wampold, & M. A. Hubble (Eds.), *The heart and soul of change* (2nd ed., pp. 239–266). Washington, D.C.: American Psychological Association.

Lambert, M. J. (2013). In M. J. Lambert (Ed.), *Bergin and Garfield's handbook of psychotherapy and behavior change* (6th ed., pp. 169–218). New York, NY: Wiley.

Lambie, G. W., Hagedorn, W. B., & Ieva, K. A. (2010). Social-cognitive development, ethical and legal knowledge, and ethical decision making of counselor education students. *Counselor Education & Supervision, 49*, 228–246.

Langer, E. J., & Abelson, R. P. (1974). A patient by any other name ...: Clinician group differences and labeling bias. *Journal of Consulting and Clinical Psychology, 42*, 4–9.

Lannin, D. G., & Scott, N. A. (2013). Social networking ethics: Developing best practices for the new small world. *Professional Psychology: Research and Practice, 44*, 135–141.

LaRoche, M. J., & Maxie, A. (2003). Ten considerations in addressing cultural differences in psychotherapy. *Professional Psychology: Research and Practice, 34*, 180–186.

Larry P. v. Riles, 495 F. Supp. at 971. (1979).

Lasky, G. B., & Riva, M. T. (2006). Confidentiality and privileged communication in group psychotherapy. *International Journal of Group Psychotherapy, 56*, 455–476.

Lawrence, G., & Kurpius, S. E. R. (2000). Legal and ethical issues involved when counseling minors in nonschool settings. *Journal of Counseling & Development, 78*, 130–136.

Lawson, G., & Myers, J. E. (2011). Wellness, professional quality of life, and career-sustaining behaviors: What keeps us well? *Journal of Counseling & Development, 89*, 163–171.

Lawson, G., & Venart, B. (2003). Preventing counselor impairment: Vulnerability, wellness, and resistance. Retrieved from http://www.counseling.org/wellness_taskforce/PDF/ACA_taskforce_vista.pdf

Layman, M. J., & McNamara, J. R. (1997). Remediation revisited. *Professional Psychology: Research and Practice, 28*, 304–305.

Lazarus, A., & Zur, O. (2002). *Dual relationships and psychotherapy.* New York, NY: Springer.

Lazovsky, R. (2008). Maintaining confidentiality with minors: Dilemmas of school counselors. *Professional School Counseling, 11*, 335–346.

Lear, C. M. (1997). Nonsexual dual relationships: How do therapists decide? *Dissertation Abstracts International: Section A, The Humanities and Social Sciences, 58*(7), 3320.

Lee, J., Lim, N., Yang, E., & Lee, S. M. (2011). Antecedents and consequences of three dimensions of burnout in psychotherapists: A meta-analysis. *Professional Psychology: Research and Practice, 42*, 252–258.

Legal Opinions of the California State Attorney General. (2011). Opinion # 08-509. Retrieved from http://oag.ca.gov/system/files/opinions/pdfs/08-509.pdf

Lehavot, K., Barnett, J. E., & Powers, D. (2010). Psychotherapy, professional relationships, and ethical considerations in the MySpace generation. *Professional Psychology: Research and Practice, 41*, 160–166.

Lent, J. C., & Schwartz, R. C. (2012). The impact of work setting, demographic characteristics, and personality factors related to burnout among professional counselors. *Journal of Mental Health Counseling, 34*, 355–372.

Lenz, A. S., Oliver, M., & Nelson, K W. (2011). In-person and computer-mediated distance group supervision: A case study. Retrieved from http://counselingoutfitters.com/vistas/vistas11/Article_67.pdf

Leong, F. T. L., & Gupta, A. (2008). Culture and race in counseling and psychotherapy: A critical review of the literature. In S. D. Brown & R. W. Lent, (Eds.), *Handbook of counseling psychology* (4th ed., pp. 320–337). Hoboken, NJ: Wiley.

Leong, F. T. L., & Wagner, N. S. (1994). Cross-cultural counseling supervision: What do we know? What do we want to know? *Counselor Education and Supervision, 34*, 117–131.

Leong, G. B., Eth, S., & Silva, J. A. (1992). The psychotherapist as witness for the prosecution: The criminalization of *Tarasoff*. *American Journal of Psychiatry, 149*, 1011–1015.

Lerman, H., & Porter, N. (1990). *Feminist ethics in psychotherapy.* New York, NY: Springer.

Leszcz, M., & Kobos, J. C. (2008). Evidence-based group

psychotherapy: Using AGPA's practice guidelines to enhance clinical effectiveness. *Journal of Clinical Psychology*, *64*, 1238–1260.

Levenson, J. L. (1986). When a colleague behaves unethically: Guidelines for intervention. *Journal of Counseling & Development*, *64*, 315–317.

Levine, M., Anderson, E., Terreti, L., Sharma, A., Steinberg, K. L., & Wallach, L. (1991, August). *Mandated reports and therapy in the context of the child protection system*. Paper presented at the annual meeting of the American Psychological Association, San Francisco, CA.

Levine, M., & Doueck, H. J. (1995). *The impact of mandated reporting on the therapeutic process: Picking up the pieces*. Thousand Oaks, CA: Sage.

Levy, C. (1974). On the development of a code of ethics. *Social Work*, *19*, 207–216.

Levy, R. B. (1973). *I can only touch you now*. Englewood Cliffs, NJ: Prentice Hall.

Lewis, J. A., & Mellman, S. (1999). Ethics and family therapy: Issues of gender. In P. Stevens (Ed.), *Ethical casebook for the practice of marriage and family counseling* (pp. 93–102). Alexandria, VA: American Counseling Association.

Lewis, M. W., & Lewis, A. C. (1996). Peer helping programs: Helper role, supervisor training, and suicidal behavior. *Journal of Counseling & Development*, *74*, 307–313.

Lewis, N. A. (2005, June 24). Interrogators cite doctors' aid at Guantanamo. *New York Times*, p. A1. Retrieved from http://tinyurl.com/39gqqh

Lichtenberg, J. L., & Goodyear, R. (2012). Informal, incidental, and deliberate continuing education. In J. M. Taylor, & G. J. Neimeyer (Eds.). *Continuing Professional Development and Lifelong Learning: Issues, Impacts and Outcomes* (pp. 71–80). New York, NY: Nova Science.

Lindsay, G., & Clarkson, P. (1999). Ethical dilemmas of psychotherapists. *Psychologist*, *12*, 182–185.

Lindsey, C. R., & Kalafat, J. (1998). Adolescents' views of preferred helper characteristics and barriers to seeking help. *Journal of Educational and Psychological Consultation*, *9*, 171–193.

Lindsey, R. T. (1985, August). *Moral sensitivity: The relationship between training and experience*. Paper presented at the annual meeting of the American Psychological Association, Los Angeles, CA.

Linstrum, K. S. (2005). The effects of training on ethical decision making skills as a function of moral development and context in master-level counseling students. *Section A, The Humanities and Social Sciences*, *65*(9), 3289.

Lloyd, A. (1992). Dual relationship problems in counselor education. In B. Herlihy & G. Corey (Eds.), *Dual relationships in counseling* (pp. 59–64). Alexandria, VA: American Counseling Association.

LoBello, S. G., & Zachar, P. (2007). Psychological test sales and internet auctions: Ethical considerations for dealing with obsolete or unwanted test materials. *Professional Psychology: Research and Practice*, *38*, 68–70.

Lockyer, B., & Duncan, S. D. (2004). *California Attorney General Opinion #04–112*.

Lonborg, S. D., & Bowen, N. (2004). Counselors, communities, and spirituality: Ethical and multicultural considerations. *Professional School Counseling*, *7*, 318–325.

Lonner, W. J., & Ibrahim, F. A. (1996). Appraisal and assessment in cross-cultural counseling. In P. B. Pedersen, J. G. Draguns, W. J. Lonner, & J. E. Trimble (Eds.), *Counseling Across Cultures* (5th ed., pp. 293–322). Thousand Oaks, CA: Sage.

Lopez, S. R., & Guarnaccia, P. J. (2005). Cultural dimensions of psychopathology: The social world's impact on mental illness. In J. E. Maddux & B. A. Winstead (Eds.), *Psychopathology: Foundations for a contemporary understanding* (pp. 19–38). Mahwah, NJ: Lawrence Erlbaum.

Louisiana v. Atterberry. (1995). 664 So2d 1216.

Lowe, J., Pomerantz, A. M., & Pettibone, J. C. (2007). The influence of payment method on psychologists' diagnostic decisions: Expanding the range of presenting problems. *Ethics & Behavior*, *17*, 83–93.

Lowman, R. L. (Ed.). (2006). *The ethical practice of psychology in organizations*. Washington, D.C.: American Psychological Association.

Lowman, R. L. (2012). The scientist-practitioner consulting psychologist. *Consulting psychology journal: Practice and research*, *64*, 151–156.

Luepker, E. T. (1999). Effects of practitioners' sexual misconduct: A follow-up study. *Journal of the American Academy of Psychiatry and the Law*, *27*, 51–63.

Lum, D. (1992). *Social work practice with people of color: A process-stage approach* (2nd ed.). Pacific Grove, CA: Brooks/Cole.

Mabe, A. R., & Rollin, S. A. (1986). The role of a code of ethical standards in counseling. *Journal of Counseling & Development*, *64*, 294–297.

MacCluskie, K. M., & Ingersoll, R. E. (2000). *Becoming a 21st century agency counselor*. Pacific Grove, CA: Brooks/Cole.

Maddux, J. E., & Winstead, B. A. (2007). (Eds.). *Psychopathology: Foundations for a contemporary understanding*. Mahwah, NJ: Lawrence Erlbaum.

Magnuson, S., Wilcoxon, S. A., & Norem, K. (2000). A profile of lousy supervisors: Experienced counselors' perspectives. *Counselor Education and Supervision*, *39*, 189–202.

Maheu, M. M., & Gordon, B. I. (2000). Counseling and therapy on the Internet. *Professional Psychology: Research and Practice*, *31*, 484–489.

Maheu, M. M., Whitten, P., & Allen, A. (2001). *E-health, telehealth, and telemedicine: A guide to start-up and success*. San Francisco, CA: Jossey-Bass.

Mahoney, M. (1997). Psychotherapists' personal problems and self-care patterns. *Professional Psychology: Research and Practice*, *28*, 14–16.

Mallen, M. J., Vogel, D. L., & Rochlen, A. B. (2005). The practical aspects of online counseling: Ethics, training, technology, and competency. *Counseling Psychologist*, *33*, 776–818.

Malley, P., Gallagher, R., & Brown, S. (1992). Ethical problems in university and college counseling centers: A Delphi study. *Journal of College Student Development*, *33*, 238–244.

Malphurs, J. E., Eisdorfer, C., & Cohen, D. (2001). Antecedents of homicide-suicide and suicide in older married men. *American Journal of Geriatric Psychiatry*, *9*, 49–57.

Manderscheid, R., & Barrett, S. (Eds.). (1991). *Mental health in the United States, 1987* (National Institute of Mental Health, DHHS Publication No. ADM-87-1518). Washington, D.C.: U.S. Government Printing Office.

Manese, J. E., Wu, J. T., & Nepomuceno, C. A. (2001). The effect of training on multicultural counseling competencies: An exploratory study over a ten-year period. *Journal of Multicultural Counseling and Development*, *29*, 31–40.

Mann, L., Harmoni, R., & Power, C. (1989). Adolescent decision making: The development of competence. *Journal of Adolescence*, *12*, 265–278.

Mannheim, C. I., Sancilio, M., Phipps-Yonas, S., Brunnquell, D., Somers, P., Farseth, G., & Ninonuevo, F. (2002). Ethical ambiguities in the practice of child clinical psychology. *Professional Psychology: Research and Practice*, *33*, 24–29.

Marcan, S., & Shapiro, D. (1998). The role of personal therapy for therapists: A review. *British Journal of Medical Psychology*, *71*, 13–25.

Marcan, S., Stiles, W. B., & Smith, J. A. (1999). How does personal therapy affect therapists' practice? *Journal of Counseling Psychology*, *46*, 419–431.

Marecek, J. (1993). Disappearance, silences, and anxious rhetoric: Gender in abnormal psychology textbooks. *Journal of Theoretical and Philosophical Psychology*, *13*, 115–123.

Margolin, G. (1982). Ethical and legal considerations in marital and family therapy. *American Psychologist*, *37*, 788–801.

Margolis, R. D., & Zweben, J. E. (2011). *Treating patients with alcohol and other drug problems: An integrated approach*. Washington, D.C.: American Psychological Association.

Marsella, A. J., & Kaplan, A. (2002). Cultural considerations for understanding, assessing and treating depressive experience. In M. A. Reinecke & M. R. Davison (Eds.), *Comparative treatment of depression* (pp. 47–78). New York, NY: Springer.

Marsh, J. E. (2003). Empirical support for the United States Supreme Court's protection of the psychotherapist-patient privilege. *Ethics & Behavior*, *13*, 385–400.

Martindale, S. J., Chambers, E., & Thompson, A. R. (2009). Clinical psychology service users' experiences of confidentiality and informed consent. *Psychology and Psychotherapy: Theory, Research, and Practice*, *82*, 335–368.

Martineau, H. (1837). *Society in America* (Vol. 3). New York, NY: Saunders & Otley.

Martinson, B. C., Anderson, M. S., & de Vries, R. (2005). Scientists behaving badly. *Nature*, *435*, 737–738.

Marzillier, J. (1993). Ethical issues in psychotherapy: The importance of informed consent. *Clinical Psychology Forum*, *54*, 33–37.

Maslach, C., & Jackson, S. E. (1986). *Maslach burnout inventory: Manual* (2nd ed.). Palo Alto, CA: Consulting Psychologists Press.

Massachusetts Commission on Gay, Lesbian, Bisexual, and Transgender Youth. Massachusetts high school students and sexual orientation: Results of the 2007 youth risk behavior survey. Retrieved from http://www.mass.gov/cgly/yrbs07.pdf

Massachusetts Governor's Commission on Gay and Lesbian Youth. (1993). Breaking the silence in schools and families. Retrieved from http://www.mass.gov/cgly/PublicationsoftheCommission.html

Matarazzo, J. D. (1986). Computerized clinical psychological test interpretations: Unvalidated plus all mean and no sigma. *American Psychologist*, *41*, 14–24.

Mathews, B., & Kenny, M. C. (2008). Mandatory reporting legislation in the United States, Canada, and Australia: A cross-jurisdictional review of key features, differences, and issues. *Child Maltreatment*, *13*, 50–63.

Mattison, D., Jayaratne, S., & Croxton, T. (2002). Client or former client? Implications of ex-client definition on social work practice. *Social Work*, *47*, 55–64.

May, W. F. (1984). The virtues in a professional setting. *Soundings*, *67*, 245–266.

McAdams, C. R., III, & Foster, V. A. (2000). Client suicide: Its frequency and impact on counselors. *Journal of Mental Health Counseling*, *22*, 107–121.

McAdams, C. R., III, Foster, V. A., & Ward, T. J. (2007). Remediation and dismissal policies in counselor education: Lessons learned from a challenge in federal court. *Counselor Education and Supervision*, *46*, 212–229.

McAdams, C. R., III, & Wyatt, K. L. (2010). The regulation of technology assisted distance counseling and supervision in the United States: An analysis of current status, trends, and implications. *Counselor Education and Supervision*, *49*, 179–191.

McCann, I. L., & Pearlman, L. A. (1990). Vicarious traumatization: A framework for the psychological effects of working with victims. *Journal of Traumatic Stress*, *3*, 131–149.

McCarthy, M. M., & Sorenson, G. P. (1993). School counselors and consultants: Legal duties and liabilities. *Journal of Counseling & Development*, *72*, 159–167.

McCarthy, P., Kulakowski, D., & Kenfield, J. (1994). Clinical supervision practices of licensed psychologists. *Professional Psychology: Research and Practice*, *25*, 177–181.

McCarthy, P., Sugden, S., Koker, M., Lamendola, F., Maurer, S., & Renninger, S. (1995). A practical guide to informed consent in clinical supervision. *Counselor Education and Supervision*, *35*, 130–138.

McCarthy, R. (1998, August). Behavioral health: Don't ignore, integrate. *Business and Health*, pp. 46, 51.

McCartney, J. (1966). Overt transference. *Journal of Sex Research*, *2*, 227–237.

McCauley, M., Hughes, J. H., & Liebling-Kalifani, H. (2008). Ethical considerations for military clinical psychologists: A review of selected literature. *Military Psychology*, *20*, 7–20.

McCollum, E. E., & Stith, S. M. (2011). Conjoint couples treatment and intimate partner violence: Best practices. In J. L. Wetchler (Ed.), *Handbook of clinical issues in couple therapy* (pp. 115–128). New York, NY: Routledge.

McConnell, W. A., & Kerbs, J. J. (1993). Providing feedback in research with human subjects. *Professional Psychology: Research and Practice, 24*, 266–270.

McDivitt, K. L. (2001). Ethics in group work with children and adolescents. *Dissertation Abstracts International: Section A, The Humanities and Social Sciences, 61*(12), 4673.

McFarland, W. P. (1998). Gay, lesbian, and bisexual student suicide. *Professional School Counseling, 1*, 26–29.

McFarland, W. P., & Dupuis, M. (2001). The legal duty to protect gay and lesbian students from violence in school. *Professional School Counseling, 4*, 171–179.

McGannon, W. M., Carey, J., & Dimmitt, C. (2005). The current status of school counseling outcome research. *Research Monograph Number 2*, Center for School Counseling Outcome Research, Amherst, MA.

McGoldrick, M., Giordano, J., & Garcia-Preto, N. (2005). *Ethnicity and family therapy*. New York, NY: Guilford.

McGuire, J., Nieri, D., Abbott, D., Sheridan, K., & Fisher, R. (1995). Do *Tarasoff* principles apply in AIDS-related psychotherapy? Ethical decision making and the role of therapist homophobia and perceived client dangerousness. *Professional Psychology: Research and Practice, 26*, 608–611.

McKeown, R. E., Cuffe, S. P., & Schultz, R. M. (2006). U.S. suicide rates by age group, 1970–2002: An examination of recent trends. *American Journal of Public Health, 96*, 1744–1761.

McLaughlin, J. E. (2002). Reducing diagnostic bias. *Journal of Mental Health Counseling, 24*, 256–269.

McLean, S., Wade, T. D., & Encel, J. S. (2003). The contribution of therapist beliefs to psychological distress in therapists: An investigation of vicarious traumatization, burnout and symptoms of avoidance and intrusion. *Behavioral and Cognitive Psychotherapy, 31*, 417–428.

McMinn, M. R., Bearse, J., Heyne, L. K., Smithberger, A., & Erb, A. (2011). Technology and independent practice: Survey findings and implications. *Professional Psychology: Research and Practice, 42*, 176–184.

McMinn, M. R., Ellens, B. M., & Soref, E. (1999). Ethical perspectives and practice behaviors involving computer-based test interpretation. *Assessment, 9*, 71–77.

McNeil-Haber, F. M. (2004). Ethical considerations in the use of nonerotic touch in psychotherapy with children. *Ethics & Behavior, 14*, 123–140.

McRoy, R. G., Freeman, E. M., Logan, S. L., & Blackmon, B. (1986). Cross-cultural field supervision: Implications for social work education. *Journal of Social Work Education, 22*, 50–56.

Meara, N. M., Schmidt, L. D., & Day, J. D. (1996). Principles and virtues: A foundation for ethical decisions, policies and character. *The Counseling Psychologist, 24*, 4–77.

Medau, I, Jox, R. J., & Reiter-Theil, S. (2013). How psychotherapists handle treatment errors – an ethical analysis. *BMC Medical Ethics, 14*, 50–59.

Meehl, P. E. (1960). The cognitive activity of the clinician. *American Psychologist, 15*, 19–27.

Meer, D., & VandeCreek, L. D. (2002). Cultural considerations in release of information. *Ethics & Behavior, 12*, 143–156.

Mehr, K. E., Ladany, N., & Caskie, G. I. L. (2010). Trainee nondisclosure in supervision: What are they not telling you? *Counselling & Psychotherapy Research, 10*, 103–113.

Melchert, T. P., & Patterson, M. M. (1999). Duty to warn and interventions with HIV-positive clients. *Professional Psychology: Research and Practice, 30*, 180–186.

Melito, R. (2003). Values in the role of the family therapist: Self determination and justice. *Journal of Marital and Family Therapy, 29*, 3–11.

Melton, G. B. (1981). Children's participation in treatment planning: Psychological and legal issues. *Professional Psychology: Research and Practice, 12*, 246–252.

Melton, G. B. (1994). Expert opinions: Not for cosmic understanding. In B. D. Sales & G. B. Vandenbos (Eds.), *Psychology in litigation and legislation* (pp. 55–100). Washington, D.C.: American Psychological Association.

Melton, G. B., Goodman, G. S., Kalichman, S. C., Levine, M., Saywitz, K. J., & Koocher, G. P. (1995). Empirical research on child maltreatment and the law. *Journal of Clinical Child Psychology, 24*(Suppl.), 47–77.

Menninger, K. (1958). *Theory of psychoanalytic technique*. New York, NY: Basic Books.

Merlone, L. (2005). Report keeping and the school counselor. *Professional School Counseling, 8*, 372–376.

Merta, R. J. (1995). Group work: Multicultural perspectives. In J. G. Ponterotto, J. M. Casas, L. A. Suzuki, & C. M. Alexander (Eds.), *Handbook of multicultural counseling* (pp. 567–585). Newbury Park, CA: Sage.

Merta, R. J., & Sisson, J. A. (1991). The experiential group: An ethical and professional dilemma. *The Journal for Specialists in Group Work, 16*, 236–245.

Merta, R., Wolfgang, L., & McNeil, K. (1993). Five models for using the experiential group in the preparation of group counselors. *The Journal for Specialists in Group Work, 18*, 200–207.

Meyers, C. J. (1991). Where the protective privilege ends: California changes the rules for dangerous psychotherapy patients. *Journal of Psychiatry and the Law, 19*, 5–31.

Michaels, M. H. (2006). Ethical considerations in writing psychological assessment reports. *Journal of Clinical Psychology, 62*, 47–58.

Miller, D. J., & Hersen, M. (1992). *Research fraud in the behavioral and biomedical sciences*. New York, NY: Wiley.

Miller, D. J., & Thelen, M. H. (1986). Knowledge and beliefs about confidentiality in psychotherapy. *Professional Psychology: Research and Practice, 17*, 15–19.

Miller, G. M., & Larrabee, M. J. (1995). Sexual intimacy in counselor education and supervision: A national survey. *Counselor Education and Supervision, 34*, 332–343.

Miller, I. J. (1995). Managed care is harmful to outpatient mental health services: A call for accountability. *Professional Psychology: Research and Practice*, *27*, 349–363.

Miller, I. J. (1996). Ethical and liability issues concerning invisible rationing. *Professional Psychology: Research and Practice*, *27*, 583–587.

Miller, T. R., Scott, R., & Searight, H. R. (1990). Ethics for marital and family therapy and subsequent training issues. *Family Therapy*, *17*, 163–171.

Milliken, T. F., & Neukrug, E. S. (2009). Perceptions of ethical behavior: A survey of human service professionals. *Human Services Education*, *29*, 35–48.

Minneapolis Foundation. (2004). Immigration in Minnesota: Discovering common ground. Retrieved from http://www.minneapolisfoundation.org/immigration/immigrationbrochure.pdf

Mintz, L. B., Rideout, C. A., & Bartells, K. M. (1994). A national survey of interns' perceptions of their preparation for counseling women and of the atmosphere of their graduate education. *Professional Psychology: Research and Practice*, *25*, 221–227.

Minuchin, S. (1974). *Families and family therapy*. Cambridge, MA: Harvard University Press.

Mitchell, C. W., Disque, J. G., & Robertson, P. (2002). When parents want to know: Responding to parental demands for confidential information. *Professional School Counseling*, *6*, 156–161.

Mitchell, R. W. (2007). *Documentation in counseling records* (3rd ed.). Alexandria, VA: American Counseling Association.

Mitrevski, J. P., & Chamberlain, J. R. (2006). Psychotherapist-patient privilege: Applying *Jaffee v. Redmond:* Communications to a psychotherapist are not privileged if they occur outside the course of diagnosis or treatment. *Journal of the American Academy of Psychiatry and the Law*, *34*, 245–246.

Moessner, C. (2007). Cyberbullying. Harris Interactive. Retrieved from http://www.ncpc.org/resources/files/pdf/bullying/Cyberbullying%20Trends%20-%20Tudes.pdf

Moleski, S. M., & Kiselica, M. S. (2005). Dual relationships: A continuum ranging from the destructive to the therapeutic. *Journal of Counseling & Development*, *83*, 3–11.

Moline, M. E., Williams, G. T., & Austin, K. M. (1998). *Documenting psychotherapy: Essentials for mental health practitioners*. Thousand Oaks, CA: Sage.

Monahan, J. (1993). Limiting therapist exposure to *Tarasoff* liability: Guidelines for risk management. *American Psychologist*, *48*, 242–250.

Monahan, J. (2008). Structured risk assessment of violence. In J. Monahan (Ed.), *Textbook of violence assessment and management* (pp. 17–33). Arlington, VA: American Psychiatric Press.

Moncrieff, J. (2009). The pharmaceutical industry and the construction of psychiatric diagnoses. *Journal of Ethics in Mental Health*, *4*(1, Suppl.), 1–4.

Montgomery, B. (1996). Ohio Attorney General Opinion #96–029.

Montgomery, L. M., Cupit, B. E., & Wimberley, T. K. (1999). Complaints, malpractice, and risk management: Professional issues and personal experiences. *Professional Psychology: Research and Practice*, *30*, 402–410.

Morey, R., Miller, C., Fulton, R., Rosen, L., & Daly, J. (1989). Peer counseling: Students served, problems discussed, overall satisfaction, and perceived helpfulness. *The School Counselor*, *37*, 137–143.

Morran, D., Stockton, R., & Bond, L. (1991). Delivery of positive and corrective feedback in counseling groups. *Journal of Counseling Psychology*, *38*, 410–414.

Morrow-Bradley, C., & Elliott, R. (1986). Utilization of psychotherapy research by practicing psychotherapists. *American Psychologist*, *41*, 188–197.

Moye, J., Karel, M. J., & Armesto, J. C. (2007). In A. M. Goldstein (Ed.), *Forensic psychology: Emerging topics and expanding roles* (pp. 260–293). Hoboken, NJ: Wiley.

Moyer, M., & Sullivan, J. (2008). Student risk-taking behaviors: When do school counselors break confidentiality? *Professional School Counseling*, *11*, 236–245.

Mullen, P. R., Griffith, C., Greene, J. H., & Lambie, G. W. (2014). Social media and professional school counselors. *Journal of School Counseling*, *12*, 1–38.

Murphy, M. J., DeBernardo, C. R., & Shoemaker, W. E. (1998). Impact of managed care on independent practice and professional ethics: A survey of independent practitioners. *Professional Psychology: Research and Practice*, *29*, 43–51.

Murphy-Shigematsu, S. (2010). Microaggressions by supervisors of color. *Training and Education in Professional Psychology*, *4*, 16–18.

Myers, J. E. B. (1991). When the parents are at war: How to get the child's side of the story. *Family Advocate*, *14*, 36–48.

Myrick, R. D., Highland, W. H., & Sabella, R. A. (1995). Peer helpers and perceived effectiveness. *Elementary School Guidance and Counseling*, *29*, 278–288.

Nachanami, I., & Somer, E. (2007). Women sexually victimized in psychotherapy speak out: The dynamics and outcome of therapist-client sex. *Women and Therapy*, *30*, 1–17.

Nadal, K. L., Griffin, K. E., Wong, Y., Hamit, S., & Rasmus, M. (2014). The impact of racial microaggressions on mental health: Counseling implications for clients of color. *Journal of Counseling & Development*, *92*, 57–66.

Naglieri, J. A., Drasgow, F., Schmit, M., Handler, L., Prifitera, A., Margolis, A., & Velasquez, R. (2004). Psychological testing on the Internet: New problems, old issues. *American Psychologist*, *59*, 150–162.

Nagy, T. F. (2005). *Ethics in plain English: An illustrative casebook for psychologists* (2nd ed.). Washington, D.C.: American Psychological Association.

Napier, A., & Whitaker, C. (1978). *The family crucible*. New York, NY: Harper & Row.

Narvaez, D., & Rest, J. R. (1994). The four components of acting morally. In W. Kurtines & J. Gewirtz (Eds.), *Moral behavior and moral development: An introduction* (pp. 385–400). New York, NY: McGraw-Hill.

Narvaez, D., & Vaydich, J. L. (2008). Moral development and behavior under the spotlight of the neurobiological sciences. *Journal of Moral Education*, *37*, 289–312.

Natanson v. Kline, 186 Kans. 393, *406*, 350P. 2d 1093. (1960).

National Academy of Neuropsychology. (2000). Official position statement on test security. *Archives of Clinical Neuropsychology*, *15*, 383–386.

National Assessment of Adult Literacy. (2003). Key findings. Retrieved from http://nces.ed.gov/naal/kf_demographics.asp

National Association of Alcohol and Drug Abuse Counselors (NAADAC). (2011). Code of ethics. Retrieved from http://www.naadac.org/resources/codeofethics

National Association of School Psychologists (NASP). (2010). Principles for professional ethics. Retrieved from http://www.nasponline.org/standards/2010standards.aspx

National Association of Social Workers (NASW). (1994/2003). Client self-determination in end-of-life decisions. *Social Work Speaks* (6th ed., pp. 46–49). Washington, D.C.: NASW Press.

National Association of Social Workers (NASW). (2008). Code of ethics. Retrieved from http://www.socialworkers.org/pubs/code/code.asp

National Association of Social Work (NASW). (n.d.). Professional review case data. Retrieved from http://www.socialworkers.org/nasw/ethics/reviewcasedata.asp

National Board for Certified Counselors (NBCC). (2005). Code of ethics. Retrieved from http://www.nbcc.org/Assets/Ethics/nbcc-codeofethics.pdf

National Board for Certified Counselors (NBCC). (2012). Understanding NBCC certifications. Retrieved from http://www.nbcc.org/ourcertifications

National Board for Certified Counselors (NBCC). (2013). Policy regarding the provision of distance professional services. Retrieved from http://www.nbcc.org/Assets/Ethics/NBCCPolicyRegardingPracticeofDistanceCounselingBoard.pdf

National Career Development Association (NCDA). (2007). Code of ethics. Retrieved from http://associationdatabase.com/aws/NCDA/asset_manager/get_file/3395

National Career Development Association (NCDA). (2009, October 2). Career counseling competencies. Retrieved from http://www.ncda.org/aws/NCDA/pt/sd/news_article/37798/_self/layout_ccmsearch/true

National Career Development Association (NCDA). (2010). Career counselor assessment and evaluation competencies. Retrieved from http://www.ncda.org/aws/NCDA/asset_manager/get_file/18143/aace-ncda_assmt_eval_competencies

National Career Development Association (NCDA). (2014). Multicultural career counseling minimum competencies. Retrieved from http://associationdatabase.com/aws/NCDA/pt/sp/guidelines

National Institute of Allergy and Infectious Diseases, National Institute of Health. (2013). National Healthcare Disparities Report. Retrieved from http://www.ahrq.gov/research/findings/nhqrdr/nhdr13/2013nhdr.pdf

National Institute of Mental Health (NIMH). (1980). *Hispanic Americans and mental health services: A comparison of Hispanic, Black and White admissions to selected mental health facilities, 1975. (DHHS Publication No. ADM 80–1006)*. Washington, D.C.: U.S. Government Printing Office.

Navin, S., Beamish, P., & Johanson, G. (1995). Ethical practices of field-based mental health counselor supervisors. *Journal of Mental Health Counseling*, *17*, 243–253.

Negash, S. M., & Hecker, S. L. (2010). Ethical issues endemic to couple and family therapy. In S. L. Hecker (Ed.), *Ethics and professional issues in couple and family therapy* (pp. 225–241). New York, NY: Routledge.

Neimeyer, G. J., Taylor, J. M., & Orwig, J. (2013). Do continuing education mandates matter? An exploratory study of the relationship between CE regulations and disciplinary actions. *Professional Psychology: Research & Practice*, *44*(2), 99–104.

Neimeyer, G. J., Taylor, J. M., & Philip, D. (2010). Continuing education in psychology: Patterns of participation and perceived outcomes among mandated and nonmandated psychologists. *Professional Psychology: Research and Practice*, *41*, 435–441.

Neimeyer, G. J., Taylor, J. M., & Rozensky, R. H. (2012). The diminishing durability of professional knowledge in psychology: A Delphi poll of specialties and proficiencies. *Professional Psychology: Research and Practice*, *43*, 364–371.

Neimeyer, G. J., Taylor, J. M., & Rozensky, R. H. & Cox, D. R. (2014). The diminishing durability of knowledge in professional psychology: A second look at specializations. *Professional Psychology: Research and Practice*, *45*, 92–103.

Neimeyer, G. J., Taylor, J. M., & Wear, D. M. (2011). Continuing education in professional psychology: Do ethics mandates really matter? *Ethics & Behavior*, *21*, 165–172.

Neimeyer, G. J., Taylor, J. M., & Zemansky, M., & Rothke, S. E. (2013). Do mandates matter? The impact of continuing education mandates on participation in continuing professional development activities. *Professional Psychology: Research and Practice*, *44*, 105–111.

Nelson, E., Bui, T. N., & Velasquez, S. E. (2011). Telepsychology: Research and practice overview. *Child and Adolescent Psychiatric Clinics of North America*, *20*, 67–79,

Nelson, J. A., Nichter, M., & Henriksen, R. (2010). On-line supervision and face-to-face supervision in the counseling internship: An exploratory study of similarities and differences. Retrieved from http://counselingoutfitters.com/vistas/vistas10/Article_46.pdf

Nelson, P. A. (2007). Striving for competence in the assessment of competence: Psychology's professional education and credentialing journey of public accountability. *Training and Education in Professional Psychology*, *1*, 3–12.

Nerison, R. M. (1992). Dual client-therapist relationships: Incidence and consequences to clients. *Dissertation Abstracts International: Section B, The Sciences and Engineering*, *54*(4), 1107.

Nessman, A., & Herndon, P. (2000, December). New Jersey settlement offers strong protections for psychologists. *APA Monitor, 31*, 20–21.

Neufeldt, S. A., & Nelson, M. L. (1999). When is counseling an appropriate and ethical supervision function? *Clinical Supervisor, 18*, 125–135.

Neukrug, E. S., & Milliken, T. (2011). Counselors' perceptions of ethical behaviors. *Journal of Counseling & Development, 89*, 206–216.

Neukrug, E. S., Milliken, T., & Walden, S. (2001). Ethics complaints against credentials counselors: An updated survey of state licensing boards. *Counselor Education and Supervision, 41*, 57–70.

Nevas, D. B., & Farber, B. A. (2001). Parents' attitudes toward their child's therapist and therapy. *Professional Psychology: Research and Practice, 32*, 165–170.

Newman, J. L. (1993). Ethical issues in consultation. *Journal of Counseling & Development, 72*, 148–156.

Newman, J. L., Robinson-Kurpius, S. E., & Fuqua, D. R. (2002). Issues in the ethical practice of consulting psychology. In R. L. Lowman (Ed.), *The California School of Organizational Studies: Handbook of organizational consulting psychology: A comprehensive guide to theory, skills, and techniques.* (pp. 733–758). San Francisco, CA: Jossey-Bass.

Newman, M. L., & Greenway, P. (1997). Therapeutic effects of providing MMPI-2 test feedback to clients at a university counseling service: A collaborative approach. *Psychological Assessment, 9*, 122–131.

Newman, R., & Bricklin, P. M. (1991). Parameters of managed mental health care: Legal, ethical and professional guidelines. *Professional Psychology: Research and Practice, 22*, 26–35.

Newton, L. (1989). *Ethics in America study guide*. Englewood Cliffs, NJ: Prentice Hall.

Nguyen, T., & Nguyen, D. (2006). Authorship ethics: Issues and suggested guidelines for the helping professions. *Counseling and Values, 50*, 208–216.

Nichols, L. H. (2003). Ethical decision-making in therapists with HIV-positive patients in duty-to-protect situations. *Dissertation Abstracts International: Section B, The Sciences and Engineering, 64*(2), 971.

Nickell, N. J., Hecker, L. L., Ray, R. E., & Bercik, J. (1995). Marriage and family therapists' sexual attraction to clients: An exploratory study. *American Journal of Family Therapy, 23*, 315–327.

Nicolosi, J., Byrd, A. D., & Potts, R. W. (2000). Retrospective self-reports of changes in homosexual orientation: A consumer survey of conversion therapy clients. *Psychological Reports, 86*, 1071–1088.

Nigro, T. (2004a). Dual relationships in counseling: A survey of British Columbian counselors. *Canadian Journal of Counseling, 38*, 36–53.

Nigro, T. (2004b). Counselors' experiences with problematic dual relationships. *Ethics & Behavior, 14*, 51–64.

No Child Left Behind Act of 2001, 20 U.S.C. 6301 et seq. Retrieved from http://www.ed.gov/policy/elsec/leg/esea02/index.html

Nodding, N. (1984). *Caring*. Berkeley: University of California.

Noel, B., & Watterson, K. (1992). *You must be dreaming*. New York, NY: Poseidon.

Noel, M. M. (2008). Sexual misconduct by psychologists: Who reports it? *Dissertation Abstracts International: Section B, The Sciences and Engineering, 68*(10), 5975.

Norcross, J. C. (2000). Psychotherapist self-care: Practitioner-tested, research-informed strategies. *Professional Psychology: Research and Practice, 31*, 710–713.

Norcross, J. C. (2011). *Psychotherapy relationships that work: Evidence-based responsiveness* (2nd ed.). Washington, D.C.: American Psychological Association.

Norcross, J. C., Beutler, L. E., & Levant, R. F. (Eds.). (2005). *Evidence-based practice in mental health: Debate and dialogue on the fundamental questions* (pp. 3–12). Washington, D.C.: American Psychological Association.

Norcross, J. C., & Guy, J. D., Jr. (2007). *Leaving it at the office*. New York, NY: Guilford.

Norcross, J. C., Hedges, M., & Castle, P. H. (2002). Psychologists conducting psychotherapy in 2001: A study of Division 29 membership. *Psychotherapy: Theory, Research, Practice, Training, 39*, 97–102.

Norman, G. (1985). Defining competence: A methodological review. In V. Neufeld & G. Norman (Eds.), *Assessing clinical competence*. New York, NY: Springer.

Nowell, D., & Spruill, J. (1993). If it's not absolutely confidential, will information be disclosed? *Professional Psychology: Research and Practice, 24*, 367–369.

Nuttgens, S., & Chang, J. (2013). Moral distress within the supervisory relationship: Implications for practice and research. *Counselor Education & Supervision, 52*, 284–296.

Oberlander, L. B. (1995). Ethical responsibilities in child custody evaluations: Implications for evaluation methodology. *Ethics & Behavior, 5*, 311–332.

O'Brien, J. M. (2011). Wounded healer: Psychotherapist grief over a client's death. *Professional Psychology: Research and Practice, 42*, 236–243.

Office for Protection from Research Risks, Protection of Human Subjects. (1991, June 18). Protection of human subjects: Title 45, Code of Federal Regulations, Part 46 (GPO 1992 O-307–551). *OPOR Reports*, 4–17.

Office of Special Education and Rehabilitation Services, U.S. Department of Health and Human Services. Early warning, timely response: A guide to safe schools. Retrieved from http://www.ed.gov/about/offices/list/osers/osep/gtss.html

Ohio Board of Psychology. (2003). When clients are in domestic relations litigation psychologists must proceed with caution. Retrieved from http://psychology.ohio.gov/pdfs/ALERT2003revised.pdf

Ohio Board of Psychology. (2011). Telepsychology rules. Retrieved from http://www.psychology.ohio.gov/pdfs/ALL NEW TELEPSYCH RULES FOR WEB.pdf.

Ohio Psychological Association (OPA). (2008). Telepsychology guidelines. Retrieved from http://www.ohpsych.org/psychologists/files/2011/06/OPATelepsychologyGuidelines41710.pdf

Ohio Rev. Code § 2305.51. (1999).

Ohio Revised Code § 3701.74. (2011).

Oleszko v. State Compensation Insurance Fund, 243F.3d 1154 (9th Cir. 2001).

Orlinsky, D. E., Ambuhl, H., Ronnestad, M. H., Davis, J., Gerin, P., Davis, M., & Eunsun, J. (1999). Development of psychotherapists: Concepts, questions, and methods of a collaborative International study. *Psychotherapy Research, 9*, 127–153.

Orlinsky, D. E., & Rommestad, M. H. (2005). *How psychotherapists develop: A study of therapeutic work and professional growth.* Washington, D.C.: American Psychological Association.

Orme, D. R., & Doerman, A. L. (2001). Ethical dilemmas and U.S. Air Force clinical psychologists: A survey. *Professional Psychology: Research and Practice, 32*, 305–311.

Orr, T. J. (2000). Psychologists' perceptions of managed mental health care practice: Implications for burnout. *Dissertation Abstracts International: Section B, The Sciences and Engineering, 61*(8), 3287.

Osipow, S., & Fitzgerald, L. F. (1986). An occupational analysis of counseling psychology: How special is the specialty? *American Psychologist, 41*, 535–545.

Otto, R. K., & Douglas, K. S. (Eds.). (2010). *Handbook of violence risk assessment*. New York, NY: Routledge.

Overholser, J. C., & Fine, M. A. (1990). Defining the boundaries of professional competence: Managing subtle cases of clinical incompetence. *Professional Psychology: Research and Practice*, 21, 462–469.

Owen, J. J., Tao, K., Leach, M. M., & Rodolfa, E. (2011). Clients' perceptions of their psychotherapists' multicultural orientation. *Psychotherapy: Theory, Research, Practice, Training, 44*, 274–282.

Owen, J. J., Wong, Y. J., & Rodolfa, E. (2009). Empirical search for psychotherapists' gender competence in psychotherapy. *Psychotherapy: Theory, Research, Practice, Training, 46*, 448–458.

Pabian, Y. L., Welfel, E. R., & Beebe, R. S. (2009). Psychologists' knowledge and application of state laws in *Tarasoff*-type situations. *Professional Psychology: Research and Practice*, 40, 8–14.

Pack-Brown, S. P., Thomas, T. L., & Seymour, J. M. (2008). Infusing professional ethics in to counselor education programs: A multicultural/social justice perspective. *Journal of Counseling & Development, 86*, 296–302.

Packman, W. L., & Harris, E. A. (1998). Legal issues and risk management in suicidal patients. In B. Bongar, A. L. Berman, R. W. Maris, E. A. Harris, & W. L. Packman (Eds.), *Risk management with suicidal patients* (pp. 150–186). New York, NY: Guilford.

Pais, S., Piercy, F., & Miller, J. (1998). Factors related to family therapists' breaking confidence when clients disclose high-risks-to-HIV/AIDS sexual behaviors. *Journal of Marital and Family Therapy, 24*, 457–472.

Palma, T. V., & Iannelli, R. J. (2002). Therapeutic reactivity to confidentiality with HIV positive clients: Bias or epidemiology? *Ethics & Behavior, 12*, 353–370.

Palmiter, D., & Renjilian, D. (2003). Clinical Web pages: Do they meet expectations? *Professional Psychology: Research and Practice, 34*, 164–169.

Paludi, M. A. (2008). *Understanding and preventing campus violence*. New York, NY: Praeger.

Paradise, L. V., & Kirby, P. C. (1990). Some perspectives on the legal liability of group counseling in private practice. *Journal for Specialists in Group Work, 15*, 114–118.

Parish, M., & Eagle, M. N. (2003). Attachment to the therapist. *Psychoanalytic psychology, 20*, 271–286.

Parker, J., Clevenger, J. E., & Sherman, J. (1997). The psychotherapist-patient privilege in group therapy. *Journal of Group Psychotherapy, Psychodrama and Sociometry*, 49, 157–160.

Pate, R. H., Jr. (1992). Are you liable? *The American Counselor, 1*, 14–19.

Patel, S. H., & Choate, L. H. (2014). Conducting child custody evaluations: Best practices for mental health counselors who are court-appointed as child custody evaluators. *Journal of Mental Health Counseling*, 36, 18–30.

Patient Protection and Affordable Care Act of 2010. (P.L. 111–148).

Patrick, K. D. (1989). Unique ethical dilemmas in counselor training. *Counselor Education and Supervision, 28*, 337–341.

Patten, C., Barnett, T., & Houlihan, D. (1991). Ethics in marital and family therapy: A review of the literature. *Professional Psychology: Research and Practice, 22*, 171–175.

Patterson, J. (2011, May 20). Bullies with byte. *Counseling Today*. Retrieved from http://ct.counseling.org/2011/06/

Paul, G., & Herbert, P. B. (2005). Court-ordered psychotherapy and the privilege against self-incrimination. *Journal of the American Academy of Psychiatry and Law, 33*, 563–564.

Pavkov, T. W., Lewis, D. A., & Lyons, J. S. (1989). Psychiatric diagnosis and racial bias: An empirical investigation. *Professional Psychology: Research and Practice, 20*, 364–368.

Pear, R. (2008, October, 5). Bailout provides more mental health coverage. *New York Times*. Retrieved from http://www.nytimes.com/2008/10/06/washington/06mental.html?em

Pearson, B., & Piazza, N. (1997). Classification of dual relationships in the helping professions. *Counselor Education and Supervision, 37*, 89–99.

Pedersen, P. B. (1991a). The multicultural perspective as a fourth force in counseling. *Journal of Mental Health Counseling, 12*, 93–95.

Pedersen, P. B. (1991b). Multiculturalism as a generic approach to counseling. *Journal of Counseling & Development, 70*, 3–14.

Pedersen, P. B. (1994). *A handbook for developing multicultural awareness* (2nd ed.). Alexandria, VA: American Counseling Association.

Pedersen, P. B. (1997). The cultural context of the American Counseling Association code of ethics. *Journal of Counseling & Development, 76*, 23–28.

Pedersen, P. B. (2001). Cross-cultural ethical guidelines. In J. B. Ponterotto, J. M. Casas, L. A. Suzuki, & C. M. Alexander (Eds.), *Handbook of multicultural counseling* (2nd ed., pp. 34–50). Thousand Oaks, CA: Sage.

Pedersen, P. B., & Carey, J. C. (Eds.). (2003). *Multicultural counseling in schools: A practical handbook*. Needham Heights, MA: Allyn & Bacon.

Pedersen, P. B., Crethar, H., & Carlson, J. (2008). *Inclusive cultural empathy; Making relationships central in counseling and psychotherapy*. Washington, D.C.: American Psychological Association.

Pedersen, P. B., Draguns, J. G., Lonner, W. J., & Trimble, J. E. (2007). *Counseling across cultures* (6th ed.). Thousand Oaks, CA: Sage.

Pepper, R. S. (2003). Confidentiality and dual relationships in group psychotherapy. *International Journal of Group Psychotherapy*, *54*, 103–114.

Perfect, T. J., & Stark I. J. (2008). Why do I always have the best ideas? The role of idea quality in unconscious plagiarism. *Memory*, *16*, 386–394.

Perry, J. L., & Dess, N. K. (2012). Laboratory animal research ethics: A practical educational approach. In S. J. Knapp, M. M. Gottlieb, Handelsman, M. M., & VandeCreek, L. D. D. *APA handbook of ethics in psychology* (Vol. 2, pp. 423–440). Washington, D.C.: American Psychological Association.

Peters, R. H., & Murrin, M. R. (2000). Effectiveness of treatment-based drug courts in reducing criminal recidivism. *Criminal Justice and Behavior*, *27*, 72–96.

Peterson, C. (1996). Common problem areas and their causes resulting in disciplinary action. In L. J. Bass, S. T. DeMers, J. R. P. Ogloff, C. Peterson, J. L. Pettifor, R. P. Reaves, T. (Eds.), *Professional conduct and discipline in psychology* (pp. 71–89). Washington, D.C.: American Psychological Association.

Peterson, C. H., Lomas, G. I., Neukrug, E. S., & Bonner, M. W. (2014). Assessment use by counselors in the United States: Implications for policy and practice. *Journal of Counseling & Development*, *92*, 90–98.

Peterson, J. S., Goodman, R., Keller, T., & McCauley, A. (2004). Teachers and non-teachers as school counselors: Reflections on the internship experience. *Professional School Counseling*, *7*, 246–255.

Peterson, M. B. (2001). Recognizing concerns about how some licensing boards are treating psychologists. *Professional Psychology: Research and Practice*, *32*, 339–340.

Pettifor, J. J. (2004). Professional ethics across national boundaries. *European Psychologist*, *9*, 264–272.

Phelan, J. E. (2007). Membership expulsions for ethical violations from major counseling, psychology, and social work organizations in the United States: A 10-year analysis. *Psychological Reports*, *101*, 145–152.

Phelan, J. E. (2009). Exploring the use of touch in the psychotherapeutic setting: A phenomenological review. *Psychotherapy: Theory, Research, Practice, Training*, *46*, 97–111.

Phelps, R., Eisman, E. J., & Kohut, J. (1998). Psychological practice and managed care: Results of the CAPP practitioner survey. *Professional Psychology: Research and Practice*, *29*, 31–36.

Phillips, S. B. (2011). Up close and personal: A consideration of the role of personal therapy in the development of the psychotherapist. In R. H. Klein, H. S. Bernard, & V. L. Schemmer (Eds.), *On becoming a psychotherapist* (144–164). New York, NY: Oxford.

Piazza, N. J., & Baruth, N. E. (1990). Client record guidelines. *Journal of Counseling & Development*, *68*, 313–316.

Pipes, R. B., Blevins, T., & Kluck, A. (2008). Confidentiality, ethics, and informed consent. *American Psychologist*, *63*, 623–624.

Pittinger, D. J. (2002). Deception in research: distinctions and solutions from the perspective of utilitarianism. *Ethics & Behavior*, *12*, 117–142.

Podbelski, J., & Weisgerber, K. (1988, August). *Differences in moral sensitivity of master's level counselors*. Paper presented at the annual meeting of the American Psychological Association, Atlanta, GA.

Pomerantz, A. M. (2005). Increasingly informed consent: Discussing distinct aspects of psychotherapy at different points in time. *Ethics & Behavior*, *15*, 351–360.

Pomerantz, A. M. (2012). Informed consent to psychotherapy (empowered collaboration). In S. J. Knapp, M. M. Gottlieb, M. M. Handelsman, & VandeCreek, L. D. (Eds.), *APA handbook of ethics in psychology* (Vol. 1, pp. 311–332). Washington, D.C.: American Psychological Association.

Pomerantz, A. M., & Handelsman, M. M. (2004). Informed consent revisited: An updated written question format. *Professional Psychology: Research and Practice*, *35*, 201–205.

Pomerantz, A. M., Ross, M. J., Gfeller, J. D., & Hughes, H. (1998). Ethical beliefs of psychotherapists: Scientific findings. *Journal of Contemporary Psychotherapy*, *28*, 35–44.

Pomerantz, A. M., & Segrist, J. (2006). The influence of payment method on psychologists' diagnostic decisions regarding minimally impaired clients. *Ethics & Behavior*, *16*, 253–263.

Ponterotto, J. G., Casas, J. M., Suzuki, L. A., & Alexander, C. M. (Eds.). (2009). *Handbook of multicultural counseling*. Thousand Oaks, CA: Sage.

Ponton, L. (1996). Sexual harassment of children and girls. In D. K. Shier (Ed.), *Sexual harassment in the workplace and academia: Psychiatric issues* (pp. 181–201). Washington, D.C.: American Psychiatric Association.

Ponton, R. F., & Duba, D. (2009). The ACA code of ethics: Articulating counseling's professional covenant. *Journal of Counseling & Development*, *87*, 117–121.

Pope, K. S. (1988). How clients are harmed by sexual contact with mental health professionals. *Journal of Counseling & Development*, *67*, 222–226.

Pope, K. S. (1989). Therapists who become sexually intimate with a patient: Classifications, dynamics, recidivism, and rehabilitation. *Independent Practitioner*, *9*, 28–34.

Pope, K. S. (1990a). Therapist-patient sex as sex abuse: Six scientific, professional and practical dilemmas in addressing victimization and rehabilitation. *Professional Psychology: Research and Practice*, *21*, 227–239.

Pope, K. S. (1990b). Therapist-patient sexual involvement: A review of the research. *Clinical Psychology Review*, *10*, 477–490.

Pope, K. S. (1992). Responsibilities in providing psychological test feedback to clients. *Psychological Assessment*, *4*, 268–271.

Pope, K. S. (1994). *Sexual involvement with therapists: Patient assessment, subsequent therapy, forensics.*

Washington, D.C.: American Psychological Association.

Pope, K. S., & Bajt, T. R. (1988). When laws and values conflict: A dilemma for psychologists. *American Psychologist, 43*, 828.

Pope, K. S., & Bouhoutsos, J. C. (1986). *Sexual intimacies between therapists and patients*. New York, NY: Praeger.

Pope, K. S., & Gutheil, T. G. (2008). The American Psychological Association and detainee interrogations: Unanswered questions. *Psychiatric Times, 25*, 16–17. Retrieved from http://kspope.com/interrogation/detainee.php

Pope, K. S., & Keith-Spiegel, P. (2008). A practical approach to boundaries in psychotherapy: Making decisions, bypassing blunders, and mending fences. *Journal of Clinical Psychology, 64*, 638–652.

Pope, K. S., Keith-Spiegel, P. S., & Tabachnick, B. G. (1986). Sexual attraction to clients: The human therapist and the (sometimes) inhuman training system. *American Psychologist, 41*, 147–158.

Pope, K. S., Levenson, H., & Schover, L. R. (1979). Sexual intimacy in psychology training. Results and implications of a national survey. *American Psychologist, 34*, 682–689.

Pope, K. S., Sonne, J. L., & Greene, B. (2006). *What therapists don't talk about and why: Understanding taboos that hurt us and our clients*. Washington, D.C.: American Psychological Association.

Pope, K. S., Sonne, J. L., & Holroyd, J. (1993). *Sexual feelings in psychotherapy: Explorations for therapists and therapists-in-training*. Washington, D.C.: American Psychological Association.

Pope, K. S., & Tabachnick, B. G. (1993). Therapists' anger, hate, fear, and sexual feelings. National survey of therapist responses, client characteristics, critical events, formal complaints, and training. *Professional Psychology: Research and Practice, 24*, 142–152.

Pope, K. S., Tabachnick, B. G., & Keith-Spiegel, P. S. (1987). Ethics of practice: The beliefs and behaviors of psychologists as therapists. *American Psychologist, 42*, 993–1006.

Pope, K. S., & Vasquez, M. J. T. (2005). *How to survive and thrive as a therapist*. Washington, D.C.: American Psychological Association.

Pope, K. S., & Vasquez, M. J. T. (2011). *Ethics in psychotherapy and counseling* (4th ed.). San Francisco, CA: Jossey-Bass.

Pope, K. S., & Vetter, V. A. (1991). Prior therapist-patient sexual involvement among patients seen by psychologists. *Psychotherapy: Theory/Research/Practice/Training, 28*, 429–438.

Pope, K. S., & Vetter, V. A. (1992). Ethical dilemmas encountered by members of the American Psychological Association. *American Psychologist, 47*, 397–411.

Pope-Davis, D. & Coleman, H. (Eds.). *The intersection of race, class, and gender in multicultural counseling*. Thousand Oaks, CA: Sage.

Powell, M. P., & Vacha-Haase, T. (1994). Issues related to research with children: What counseling psychologists need to know. *The Counseling Psychologist, 22*, 444–453.

Price, J. H., & Teljohann, S. K. (1991). School counselor perceptions of adolescent homosexuals. *Journal of School Health, 61*, 433–438.

Procidano, M. E., Busch-Rossnagel, N. A., Reznikoff, M., & Geisinger, K. F. (1995). Responding to graduate students' professional deficiencies: A national survey. *Journal of Clinical Psychology, 51*, 426–433.

Prosek, E. A., Holm, J. M., & Daly, C. M. (2013). Benefits of required counseling for counseling students. *Counselor Education and Supervision, 52*, 242–250.

Pryzwansky, W., & Wendt, R. N. (1999). *Professional and ethical issues in psychology*. New York, NY: W. W. Norton.

Pulakos, J. (1994). Incidental encounters between therapists and clients: The client's perspective. *Professional Psychology: Research and Practice, 25*, 300–303.

Rabasca, L. (2000, March). Attracting more minority students to psychology programs. *APA Monitor, 31, 56*. Retrieved from http://www.apa.org/monitor/mar00/muse.html

Rabinowitz, J., & Efron, N. J. (1997). Diagnosis, dogmatism, and rationality. *Journal of Mental Health Counseling, 19*, 40–56.

Radden, J., & Sadler, J. Z. (2010). *The virtuous psychiatrist: Character ethics in psychiatric practice*. New York, NY: Oxford.

Radeke, J. T., & Mahoney, M. J. (2000). Comparing the personal lives of psychotherapists and research psychologists. *Professional Psychology: Research and Practice, 31*, 284–292.

Rae, W. A., & Worchel, F. F. (1991). Ethical beliefs and behaviors of pediatric psychologists: A survey. *Journal of Pediatric Psychology, 16*, 727–745.

Ragusea, S. A. (2002). A professional living will for psychologists and other mental health professionals. In L. VandeCreek & T. L. Jackson (Eds.), *Innovations in clinical practice: A sourcebook* (Vol. 20, pp. 301–305). Sarasota, FL: Professional Resource Exchange.

Ragusea, S. A. (2012). The more things change, the more they stay the same: Ethical issues in the provision of telehealth. In S. J. Knapp, M. C. Gottlieb, M. M. Handelsman, & L. D. VandeCreek (Eds.), *APA handbook of ethics in psychology* (Vol. 2, pp. 183–198). Washington, D.C.: American Psychological Association.

Raimy, V. (1975). *Misunderstandings of the self*. San Francisco, CA: Jossey-Bass.

Ramisch, J. (2010). Ethical issues in clinical practice. In L. Heckler (Ed.), *Ethics and professional issues in couple and family therapy* (pp. 203–224). New York, NY: Routledge.

Ramos-Sanchez, L., Esnil, E., Goodwin, A., Riggs, S., Touster, L. O., Wright, L. K., … Rodolfa, E. (2002). Negative supervisory events: Effects on supervision and supervisory alliance. *Professional Psychology: Research and Practice, 33*, 197–202.

Randazzo, M. R., & Keeney, M. (2009). Threats against public officials: Considerations for risk assessment, reporting, and intervention. In J. L. Werth, E. R. Welfel, & G. A. H. Benjamin (Eds.), *The duty to protect: Ethical, legal, and professional responsibilities of mental health professionals* (pp. 111–126). Washington, D.C.: American Psychological Association.

Raquepaw, J., & Miller, R. S. (1989). Psychotherapist burnout: A componential analysis. *Professional Psychology: Research and Practice, 20*, 32–36.

Reamer, F. G. (1995). Malpractice claims against social workers: First facts. *Social Work, 40*, 595–601.

Reaves, R. P., & Ogloff, J. R. P. (1996). Liability for professional misconduct. In L. J. Bass, S. T. DeMers, J. R. P. Peterson, J. L. Pettifor, P. Reaves, T. Retfalvi, N. P. Simon, C. Sinclair, & R. M. Tipton (Eds.), *Professional conduct and discipline in psychology* (pp. 117–142). Washington, D.C.: American Psychological Association.

Recupero, P. R., & Rainey, S. E. (2006). Characteristics of e-therapy websites. *Journal of Clinical Psychiatry, 67*, 1435–1440.

Reed, G. M. (2006). What qualifies as evidence of effective practice? In J. C. Norcross, L. E. Beutler, & R. F. Levant (Eds.), *Evidence-based practice in mental health* (pp. 13–23). Washington, D.C.: American Psychological Association.

Reed, G. M., & Eisman, E. J. (2007). Uses and misuses of evidence: Managed care, treatment guidelines, and outcomes measurement in professional practice. In C. D. Goodheart, A. E. Kazdin, & R. J. Sternberg (Eds.), (2007). *Evidence based psychotherapy: Where research and practice meet* (pp. 13–35). Washington, D.C.: American Psychological Association.

Regehr, C., & Glancy, G. (1995). Sexual exploitation of patients: Issues for colleagues. *American Journal of Orthopsychiatry, 65*, 194–202.

Reid, K. (2001). Iowa's high court holds counselors liable. *Education Week*. Retrieved from http://www.edweek.org/ew/articles/2001/05/02/33guide.h20.html

Reiner, S. M., Colbert, R. D., & Prusse, R. (2009). Teacher perceptions of the professional school counselor role: A national study. *Professional School Counseling, 12*, 324–332.

Reis, C., & Cornell, D. (2008). An evaluation of suicide gatekeeper training for school counselors and teachers. *Professional School Counseling, 11*, 386–394.

Remafedi, G. (1999). Sexual orientation and youth suicide. *Journal of the American Medical Association, 282*, 1291–1292.

Remley, T. P., Jr., & Herlihy, B. J. (2013). *Ethical, legal, and professional issues in counseling* (3rd ed.). Upper Saddle River, NJ: Pearson.

Remley, T. P., Jr., Herlihy, B. J., & Herlihy, S. B. (1997). The U.S. Supreme Court decision in *Jaffee v. Redmond*: Implications for counselors. *Journal of Counseling & Development, 75*, 213–218.

Remley, T. P., Jr., & Sparkman, L. B. (1993). Student suicides: The counselor's limited legal liability. *The School Counselor, 40*, 164–169.

Renninger, S. M., Veach, P. M., & Bagdade, P. (2002). Psychologists' knowledge, opinions, and decision-making processes regarding child abuse and neglect reporting laws. *Professional Psychology: Research and Practice, 33*, 19–23.

Rest, J. R. (1983). Morality. In J. Flavell & E. Markman (Eds.), *Cognitive development*. In P. Mussen (General Ed.), *Manual of child psychology* (Vol. 4, pp. 550–629). New York, NY: Wiley.

Rest, J. R. (1984). Research on moral development: Implications for training counseling psychologists. *The Counseling Psychologist, 12*, 19–29.

Rest, J. R. (1994). Background: Theory and research. In J. R. Rest & D. Narvaez (Eds.), *Moral development in the professions: Psychology and applied ethics* (pp. 1–26). Hillsdale, NJ: Lawrence Erlbaum.

Rhule, D. M. (2005). Take care to do no harm: Harmful interventions for youth problem behavior. *Professional Psychology: Research and Practice, 36*, 618–625.

Ridley, C. R. (2005). *Overcoming unintentional racism in counseling: A practitioner's guide to intentional intervention* (2nd ed.). Thousand Oaks, CA: Sage.

Ridley, C. R., Li, L., & Hill, C. L. (1998). Multicultural assessment: Reexamination, reconceptualization, and practical application. *The Counseling Psychologist, 26*, 827–910.

Ridley, C. R., Liddle, M. C., Hill, C. L., & Li, L. C. (2001). Ethical decision making in multicultural counseling. In J. G. Ponterotto, J. M. Casas, L. A. Suzuki, & C. M. Alexander (Eds.), *Handbook of multicultural counseling* (pp. 165–188). Newbury Park, CA: Sage.

Riester, A. E. (2002). Group counseling in the American high school. In S. Aronson & S. Scheidlinger (Eds.), *Group treatment of adolescents in context: Outpatient, inpatient, and school* (pp. 191–203). Madison, CT: International Universities Press.

Rings, J., Genuchi, M., Hall, M., Angelo, M., & Cornish, J. (2009). Is there consensus among predoctoral internship training directors regarding clinical supervision competencies? A descriptive analysis. *Training and Education in Professional Psychology, 3*, 140–147.

Ritchie, M. H., & Huss, S. N. (2000). Recruitment and screening of minors for group counseling. *Journal for Specialists in Group Work, 25*, 145–156.

Ritter, K. Y., & Terndrup, A. I. (2002). *Handbook of affirmative psychotherapy with lesbians and gay men*. New York, NY: Guilford.

Roback, H. B. (2000). Adverse outcomes in group psychotherapy: Risk factors, preventions, and research directions. *Journal of Psychotherapy: Research and Practice, 9*, 113–122.

Roback, H. B., Ochoa, E., Bloch, F., & Purdon, S. (1992). Guarding confidentiality in clinical groups: The therapist's dilemma. *International Journal of Group Psychotherapy, 42*, 81–103.

Roberts, L. W., Battaglia, J., & Epstein, R. S. (1999). Frontier ethics: Mental health care needs and ethical dilemmas in rural communities. *Psychiatric Services, 50*, 497–503.

Roberts, L. W., & Geppert, C. (Eds.). (2008). *The book of ethics: Expert guidance for professionals who treat addiction*. Center City, MN: Hazelden Publishing.

Roberts-Dobie, S., & Donatelle, R. J. (2007). School Counselors and Student Self-Injury. *The Journal of School Health, 77*, 257–264.

Robertson, J., & Fitzgerald, L. F. (1990). The (mis)treatment of men: Effects of client gender role and life style on diagnosis and attribution of pathology. *Journal of Counseling Psychology, 37*, 3–9.

Robinson, W. L., & Reid, P. T. (1985). Sexual intimacies in psychology revisited. *Professional Psychology: Research and Practice, 16*, 512–520.

Rodolfa, E., Hall, T., Holms, V., Davena, A., Komatz, D., Antunez, M., & Hall, A. (1994). The management of sexual feelings in therapy. *Professional Psychology: Research and Practice, 25*, 168–172.

Roesch, R., Zapf, P. A., & Hart, S. D. (2010). *Forensic psychology and law*. Hoboken, NJ: Wiley.

Rogers, J. R., Gueulette, C. M., Abbey-Hines, J., Carney, J. V., & Werth, J. L. (2001). Rational suicide: An empirical investigation of counselor attitudes. *Journal of Counseling & Development, 80*, 493–502.

Rogers, N. M. (2011). Intimate boundaries: Therapists' perception and experience of erotic transference within the therapeutic relationship. *Counseling and Psychotherapy Research, 11*, 266–274.

Rogers, W. H., Wells, K. B., Meredith, L. S., Sturm, R., & Burman, A. (1993). Outcomes for adult outpatients with depression under pre-paid or fee-for-service financing. *Archives for General Psychiatry, 50*, 517–525.

Rohrbaugh, J. B. (1992). Lesbian families: Clinical issues and theoretical implications. *Professional Psychology: Research and Practice, 23*, 467–473.

Rokop, J. J. (2003). The effects of CPS mandated reporting on the therapeutic relationship: The client's perspective. *Dissertation Abstracts International: Section B, The Sciences and Engineering, 64*(5), 135.

Rooney, R. (2001). Guidelines for counseling mandated and nonvoluntary clients. In E. R. Welfel & R. E. Ingersoll (Eds.), *The mental health desk reference: A practice-based guide to diagnosis, treatment, and professional ethics* (pp. 94–98). New York, NY: Wiley.

Rorschach, H. (1951). *Psychodiagnostics*. New York, NY: Grune & Stratton.

Rosen, L. D., & Weil, M. M. (1996). Psychologists and technology: A look at the future. *Professional Psychology: Research and Practice, 27*, 635–637.

Rosenhan, D. L. (1973). On being sane in insane places. *Science, 179*, 250–258.

Rosenthal, R. (1994). Science and ethics in conducting, analyzing, and reporting psychological research. *Psychological Science, 5*, 127–133.

Ross, D. M. (2003). *Childhood bullying, teasing, and violence: What school personnel, other professionals, and parents can do*. Alexandria, VA: American Counseling Association.

Rovero, M. V. (2004). A study of burnout in elementary, middle and secondary school counselors. *Dissertation Abstracts International: Section A, The Humanities and Social Sciences, 64*(10), 3204.

Rowan, J. (2000). Research ethics. *International Journal of Psychotherapy, 5*, 103–111.

Rowley, W. J., & MacDonald, D. (2001). Counseling and the law: A cross-cultural perspective. *Journal of Counseling & Development, 79*, 422–429.

Roy v. Hartogs, 366 NY, S2d 297. (1975).

Royer, R. I. (1985). *Ethical orientation of mental health practitioners: A comparative study*. Paper presented at the annual meeting of the American Psychological Association, Los Angeles, CA.

Roysircar, G. (2005). Culturally sensitive assessment, diagnosis, and guidelines. In M. G. Constantine & D. W. Sue (Eds.), *Strategies for building multicultural competence in mental health and educational settings* (pp. 19–38). New York, NY: Wiley.

Rozovsky. F. A. (2011). *Consent to treatment: A practical guide*. New York, NY: Aspen.

Rubin, L. J., Hampton, B. R., & McManus, P. W. (1997). Sexual harassment of students by professional psychology educators: A national survey. *Sex Roles, 37*, 753–771.

Rubinson, E., Asnis, G. M., Harkavy, S., & Friedman, J. M. (1988). Knowledge of the diagnostic criteria for major depression: A survey of mental health professionals. *Journal of Nervous and Mental Disease, 176*, 480–484.

Ruebensaal, D. M. (2006). Attitudes and practices of school counselors and school psychologists with lesbian and gay male youth. *Dissertation Abstracts International: Section B, The Sciences and Engineering, 67*(5), 1660.

Rummell, C. M., & Joyce, N. R. (2010). "So wat do u want to wrk on 2day?": The ethical implications of online counseling. *Ethics & Behavior, 20*(6), 482–496.

Rupert, P. A., & Baird, K. A. (2004). Managed care and the independent practice of psychology. *Professional Psychology: Research and Practice, 35*, 185–191.

Rupert, P. A., & Kent, J. S. (2007). Gender and work setting differences in career-sustaining behaviors and burnout among professional psychologists. *Professional Psychology: Research and Practice, 38*, 88–96.

Rupert, P. A., & Morgan, D. J. (2005). Work setting and burnout among professional psychologists. *Professional Psychology: Research and Practice, 36*, 544–550.

Rutter, P. (1989). *Sex in the forbidden zone: When men in power—therapists, doctors, clergy, teachers and others—betray women's trust*. Los Angeles, CA: Tarcher.

Ryan, C., Huebner, D., Diaz, R. M., & Sanchez, J. (2009). Family rejection as a predictor of negative health outcomes in white and Latino lesbian, gay, and bisexual young adults. *Pediatrics, 123*, 346–352.

Sadeghi, M., Fischer, J. M., & House, S. G. (2003). Ethical dilemmas in multicultural counseling. *Journal of Multicultural Counseling and Development, 31*, 179–191.

Sales, B. D., DeKraai, M. D., Hall, S. R., & Duvall, J. C. (2008). Child therapy and the law. In R. J. Morris & T. R. Kratochwill (Eds.), *The practice of child therapy* (pp. 519–542). New York, NY: Lawrence Erlbaum.

Sales, B. D., & Folkman, S. (Eds.). (2000). *Ethics in research with human participants*. Washington, D.C.: American Psychological Association.

Sales, B. D., & Lavin, M. (2000). Identifying conflicts of interest and resolving ethical dilemmas. In B. D. Sales & S. Folkman (Eds.), *Ethics in research with human participants* (pp. 109–128). Washington, D.C.: American Psychological Association.

Salisbury, W. A., & Kinnier, R. T. (1996). Posttermination friendship between counselors and clients. *Journal of Counseling & Development, 74*, 495–500.

Salter, D. S., & Salter, B. R. (2012). Competence with diverse populations. In S. J. Knapp, M. C. Gottlieb, M. M. Handelsman, & L. D. VandeCreek (Eds.), *APA handbook of ethics in psychology* (Vol. 1, pp. 217–239). Washington, D.C.: American Psychological Association.

Sampson, K. (1993). The use and misuse of expert evidence in courts. *Judicature*, *77*, 68–76.

Sanabria, S., & Freeman, L. T. (2008). Report of the CA Ethics Committee: 2006–2007. *Journal of Counseling & Development*, *86*, 249–252.

Sanchez, L. M., & Turner, M. (2003). Practicing psychology in the era of managed care: Implications for practice and training. *American Psychologist*, *58*, 116–129.

Sandhi, D. S., & Aspy, C. B. (2000). *Violence in American schools: A practical guide for counselors*. Alexandria, VA: American Counseling Association.

Sank, L. I. (1997). Taking on managed care: One reviewer at a time. *Professional Psychology: Research and Practice*, *28*, 548–554.

Santhiveeran, J. (2009). Compliance of social work E-therapy websites to the NASW code of ethics. *Social Work in Health Care*, *48*, 1–13.

Sawyer, D., Gale, J., & Lambert, D. (2006). Rural and frontier mental and behavioral health care: Barriers, effective policy strategies, best practices. Retrieved from http://narmh.org/publications/archives/rural_frontier.pdf

Schank, J. A., Helbok, C. M., Haldeman, D. C., & Gallardo, M. E. (2010). Challenges and benefits of ethical small-community practice. *Professional Psychology: Research and Practice*, *41*, 502–510.

Schank, J. A., & Skovholt, T. M. (1997). Dual-relationship dilemmas of rural and small community psychologists. *Professional Psychology: Research and Practice*, *28*, 44–49.

Schank, J. A., & Skovholt, T. M. (2006). *Ethical practices in small communities*. Washington, D.C.: American Psychological Association.

Scheiderer, E. M. (2011). Elder abuse: Ethical and related considerations for professionals in psychology. *Ethics & Behavior*, *22*, 78–87.

Schellenberg, R. C., & Parks-Savage, A. (2007). Reducing levels of elementary school violence with peer mediation. *Professional School Counseling*, *10*, 475–481.

Schloendorff v. Society of New York Hospital. (1914). 105 N.E. 92, 93.

Schoener, G. R., & Gonsiorek, J. (1988). Assessment and development of rehabilitation plans for counselors who have sexually exploited their clients. *Journal of Counseling & Development*, *67*, 227–232.

Schoener, G. R., Milgrom, J., & Gonsiorek, J. (1989). Therapeutic responses to clients who have been sexually abused by psychotherapists. In G. Schoener & J. Milgrom (Eds.), *Psychotherapists' sexual involvement with clients: Intervention and prevention* (pp. 95–112). Minneapolis, MN: Walk-In Counseling Center.

Schoenfeld, L. S., Hatch, J. P., & Gonzales, J. M. (2001). Responses of psychologists to complaints filed against them with a state licensing board. *Professional Psychology: Research and Practice*, *32*, 491–495.

Schulenberg, S. E., & Yutrzenka, B. A. (2004). Ethical issues in the use of computerized assessment. *Computers in Human Behavior*, *20*, 477–490.

Schulte, J. M., & Cochrane, D. B. (1995). *Ethics of school counseling*. New York, NY: Teachers College Press.

Schulz, K. (2010). *Being wrong: Adventures in the margin of error*. New York, NY: HarperCollins.

Schwab, R., & Neukrug, E. (1994). A survey of counselor educators' ethical concerns. *Counseling and Values*, *39*, 42–55.

Schwartz, A., Rodriguez, M. M. D., Santiago-Rivera, A. L., Arredondo, P., & Field, L. D. (2010). Cultural and linguistic competence: Welcome challenges from successful diversification. *Professional Psychology: Research and Practice*, *41*, 210–220.

Schwartz, L. L. (Ed.). (1999). *Psychologists and the media: A second look*. Washington, D.C.: American Psychological Association.

Schwebel, D. C., & Hodari, A. J. (2005). Ethical principles and acculturation: Two case studies. *Ethics & Behavior*, *15*, 131–137.

Schwebel, M., Schoener, G., & Skorina, J. K. (1994). *Assisting impaired psychologists* (rev. ed.). Washington, D.C.: American Psychological Association.

Schweibert, V. L. (2000). *Mentoring: Creating connected, empowered relationships*. Alexandria, VA: American Counseling Association.

Scott, K. J., Ingram, K. M., Vitanza, S. A., & Smith, N. G. (2000). Training in supervision: A survey of current practices. *Counseling Psychologist*, *28*, 403–422.

Scott, M., Wilcox, H., Huo, Y., Turner, J. B., Fisher, P., & Shaffer, D. (2010). School-based screening for suicide risk: Balancing costs and benefits. *American Journal of Public Health*, *100*, 1648–1652.

Scott-Jones, D. (2000). Recruitment of research participants. In B. D. Sales & S. Folkman (Eds.), *Ethics in research with human participants* (pp. 27–34). Washington, D.C.: American Psychological Association.

Scrivner, R. (1997). Ethical and legal issues in lesbian, gay, and bisexual family therapy. In D. Marsh & R. D. Magee (Eds.), *Ethical and legal issues in professional practice with families* (pp. 140–160). New York, NY: Wiley.

Sehgal, R., Saules, K., Young, A., Grey, M. J., Gillem, A. R., Nabors, N. A., & Masciulli, L. (2011). Practicing what we know: Multicultural counseling competence among clinical psychology trainees and experienced multicultural psychologists. *Cultural Diversity and Ethnic Minority Psychology*, *17*, 1–10.

Sekaran, U. (1986). *Dual-career families*. San Francisco, CA: Jossey-Bass.

Seligman, M. E. P. (1995). The effectiveness of psychotherapy: The *Consumer Reports* study. *The American Psychologist*, *50*, 965–974.

Sell, J. M., Gottlieb, M. C., & Schoenfeld, L. S. (1986). Ethical considerations of social/romantic relationships with present and former clients. *Professional Psychology: Research and Practice*, *17*, 504–508.

Sexton, T. L., & Liddle, M. C. (2001). Practicing evidence-based mental health: Using research and measuring outcomes. In E. R. Welfel & R. E. Ingersoll (Eds.), *The mental health desk reference: A practice-based guide to diagnosis, treatment, and professional ethics*. New York, NY: Wiley.

Sexton, T. L., Whiston, S. C., Bleuer, J. C., & Walz, G. R. (1997). *Integrating outcome research into counseling practice and training*. Alexandria, VA: American Counseling Association.

Sexual harassment: A female counseling student's experience. (1991). *Journal of Counseling & Development, 69*, 502–506.

Shapiro, D. L., & Smith, S. R. (2011). *Malpractice in psychology*. Washington, D.C.: American Psychological Association.

Sharkin, B. S., & Plageman, P. M. (2003). What do psychologists think about mandatory continuing education? A survey of Pennsylvania practitioners. *Professional Psychology: Research and Practice, 34*, 318–323.

Shavit, N. (2005). Sexual contact between psychologists and patients. *Journal of Aggression, Maltreatment, and Trauma, 11*, 205–239.

Shaw, G. B. (1903). *Man and Superman*. London: Constable.

Shaw, H. E., & Shaw, S. F. (2006). Critical ethical issues in online counseling: Assessing current practices with an Ethical Intent Checklist. *Journal of Counseling & Development, 84*, 41–53.

Shaw, L. R., Chan, F., Lam, C. S., & McDougall, A. G. (2004). Professional disclosure practices of rehabilitation counselors. *Rehabilitation Counseling Bulletin, 48*, 38–50.

Shead, N. W., & Dobson, K. S. (2004). Psychology for sale: The ethics of advertising professional services. *Canadian Psychology, 45*, 126–136.

Shearer, R. A. (2003). Court ordered counseling: An ethical minefield for psychotherapists. *Annals of the American Psychotherapy Association, 6*, 8–11.

Shechtman, A. (2002). Child group psychotherapy in the school at the threshold of a millennium. *Journal of Counseling & Development, 80*, 293–299.

Shechtman, A., & Yanuv, H. (2001). Interpretive interventions: Feedback, confrontation, and interpretation. *Group Dynamics, 5*, 124–135.

Shen-Miller, D. S., Grus, C. L., Van Sickle, K. S., Schwartz-Mette, R., Cage, E. A., Elman, N. S., & Kaslow, N. J. (2011). Trainees' experiences with peers having competence problems: A national survey. *Training and Education in Professional Psychology, 5*, 112–121.

Shepard, M. (1972). *The love treatment*. New York, NY: Paperback Library.

Sherman, W. J., Stroessner, S. J., Conrey, F. R., & Azam, O. A. (2005). Prejudice and stereotype maintenance processes: Attention, attribution, and individuation. *Journal of Personality and Social Psychology, 89*, 607–622.

Sherry, P., Teschendorf, R., Anderson, S., & Guzman, F. (1991). Ethical beliefs and behaviors of counseling center professionals. *Journal of College Student Development, 32*, 350–358.

Shiles, M. (2009). Discriminatory referrals: Uncovering a potential ethical dilemma facing practitioners. *Ethics & Behavior, 19*, 142–155.

Shuman, D. W., & Foote, W. (1999). *Jaffee v. Redmond*'s impact: Life after the Supreme Court's recognition of a psychotherapist-patient privilege. *Professional Psychology: Research and Practice, 30*, 479–487.

Sieber, J. E., & Tolich, M. B. (2013). *Planning ethically responsible research: A guide for students and internal review boards* (2nd ed.). Newbury Park, CA: Sage.

Siegel, S. J. (1991). *What to do when psychotherapy goes wrong*. Las Vegas, NV: Priority One Consultants.

Simon, R. I. (1991). Psychological injury caused by boundary violation precursors to therapist-patient sex. *Psychiatric Annals, 21*, 614–619.

Simon, R. I. (1992). Treatment of boundary violations: Clinical, ethical and legal considerations. *Bulletin of the American Academy of Psychiatry and the Law, 20*, 269–288.

Simon, R. I., & Shuman, D. W. (2007). *Clinical manual of psychiatry and the law*. Washington, D.C.: American Psychiatric Press.

Simpson case: Confidences survive clients. (1994, September). *National Association of Social Workers Newsletter*, p. 8.

Simpson, L. E., Doss, B. D., Wheeler, J., & Christensen, A. (2007). Relationship violence among couples seeking therapy: Common couple violence or battering? *Journal of Marital and Family Therapy, 33*, 270–283.

Sinnot-Armstrong, W. (Ed.). (2008). *Moral Psychology: The Neuroscience of Morality: Emotion, Brain Disorders, and Development* (Vol. 3). Cambridge, MA: MIT Press.

Skovholt, T. M. (2001). *The resilient practitioner: Burnout prevention and self-care strategies for counselors, therapists, teachers, and health professionals*. Boston, MA: Allyn & Bacon.

Skovholt, T. M., & Starkey, M. T. (2010). The three legs of the practitioner's learning stool: Practice, research/theory, and personal life. *Journal of Contemporary Psychotherapy, 40*, 125–130.

Sleek, S. (1994, December). Ethical dilemmas plague rural practice. *APA Monitor*, 26–27.

Slimp, P. A. O., & Burian, B. K. (1994). Multiple role relationships during internship: Consequences and recommendations. *Professional Psychology: Research and Practice, 25*, 39–45.

Slovenko, R. (1980). Legal issues in psychotherapy supervision. In A. K. Hess (Ed.), *Psychotherapy supervision: Theory, research and practice* (pp. 453–473). New York, NY: Wiley.

Slovenko, R. (2000). Psychiatric opinion without examination. *Journal of Psychiatry & Law, 28*, 103–143.

Smith, A., & Duggan, M. (2013). Online dating and relationships. Pew Internet Research Project. Retrieved from http://www.pewinternet.org/2013/10/21/online-dating-relationships/

Smith, D., & Dumont F. (1995). A cautionary study: Unwarranted interpretations of the draw-a-person test. *Professional Psychology: Research and Practice, 23*, 298–303.

Smith, D., & Fitzpatrick, M. (1995). Patient-therapist boundary issues: An integrative review of theory and research. *Professional Psychology: Research and Practice, 26*, 499–506.

Smith, E. W. L., Clance, P. R., & Imes, S. (1998). *Touch in psychotherapy: Theory, research, and practice*. New York, NY: Guilford.

Smith, J. A., Pomerantz, A. M., Pettibone, H. C., & Segrist, D. J. (2012). When does a professional relationship begin? An empirical investigation. *Ethics & Behavior, 22*, 208–217.

Smith, P. L., & Moss, S. B. (2009). Psychologist impairment: What is it, how can it be prevented, and what can be done to address it? *Clinical Psychology: Science and Practice, 16*, 1–15.

Smith, R. L. (1999). Client confidentiality in marriage and family counseling. In P. Stevens (Ed.), *Ethical casebook for the practice of marriage and family counseling* (pp. 83–92). Alexandria, VA: American Counseling Association.

Smith, S. R. (1996). Malpractice liability of mental health professionals and institutions. In B. D. Sales & D. W. Shuman, D. W. (Eds.), *Law, mental health, and mental disorder* (pp. 76–98). Pacific Grove, CA: Brooks/Cole.

Smith, S. R., & Meyer, R. G. (1987). *Law, behavior and mental health policy and practice*. New York: New York University Press.

Smith, T. S., McGuire, J. M., Abbott, D. W., & Blau, B. I. (1991). Clinical ethical decision making: An investigation of the rationales used to justify doing less than one believes one should. *Professional Psychology: Research and Practice, 22*, 235–239.

Smokowski, P. R., Rose, S. D., & Bacallao, M. L. (2001). Damaging experiences in therapeutic groups: How vulnerable consumers become group casualties. *Small Group Research, 32*, 223–251.

Snyder, D. K. (2000). Computer-assisted judgment: Defining strengths and weaknesses. *Psychological Assessment, 12*, 52–60.

Sobel, S. B. (1992). Small town practice of psychotherapy: Ethical and personal dilemmas. *Psychotherapy in Private Practice, 10*, 61–69.

Society for Adolescent Medicine. (2004). Confidential health care for adolescents: Position paper of the Society for Adolescent Medicine. *Journal of Adolescent Health, 35*, 160–167.

Society for Personality Assessment (SPA). (2006). Standards for education and training in psychological assessment. *Journal of Personality Assessment, 87*, 355–357.

Society for Research in Child Development (SRCD). (2007). Ethical standards for research with children. Retrieved from http://www.srcd.org/index.php?option=com_content&task=view&id=68&Itemid=110

Sodowsky, G. R., Taffe, R. C., Gutlin, T. B., & Wise, S. L. (1994). Development of the Multicultural Counseling Inventory: A self-report measure of multicultural competencies. *Journal of Counseling Psychology, 41*, 137–148.

Soet, J., & Sevig, T. (2006). Mental health issues facing a diverse sample of college students: Results from the college student mental health survey. *NASPA Journal, 41*, 410–429.

Soisson, E. L., VandeCreek, L. D., & Knapp, S. J. (1987). Thorough record keeping: A good defense in a litigious era. *Professional Psychology: Research and Practice, 18*, 498–502.

Somberg, D. R. (1997). The influence of narcissism on psychologists' moral sensitivity. *Dissertation Abstracts International: Section B, The Sciences and Engineering, 55*(9), 5577.

Somberg, D. R., Stone, G. L., & Claiborn, C. D. (1993). Informed consent: Therapists' beliefs and practices. *Professional Psychology: Research and Practice, 24*, 153–159.

Somer, E., & Nachmani, I. (2005). Constructions of therapist-client sex: A comparative analysis of reconstructive victim reports. *Sexual Abuse: A Journal of Research and Treatment, 17*, 47–62.

Somer, E., & Saadon, M. (1999). Therapist-client sex: Clients' retrospective reports. *Professional Psychology: Research and Practice, 30*, 504–509.

Sommers-Flanagan, R. (2012). Boundaries, multiple roles, and the professional relationship. In S. J. Knapp, M. C. Gottlieb, M. M. Handelsman, & L. D. VandeCreek (Eds.), *APA handbook of ethics in psychology* (Vol. 1, pp. 241–278). Washington, D.C.: American Psychological Association.

Sommers-Flanagan, R., Elliott, D., & Sommers-Flanagan, J. (1998). Exploring the edges: Boundaries and breaks. *Ethics & Behavior, 8*, 37–48.

Sommers-Flanagan, R., & Sommers-Flanagan, J. (2007). *Becoming an ethical helping professional: Cultural and philosophical foundations*. Hoboken, NJ: Wiley.

Sonne, J. L. (1987). Proscribed sex: Counseling the patient subjected to sexual intimacy by a therapist. *Medical Aspects of Human Sexuality, 16*, 18–23.

Sonne, J. L. (1994). Multiple relationships: Does the new ethics code answer the right questions? *Professional Psychology: Research and Practice, 25*, 336–343.

Sonne, J. L. (2012). Sexualized relationships. In S. J. Knapp, M. C. Gottleib, M. M. Handelsman, & L. D. VandeCreek (Eds.), *APA handbook of ethics in psychology* (Vol. 1, pp. 291–310). Washington, D.C.: American Psychological Association.

Sonne, J. L., & Jochai, D. (2014). The "vicissitudes of love" between therapist and patient: A review of the research on romantic and sexual feelings, thoughts, and behaviors in psychotherapy. *Journal of Clinical Psychology, 70*, 182–195.

Sonne, J. L., Meyer, C., Borys, D., & Marshall, V. (1985). Clients' reactions to sexual intimacy in therapy. *American Journal of Orthopsychiatry, 55*, 183–189.

Sonne, J. L., & Pope, K. S. (1991). Treating victims of therapist-patient sexual involvement. *Psychotherapy: Theory/Research/Practice/Training, 28*, 174–187.

Sorenson, G., & Chapman, D. W. (1985). School compliance with federal law concerning the release of student records. *Educational Evaluation & Policy Analysis, 7*, 9–18.

Sorensen, J. L., Masson, C. L., Clark, W. W., & Morin, S. F. (1998). Providing public testimony: A guide for psychologists. *Professional Psychology: Research and Practice, 29*, 588–593.

Spengler, P. (2000). Does vocational overshadowing even exist? A test of the robustness of the vocational overshadowing bias. *Journal of Counseling Psychology, 47*, 342–351.

Spengler, P. M., White, M. J., Ægisdóttir, S., Maugherman, A. S., Anderson, L. A., Cook, R. S., & Rush, J. D. (2009). The meta-analysis of clinical judgment project: Effects of experience on judgment accuracy. *The Counseling Psychologist*, *37*, 350–399.

Spitzer, R. L. (1975). On pseudoscience in science, logic in remission, and psychiatric diagnosis: A critique of Rosenhan's "On being sane in insane places." *Journal of Abnormal Psychology*, *84*, 442–452.

Sporakowski, M. J., Prouty, A. M., & Habben, C. (2001). Assessment in couple and family counseling. In E. R. Welfel & R. E. Ingersoll (Eds.), *The mental health desk reference: A practice-based guide to diagnosis, treatment, and professional ethics* (pp. 372–378). New York, NY: Wiley.

Sprague, R. L. (1993). Whistleblowing: A very unpleasant avocation. *Ethics & Behavior*, *3*, 103–133.

Spruill, J., Rozensky, R. H., Stigall, T. T., Vasquez, M. J. T., Bingham, R. P., & Olvey, C. D. (2004). Becoming a competent clinician: Basic competencies in intervention. *Journal of Clinical Psychology*, *60*, 741–754.

Stadler, H. A., Willing, K. L., Eberhage, M. G., & Ward, W. H. (1988). Impairment: Implications for the counseling profession. *Journal of Counseling & Development*, *66*, 258–260.

Stahl, P. M. (1999). *Complex issues in child custody evaluations*. Thousand Oaks, CA: Sage.

Stake, J. E., & Oliver, J. (1991). Sexual contact and touching between therapist and client: A survey of psychologists' attitudes and behavior. *Professional Psychology: Research and Practice*, *22*, 297–307.

Steinberg, K. L. (1994). In the service of two masters: Psychotherapists struggle with child maltreatment reporting laws. *Dissertation Abstracts International: Section B, The Sciences and Engineering*, *55*(4), 2412.

Stenzel, C. L., & Rupert, P. A. (2004). Psychologists' use of touch in individual psychotherapy. *Psychotherapy: Theory, Research, Practice, Training*, *41*, 332–347.

Stevanovic, P., & Rupert, P. A. (2004). Career-sustaining behaviors, satisfactions, and stresses of professional psychologists. *Psychotherapy: Theory, Research, Practice, Training*, *41*, 301–309.

St. Germaine, J. (1997). Ethical practices of certified addiction counselors: A national survey of state certification boards. *Alcoholism Treatment Quarterly*, *15*, 63–72.

Stodghill, M. (2011, February 23). Patient from Duluth sues therapist, Essential Health over loan. Duluth News-Tribune (MN).

Stokes, L., & Remley, T. P., Jr. (2001). Counselors in forensic settings. In E. R. Welfel & R. E. Ingersoll (Eds.), *The mental health desk reference: A practice-based guide to diagnosis, treatment, and professional ethics* (pp. 404–411). New York, NY: Wiley.

Stokes, T. J. (1999). Sexual orientation and clinical decisions. *Dissertation Abstracts International: Section B, The Sciences and Engineering*, *59*(10), 4488.

Stoller, R. J. (1988). Patients' responses to their own case reports. *Journal of the American Psychoanalytic Association*, *36*, 371–391.

Stone, C. (2009). *School counseling principles: Ethics and law* (2nd ed.). Washington, D.C.: American School Counselor Association.

Stone, C. B. (2002). Negligence in academic advising and abortion counseling: Courts rulings and implications. *Professional School Counseling*, *6*, 28–35.

Stone, C. B. (2005). Students' self-direction and autonomy: Educating versus directing. *ASCA School Counselor*, *42*, 6–7.

Stone, C. B., & Zirkel, P. A. (2010). School counselor advocacy: When law and ethics may collide. *Professional School Counseling*, *13*(4), 244–247.

Stone, C. B., & Isaacs, M. I. (2003). Confidentiality with minors: The need for policy to promote and protect. *Journal of Educational Research*, *96*, 140–147.

Stopbullying.gov. (2014). Take action today: How mental health professionals can prevent bullying. Retrieved from http://www.stopbullying.gov/blog/2014/03/04/take-action-today-how-mental-health-professionals-can-prevent-bullying

Strom-Gottfried, K. (1999). Professional boundaries: An analysis of violations by social workers. *Families in Society*, *80*, 439–449.

Strom-Gottfried, K. (2003). Understanding adjudication: Origins, targets, and outcomes of ethics complaints. *Social Work*, *48*, 85–94.

Strom-Gottfried, K. (2008). *Ethics of practice with minors*. Chicago, IL: Lyceum.

Strozier, M., Brown, R., Fennell, M., Hardee, J., & Vogel, R. (2005). Experiences of mandated reporting among family therapists. *Contemporary Family Therapy: An International Journal*, *27*, 177–191.

Sturdivant, S. (1993). The ethics of marketing a private practice. *Psychotherapy in Private Practice*, *12*, 23–28.

Substance Abuse and Mental Health Services Administration (SAMHSA). (2010). Mental health findings. Retrieved from http://www.samhsa.gov/data/nsduh/2k10MH_Findings/

Substance Abuse and Mental Health Services Administration (SAMHSA). (2014). Health care integration initiatives. Retrieved from http://beta.samhsa.gov/health-reform/health-care-integration

Sude, M. E. (2013). Text messaging and private practice: Ethical challenges and guidelines for developing personal best practices. *Journal of Mental Health Counseling*, *25*, 211–227.

Sue, D. W. (2005). Racism and the conspiracy of silence: Presidential address. *The Counseling Psychologist*, *33*, 100–114.

Sue, D. W. (2010). *Microaggressions in everyday life: Race, gender, and sexual orientation*. Hoboken, NJ: Wiley.

Sue, D. W., Bucceri, J., Lin, A. I., Nadal, K. L., & Torino, G. C. (2007). Racial microaggressions and the Asian-American experience. *Cultural Diversity and Ethnic Minority Psychology*, *13*, 72–81.

Sue, D. W., Capodilupo, C. M., Torino, G. C., Bucceri, J. M., Holder, A. M. B., Nadal, K. L., … & Esquilin, M. (2007). Racial microaggressions in everyday life: Implications for clinical practice. *American Psychologist*, *62*, 271–286.

Sue, D. W., Ivey, A. E., & Pedersen, P. B. (1996). *A theory of multicultural counseling and therapy*. Pacific Grove, CA: Brooks/Cole.

Sue, D. W., & Sue, D. (2012). *Counseling the culturally divers: Theory and practice* (6th ed.). New York, NY: Wiley.

Sullivan, K., & Zirkel, P. (1999). Student to student sexual harassment: Which tack will the Supreme Court take in a sea of analyses? *West Education Law Reporter*, *132*, 609–628.

Sullivan, T., Martin, W. L., & Handelsman, M. M. (1993). Practical benefits of an informed-consent procedure: An empirical investigation. *Professional Psychology: Research and Practice*, *24*, 160–163.

Sutter, E., McPherson, R. H., & Geeseman, R. (2002). Contracting for supervision. *Professional Psychology: Research and Practice*, *33*, 495–498.

Suzuki, L. A., & Kugler, J. F. (2001). Multicultural assessment. In E. R. Welfel & R. E. Ingersoll (Eds.), *The mental health desk reference: A practice-based guide to diagnosis, treatment, and professional ethics* (pp. 279–285). New York, NY: Wiley.

Suzuki, L. A., Ponterotto, J. G., & Meller, P. J. (2008). *Handbook of multicultural assessment: Clinical, psychological and educational applications* (3rd ed.). San Francisco, CA: Jossey-Bass.

Swenson, L. C. (1997). *Psychology and law for the helping professions* (2nd ed.). Pacific Grove, CA: Brooks/Cole.

Szasz, T. S. (1971). The sane slave. An historical note on the use of medical diagnosis as justificatory rhetoric. *American Journal of Psychotherapy*, *25*, 228–239.

Szasz, T. S. (1973). *The second sin*. Garden City, NJ: Anchor.

Tabachnick, B. G., Keith-Spiegel, P. S., & Pope, K. S. (1991). Ethics of teaching: Beliefs and behaviors of psychologists as educators. *American Psychologist*, *46*, 506–515.

Talbert, F. S., & Pipes, R. B. (1988). Informed consent for psychotherapy: Content analysis of selected forms. *Professional Psychology: Research and Practice*, *19*, 131–132.

Tarasoff v. Regents of the University of California, 118 Cal. Rptr. 129, 529 P. 2d 533. (1974).

Tarasoff v. Regents of the University of California, 131 Cal. Rptr. 14, 551 P. 2d 334. (1976).

Tarvydas, V. M., Leahy, M. J., & Saunders, J. L. (2004). A comparison of the ethical beliefs of certified rehabilitation counselors and national certified counselors. *Rehabilitation Counseling Bulletin*, *47*, 234–246.

Taylor, L., & Adelman, H. (1998). Confidentiality: Competing principles, inevitable dilemmas. *Journal of Educational and Psychological Consultation*, *9*, 267–275.

Taylor, L., & Adelman, H. S. (1989). Reframing the confidentiality dilemma to work in children's best interests. *Professional Psychology: Research and Practice*, *20*, 79–83.

Taylor, L., & Adelman, H. S. (2001). Enlisting appropriate parental cooperation and involvement in children's mental health treatment. In E. R. Welfel & R. E. Ingersoll (Eds.), *Mental health desk reference: A practice-based guide to diagnosis, treatment, and professional ethics* (pp. 219–224). New York, NY: Wiley.

Taylor, L., Adelman, H. S., & Kaser-Boyd, N. (1984). Attitudes towards involving minors in decisions. *Professional Psychology: Research and Practice*, *15*, 436–449.

Taylor, L., McMinn, M. R., Bufford, R. K., & Change, K. B. T. (2010). Psychologists' attitudes and ethical concerns regarding the use of social networking web sites. *Professional Psychology: Research and Practice*, *41*, 153–159.

Taylor, R. E., & Gazda, G. M. (1991). Concurrent individual and group therapy: The ethical issues. *Journal of Group Psychotherapy, Psychodrama, and Sociometry*, *44*, 51–59.

Teisman, M. (1980). Convening strategies in family therapy. *Family Process*, *19*, 393–400.

Texas Health & Safety Code § 611.004(a)(2). (1995).

Thomas, J. T. (2005). Licensing board complaints: Minimizing the impact on the psychologist's defense and clinical practice. *Professional Psychology: Research and Practice*, *36*, 426–433.

Thomas, J. T. (2010). *The ethics of supervision and consultation: Practical guidance for mental health professionals*. Washington, D.C.: American Psychological Association.

Thompson, I. S., Amatea, E. S., & Thompson, E. S. (2014). Personal and contextual predictors of mental health counselors' compassion fatigue and burnout. *Journal of Mental Health Counseling*, *36*, 58–77.

Thompson, T. L. (1999). Managed care: Views, practices, and burnout of psychologists. *Dissertation Abstracts International: Section B, The Sciences and Engineering*, *60*(4), 1318.

Thoreson, R. W., Miller, M., & Krauskopf, C. J. (1989). The distressed psychologist: Prevalence and treatment considerations. *Professional Psychology: Research and Practice*, *20*, 153–158.

Thoreson, R. W., Shaughnessy, P., & Frazier, P. A. (1995). Sexual contact during and after professional relationships: Practices and attitudes of female counselors. *Journal of Counseling & Development*, *74*, 84–89.

Thoreson, R. W., Shaughnessy, P., Heppner, P. P., & Cook, S. W. (1993). Sexual contact during and after the professional relationships: Attitudes and practices of male counselors. *Journal of Counseling & Development*, *71*, 429–434.

Thorn, B. E., Shealy, R. C., & Briggs, S. D. (1993). Sexual misconduct in psychotherapy: Reactions to a consumer-oriented brochure. *Professional Psychology: Research and Practice*, *24*, 75–82.

Timmons, S., Bryant, J., Platt, R. A., & Netko, D. (2010). Ethical and clinical issues with intimate partner violence. In L. Heckler (Ed.), *Ethics and professional issues in couple and family therapy* (pp. 107–130). New York, NY: Routledge.

Tirnauer, L., Smith, E., & Foster, P. (1996). The American Academy of Psychotherapists research committee survey of members. *Voices*, *32*, 87–94.

Tjeltveit, A. C., & Gottlieb, M. C. (2010). Avoiding the road to ethical disaster: Overcoming vulnerabilities and developing resilience. *Psychotherapy: Theory, Research, Practice, Training*, *47*, 98–110.

Tobias, A. K., & Myrick, R. D. (1999). A peer facilitator-led intervention with middle school problem behavior students. *Professional School Counseling*, *3*, 27–33.

Tompkins, L., & Mehring, T. (1993). Client privacy and the school counselor: Privilege, ethics and employer policies. *The School Counselor*, *40*, 335–342.

Toporek, R. L., & Reza, J. V. (2001). Context as a critical dimension of multicultural counseling: Articulating personal, professional, and institutional competence. *Journal of Multicultural Counseling and Development*, *29*, 13–30.

Treloar, H. R. (2010). Financial and ethical considerations, for professionals in psychology. *Ethics & Behavior*, *20*, 454–465.

Treppa, J. A. (1998). A practitioner's guide to ethical decision making. In R. M. Anderson, T. L. Needels, & H. V. Hall (Eds.), *Avoiding ethical misconduct in psychology specialty areas* (pp. 26–41). Springfield, IL: Charles C. Thomas.

Trice-Black, S., Riechel, M. E. K., & Shillingford, M. A. (2013). School counselors' constructions of student confidentiality. *Journal of School Counseling*, *11*(12). Retrieved from http://jsc.montana.edu/articles/v11n12.pdf

Trippany, R. L., Kress, V. E. W., & Wilcoxon, S. A. (2004). Preventing vicarious trauma: What counselors should know when working with trauma survivors. *Journal of Counseling & Development*, *82*, 31–37.

Trippany, R. L., Wilcoxon, S. A., & Satcher, J. F. (2003). Factors influencing vicarious trauma for therapists of survivors of sexual victimization. *Journal of Trauma Practice*, 2, 47–60.

Truman v. Thomas, California, 611 p. 2d 902, 27 Cal. 3d 285. (1980).

Truscott, D. (2013, August). *Incorporating non-rational reasoning into ethics education in professional psychology*. Paper presented at the annual meeting of the American Psychological Association, Honolulu, HI.

Truscott, D., & Crook, K. H. (2013). *Ethics for the practice of psychology in Canada, Revised and expanded edition*. Edmonton, AL: University of Alberta.

Truscott, D., & Evans, J. (2001). Responding to dangerous clients. In E. R. Welfel & R. E. Ingersoll (Eds.), *The mental health desk reference: A practice-based guide to diagnosis, treatment, and professional ethics* (pp. 271–276). New York, NY: Wiley.

Truscott, D., & Evans, J. (2009). Protecting others from homicide and serious harm. In J. L. Werth, E. R. Welfel, & G. A. H. Benjamin (Eds.), *The duty to protect: Ethical, legal, and professional responsibilities of mental health professionals* (pp. 61–77). Washington, D.C.: American Psychological Association.

Truscott, D., Evans, J., & Mansell, S. (1995). Outpatient psychotherapy with dangerous clients: A model for clinical decision making. *Professional Psychology: Research and Practice*, *26*, 484–490.

Tryon, G. S., Bishop, J. L., & Hatfield, T. A. (2007). Doctoral students' beliefs about authorship credit for dissertations. *Training and Education in Professional Psychology*, *1*, 184–192.

Tubbs, P., & Pomerantz, A. M. (2001). Ethical behavior of psychologists: Changes since 1987. *Journal of Clinical Psychology*, *57*, 395–399.

Turner, S. M., DeMers, S. T., Fox, H. R., & Reed, G.M. (2001). APA's Guidelines for test user qualifications: An executive summary. *American Psychologist*, *56*, 1099–1113.

Tziporah, R., & Pace, M. (2006). Burnout among mental health professionals: Special considerations for the marriage and family therapist. *Journal of Marital and Family Therapy*, *32*, 87–99.

United Nations. (1948). Universal declaration of human rights. http://www.un.org/en/documents/udhr/

United States v. Chase, 340 F.3d 978 (9th Cir., August 22, 2003).

Urbina, S., & Anastasi, A. (1997). *Psychological testing* (7th ed.). New York, NY: Macmillan.

Urofsky, R., & Sowa, C. (2004). Ethics education in CACREP-accredited counselor education programs. *Counseling and Values*, *49*, 37–47.

Urofsky, R. I., & Engels, D. W. (2003). Philosophy, moral philosophy, and counseling ethics: Not an abstraction. *Counseling and Values*, *47*, 118–130.

U.S. Census Bureau. (2006). U.S. interim projections by age, sex, race, and Hispanic origin: 2000–2050. Retrieved from http://www.census.gov/ipc/www/usinterimproj/

U.S. Census Bureau. (2010a). Age and sex composition, 2010. Retrieved from http://www.census.gov/prod/cen2010/briefs/c2010br-03.pdf

U.S. Census Bureau. (2010b). Race and Hispanic origin in 2010. Retrieved from https://www.census.gov/content/dam/Census/library/publications/2011/demo/c2010br-02.pdf

U.S. Census Bureau. (2011). American community survey data on language use. Retrieved from https://www.census.gov/hhes/socdemo/language/data/acs/

U.S. Census Bureau. (2013). Asians the fastest growing ethic group or race in 2012. Retrieved from https://www.census.gov/newsroom/releases/archives/population/cb13-112.html

U.S. Department of Health and Human Services. (2006). Mental health and rural America 1994–2005. Retrieved from ftp://ftp.hrsa.gov/ruralhealth/RuralMentalHealth.pdf

U.S. Department of Health and Human Services. (2014). Child maltreatment 2012. Retrieved from https://www.childwelfare.gov/pubs/factsheets/canstats.cfm

Uthe-Burow, C. M. (2002). An exploratory study of ethical training as a factor of moral development. *Dissertation Abstracts International: Section A, The Humanities and Social Sciences*, *63*(8), 2312.

Vacha-Haase, T., Davenport, D. S., & Kerewsky, S. D. (2004). Problematic students: Gatekeeping practices of academic professional psychology programs. *Professional Psychology: Research and Practice*, *35*, 115–122.

Valliant, G. E. (1984). The disadvantages of DSM-III outweigh its advantages. *American Journal of Psychiatry*, *141*, 542–545.

VandeCreek, L. D., & Jackson, T. L. (Eds.). (2000). *Innovations in clinical practice: A sourcebook* (pp. 441–453). Sarasota, FL: Professional Resource Press.

VandeCreek, L. D., Knapp, S. J., & Brace, K. (1990). Mandatory continuing education for licensed psychologists: Its rationale and current implementation. *Professional Psychology: Research and Practice*, *21*, 135–140.

VandeCreek, L. D., Miars, R., & Herzog, C. (1987). Client anticipations and preferences for confidentiality of records. *Journal of Counseling Psychology*, *34*, 62–67.

Vander Kolk, C. J. (1974). The relationship of personality, values and race to anticipation of the supervisory relationship. *Rehabilitation Counseling Bulletin*, *18*, 41–46.

Vanek, C. A. (1990). Survey of ethics education in clinical and counseling psychology. *Dissertation Abstracts International: Section B, The Sciences and Engineering*, *52*(8), 5797.

VanHoose, W. H., & Kottler, J. A. (1985). *Ethical and legal issues in counseling and psychotherapy* (2nd ed.). San Francisco, CA: Jossey-Bass.

Van Horne, B. A. (2004). Psychology licensing board disciplinary actions: The realities. *Professional Psychology: Research and Practice*, *35*, 170–178.

Vansandt, C. V. (1992). An examination of the relationship between ethical work climate and moral awareness. *Dissertation Abstracts International: Section A, The Humanities and Social Sciences*, *62*(7), 2486.

Vasquez, M. J. T. (1988). Counselor client sexual contact: Implications for ethics training. *Journal of Counseling & Development*, *67*, 238–241.

Vasquez, M. J. T. (1992). Psychologist as clinical supervisor: Promoting ethical practice. *Professional Psychology: Research and Practice*, *23*, 196–202.

Vasquez, M. J. T. (2012). Social justice and civil virtue. In S. J. Knapp, M. C. Gottlieb, M. M. Handelsman, & L. D. VandeCreek (Eds.), *APA handbook of ethics in psychology* (Vol. 1, pp. 75–97). Washington, D.C.: American Psychological Association.

Vasquez, M. J. T., Bingham, R. P., & Barnett, J. E. (2008). Psychotherapy termination: Clinical and ethical responsibilities. *Journal of Clinical Psychology*, *64*, 653–665.

Vaughn, T. J. (2006). *Psychology licensure and certification: What students need to know*. Washington, D.C.: American Psychological Association.

Verges, A. (2010). Integrating contextual issues into ethical decision making. *Ethics & Behavior*, *20*, 407–507.

Vinson, J. S. (1987). Use of complaint procedures in cases of therapist-patient sexual misconduct. *Professional Psychology: Research and Practice*, *18*, 159–164.

Volker, J. M. (1983, August). *Counseling experience, moral judgment, awareness of consequences and moral sensitivity in counseling practice*. Paper presented at the annual meeting of the American Psychological Association, Toronto, Canada.

Wagner, C. (1978). Elementary school counselors' perceptions of confidentiality with children. *The School Counselor*, *25*, 240–248.

Wagner, C. (1981). Confidentiality and the school counselor. *The Personnel and Guidance Journal*, *59*, 305–310.

Wagner, L., Davis, S., & Handelsman, M. M. (1998). In search of the abominable consent form: The impact of readability and personalization. *Journal of Clinical Psychology*, *54*(1), 115–120.

Wakefield, J. C. (1992). The concept of mental disorder: On the boundary between biological facts and social values. *American Psychologist*, *47*, 373–388.

Walden v. Centers for Disease Control and Prevention. No. 1:08-cv-02278-JEC (United States District Court for the Northern District of Georgia, March 18, 2010).

Walfish, S., Barnett, J. E., Marlyere, K., & Zielke, R. (2010). "Doc, there's something I have to tell you": Patient disclosure to their psychotherapist of unprosecuted murder and other violence. *Ethics & Behavior*, *20*, 311–323.

Walfish, S., & Ducey, B. B. (2007). Readability level of Health Insurance Portability and Accountability Act Notices of Privacy Practices used by psychologists in clinical practice. *Professional Psychology: Research and Practice*, *38*, 203–207.

Walfish, S., McAlister, B., O'Donnell, P., & Lambert, M. L. (2012). An investigation of self assessment bias in mental health professionals. *Psychological Reports*, *110*, 639–644.

Wall, A. (2009). Psychology interns' perceptions of supervisor ethical behavior. *Dissertation Abstracts International: Section B, The Sciences and Engineering*, *70*(8), 3799.

Walsh, W. B., & Betz, N. E. (1995). *Tests and assessment* (3rd ed.). Englewood Cliffs, NJ: Prentice Hall.

Walter, M. I., & Handelsman, M. M. (1996). Informed consent for mental health counseling: Effects of information specificity on clients' ratings of counselors. *Journal of Mental Health Counseling*, *18*, 253–262.

Wampold, B. E. (2001). *The great psychotherapy debate*. Mahwah, NJ: Lawrence Erlbaum.

Wampold, B. E. (2010). The research evidence for common factors models: A historically situated perspective. In B. L. Duncan, S. D. Miller, B. E. Wampold, & M. A. Hubble (Eds.), *The heart and soul of change* (2nd ed., pp. 49–82). Washington, D.C.: American Psychological Association.

Wangberg, S. C., Gammon, D., & Spitznogle, K. (2007). In the eyes of the beholder: Exploring psychologists' attitudes towards and use of e-therapy in Norway. *CyberPsychology & Behavior*, *10*, 418–423.

Ward v. Polite et al. 667 F. 3d 727. (2012).

Ward v. Wilbanks, No. 09-CV-11237, Doc. 139. (E.D. Mich., July 26, 2010).

Warren, E. S. (2005). Future colleague or convenient friend. *Counseling and Values*, *49*, 141–146.

Warwick, D., & Kelman, H. (1973). Ethical issues in social intervention. In G. Zaltman (Ed.), *Processes and phenomena of social change* (pp. 377–417). New York, NY: Wiley Interscience.

Watson, C. H. (1990). Gossip and the guidance counselor: An ethical dilemma. *The School Counselor*, *38*, 34–39.

Watson, H., & Levine, M. (1989). Psychotherapy and mandated reporting of child abuse. *American Journal of Psychiatry*, *59*, 246–256.

Watson, J. C., & Sheperis, C. J. (2010). *Counselors and the right to test: Working toward professional parity*. Alexandria, VA: American Counseling Association.

Webb, K. B. (2011). Care of others and self: A suicidal patient's impact on the psychologist. *Professional*

Psychology: Research and Practice, *42*, 215–221.

Wechsler, D. (2008). *Wechsler Adult Intelligence Scale IV*. San Antonio, TX: Pearson Assessments.

Weikel, W. J., & Hughes, P. R. (1993). *The counselor as expert witness*. In T. P. Remley (Ed.), *ACA Legal Series* (Vol. 5). Alexandria, VA: American Counseling Association.

Weiner, I. B. (1989). On competence and ethicality in psychodiagnostic assessment. *Journal of Personality Assessment*, *53*, 827–831.

Weisner, C., & Matzger, H. (2003). Missed opportunities in addressing drinking behavior in medical and mental health services. *Alcoholism: Clinical and Experimental Research*, *27*, 1132–1141.

Weithorn, L. A. (1983). Involving children in decisions affecting their own welfare: Guidelines for professionals. In G. B. Melton, G. P. Koocher, & M. J. Saks (Eds.), *Children's competence to consent* (pp. 235–260). New York, NY: Plenum.

Welfel, E. R. (1992). Psychologists as ethics educators: Successes, failures, and unanswered questions. *Professional Psychology: Research and Practice*, *23*, 182–189.

Welfel, E. R. (2001). Protecting clients' rights to privacy. In E. R. Welfel & R. E. Ingersoll (Eds.), *The mental health desk reference: A practice-based guide to diagnosis, treatment, and professional ethics* (pp. 447–452). New York, NY: Wiley.

Welfel, E. R. (2005). Accepting our fallibility: A model for personal responsibility for non-egregious ethics infractions. *Counseling and Values*, *49*, 120–131.

Welfel, E. R. (2009). Emerging issues in the duty to protect. In J. L. Werth, E. R. Welfel, & G. A. H. Benjamin (Eds.), *The duty to protect: Ethical, legal, and professional considerations in risk assessment and intervention* (pp. 229–248). Washington, D.C.: American Psychological Association.

Welfel, E. R. (2012). Teaching ethics: Models, methods, and challenges. In S. J. Knapp, M. C. Gottlieb, M. M. Handelsman, & L. D. VandeCreek (Eds.), *APA handbook of ethics in psychology* (Vol. 2, pp. 277–305). Washington, D.C.: American Psychological Association.

Welfel, E. R., & Bunce, R. (2003, August). How psychotherapists use electronic communication with current clients. Presented at the annual meeting of the American Psychological Association, Toronto, Canada.

Welfel, E. R., Danzinger, P. R., & Santoro, S. (2000). Mandated reporting of abuse/maltreatment of older adults: A primer for counselors. *Journal of Counseling & Development*, *78*, 284–292.

Welfel, E. R., & Hannigan-Farley, P. (1996). Ethics education in counseling: A survey of faculty and student views. *ICA Quarterly*, *140*, 24–33.

Welfel, E. R., & Heinlen, K. T. (2001). The responsible use of technology in mental health practice. In E. R. Welfel & R. E. Ingersoll (Eds.), *The mental health desk reference: A practice-based guide to diagnosis, treatment, and professional ethics* (pp. 484–489). New York, NY: Wiley.

Welfel, E. R., & Khamush, B. (2012). *Ethical standards, credentialing, and accountability: An international perspective*. In M. Leach, M. Stevens, A. Ferrero, Y. Korkut, & G. Lindsay, G. (Eds.). *International Handbook of Psychological Ethics* (pp. 289–315). Washington, D.C.: APA Press.

Welfel, E. R., & Lipsitz, N. E. (1983). Ethical orientation of counselors: Its relationship to moral reasoning and level of training. *Counselor Education and Supervision*, *22*, 35–45.

Welfel, E. R., & Patterson, L. E. (2004). *The counseling process* (6th ed.). Pacific Grove, CA: Brooks/Cole.

Wellman, M. M. (1984). The school counselor's role in the communication of suicidal ideation by adolescents. *The School Counselor*, *32*, 104–109.

Wells, K. B., Hays, R. D., Burman, A., Rogers, W., Greenfield, S., & Ware, J. E., Jr. (1989). Detection of depressive disorder for patients receiving prepaid or fee-for-service care. Results for the medical outcomes study. *Journal of the American Medical Association*, *262*, 3298–3302.

Werth, J. L., Jr., & Blevins, D. (2008). *Decision-making near the end of life: Recent developments and future directions*. Philadelphia, PA: Routledge.

Werth, J. L., Burke, C., & Bardash, R. J. (2002). Confidentiality in end-of-life and after-death situations. *Ethics & Behavior*, *12*, 205–222.

Werth, J. L., Jr., & Richmond, J. M. (2009). End-of life decisions and the duty to protect. In J. L. Werth, Jr., E. R. Welfel, & G. A. H. Benjamin (Eds.), *The duty to protect: Ethical, legal, and professional responsibilities of mental health professionals* (pp. 195–208). Washington, D.C.: American Psychological Association.

Werth, J. L., Jr., Welfel, E. R., & Benjamin, G. A. H. (Eds.). (2009). *The duty to protect: Ethical, legal, and professional responsibilities of mental health professionals*. Washington, D.C.: American Psychological Association.

Wester, K. L. (2007). Teaching research integrity in the field of counseling. *Counselor Education and Supervision*, *46*, 199–211.

Wheeler, A. M. N., & Bertram, B. (2012). *The counselor and the law: A guide to legal and ethical practice* (6th ed.). Alexandria, VA: American Counseling Association.

Whiston, S. C., & Emerson, S. (1989). Ethical implications for supervisors in counseling of trainees. *Counselor Education and Supervision*, *28*, 318–325.

Whiteley, J. M. (1984). A historical perspective on the development of counseling psychology as a profession. In S. D. Brown & R. W. Lent (Eds.), *Handbook of counseling psychology* (pp. 3–55). New York, NY: Wiley.

Whitman, J. S., Glosoff, H. L., Kocet, M. M., & Tarvydas, V. (2006). Ethical issues related to conversion or reparative therapy. Retrieved from http://www.counseling.org/news/updates/2013/01/16/ethical-issues-related-to-conversion-or-reparative-therapy

Whittinghill, K. (2002). Ethical considerations for the use of family therapy in substance abuse treatment. *The Family Journal*, *10*, 75–78.

Whybrow, A. (2008). Coaching psychology: Coming of age?. *International Coaching Psychology Review*, *3*, 227–240.

Wierzbicki, M., Siderits, M. A., Kuchan, A. M. (2012). Ethical questions addressed by a state psychological association. *Professional Psychology: Research and Practice, 43*, 280–285.

Wiger, D. (2005). *The clinical documentation sourcebook: The complete paperwork resource for your mental health practice* (3rd ed.). Hoboken, NJ: Wiley.

Wilcoxon, S. A., & Fennel, D. L. (1983). Engaging the non-attending spouse in marital therapy through the use of therapist-initiated written communication. *Journal of Marital and Family Therapy, 9*, 199–203.

Wilcoxon, S. A., Gladding, S. T., Remley, T. P., Jr., & Huber, C. H. (2011). *Ethical, legal, and professional issues in the practice of marriage and family therapy* (5th ed.). Englewood Cliffs, NJ: Prentice Hall.

Wilcoxon, S. A., & Magnuson, S. (1999). Considerations for school counselors serving noncustodial parents: Premises and suggestions. *Professional School Counseling, 2*, 275–279.

Wilkins, M., McGuire, J. M., Abbott, D. W., & Blau, B. I. (1990). Willingness to apply understood ethical principles. *Journal of Clinical Psychology, 46*, 539–547.

Williams, G. T. (1996). A group leader's risky interventions. In B. Herlihy & G. Corey (Eds.), *ACA Ethical Standards casebook* (pp. 237–240). Alexandria, VA: American Counseling Association.

Williams, M. H. (1992). Exploitation and interference: Mapping the damage from patient-therapist sexual involvement. *American Psychologist, 47*, 412–421.

Williams, M. H. (2000). Victimized by "victims": A taxonomy of antecedents of false complaints against psychotherapists. *Professional Psychology: Research and Practice, 31*, 75–81.

Williams, P., & Anderson, S. K. (2006). *Law and ethics in coaching*. New York, NY: Wiley.

Williams, S., & Halgin, R. P. (1995). Issues in psychotherapy supervision between the white supervisor and the black supervisee. *The Clinical Supervisor, 13*, 39–61.

Willison, B. G., & Masson, R. L. (1986). The role of touch in therapy: An adjunct to communication. *Journal of Counseling & Development, 64*, 497–500.

Wilson, L. S., & Ranft, V. A. (1993). The state of ethical training for counseling psychology doctoral students. *The Counseling Psychologist, 21*, 445–456.

Wincze, J. P., Richards, J., Parsons, J., & Bailey, S. (1996). A comparative survey of therapist sexual misconduct between an American state and an Australian state. *Professional Psychology: Research and Practice, 27*, 289–294.

Winter, G. (2004, July 8). Wooing of school counselors in raising profiles and eyebrows. *New York Times*. Retrieved from http://query.nytimes.com/gst/fullpage.html?res=9804E5DF123BF93BA35754C0A9629C8B63

Wise, E. H., Hersh, M. A., & Gibson, C. M. (2012). Ethics, self care and well being for psychologists: Re-envisioning the stress-distress continuum. *Professional Psychology: Research and Practice, 43*, 487–494.

Wise, E. H., Strum, C. A., Nutt, R. L, Rodolfa, E., Schaffer, J. B., & Webb, C. (2010). Life-long learning for psychologists: Current status and a vision for the future. *Professional Psychology: Research and Practice, 41*, 288–297.

Wise, P. S., Lowery, S., & Silverglade, L. (1989). Personal counseling or counselors in training: Guidelines for supervisors. *Counselor Education and Supervision, 28*, 326–336.

Wohlberg, J. W. (2000). Sexual abuse in the therapeutic setting: What do victims really want? *Psychoanalytic Inquiry: A Topical Journal for Mental Health Professionals, 17*, 329–348.

Wolberg, L. R. (1967). *The technique of psychotherapy* (2nd ed.). New York, NY: Grune & Stratton.

Wood, B., Klein, S., Cross, H., Lammers, C., & Elliott, J. (1985). Impaired practitioners: Psychologists' opinions about prevalence and prognosis for intervention. *Professional Psychology: Research and Practice, 16*, 843–850.

Woody, R. H. (1988). *Protecting your mental health practice: How to minimize legal and financial risk*. San Francisco, CA: Jossey-Bass.

Woody, R. H. (1997). Dubious and bogus credentials in mental health practice. *Ethics & Behavior, 7*, 337–345.

Woody, R. H. (1999). Domestic violations of confidentiality. *Professional Psychology: Research and Practice, 30*, 607–610.

Woody, R. H. (2000). *Child custody: Practice standards, ethical issues, and legal safeguards for mental health professionals*. Sarasota, FL: Professional Resource Exchange.

World Health Organization (WHO). (2014). *International Statistical Classification of Diseases and Related Health Problems (ICD)*. Washington, D.C.: American Medical Association.

World Professional Association for Transgender Health. (2012). Standards of care for the health of transsexual, transgender, and gender nonconforming people. Retrieved from http://www.wpath.org/uploaded_files/140/files/Standards of Care, V7 Full Book.pdf

Wrenn, C. G. (1962). The culturally encapsulated counselor. *Harvard Educational Review, 32*, 444–449.

Wrenn, C. G. (1985). Afterword: The culturally encapsulated counselor revisited. In P. Pedersen (Ed.), *Handbook of cross-cultural counseling and therapy* (pp. 323–329). Westport, CT: Greenwood.

Wrich, J. T. (1995, March–April). Who's at risk? *EAP Digest*, pp. 19–25.

Wrightsman, L. S. (2000). *Forensic psychology*. Belmont, CA: Wadsworth.

Wylie, C. L. (2003). An investigation into burnout in the field of school psychology. *Dissertation Abstracts International: Section A, The Humanities and Social Sciences, 64*(1), 401.

Yabusaki, A. S. (2010). Clinical supervision: Dialogues on diversity. *Training and Education in Professional Psychology, 4*, 55–61.

Yalom, I. D., & Leszcz, M. (2005). *The Theory & Practice of Group Psychotherapy* (5th ed.). New York, NY: Basic Books.

Yang, M., Wong, S. C. P., & Coid, J. (2010). The efficacy of violence prediction: A meta-analytic comparison of nine risk assessment tools. *Psychological Bulletin, 136*, 740–767.

Yazvac, J. (2009). Website compliance with ethical guidelines by psychologists and professional counselors. *Dissertation Abstracts International: Section B, The Sciences and Engineering*, *70*(1), 09.

Young, E. L., & Mendez, L. M. R. (2003). The mental health professional's role in understanding, preventing, and responding to student sexual harassment. *Journal of Applied School Psychology*, *19*, 7–23.

Young, L., & Phillips, J. (2011). The paradox of moral focus. *Cognition*, *119*, 166–178.

Younggren, J. N., & Gottlieb, M. C. (2004). Managing risk when contemplating multiple relationships. *Professional Psychology: Research and Practice*, *35*, 255–260.

Younggren, J. N., & Gottlieb, M. C. (2008). Termination and abandonment: Risk and risk management. *Professional Psychology: Research and Practice*, *39*, 498–504.

Younggren, J. N., & Harris, E. (2008). Can you keep a secret? Confidentiality in psychotherapy. *Journal of Clinical Psychology*, *64*, 589–600.

Yuen, E. K., Goetter, E. M., Herbert, J. D., & Forman, E. M. (2012). Challenges and opportunities in Internet-mediated telemental health. *Professional psychology: Research and Practice*, *43*, 1–8.

Zakrzewski, R. F. (2006). A national survey of American Psychological Association student affiliates' involvement and ethical training in psychology educator-student sexual relationships. *Professional Psychology: Research and Practice*, *37*, 724–730.

Zane, M. (1990, January 27). $1.5 million verdict against doctor who seduced patient. *San Francisco Chronicle*, p. 4.

Zayas, L. H., Torres, L. R., Malcolm, J., & DesRosiers, F. S. (1996). Clinicians' definitions of ethnically sensitive therapy. *Professional Psychology: Research and Practice*, *27*, 78–82.

Zeranski, L., & Halgin, R. P. (2011). Ethical issues in elder abuse reporting: A professional psychologist's guide. *Professional Psychology: Research and Practice*, *42*, 294–300.

Zuckerman, E. L. (2008). *The paper office: Forms, guidelines, resources* (3rd ed.). New York, NY: Guilford.

Zur, O. (2007). *Boundaries in psychotherapy: Ethical and clinical explorations* (pp. 83–98). Washington, D.C.: American Psychological Association.

Zur, O., & Anderson, S. J. (2006). Multiple role relationships in coaching. In P. Williams & S. K. Anderson (Eds.), *Law and ethics in coaching: How to avoid and solve difficult problems in your practice* (pp. 126–139). Hoboken, NJ: Wiley.

American Counseling Association, Code of Ethics and Standards of Practice

APPENDIX **A**

ACA Code of Ethics Preamble

The American Counseling Association (ACA) is an educational, scientific, and professional organization whose members work in a variety of settings and serve in multiple capacities. Counseling is a professional relationship that empowers diverse individuals, families, and groups to accomplish mental health, wellness, education, and career goals.

Professional values are an important way of living out an ethical commitment. The following are core professional values of the counseling profession:

1. enhancing human development throughout the life span;
2. honoring diversity and embracing a multicultural approach in support of the worth, dignity, potential, and uniqueness of people within their social and cultural contexts;
3. promoting social justice;
4. safeguarding the integrity of the counselor–client relationship; and
5. practicing in a competent and ethical manner.

These professional values provide a conceptual basis for the ethical principles enumerated below. These principles are the foundation for ethical behavior and decision making. The fundamental principles of professional ethical behavior are

- *autonomy*, or fostering the right to control the direction of one's life;
- *nonmaleficence*, or avoiding actions that cause harm;
- *beneficence*, or working for the good of the individual and society by promoting mental health and well-being;
- *justice*, or treating individuals equitably and fostering fairness and equality;
- *fidelity*, or honoring commitments and keeping promises, including fulfilling one's responsibilities of trust in professional relationships; and

- *veracity*, or dealing truthfully with individuals with whom counselors come into professional contact.

ACA Code of Ethics Purpose

The *ACA Code of Ethics* serves six main purposes:

1. The *Code* sets forth the ethical obligations of ACA members and provides guidance intended to inform the ethical practice of professional counselors.
2. The *Code* identifies ethical considerations relevant to professional counselors and counselors-in-training.
3. The *Code* enables the association to clarify for current and prospective members, and for those served by members, the nature of the ethical responsibilities held in common by its members.
4. The *Code* serves as an ethical guide designed to assist members in constructing a course of action that best serves those utilizing counseling services and establishes expectations of conduct with a primary emphasis on the role of the professional counselor.
5. The *Code* helps to support the mission of ACA.
6. The standards contained in this *Code* serve as the basis for processing inquiries and ethics complaints concerning ACA members.

The *ACA Code of Ethics* contains nine main sections that address the following areas:

Section A: The Counseling Relationship

Section B: Confidentiality and Privacy

Section C: Professional Responsibility

Section D: Relationships With Other Professionals

Section E: Evaluation, Assessment, and Interpretation

Section F: Supervision, Training, and Teaching

Section G: Research and Publication

Section H: Distance Counseling, Technology, and Social Media

Section I: Resolving Ethical Issues

Each section of the *ACA Code of Ethics* begins with an introduction. The introduction to each section describes the ethical behavior and responsibility to which counselors aspire. The introductions help set the tone for each particular section and provide a starting point that invites reflection on the ethical standards contained in each part of the *ACA Code of Ethics*. The standards outline professional responsibilities and provide direction for fulfilling those ethical responsibilities.

When counselors are faced with ethical dilemmas that are difficult to resolve, they are expected to engage in a care-fully considered ethical decision-making process, consulting available resources as needed. Counselors acknowledge that resolving ethical issues is a process; ethical reasoning includes consideration of professional values, professional ethical principles, and ethical standards.

Counselors' actions should be consistent with the spirit as well as the letter of these ethical standards. No specific ethical decision-making model is always most effective, so counselors are expected to use a credible model of decision making that can bear public scrutiny of its application. Through a chosen ethical decision-making process and evaluation of the context of the situation, counselors work collaboratively with clients to make decisions that promote clients' growth and development. A breach of the standards and principles provided herein does not necessarily constitute legal liability or violation of the law; such action is established in legal and judicial proceedings.

The glossary at the end of the *Code* provides a concise description of some of the terms used in the *ACA Code of Ethics*.

Section A: The Counseling Relationship

Introduction

Counselors facilitate client growth and development in ways that foster the interest and welfare of clients and promote formation of healthy relationships. Trust is the cornerstone of the counseling relationship, and counselors have the responsibility to respect and safeguard the client's right to privacy and confidentiality. Counselors actively attempt to understand the diverse cultural backgrounds of the clients they serve. Counselors also explore their own cultural identities and how these affect their values and beliefs about the counseling process. Additionally, counselors are encouraged to contribute to society by devoting a portion of their professional activities for little or no financial return (*pro bono publico*).

A.1. Client Welfare

A.1.a. Primary Responsibility

The primary responsibility of counselors is to respect the dignity and promote the welfare of clients.

A.1.b. Records and Documentation

Counselors create, safeguard, and maintain documentation necessary for rendering professional services. Regardless of the medium, counselors include sufficient and timely documentation to facilitate the delivery and continuity of services. Counselors take reasonable steps to ensure that documentation accurately reflects client progress and services provided. If amendments are made to records and documentation, counselors take steps to properly note the amendments according to agency or institutional policies.

A.1.c. Counseling Plans

Counselors and their clients work jointly in devising counseling plans that offer reasonable promise of success and are consistent with the abilities, temperament, developmental level, and circumstances of clients. Counselors and clients regularly review and revise counseling plans to assess their continued viability and effectiveness, respecting clients' freedom of choice.

A.1.d. Support Network Involvement

Counselors recognize that support networks hold various meanings in the lives of clients and consider enlisting the support, understanding, and involvement of others (e.g., religious/spiritual/community leaders, family members, friends) as positive resources, when appropriate, with client consent.

A.2. Informed Consent in the Counseling Relationship

A.2.a. Informed Consent

Clients have the freedom to choose whether to enter into or remain in a counseling relationship and need adequate information about the counseling process and the counselor. Counselors have an obligation to review in writing and verbally with clients the rights and responsibilities of both counselors and clients. Informed consent is an ongoing part of the counseling process, and counselors appropriately document discussions of informed consent throughout the counseling relationship.

A.2.b. Types of Information Needed

Counselors explicitly explain to clients the nature of all services provided. They inform clients about issues such as, but not limited to, the following: the purposes, goals, techniques, procedures, limitations, potential risks, and benefits of services; the counselor's qualifications, credentials, relevant experience, and approach to counseling; continuation of services upon the incapacitation or death of the counselor; the role of technology; and other pertinent information. Counselors take steps to ensure that clients understand the implications of diagnosis and the intended use of tests and reports. Additionally, counselors inform clients about fees and billing arrangements, including procedures for nonpayment of fees. Clients have the right to confidentiality and to be provided with an explanation of its limits (including how supervisors and/or treatment or interdisciplinary team professionals are involved), to obtain clear information about their records, to participate in the ongoing counseling plans, and to refuse any services or modality changes and to be advised of the consequences of such refusal.

A.2.c. Developmental and Cultural Sensitivity

Counselors communicate information in ways that are both developmentally and culturally appropriate. Counselors use clear and understandable language when discussing issues related to informed consent. When clients have difficulty understanding the language that counselors use, counselors provide necessary services (e.g., arranging for a qualified interpreter or translator) to ensure comprehension by clients. In collaboration with clients, counselors consider cultural implications of informed consent procedures and, where possible, counselors adjust their practices accordingly.

A.2.d. Inability to Give Consent

When counseling minors, incapacitated adults, or other persons unable to give voluntary consent, counselors seek the assent of clients to services and include them in decision making as appropriate. Counselors recognize the need to balance the ethical rights of clients to make choices, their capacity to give consent or assent to receive services, and parental or familial legal rights and responsibilities to protect these clients and make decisions on their behalf.

A.2.e. Mandated Clients

Counselors discuss the required limitations to confidentiality when working with clients who have been mandated for counseling services. Counselors also explain what type of information and with whom that information is shared prior to the beginning of counseling. The client may choose to refuse services. In this case, counselors will, to the best of their ability, discuss with the client the potential consequences of refusing counseling services.

A.3. Clients Served by Others

When counselors learn that their clients are in a professional relationship with other mental health professionals, they request release from clients to inform the other professionals and strive to establish positive and collaborative professional relationships.

A.4. Avoiding Harm and Imposing Values

A.4.a. Avoiding Harm

Counselors act to avoid harming their clients, trainees, and research participants and to minimize or to remedy unavoidable or unanticipated harm.

A.4.b. Personal Values

Counselors are aware of—and avoid imposing—their own values, attitudes, beliefs, and behaviors. Counselors respect the diversity of clients, trainees, and research participants and seek training in areas in which they are at risk of imposing their values onto clients, especially when the counselor's values are inconsistent with the client's goals or are discriminatory in nature.

A.5. Prohibited Noncounseling Roles and Relationships

A.5.a. Sexual and/or Romantic Relationships Prohibited

Sexual and/or romantic counselor-client interactions or relationships with current clients, their romantic partners, or their family members are prohibited. This prohibition applies to both in-person and electronic interactions or relationships.

A.5.b. Previous Sexual and/or Romantic Relationships

Counselors are prohibited from engaging in counseling relationships with persons with whom they have had a previous sexual and/or romantic relationship.

A.5.c. Sexual and/or Romantic Relationships With Former Clients

Sexual and/or romantic counselor– client interactions or relationships with former clients, their romantic partners, or their family members are prohibited for a period of 5 years following the last professional contact. This prohibition applies to both in-person and electronic interactions or relationships. Counsel-ors, before engaging in sexual and/or romantic interactions or relationships with former clients, their romantic partners, or their family members, demonstrate forethought and document (in written form) whether the interaction or relationship can be viewed as exploitive in any way and/or whether there is still potential to harm the former client; in cases of potential exploitation and/or harm, the counselor avoids entering into such an interaction or relationship.

A.5.d. Friends or Family Members

Counselors are prohibited from engaging in counseling relationships with friends or family members with whom they have an inability to remain objective.

A.5.e. Personal Virtual Relationships With Current Clients

Counselors are prohibited from engaging in a personal virtual relationship with individuals with whom they have a current counseling relationship (e.g., through social and other media).

A.6. Managing and Maintaining Boundaries and Professional Relationships

A.6.a. Previous Relationships

Counselors consider the risks and benefits of accepting as clients those with whom they have had a previous relationship. These potential clients may include individuals with whom the counselor has had a casual, distant, or past relationship. Examples include mutual or past membership in a professional association, organization, or community. When counselors accept these clients, they take appropriate professional precautions such as informed consent, consultation, supervision, and documentation to ensure that judgment is not impaired and no exploitation occurs.

A.6.b. Extending Counseling Boundaries

Counselors consider the risks and benefits of extending current counseling relationships beyond conventional parameters. Examples include attending a client's formal ceremony (e.g., a wedding/commitment ceremony or graduation), purchasing a service or product provided by a client (excepting unrestricted bartering), and visiting a client's ill family member in the hospital. In extending these boundaries, counselors take appropriate professional precautions such as informed consent, consultation, supervision, and documentation to ensure that judgment is not impaired and no harm occurs.

A.6.c. Documenting Boundary Extensions

If counselors extend boundaries as described in A.6.a. and A.6.b., they must officially document, prior to the interaction (when feasible), the rationale for such an interaction, the potential benefit, and anticipated consequences for the client or former client and other individuals significantly involved with the client or former client. When un-intentional harm occurs to the client or former client, or to an individual significantly involved with the client or former client, the counselor must show evidence of an attempt to remedy such harm.

A.6.d. Role Changes in the Professional Relationship

When counselors change a role from the original or most recent contracted relationship, they obtain informed consent from the client and explain the client's right to refuse services related to the change. Examples of role changes include, but are not limited to

1. changing from individual to relationship or family counseling, or vice versa;
2. changing from an evaluative role to a therapeutic role, or vice versa; and
3. changing from a counselor to a mediator role, or vice versa.

Clients must be fully informed of any anticipated consequences (e.g., financial, legal, personal, therapeutic) of counselor role changes.

A.6.e. Nonprofessional Interactions or Relationships (Other Than Sexual or Romantic Interactions or Relationships)

Counselors avoid entering into nonprofessional relationships with former clients, their romantic partners, or their family members when the interaction is potentially harmful to the client. This applies to both in-person and electronic interactions or relationships.

A.7. Roles and Relationships at Individual, Group, Institutional, and Societal Levels

A.7.a. Advocacy

When appropriate, counselors advocate at individual, group, institutional, and societal levels to address potential barriers and obstacles that inhibit access and/or the growth and development of clients.

A.7.b. Confidentiality and Advocacy

Counselors obtain client consent prior to engaging in advocacy efforts on behalf of an identifiable client to improve the provision of services and to work toward removal of systemic barriers or obstacles that inhibit client access, growth, and development.

A.8. Multiple Clients

When a counselor agrees to provide counseling services to two or more persons who have a relationship, the counselor clarifies at the outset which person or persons are clients and the nature of the relationships the counselor will have with each involved person. If it becomes apparent that the counselor may be called upon to perform potentially conflicting roles, the counselor will clarify, adjust, or withdraw from roles appropriately.

A.9. Group Work

A.9.a. Screening

Counselors screen prospective group counseling/therapy participants. To the extent possible, counselors select members whose needs and goals are compatible with the goals of the group, who will not impede the group process, and whose well-being will not be jeopardized by the group experience.

A.9.b. Protecting Clients

In a group setting, counselors take reasonable precautions to protect clients from physical, emotional, or psychological trauma.

A.10. Fees and Business Practices

A.10.a. Self-Referral

Counselors working in an organization (e.g., school, agency, institution) that provides counseling services do not refer clients to their private practice unless the policies of a particular organization make explicit provisions for self-referrals. In such instances, the clients must be informed of other options open to them should they seek private counseling services.

A.10.b. Unacceptable Business Practices

Counselors do not participate in fee splitting, nor do they give or receive commissions, rebates, or any other form of remuneration when referring clients for professional services.

A.10.c. Establishing Fees

In establishing fees for professional counseling services, counselors consider the financial status of clients and locality. If a counselor's usual fees create undue hardship for the client, the counselor may adjust fees, when legally permissible, or assist the client in locating comparable, affordable services.

A.10.d. Nonpayment of Fees

If counselors intend to use collection agencies or take legal measures to collect fees from clients who do not pay for services as agreed upon, they include such information in their informed consent documents and also inform clients in a timely fashion of intended actions and offer clients the opportunity to make payment.

A.10.e. Bartering

Counselors may barter only if the bartering does not result in exploitation or harm, if the client requests it, and if such arrangements are an accepted practice among professionals in the community. Counselors consider the cultural implications of bartering and discuss relevant concerns with clients and document such agreements in a clear written contract.

A.10.f. Receiving Gifts

Counselors understand the challenges of accepting gifts from clients and recognize that in some cultures, small gifts are a token of respect and gratitude. When determining whether to accept a gift from clients, counselors take into account the therapeutic relationship, the monetary value of the gift, the client's motivation for giving the gift, and the counselor's motivation for wanting to accept or decline the gift.

A.11. Termination and Referral

A.11.a. Competence Within Termination and Referral

If counselors lack the competence to be of professional assistance to clients, they avoid entering or continuing counseling relationships. Counselors are knowledgeable about culturally and clinically appropriate referral resources and suggest these alternatives. If clients decline the suggested referrals, counselors discontinue the relationship.

A.11.b. Values Within Termination and Referral

Counselors refrain from referring prospective and current clients based solely on the counselor's personally held values, attitudes, beliefs, and behaviors. Counselors respect the diversity of clients and seek training in areas in which they are at risk of imposing their values onto clients, especially when the counselor's values are inconsistent with the client's goals or are discriminatory in nature.

A.11.c. Appropriate Termination

Counselors terminate a counseling relationship when it becomes reasonably apparent that the client no longer needs assistance, is not likely to benefit, or is being harmed by continued counseling. Counselors may terminate counseling when in jeopardy of harm by the client or by another person with whom the client has a relationship, or when clients do not pay fees as agreed upon. Counselors provide pretermination counseling and recommend other service providers when necessary.

A.11.d. Appropriate Transfer of Services

When counselors transfer or refer clients to other practitioners, they ensure that appropriate clinical and administrative processes are completed and open communication is maintained with both clients and practitioners.

A.12. Abandonment and Client Neglect

Counselors do not abandon or neglect clients in counseling. Counselors assist in making appropriate arrangements for the continuation of treatment, when necessary, during interruptions such as vacations, illness, and following termination.

Section B: Confidentiality and Privacy

Introduction

Counselors recognize that trust is a cornerstone of the counseling relationship. Counselors aspire to earn the trust of clients by creating an ongoing partnership, establishing and upholding appropriate boundaries, and maintaining confidentiality. Counselors communicate the parameters of confidentiality in a culturally competent manner.

B.1. Respecting Client Rights

B.1.a. Multicultural/Diversity Considerations

Counselors maintain awareness and sensitivity regarding cultural meanings of confidentiality and privacy. Counselors respect differing views toward disclosure of information. Counselors hold ongoing discussions with clients as to how, when, and with whom information is to be shared.

B.1.b. Respect for Privacy

Counselors respect the privacy of prospective and current clients. Counselors request private information from clients only when it is beneficial to the counseling process.

B.1.c. Respect for Confidentiality

Counselors protect the confidential information of prospective and current clients. Counselors disclose information only with appropriate consent or with sound legal or ethical justification.

B.1.d. Explanation of Limitations

At initiation and throughout the counseling process, counselors inform clients of the limitations of confidentiality and seek to identify situations in which confidentiality must be breached.

B.2. Exceptions

B.2.a. Serious and Foreseeable Harm and Legal Requirements

The general requirement that counselors keep information confidential does not apply when disclosure is required to protect clients or identified others from serious and foreseeable harm or when legal requirements demand that confidential information must be revealed. Counselors consult with other professionals when in doubt as to the validity of an exception. Additional considerations apply when addressing end-of-life issues.

B.2.b. Confidentiality Regarding End-of-Life Decisions

Counselors who provide services to terminally ill individuals who are considering hastening their own deaths have the option to maintain confidentiality, depending on applicable laws and the specific circumstances of the situation and after seeking consultation or supervision from appropriate professional and legal parties.

B.2.c. Contagious, Life-Threatening Diseases

When clients disclose that they have a disease commonly known to be both communicable and life threatening, counselors may be justified in disclosing information to identifiable third parties, if the parties are known to be at serious and foreseeable risk of contracting the disease. Prior to making a disclosure, counselors assess the intent of clients to inform the third parties about their disease or to engage in any behaviors that may be harmful to an identifiable third party. Counselors adhere to relevant state laws concerning disclosure about disease status.

B.2.d. Court-Ordered Disclosure

When ordered by a court to release confidential or privileged information without a client's permission, counselors seek to obtain written, informed consent from the client or take steps to prohibit the disclosure or have it limited as narrowly as possible because of potential harm to the client or counseling relationship.

B.2.e. Minimal Disclosure

To the extent possible, clients are informed before confidential information is disclosed and are involved in the disclosure decision-making process. When circumstances require the disclosure of confidential information, only essential information is revealed.

B.3. Information Shared With Others

B.3.a. Subordinates

Counselors make every effort to ensure that privacy and confidentiality of clients are maintained by subordinates, including employees, supervisees, students, clerical assistants, and volunteers.

B.3.b. Interdisciplinary Teams

When services provided to the client involve participation by an interdisciplinary or treatment team, the client will be informed of the team's existence and composition, information being shared, and the purposes of sharing such information.

B.3.c. Confidential Settings

Counselors discuss confidential information only in settings in which they can reasonably ensure client privacy.

B.3.d. Third-Party Payers

Counselors disclose information to third-party payers only when clients have authorized such disclosure.

B.3.e. Transmitting Confidential Information

Counselors take precautions to ensure the confidentiality of all information transmitted through the use of any medium.

B.3.f. Deceased Clients

Counselors protect the confidentiality of deceased clients, consistent with legal requirements and the documented preferences of the client.

B.4. Groups and Families

B.4.a. Group Work

In group work, counselors clearly explain the importance and parameters of confidentiality for the specific group.

B.4.b. Couples and Family Counseling

In couples and family counseling, counselors clearly define who is considered "the client" and discuss expectations and limitations of confidentiality. Counselors seek agreement and document in writing such agreement among all involved parties regarding the confidentiality of information. In the absence of an agreement to the contrary, the couple or family is considered to be the client.

B.5. Clients Lacking Capacity to Give Informed Consent

B.5.a. Responsibility to Clients

When counseling minor clients or adult clients who lack the capacity to give voluntary, informed consent, counselors protect the confidentiality of information received—in any medium—in the counseling relationship as specified by federal and state laws, written policies, and applicable ethical standards.

B.5.b. Responsibility to Parents and Legal Guardians

Counselors inform parents and legal guardians about the role of counselors and the confidential nature of the counseling relationship, consistent with current legal and custodial arrangements. Counselors are sensitive to the cultural diversity of families and respect the inherent rights and responsibilities of parents/guardians regarding the welfare of their children/charges according to law. Counselors work to establish, as appropriate, collaborative relationships with parents/guardians to best serve clients.

B.5.c. Release of Confidential Information

When counseling minor clients or adult clients who lack the capacity to give voluntary consent to release confidential information, counselors seek permission from an appropriate third party to disclose information. In such instances, counselors inform clients consistent with their level of understanding and take appropriate measures to safeguard client confidentiality.

B.6. Records and Documentation

B.6.a. Creating and Maintaining Records and Documentation

Counselors create and maintain records and documentation necessary for rendering professional services.

B.6.b. Confidentiality of Records and Documentation

Counselors ensure that records and documentation kept in any medium are secure and that only authorized persons have access to them.

B.6.c. Permission to Record

Counselors obtain permission from clients prior to recording sessions through electronic or other means.

B.6.d. Permission to Observe

Counselors obtain permission from clients prior to allowing any person to observe counseling sessions, review session transcripts, or view recordings of sessions with supervisors, faculty, peers, or others within the training environment.

B.6.e. Client Access

Counselors provide reasonable access to records and copies of records when requested by competent clients. Counselors limit the access of clients to their records, or portions of their records, only when there is compelling evidence that such access would cause harm to the client. Counselors document the request of clients and the rationale for withholding some or all of the records in the files of clients. In situations involving multiple clients, counselors provide individual clients with only those parts of records that relate directly to them and do not include confidential information related to any other client.

B.6.f. Assistance With Records

When clients request access to their records, counselors provide assistance and consultation in interpreting counseling records.

B.6.g. Disclosure or Transfer

Unless exceptions to confidentiality exist, counselors obtain written permission from clients to disclose or transfer records to legitimate third parties. Steps are taken to ensure that receivers of counseling records are sensitive to their confidential nature.

B.6.h. Storage and Disposal After Termination

Counselors store records following termination of services to ensure reasonable future access, maintain records in accordance with federal and state laws and statutes such as licensure laws and policies governing records, and dispose of client records and other sensitive materials in a manner that protects client confidentiality. Counselors apply careful discretion and deliberation before destroying records that may be needed by a court of law, such as notes on child abuse, suicide, sexual harassment, or violence.

B.6.i. Reasonable Precautions

Counselors take reasonable precautions to protect client confidentiality in the event of the counselor's termination of practice, incapacity, or death and appoint a records custodian when identified as appropriate.

B.7. Case Consultation

B.7.a. Respect for Privacy

Information shared in a consulting relationship is discussed for professional purposes only. Written and oral reports present only data germane to the purposes of the consultation, and every effort is made to protect client identity and to avoid undue invasion of privacy.

B.7.b. Disclosure of Confidential Information

When consulting with colleagues, counselors do not disclose confidential information that reasonably could lead to the identification of a client or other person or organization with whom they have a confidential relationship unless they have obtained the prior consent of the person or organization or the disclosure cannot be avoided. They disclose information only to the extent necessary to achieve the purposes of the consultation.

Section C: Professional Responsibility

Introduction

Counselors aspire to open, honest, and accurate communication in dealing with the public and other professionals. Counselors facilitate access to counseling services, and they practice in a nondiscriminatory manner within the boundaries of professional and personal competence; they also have a responsibility to abide by the *ACA Code of Ethics*. Counselors actively participate in local, state, and national associations that foster the development and improvement of counseling. Counselors are expected to advocate to promote changes at the individual, group, institutional, and societal levels that improve the quality of life for individuals and groups and remove potential barriers to the provision or access of appropriate services being offered. Counselors have a responsibility to the public to engage in counseling practices that are based on rigorous re-search methodologies. Counselors are encouraged to contribute to society by devoting a portion of their professional activity to services for which there is little or no financial return (*pro bono publico*). In addition, counselors engage in self-care activities to maintain and promote their own emotional, physical, mental, and spiritual well-being to best meet their professional responsibilities.

C.1. *Knowledge of and Compliance With Standards*

Counselors have a responsibility to read, understand, and follow the *ACA Code of Ethics* and adhere to applicable laws and regulations.

C.2. *Professional Competence*

C.2.a. Boundaries of Competence

Counselors practice only within the boundaries of their competence, based on their education, training, supervised experience, state and national professional credentials, and appropriate professional experience. Whereas multicultural counseling competency is required across all counseling specialties, counselors gain knowledge, personal awareness, sensitivity, dispositions, and skills pertinent to being a culturally competent counselor in working with a diverse client population.

C.2.b. New Specialty Areas of Practice

Counselors practice in specialty areas new to them only after appropriate education, training, and supervised experience. While developing skills in new specialty areas, counselors take steps to ensure the competence of their work and protect others from possible harm.

C.2.c. Qualified for Employment

Counselors accept employment only for positions for which they are qualified given their education, training, supervised experience, state and national professional credentials, and appropriate professional experience. Counselors hire for professional counseling positions only individuals who are qualified and competent for those positions.

C.2.d. Monitor Effectiveness

Counselors continually monitor their effectiveness as professionals and take steps to improve when necessary. Counselors take reasonable steps to seek peer supervision to evaluate their efficacy as counselors.

C.2.e. Consultations on Ethical Obligations

Counselors take reasonable steps to consult with other counselors, the ACA Ethics and Professional Standards Department, or related professionals when they have questions regarding their ethical obligations or professional practice.

C.2.f. Continuing Education

Counselors recognize the need for continuing education to acquire and maintain a reasonable level of awareness of current scientific and professional information in their fields of activity. Counselors maintain their competence in the skills they use, are open to new procedures, and remain informed regarding best practices for working with diverse populations.

C.2.g. Impairment

Counselors monitor themselves for signs of impairment from their own physical, mental, or emotional problems and refrain from offering or providing professional services when impaired. They seek assistance for problems that reach the level of professional impairment, and, if necessary, they limit, suspend, or terminate their professional responsibilities until it is determined that they may safely resume their work. Counselors assist colleagues or supervisors in recognizing their own professional impairment and provide consultation and assistance when war-ranted with colleagues or supervisors showing signs of impairment and intervene as appropriate to prevent imminent harm to clients.

C.2.h. Counselor Incapacitation, Death, Retirement, or Termination of Practice

Counselors prepare a plan for the transfer of clients and the dissemination of records to an identified colleague or records custodian in the case of the counselor's incapacitation, death, retirement, or termination of practice.

C.3. Advertising and Soliciting Clients

C.3.a. Accurate Advertising

When advertising or otherwise representing their services to the public, counselors identify their credentials in an accurate manner that is not false, misleading, deceptive, or fraudulent.

C.3.b. Testimonials

Counselors who use testimonials do not solicit them from current clients, former clients, or any other persons who may be vulnerable to undue influence. Counselors discuss with clients the implications of and obtain permission for the use of any testimonial.

C.3.c. Statements by Others

When feasible, counselors make reasonable efforts to ensure that statements made by others about them or about the counseling profession are accurate.

C.3.d. Recruiting Through Employment

Counselors do not use their places of employment or institutional affiliation to recruit clients, supervisors, or consultees for their private practices.

C.3.e. Products and Training Advertisements

Counselors who develop products related to their profession or conduct workshops or training events ensure that the advertisements concerning these products or events are accurate and disclose adequate information for consumers to make informed choices.

C.3.f. Promoting to Those Served

Counselors do not use counseling, teaching, training, or supervisory relationships to promote their products or training events in a manner that is deceptive or would exert undue influence on individuals who may be vulnerable. However, counselor educators may adopt textbooks they have authored for instructional purposes.

C.4. *Professional Qualifications*

C.4.a. Accurate Representation

Counselors claim or imply only professional qualifications actually completed and correct any known misrepresentations of their qualifications by others. Counselors truthfully represent the qualifications of their professional colleagues. Counselors clearly distinguish between paid and volunteer work experience and accurately describe their continuing education and specialized training.

C.4.b. Credentials

Counselors claim only licenses or certifications that are current and in good standing.

C.4.c. Educational Degrees

Counselors clearly differentiate between earned and honorary degrees.

C.4.d. Implying Doctoral-Level Competence

Counselors clearly state their highest earned degree in counseling or a closely related field. Counselors do not imply doctoral-level competence when possessing a master's degree in counseling or a related field by referring to them-selves as "Dr." in a counseling context when their doctorate is not in counseling or a related field. Counselors do not use "ABD" (all but dissertation) or other such terms to imply competency.

C.4.e. Accreditation Status

Counselors accurately represent the accreditation status of their degree program and college/university.

C.4.f. Professional Membership

Counselors clearly differentiate between current, active memberships and former memberships in associations. Members of ACA must clearly differentiate between professional membership, which implies the possession of at least a master's degree in counseling, and regular membership, which is open to individuals whose interests and activities are consistent with those of ACA but are not qualified for professional membership.

C.5. *Nondiscrimination*

Counselors do not condone or engage in discrimination against prospective or current clients, students, employees, supervisees, or research participants based on age, culture, disability, ethnicity, race, religion/spirituality, gender, gender identity, sexual orientation, marital/partnership status, language preference, socioeconomic status, immigration status, or any basis proscribed by law.

C.6. *Public Responsibility*

C.6.a. Sexual Harassment

Counselors do not engage in or condone sexual harassment. Sexual harassment can consist of a single intense or severe act, or multiple persistent or pervasive acts.

C.6.b. Reports to Third Parties

Counselors are accurate, honest, and objective in reporting their professional activities and judgments to appropriate third parties, including courts, health insurance companies, those who are the recipients of evaluation reports, and others.

C.6.c. Media Presentations

When counselors provide advice or comment by means of public lectures, demonstrations, radio or television programs, recordings, technology-based applications, printed articles, mailed material, or other media, they take reasonable precautions to ensure that

1. the statements are based on appropriate professional counseling literature and practice,
2. the statements are otherwise consistent with the *ACA Code of Ethics*, and
3. the recipients of the information are not encouraged to infer that a professional counseling relationship has been established.

C.6.d. Exploitation of Others

Counselors do not exploit others in their professional relationships.

C.6.e. Contributing to the Public Good (*Pro Bono Publico*)

Counselors make a reasonable effort to provide services to the public for which there is little or no financial return (e.g., speaking to groups, sharing professional information, offering reduced fees).

C.7. Treatment Modalities

C.7.a. Scientific Basis for Treatment

When providing services, counselors use techniques/procedures/modalities that are grounded in theory and/or have an empirical or scientific foundation.

C.7.b. Development and Innovation

When counselors use developing or innovative techniques/procedures/modalities, they explain the potential risks, benefits, and ethical considerations of using such techniques/procedures/modalities. Counselors work to minimize any potential risks or harm when using these techniques/procedures/modalities.

C.7.c. Harmful Practices

Counselors do not use techniques/procedures/modalities when substantial evidence suggests harm, even if such services are requested.

C.8. Responsibility to Other Professionals

C.8.a. Personal Public Statements

When making personal statements in a public context, counselors clarify that they are speaking from their personal perspectives and that they are not speaking on behalf of all counselors or the profession.

Section D: Relationships With Other Professionals

Introduction

Professional counselors recognize that the quality of their interactions with colleagues can influence the quality of services provided to clients. They work to become knowledgeable about colleagues within and outside the field of counseling. Counselors develop positive working relationships and systems of communication with colleagues to enhance services to clients.

D.1. Relationships With Colleagues, Employers, and Employees

D.1.a. Different Approaches

Counselors are respectful of approaches that are grounded in theory and/or have an empirical or scientific foundation but may differ from their own. Counselors acknowledge the expertise of other professional groups and are respectful of their practices.

D.1.b. Forming Relationships

Counselors work to develop and strengthen relationships with colleagues from other disciplines to best serve clients.

D.1.c. Interdisciplinary Teamwork

Counselors who are members of interdisciplinary teams delivering multifaceted services to clients remain focused on how to best serve clients. They participate in and contribute to decisions that affect the well-being of clients by drawing on the perspectives, values, and experiences of the counseling profession and those of colleagues from other disciplines.

D.1.d. Establishing Professional and Ethical Obligations

Counselors who are members of interdisciplinary teams work together with team members to clarify professional and ethical obligations of the team as a whole and of its individual members. When a team decision raises ethical concerns, counselors first attempt to resolve the concern within the team. If they cannot reach resolution among team members, counselors pursue other avenues to address their concerns consistent with client well-being.

D.1.e. Confidentiality

When counselors are required by law, institutional policy, or extraordinary circumstances to serve in more than one role in judicial or administrative proceedings, they clarify role expectations and the parameters of confidentiality with their colleagues.

D.1.f. Personnel Selection and Assignment

When counselors are in a position requiring personnel selection and/or assigning of responsibilities to others, they select competent staff and assign responsibilities compatible with their skills and experiences.

D.1.g. Employer Policies

The acceptance of employment in an agency or institution implies that counselors are in agreement with its general policies and principles. Counselors strive to reach agreement with employers regarding acceptable standards of client care and professional conduct that allow for changes in institutional policy conducive to the growth and development of clients.

D.1.h. Negative Conditions

Counselors alert their employers of inappropriate policies and practices. They attempt to effect changes in such policies or procedures through constructive action within the organization. When such policies are potentially disruptive or damaging to clients or may limit the effectiveness of services provided and change cannot be affected, counselors take appropriate further action. Such action may include referral to appropriate certification, accreditation, or state licensure organizations, or voluntary termination of employment.

D.1.i. Protection From Punitive Action

Counselors do not harass a colleague or employee or dismiss an employee who has acted in a responsible and ethical manner to expose inappropriate employer policies or practices.

D.2. Provision of Consultation Services

D.2.a. Consultant Competency

Counselors take reasonable steps to ensure that they have the appropriate resources and competencies when providing consultation services. Counselors provide appropriate referral resources when requested or needed.

D.2.b. Informed Consent in Formal Consultation

When providing formal consultation services, counselors have an obligation to review, in writing and verbally, the rights and responsibilities of both counselors and consultees. Counselors use clear and understandable language to inform all parties involved about the purpose of the services to be provided, relevant costs, potential risks and benefits, and the limits of confidentiality.

Section E: Evaluation, Assessment, and Interpretation

Introduction

Counselors use assessment as one component of the counseling process, taking into account the clients' personal and cultural context. Counselors promote the well-being of individual clients or groups of clients by developing and using appropriate educational, mental health, psychological, and career assessments.

E.1. General

E.1.a. Assessment

The primary purpose of educational, mental health, psychological, and career assessment is to gather information regarding the client for a variety of purposes, including, but not limited to, client decision making, treatment planning, and forensic proceedings. Assessment may include both qualitative and quantitative methodologies.

E.1.b. Client Welfare

Counselors do not misuse assessment results and interpretations, and they take reasonable steps to prevent others from misusing the information provided. They respect the client's right to know the results, the interpretations made, and the bases for counselors' conclusions and recommendations.

E.2. Competence to Use and Interpret Assessment Instruments

E.2.a. Limits of Competence

Counselors use only those testing and assessment services for which they have been trained and are competent. Counselors using technology-assisted test interpretations are trained in the construct being measured and the specific instrument being used prior to using its technology-based application. Counselors take reasonable measures to ensure the proper use of assessment techniques by persons under their supervision.

E.2.b. Appropriate Use

Counselors are responsible for the appropriate application, scoring, interpretation, and use of assessment instruments relevant to the needs of the client, whether they score and interpret such assessments themselves or use technology or other services.

E.2.c. Decisions Based on

Counselors responsible for decisions involving individuals or policies that are based on assessment results have a thorough understanding of psychometrics.

E.3. Informed Consent in Assessment

E.3.a. Explanation to Clients

Prior to assessment, counselors explain the nature and purposes of assessment and the specific use of results by potential recipients. The explanation will be given in terms and language that the client (or other legally authorized person on behalf of the client) can understand.

E.3.b. Recipients of Results

Counselors consider the client's and/or examinee's welfare, explicit understandings, and prior agreements in determining who receives the assessment results. Counselors include accurate and appropriate interpretations with any release of individual or group assessment results.

E.4. Release of Data to Qualified Personnel

Counselors release assessment data in which the client is identified only with the consent of the client or the client's legal representative. Such data are released only to persons recognized by counselors as qualified to interpret the data.

E.5. Diagnosis of Mental Disorders

E.5.a. Proper Diagnosis

Counselors take special care to provide proper diagnosis of mental disorders. Assessment techniques (including personal interviews) used to determine client care (e.g., locus of treatment, type of treatment, recommended follow-up) are carefully selected and appropriately used.

E.5.b. Cultural Sensitivity

Counselors recognize that culture affects the manner in which clients' problems are defined and experienced. Clients' socioeconomic and cultural experiences are considered when diagnosing mental disorders.

E.5.c. Historical and Social Prejudices in the Diagnosis of Pathology

Counselors recognize historical and social prejudices in the misdiagnosis and or others.

E.5.d. Refraining From Diagnosis

Counselors may refrain from making and/or reporting a diagnosis if they believe that it would cause harm to the client or others. Counselors carefully consider both the positive and negative implications of a diagnosis.

E.6. Instrument Selection

E.6.a. Appropriateness of Instruments

Counselors carefully consider the validity, reliability, psychometric limitations, and appropriateness of instruments when selecting assessments and, when possible, use multiple forms of assessment, data, and/or instruments in forming conclusions, diagnoses, or recommendations.

E.6.b. Referral Information

If a client is referred to a third party for assessment, the counselor provides specific referral questions and sufficient objective data about the client to ensure that appropriate assessment instruments are utilized.

E.7. Conditions of Assessment Administration

E.7.a. Administration Conditions

Counselors administer assessments under the same conditions that were established in their standardization. When assessments are not administered under standard conditions, as may be necessary to accommodate clients with disabilities, or when unusual behavior or irregularities occur during the administration, those conditions are noted in interpretation, and the results may be designated as invalid or of questionable validity.

E.7.b. Provision of Favorable Conditions

Counselors provide an appropriate environment for the administration of assessments (e.g., privacy, comfort, freedom from distraction).

E.7.c. Technological Administration

Counselors ensure that technologically administered assessments function properly and provide clients with accurate results.

E.7.d. Unsupervised Assessments

Unless the assessment instrument is designed, intended, and validated for self-administration and/or scoring, counselors do not permit unsupervised use.

E.8. Multicultural Issues/Diversity in Assessment

Counselors select and use with caution assessment techniques normed on populations other than that of the client. Counselors recognize the effects of age, color, culture, disability, ethnic group, gender, race, language preference, religion, spirituality, sexual orientation, and socioeconomic status on test administration and interpretation, and they place test results in proper perspective with other relevant factors.

E.9. Scoring and Interpretation of Assessments

E.9.a. Reporting

When counselors report assessment results, they consider the client's personal and cultural background, the level of the client's understanding of the results, and the impact of the results on the client. In reporting assessment results, counselors indicate reservations that exist regarding validity or reliability due to circumstances of the assessment or inappropriateness of the norms for the person tested.

E.9.b. Instruments With Insufficient Empirical Data

Counselors exercise caution when interpreting the results of instruments not having sufficient empirical data to support respondent results. The specific purposes for the use of such instruments are stated explicitly to the examinee. Counselors qualify any conclusions, diagnoses, or recommendations made that are based on assessments or instruments with questionable validity or reliability.

E.9.c. Assessment Services

Counselors who provide assessment, scoring, and interpretation services to support the assessment process confirm the validity of such interpretations. They accurately describe the purpose, norms, validity, reliability, and applications of the procedures and any special qualifications applicable to their use. At all times, counselors maintain their ethical responsibility to those being assessed.

E.10. Assessment Security

Counselors maintain the integrity and security of tests and assessments consistent with legal and contractual obligations. Counselors do not appropriate, reproduce, or modify published assessments or parts thereof without acknowledgment and permission from the publisher.

E.11. Obsolete Assessment and Outdated Results

Counselors do not use data or results from assessments that are obsolete or outdated for the current purpose (e.g., noncurrent versions of assessments/instruments). Counselors make every effort to prevent the misuse of obsolete measures and assessment data by others.

E.12. Assessment Construction

Counselors use established scientific procedures, relevant standards, and current professional knowledge for assessment design in the development, publication, and utilization of assessment techniques.

E.13. Forensic Evaluation: Evaluation for Legal Proceedings

E.13.a. Primary Obligations

When providing forensic evaluations, the primary obligation of counselors is to produce objective findings that can be substantiated based on information and techniques appropriate to the evaluation, which may include examination of the individual and/or review of records. Counselors form professional opinions based on their professional knowledge and expertise that can be supported by the data gathered in evaluations. Counselors define the limits of their reports or testimony, especially when an examination of the individual has not been conducted.

E.13.b. Consent for Evaluation

Individuals being evaluated are informed in writing that the relationship is for the purposes of an evaluation and is not therapeutic in nature, and entities or individuals who will receive the evaluation report are identified. Counselors who perform forensic evaluations obtain written consent from those being evaluated or from their legal representative unless a court orders evaluations to be conducted without the written consent of the individuals being evaluated. When children or adults who lack the capacity to give voluntary consent are being evaluated, informed written consent is obtained from a parent or guardian.

E.13.c. Client Evaluation Prohibited

Counselors do not evaluate current or former clients, clients' romantic partners, or clients' family members for forensic purposes. Counselors do not counsel individuals they are evaluating.

E.13.d. Avoid Potentially Harmful Relationships

Counselors who provide forensic evaluations avoid potentially harmful professional or personal relationships with family members, romantic partners, and close friends of individuals they are evaluating or have evaluated in the past.

Section F: Supervision, Training, and Teaching

Introduction

Counselor supervisors, trainers, and educators aspire to foster meaningful and respectful professional relationships and to maintain appropriate boundaries with supervisees and students in both face-to-face and electronic formats. They have theoretical and pedagogical foundations for their work; have knowledge of supervision models; and aim to be fair, accurate, and honest in their assessments of counselors, students, and supervisees.

F.1. Counselor Supervision and Client Welfare

F.1.a. Client Welfare

A primary obligation of counseling supervisors is to monitor the services provided by supervisees. Counseling supervisors monitor client welfare and supervisee performance and professional development. To fulfill these obligations, supervisors meet regularly with supervisees to review the supervisees' work and help them become prepared to serve a range of diverse clients. Supervisees have a responsibility to understand and follow the *ACA Code of Ethics*.

F.1.b. Counselor Credentials

Counseling supervisors work to ensure that supervisees communicate their qualifications to render services to their clients.

F.1.c. Informed Consent and Client Rights

Supervisors make supervisees aware of client rights, including the protection of client privacy and confidentiality in the counseling relationship. Supervisees provide clients with professional disclosure information and inform them of how the supervision process influences the limits of confidentiality. Supervisees make clients aware of who will have access to records of the counseling relationship and how these records will be stored, transmitted, or otherwise reviewed.

F.2. Counselor Supervision Competence

F.2.a. Supervisor Preparation

Prior to offering supervision services, counselors are trained in supervision methods and techniques. Counselors who offer supervision services regularly pursue continuing education activities, including both counseling and supervision topics and skills.

F.2.b. Multicultural Issues/Diversity in Supervision

Counseling supervisors are aware of and address the role of multiculturalism/diversity in the supervisory relationship.

F.2.c. Online Supervision

When using technology in supervision, counselor supervisors are competent in the use of those technologies. Supervisors take the necessary precautions to protect the confidentiality of all information transmitted through any electronic means.

F.3. Supervisory Relationship

F.3.a. Extending Conventional Supervisory Relationships

Counseling supervisors clearly define and maintain ethical professional, personal, and social relationships with their supervisees. Supervisors consider the risks and benefits of extending current supervisory relationships in any form beyond conventional parameters. In extending these boundaries, supervisors take appropriate professional precautions to ensure that judgment is not impaired and that no harm occurs.

F.3.b. Sexual Relationships

Sexual or romantic interactions or relationships with current supervisees are prohibited. This prohibition applies to both in-person and electronic interactions or relationships.

F.3.c. Sexual Harassment

Counseling supervisors do not con-done or subject supervisees to sexual harassment.

F.3.d. Friends or Family Members

Supervisors are prohibited from engaging in supervisory relationships with individuals with whom they have an inability to remain objective.

F.4. Supervisor Responsibilities

F.4.a. Informed Consent for Supervision

Supervisors are responsible for incorporating into their supervision the principles of informed consent and participation. Supervisors inform supervisees of the policies and procedures to which supervisors are to adhere and the mechanisms for due process appeal of individual supervisor actions. The issues unique to the use of distance supervision are to be included in the documentation as necessary.

F.4.b. Emergencies and Absences

Supervisors establish and communicate to supervisees procedures for contacting supervisors or, in their absence, alternative on-call supervisors to assist in handling crises.

F.4.c. Standards for Supervisees

Supervisors make their supervisees aware of professional and ethical standards and legal responsibilities.

F.4.d. Termination of the Supervisory Relationship

Supervisors or supervisees have the right to terminate the supervisory relationship with adequate notice. Reasons for considering termination are discussed, and both parties work to resolve differences. When termination is warranted, supervisors make appropriate referrals to possible alternative supervisors.

F.5. Student and Supervisee Responsibilities

F.5.a. Ethical Responsibilities

Students and supervisees have a responsibility to understand and follow the *ACA Code of Ethics*. Students and supervisees have the same obligation to clients as those required of professional counselors.

F.5.b. Impairment

Students and supervisees monitor themselves for signs of impairment from their own physical, mental, or emotional problems and refrain from offering or providing professional services when such impairment is likely to harm a client or others. They notify their faculty and/or supervisors and seek assistance for problems that reach the level of professional impairment, and, if necessary, they limit, suspend, or terminate their professional responsibilities until it is determined that they may safely resume their work.

F.5.c. Professional Disclosure

Before providing counseling services, students and supervisees disclose their status as supervisees and explain how this status affects the limits of confidentiality. Supervisors ensure that clients are aware of the services rendered and the qualifications of the students and supervisees rendering those services. Students and supervisees obtain client permission before they use any information concerning the counseling relationship in the training process.

F.6. Counseling Supervision Evaluation, Remediation, and Endorsement

F.6.a. Evaluation

Supervisors document and provide supervisees with ongoing feedback regarding their performance and schedule periodic formal evaluative sessions throughout the supervisory relationship.

F.6.b. Gatekeeping and Remediation

Through initial and ongoing evaluation, supervisors are aware of supervisee limitations that might impede performance. Supervisors assist supervisees in securing remedial assistance when needed. They recommend dismissal from training programs, applied counseling settings, and state or voluntary professional credentialing processes when those supervisees are unable to demonstrate that they can provide competent professional services to a range of diverse clients. Supervisors seek consultation and document their decisions to dismiss or refer supervisees for assistance. They ensure that supervisees are aware of options available to them to address such decisions.

F.6.c. Counseling for Supervisees

If supervisees request counseling, the supervisor assists the supervisee in identifying appropriate services. Supervisors do not provide counseling services to supervisees. Supervisors address interpersonal competencies in terms of the impact of these issues on clients, the supervisory relationship, and professional functioning.

F.6.d. Endorsements

Supervisors endorse supervisees for certification, licensure, employment, or completion of an academic or training program only when they believe that supervisees are qualified for the endorsement. Regardless of qualifications, supervisors do not endorse supervisees whom they believe to be impaired in any way that would interfere with the performance of the duties associated with the endorsement.

F.7. Responsibilities of Counselor Educators

F.7.a. Counselor Educators

Counselor educators who are responsible for developing, implementing, and supervising educational programs are skilled as teachers and practitioners. They are knowledgeable regarding the ethical, legal, and regulatory aspects of the profession; are skilled in applying that knowledge; and make students and supervisees aware of their responsibilities. Whether in traditional, hybrid, and/or online formats, counselor educators conduct counselor education and training programs in an ethical manner and serve as role models for professional behavior.

F.7.b. Counselor Educator Competence

Counselors who function as counselor educators or supervisors provide instruction within their areas of knowledge and competence and provide instruction based on current information and knowledge available in the profession. When using technology to deliver instruction, counselor educators develop competence in the use of the technology.

F.7.c. Infusing Multicultural Issues/Diversity

Counselor educators infuse material related to multiculturalism/diversity into all courses and workshops for the development of professional counselors.

F.7.d. Integration of Study and Practice

In traditional, hybrid, and/or online formats, counselor educators establish education and training programs that integrate academic study and supervised practice.

F.7.e. Teaching Ethics

Throughout the program, counselor educators ensure that students are aware of the ethical responsibilities and standards of the profession and the ethical responsibilities of students to the profession. Counselor educators infuse ethical considerations throughout the curriculum.

F.7.f. Use of Case Examples

The use of client, student, or supervisee information for the purposes of case examples in a lecture or classroom setting is permissible only when (a) the client, student, or supervisee has reviewed the material and agreed to its presentation or (b) the information has been sufficiently modified to obscure identity.

F.7.g. Student-to-Student Supervision and Instruction

When students function in the role of counselor educators or supervisors, they understand that they have the same ethical obligations as counselor educators, trainers, and supervisors. Counselor educators make every effort to ensure that the rights of students are not compromised when their peers lead experiential counseling activities in traditional, hybrid, and/or online formats (e.g., counseling groups, skills classes, clinical supervision).

F.7.h. Innovative Theories and Techniques

Counselor educators promote the use of techniques/procedures/modalities that are grounded in theory and/or have an empirical or scientific foundation. When counselor educators discuss developing or innovative techniques/procedures/modalities, they explain the potential risks, benefits, and ethical considerations of using such techniques/procedures/modalities.

F.7.i. Field Placements

Counselor educators develop clear policies and provide direct assistance within their training programs regarding appropriate field placement and other clinical experiences. Counselor educators provide clearly stated roles and responsibilities for the student or supervisee, the site supervisor, and the program supervisor. They confirm that site supervisors are qualified to provide supervision in the formats in which services are provided and inform site supervisors of their professional and ethical responsibilities in this role.

F.8. Student Welfare

F.8.a. Program Information and Orientation

Counselor educators recognize that program orientation is a developmental process that begins upon students' initial contact with the counselor education program and continues throughout the educational and clinical training of students. Counselor education faculty provide prospective and current students with information about the counselor education program's expectations, including

1. the values and ethical principles of the profession;
2. the type and level of skill and knowledge acquisition required for successful completion of the training;
3. technology requirements;
4. program training goals, objectives, and mission, and subject matter to be covered;
5. bases for evaluation;
6. training components that encourage self-growth or self-disclosure as part of the training process;
7. the type of supervision settings and requirements of the sites for required clinical field experiences;
8. student and supervisor evaluation and dismissal policies and procedures; and
9. up-to-date employment prospects for graduates.

F.8.b. Student Career Advising

Counselor educators provide career advisement for their students and make them aware of opportunities in the field.

F.8.c. Self-Growth Experiences

Self-growth is an expected component of counselor education. Counselor educators are mindful of ethical principles when they require students to engage in self-growth experiences. Counselor educators and supervisors inform students that they have a right to decide what information will be shared or withheld in class.

F.8.d. Addressing Personal Concerns

Counselor educators may require students to address any personal concerns that have the potential to affect professional competency.

F.9. Evaluation and Remediation

F.9.a. Evaluation of Students

Counselor educators clearly state to students, prior to and throughout the training program, the levels of competency expected, appraisal methods, and timing of evaluations for both didactic and clinical competencies. Counselor educators provide students with ongoing feedback regarding their performance throughout the training program.

F.9.b. Limitations

Counselor educators, through ongoing evaluation, are aware of and address the inability of some students to achieve counseling competencies. Counselor educators do the following:

1. assist students in securing remedial assistance when needed,
2. seek professional consultation and document their decision to dismiss or refer students for assistance, and
3. ensure that students have recourse in a timely manner to address decisions requiring them to seek assistance or to dismiss them and provide students with due process according to institutional policies and procedures.

F.9.c. Counseling for Students

If students request counseling, or if counseling services are suggested as part of a remediation process, counselor educators assist students in identifying appropriate services.

F.10. Roles and Relationships Between Counselor Educators and Students

F.10.a. Sexual or Romantic Relationships

Counselor educators are prohibited from sexual or romantic interactions or relationships with students currently enrolled in a counseling or related program and over whom they have power and authority. This prohibition applies to both in-person and electronic interactions or relationships.

F.10.b. Sexual Harassment

Counselor educators do not condone or subject students to sexual harassment.

F.10.c. Relationships With Former Students

Counselor educators are aware of the power differential in the relationship between faculty and students. Faculty members discuss with former students potential risks when they consider engaging in social, sexual, or other intimate relationships.

F.10.d. Nonacademic Relationships

Counselor educators avoid nonacademic relationships with students in which there is a risk of potential harm to the student or which may compromise the training experience or grades assigned. In addition, counselor educators do not accept any form of professional services, fees, commissions, reimbursement, or remuneration from a site for student or supervisor placement.

F.10.e. Counseling Services

Counselor educators do not serve as counselors to students currently enrolled in a counseling or related program and over whom they have power and authority.

F.10.f. Extending Educator–Student Boundaries

Counselor educators are aware of the power differential in the relationship between faculty and students. If they believe that a nonprofessional relationship with a student may be potentially beneficial to the student, they take pre-cautions similar to those taken by counselors when working with clients. Examples of potentially beneficial interactions or relationships include, but are not limited to, attending a formal ceremony; conducting hospital visits; providing support during a stressful event; or maintaining mutual membership in a professional association, organization, or community. Counselor educators discuss with students the rationale for such interactions, the potential benefits and drawbacks, and the anticipated consequences for the student. Educators clarify the specific nature and limitations of the additional role(s) they will have with the student prior to engaging in a nonprofessional relationship. Nonprofessional relationships with students should be time limited and/or context specific and initiated with student consent.

F.11. Multicultural/Diversity Competence in Counselor Education and Training Programs

F.11.a. Faculty Diversity

Counselor educators are committed to recruiting and retaining a diverse faculty.

F.11.b. Student Diversity

Counselor educators actively attempt to recruit and retain a diverse student body. Counselor educators demonstrate commitment to multicultural/diversity competence by recognizing and valuing the diverse cultures and types of abilities that students bring to the training experience. Counselor educators provide appropriate accommodations that enhance and support diverse student well-being and academic performance.

F.11.c. Multicultural/Diversity Competence

Counselor educators actively infuse multicultural/diversity competency in their training and supervision practices. They actively train students to gain awareness, knowledge, and skills in the competencies of multicultural practice.

Section G: Research and Publication

Introduction

Counselors who conduct research are encouraged to contribute to the knowledge base of the profession and promote a clearer understanding of the conditions that lead to a healthy and more just society. Counselors support the efforts of researchers by participating fully and willingly whenever possible. Counselors minimize bias and respect diversity in designing and implementing research.

G.1. Research Responsibilities

G.1.a. Conducting Research

Counselors plan, design, conduct, and report research in a manner that is consistent with pertinent ethical principles, federal and state laws, host institutional regulations, and scientific standards governing research.

G.1.b. Confidentiality in Research

Counselors are responsible for understanding and adhering to state, federal, agency, or institutional policies or applicable guidelines regarding confidentiality in their research practices.

G.1.c. Independent Researchers

When counselors conduct independent research and do not have access to an institutional review board, they are bound to the same ethical principles and federal and state laws pertaining to the review of their plan, design, conduct, and reporting of research.

G.1.d. Deviation From Standard Practice

Counselors seek consultation and observe stringent safeguards to protect the rights of research participants when research indicates that a deviation from standard or acceptable practices may be necessary.

G.1.e. Precautions to Avoid Injury

Counselors who conduct research are responsible for their participants' welfare throughout the research process and should take reasonable precautions to avoid causing emotional, physical, or social harm to participants.

G.1.f. Principal Researcher Responsibility

The ultimate responsibility for ethical research practice lies with the principal researcher. All others involved in the research activities share ethical obligations and responsibility for their own actions.

G.2. *Rights of Research Participants*

G.2.a. Informed Consent in Research

Individuals have the right to decline requests to become research participants. In seeking consent, counselors use language that

1. accurately explains the purpose and procedures to be followed;
2. identifies any procedures that are experimental or relatively untried;
3. describes any attendant discomforts, risks, and potential power differentials between researchers and participants;
4. describes any benefits or changes in individuals or organizations that might reasonably be expected;
5. discloses appropriate alternative procedures that would be advantageous for participants;
6. offers to answer any inquiries concerning the procedures;
7. describes any limitations on confidentiality;
8. describes the format and potential target audiences for the dissemination of research findings; and
9. instructs participants that they are free to withdraw their consent and discontinue participation in the project at any time, without penalty.

G.2.b. Student/Supervisee Participation

Researchers who involve students or supervisees in research make clear to them that the decision regarding participation in research activities does not affect their academic standing or supervisory relationship. Students or supervisees who choose not to participate in research are provided with an appropriate alternative to fulfill their academic or clinical requirements.

G.2.c. Client Participation

Counselors conducting research involving clients make clear in the informed consent process that clients are free to choose whether to participate in research activities. Counselors take necessary precautions to protect clients from adverse consequences of declining or withdrawing from participation.

G.2.d. Confidentiality of Information

Information obtained about research participants during the course of re-search is confidential. Procedures are implemented to protect confidentiality.

G.2.e. Persons Not Capable of Giving Informed Consent

When a research participant is not capable of giving informed consent, counselors provide an appropriate explanation to, obtain agreement for participation from, and obtain the appropriate consent of a legally authorized person.

G.2.f. Commitments to Participants

Counselors take reasonable measures to honor all commitments to research participants.

G.2.g. Explanations After Data Collection

After data are collected, counselors provide participants with full clarification of the nature of the study to re-move any misconceptions participants might have regarding the research. Where scientific or human values justify delaying or withholding information, counselors take reasonable measures to avoid causing harm.

G.2.h. Informing Sponsors

Counselors inform sponsors, institutions, and publication channels regarding research procedures and outcomes. Counselors ensure that appropriate bodies and authorities are given pertinent information and acknowledgment.

G.2.i. Research Records Custodian

As appropriate, researchers prepare and disseminate to an identified colleague or records custodian a plan for the transfer of research data in the case of their incapacitation, retirement, or death.

G.3. *Managing and Maintaining Boundaries*

G.3.a. Extending Researcher–Participant Boundaries

Researchers consider the risks and benefits of extending current research relationships beyond conventional parameters. When a nonresearch interaction between the researcher and the research participant may be potentially beneficial, the researcher must document, prior to the interaction (when feasible), the rationale for such an interaction, the potential benefit, and anticipated consequences for the research participant. Such interactions should be initiated with appropriate consent of the research participant. Where unintentional harm occurs to the research participant, the researcher must show evidence of an attempt to remedy such harm.

G.3.b. Relationships With Research Participants

Sexual or romantic counselor – research participant interactions or relationships with current research participants are prohibited. This prohibition applies to both in-person and electronic interactions or relationships.

G.3.c. Sexual Harassment and Research Participants

Researchers do not condone or subject research participants to sexual harassment.

G.4. Reporting Results

G.4.a. Accurate Results

Counselors plan, conduct, and report research accurately. Counselors do not engage in misleading or fraudulent re-search, distort data, misrepresent data, or deliberately bias their results. They describe the extent to which results are applicable for diverse populations.

G.4.b. Obligation to Report Unfavorable Results

Counselors report the results of any research of professional value. Results that reflect unfavorably on institutions, programs, services, prevailing opinions, or vested interests are not withheld.

G.4.c. Reporting Errors

If counselors discover significant errors in their published research, they take reasonable steps to correct such errors in a correction erratum or through other appropriate publication means.

G.4.d. Identity of Participants

Counselors who supply data, aid in the research of another person, report research results, or make original data available take due care to disguise the identity of respective participants in the absence of specific authorization from the participants to do otherwise. In situations where participants self-identify their involvement in research studies, researchers take active steps to ensure that data are adapted/changed to protect the identity and welfare of all parties and that discussion of results does not cause harm to participants.

G.4.e. Replication Studies

Counselors are obligated to make available sufficient original research information to qualified professionals who may wish to replicate or extend the study.

G.5. Publications and Presentations

G.5.a. Use of Case Examples

The use of participants', clients', students', or supervisees' information for the purpose of case examples in a presentation or publication is permissible only when (a) participants, clients, students, or supervisees have reviewed the material and agreed to its presentation or publication or (b) the information has been sufficiently modified to obscure identity.

G.5.b. Plagiarism

Counselors do not plagiarize; that is, they do not present another person's work as their own.

G.5.c. Acknowledging Previous Work

In publications and presentations, counselors acknowledge and give recognition to previous work on the topic by others or self.

G.5.d. Contributors

Counselors give credit through joint authorship, acknowledgment, footnote statements, or other appropriate means to those who have contributed significantly to research or concept development in accordance with such contributions. The principal contributor is listed first, and minor technical or professional contributions are acknowledged in notes or introductory statements.

G.5.e. Agreement of Contributors

Counselors who conduct joint research with colleagues or students/supervisors establish agreements in advance regarding allocation of tasks, publication credit, and types of acknowledgment that will be received.

G.5.f. Student Research

Manuscripts or professional presentations in any medium that are substantially based on a student's course papers, projects, dissertations, or theses are used only with the student's permission and list the student as lead author.

G.5.g. Duplicate Submissions

Counselors submit manuscripts for consideration to only one journal at a time. Manuscripts that are published in whole or in substantial part in one journal or published work are not submitted for publication to another publisher without acknowledgment and permission from the original publisher.

G.5.h. Professional Review

Counselors who review material submitted for publication, research, or other scholarly purposes respect the confidentiality and proprietary rights of those who submitted it. Counselors make publication decisions based on valid and defensible standards. Counselors review article submissions in a timely manner and based on their scope and competency in research methodologies. Counselors who serve as reviewers at the request of editors or publishers make every effort to only review materials that are within their scope of competency and avoid personal biases.

Section H: Distance Counseling, Technology, and Social Media

Introduction

Counselors understand that the profession of counseling may no longer be limited to in-person, face-to-face interactions. Counselors actively attempt to understand the evolving nature of the profession with regard to distance counseling, technology, and social media and how such resources may be used to better serve their clients. Counselors strive to become knowledgeable about these resources. Counselors understand the additional concerns related to the use of distance counseling, technology, and social media and make every attempt to protect confidentiality and meet any legal and ethical requirements for the use of such resources.

H.1. Knowledge and Legal Considerations

H.1.a. Knowledge and Competency

Counselors who engage in the use of distance counseling, technology, and/or social media develop knowledge and skills regarding related technical, ethical, and legal considerations (e.g., special certifications, additional course work).

H.1.b. Laws and Statutes

Counselors who engage in the use of distance counseling, technology, and social media within their counseling practice understand that they may be subject to laws and regulations of both the counselor's practicing location and the client's place of residence. Counselors ensure that their clients are aware of pertinent legal rights and limitations governing the practice of counseling across state lines or international boundaries.

H.2. Informed Consent and Security

H.2.a. Informed Consent and Disclosure

Clients have the freedom to choose whether to use distance counseling, social media, and/or technology within the counseling process. In addition to the usual and customary protocol of informed consent between counselor and client for face-to-face counseling, the following issues, unique to the use of distance counseling, technology, and/or social media, are addressed in the informed consent process:

- distance counseling credentials, physical location of practice, and contact information;
- risks and benefits of engaging in the use of distance counseling, technology, and/or social media;
- possibility of technology failure and alternate methods of service delivery;
- anticipated response time;
- emergency procedures to follow when the counselor is not available;
- time zone differences;
- cultural and/or language differences that may affect delivery of services;
- possible denial of insurance benefits; and
- social media policy.

H.2.b. Confidentiality Maintained by the Counselor

Counselors acknowledge the limitations of maintaining the confidentiality of electronic records and transmissions. They inform clients that individuals might have authorized or unauthorized access to such records or transmissions (e.g., colleagues, supervisors, employees, information technologists).

H.2.c. Acknowledgment of Limitations

Counselors inform clients about the inherent limits of confidentiality when using technology. Counselors urge clients to be aware of authorized and/or unauthorized access to information disclosed using this medium in the counseling process.

H.2.d. Security

Counselors use current encryption standards within their websites and/or technology-based communications that meet applicable legal requirements. Counselors take reasonable precautions to ensure the confidentiality of information transmitted through any electronic means.

H.3. Client Verification

Counselors who engage in the use of distance counseling, technology, and/or social media to interact with clients take steps to verify the client's identity at the beginning and throughout the therapeutic process. Verification can include, but is not limited to, using code words, numbers, graphics, or other nondescript identifiers.

H.4. Distance Counseling Relationship

H.4.a. Benefits and Limitations

Counselors inform clients of the benefits and limitations of using technology applications in the provision of counseling services. Such technologies include, but are not limited to, computer hardware and/or software, telephones and applications, social media and Internet-based applications and other audio and/or video communication, or data storage devices or media.

H.4.b. Professional Boundaries in Distance Counseling

Counselors understand the necessity of maintaining a professional relationship with their clients. Counselors discuss and establish professional boundaries with clients regarding the appropriate use and/or application of technology and the limitations of its use within the counseling relationship (e.g., lack of confidentiality, times when not appropriate to use).

H.4.c. Technology-Assisted Services

When providing technology-assisted services, counselors make reasonable efforts to determine that clients are intellectually, emotionally, physically, linguistically, and functionally capable of using the application and that the application is appropriate for the needs of the client. Counselors verify that clients understand the purpose and operation of technology applications and follow up with clients to correct possible misconceptions, discover appropriate use, and assess subsequent steps.

H.4.d. Effectiveness of Services

When distance counseling services are deemed ineffective by the counselor or client, counselors consider delivering services face-to-face. If the counselor is not able to provide face-to-face services (e.g., lives in another state), the counselor assists the client in identifying appropriate services.

H.4.e. Access

Counselors provide information to clients regarding reasonable access to pertinent applications when providing technology-assisted services.

H.4.f. Communication Differences in Electronic Media

Counselors consider the differences between face-to-face and electronic communication (nonverbal and verbal cues) and how these may affect the counseling process. Counselors educate clients on how to prevent and address potential misunderstandings arising from the lack of visual cues and voice intonations when communicating electronically.

H.5. Records and Web Maintenance

H.5.a. Records

Counselors maintain electronic records in accordance with relevant laws and statutes. Counselors inform clients on how records are maintained electronically. This includes, but is not limited to, the type of encryption and security assigned to the records, and if/for how long archival storage of transaction records is maintained.

H.5.b. Client Rights

Counselors who offer distance counseling services and/or maintain a professional website provide electronic links to relevant licensure and professional certification boards to protect consumer and client rights and address ethical concerns.

H.5.c. Electronic Links

Counselors regularly ensure that electronic links are working and are professionally appropriate.

H.5.d. Multicultural and Disability Considerations

Counselors who maintain websites provide accessibility to persons with disabilities. They provide translation capabilities for clients who have a different primary language, when feasible. Counselors acknowledge the imperfect nature of such translations and accessibilities.

H.6. Social Media

H.6.a. Virtual Professional Presence

In cases where counselors wish to maintain a professional and personal presence for social media use, separate professional and personal web pages and profiles are created to clearly distinguish between the two kinds of virtual presence.

H.6.b. Social Media as Part of Informed Consent

Counselors clearly explain to their clients, as part of the informed consent procedure, the benefits, limitations, and boundaries of the use of social media.

H.6.c. Client Virtual Presence

Counselors respect the privacy of their clients' presence on social media unless given consent to view such information.

H.6.d. Use of Public Social Media

Counselors take precautions to avoid disclosing confidential information through public social media.

Section I: Resolving Ethical Issues

Introduction

Professional counselors behave in an ethical and legal manner. They are aware that client welfare and trust in the profession depend on a high level of professional conduct. They hold other counselors to the same standards and are willing to take appropriate action to ensure that standards are upheld. Counselors strive to resolve ethical dilemmas with direct and open communication among all parties involved and seek consultation with colleagues and supervisors when necessary. Counselors incorporate ethical practice into their daily professional work and engage in ongoing professional development regarding current topics in ethical and legal issues in counseling. Counselors become familiar with the ACA Policy and Procedures for Processing Complaints of Ethical Violations* and use it as a reference for assisting in the enforcement of the *ACA Code of Ethics*.

---

*See the American Counseling Association web site at http://www.counseling.org/knowledge-center/ethics

I.1. Standards and the Law

I.1.a. Knowledge

Counselors know and understand the *ACA Code of Ethics* and other applicable ethics codes from professional organizations or certification and licensure bodies of which they are members. Lack of knowledge or misunderstanding of an ethical responsibility is not a defense against a charge of unethical conduct.

I.1.b. Ethical Decision Making

When counselors are faced with an ethical dilemma, they use and document, as appropriate, an ethical decision-making model that may include, but is not limited to, consultation; consideration of relevant ethical standards, principles, and laws; generation of potential courses of action; deliberation of risks and benefits; and selection of an objective decision based on the circumstances and welfare of all involved.

I.1.c. Conflicts Between Ethics and Laws

If ethical responsibilities conflict with the law, regulations, and/or other governing legal authority, counselors make known their commitment to the *ACA Code of Ethics* and take steps to resolve the conflict. If the conflict cannot be resolved using this approach, counselors, acting in the best interest of the client, may adhere to the requirements of the law, regulations, and/or other governing legal authority.

I.2. Suspected Violations

I.2.a. Informal Resolution

When counselors have reason to believe that another counselor is violating or has violated an ethical standard and substantial harm has not occurred, they attempt to first resolve the issue informally with the other counselor if feasible, provided such action does not violate confidentiality rights that may be involved.

I.2.b. Reporting Ethical Violations

If an apparent violation has substantially harmed or is likely to substantially harm a person or organization and is not appropriate for informal resolution or is not resolved properly, counselors take further action depending on the situation. Such action may include referral to state or national committees on professional ethics, voluntary national certification bodies, state licensing boards, or appropriate institutional authorities. The confidentiality rights of clients should be considered in all actions. This standard does not apply when counselors have been retained to review the work of another counselor whose professional conduct is in question (e.g., consultation, expert testimony).

I.2.c. Consultation

When uncertain about whether a particular situation or course of action may be in violation of the *ACA Code of Ethics*, counselors consult with other counselors who are knowledgeable about ethics and the *ACA Code of Ethics*, with colleagues, or with appropriate authorities, such as the ACA Ethics and Professional Standards Department.

I.2.d. Organizational Conflicts

If the demands of an organization with which counselors are affiliated pose a conflict with the *ACA Code of Ethics*, counselors specify the nature of such conflicts and express to their supervisors or other responsible officials their commitment to the *ACA Code of Ethics* and, when possible, work through the appropriate channels to address the situation.

I.2.e. Unwarranted Complaints

Counselors do not initiate, participate in, or encourage the filing of ethics complaints that are retaliatory in nature or are made with reckless disregard or willful ignorance of facts that would disprove the allegation.

I.2.f. Unfair Discrimination Against Complainants and Respondents

Counselors do not deny individuals employment, advancement, admission to academic or other programs, tenure, or promotion based solely on their having made or their being the subject of an ethics complaint. This does not preclude taking action based on the outcome of such proceedings or considering other appropriate information.

I.3. Cooperation With Ethics Committees

Counselors assist in the process of enforcing the *ACA Code of Ethics*. Counselors cooperate with investigations, proceedings, and requirements of the ACA Ethics Committee or ethics committees of other duly constituted associations or boards having jurisdiction over those charged with a violation.

Source: Reprinted with permission from American Counseling Association.

APPENDIX B

American Psychological Association, Ethical Principles of Psychologists and Code of Conduct

Introduction and Applicability

The American Psychological Association's (APA's) Ethical Principles of Psychologists and Code of Conduct (hereinafter referred to as the Ethics Code) consists of an Introduction, a Preamble, five General Principles (A–E), and specific Ethical Standards. The Introduction discusses the intent, organization, procedural considerations, and scope of application of the Ethics Code. The Preamble and General Principles are aspirational goals to guide psychologists toward the highest ideals of psychology. Although the Preamble and General Principles are not themselves enforceable rules, they should be considered by psychologists in arriving at an ethical course of action. The Ethical Standards set forth enforceable rules for conduct as psychologists. Most of the Ethical Standards are written broadly, in order to apply to psychologists in varied roles, although the application of an Ethical Standard may vary depending on the context. The Ethical Standards are not exhaustive. The fact that a given conduct is not specifically addressed by an Ethical Standard does not mean that it is necessarily either ethical or unethical.

This Ethics Code applies only to psychologists' activities that are part of their scientific, educational, or professional roles as psychologists. Areas covered include but are not limited to the clinical, counseling, and school practice of psychology; research; teaching; supervision of trainees; public service; policy development; social intervention; development of assessment instruments; conducting assessments; educational counseling; organizational consulting; forensic activities; program design and evaluation; and administration. This Ethics Code applies to these activities across a variety of contexts, such as in person, postal, telephone, internet, and other electronic transmissions. These activities shall be distinguished from the purely private conduct of psychologists, which is not within the purview of the Ethics Code.

Membership in the APA commits members and student affiliates to comply with the standards of the APA Ethics Code and to the rules and procedures used to enforce them. Lack of awareness or misunderstanding of an Ethical Standard is not itself a defense to a charge of unethical conduct.

The procedures for filing, investigating, and resolving complaints of unethical conduct are described in the current Rules and Procedures of the APA Ethics Committee. APA may impose sanctions on its members for violations of the standards of the Ethics Code, including termination of APA membership, and may notify other bodies and individuals of its actions. Actions that violate the standards of the Ethics Code may also lead to the imposition of sanctions on psychologists or students whether or not they are APA members by bodies other than APA, including state psychological associations, other professional groups, psychology boards, other state or federal agencies, and payors for health services. In addition, APA may take action against a member after his or her conviction of a felony, expulsion or suspension from an affiliated state psychological association, or suspension or loss of licensure. When the sanction to be imposed by APA is less than expulsion, the 2001 Rules and Procedures do not guarantee an opportunity for an in-person hearing, but generally provide that complaints will be resolved only on the basis of a submitted record.

The Ethics Code is intended to provide guidance for psychologists and standards of professional conduct that can be applied by the APA and by other bodies that choose to adopt them. The Ethics Code is not intended to be a basis of civil liability. Whether a psychologist has violated the Ethics Code standards does not by itself determine whether the psychologist is legally liable in a court action, whether a contract is enforceable, or whether other legal consequences occur.

The modifiers used in some of the standards of this Ethics Code (e.g., reasonably, appropriate, potentially) are included in the standards when they would (1) allow professional judgment on the part of psychologists, (2) eliminate injustice or inequality that would occur without the modifier, (3) ensure applicability across the broad range of activities conducted by psychologists, or (4) guard against a set of rigid rules that might be quickly outdated. As used in this Ethics Code, the term reasonable means the prevailing professional judgment of psychologists engaged in similar activities in similar circumstances, given the knowledge the psychologist had or should have had at the time.

In the process of making decisions regarding their professional behavior, psychologists must consider this Ethics Code in addition to applicable laws and psychology board regulations. In applying the Ethics Code to their professional work, psychologists may consider other materials and guidelines that have been adopted or endorsed by scientific and professional psychological organizations and the dictates of their own conscience, as well as consult with others within the field. If this Ethics Code establishes a higher standard of conduct than is required by law, psychologists must meet the higher ethical standard. If psychologists' ethical responsibilities conflict with law, regulations, or other governing legal authority, psychologists make known their commitment to this Ethics Code and take steps to resolve the conflict in a responsible manner. If the conflict is unresolvable via such means, psychologists may adhere to the requirements of the law, regulations, or other governing authority in keeping with basic principles of human rights.

Preamble

Psychologists are committed to increasing scientific and professional knowledge of behavior and people's understanding of themselves and others and to the use of such knowledge to improve the condition of individuals, organizations, and society. Psychologists respect and protect civil and human rights and the central importance of freedom of inquiry and expression in research, teaching, and publication. They strive to help the public in developing informed judgments and choices concerning human behavior. In doing so, they perform many roles, such as researcher, educator, diagnostician, therapist, supervisor, consultant, administrator, social interventionist, and expert witness. This Ethics Code provides a common set of principles and standards upon which psychologists build their professional and scientific work.

This Ethics Code is intended to provide specific standards to cover most situations encountered by psychologists. It has as its goals the welfare and protection of the individuals and groups with whom psychologists work and the education of members, students, and the public regarding ethical standards of the discipline.

The development of a dynamic set of ethical standards for psychologists' work-related conduct requires a personal commitment and lifelong effort to act ethically; to encourage ethical behavior by students, supervisees, employees, and colleagues; and to consult with others concerning ethical problems.

General Principles

This section consists of General Principles. General Principles, as opposed to Ethical Standards, are aspirational in nature. Their intent is to guide and inspire psychologists toward the very highest ethical ideals of the profession. General Principles, in contrast to Ethical Standards, do not represent obligations and should not form the basis for imposing sanctions. Relying upon General Principles for either of these reasons distorts both their meaning and purpose.

Principle A: Beneficence and Nonmaleficence

Psychologists strive to benefit those with whom they work and take care to do no harm. In their professional actions, psychologists seek to safeguard the welfare and rights of those with whom they interact professionally and other affected persons, and the welfare of animal subjects of research. When conflicts occur among psychologists' obligations or concerns, they attempt to resolve these conflicts in a responsible fashion that avoids or minimizes harm. Because psychologists' scientific and professional judgments and actions may affect the lives of others, they are alert to and guard against personal, financial, social, organizational, or political factors that might lead to misuse of their influence. Psychologists strive to be aware of the possible effect of their own physical and mental health on their ability to help those with whom they work.

Principle B: Fidelity and Responsibility

Psychologists establish relationships of trust with those with whom they work. They are aware of their professional and scientific responsibilities to society and to the specific communities in which they work. Psychologists uphold professional standards of conduct, clarify their professional roles and obligations, accept appropriate responsibility for their behavior, and seek to manage conflicts of interest that could lead to exploitation or harm. Psychologists consult with, refer to, or cooperate with other professionals and institutions to the extent needed to serve the best interests of those with whom they work. They are concerned about the ethical compliance of their colleagues' scientific and professional conduct. Psychologists strive to contribute a portion of their professional time for little or no compensation or personal advantage.

Principle C: Integrity

Psychologists seek to promote accuracy, honesty, and truthfulness in the science, teaching, and practice of psychology. In these activities psychologists do not steal, cheat, or engage in fraud, subterfuge, or intentional misrepresentation of fact. Psychologists strive to keep their promises and to avoid unwise or unclear commitments. In situations in which deception may be ethically justifiable to maximize benefits and minimize harm, psychologists have a serious obligation to consider the need for, the possible consequences of, and their responsibility to correct any resulting mistrust or other harmful effects that arise from the use of such techniques.

Principle D: Justice

Psychologists recognize that fairness and justice entitle all persons to access to and benefit from the contributions of psychology and to equal quality in the processes, procedures, and services being conducted by psychologists. Psychologists exercise reasonable judgment and take precautions to ensure that their potential biases, the boundaries of their competence, and the limitations of their expertise do not lead to or condone unjust practices.

Principle E: Respect for People's Rights and Dignity

Psychologists respect the dignity and worth of all people, and the rights of individuals to privacy, confidentiality, and self-determination. Psychologists are aware that special safeguards may be necessary to protect the rights and welfare of persons or communities whose vulnerabilities impair autonomous decision making. Psychologists are aware of and respect cultural, individual, and role differences, including those based on age, gender, gender identity, race, ethnicity, culture, national origin, religion, sexual orientation, disability, language, and socioeconomic status and consider these factors when working with members of such groups. Psychologists try to eliminate the effect on their work of biases based on those factors, and they do not knowingly participate in or condone activities of others based upon such prejudices.

Ethical Standards

1. Resolving Ethical Issues

1.01 Misuse of Psychologists' Work

If psychologists learn of misuse or misrepresentation of their work, they take reasonable steps to correct or minimize the misuse or misrepresentation.

1.02 Conflicts Between Ethics and Law, Regulations, or Other Governing Legal Authority

If psychologists' ethical responsibilities conflict with law, regulations, or other governing legal authority, psychologists clarify the nature of the conflict, make known their commitment to the Ethics Code, and take reasonable steps to resolve the conflict consistent with the General Principles and Ethical Standards of the Ethics Code. Under no circumstances may this standard be used to justify or defend violating human rights.

1.03 Conflicts Between Ethics and Organizational Demands

If the demands of an organization with which psychologists are affiliated or for whom they are working are in conflict with this Ethics Code, psychologists clarify the nature of the conflict, make known their commitment to the Ethics Code, and take reasonable steps to resolve the conflict consistent with the General Principles and Ethical Standards of the Ethics Code. Under no circumstances may this standard be used to justify or defend violating human rights.

1.04 Informal Resolution of Ethical Violations

When psychologists believe that there may have been an ethical violation by another psychologist, they attempt to resolve the issue by bringing it to the attention of that individual, if an informal resolution appears appropriate and the intervention does not violate any confidentiality rights that may be involved. (See also Standards 1.02, Conflicts Between Ethics and Law, Regulations, or Other Governing Legal Authority, and 1.03, Conflicts Between Ethics and Organizational Demands.)

1.05 Reporting Ethical Violations

If an apparent ethical violation has substantially harmed or is likely to substantially harm a person or organization and is not appropriate for informal resolution under Standard 1.04, Informal Resolution of Ethical Violations, or is not resolved properly in that fashion, psychologists take further action appropriate to the situation. Such action might include referral to state or national committees on professional ethics, to state licensing boards, or to the appropriate institutional authorities. This standard does not apply when an intervention would violate confidentiality rights or when psychologists have been retained to review the work of another psychologist whose professional conduct is in question. (See also Standard 1.02, Conflicts Between Ethics and Law, Regulations, or Other Governing Legal Authority.)

1.06 Cooperating With Ethics Committees

Psychologists cooperate in ethics investigations, proceedings, and resulting requirements of the APA or any affiliated state psychological association to which they belong. In doing so, they address any confidentiality issues. Failure to cooperate is itself an ethics violation. However, making a request for deferment of adjudication of an ethics complaint pending the outcome of litigation does not alone constitute noncooperation.

1.07 Improper Complaints

Psychologists do not file or encourage the filing of ethics complaints that are made with reckless disregard for or willful ignorance of facts that would disprove the allegation.

1.08 Unfair Discrimination Against Complainants and Respondents

Psychologists do not deny persons employment, advancement, admissions to academic or other programs, tenure, or promotion, based solely upon their having made or their being the subject of an ethics complaint. This does not preclude taking action based upon the outcome of such proceedings or considering other appropriate information.

2. *Competence*

2.01 Boundaries of Competence

(a) Psychologists provide services, teach, and conduct research with populations and in areas only within the boundaries of their competence, based on their education, training, supervised experience, consultation, study, or professional experience.

(b) Where scientific or professional knowledge in the discipline of psychology establishes that an understanding of factors associated with age, gender, gender identity, race, ethnicity, culture, national origin, religion, sexual orientation, disability, language, or socioeconomic status is essential for effective implementation of their services or research, psychologists have or obtain the training, experience, consultation, or supervision necessary to ensure the competence of their services, or they make appropriate referrals, except as provided in Standard 2.02, Providing Services in Emergencies.

(c) Psychologists planning to provide services, teach, or conduct research involving populations, areas, techniques, or technologies new to them undertake relevant education, training, supervised experience, consultation, or study.

(d) When psychologists are asked to provide services to individuals for whom appropriate mental health services are not available and for which psychologists have not obtained the competence necessary, psychologists with closely related prior training or experience may provide such services in order to ensure that services are not denied if they make a reasonable effort to obtain the competence required by using relevant research, training, consultation, or study.

(e) In those emerging areas in which generally recognized standards for preparatory training do not yet exist, psychologists nevertheless take reasonable steps to ensure the competence of their work and to protect clients/patients, students, supervisees, research participants, organizational clients, and others from harm.

(f) When assuming forensic roles, psychologists are or become reasonably familiar with the judicial or administrative rules governing their roles.

2.02 Providing Services in Emergencies

In emergencies, when psychologists provide services to individuals for whom other mental health services are not available and for which psychologists have not obtained the necessary training, psychologists may provide such services in order to ensure that services are not denied. The services are discontinued as soon as the emergency has ended or appropriate services are available.

2.03 Maintaining Competence

Psychologists undertake ongoing efforts to develop and maintain their competence.

2.04 Bases for Scientific and Professional Judgments

Psychologists' work is based upon established scientific and professional knowledge of the discipline. (See also Standards 2.01e, Boundaries of Competence, and 10.01b, Informed Consent to Therapy.)

2.05 Delegation of Work to Others

Psychologists who delegate work to employees, supervisees, or research or teaching assistants or who use the services of others, such as interpreters, take reasonable steps to (1) avoid delegating such work to persons who have a multiple relationship with those being served that would likely lead to exploitation or loss of objectivity; (2) authorize only those responsibilities that such persons can be expected to perform competently on the basis of their education, training, or experience, either independently or with the level of supervision being provided; and (3) see that such persons perform these services competently. (See also Standards 2.02, Providing Services in Emergencies; 3.05, Multiple Relationships; 4.01, Maintaining Confidentiality; 9.01, Bases for Assessments; 9.02, Use of Assessments; 9.03, Informed Consent in Assessments; and 9.07, Assessment by Unqualified Persons.)

2.06 Personal Problems and Conflicts

(a) Psychologists refrain from initiating an activity when they know or should know that there is a substantial likelihood that their personal problems will prevent them from performing their work-related activities in a competent manner.

(b) When psychologists become aware of personal problems that may interfere with their performing work-related duties adequately, they take appropriate measures, such as obtaining professional consultation or assistance, and determine whether they should limit, suspend, or terminate their work-related duties. (See also Standard 10.10, Terminating Therapy.)

3. *Human Relations*

3.01 Unfair Discrimination

In their work-related activities, psychologists do not engage in unfair discrimination based on age, gender, gender identity, race, ethnicity, culture, national origin, religion, sexual orientation, disability, socioeconomic status, or any basis proscribed by law.

3.02 Sexual Harassment

Psychologists do not engage in sexual harassment. Sexual harassment is sexual solicitation, physical advances, or verbal or nonverbal conduct that is sexual in nature, that occurs in connection with the psychologist's activities or roles as a psychologist, and that either (1) is unwelcome, is offensive, or creates a hostile workplace or educational environment, and the psychologist knows or is told this or (2) is sufficiently severe or intense to be abusive to a reasonable person in the context. Sexual harassment can consist of a single intense or severe act or of multiple persistent or pervasive acts. (See also Standard 1.08, Unfair Discrimination Against Complainants and Respondents.)

3.03 Other Harassment

Psychologists do not knowingly engage in behavior that is harassing or demeaning to persons with whom they interact in their work based on factors such as those persons' age, gender, gender identity, race, ethnicity, culture, national origin, religion, sexual orientation, disability, language, or socioeconomic status.

3.04 Avoiding Harm

Psychologists take reasonable steps to avoid harming their clients/patients, students, supervisees, research participants, organizational clients, and others with whom they work, and to minimize harm where it is foreseeable and unavoidable.

3.05 Multiple Relationships

(a) A multiple relationship occurs when a psychologist is in a professional role with a person and (1) at the same time is in another role with the same person, (2) at the same time is in a relationship with a person closely associated with or related to the person with whom the psychologist has the professional relationship, or (3) promises to enter into another relationship in the future with the person or a person closely associated with or related to the person.

A psychologist refrains from entering into a multiple relationship if the multiple relationship could reasonably be expected to impair the psychologist's objectivity, competence, or effectiveness in performing his or her functions as a psychologist, or otherwise risks exploitation or harm to the person with whom the professional relationship exists.

Multiple relationships that would not reasonably be expected to cause impairment or risk exploitation or harm are not unethical.

(b) If a psychologist finds that, due to unforeseen factors, a potentially harmful multiple relationship has arisen, the psychologist takes reasonable steps to resolve it with due regard for the best interests of the affected person and maximal compliance with the Ethics Code.

(c) When psychologists are required by law, institutional policy, or extraordinary circumstances to serve in more than one role in judicial or administrative proceedings, at the outset they clarify role expectations and the extent of confidentiality and thereafter as changes occur. (See also Standards 3.04, Avoiding Harm, and 3.07, Third-Party Requests for Services.)

3.06 Conflict of Interest

Psychologists refrain from taking on a professional role when personal, scientific, professional, legal, financial, or other interests or relationships could reasonably be expected to (1) impair their objectivity, competence, or effectiveness in performing their functions as psychologists or (2) expose the person or organization with whom the professional relationship exists to harm or exploitation.

3.07 Third-Party Requests for Services

When psychologists agree to provide services to a person or entity at the request of a third party, psychologists attempt to clarify at the outset of the service the nature of the relationship with all individuals or organizations involved. This clarification includes the role of the psychologist (e.g., therapist, consultant, diagnostician, or expert witness), an identification of who is the client, the probable uses of the services provided or the information obtained, and the fact that there may be limits to confidentiality. (See also Standards 3.05, Multiple Relationships, and 4.02, Discussing the Limits of Confidentiality.)

3.08 Exploitative Relationships

Psychologists do not exploit persons over whom they have supervisory, evaluative, or other authority such as clients/patients, students, supervisees, research participants, and employees. (See also Standards 3.05, Multiple Relationships; 6.04, Fees and Financial Arrangements; 6.05, Barter With Clients/Patients; 7.07, Sexual Relationships With Students and Supervisees; 10.05, Sexual Intimacies With Current Therapy Clients/Patients; 10.06, Sexual Intimacies With Relatives or Significant Others of Current Therapy Clients/Patients; 10.07, Therapy With Former Sexual Partners; and 10.08, Sexual Intimacies With Former Therapy Clients/ Patients.)

3.09 Cooperation With Other Professionals

When indicated and professionally appropriate, psychologists cooperate with other professionals in order to serve their clients/patients effectively and appropriately. (See also Standard 4.05, Disclosures.)

3.10 Informed Consent

(a) When psychologists conduct research or provide assessment, therapy, counseling, or consulting services in person or via electronic transmission or other forms of communication, they obtain the informed consent of the individual or individuals using language that is reasonably understandable to that person or persons except when conducting such activities without consent is mandated by law or governmental regulation or as otherwise provided in this Ethics Code. (See also Standards 8.02, Informed Consent to Research; 9.03, Informed Consent in Assessments; and 10.01, Informed Consent to Therapy.)

(b) For persons who are legally incapable of giving informed consent, psychologists nevertheless (1) provide an appropriate explanation, (2) seek the individual's assent, (3) consider such persons' preferences and best interests, and (4) obtain appropriate permission from a legally authorized person, if such substitute consent is permitted or required by law. When consent by a legally authorized person is not permitted or required by law, psychologists take reasonable steps to protect the individual's rights and welfare.

(c) When psychological services are court ordered or otherwise mandated, psychologists inform the individual of the nature of the anticipated services, including whether the services are court ordered or mandated and any limits of confidentiality, before proceeding.

(d) Psychologists appropriately document written or oral consent, permission, and assent. (See also Standards 8.02, Informed Consent to Research; 9.03, Informed Consent in Assessments; and 10.01, Informed Consent to Therapy.)

3.11 Psychological Services Delivered To or Through Organizations

(a) Psychologists delivering services to or through organizations provide information beforehand to clients and when appropriate those directly affected by the services about (1) the nature and objectives of the services, (2) the intended recipients, (3) which of the individuals are clients, (4) the relationship the psychologist will have with each person and the organization, (5) the probable uses of services provided and information obtained, (6) who will have access to the information, and (7) limits of confidentiality. As soon as feasible, they provide information about the results and conclusions of such services to appropriate persons.

(b) If psychologists will be precluded by law or by organizational roles from providing such information to particular individuals or groups, they so inform those individuals or groups at the outset of the service.

3.12 Interruption of Psychological Services

Unless otherwise covered by contract, psychologists make reasonable efforts to plan for facilitating services in the event that psychological services are interrupted by factors such as the psychologist's illness, death, unavailability, relocation, or retirement or by the client's/patient's relocation or financial limitations. (See also Standard 6.02c, Maintenance, Dissemination, and Disposal of Confidential Records of Professional and Scientific Work.)

4. Privacy and Confidentiality

4.01 Maintaining Confidentiality

Psychologists have a primary obligation and take reasonable precautions to protect confidential information obtained through or stored in any medium, recognizing that the extent and limits of confidentiality may be regulated by law or established by institutional rules or professional or scientific relationship. (See also Standard 2.05, Delegation of Work to Others.)

4.02 Discussing the Limits of Confidentiality

(a) Psychologists discuss with persons (including, to the extent feasible, persons who are legally incapable of giving informed consent and their legal representatives) and organizations with whom they establish a scientific or professional relationship (1) the relevant limits of confidentiality and (2) the foreseeable uses of the information generated through their psychological activities. (See also Standard 3.10, Informed Consent.)

(b) Unless it is not feasible or is contraindicated, the discussion of confidentiality occurs at the outset of the relationship and thereafter as new circumstances may warrant.

(c) Psychologists who offer services, products, or information via electronic transmission inform clients/patients of the risks to privacy and limits of confidentiality.

4.03 Recording

Before recording the voices or images of individuals to whom they provide services, psychologists obtain permission from all such persons or their legal representatives. (See also Standards 8.03, Informed Consent for Recording Voices and Images in Research; 8.05, Dispensing With Informed Consent for Research; and 8.07, Deception in Research.)

4.04 Minimizing Intrusions on Privacy

(a) Psychologists include in written and oral reports and consultations, only information germane to the purpose for which the communication is made.

(b) Psychologists discuss confidential information obtained in their work only for appropriate scientific or professional purposes and only with persons clearly concerned with such matters.

4.05 Disclosures

(a) Psychologists may disclose confidential information with the appropriate consent of the organizational client, the individual client/patient, or another legally authorized person on behalf of the client/patient unless prohibited by law.

(b) Psychologists disclose confidential information without the consent of the individual only as mandated by law, or where permitted by law for a valid purpose such as to (1) provide needed professional services; (2) obtain appropriate professional consultations; (3) protect the client/patient, psychologist, or others from harm; or (4) obtain payment for services from a client/patient, in which instance disclosure is limited to the minimum that is necessary to achieve the purpose. (See also Standard 6.04e, Fees and Financial Arrangements.)

4.06 Consultations

When consulting with colleagues, (1) psychologists do not disclose confidential information that reasonably could lead to the identification of a client/patient, research participant, or other person or organization with whom they have a confidential relationship unless they have obtained the prior consent of the person or organization or the disclosure cannot be avoided, and (2) they disclose information only to the extent necessary to achieve the purposes of the consultation. (See also Standard 4.01, Maintaining Confidentiality.)

4.07 Use of Confidential Information for Didactic or Other Purposes

Psychologists do not disclose in their writings, lectures, or other public media, confidential, personally identifiable information concerning their clients/patients, students, research participants, organizational clients, or other recipients of their services that they obtained during the course of their work, unless (1) they take reasonable steps to disguise the person or organization, (2) the person or organization has consented in writing, or (3) there is legal authorization for doing so.

5. *Advertising and Other Public Statements*

5.01 Avoidance of False or Deceptive Statements

(a) Public statements include but are not limited to paid or unpaid advertising, product endorsements, grant applications, licensing applications, other credentialing applications, brochures, printed matter, directory listings, personal résumés or curricula vitae, or comments for use in media such as print or electronic transmission, statements in legal proceedings, lectures and public oral presentations, and published materials. Psychologists do not knowingly make public statements that are false, deceptive, or fraudulent concerning their research, practice, or other work activities or those of persons or organizations with which they are affiliated.

(b) Psychologists do not make false, deceptive, or fraudulent statements concerning (1) their training, experience, or competence; (2) their academic degrees; (3) their credentials; (4) their institutional or association affiliations; (5) their services; (6) the scientific or clinical basis for, or results or degree of success of, their services; (7) their fees; or (8) their publications or research findings.

(c) Psychologists claim degrees as credentials for their health services only if those degrees (1) were earned from a regionally accredited educational institution or (2) were the basis for psychology licensure by the state in which they practice.

5.02 Statements by Others

(a) Psychologists who engage others to create or place public statements that promote their professional practice, products, or activities retain professional responsibility for such statements.
(b) Psychologists do not compensate employees of press, radio, television, or other communication media in return for publicity in a news item. (See also Standard 1.01, Misuse of Psychologists' Work.)
(c) A paid advertisement relating to psychologists' activities must be identified or clearly recognizable as such.

5.03 Descriptions of Workshops and Non-Degree-Granting Educational Programs

To the degree to which they exercise control, psychologists responsible for announcements, catalogs, brochures, or advertisements describing workshops, seminars, or other non-degree-granting educational programs ensure that they accurately describe the audience for which the program is intended, the educational objectives, the presenters, and the fees involved.

5.04 Media Presentations

When psychologists provide public advice or comment via print, internet, or other electronic transmission, they take precautions to ensure that statements (1) are based on their professional knowledge, training, or experience in accord with appropriate psychological literature and practice; (2) are otherwise consistent with this Ethics Code; and (3) do not indicate that a professional relationship has been established with the recipient. (See also Standard 2.04, Bases for Scientific and Professional Judgments.)

5.05 Testimonials

Psychologists do not solicit testimonials from current therapy clients/patients or other persons who because of their particular circumstances are vulnerable to undue influence.

5.06 In-Person Solicitation

Psychologists do not engage, directly or through agents, in uninvited in-person solicitation of business from actual or potential therapy clients/patients or other persons who because of their particular circumstances are vulnerable to undue influence. However, this prohibition does not preclude (1) attempting to implement appropriate collateral contacts for the purpose of benefiting an already engaged therapy client/patient or (2) providing disaster or community outreach services.

6. *Record Keeping and Fees*

6.01 Documentation of Professional and Scientific Work and Maintenance of Records

Psychologists create, and to the extent the records are under their control, maintain, disseminate, store, retain, and dispose of records and data relating to their professional and scientific work in order to (1) facilitate provision of services later by them or by other professionals, (2) allow for replication of research design and analyses, (3) meet institutional requirements, (4) ensure accuracy of billing and payments, and (5) ensure compliance with law. (See also Standard 4.01, Maintaining Confidentiality.)

6.02 Maintenance, Dissemination, and Disposal of Confidential Records of Professional and Scientific Work

(a) Psychologists maintain confidentiality in creating, storing, accessing, transferring, and disposing of records under their control, whether these are written, automated, or in any other medium. (See also Standards 4.01, Maintaining Confidentiality, and 6.01, Documentation of Professional and Scientific Work and Maintenance of Records.)

(b) If confidential information concerning recipients of psychological services is entered into databases or systems of records available to persons whose access has not been consented to by the recipient, psychologists use coding or other techniques to avoid the inclusion of personal identifiers.

(c) Psychologists make plans in advance to facilitate the appropriate transfer and to protect the confidentiality of records and data in the event of psychologists' withdrawal from positions or practice. (See also Standards 3.12, Interruption of Psychological Services, and 10.09, Interruption of Therapy.)

6.03 Withholding Records for Nonpayment

Psychologists may not withhold records under their control that are requested and needed for a client's/patient's emergency treatment solely because payment has not been received.

6.04 Fees and Financial Arrangements

(a) As early as is feasible in a professional or scientific relationship, psychologists and recipients of psychological services reach an agreement specifying compensation and billing arrangements.

(b) Psychologists' fee practices are consistent with law.

(c) Psychologists do not misrepresent their fees.

(d) If limitations to services can be anticipated because of limitations in financing, this is discussed with the recipient of services as early as is feasible. (See also Standards 10.09, Interruption of Therapy, and 10.10, Terminating Therapy.)

(e) If the recipient of services does not pay for services as agreed, and if psychologists intend to use collection agencies or legal measures to collect the fees, psychologists first inform the person that such measures will be taken and provide that person an opportunity to make prompt payment. (See also Standards 4.05, Disclosures; 6.03, Withholding Records for Nonpayment; and 10.01, Informed Consent to Therapy.)

6.05 Barter With Clients/Patients

Barter is the acceptance of goods, services, or other nonmonetary remuneration from clients/patients in return for psychological services. Psychologists may barter only if (1) it is not clinically contraindicated, and (2) the resulting arrangement is not exploitative. (See also Standards 3.05, Multiple Relationships, and 6.04, Fees and Financial Arrangements.)

6.06 Accuracy in Reports to Payors and Funding Sources

In their reports to payors for services or sources of research funding, psychologists take reasonable steps to ensure the accurate reporting of the nature of the service provided or research conducted, the fees, charges, or payments, and where applicable, the identity of the provider, the findings, and the diagnosis. (See also Standards 4.01, Maintaining Confidentiality; 4.04, Minimizing Intrusions on Privacy; and 4.05, Disclosures.)

6.07 Referrals and Fees

When psychologists pay, receive payment from, or divide fees with another professional, other than in an employer-employee relationship, the payment to each is based on the services provided (clinical, consultative, administrative, or other) and is not based on the referral itself. (See also Standard 3.09, Cooperation With Other Professionals.)

7. *Education and Training*

7.01 Design of Education and Training Programs

Psychologists responsible for education and training programs take reasonable steps to ensure that the programs are designed to provide the appropriate knowledge and proper experiences, and to meet the requirements for licensure, certification, or other goals for which claims are made by the program. (See also Standard 5.03, Descriptions of Workshops and Non-Degree-Granting Educational Programs.)

7.02 Descriptions of Education and Training Programs

Psychologists responsible for education and training programs take reasonable steps to ensure that there is a current and accurate description of the program content (including participation in required course-or program-related counseling, psychotherapy, experiential groups, consulting projects, or community service), training goals and objectives, stipends and benefits, and requirements that must be met for satisfactory completion of the program. This information must be made readily available to all interested parties.

7.03 Accuracy in Teaching

(a) Psychologists take reasonable steps to ensure that course syllabi are accurate regarding the subject matter to be covered, bases for evaluating progress, and the nature of course experiences. This standard does not preclude an instructor from modifying course content or requirements when the instructor considers it pedagogically necessary or desirable, so long as students are made aware of these modifications in a manner that enables them to fulfill course requirements. (See also Standard 5.01, Avoidance of False or Deceptive Statements.)

(b) When engaged in teaching or training, psychologists present psychological information accurately. (See also Standard 2.03, Maintaining Competence.)

7.04 Student Disclosure of Personal Information

Psychologists do not require students or supervisees to disclose personal information in course-or program-related activities, either orally or in writing, regarding sexual history, history of abuse and neglect, psychological treatment, and relationships with parents, peers, and spouses or significant others except if (1) the program or training facility has clearly identified this requirement in its admissions and program materials or (2) the information is necessary to evaluate or obtain assistance for students whose personal problems could reasonably be judged to be preventing them from performing their training-or professionally related activities in a competent manner or posing a threat to the students or others.

7.05 Mandatory Individual or Group Therapy

(a) When individual or group therapy is a program or course requirement, psychologists responsible for that program allow students in undergraduate and graduate programs the option of selecting such therapy from practitioners unaffiliated with the program. (See also Standard 7.02, Descriptions of Education and Training Programs.)

(b) Faculty who are or are likely to be responsible for evaluating students' academic performance do not themselves provide that therapy. (See also Standard 3.05, Multiple Relationships.)

7.06 Assessing Student and Supervisee Performance

(a) In academic and supervisory relationships, psychologists establish a timely and specific process for providing feedback to students and supervisees. Information regarding the process is provided to the student at the beginning of supervision.

(b) Psychologists evaluate students and supervisees on the basis of their actual performance on relevant and established program requirements.

7.07 Sexual Relationships With Students and Supervisees

Psychologists do not engage in sexual relationships with students or supervisees who are in their department, agency, or training center or over whom psychologists have or are likely to have evaluative authority. (See also Standard 3.05, Multiple Relationships.)

8. Research and Publication

8.01 Institutional Approval

When institutional approval is required, psychologists provide accurate information about their research proposals and obtain approval prior to conducting the research. They conduct the research in accordance with the approved research protocol.

8.02 Informed Consent to Research

(a) When obtaining informed consent as required in Standard 3.10, Informed Consent, psychologists inform participants about (1) the purpose of the research, expected duration, and procedures; (2) their right to decline to participate and to withdraw from the research once participation has begun; (3) the foreseeable consequences of declining or withdrawing; (4) reasonably foreseeable factors that may be expected to influence their willingness to participate such as potential risks, discomfort, or adverse effects; (5) any prospective research benefits; (6) limits of confidentiality; (7) incentives for participation; and (8) whom to contact for questions about the research and research participants' rights. They provide opportunity for the prospective participants to ask questions and receive answers. (See also Standards 8.03, Informed Consent for Recording Voices and Images in Research; 8.05, Dispensing With Informed Consent for Research; and 8.07, Deception in Research.)

Psychologists maintain confidentiality in creating, storing, accessing, transferring, and disposing of records. Psychologists conducting intervention research involving the use of experimental treatments clarify to participants at the outset of the research (1) the experimental nature of the treatment; (2) the services that will or will not be available to the control group(s) if appropriate; (3) the means by which assignment to treatment and control groups will be made; (4) available treatment alternatives if an individual does not wish to participate in the research or wishes to withdraw once a study has begun; and (5) compensation for or monetary costs of participating including, if appropriate, whether reimbursement from the participant or a third-party payor will be sought. (See also Standard 8.02a, Informed Consent to Research.)

8.03 Informed Consent for Recording Voices and Images in Research

Psychologists obtain informed consent from research participants prior to recording their voices or images for data collection unless (1) the research consists solely of naturalistic observations in public places, and it is not anticipated that the recording will be used in a manner that could cause personal identification or harm, or (2) the research design includes deception, and consent for the use of the recording is obtained during debriefing. (See also Standard 8.07, Deception in Research.)

8.04 Client/Patient, Student, and Subordinate Research Participants

(a) When psychologists conduct research with clients/patients, students, or subordinates as participants, psychologists take steps to protect the prospective participants from adverse consequences of declining or withdrawing from participation.

(b) When research participation is a course requirement or an opportunity for extra credit, the prospective participant is given the choice of equitable alternative activities.

8.05 Dispensing With Informed Consent for Research

Psychologists may dispense with informed consent only (1) where research would not reasonably be assumed to create distress or harm and involves (a) the study of normal educational practices, curricula, or classroom management methods conducted in educational settings; (b) only anonymous questionnaires, naturalistic observations, or archival research for which disclosure of responses would not place participants at risk of criminal or civil liability or damage their financial standing, employability, or reputation, and confidentiality is protected; or (c) the study of factors related to job or organization effectiveness conducted in organizational settings for which there is no risk to participants' employability, and confidentiality is protected or (2) where otherwise permitted by law or federal or institutional regulations.

8.06 Offering Inducements for Research Participation

(a) Psychologists make reasonable efforts to avoid offering excessive or inappropriate financial or other inducements for research participation when such inducements are likely to coerce participation.

(b) When offering professional services as an inducement for research participation, psychologists clarify the nature of the services, as well as the risks, obligations, and limitations. (See also Standard 6.05, Barter With Clients/Patients.)

8.07 Deception in Research

(a) Psychologists do not conduct a study involving deception unless they have determined that the use of deceptive techniques is justified by the study's significant prospective scientific, educational, or applied value and that effective nondeceptive alternative procedures are not feasible.

(b) Psychologists do not deceive prospective participants about research that is reasonably expected to cause physical pain or severe emotional distress.

(c) Psychologists explain any deception that is an integral feature of the design and conduct of an experiment to participants as early as is feasible, preferably at the conclusion of their participation, but no later than at the conclusion of the data collection, and permit participants to withdraw their data. (See also Standard 8.08, Debriefing.)

8.08 Debriefing

(a) Psychologists provide a prompt opportunity for participants to obtain appropriate information about the nature, results, and conclusions of the research, and they take reasonable steps to correct any misconceptions that participants may have of which the psychologists are aware.

(b) If scientific or humane values justify delaying or withholding this information, psychologists take reasonable measures to reduce the risk of harm.

(c) When psychologists become aware that research procedures have harmed a participant, they take reasonable steps to minimize the harm.

8.09 Humane Care and Use of Animals in Research

(a) Psychologists acquire, care for, use, and dispose of animals in compliance with current federal, state, and local laws and regulations, and with professional standards.

(b) Psychologists trained in research methods and experienced in the care of laboratory animals supervise all procedures involving animals and are responsible for ensuring appropriate consideration of their comfort, health, and humane treatment.

(c) Psychologists ensure that all individuals under their supervision who are using animals have received instruction in research methods and in the care, maintenance, and handling of the species being used, to the extent appropriate to their role. (See also Standard 2.05, Delegation of Work to Others.)

(d) Psychologists make reasonable efforts to minimize the discomfort, infection, illness, and pain of animal subjects.

(e) Psychologists use a procedure subjecting animals to pain, stress, or privation only when an alternative procedure is unavailable and the goal is justified by its prospective scientific, educational, or applied value.

(f) Psychologists perform surgical procedures under appropriate anesthesia and follow techniques to avoid infection and minimize pain during and after surgery.

(g) When it is appropriate that an animal's life be terminated, psychologists proceed rapidly, with an effort to minimize pain and in accordance with accepted procedures.

8.10 Reporting Research Results

(a) Psychologists do not fabricate data. (See also Standard 5.01a, Avoidance of False or Deceptive Statements.)

(b) If psychologists discover significant errors in their published data, they take reasonable steps to correct such errors in a correction, retraction, erratum, or other appropriate publication means.

8.11 Plagiarism

Psychologists do not present portions of another's work or data as their own, even if the other work or data source is cited occasionally.

8.12 Publication Credit

(a) Psychologists take responsibility and credit, including authorship credit, only for work they have actually performed or to which they have substantially contributed. (See also Standard 8.12b, Publication Credit.)

(b) Principal authorship and other publication credits accurately reflect the relative scientific or professional contributions of the individuals involved, regardless of their relative status. Mere possession of an institutional position, such as department chair, does not justify authorship credit. Minor contributions to the research or to the writing for publications are acknowledged appropriately, such as in footnotes or in an introductory statement.

(c) Except under exceptional circumstances, a student is listed as principal author on any multiple-authored article that is substantially based on the student's doctoral dissertation. Faculty advisors discuss publication credit with students as early as feasible and throughout the research and publication process as appropriate. (See also Standard 8.12b, Publication Credit.)

8.13 Duplicate Publication of Data

Psychologists do not publish, as original data, data that have been previously published. This does not preclude republishing data when they are accompanied by proper acknowledgment.

8.14 Sharing Research Data for Verification

(a) After research results are published, psychologists do not withhold the data on which their conclusions are based from other competent professionals who seek to verify the substantive claims through reanalysis and who intend to use such data only for that purpose, provided that the confidentiality of the participants can be protected and unless legal rights concerning proprietary data preclude their release. This does not preclude psychologists from requiring that such individuals or groups be responsible for costs associated with the provision of such information.

(b) Psychologists who request data from other psychologists to verify the substantive claims through reanalysis may use shared data only for the declared purpose. Requesting psychologists obtain prior written agreement for all other uses of the data.

8.15 Reviewers

Psychologists who review material submitted for presentation, publication, grant, or research proposal review respect the confidentiality of and the proprietary rights in such information of those who submitted it.

9. Assessment

9.01 Bases for Assessments

(a) Psychologists base the opinions contained in their recommendations, reports, and diagnostic or evaluative statements, including forensic testimony, on information and techniques sufficient to substantiate their findings. (See also Standard 2.04, Bases for Scientific and Professional Judgments.)

(b) Except as noted in 9.01c, psychologists provide opinions of the psychological characteristics of individuals only after they have conducted an examination of the individuals adequate to support their statements or conclusions. When, despite reasonable efforts, such an examination is not practical, psychologists document the efforts they made and the result of those efforts, clarify the probable impact of their limited information on the reliability and validity of their opinions, and appropriately limit the nature and extent of their conclusions or recommendations. (See also Standards 2.01, Boundaries of Competence, and 9.06, Interpreting Assessment Results.)

(c) When psychologists conduct a record review or provide consultation or supervision and an individual examination is not warranted or necessary for the opinion, psychologists explain this and the sources of information on which they based their conclusions and recommendations.

9.02 Use of Assessments

(a) Psychologists administer, adapt, score, interpret, or use assessment techniques, interviews, tests, or instruments in a manner and for purposes that are appropriate in light of the research on or evidence of the usefulness and proper application of the techniques.

(b) Psychologists use assessment instruments whose validity and reliability have been established for use with members of the population tested. When such validity or reliability has not been established, psychologists describe the strengths and limitations of test results and interpretation.

(c) Psychologists use assessment methods that are appropriate to an individual's language preference and competence, unless the use of an alternative language is relevant to the assessment issues.

9.03 Informed Consent in Assessments

(a) Psychologists obtain informed consent for assessments, evaluations, or diagnostic services, as described in Standard 3.10, Informed Consent, except when (1) testing is mandated by law or governmental regulations; (2) informed consent is implied because testing is conducted as a routine educational, institutional, or organizational activity (e.g., when participants voluntarily agree to assessment when applying for a job); or (3) one purpose of the testing is to evaluate decisional capacity. Informed consent includes an explanation of the nature and purpose of the assessment, fees, involvement of third parties, and limits of confidentiality and sufficient opportunity for the client/patient to ask questions and receive answers.

(b) Psychologists inform persons with questionable capacity to consent or for whom testing is mandated by law or governmental regulations about the nature and purpose of the proposed assessment services, using language that is reasonably understandable to the person being assessed.

(c) Psychologists using the services of an interpreter obtain informed consent from the client/patient to use that interpreter, ensure that confidentiality of test results and test security are maintained, and include in their recommendations, reports, and diagnostic or evaluative statements, including forensic testimony, discussion of any limitations on the data obtained. (See also Standards 2.05, Delegation of Work to Others; 4.01, Maintaining Confidentiality; 9.01, Bases for Assessments; 9.06, Interpreting Assessment Results; and 9.07, Assessment by Unqualified Persons.)

9.04 Release of Test Data

(a) The term test data refers to raw and scaled scores, client/patient responses to test questions or stimuli, and psychologists' notes and recordings concerning client/ patient statements and behavior during an examination. Those portions of test materials that include client/patient responses are included in the definition of test data. Pursuant to a client/patient release, psychologists provide test data to the client/patient or other persons identified in the release. Psychologists may refrain from releasing test data to protect a client/patient or others from substantial harm or misuse or misrepresentation of the data or the test, recognizing that in many instances release of confidential information under these circumstances is regulated by law. (See also Standard 9.11, Maintaining Test Security.)

(b) In the absence of a client/patient release, psychologists provide test data only as required by law or court order.

9.05 Test Construction

Psychologists who develop tests and other assessment techniques use appropriate psychometric procedures and current scientific or professional knowledge for test design, standardization, validation, reduction or elimination of bias, and recommendations for use.

9.06 Interpreting Assessment Results

When interpreting assessment results, including automated interpretations, psychologists take into account the purpose of the assessment as well as the various test factors, test-taking abilities, and other characteristics of the person being assessed, such as situational, personal, linguistic, and cultural differences, that might affect psychologists' judgments or reduce the accuracy of their interpretations. They indicate any significant limitations of their interpretations. (See also Standards 2.01b and c, Boundaries of Competence, and 3.01, Unfair Discrimination.)

9.07 Assessment by Unqualified Persons

Psychologists do not promote the use of psychological assessment techniques by unqualified persons, except when such use is conducted for training purposes with appropriate supervision. (See also Standard 2.05, Delegation of Work to Others.)

9.08 Obsolete Tests and Outdated Test Results

(a) Psychologists do not base their assessment or intervention decisions or recommendations on data or test results that are outdated for the current purpose.
(b) Psychologists do not base such decisions or recommendations on tests and measures that are obsolete and not useful for the current purpose.

9.09 Test Scoring and Interpretation Services

(a) Psychologists who offer assessment or scoring services to other professionals accurately describe the purpose, norms, validity, reliability, and applications of the procedures and any special qualifications applicable to their use.
(b) Psychologists select scoring and interpretation services (including automated services) on the basis of evidence of the validity of the program and procedures as well as on other appropriate considerations. (See also Standard 2.01b and c, Boundaries of Competence.)
(c) Psychologists retain responsibility for the appropriate application, interpretation, and use of assessment instruments, whether they score and interpret such tests themselves or use automated or other services.

9.10 Explaining Assessment Results

Regardless of whether the scoring and interpretation are done by psychologists, by employees or assistants, or by automated or other outside services, psychologists take reasonable steps to ensure that explanations of results are given to the individual or designated representative unless the nature of the relationship precludes provision of an explanation of results (such as in some organizational consulting, preemployment or security screenings, and forensic evaluations), and this fact has been clearly explained to the person being assessed in advance.

9.11 Maintaining Test Security

The term test materials refers to manuals, instruments, protocols, and test questions or stimuli and does not include test data as defined in Standard 9.04, Release of Test Data. Psychologists make reasonable efforts to maintain the integrity and security of test materials and other assessment techniques consistent with law and contractual obligations, and in a manner that permits adherence to this Ethics Code.

10. Therapy

10.01 Informed Consent to Therapy

(a) When obtaining informed consent to therapy as required in Standard 3.10, Informed Consent, psychologists inform clients/patients as early as is feasible in the therapeutic relationship about the nature and anticipated course of therapy, fees, involvement of third parties, and limits of confidentiality and provide sufficient opportunity for the client/patient to ask questions and receive answers. (See also Standards 4.02, Discussing the Limits of Confidentiality, and 6.04, Fees and Financial Arrangements.)

(b) When obtaining informed consent for treatment for which generally recognized techniques and procedures have not been established, psychologists inform their clients/patients of the developing nature of the treatment, the potential risks involved, alternative treatments that may be available, and the voluntary nature of their participation. (See also Standards 2.01e, Boundaries of Competence, and 3.10, Informed Consent.)

(c) When the therapist is a trainee and the legal responsibility for the treatment provided resides with the supervisor, the client/patient, as part of the informed consent procedure, is informed that the therapist is in training and is being supervised and is given the name of the supervisor.

10.02 Therapy Involving Couples or Families

(a) When psychologists agree to provide services to several persons who have a relationship (such as spouses, significant others, or parents and children), they take reasonable steps to clarify at the outset (1) which of the individuals are clients/patients and (2) the relationship the psychologist will have with each person. This clarification includes the psychologist's role and the probable uses of the services provided or the information obtained. (See also Standard 4.02, Discussing the Limits of Confidentiality.)

(b) If it becomes apparent that psychologists may be called on to perform potentially conflicting roles (such as family therapist and then witness for one party in divorce proceedings), psychologists take reasonable steps to clarify and modify, or withdraw from, roles appropriately. (See also Standard 3.05c, Multiple Relationships.)

10.03 Group Therapy

When psychologists provide services to several persons in a group setting, they describe at the outset the roles and responsibilities of all parties and the limits of confidentiality.

10.04 Providing Therapy to Those Served by Others

In deciding whether to offer or provide services to those already receiving mental health services elsewhere, psychologists carefully consider the treatment issues and the potential client's/patient's welfare. Psychologists discuss these issues with the client/patient or another legally authorized person on behalf of the client/patient in order to minimize the risk of confusion and conflict, consult with the other service providers when appropriate, and proceed with caution and sensitivity to the therapeutic issues.

10.05 Sexual Intimacies With Current Therapy Clients/Patients

Psychologists do not engage in sexual intimacies with current therapy clients/patients.

10.06 Sexual Intimacies With Relatives or Significant Others of Current Therapy Clients/Patients

Psychologists do not engage in sexual intimacies with individuals they know to be close relatives, guardians, or significant others of current clients/patients. Psychologists do not terminate therapy to circumvent this standard.

10.07 Therapy With Former Sexual Partners

Psychologists do not accept as therapy clients/patients persons with whom they have engaged in sexual intimacies.

10.08 Sexual Intimacies With Former Therapy Clients/Patients

(a) Psychologists do not engage in sexual intimacies with former clients/patients for at least two years after cessation or termination of therapy.

(b) Psychologists do not engage in sexual intimacies with former clients/patients even after a two-year interval except in the most unusual circumstances. Psychologists who engage in such activity after the two years following cessation or termination of therapy and of having no sexual contact with the former client/patient bear the burden of demonstrating that there has been no exploitation, in light of all relevant factors, including (1) the amount of time that has passed since therapy terminated; (2) the nature, duration, and intensity of the therapy; (3) the circumstances of termination; (4) the client's/patient's personal history; (5) the client's/patient's current mental status; (6) the likelihood of adverse impact on the client/patient; and (7) any statements or actions made by the therapist during the course of therapy suggesting or inviting the possibility of a posttermination sexual or romantic relationship with the client/patient. (See also Standard 3.05, Multiple Relationships.)

10.09 Interruption of Therapy

When entering into employment or contractual relationships, psychologists make reasonable efforts to provide for orderly and appropriate resolution of responsibility for client/patient care in the event that the employment or contractual relationship ends, with paramount consideration given to the welfare of the client/patient. (See also Standard 3.12, Interruption of Psychological Services.)

10.10 Terminating Therapy

(a) Psychologists terminate therapy when it becomes reasonably clear that the client/patient no longer needs the service, is not likely to benefit, or is being harmed by continued service.

(b) Psychologists may terminate therapy when threatened or otherwise endangered by the client/patient or another person with whom the client/patient has a relationship.

(c) Except where precluded by the actions of clients/patients or third-party payors, prior to termination psychologists provide pretermination counseling and suggest alternative service providers as appropriate.

Source: Copyright © 2010 by the American Psychological Association. Reproduced with permission.

APPENDIX C

American School Counselors Association, Ethical Standards for School Counselors

Preamble

The American School Counselor Association (ASCA) is a professional organization whose members are school counselors certified/licensed in school counseling with unique qualifications and skills to address all students' academic, personal/social and career development needs. Members are also school counseling program directors/supervisors and counselor educators. These ethical standards are the ethical responsibility of school counselors. School counseling program directors/supervisors should know them and provide support for practitioners to uphold them. School counselor educators should know them, teach them to their students and provide support for school counseling candidates to uphold them.

Professional school counselors are advocates, leaders, collaborators and consultants who create opportunities for equity in access and success in educational opportunities by connecting their programs to the mission of schools and subscribing to the following tenets of professional responsibility:

- Each person has the right to be respected, be treated with dignity and have access to a comprehensive school counseling program that advocates for and affirms all students from diverse populations including: ethnic/racial identity, age, economic status, abilities/disabilities, language, immigration status, sexual orientation, gender, gender identity/expression, family type, religious/spiritual identity and appearance.
- Each person has the right to receive the information and support needed to move toward self-direction and self-development and affirmation within one's group identities, with special care being given to students who have historically not received adequate educational services, e.g., students of color, students living at a low socio-economic status, students with disabilities and students from non-dominant language backgrounds.

- Each person has the right to understand the full magnitude and meaning of his/her educational choices and how those choices will affect future opportunities.
- Each person has the right to privacy and thereby the right to expect the school-counselor/student relationship to comply with all laws, policies and ethical standards pertaining to confidentiality in the school setting.
- Each person has the right to feel safe in school environments that school counselors help create, free from abuse, bullying, neglect, harassment or other forms of violence.

In this document, ASCA specifies the principles of ethical behavior necessary to maintain the high standards of integrity, leadership and professionalism among its members. The Ethical Standards for School Counselors were developed to clarify the nature of ethical responsibilities held in common by school counselors, supervisors/directors of school counseling programs and school counselor educators. The purposes of this document are to:

- Serve as a guide for the ethical practices of all professional school counselors, supervisors/directors of school counseling programs and school counselor educators regardless of level, area, population served or membership in this professional association;
- Provide self-appraisal and peer evaluations regarding school counselors' responsibilities to students, parents/guardians, colleagues and professional associates, schools, communities and the counseling profession; and
- Inform all stakeholders, including students, parents and guardians, teachers, administrators, community members and courts of justice, of best ethical practices, values and expected behaviors of the school counseling professional.

A.1. Responsibilities to Students

Professional school counselors:

(a) Have a primary obligation to the students, who are to be treated with dignity and respect as unique individuals.
(b) Are concerned with the educational, academic, career, personal and social needs and encourage the maximum development of every student.
(c) Respect students' values, beliefs and cultural background and do not impose the school counselor's personal values on students or their families.
(d) Are knowledgeable of laws, regulations and policies relating to students and strive to protect and inform students regarding their rights.
(e) Promote the welfare of individual students and collaborate with them to develop an action plan for success.
(f) Consider the involvement of support networks valued by the individual students.
(g) Understand that professional distance with students is appropriate, and any sexual or romantic relationship with students whether illegal in the state of practice is considered a grievous breach of ethics and is prohibited regardless of a student's age.
(h) Consider the potential for harm before entering into a relationship with former students or one of their family members.

A.2. Confidentiality

Professional school counselors:

(a) Inform individual students of the purposes, goals, techniques and rules of procedure under which they may receive counseling. Disclosure includes the limits of confidentiality in a developmentally appropriate manner. Informed consent requires competence on the part of students to understand the limits of confidentiality and therefore, can be difficult to obtain from students of a certain developmental level. Professionals are aware that even though every attempt is made to obtain informed consent it is not always possible and when needed will make counseling decisions on students' behalf.

(b) Explain the limits of confidentiality in appropriate ways such as classroom guidance lessons, the student handbook, school counseling brochures, school Web site, verbal notice or other methods of student, school and community communication in addition to oral notification to individual students.

(c) Recognize the complicated nature of confidentiality in schools and consider each case in context. Keep information confidential unless legal requirements demand that confidential information be revealed or a breach is required to prevent serious and foreseeable harm to the student. Serious and foreseeable harm is different for each minor in schools and is defined by students' developmental and chronological age, the setting, parental rights and the nature of the harm. School counselors consult with appropriate professionals when in doubt as to the validity of an exception.

(d) Recognize their primary obligation for confidentiality is to the students but balance that obligation with an understanding of parents'/guardians' legal and inherent rights to be the guiding voice in their children's lives, especially in value-laden issues. Understand the need to balance students' ethical rights to make choices, their capacity to give consent or assent and parental or familial legal rights and responsibilities to protect these students and make decisions on their behalf.

(e) Promote the autonomy and independence of students to the extent possible and use the most appropriate and least intrusive method of breach. The developmental age and the circumstances requiring the breach are considered and as appropriate students are engaged in a discussion about the method and timing of the breach.

(f) In absence of state legislation expressly forbidding disclosure, consider the ethical responsibility to provide information to an identified third party who, by his/her relationship with the student, is at a high risk of contracting a disease that is commonly known to be communicable and fatal. Disclosure requires satisfaction of all of the following conditions:

- Student identifies partner or the partner is highly identifiable
- School counselor recommends the student notify partner and refrain from further high-risk behavior
- Student refuses
- School counselor informs the student of the intent to notify the partner
- School counselor seeks legal consultation from the school district's legal representative in writing as to the legalities of informing the partner

(g) Request of the court that disclosure not be required when the release of confidential information may potentially harm a student or the counseling relationship.
(h) Protect the confidentiality of students' records and release personal data in accordance with prescribed federal and state laws and school policies including the laws within the Family Education Rights and Privacy Act (FERPA). Student information stored and transmitted electronically is treated with the same care as traditional student records. Recognize the vulnerability of confidentiality in electronic communications and only transmit sensitive information electronically in a way that is untraceable to students' identity. Critical information such as a student who has a history of suicidal ideation must be conveyed to the receiving school in a personal contact such as a phone call.

A.3. Academic, Career/College/Post-Secondary Access and Personal/ Social Counseling Plans

Professional school counselors:

(a) Provide students with a comprehensive school counseling program that parallels the ASCA National Model with emphasis on working jointly with all students to develop personal/social, academic and career goals.
(b) Ensure equitable academic, career, post-secondary access and personal/social opportunities for all students through the use of data to help close achievement gaps and opportunity gaps.
(c) Provide and advocate for individual students' career awareness, exploration and post-secondary plans supporting the students' right to choose from the wide array of options when they leave secondary education.

A.4. Dual Relationships

Professional school counselors:

(a) Avoid dual relationships that might impair their objectivity and increase the risk of harm to students (*e.g.*, counseling one's family members or the children of close friends or associates). If a dual relationship is unavoidable, the school counselor is responsible for taking action to eliminate or reduce the potential for harm to the student through use of safeguards, which might include informed consent, consultation, supervision and documentation.
(b) Maintain appropriate professional distance with students at all times.
(c) Avoid dual relationships with students through communication mediums such as social networking sites.
(d) Avoid dual relationships with school personnel that might infringe on the integrity of the school counselor/student relationship.

A.5. Appropriate Referrals

Professional school counselors:

(a) Make referrals when necessary or appropriate to outside resources for student and/or family support. Appropriate referrals may necessitate informing both parents/guardians and students of applicable resources and making proper plans for transitions with minimal interruption of services. Students retain the right to discontinue the counseling relationship at any time.

(b) Help educate about and prevent personal and social concerns for all students within the school counselor's scope of education and competence and make necessary referrals when the counseling needs are beyond the individual school counselor's education and training. Every attempt is made to find appropriate specialized resources for clinical therapeutic topics that are difficult or inappropriate to address in a school setting such as eating disorders, sexual trauma, chemical dependency and other addictions needing sustained clinical duration or assistance.

(c) Request a release of information signed by the student and/or parents/guardians when attempting to develop a collaborative relationship with other service providers assigned to the student.

(d) Develop a reasonable method of termination of counseling when it becomes apparent that counseling assistance is no longer needed or a referral is necessary to better meet the student's needs.

A.6. *Group Work*

Professional school counselors:

(a) Screen prospective group members and maintain an awareness of participants' needs, appropriate fit and personal goals in relation to the group's intention and focus. The school counselor takes reasonable precautions to protect members from physical and psychological harm resulting from interaction within the group.

(b) Recognize that best practice is to notify the parents/guardians of children participating in small groups.

(c) Establish clear expectations in the group setting, and clearly state that confidentiality in group counseling cannot be guaranteed. Given the developmental and chronological ages of minors in schools, recognize the tenuous nature of confidentiality for minors renders some topics inappropriate for group work in a school setting.

(d) Provide necessary follow up with group members, and document proceedings as appropriate.

(e) Develop professional competencies, and maintain appropriate education, training and supervision in group facilitation and any topics specific to the group.

(f) Facilitate group work that is brief and solution-focused, working with a variety of academic, career, college and personal/social issues.

A.7. *Danger to Self or Others*

Professional school counselors:

(a) Inform parents/guardians and/or appropriate authorities when a student poses a danger to self or others. This is to be done after careful deliberation and consultation with other counseling professionals.

(b) Report risk assessments to parents when they underscore the need to act on behalf of a child at risk; never negate a risk of harm as students sometimes deceive in order to avoid further scrutiny and/or parental notification.
(c) Understand the legal and ethical liability for releasing a student who is in danger to self or others without proper and necessary support for that student.

A.8. Student Records

Professional school counselors:

(a) Maintain and secure records necessary for rendering professional services to the student as required by laws, regulations, institutional procedures and confidentiality guidelines.
(b) Keep sole-possession records or individual student case notes separate from students' educational records in keeping with state laws.
(c) Recognize the limits of sole-possession records and understand these records are a memory aid for the creator and in absence of privileged communication may be subpoenaed and may become educational records when they are shared or are accessible to others in either verbal or written form or when they include information other than professional opinion or personal observations.
(d) Establish a reasonable timeline for purging sole-possession records or case notes. Suggested guidelines include shredding sole possession records when the student transitions to the next level, transfers to another school or graduates. Apply careful discretion and deliberation before destroying sole-possession records that may be needed by a court of law such as notes on child abuse, suicide, sexual harassment or violence.
(e) Understand and abide by the Family Education Rights and Privacy Act (FERPA, 1974), which safeguards student's records and allows parents to have a voice in what and how information is shared with others regarding their child's educational records.

A.9. Evaluation, Assessment and Interpretation

Professional school counselors:

(a) Adhere to all professional standards regarding selecting, administering and interpreting assessment measures and only utilize assessment measures that are within the scope of practice for school counselors and for which they are trained and competent.
(b) Consider confidentiality issues when utilizing evaluative or assessment instruments and electronically based programs.
(c) Consider the developmental age, language skills and level of competence of the student taking the assessments before assessments are given.
(d) Provide interpretation of the nature, purposes, results and potential impact of assessment/evaluation measures in language the students can understand.
(e) Monitor the use of assessment results and interpretations, and take reasonable steps to prevent others from misusing the information.

(f) Use caution when utilizing assessment techniques, making evaluations and interpreting the performance of populations not represented in the norm group on which an instrument is standardized.

(g) Assess the effectiveness of their program in having an impact on students' academic, career and personal/social development through accountability measures especially examining efforts to close achievement, opportunity and attainment gaps.

A.10. Technology

Professional school counselors:

(a) Promote the benefits of and clarify the limitations of various appropriate technological applications. Professional school counselors promote technological applications (1) that are appropriate for students' individual needs, (2) that students understand how to use and (3) for which follow-up counseling assistance is provided.

(b) Advocate for equal access to technology for all students, especially those historically underserved.

(c) Take appropriate and reasonable measures for maintaining confidentiality of student information and educational records stored or transmitted through the use of computers, facsimile machines, telephones, voicemail, answering machines and other electronic or computer technology.

(d) Understand the intent of FERPA and its impact on sharing electronic student records.

(e) Consider the extent to which cyberbullying is interfering with students' educational process and base guidance curriculum and intervention programming for this pervasive and potentially dangerous problem on research-based and best practices.

A.11. Student Peer Support Program

Professional school counselors:

(a) Have unique responsibilities when working with peer-helper or student-assistance programs and safeguard the welfare of students participating in peer-to-peer programs under their direction.

(b) Are ultimately responsible for appropriate training and supervision for students serving as peer-support individuals in their school counseling programs.

B. Responsibilities to Parents/Guardians

B.1. Parent Rights and Responsibilities

Professional school counselors:

(a) Respect the rights and responsibilities of parents/guardians for their children and endeavor to establish, as appropriate, a collaborative relationship with parents/guardians to facilitate students' maximum development.

(b) Adhere to laws, local guidelines and ethical standards of practice when assisting parents/guardians experiencing family difficulties interfering with the student's effectiveness and welfare.
(c) Are sensitive to diversity among families and recognize that all parents/guardians, custodial and noncustodial, are vested with certain rights and responsibilities for their children's welfare by virtue of their role and according to law.
(d) Inform parents of the nature of counseling services provided in the school setting.
(e) Adhere to the FERPA act regarding disclosure of student information.
(f) Work to establish, as appropriate, collaborative relationships with parents/guardians to best serve student.

B.2. Parents/Guardians and Confidentiality

Professional school counselors:

(a) Inform parents/guardians of the school counselor's role to include the confidential nature of the counseling relationship between the counselor and student.
(b) Recognize that working with minors in a school setting requires school counselors to collaborate with students' parents/guardians to the extent possible.
(c) Respect the confidentiality of parents/guardians to the extent that is reasonable to protect the best interest of the student being counseled.
(d) Provide parents/guardians with accurate, comprehensive and relevant information in an objective and caring manner, as is appropriate and consistent with ethical responsibilities to the student.
(e) Make reasonable efforts to honor the wishes of parents/guardians concerning information regarding the student unless a court order expressly forbids the involvement of a parent(s). In cases of divorce or separation, school counselors exercise a good-faith effort to keep both parents informed, maintaining focus on the student and avoiding supporting one parent over another in divorce proceedings.

C. Responsibilities to Colleagues and Professional Associates

C.1. Professional Relationships

Professional school counselors, the school counseling program director/site supervisor and the school counselor educator:

(a) Establish and maintain professional relationships with faculty, staff and administration to facilitate an optimum counseling program.
(b) Treat colleagues with professional respect, courtesy and fairness.
(c) Recognize that teachers, staff and administrators who are highfunctioning in the personal and social development skills can be powerful allies in supporting student success. School counselors work to develop relationships with all faculty and staff in order to advantage students.
(d) Are aware of and utilize related professionals, organizations and other resources to whom the student may be referred.

C.2. Sharing Information with Other Professionals

Professional school counselors:

(a) Promote awareness and adherence to appropriate guidelines regarding confidentiality, the distinction between public and private information and staff consultation.
(b) Provide professional personnel with accurate, objective, concise and meaningful data necessary to adequately evaluate, counsel and assist the student.
(c) Secure parental consent and develop clear agreements with other mental health professionals when a student is receiving services from another counselor or other mental health professional in order to avoid confusion and conflict for the student and parents/guardians.
(d) Understand about the "release of information" process and parental rights in sharing information and attempt to establish a cooperative and collaborative relationship with other professionals to benefit students.
(e) Recognize the powerful role of ally that faculty and administration who function high in personal/social development skills can play in supporting students in stress, and carefully filter confidential information to give these allies what they "need to know" in order to advantage the student. Consultation with other members of the school counseling profession is helpful in determining need-to-know information. The primary focus and obligation is always on the student when it comes to sharing confidential information.
(f) Keep appropriate records regarding individual students, and develop a plan for transferring those records to another professional school counselor should the need occur. This documentation transfer will protect the confidentiality and benefit the needs of the student for whom the records are written.

C.3. Collaborating and Educating Around the Role of the School Counselor

The school counselor, school counseling program supervisor/director and school counselor educator:

(a) Share the role of the school counseling program in ensuring data-driven academic, career/college and personal/social success competencies for every student, resulting in specific outcomes/indicators with all stakeholders.
(b) Broker services internal and external to the schools to help ensure every student receives the benefits of a school counseling program and specific academic, career/college and personal/social competencies.

D. Responsibilities to School, Communities and Families

D.1. Responsibilities to the School

Professional school counselors:

(a) Support and protect students' best interest against any infringement of their educational program.

(b) Inform appropriate officials, in accordance with school policy, of conditions that may be potentially disruptive or damaging to the school's mission, personnel and property while honoring the confidentiality between the student and the school counselor.
(c) Are knowledgeable and supportive of their school's mission, and connect their program to the school's mission.
(d) Delineate and promote the school counselor's role, and function as a student advocate in meeting the needs of those served. School counselors will notify appropriate officials of systemic conditions that may limit or curtail their effectiveness in providing programs and services.
(e) Accept employment only for positions for which they are qualified by education, training, supervised experience, state and national professional credentials and appropriate professional experience.
(f) Advocate that administrators hire only qualified, appropriately trained and competent individuals for professional school counseling positions.
(g) Assist in developing: (1) curricular and environmental conditions appropriate for the school and community; (2) educational procedures and programs to meet students' developmental needs; (3) a systematic evaluation process for comprehensive, developmental, standards-based school counseling programs, services and personnel; and (4) a data-driven evaluation process guiding the comprehensive, developmental school counseling program and service delivery.

D.2. Responsibility to the Community

Professional school counselors:

(a) Collaborate with community agencies, organizations and individuals in students' best interest and without regard to personal reward or remuneration.
(b) Extend their influence and opportunity to deliver a comprehensive school counseling program to all students by collaborating with community resources for student success.
(c) Promote equity for all students through community resources.
(d) Are careful not to use their professional role as a school counselor to benefit any type of private therapeutic or consultative practice in which they might be involved outside of the school setting.

E. Responsibilities to Self

E.1. Professional Competence

Professional school counselors:

(a) Function within the boundaries of individual professional competence and accept responsibility for the consequences of their actions.
(b) Monitor emotional and physical health and practice wellness to ensure optimal effectiveness. Seek physical or mental health referrals when needed to ensure competence at all times.

(c) Monitor personal responsibility and recognize the high standard of care a professional in this critical position of trust must maintain on and off the job and are cognizant of and refrain from activity that may lead to inadequate professional services or diminish their effectiveness with school community members Professional and personal growth are ongoing throughout the counselor's career.

(d) Strive through personal initiative to stay abreast of current research and to maintain professional competence in advocacy, teaming and collaboration, culturally competent counseling and school counseling program coordination, knowledge and use of technology, leadership, and equity assessment using data.

(e) Ensure a variety of regular opportunities for participating in and facilitating professional development for self and other educators and school counselors through continuing education opportunities annually including: attendance at professional school counseling conferences; reading *Professional School Counseling* journal articles; facilitating workshops for education staff on issues school counselors are uniquely positioned to provide.

(f) Enhance personal self-awareness, professional effectiveness and ethical practice by regularly attending presentations on ethical decision-making. Effective school counselors will seek supervision when ethical or professional questions arise in their practice.

(g) Maintain current membership in professional associations to ensure ethical and best practices.

E.2. Multicultural and Social Justice Advocacy and Leadership

Professional school counselors:

(a) Monitor and expand personal multicultural and social justice advocacy awareness, knowledge and skills. School counselors strive for exemplary cultural competence by ensuring personal beliefs or values are not imposed on students or other stakeholders.

(b) Develop competencies in how prejudice, power and various forms of oppression, such as ableism, ageism, classism, familyism, genderism, heterosexism, immigrationism, linguicism, racism, religionism and sexism, affect self, students and all stakeholders.

(c) Acquire educational, consultation and training experiences to improve awareness, knowledge, skills and effectiveness in working with diverse populations: ethnic/racial status, age, economic status, special needs, ESL or ELL, immigration status, sexual orientation, gender, gender identity/expression, family type, religious/spiritual identity and appearance.

(d) Affirm the multiple cultural and linguistic identities of every student and all stakeholders. Advocate for equitable school and school counseling program policies and practices for every student and all stakeholders including use of translators and bilingual/multilingual school counseling program materials that represent all languages used by families in the school community, and advocate for appropriate accommodations and accessibility for students with disabilities.

(e) Use inclusive and culturally responsible language in all forms of communication.
(f) Provide regular workshops and written/digital information to families to increase understanding, collaborative two-way communication and a welcoming school climate between families and the school to promote increased student achievement.
(g) Work as advocates and leaders in the school to create equity-based school counseling programs that help close any achievement, opportunity and attainment gaps that deny all students the chance to pursue their educational goals.

F. Responsibilities to the Profession

F.1. Professionalism

Professional school counselors:

(a) Accept the policies and procedures for handling ethical violations as a result of maintaining membership in the American School Counselor Association.
(b) Conduct themselves in such a manner as to advance individual ethical practice and the profession.
(c) Conduct appropriate research, and report findings in a manner consistent with acceptable educational and psychological research practices. School counselors advocate for the protection of individual students' identities when using data for research or program planning.
(d) Seek institutional and parent/guardian consent before administering any research, and maintain security of research records.
(e) Adhere to ethical standards of the profession, other official policy statements, such as ASCA's position statements, role statement and the ASCA National Model and relevant statutes established by federal, state and local governments, and when these are in conflict work responsibly for change.
(f) Clearly distinguish between statements and actions made as a private individual and those made as a representative of the school counseling profession.
(g) Do not use their professional position to recruit or gain clients, consultees for their private practice or to seek and receive unjustified personal gains, unfair advantage, inappropriate relationships or unearned goods or services.

F.2. Contribution to the Profession

Professional school counselors:

(a) Actively participate in professional associations and share results and best practices in assessing, implementing and annually evaluating the outcomes of data-driven school counseling programs with measurable academic, career/college and personal/social competencies for every student.
(b) Provide support, consultation and mentoring to novice professionals.
(c) Have a responsibility to read and abide by the ASCA Ethical Standards and adhere to the applicable laws and regulations.

F.3. Supervision of School Counselor Candidates Pursuing Practicum and Internship Experiences:

Professional school counselors:

(a) Provide support for appropriate experiences in academic, career, college access and personal/social counseling for school counseling interns.
(b) Ensure school counselor candidates have experience in developing, implementing and evaluating a data-driven school counseling program model, such as the ASCA National Model.
(c) Ensure the school counseling practicum and internship have specific, measurable service delivery, foundation, management and accountability systems.
(d) Ensure school counselor candidates maintain appropriate liability insurance for the duration of the school counseling practicum and internship experiences.
(e) Ensure a site visit is completed by a school counselor education faculty member for each practicum or internship student, preferably when both the school counselor trainee and site supervisor are present.

F.4. Collaboration and Education about School Counselors and School Counseling Programs with other Professionals

School counselors and school counseling program directors/supervisors collaborate with special educators, school nurses, school social workers, school psychologists, college counselors/admissions officers, physical therapists, occupational therapists and speech pathologists to advocate for optimal services for students and all other stakeholders.

G. Maintenance of Standards

Professional school counselors are expected to maintain ethical behavior at all times.

G.1. When there exists serious doubt as to the ethical behavior of a colleague(s) the following procedure may serve as a guide:

1. The school counselor should consult confidentially with a professional colleague to discuss the nature of a complaint to see if the professional colleague views the situation as an ethical violation.
2. When feasible, the school counselor should directly approach the colleague whose behavior is in question to discuss the complaint and seek resolution.
3. The school counselor should keep documentation of all the steps taken.
4. If resolution is not forthcoming at the personal level, the school counselor shall utilize the channels established within the school, school district, the state school counseling association and ASCA's Ethics Committee.
5. If the matter still remains unresolved, referral for review and appropriate action should be made to the Ethics Committees in the following sequence:
    - State school counselor association
    - American School Counselor Association

6. The ASCA Ethics Committee is responsible for:
   - Educating and consulting with the membership regarding ethical standards
   - Periodically reviewing and recommending changes in code
   - Receiving and processing questions to clarify the application of such standards. Questions must be submitted in writing to the ASCA Ethics Committee chair.
   - Handling complaints of alleged violations of the ASCA Ethical Standards for School Counselors. At the national level, complaints should be submitted in writing to the ASCA Ethics Committee, c/o the Executive Director, American School Counselor Association, 1101 King St., Suite 625, Alexandria, VA 22314.

G.2. When school counselors are forced to work in situations or abide by policies that do not reflect the ethics of the profession, the school counselor works responsibly through the correct channels to try and remedy the condition.

G.3. When faced with any ethical dilemma school counselors, school counseling program directors/supervisors and school counselor educators use an ethical decision-making model such as Solutions to Ethical Problems in Schools (STEPS) (Stone, 2001):

1. *Define the problem emotionally and intellectually*
2. *Apply the ASCA Ethical Standards and the law*
3. *Consider the students' chronological and developmental levels*
4. *Consider the setting, parental rights and minors' rights*
5. *Apply the moral principles*
6. *Determine Your potential courses of action and their consequences*
7. *Evaluate the selected action*
8. *Consult*
9. *Implement the course of action*

Source: Reprinted with permission from Kathleen Rakestraw, ASCA.

APPENDIX D

List of Specialized Ethics Codes and Guidelines in Mental Health Disciplines

American Academy of Clinical Neuropsychology (AACN). (2007). Practice guidelines for neuropsychological assessment and consultation. *The Clinical Neuropsychologist*, *21*, 209–231.

American Association for Marriage and Family Therapy (AAMFT). (2012). Code of ethics. Retrieved from http://www.aamft.org/imis15/content/legal_ethics/code_of_ethics.aspx

American Association of Christian Counselors. (AACC). (2004). AACC Code of ethics. Retrieved from http://www.aacc.net/about-us/code-of-ethics/

American Association of Pastoral Counselors (AAPC). (2012). Code of ethics. Retrieved from http://www.aapc.org/about-us/code-of-ethics

American Association of Sexuality Educators, Counselors, and Therapists (AASECT). (2004). Code of ethics. Retrieved from http://www.aasect.org/sites/default/files/documents/Code%20of%20Ethics%20and%20Conduct.pdf

American Association of State Counseling Boards (AASCB). (2007). Approved supervisor model. Retrieved from http://www.aascb.org/aws/AASCB/asset_manager/get_file/37297

American College Personnel Association (ACPA). (2006). Statement of ethical principles and standards. Retrieved from http://www.acpa.nche.edu/sites/default/files/Ethical_Principles_Standards.pdf

American Counseling Association (ACA). (1999). The layperson's guide to professional ethics. Washington, D.C.: Author.

American Counseling Association. (2014). Code of ethics. Retrieved from http://www.counseling.org/resources/aca-code-of-ethics.pdf

American Counseling Association (ACA) and the Association for Lesbian, Gay, Bisexual, and Transgender Issues in Counseling (ALGBTI). (2009). Competencies for counseling transgender clients. Retrieved from http://www.counseling.org/Resources/Competencies/ALGBTIC_Competencies.pdf

American Counseling Association (ACA) and the Association for Lesbian, Gay, Bisexual, and Transgender Issues in Counseling (ALGBTI). (2012). Competencies for counseling with lesbian, gay, bisexual, queer, questioning, intersex and ally individuals. Retrieved from http://www.counseling.org/docs/competencies/algbtic-competencies-for-counseling-lgbqqia-individuals.pdf?sfvrsn=6

American Group Psychotherapy Association (AGPA). (2002). AGPA and NRCGP guidelines for ethics. Retrieved from http://www.agpa.org/home/practice-resources/ethics-in-group-therapy

American Group Psychotherapy Association (AGPA). (2007). Practice guidelines for group psychotherapy. Retrieved from http://www.agpa.org/home/practice-resources/practice-guidelines-for-group-psychotherapy

American Medical Association (AMA). (2001). Principles of medical ethics. Retrieved from http://www.ama-assn.org/ama/pub/physician-resources/medical-ethics/code-medical-ethics/principles-medical-ethics.page

American Medical Informatics Association. (2006). Statement of ethical principles and standards. Retrieved from http://www.amia.org/about-amia/ethics

American Mental Health Counselors Association (AMHCA). (2010). Code of ethics for mental health counselors. Retrieved from http://www.amhca.org/assets/news/AMHCA_Code_of_Ethics_2010_w_pagination_cxd_51110.pdf

American Music Therapy Association (AMTA). (2008). Code of ethics. Retrieved from http://www.musictherapy.org/about/ethics/

American Psychiatric Association. (1999). Psychotherapy and managed care position statement. Retrieved from http://www.psychiatry.org/advocacy–newsroom/position-statements

American Psychiatric Association. (2009). Principles of medical ethics with annotations especially applicable to psychiatry. Retrieved from http://www.psychiatry.org/File%20Library/Practice/Ethics%20Documents/principles2013–final.pdf

American Psychoanalytic Association (APsaA). (2009). Principles and standards of ethics for psychoanalysts. Retrieved from http://www.apsa.org/About_APsaA/Ethics_Code.aspx

American Psychological Association (APA). (1981). Specialty guidelines for the delivery of services: Clinical psychologists, counseling psychologists, organizational/industrial psychologists, school psychologists. Washington, D.C.: Author.

American Psychological Association (APA). (1994). Guidelines for child custody evaluations in divorce proceedings. *American Psychologist*, *49*, 677–680.

American Psychological Association (APA). (1997). What practitioners should know about working with older adults. Retrieved from http://www.apa.org/pi/aging/resources/guides/practitioners-should-know.aspx

American Psychological Association (APA). (1999). Rights and responsibilities of test takers: Guidelines and expectations. Retrieved from http://www.apa.org/science/ttrr.html

American Psychological Association (APA). (1999). *Suggestions for psychologists working with the media*. Washington, D.C.: Author.

American Psychological Association (APA). (1999). *Warning signs: A youth anti-violence initiative*. Washington, D.C.: Retrieved from http://www.apahelpcenter.org/.featuredtopics/feature.php?id=38

American Psychological Association (APA). (2001). Appropriate use of high stakes testing in our nation's schools. Retrieved from http://www.apa.org/pubs/info/brochures/testing.aspx

American Psychological Association (APA). (2001). APA's Council of Representatives passes resolution on assisted suicide. Retrieved from http://www.apa.org/monitor/apr01/council.aspx

American Psychological Association (APA). (2001). Guidelines for test user qualifications: An executive summary. *American Psychologist*, *56*, 1099–1113.

American Psychological Association (APA). (2003). Guidelines on multicultural education, training, research, practice, and organizational change for psychologists. *American Psychologist*, *58*, 377–402.

American Psychological Association (APA). (2005). Statement on the use of secure psychological tests in the education of graduate and undergraduate psychology students. Retrieved from http://www.apa.org/science/leadership/tests/test-security.aspx

American Psychological Association (APA). (2007). Guidelines for psychological practice with girls and women. Retrieved from http://www.apa.org/practice/guidelines/girls-and-women.pdf

American Psychological Association (APA). (2007). Statement on third party observers in psychological testing and assessment: A framework for decision making. Retrieved from http://www.apa.org/science/programs/testing/third-party-observers.pdf

American Psychological Association (APA). (2007). Record keeping guidelines. Retrieved from http://www.apa.org/practice/recordkeeping.pdf

American Psychological Association (APA). (2007). Reaffirmation of the American Psychological Association position against torture and other cruel, inhuman, or degrading treatment or punishment and its application to individuals defined in the United States code as "enemy combatants." Retrieved from http://www.apa.org/about/policy/torture.aspx

American Psychological Association. (2009). Appropriate therapeutic responses to sexual orientation. Retrieved from http://www.apa.org/pi/lgbt/resources/therapeutic-response.pdf

American Psychological Association (APA). (2010). Ethical principles of psychologists and code of conduct. Washington, D.C.: Retrieved from http://www.apa.org/ethics/code.html

American Psychological Association (APA). (2010). Guidelines for child custody evaluations in family law proceedings. *American Psychologist*, *65*, 863–867.

American Psychological Association (APA). (2011). Guidelines for psychological practice in health care delivery systems. *American Psychologist*, *68*, 1–6.

American Psychological Association (APA). (2011). Practice guidelines for LGB clients. Retrieved from http://www.apa.org/pi/lgbt/resources/guidelines.aspx

American Psychological Association (APA). (2011). Practice guidelines regarding psychologists' involvement in pharmacological issues. *American Psychologist*, *66*, 835–849.

American Psychological Association (APA). (2012). Guidelines for ethical conduct in the care and use of nonhuman animals in research. Retrieved from http://apa.org/science/leadership/care/guidelines.aspx?item=1

American Psychological Association. (2013). Guidelines for the practice of telepsychology. Retrieved from http://www.apapracticecentral.org/ce/guidelines/telepsychology-guidelines.pdf

American Psychological Association. (2013). Guidelines for the undergraduate psychology major. Retrieved from http://www.apa.org/ed/precollege/about/psymajor-guidelines.pdf

American Psychological Association. (2013). Specialty guidelines for forensic psychology. Retrieved from http://www.apa.org/practice/guidelines/forensic-psychology.pdf

American Psychological Association. (2013). Guidelines for psychological evaluation in child protection matters. Retrieved from https://www.apa.org/practice/guidelines/child-protection.pdf and available at *American Psychologist*, *68*, 20–31.

American Psychological Association (APA). (2014). Guidelines for psychological practice with older adults. *American Psychologist*, *69*, 34–65.

American Psychological Association (APA). (2014). Guidelines for prevention. *American Psychologist*, *69*, 285–296.

American Psychological Association (APA), Board of Educational Affairs. (2013). Preparing professional psychologists to serve a diverse public. Retrieved from http://www.apa.org/pi/lgbt/resources/policy/diversity-preparation.aspx

American Psychological Association (APA), Board of Professional Affairs. (1999). Guidelines for psychological evaluations in child protection matters. *American Psychologist*, *54*, 586–593.

American Psychological Association (APA), Committee on Legal Issues. (2006). Strategies for private practitioners coping with subpoenas or compelled testimony for client records or test data. *Professional Psychology: Research and Practice*, *37*, 215–222.

American Psychological Association (APA), Committee on Professional Practice and Standards. (1995). Twenty-four questions (and answers) about professional practice in the area of child abuse. *Professional Psychology: Research and Practice*, *26*, 377–383.

American Psychological Association (APA), Committee on Psychological Testing and Assessment. (1996). Statement on the disclosure of test data. *American Psychologist*, *51*, 644–648.

American Psychological Association (APA), Committee on Women in Psychology. (1989). If sex enters into the psychotherapy relationship. *Professional Psychology: Research and Practice*, *20*, 112–115.

American School Counselor Association (ASCA). (2010). Ethical standards for school counselors. Retrieved from http://www.schoolcounselor.org/asca/media/asca/Resource Center/Legal and Ethical Issues/Sample Documents/EthicalStandards2010.pdf

Association for Counselor Education and Supervision (ACES). (1990). Standards for counseling supervisors. *Journal of Counseling and Development*, *69*, 30–32.

Association for Counselor Education and Supervision (ACES). (1993). Ethical guidelines for counseling supervisors. *Counselor Education and Supervision*, *34*, 270–276.

Association for Counselor Education and Supervision (ACES). (1999). Guidelines for online instruction in counselor education. Alexandria, VA: Author.

Association for Counselor Education and Supervision (ACES). (2009). Guidelines for research mentorship in counseling/counselor education. Retrieved from http://www.acesonline.net/wp-content/uploads/2010/12/ACES-research-mentorship-guidelines.pdf

Association for Multicultural Counseling and Development. (1996). Multicultural counseling competencies. Retrieved from http://www.counseling.org/docs/competencies/multcultural_competencies.pdf?sfvrsn=5

Association for Specialists in Group Work (ASGW). (2000). Professional standards for the training of group workers. Retrieved from http://www.asgw.org/PDF/training_standards.pdf

Association for Specialists in Group Work (ASGW). (2007). Best practice guidelines. Retrieved from http://www.asgw.org/pdf/best_practices.pdf

Association for Specialists in Group Work (ASGW). (2012). Multicultural and social justice competence principles for group workers. Retrieved from http://www.asgw.org/pdf/ASGW_MC_SJ_Priniciples_Final_ASGW.pdf

Association of State and Provincial Psychology Boards (ASPPB). (2005). Code of conduct. Retrieved from http://www.asppb.org/publications/model/conduct.aspx

Association of State and Provincial Psychology Boards (ASPPB). (2009). Guidelines on practicum experience for licensure. Retrieved from https://c.ymcdn.com/sites/asppb.site-ym.com/resource/resmgr/guidelines/final_prac_guidelines_1_31_0.pdf

Australian Psychological Society. (2007). Code of ethics. Retrieved from http://www.psychology.org.au/about/ethics/

British Association for Counselling and Psychotherapy. (2001). Ethical framework for good practice in counselling and psychotherapy. Retrieved from http://www.bacp.co.uk/ethical_framework/

Canadian Counselling and Psychotherapy Association. (2007). Code of ethics. Retrieved from http://www.ccpa-accp.ca/_documents/CodeofEthics_en_new.pdf

Canadian Psychological Association. (2000). Canadian code of ethics for psychologists (3rd ed.). Retrieved from http://www.cpa.ca/aboutcpa/committees/ethics/codeofethics

Canadian Psychological Association. (2006). Draft ethical guidelines for psychologists providing psychological services via electronic media. Retrieved from http://www.cpa.ca/docs/File/Ethics/Draft_Guidelines_EServices_31Oct2013.pdf

Canadian Psychological Association. (2010). A resource guide for psychologists: Ethical supervision in teaching, research, practice and supervision. Retrieved from http://www.cpa.ca/docs/File/Ethics/COEresGuideSuperAppNov2010Rev14June2011.pdf

Commission on Rehabilitation Counselor Certification (CRCC). (2010). Code of professional ethics for rehabilitation counselors. Retrieved from https://www.crccertification.com/filebin/pdf/CRCC_COE_1-1-10_Rev12-09.pdf

Committee on Ethical Guidelines for Forensic Psychologists. (1991). Specialty guidelines for forensic psychologists. *Law and Human Behavior*, *15*, 655–665.

Employee Assistance Professionals Association (EAPA). (2009). Code of ethics. Retrieved from http://www.eapassn.org/files/public/EAPACodeofEthics0809.pdf

International Association of Marriage and Family Counselors (IAMFC). (2005). Ethical code for the International Association of Marriage and Family Counseling. *The Family Journal*, *14*, 92–98.

International Coaches Association. (2003). Code of ethics. Retrieved from http://www.certifiedcoach.org/index.php/about_iac/iac_code_of_ethics/

International Society for Coaching Psychology. (2011). Ethics. Retrieved from http://www.isfcp.net/ethics.htm

International Testing Commission (ITC). (2005). Guidelines on computer-based and Internet-delivered testing. Retrieved from http://www.intestcom.org/Downloads/ITC Guidelines on Computer-version 2005 approved.pdf

International Union of Psychological Science. (2008). Universal declaration of ethical principles for psychologists. Retrieved from http://www.iupsys.net/about/governance/universal-declaration-of-ethical-principles-for-psychologists.html

National Academy of Neuropsychology. (2000). Official position statement on test security. *Archives of Clinical Neuropsychology*, *15*, 383–386.

National Association of Alcohol and Drug Abuse Counselors (NAADAC). (2011). Code of ethics. Retrieved from http://www.naadac.org/resources/codeofethics

National Association of School Psychologists (NASP). (2010). Principles for professional ethics. Retrieved from http://www.nasponline.org/standards/2010standards.aspx

National Association of Social Workers (NASW). (2008). Code of ethics. Retrieved from http://www.socialworkers.org/pubs/code/code.asp

National Board for Certified Counselors (NBCC). (2005). Code of ethics. Retrieved from http://www.nbcc.org/Assets/Ethics/nbcc-codeofethics.pdf

National Board for Certified Counselors (NBCC). (2013). Policy regarding the provision of distance professional services. Retrieved from http://www.nbcc.org/Assets/Ethics/NBCCPolicyRegardingPracticeofDistanceCounselingBoard.pdf

National Career Development Association (NCDA). (2007). Code of ethics. Retrieved from http://associationdatabase.com/aws/NCDA/asset_manager/get_file/3395

National Career Development Association (NCDA). (2009). Career counseling competencies. Retrieved from http://www.ncda.org/aws/NCDA/pt/sd/news_article/37798/_self/layout_ccmsearch/true

National Career Development Association (NCDA). (2010). Career counselor assessment and evaluation competencies. Retrieved from http://www.ncda.org/aws/NCDA/asset_manager/get_file/18143/aace-ncda_assmt_eval_competencies

National Career Development Association (NCDA). (2014). Multicultural career counseling minimum competencies. Retrieved from http://associationdatabase.com/aws/NCDA/pt/sp/guidelines

Ohio Psychological Association (OPA). (2008). Telepsychology guidelines. Retrieved from http://www.ohpsych.org/psychologists/files/2011/06/OPATelepsychologyGuidelines41710.pdf

Society for Personality Assessment (SPA). (2006). Standards for education and training in psychological assessment. *Journal of Personality Assessment*, *87*, 355–357.

Society for Research in Child Development (SRCD). (2007). Ethical standards for research with children. Retrieved from http://www.srcd.org/index.php?option=com_content&task=view&id=68&Itemid=110

World Professional Association for Transgender Health. (2012). Standards of care for the health of transsexual, transgender, and gender nonconforming people. Retrieved from http://www.wpath.org/uploaded_files/140/files/Standards%20of%20Care,%20V7 Full Book.pdf

For additional international codes of ethics, see http://www.kspope.com/ethcodes/index.php

Author Index

Subject Index